THE
Life and Times
OF
Menachem Begin

Other Books by Amos Perlmutter

ISRAEL: THE PARTITIONED STATE

MODERN AUTHORITARIANISM

POLITICAL ROLES AND MILITARY RULERS

POLITICS AND THE MILITARY IN ISRAEL: 1967–77

THE MILITARY AND POLITICS IN MODERN TIMES

EGYPT, THE PRAETORIAN STATE

ANATOMY OF POLITICAL INSTITUTIONALIZATION:
THE CASE OF ISRAEL AND SOME COMPARATIVE ANALYSIS

MILITARY AND POLITICS IN ISRAEL:
NATION BUILDING AND ROLE EXPANSION

THE
Life and Times
OF
Menachem Begin

AMOS PERLMUTTER

Doubleday & Company, Inc.
Garden City, New York
1987

Part One

THE POLAND YEARS
1925–42

1

Menachem Begin: An Overview

A tremor went through Israel, the Middle East, and the world at large on May 17, 1977, when Menachem Begin was elected Prime Minister of Israel. The tremor was made up in almost equal parts of trepidation, incredulity, and astonishment, depending on the vantage point from which the event was being perceived.

Surely a small part of that tremor must have been felt by this bespectacled, slight, and balding man, although he himself, calm in the spotlight, did not perceive the moment as the high-water mark of his life.

Begin's victory was the culmination of an election that had already defied belief, an election as untypical in its outcome as in its conduct. The Labor candidate, the reigning Prime Minister Yitzhak Rabin, a war hero with impeccable credentials, had been forced to withdraw from the head of the ticket because of a corruption scandal. His successor, Shimon Peres, a superb behind-the-scenes manager, lacked the one quality which might have pulled it off for Labor—charisma. The winning candidate, who had plenty of charisma, appeared at one point to be at death's door, after suffering a serious heart attack.

In a way, Begin's victory for himself and his Likud coalition was typical of the man's political life—it was an act of willful, dogged survival and perseverance. The victory stunned the rest of the world as much as it did Israel. It ended the unbroken hold of the Labor Party, which had dominated Israel's politics from the beginning of its existence as a nation. To appreciate the enormity of the event, one has only to imagine that Harold Stassen, after decades of trying, had suddenly emerged victorious over the established Republican and Democratic parties. Since Israel had gained its independence in 1948, Begin had entered every election as the principal opposition to Labor; dutifully, with no perceptible impact, he lost every election, falling without a ripple before some of the giants of Israel's history—David Ben Gurion, his life-long antagonist; Levi Eshkol; and Golda Meir.

To the rest of the world, Begin seemed to have popped out of nowhere, an anomaly who had "suddenly" and "miraculously" emerged as a major political force. Little was known about him, except in terms of clichés —he was thought of as a "terrorist" who had been responsible for the bombing of the King David Hotel in 1947, an irresponsible militarist, perhaps even a Fascist. Experts around the world feared for the prospects of peace in the Middle East.

Within Israel, Laborites, caught by surprise, were disappointed, but most of them, from Rabin to Peres to Allon, saw Begin's election as a temporary setback. Nevertheless, Begin's election was a culmination of changes which had been building up ever since the 1973 Yom Kippur War and perhaps even the 1967 Six-Day War, a symptom of a decade of significant changes that had been transforming Israel. That country's confidence, once so high after the stunning military victory of 1967, had been badly shattered after the near-miss of the 1973 war. Its economy, now incestuously tied to a ballooning military machine and to its security concerns, was beginning to become unglued. The Labor Party and all of its symbols—its spirit of elitism, pioneerism, socialistic liberalism, its cosmopolitan attitude toward the world at large—was being challenged by newer forces fueled by a growing population of alienated Sephardic Jews. Like the unrepentant Begin, they saw themselves as outsiders in their homeland.

These new Israelis were ill at ease in the international scene, and their resentment often translated itself into defiance. The tie that bound Begin to his new-found constituency was a visionary and rhapsodic belief in Eretz Israel (the Land of Israel), the inclusion in Israel of the ancient lands of Judea and Samaria. In modern terms, this meant that land acquired by force in the 1967 war—land in Palestine, the West Bank, and Gaza, heavily populated by Palestinians—was to become part of Israel. For Begin, these were not newly acquired territories, but rather regained ones, and they meant redemption. To the rest of the world, they meant new Israeli settlements.

The war of 1967 had quadrupled the size of Israel. It brought under Israeli control not only the West Bank and Gaza, but also Jerusalem, the Sinai and the Golan Heights. The Laborites, as firmly committed to settlement and as security-conscious as their opponents, nevertheless looked at the new territories hesitatingly, as if they were poisoned gifts. In the minds of men like Moshe Dayan and Yitzhak Rabin, these territories were a way to push the Arab enemy farther from Israel's frontiers and at the same time to assure, through compromise and force, potential peace with their adversaries. They were flawed with the potential for more conflict, but they shone with the potential for peace.

To Begin, the West Bank and Gaza were as much a part of Israel as Tel Aviv and Jerusalem. The right of history, ancient and modern, declared the territories part of the state. He spoke of them with a passion which was totally uncompromising yet entirely heartfelt and real. His position on the acquired territories and the strident, shrill notes of his rhetoric, as well as his duly noted reputation for fantasies and outspoken hostility to the Arab enemy, made him unattractive to the West, and particularly to Israel's traditional big-power ally and protector, the United States.

The hide-bound political machinery of the Labor Party still tended to view Begin with contempt. They sat back, haggled among themselves, and waited for the inevitable collapse of his government, which they believed was not long in coming. But Labor had to wait for six long, eventful, and shattering years (1977–83), and by then it was in no political shape to challenge either Begin or his successor, Yitzhak Shamir.

Labor did mount one serious challenge against Begin in the 1981 elections, but did not manage to topple him. In the middle of September 1983, Begin did the job himself by bluntly announcing he would step down. He formally resigned on September 15, 1983.

Begin's resignation, an event with thunderous political reverberations, was conducted in silence. It seemed that Begin willed himself to disappear. There were no emotional television appearances; the formal resignation itself was delivered unceremoniously by Cabinet Secretary Dan Meridor to President Chaim Herzog. Begin himself remained in seclusion and silent, reportedly ill and frail. He seemed to have lost all interest in the outside world, a mood which had been gathering steadily throughout the long, frustrating, and inconclusive summer.

After seven years of tumult and shouting, after a reign that was loudly punctuated by events which rocked the Middle East with repeated hammer-blows of significant change, Begin was determined to turn into a ghost, a political mute. Over those seven years, Begin had managed to change the physical map of Israel; he had changed irrevocably its political climate and the way the country saw itself. He had brought Israel respect and prestige; he had brought it glory. He had also brought it shame, and since he was uncharacteristically silent, bearing all the ashen marks of a defeated, depleted man who was no longer in control of events and had therefore decided to bow out. "I cannot go any longer," he told friends who tried to dissuade him.

It is easy enough to say Begin was ill, worn-out, tired, depressed, and still grieving over the death a year earlier of his wife Aliza. All of this is no doubt true. It was obvious to those who saw Begin in the months just before his resignation that his fire had cooled, the visionary flame had begun to dim. It was also obvious, by the time Begin resigned, that Israel itself seemed at a standstill. A kind of miasma and depression had enveloped the country, too.

The economy worsened day by day and headed toward disaster. Lebanon was increasingly becoming a tortuous maze, not only for Israel but also for the United States and the sundry Christians, Phalangists, Palestinians and radical Shiites who conducted a daily bloodbath in the streets of Beirut and the Shouf mountains. Each week brought word of new Israeli casualties; the news pecked away at a nation's and a Prime Minister's morale. The harsh findings of the commission inquiry into the Sabra-Shatila massacre had covered everyone—Begin, Shamir, the belligerent Defense Minister Ariel Sharon, and the proud Israeli defense forces—with a layer of shame. The country was restive, moribund, and more divided than it had ever been in its brief history.

For Begin, the days of glory, the days of shaping history with decisive, defiant acts, were over. His tenure seemed to end, ironically, with a defeated sigh instead of the bursts of accomplishment, controversy, and action which characterized the preceding seven years.

It is impossible, after looking at the events of Begin's seven-year tenureship, not to acknowledge that he had a huge impact on the times. To the consternation of most of the Arab world, and to the surprise of many others, Begin stood face to face with Egyptian President Anwar Sadat, only six months after he was elected, and that occasion was the start of a process that culminated in the Egyptian-Israeli Peace Treaty and the Camp David Agreement, events which were viewed by many as the first block in a brick-by-brick building of a general Middle East peace. It was a courageous political act on the part of Begin and Sadat. It was an act by statesmen who faced heated opposition. Begin's opposition included Yitzhak Shamir and Defense Minister Moshe Arens, both of whom voted against the Camp David Agreements.

Begin was a most unusual politician and a most unusual Prime Minister who defied convention and common practice. In fact, he defied just about everyone. Begin (who had served ably in a National Unity Government between 1967 and 1970), set the tone of his tenureship by naming Moshe Dayan, a Labor stalwart and a restraining influence, as his Foreign Minister. Dayan and Ezer Weizman, the latter for a time Defense Minister, had a considerable reigning influence on Begin, especially during Camp David, lasting until they could no longer check or abide Begin's settlements policy in the West Bank. Begin was steely and fervent when it came to the West Bank; he pursued the dream of Eretz Israel with a singlemindedness rare even in a country that has produced more than its share of willful political leaders.

Begin's settlements policy, combined with a combative, strike-first attitude toward Israel's Arab enemies, began to slowly strain relations between

Israel and the United States. President Jimmy Carter chafed and gritted his teeth when Begin sent tanks into southern Lebanon in 1978 to devastate PLO strongholds. Israel's relationship with the United States became further strained even under Reagan, an avowed opponent of the terrorist PLO and Israel's best champion in the White House since Harry Truman, when in June of 1981 Israeli jets blasted an Iraqi nuclear reactor. The Israelis later conducted a cold-blooded raid against PLO headquarters in Beirut, with heavy civilian casualties.

By that time, all the checks were gone. With the help of the aggressive Ariel Sharon, Begin survived a hair-raising 1981 election and rewarded Sharon with the Defense Ministership. That may well have been Begin's biggest mistake, for it led directly to the craggy hills of Lebanon and the battered streets of Beirut.

If one were to draw a graph of the reign of Menachem Begin as Prime Minister, one could start at zero, point sharply upward with Camp David, then note a slight rise in the wake of the bombing of the nuclear reactor in Iraq, the line sinking until just before the 1981 election, then sharply rising again, reaching an apex as Israel began its incursion into Lebanon.

The war in Lebanon, which Sharon had promised would be quick, decisive, and limited, turned out to be long and painful. In fact, the high-water mark of Begin's tenureship was the first few days of the Lebanese war, when Israeli forces defeated Syrian forces, then proceeded to rout and scatter PLO units all over southern Lebanon. Once the Israeli thrust veered toward Beirut, with a kind of slow, awesome inevitability, Begin's fate, it now seems, was sealed. All of his objectives, and more to the point, Sharon's careful and grandiose plans, unraveled as Israel finally realized the limits of military solutions to political problems. Sharon had hoped to set up a Christian-dominated government, through which he hoped to shatter the PLO once and for all. All of those hopes were undone the longer the war dragged on. The final blow was the assassination of the pro-Israeli Lebanese President Bashir Gemayel and the act of revenge that followed it—the Sabra-Shatila massacre. There was no decisive victory, very little honor, and a growing dissatisfaction and disgust at home as the casualties mounted daily.

In the end of his career, his most cherished dream remained unfulfilled, a nonachievement which pleased others, but which blighted Begin's soul. After the Egyptian-Israeli Peace Treaty, a watershed event by any judgment, he was asked how he wanted to be remembered in the annals of history. (Begin does surely want to be remembered.) "I want to be remembered as the man who set the borders of Eretz Yisrael for all eternity."[1] He meant the incorporation and reclamation of Judea and Samaria—which may happen with the cumulative impact of Israeli settlements in the West Bank, but not in Begin's lifetime.

In the aftermath of what appears to be failure, how does one assess

Menachem Begin? Certainly, by any available criteria, he was a man who had a tremendous impact on his time, in a positive and a negative way. He was also a man curiously out of his time, a throwback, a visionary who tended to look backward, over his shoulder. When one looks at Begin's life, a stream of contradictions and ironies runs through it. There is a tendency to pigeonhole him in a particular role, to fasten the straightjacket of cliché on him; yet he eludes the attempt. More than any of Israel's leaders, he is shrouded in complexity, in double meanings and clashing tendencies.

Always, he has been a man of controversy. To many, he incarnated the best and the worst of Israel. No one, whether Jew, Gentile or Arab, has managed to remain indifferent to him. He has been likened to a sphinx, called "a windbag" by David Ben Gurion, a champion of peace by Sadat, a threat to peace by Carter.

More than anything, however, he appears as the great man pushed to the edge of tragedy and despair. There is almost something biblical about his life and career, as if he were some ancient prophet tested time and again by a capricious and stern God. The ancient biblical heroes and prophets of the Old Testament endured and sometimes triumphed, but often died unfulfilled, their dreams unconstructed. Begin evokes them with his rhetoric, his defiance, his acute and eloquent description of Jewish suffering, which he often personalized and took upon himself as a mantle of justification.

Tragedy and a curious unfulfillment lie at the core of most of the great men of Zionism, who died just as Zionism became engaged in a fratricidal internal struggle that threatened to destroy it. Herzl died as the Zionist movement was threatened by the Uganda controversy. Chaim Weizmann, the long-time president of the World Zionist Organization, an urbane man who was at home in the diplomatic corridors of Europe and a guiding force behind the Balfour Declaration, which formed the spurious basis for the creation of a Jewish Palestinian homeland, died an isolated man, his latter years marked by a bitter struggle for power with Ben Gurion. His dogged and unflinching faith in British honor and power left him discredited and powerless. Jabotinsky, too, died as Revisionism, Betar, and Etzel were being torn asunder by strife.

Ben Gurion, the man generally given credit for being the founder and father of modern Israel faded from the scene in semidisgrace, after being shunted aside in the wake of a bitter political battle in the early 1960s, a political outcast from the party he helped to create.

So it goes. The list is long, full of flawed and great men reaching peaks of fame and glory, undone by fate and by their own hubris. Moshe Sharett, an effective diplomat, proved to be an ineffectual Prime Minister, destroyed by his rivals as well as by his own mild perplexing nature. Levi Eshkol died in the wake of Israel's greatest military triumph in 1968. Golda Meir left office dying and disillusioned after the near-disastrous Yom Kippur War.

Rabin, the shining war hero, was tarnished by scandals when he became Prime Minister, a job that he had neither the skills nor the diversified qualities to fulfill. He fell short of his potential for real greatness. Ariel Sharon's sheer courage and tactical ability made him one of Israel's greatest generals, but his hubris and pride, his overweening ambition, and his very justified image as a brutal man have blotted his reputation irrevocably.

So it is with Begin. A list of his accomplishments and virtues side by side with his failures and flaws would come out perfectly aligned. In Begin's life, achievement always ran head on into defeat. Again the recurring images are from the Bible—like Moses, who was denied the Promised Land after years of struggle, Begin was exiled in the political wilderness, returning again and again.

Whatever one might say about Begin, he had all the earmarks of greatness, yet he suffered from living in a time of greater men. Throughout his life, he was haunted by the images of two giants: one his mentor, Zeev Jabotinsky[2], the founder of Revisionist Zionism; the other his political rival, David Ben Gurion,[3] who often despised Begin but whom Begin always respected, emulated and imitated. Deep in his heart, Begin believed he never quite measured up to either man, and the long shadows they threw threatened him even long after their deaths.

The odd quality about this curious form of hero worship tinged by bitterness and envy is that Begin is so startlingly different from both men.

Jabotinsky was the founder and patron saint of Revisionist Zionism. His movement was the antithesis of the pragmatic Socialist Zionism led by Ben Gurion and became its sharp antagonist and rival for the hearts and minds of Zionism in Palestine. Jabotinsky's aim was not only a Jewish state and homeland, but a homeland that encompassed the two banks of the Jordan River—Eretz Israel, the Land of Israel. With its aim, it had a biblical strain, and it marched to the music of other times, not the convoluted and pragmatic discordancy of the twentieth century. Thus it completely ignored the reality of the Arab question. With Begin at its head, it would challenge and rise up against the British presence in Palestine.

Jabotinsky was a tribune of radical Zionism, a Renaissance man who was an indefatigable and cogent speaker, a man of immense gifts, a writer who wrote and spoke seven languages, a novelist, an urbane and almost quintessential European who came out of the nineteenth-century Russian intelligentsia, a man of undeniable charisma. Begin was then a provincial leader of Betar, a Revisionist Zionist youth movement in Poland. When he first met Jabotinsky, he was enthralled—he had found his leader and mentor —but it was a little like staring in awe at a distant mountaintop.

Jabotinsky was indeed distant, a vain man who would never stoop to informality with a subordinate. He abhorred small talk, treating his followers as enlisted soldiers in a cause. His relationship with Begin was that of a master to a pupil, and Jabotinsky never let Begin forget it. Jabotinsky was worldly and urbane; Begin was an ungainly young man, a rabble rouser without subtlety and eloquence in his speech, an impassioned man who would never pass for an intellectual. Where Jabotinsky's writing was precise, stately, and marked with grace and style, Begin's is heavily burdened with rhetoric, dying a plodding death on the printed page.

By the time Begin had become High Commissioner of Betar in Poland in March 1939, Jabotinsky's movement was coming asunder, its more radical members impatient, militant and ready to fight the British for their homeland. But Jabotinsky still retained the power and charisma that could chastise the presumptuous rebels in 1938. At a Betar executive committee meeting in Warsaw, he laconically dismissed the idea that Betar (and Revisionism) should become a military organization. He challenged the defenders of illegal militarism that Begin had reluctantly joined. Begin suggested that Betar should now follow the "military Zionism" phase, as the Irish did and as the Italians did under Garibaldi. Jabotinsky replied in anger that this was chatter *(pilpulim)*. He asked Begin how Begin would bring Betar soldiers to Palestine without the good will of foreigners. "Yours is the whistle of a door,"[4] he said.

This was a sharp and cold rebuke, and it must have stung Begin, who still revered his mentor and would always do so. Begin, however, was loyal; he took over the leaderless Betar organization in Poland during World War II and remained true to the tenets of Revisionism—whose core is liberated and complete Eretz Israel. Begin kept faith with Jabotinsky long after the latter's death in 1940. In fact, in the 1960s, Begin repeatedly pleaded with Labor to have Jabotinsky's body interred in Israel's Mount Herzl, near Jerusalem, and he finally succeeded. And on the eve of the 1967 war, Begin visited Jabotinsky's grave to pay homage, like the good Betar soldier that he remained. "Sir," he reportedly said, "head of Betar, we have come to inform you that one of your followers is now serving as a minister in the government of Israel."[5]

The differences between Ben Gurion and Begin are even more sharply defined, because they strike at the heart of what Begin really is, as well as what he aspired to be. Their paths crossed again and again, always in antagonism. Ben Gurion was always the victor; Begin was the loser for the sake of his ideal, the greater Israel.

Ben Gurion was to be the founder of the modern state of Israel, and he was Revisionist Zionism's bitterest Zionist enemy. He repeatedly thwarted its efforts to become a political force in Palestine. He sought to restrict immigration of Revisionists from Poland in the 1930s, correctly seeing the potential influx as Revisionist recruits. He helped tarnish Revisionism with the taint of terrorism and murder, and even risked a Jewish civil war with its adherents in the midst of the fight for independence. Begin, refusing to shed Jewish blood, backed down. Thus, in July 1948, Ben Gurion sank the supply ship *Altalena,* which was carrying arms for Begin's Etzel underground members. The *Altalena* incident assured that Etzel and whatever political party Begin might head would be relegated to the background of Israeli politics for at least two decades.

Ben Gurion treated Begin with such undisguised contempt that in all the time Begin served in the Knesset, Ben Gurion referred to him "as that member of the Knesset sitting next to M. K. Bader" (Begin's deputy in the Knesset). This was Ben Gurion's pointed way of totally dismissing Begin's importance as a politician.

Ben Gurion seemed almost to loathe Begin, but Begin secretly admired Ben Gurion. He saw Ben Gurion's achievements as milestones to be surpassed. Ben Gurion was indeed the founder of the state; Begin, as Prime Minister, would go further and bring the peace to Israel; he would achieve Israel's final security and reclaim Eretz Israel.

Yet the two men could never be compared. Begin was something new in Israeli history and politics. Ben Gurion, and those who came after him, were of the generation that emigrated to Palestine in the early 1900s. They were pioneers who literally forged the country with their hands, whose dominant roots were in Palestine, not Europe.

Begin was Israel's first Prime Minister to represent the classic Diaspora European Jew, whose route to Israel was entirely different from the early settlers.

Begin grew up in a typically middle class, bourgeois Jewish family in the Brest-Litovsk district of south central Poland at the height of Poland's nationalism and anti-Semitism; he became imbued with Jewish nationalism. While the Socialist Zionists struggled to survive in Palestine amid Arab rioting, Begin, as the shadow of Nazism crept toward Poland, was making his way up the Betar chain of command.

He experienced the early phase of the Holocaust firsthand, losing most of his family to the Nazi slaughter. In the war years he himself narrowly escaped extinction and suffered the pain of imprisonment in the Russian Gulag. Finally, he made his way to Palestine as a member of the Polish Army.

The Holocaust is an indelible part of Begin's political, emotional, and rhetorical makeup precisely because he experienced it directly, as opposed to the Palestinian Jews, who did not. It is not startling to hear an Israeli Prime Minister repeatedly invoke the memory of the Holocaust in his justification for military acts. But Begin is entirely sincere, entirely impassioned and entirely haunted. The history of the Jews for Begin is clear—it is the history of the knout, the pogrom, the auto-da-fé, the extermination, and the Holocaust. As a member of the Knesset, Begin was so violent in his opposition to the acceptance of German restitution in the middle 1950s that he called for large-scale demonstrations that very nearly became full-scale riots outside the Knesset during the debate.

In Begin's mind, the Holocaust became a metaphor for the sufferings of Jews throughout history, and he used the metaphor often. When he saw opposition and criticism from the outside world for his acts, he painted that opposition with the broad strokes of anti-Semitism. By identifying with the Holocaust in its enormity, Begin sought to dishonor opposition and criticism. In 1981, when Israel destroyed a nuclear reactor near Baghdad, Begin's justification was prompt and impassioned: "There will not be another Holocaust in history . . . never again, never again."[6]

He took the Palestine Liberation Organization's vow to destroy Israel at face value, even though it might seem that the PLO lacked the means to carry out that vow. To Begin, it was an ill-disguised call for another Holocaust, and so he set about destroying the PLO threat ruthlessly and efficiently, a policy that would eventually land him in the quagmire that was Lebanon.

His insularity, his defensiveness, his almost bristling stance against anything that smacked of criticism, always had its roots in the horrors of the Holocaust. It also served him badly, for it made him seem nakedly and coldly insensitive and paranoid, never more so than when he labeled the world's harsh reaction to the Sabra-Shatila massacre as "a blood libel"—alluding to century-old anti-Semitic accusations that Jews murdered Christian children at Passover. Apparently oblivious to the horror of the event, Begin commented, "Goyim kill goyim and they blame the Jews".

There is a kind of moral outrage in these utterances that is as contradictory as everything else about Begin. At their best they sound eloquent, a stirring reminder of events much of the world wants to forget. At their worst they sound shrill, pathological, and unforgivably insensitive.

This pattern was also evident in his attitude about the Arabs and the Arab problem. On the level of statesmanship, he forged a close relationship with the suave, debonair, and vain Anwar al-Sadat. Together with President Carter they forged the Egyptian-Israeli Peace Treaty, an event that was at least partly spurred by the relationship between the two men.

Yet when Begin looks at the Arab world as a whole, he primarily sees a threat, an unformed, shadowy, hostile, enemy. Much of this reaction is rooted in the attitude of Revisionist Zionism itself, whose followers seemed to think that the Arabs would go away peaceably, that their nationalism was not genuine and not to be taken seriously. This of course was as naive as it sounds. The hope was that aggressive Jewish settlements, and Arab weaknesses and divisiveness, would force the Arabs to emigrate. Behind that seemingly "peaceful" intention lurked the aggressive policy of evacuating and exiling the Palestinians.

Begin has always remained insular. For a man who can speak eloquently about Jewish sufferings, and appear to feel it in his heart and soul, he is curiously indifferent to the sufferings of others, especially when the victims are Arabs. Read his testimony before the Commission Inquiry into the Sabra-Shatila Massacre, and you note an almost businesslike detachment, as if he were delivering reports to a corporate board meeting. Begin remained indifferent to the victims of Sabra-Shatila; they blurred into a single body, the Arabs, for whom he had no tears to shed, for whom no outrage touched him.

Begin remains profoundly ignorant about Arab customs, culture, and aspirations. He sees only one thing: the dire threat they represent to Israel. The PLO are Nazis. Arafat is Hitler.

This peacemaker, who does not appear to understand or want to understand his enemy, is a man who was overly enamored of all things military. Much as the Nazi war machine blistered his rage, he loves the trappings that smack of radical nationalism. Thus, the Betar units in Poland were patterned by Jabotinsky after similar Polish military units that were decidedly radical-nationalist, some even fascist and rabidly anti-Semitic. He and his movement were more than once accused of Fascist tendencies by his political enemies because he roamed the streets in a huge car, flanked by motorcyclists with an obviously military bearing.

Begin has an evident flair for propaganda and the management of symbols. He showed this in his strategy as Etzel commander in the underground's battle against the British, a battle which he bombastically called "The Revolt." Thus, the flogging of British military personnel, the Acre raid, the bombing of the King David Hotel, and the hanging of the British sergeants were all highly symbolic acts aimed to persuade the Jews and to punish the British. They provoked outrage and condemnation from the world at large and from the moderate Zionists, but they also evoked a certain amount of pride. More than that, they humbled and angered British pride and therefore they were surely a significant contribution to the struggle for independence.

His emotional detachment from the suffering of non-Jews hurt him then and hurts him today. The Etzel attack on Dir Yassin, a Palestinian village that became a staging point for Arab irregulars against Jewish Jerusalem, was a disaster and smacked of massacre, and it would reverberate decades later at Sabra-Shatila.

It was an example of Begin's faith in military solutions to diplomatic problems. That faith would undo him when he ventured into Lebanon, guided by Sharon.

Begin, over the years, has been labeled a Fascist, a threat to Israeli democracy and a militarist, but in fact he was a democrat, a liberal and a parliamentary politician.

Begin was loyal, both to democratic institutions and to Israel. Thus, he bowed after a bitter struggle in the *Altalena* affair, dooming himself for years to second-rate status as a politician. Thus he also dutifully and proudly joined a National Unity Government during the 1967 crisis, laying aside political scars and enmities. He was both a survivor and a loyalist.

His tenacity served him well. Like a jack-in-the-box, battered but still jaunty, he would reappear and finally prevail. He often despaired, because at heart he is a loner, a romantic, and sees himself as a Last Mohican.

All of his flaws and all of his virtues brought him to the apex of Israeli politics and also to that strangely silent moment of resignation. By that time, his friends and many of his political enemies were dead. Gone too was his wife Aliza, the only person he genuinely trusted.

Begin was a man oddly out of step with his times, a man whose life is modern and ancient all at once. He was a superb propagandist, a manipulator and a master parliamentary orator, as befits his legalistic nature. But he also harkens back to a different time, one he often evokes in words and spirit. For Begin, the lands of ancient Israel and its history of heroic deeds still exists. He speaks of the dangers that have always threatened to swallow the Jewish people. An East European Diaspora Jew, he became the hero of a new generation of volatile Israeli Sephardim—Jews, born in Arab-Moslem countries who unleashed forces he could barely control, and which burst after he retired.

An accumulation of contradictions such as those that exist in a man like Menachem Begin amounts to a mystery. Perhaps the deepest mystery of all is that loud silence that surrounded his resignation. In order to probe the mystery and the contradiction, in order to set off on a journey through Begin's life and time, we shall begin at the end, in the time of that strange silence.

2

September 1983: Collapse[1]

It would be a day like any other day, with a singular difference—a difference about which he had told no one, not even his closest advisers. The people he might have told—his wife Aliza, his closest Etzel comrades—were dead, and, in may ways, so was Begin.

On September 14 he woke as always around 5 A.M., with the first light of day filtering into the second-story room on Balfour Street the Prime Minister's mansion in Jerusalem. If he chose, he could look outside his window and see the protesters, a constant reminder of one of his legacies—the war in Lebanon. Almost all of them "Peace Now" adherents, they kept a constant vigil of protest on the pavement, carrying placards denoting the number of Israeli dead in Lebanon, which had risen to 554 by that particular day.

For three months, ever since Begin had abruptly announced his intention to resign, Israel had remained in a state of political suspended animation. When Begin named Foreign Minister Yitzhak Shamir as his successor, the old diminutive Lehi terrorist was catapulted by Begin to a step away from the top political job in Israel. Yet Begin had not made it official by formally tendering his resignation to the President of Israel. He still held the reins of government, still attended cabinet meetings, still made decisions, although in an atmosphere of silence and stillness.

Rumors, as always, abounded. Begin was deathly ill, he was deranged, he was in deep mourning, he would quit, he would not quit. Herut party members, old friends, and members of the fragile coalition which held the Likud government together pleaded with him to remain in office. Begin was still the most charismatic man in Israeli politics. The Herut-Likud men waiting in the wings—Yitzhak Shamir, the ultimate technocrat; Defense Minister Moshe Arens; the passive but ambitious Deputy Prime Minister David Levy—and the men of the opposition, Shimon Peres and former Prime Minister Yitzhak Rabin. All paled beside Begin, who could still arouse deep feelings within the body politic. Shamir, for one, was not above using Begin's reflected charisma and the hypnotic power he held over Israeli voters. In speeches defending Likud economic policies, policies which had brought Israel to the brink of disaster, whenever Shamir invoked Begin's name he was rewarded with a deep, rumbling cheer that defied common sense and swallowed up issues.

The constant pleadings from Begin's political cohorts for him to stay in office came not so much out of loyalty and affection as out of fear of retribution at the polls. The small splinter groups which were the pivots of the coalition—the National Religious Party and the Renaissance Party—wanted Begin to remain because they did not want to face the electorate. All the polls showed that they could be swept away in the devisive political atmosphere, another of Begin's legacies.

As Begin listened to the morning radio bulletins from the BBC, unconsciously following a ritual that dated back to his days as Etzel's underground leader, his mind was already made up. He had been on the brink of calling it quits many times during a fabled career, and always there had been someone—cronies, Aliza—to pull him out of his depression, to buck him up. Begin has always needed a good deal of persuasion and emotional pleading. It was Arieh Ben Eliezer, an Etzel commander in 1943, who persuaded Begin to take over Etzel, and it took Aliza's urgings for him to stay with Herut in 1951 and the pleas of Benny (Benyamin Zeev) when he was ready to throw in the towel and retire to a career of being just another lawyer.

Begin's health or, more to the point, his depressions have been kept under wraps but are a necessary topic for discussion. His 1982–83 bout of depression was not his first. He must have suffered from depression in Vilna in 1940, in 1951 and again in 1981 just before the election. The signs are of a manic-depressive, but we have no medical record of it, at least before 1977. If there is a record, it is kept a secret and well guarded.

This time he did not recover before it became known. The pressure upon him became too much. The disappointment, grief and confusion ran too deep, and there was no person to change his mind, no reservoir of strength or infusion of energy to make him rise again as he had so often in the past.

By the following day, Begin would no longer be Prime Minister of Israel and he would take the first steps toward his sought-after anonymity. He had served 2,251 days in office, the longest tenure of any Israeli Prime Minister except that of his old rival, David Ben Gurion. A remarkable career, spanning five decades, was ending. It marked the political passing of a man who, again with the exception of Ben Gurion, had influenced the history of Israel and reshaped the map of the Middle East more than any other political figure.

The formal resignation—delivered not by Begin but unceremoniously by Begin's Cabinet Secretary Dan Meridor—would also put an end to the rumors, the speculation, and the gossip, a climate which had surrounded Begin from the start of his tenureship as Prime Minister.

Much of the rumor industry focused on the state of his health and the state of Begin's mind, the subject of discussion throughout his career but especially during his Prime Ministership. His heart had always been fragile, and his state of mind seemed always to be in a pendulum swing, running from deep depression to periods of frantic activity. His close lieutenants in his last phase went to great lengths to cover up and make excuses for his frailty. As late as December 1983, they insisted that throughout his reign as Prime Minister, Begin's mental, physical and intellectual faculties were in top shape. The rumor mills continued to be fed glowing reports by Begin's top lieutenant Yehiel Kadishai and his press officer, Uri Porath, both of whom knew otherwise.[2]

His health was always the subject of speculation, no more so than in the 1977 election, surely one of the most startling and dramatic in Israel's history. In March of 1977, at the height of a heated campaign, Begin fell victim to a serious heart attack and all but disappeared from sight. There were rumors that he was near death. In his stead, the suave Ezer Weizman took over the campaign, a switch which resulted in a stunning Begin-Likud victory. Weizman used slick American-style campaign tactics.

Many Laborites, perhaps showing sour grapes, felt Begin's prolonged absence from the campaign perversely assured his victory and prevented him from losing for a ninth time. Rabin, who was forced to resign the Prime Ministership during the middle of the campaign, told me "his absence removed the spirit of demagoguery from the campaign."

Begin was Lazarus-like. He came back to end the campaign vigorously and in triumph. He then embarked on an epoch-making term, which culminated in the Egyptian-Israeli Peace Treaty.

But sometime in March of 1979, during the Egyptian-Israeli negotiations, Begin suffered more complications stemming from his heart condition, and lost 30 percent of his sight. From then on, an ambulance and a medical team headed by Begin's private physician, Dr. Marvin Gotesman, accompanied him wherever he went.

Again, between April and June of 1981, just before the second general elections, Begin all but disappeared. The rumors started again—Begin was depressed, he was ill, he was frail. But like a sleeping lion, Begin was roused to the campaign fight, defying polls which showed him and Likud twenty seats behind Labor and its candidate, Shimon Peres. Begin, with the help of the popular Sharon, took to the hustings with singular passion and energy, and squeaked to victory.

But the health issue remained. The liberal critics of the daily *Haaretz* continued to needle Begin, not only for his policies and leadership style, but also about his health. Columnist Yoel Marcus openly questioned Begin's ability to properly function as Prime Minister.[3] Stung, Begin replied in an open letter in *Haaretz* under the heading of "My Policy Concerning My Health." He wrote a detailed, minute-by-minute description of his health problems, comparing them to a broken leg that caused him pain but from which he was recovering. He wrote pompously and stoically, sounding like both a statesman and martyr. He wrote Marcus: "You can be assured . . . concerning my health that I am like a wounded soldier of Israel continuing my mission for peace and prosperity."[4] If his health ever prevented him from fulfilling his duties, he cautioned, he would not stay in office. Of the three promises—peace, prosperity, and the promise to quit—Begin would deliver only the latter.

His reassurances did not stop the speculations and rumors, and rightly so. From 1981, not a month went by without a story in the press on the state of his physical or mental health. However, the war in Lebanon changed everything, for it brought about a real psychic, emotional, and political collapse.

Lebanon sapped Begin of his strength, energy, spirit, and faith. It left him bitter, disappointed, adrift, and feeling betrayed.

Assured by Sharon and Chief of Staff Rafael (Raful) Eitan, Begin envisioned the invasion of Lebanon as a way of destroying the PLO and buying time for the annexation of a complete Eretz Israel. The operation would be swift, short, and decisive, with a minimum number of casualties. Sharon, as we have seen, had other plans. For Begin Lebanon would prove to be the final straw; the war was a disaster.

Begin's final decline could be traced to the day when the war began to drag, when fighting had grown out of all proportions to Begin's initial vision. Begin was worried and out of touch, but most senior Israeli Defense Forces (IDF) officers were angry—not so much at Begin as at Sharon. Over a hundred senior IDF commanders, from colonel on up, got together in an angry meeting with Eitan and presented a condemnation of Sharon. Eitan, no Sharon fan, was nevertheless a professional soldier, and called off the meeting. He rescheduled it for the next day, when Sharon could be present. The meeting amounted to an officers' revolt. It ran for an interminable and heated eight hours, during which time some of the officers present demanded Sharon's resignation. They accused him of getting the army into an unwinnable, overextended, and never-ending war. In effect, they accused Sharon of lying, not only to them but to the Prime Minister, all of which was true. Sharon, steeled by his arrogance and stubbornness, weathered the storm.

When Begin saw the minutes of the meeting the following day, he was stunned. According to eyewitnesses, he went into shock. What he was reading showed clearly that many of IDF's best and most loyal commanders had lost their faith in his ability to harness the aggressive Sharon.[5]

Begin, whose worship of things military knew no bounds, was severely wounded. He understood that his own, not Sharon's credibility, was on the line, because he was responsible for Sharon's actions. If he could not see through Sharon's machinations, then he was clearly seen as a fool and negligent in the eyes of the officers.

Begin was accustomed to showering superlatives on his officers, and although they did not have the same affection and respect for him as they had for Ben Gurion, they nevertheless treated him with dignity. That was all a thing of the past now. The men whom he once described as "those wonderful modern biblical heroes," clearly had lost confidence in his leadership.

Sharon was not a creature of Begin's making, and Begin had always felt ambivalent about him. Long before Lebanon, he had said of his Defense Minister—"Sharon is a great general . . . and a vicious character." In September 1982, Begin was asked if he considered Sharon a "statesman." He was noncommittal. "He is a professional, a great general,"[6] Begin insisted.

Begin's increasing remoteness and lack of control could be traced from the meeting of the IDF command. He sensed a morass and retreated from it, so much so that he hardly noticed Sabra-Shatila and remained unaffected by it.[7] His insensitivity to the massacre was appalling to many.

Bashir Gemayel's assassination, Sharon's deviousness, and Sabra-Shatila were devastating blows, but more was to come. Having fallen victim to the war he had initiated, he was now dealt a personal tragedy. His wife Aliza, the one person he genuinely trusted in his world, died of lung cancer on November 14, 1982, while Begin was in Los Angeles. Crying on the telephone, he talked with his daughter Lea while his doctor stood close by his side. "I shall remember you going after me on an unseen desert," he recited from Proverbs over the telephone.[8]

He withdrew deeper into himself and surfaced only during the furor over the Kahan Commission report, which was the final straw. He was stung by the criticism of him in the report: "For two days . . . he showed absolutely no interest in the camps . . . His lack of involvement casts on him a certain degree of responsibility." Begin was now forced to decide what to do with Sharon, for whom he still felt a great deal of personal loyalty.

It was an agonizing, exhausting and turbulent period, helped not a bit by Sharon's recalcitrance and unwillingness to step down, in spite of a strong suggestion from the commission to do so. Begin, one colleague explained, "is in a dilemma. He respects the judges and the judicial system. Yet he doesn't want to fire Sharon. He doesn't want to be the man to do it . . . He respects a good soldier. And to him Arik is a good soldier."[9]

The crisis involved the whole nation. Begin saw the spectacle of an Israel torn and divided to the point of fury. While the cabinet members debated furiously, "Peace Now" adherents, the left-centered anti-war movement, demonstrated outside. A grenade exploded in their midst, killing one person and injuring nine others, including the son of Interior Minister Yosef Burg, Avraham. Israel was divided, and clearly Begin had no one but himself to blame.

Begin shunned responsibility for Lebanon; if he looked at the situation there, he would have been confronted by the bloody dust of all his dreams. He visited Lebanon only one time. He did not visit a single wounded Israeli soldier. He agonized over the mounting casualty rate, but refused to confront their reality. When the nation needed a leader most, even though he fulfilled his nominal duties as Prime Minister, he was simply not there.

When the storm broke ("There is hysteria out there," one Knesset member said), Begin was puzzled. "We've known worse crises," he said. He was wrong.[10]

Beginning with Lebanon and running through the February commission crisis of 1983, the decline in Begin was noticeable. Predictably, the rumor mills set to work again, but the focus this time was more on his mental health than his physical frailty. One seemed to contribute to the other.

As 1983 wound into summer and Lebanon dragged like a heavy anchor on both the nation and Begin's psyche, new words were beginning to creep into the descriptions of the increasingly hermetical Prime Minister, words like "depression, self-flagellation." Graphologists studying his signature saw "deep signs of remorse, torment, and affliction."[11]

Porath and Kadishai, his closest advisers, covered for him throughout his steady decline. They reacted sharply to a February 1982 Washington *Post* story, which claimed that Begin seemed "to be suffering from a depression from which he can't recover." Porath called the story "gossip, a vicious act of malice . . . These people, they themselves are in a depression."[12]

Porath conceded that Begin had difficulty sitting in one place for long periods of time, but added that "there was not a single important issue in which the Prime Minister did not take part."[13]

Nevertheless, over the last hundred days of his tenureship, Begin became a recluse of sorts, even though he made regular appearances in the Knesset. He had changed visibly. I saw him on August 12 and 20 of 1983. I found him frail, his clothes hanging loosely on him, his handshake weak and brief.

Porath and Kadishai, however, acted as if nothing were wrong, and put on an air of frivolity. While the casualties continued in Lebanon and the shekel tripled from 46 to 120 to the dollar, Kadishai deceptively acted like a clown to cover up his real power: both he and Porath were instrumental in hiding Begin's fading will and capacities from the public.

Begin's schedule before the announcement of his resignation consisted of working for a few hours, and, in the afternoon, taking an extended nap or retiring for the day, except when he attended Sunday cabinet meetings. He was loathe to conduct face-to-face meetings; he put off old friends and avoided important business.

By the time he announced his resignation, he was already a tortured, gaunt man, and he became even more so afterward. It was reported that he had grown a beard and that he had gone into seclusion. No one saw him. Between September and November of 1983, not a single picture of Begin was taken.

Nor was any picture taken on the day of his last cabinet meeting, or on the day of his formal resignation.

By November 14, he had already made up his mind, irrevocably. It must have been a haunting day for him, normal on the surface but indelible, unusual underneath, full of routine but weighted down by memory.

The place was full of ghosts, people who should have been there and were not. The reception room in the Prime Minister's residence was empty of friends, inhabited only by some persistent and curious reporters.

While the BBC chattered aimlessly, Begin was served tea by his daughter Lea, another routine altered poignantly of late—it was Aliza who always brought him his first cup of morning tea. The crackle of the BBC reminded him of his Etzel days, when he learned English by listening to the radio in one hideout or another.

He moved to a desk in the corner of his second-floor office and began the daily ritual of reading the morning Hebrew papers, beginning with the *al-Hamishmar, Haaretz, Maariv, Yediot Aharonot,* and ending with the Herut weekly *Min Haaretz.* From there, he moved to the European *International Herald Tribune.* In the hours before the cabinet meeting at 8 A.M., he half-heartedly underlined items of interest for his staff to pursue.

Downstairs his driver, Menachem Ramati, was already waiting for him, attaché case in hand. Begin looked at the Prime Minister's car fondly. It is American and can best be described as a clunker which is kept in top condition. On this day, Ramati was having trouble starting the car. The ten-year-old Ford was an inheritance from Rabin. Begin smiled at the coughing engine. "I don't want a new car, Menachem," he told his driver. "This one will do."[14] Begin never did care about things, except for books.

In his office, Kadishai and Porath were waiting. Kadishai, who was not in on Begin's decision, was smiling his usual jovial, pasteboard smile. Begin looked tired and thin. He said little, and did not comment about his successor-to-be Shamir. In fact, he hardly said anything at all.

At 8:15 A.M., Defense Minister Moshe Arens arrived. He was brisk and all business for the briefing, whose contents were almost an inventory of Israel's problems and a reminder of Begin's biggest failure: Lebanon. Arens began to brief him, and the news was mostly bad.

There was trouble with the Druze in the Shouf mountains. The Shiites in the South were beginning to mount a resistance movement aimed at the Israeli occupiers. The senior IDF commanders were unhappy and bristling. Because of Lebanon, there had been no proper training for two years and the yearly exercises had to be postponed. The IDF commanders were unhappy over the army's role as an occupier and the whole idea of a continued war. The ill feeling had spread through the nation. General Amos Yaron, head of manpower, reported problems with Kibbutzim inductees, who were singularly unenthusiastic about joining elite units which once had to turn away volunteers. Yaron was the divisional commander of the troops who had encircled the Palestinian camps at Sabra-Shatila, a fact of which Begin did not need to be reminded.

Arens noted that IDF officers, once the heroes of the nation, were being treated with less enthusiasm, less adulation. With that glum fact in their minds, he decided on a retreat from the Shouf mountains and the establishment of a temporary line of defense on the Awali River.

By 9 A.M., Matti Shmulevitz, a director general of the Prime Minister's office, and Porath arrived to escort Begin to the cabinet room. Shmulevitz was a visible reminder of the underground, a man who allegedly was one of the Lehi terrorists who killed Count Bernadotte.

Begin walked slowly, supported by Porath, and took his place at the head of the table. None of those present, including Shamir and Levy, knew that he had already decided to formally resign. It was a quiet, depressing session. There were no jokes, no small talk, no smiles. Halfway through the meeting, Colonel Azriel Nevo handed Begin a note full of urgent requests for immediate approval. Begin read the notes, but didn't do anything.

At 10:30 A.M., the cabinet meeting was over. By any standards, it was a short meeting. Meetings have been known to drag on late into the afternoon and sometimes the evening, but not on this day. Begin acted like a man at a banquet without an appetite.

At the end of the meeting Ramati escorted Begin back to his office, where most of his appointments had already been kept by his successor-to-be. He declined to sit at his desk and moved to the sofa instead. "I feel more comfortable there," he said. For the next two hours, he read a variety of telexes, memos, and reports from Mossad.

From time to time, there was a polite knock on the door as his advisers discreetly tried to check on his health. He ignored them. Fatigue was already beginning to overtake him, and by 1:30 P.M., he was ready to go home. His unmarried daughter Lea waited for him, and had already prepared his favorite lunch—boiled chicken with vegetable, a dietary regimen which also happened to meet his doctor's orders. Finished with lunch, he took a long nap until 4 P.M. when a packet of reports, prepared by Kadishai, awaited his approval.[15]

Slowly he paced through the second-floor room, sparsely decorated by former Prime Ministers. Until 6 P.M., he listened to the radio, then began writing letters, an activity he loves. He writes them in his illegible handwriting which can only be decoded by Kadishai or his private secretary.

This time the task of writing exhausted him, so he turned to reading. Begin has always been a bookish man, and during his seclusion, he increasingly turned to books about World War II and the politics of the 1930s. Then he struggled through the memoirs of Brzezinski and Kissinger, trying to reach through the printed page to the place where history would place him.

He read to midnight and retired, his decision firm in his mind.

On September 15, reporters again hung around him, nagging to find out whether or not he would see President Chaim Herzog. He remained noncommittal for the moment, even though all his Etzel cronies, the Herut stalwarts, and Shamir were anxiously awaiting his decision. They were fearful about their electoral prospects without Begin to guide them. The truth of the matter was that Begin really didn't care anymore about the party or the future. Aliza was dead and so was Simcha Ehrlich, the deputy leader of the Liberals who was one of his closest friends. Begin retained no comparable love or respect for his remaining cronies, for old-timers like Shamir or newcomers like Dan Meridor.

Still stung by Sharon's "betrayal," he trusted no one and cared about few. On the day of his formal resignation, he recalled a political cartoon in *Maariv* that had portrayed him as a sheriff who has discarded his badge and guns as Rabin and Peres struggle over them on the floor. He joked with Kadishai: "What does Peres want with my pistols?"

He looked at the wall of pictures and mementos. "Don't forget to take down my portraits of Herzl and Jabotinsky in my office," he said. "Bring my Etzel Certificate number three and my family portrait."

In his office were portraits of Ben Gurion, Sharett, Eshkol, Meir, and Rabin, all former Prime Ministers. He looked at them wistfully. "Do you think there's space up there for my portrait?"[16] he asked.

He left his office still unsure, doubtful of his historical role. He headed for his son's home, which overlooks the village of Dir Yassin.

3

Begin's Poland[1]

Throughout his tenureship as Prime Minister of Israel, Menachem Begin styled himself as a major Israeli leader, a messiah-savior come to restore Eretz Israel in a modern form. But in terms of the real as opposed to the imagined Israel, he was a throwback and an aberration.

Begin was a surviving member of a nearly vanished Jewish type—the Polish Diaspora Jew. Although he was Prime Minister of Israel for seven years, he was a stranger in a strange adopted land, a man whose biblical-East-European rhetoric managed to attract a following totally alien to his own background, but one which propelled him to power.

Unlike most of Israel's founders and leaders, past and present, Begin spent half of his life in Poland, the wellspring of European Jewry.

By contrast, David Ben Gurion, who left Poland in 1904 at the age of nineteen, spent the majority of his adult life in Palestine, where he forged his following and founded a state. The preponderance of Laborites and Kibbutzim—early pioneers like Tabenkin, Eshkol and Golda Meir, and later Dayan, Peres and Rabin—were either early Polish or Russian immigrants to Palestine, or the sons of immigrants. Their concerns, ambitions, and battles were all centered on the new land that would become Israel; their European pasts became distant memory.

Begin's ideas and phobias, his dreams and inclinations were forged in the small shtetlach and villages of Poland, in the schools and universities of Warsaw and in the war-ravaged streets of Brest-Litovsk (known as Brisk). He came to manhood in a resurgent but highly anti-Semitic Poland and in the bisecting shadows cast by two world wars.

In 1920, after the First World War, Poland achieved its independence, ending one hundred fifty years of occupation by Russia, Prussia and Austria.

With independence came a new Polish patriotism tainted by anti-Semitism: Traditional religious anti-Semitism was now replaced by political anti-Semitism, and Brisk did not escape it.

In Begin's rhetoric and posturing can be heard echoes of this pre–World War II Poland. His dream of Eretz Israel was first nurtured at his father's knee, in an atmosphere at once Zionist and highly traditionalist. Later it would be further refined under the tutelage of Zeev Jabotinsky. The harrowing and impassioned references to the Holocaust which color so much of Begin's rhetoric came from firsthand experience.

Even though Jewish life has been eradicated from the Polish landscape, even though the Jewish world that constituted almost half of Begin's life no longer exists, except as tragic history and as a reminder, the impressions of Jewish life in Poland are still present in Begin's consciousness.

But it is not only Jewish life in Poland which clung to Begin like a faithful coat. Poland itself, its politics and nationalism stayed with him. In Begin's political history, there is a strong sense of identification with Poland; his strident fascination for all things military is a throwback to the militant nationalism which pervaded Poland between the two world wars. As a political leader he in fact chose to adopt many of the outer trappings of Polish nationalism and militarism. To understand this early Begin, it is necessary to examine all these forces.

Until the Holocaust, the Jews in Poland were the major component of European Jewry. The predominantly Catholic Poles and the Jews shared a unique trauma and a unique yearning. Both were peoples with an uncommonly vivid sense of themselves in historical reality, both peoples who did not exist as nations in the present. It is ironic that the Jews would eventually succeed at becoming independent and that the Poles are still dominated by the Russians, or their surrogates.

The similarities in the search for nationhood on the part of the Jews and Poles are striking. The Jews enjoyed real nationhood only once, during the biblical days to which Begin harkens so much. Then, in the wake of World War I, with the formulation of the Balfour Declaration, the glimmer of a Jewish nation as a possible reality reappeared. In between those periods Jews were scattered all over the world, a people of no nation, but a people with a strong sense of unity, identity and self.

Likewise, except in times that seem at least as ancient to them as the biblical days to the Jews, and except for the brief period between the two wars, Poland has never existed as an independent nation, without masters, with borders clearly defined and permanent.

Poland's biblical days, its golden age, was in the sixteenth century; it was all downhill after that, or as one historian aptly says: "The Polish drama lies in an unprecedented descent from national grandeur to national annihilation."[2]

The Poles recognize their lack of independent nationhood today. Rising from a sea of red Solidarity banners in 1983 was the anthem, "Let Poland Be Poland." The Poles still have masters.

The "nation" of Poland which dominated Eastern Europe for a major part of the sixteenth century was a remarkable state. It comprised modern Poland, Lithuania, and large chunks of the Ukraine. More importantly, long before the French discovered the Universal Rights of Man, the Poles, with power held in the hands of a very independent-minded group of landed nobility, were practicing a form of republicanism that was new to Europe. The nobility, or szlachta, were the ultimate power in the new Polish commonwealth by the 1500s. Although Poland would become predominantly wedded to the Catholic Church, it was remarkable then for its religious variety and tolerance. Poland, as one historian put it, was a "democracy of nobles."

This idyllic period during the 1600s, when Poland constituted one of the largest nation-states of Europe, did not last. This nation, with its revolutionary form of republicanism, fell victim to the revolutionary wars of the eighteenth century and the political rivalries of powers greater than Poland. It fragmented as much from its neighbors' avariciousness as from its internal unrest. It had its own revolution, but that revolution brought about not liberty, but ruin. Poland was first carved up in 1772. In 1793, the Prussians and Russians, both imperial powers, moved in to crush Poland and reduced it to a rump state in a series of partitions. A revolt (led by American Revolutionary War hero Tadeusz Kościuszko) followed and was crushed, leading to still another partition in 1795, this time among Russia, Prussia and Austro-Hungary.

These three partitions resulted in a fragmented, polyglot and diverse, but formless Poland. In the West, the mineral-rich districts of Pomorze, Poznan, and Silesia went to the Prussians. The southeastern portion, mainly Galicia, went to the Austro-Hungarian empire. The eastern part of Poland, mainly the Kresy (borderlands) and the peripheries of Polish Lithuania, Belorussia, and Volyna went to the Russian Romanovs. Between 1815 and 1863, a Central Poland was established by the Congress of Vienna after the defeat of Napoleon. It was ostensibly autonomous, with its own army, parliament and constitutional monarch, but it was actually under the domination of Russia.

In each part of the thoroughly divided Poland, a huge mix of diverse peoples, customs, traditions and political activities existed, varying from area to area.

In Prussian Poland, the Poles went through a process of Germanization; it was also in Prussian Poland that a virulent form of nationalism sprouted.

In the more relaxed, relatively tolerant and diverse Austro-Hungarian empire of the Hapsburgs, the Poles flourished and became privileged nationals on an equal basis with Hungarians and Germans. Galicia became semi-autonomous. The Poles played a conspicuous role among the Hapsburg elite in the bureaucracy and military. Nationalism here was not a political force.

This was not the case in the Russian portion of Poland, where the Poles continuously and futilely resisted. Congress Poland, the autonomous area of Russian Poland, was also a hotbed of repeated revolt.

What kept the idea of Poland together throughout this period of non-nationhood and fragmentation was its still flourishing landed gentry. The Roman Catholic church, too, became ever more influential in rallying the remnants of resistance, a situation that still prevails.

Different patterns—political, sociological and economic—emerged in the various parts of partitioned Poland. Ethnic groups submerged themselves while retaining their own characteristics. The intensity of domination varied from place to place. Poles became Germanized, or took on Russian and Austrian identities, and the various ethnic groups that comprised the dismembered state splintered into separate identities—the Lithuanians, Belorussians, Ukrainians, Germans, Armenians, Tartars, and Jews developed their own nationalism.

Successful economic conditions flourished in Prussian Poland; poverty was the norm in the Kresy and Eastern Galicia. The Western Poles maintained a strong sense of regional identity, but the Austrian Poles all but submerged themselves into the Empire. In Congress Poland and in the Eastern periphery of Poland, Jews, Lithuanians and Ukrainians struggled to maintain themselves in the economic hinterlands.

The status of a polyglot people with split allegiances dreaming of nationhood would remain until the victors of World War I dismembered the vestiges of the three empires. Poland emerged, like many Eastern European states, from the redrawing of the European map.

In 1918–21, the new state of Poland comprised three major areas formerly dominated by the Austrian, Prussian, and Russian Empires. In the west, the Duchy of Silesia, Posen, and Western Galicia, formerly Prussia. The Kingdom of Poland, central Poland, formerly Russia, Eastern Galacia, formerly Austria and Eastern Poland (middle Lithuania, Bielorussia) formerly Russia.

After the Great War and the heady victory over the Bolsheviks, nationalism reared its head in Poland. So did a violent form of anti-Semitism. This climate lasted until the coup d'etat by Józef Pilsudski in 1926. Strangely enough, in spite of the crackdown on Jews in the early 1920s, in spite of the violent riots, killings, and destruction of property, the Jewish population of Poland were caught up in Poland's giddy nationalism, but it was of a very different sort.

Although the Polish Jews were also searching for a sense of nationhood, like the various sections in the Polish body politic, they were divided in their goals. A strong and highly visible minority in a nation full of minorities—they constituted over 10 percent of a total population of twenty-seven million. After the Ukrainians, the Jews comprised the second largest minority in Poland. But that percentage was skewed, because it rose dramatically in urban areas. Fifty percent of the Jews tended to live in central or Congress Poland, and whereas the Jews made up only a small percentage of the countryside population, they dominated the cities. Thus, 30 percent of the population of Warsaw in 1931 (352,659) was Jewish. Jews were also a strong factor in such smaller urban centers as Lodz, Lvov, Cracow, Vilna, Czestochowa, Lublin and Sosnowiec. In fact, 80.9 percent of all Jews lived in cities. The rest were scattered in small shtetlach with an entirely different set of traditions and values.

The Jews of Poland also tended to have certain economic characteristics. They figured strongly and disproportionately in commerce and trade, while making up only a minuscule portion of workers in the agricultural and heavy industry areas.

Thus, one did not find very many Jewish miners, partly because of the government's exclusionary policies, but also because of tradition. There were tremendous numbers of Jewish peddlers, tailors and shopkeepers. The typical Jewish workers were tailors who barely survived on a subsistence wage. The typical Jewish middle-class person was a small shopkeeper or the owner of a stall in a street market. Economically, Jews tended to group near the bottom or the middle. The avenues of a career in government were closed to them, again because of the government's restrictive policies.

The Jews were in relatively high profile. In Poland, more than anywhere else, the questions of Jewish identity, aspirations and political orientation came into full flower, and the Polish response to the Jews in their midst was markedly different from the past. Jews had long been debating the issue of assimilation vs. nationhood, whether or not to become a part of the nation in which they resided. Should they be genuinely Polish or seek a nation of their own?

The debate had been building over centuries.

Since early in the twelfth century, the Jews of East Central Europe had undergone endless and turbulent ups and downs as they were swept up in the imperial ambitions and strife of numerous empires and conquering peoples. At one time or another, they lived under or at the mercy of Poles, Ukrainians, Belorussians, Latvians, Russians, Lithuanians and Germans.

By the sixteenth century, Jewish life had become governed by a "national" organization of Jews, a conference of four states that conducted religious affairs and was responsible for Jewish education and culture. The conference established and ran religious schools and seminaries (*Heder* and

Yeshiva) under the domination of the Rabbinate, the highest Jewish authority. Except for periodic messianic movements, Rabbinical authority was never seriously challenged until the middle of the nineteenth century, when strong responses to the Jews' condition of statelessness, dependence, and repression began to emerge.

The responses were basic: assimilationist, which saw the solution in almost total integration into the state; autonomist, which sought Jewish autonomy *within* the state and focused on gaining political and civil rights; and Zionist, with all its variations, from total autonomy within the state to emigration to Palestine and the creation of a Jewish homeland.

Dr. Leon Pinsker, a Zionist, saw the problem of the Jews' existence clearly. "Wherever the Jews reside," he wrote, "they cannot be assimilated, they cannot be readily digested by the nation." Assimilation, he contended, was no solution. Natives feared the Jews because they were "ghosts," not a nation. He saw Judeophobia as a European disease, a psychic aberration, a hereditary illness that had been transmitted for thousands of years. It would not pass, he warned.

Pinsker saw the Jews as "alien everywhere," making a mockery of assimilation. "Ill treatment," he said, "is a blow dealt to our faces. We can neither live nor die."[3]

The solution for Pinsker and others like him was a Jewish national home. It was not enough to obtain civil rights, and it was certainly dreamlike and unrealistic to await the Messiah, as the rabbinical movement taught.[4] "We finally," he said prophetically, "must have a home." Home to the fledgling Zionist movement was Palestine.

The growing political awareness of East European Jews began with a Jewish Enlightenment, known in Jewish history as the *Haskalah.* This movement sprang up from the French Revolution, gained momentum in the Napoleonic era, and then rolled west and east, capturing the imagination of Jewish intellectuals. To them, Haskalah spelled emancipation, an awakening and a hope for progress.

In the vanguard was the Haskalah's acknowledged father, Moses Mendelssohn, a German Jewish philosopher whose views were a rationally thought-out espousal of assimilation. He preached the idea of the virtuous Jew. Inherent in his ideas was a revolt against the orthodoxy and obscurantism of Rabbinicalism. This movement saw Judaism primarily as a religion, not a nationalist movement. Mendelssohn's motto was "Be a Jew at home and a gentile outside." The new Jew, while he was being a good citizen, would also clamor for legal, civic and religious rights.

Haskalah was a fresh intellectual wind from Germany, which was more affluent than Poland. In Poland, Haskalah took on a different aspect, more inwardly directed, less concerned with changes in prayer and style of worshipping. The movement in Poland focused on rediscovery, and sparked a resurgence of Hebrew literature and love of the Hebrew language. It also sparked a move toward autonomy, signaling the beginning of a struggle for civil rights in Poland.

The Zionists, with an eye toward establishing a homeland, were less enthusiastic about civil rights. "Regrettably," writes Norman Davies, the English historian of modern Poland, "the condition of Polish Jewry is often described out of context. It has always lain in the interests of the Zionist movement, which sought to persuade the Jews to leave their homes in Poland, to paint Polish life in the most unfavorable colours." However, the Zionist viewpoint was hardly representative of the Jewish masses. Many Jews resigned themselves to joining the struggle for rights in Poland. A network of Jewish publications sprouted up, the voices of diverse political movements and organizations.

All of this activity was shaped and sparked by the results of Polish independence, from which the Jews took an unjustified amount of hope.

The growth of Jewish political parties in the Polish provinces, for example, marks a striking parallel with the Polish politics of the time. The demands of the Zionists for a national secular homeland also matched those of the Polish National Democrats, whose ambivalent relationship to the Church matched the Zionist's ambivalence toward traditional Judaism. Yet this was the prime anti-Semitic party. The 1920s, and even more so the 1930s, was a fractious time for Jewish causes, as groups and organizations rose only to split asunder into warring factions. Division over the issues of assimilation, Zionism, secularism, Marxism and nationalism, and traditionalism produced a large number of political followings. On the left were the Poale Zion Party, which was split between Zionists and Marxists and the anti-Zionist Marxist *Bund.* The moderates were represented by the Youth of Zion Party. The centrist Zionist parties included the religious Mizrachi and the Folkspartei. The anti-Zionists were led by the Orthodox Agudas Yisroel. All of them, including Zeev Jabotinsky's Revisionist Zionists, sprouted youth parties and dissident movements.

To get a clear picture of divisive Jewish politics, which were much like those of the bitterly divided Polish political parties, one has only to look at the various splinter groups that emerged under the banner of Zionism: There were six Zionist-socialist or Zionist-labor parties and five general Zionist parties. All of them had splinter groups and youth movements. How did they become so prominent?

When change swept over the Jewish community at the end of World War I, the traditional synagogue was no longer the cultural and political center. This center shifted to the youth and to the various youth movements that had emerged. The ideologues of Socialist Zionism, religious Zionism, and Revisionist Zionism saw their national successors within the youth movement.

It was vastly different to belong to a youth movement than to belong to a boys' club or boy scout group. The youth movements mobilized and imbued young people with the ideas, ideology and goals of the movement itself.

The movements were multivaried, multipolitical, and multiideological, and sprouted up continuously among all ranks of Zionism. They attracted primarily the offspring of the middle and artisan class. The clubs met two to three times a week, after school and in the early evening. The meetings included a program of recreation, poetry, literature readings, discussions and conversations of a political nature. The spirit of the youth movements touched Poles and Jews alike.

The Zionist youth movements emphasized the learning of Hebrew, the celebration of Jewish Nationalist holidays, and the veneration of the ideology and personalities of its leaders.

To attract and recruit new members, the youth movements organized sports and summer camps, where Zionist *achshara* (preparation) took place. Next to home life, these movements became the vehicle for Zionist education. Frequently they published their own newspapers and magazines. Belonging to the movement guaranteed community approval and participation.

Dov Zeev Begin also felt that his son Menachem should join a movement, but one that was the least ideologically inclined and most proper. Begin began with Hashomer Hatzair, which was far removed from proper. Initially, it was a boy scout movement displaying none of its fervor for the land of Palestine until much later. It became a stridently Marxist movement by the late 1920s.

Much of this heated political activity was sparked by Polish independence. The Jews were swept up in the euphoria over Polish nationhood; in 1919, Allied leaders at the Paris Conference aware of the need to provide international guarantees to minorities in the successor states succeeded in forcing the reluctant Poles to sign a Minorities Charter with the victorious powers.

Two of the articles dealt directly with the Jews. Jews were to have their own schools, controlled by Jewish authorities and funded by the state. The second statute forbade the authorities to compel Jews to violate the Sabbath.

The reality proved to be unsettling. The Poles resented the Charter and were aghast at the prospect of any sort of Jewish autonomy within Poland. While many Zionists improbably saw the document as some sort of civil rights Magna Carta, the Poles saw it as a usurpation of their national right and set about stifling any prospect of Jewish autonomy.

Jews were indeed allowed to establish Yiddish and Hebrew language schools of their own, but the state did not pay for them and made life difficult for such schools. The government made sure that graduates of Jewish schools could not enter Polish universities.

The years immediately after World War I were trying times for the Jews of Poland, as Poles grew increasingly hostile toward them. There was systematic discrimination and widespread anti-Semitic violence. The new pogroms, beginning in Lvov in 1918, in which Polish troops were allowed to kill Jews and loot property, were typical. According to the leading Hebrew newspaper of the day, it was an ironic apocalypse. "In this hour," a lead editorial stated, "the hour of the rebirth and reunification of Poland, the hour of Poland's victory over her enemies, who arose to tear away from her the city of Lvov—in this hour we Jews sit and mourn for our victims, the victims of the terrible pogroms, the slaughtered and murdered."

For many Jews, Pilsudski, the leading Polish political figure, represented a form of salvation. Second to him was his rival and antagonist, Roman Dmowski, the anti-Semitic leader of the National Democrats.

Dmowski was rabidly nationalistic, conservative, and anti-Semitic. In the eyes of his followers he was a Polish patriot, but for Dmowski, Poland did not include the Jews.

Dmowski exploited anti-Semitism for political purposes. He described the "Jewish danger," posed by potential assimilation: ". . . in the character of this race [the Jews] so many different values, strange to our moral constitution and harmful to our life, have accumulated that assimilation with a larger number of Jews would destroy us, replacing with decadent elements those young creative foundations upon which we are building our future."[5]

Jews, he warned, would undermine the Polish national character. Dmowski argued like the Nazis that the Jews "instinctively seek to destroy the European environment." They are, he shouted, our society's "lethal enemy and they must be gotten rid of."

By contrast, Pilsudski was tolerant. Although he was not by any stretch of the imagination the champion of Jews, under his rule, beginning in 1926, Jews in Poland enjoyed something of a golden age. More importantly, Pilsudski's concept of coupling nationalistic aspirations with military action made him a hero of the Revisionist stamp.

Marshall Józef Pilsudski, a figure revered by many Jews, declared the Second Polish Republic. Poland, he announced, would be for the Poles once again.

First, Pilsudski and his fledgling army had to survive a military threat from the new Bolshevik regime in Moscow, which was casting the red shadow of Communism all over Europe. As Poland had been the savior of Europe against the Turks in the sixteenth century, Pilsudski and the Poles now stood as the savior of Europe against the rising tide of Bolshevism. The red surge actually broke up at the gates of Warsaw, where Pilsudski, with some daring military tactics, won a decisive battle. The victory strengthened the mythology and charisma of Pilsudski, but it also made the various political powers in Poland wary of him. The 1921 constitution, ostensibly liberal and democratic, was not so much a whiff of democratic springtime as it was a tactic to keep Pilsudski out of power. In this, it did not succeed. Pilsudski, with the help of his fellow officers, took power in a coup d'état in 1926, thus ending the Republic and implementing a strong federalist concept that was at once autocratic and tolerant, a form of benevolent despotism.

His principal success, his historical astuteness, was that he understood that Poland was a multinational, multiethnic land. As a Lithuanian Pole, he understood that the polyglot national state must accommodate its minorities. His legacy, however, was not only Federalism, but also the coup d'état. Unfortunately his successors turned out to be small men, incompetent and not nearly strong enough to offer serious resistance to the challenge of Hitler.

What Zionists like Jabotinsky admired about Pilsudski, however, was not his concepts of government, but his success with arms. They gaped in awe at the creation of Polish legions and Jabotinsky and Yoseph Trumpeldor created the Jewish Legions of World War I in their image. Above all, they admired and emulated Pilsudski's use of arms and military might to achieve the aims of nationalism.

Pilsudski, as commander of the Polish Legions, and as the hero of the war against Russia, was the Polish equivalent of a Garibaldi, whom Jabotinsky also admired greatly. Begin, too, like all Betarim, respected and admired Pilsudski.

Like Begin, he was an underground fighter and was imprisoned in Siberia. Also like Begin, he was a student in schools where his identity (as a Pole) was forcibly submerged. He was also a military hero (which Begin was not), the organizer and leader of a Polish legion which fought alongside Austro-Hungarian troops. So strong was the Zionists' admiration that when Pilsudski died in 1935, hordes of Betarim showed up in full uniform to honor the old marshall.

In Brisk, Eastern Poland, where Begin was born and intermittently grew up, the Jews played the role of the middleman as they did in many cities in Poland. They had developed their own political institutions, including two gymnasiums, two *Tarbut*—one modern and secular, the other traditional and orthodox. The Jewish organizations in Brisk ran the high schools and the medical, cultural and welfare institutions, very much as these institutions would later develop in Palestine. At the time, Zionism was just beginning to emerge as a philosophical, cultural and political force, albeit a divided one.

Begin often likes to reminisce about his childhood. When he talks about Brisk and the Jewish life of that time, he tends to imbue it with romantic hues and tones, alternating with the bitterness of a Jew living in the world of goyim. The memories are exaggerated, vivid, and not always tightly embraced by the truth.

"I have never asked whether it would be wise for me to fly to Johannesburg or New York (long-time strongholds of Betar)," he once said when talking about Poland at great length. "But I wonder if I will return to visit the city [Brisk] where I spent my sunnier days. It's possible the house mixed with love and sorrow is still there. Would I come back home to streets where there are no answers to be heard? Only shadows will greet me. No one could even take me to the cemetery since the generation of the Holocaust were not lucky, enough to be buried. But there, I see the house in which we lived after Polish independence, on the street named after one of the old kings—[Zygmunt I, 1506–48]. In that street I passed my childhood, my semichildhood . . . When I was a boy, I was thrown into the total human revolution, World War I. I remember the first time I saw the bayonets of a Soviet soldier, in 1920 . . . In that street on Zygmunt Street, a little child's eyes saw not one goyim regime, but one goyim regime after another. The pogroms did not skip our home. I remember when my father was called to another street where soldiers were marching to celebrate Polish Independence. My father left, and the rumors were that he would not return, that he had been shot. In fact, one of the soldiers pointed a gun at my father, but missed his target. The rumor chilled my blood. . . ."

"That house on Zygmunt Street, what terrible and holy remains are amongst its walls. Here is a small wooden house that is about to collapse, there I learned my first Hebrew, and in unison with other small children, I recited *Kometz Aleph-A* [the ABCs] . . . Here is the two-story house where I was taught to think in Hebrew. Here was the synagogue that was always set in darkness; here was the stooped and black-eyed Rabbi, who taught us how to hold the shawl for two.

And, at the end of the city, I remember that red-bricked, big, terrible house where we learned the foreigner's language [Polish], and the hatred of Israel. The children of the goyim in their hundreds, the Jewish children in their tens. We bought knowledge with a price, being beaten day after day, insulted, shoved, but through all this we learned to defend ourselves against those who insult us. Yet on the other side of town, there was a white brick house, a school, not Jewish, not goyim. There we were not beaten, but we fought, and that was also symbolic of our patient defense of the uniqueness of Israel . . . Thereafter, I learned—to love Jews—not to be afraid of the goyim, and that it was good that a man carried his burdens when already young."[6]

Here is a vividly nostalgic picture of the budding rebel and leader, influenced by a beloved and rebellious father, witness to great events. This young Begin was not yet much of a rebel, although he lived in tumultuous times, and great events rippled over his home and family. He was not much of a leader or even very prescient until the middle of his life.

Begin's father, Dov Zeev Begin, was more of a rebel than his son, but he was first and foremost a pragmatist and survivor. He was born into a family of nine children, the son of David Eliezer, a prosperous lumber merchant who had started out in the nearby district of Polsha before moving to Brisk. David Eliezer lived in a large house and ran a far-flung business that reached as far as Warsaw and Danzig, considerable distances for the time. Dov Zeev was a brilliant Yeshiva student and a briefly rebellious son.

At the age of seventeen, he tried to run away from home to study medicine in Berlin. He never got past the railroad station, where his father found him waiting for the train and quickly took him home. Somewhat cowed, Dov Zeev became his father's assistant in the lumber business and got to see the great wide world in a more practical manner, traveling with his father throughout Poland and Germany. These trips were revelations for the young, traditionally educated Jewish boy, revelations which pierced the barriers and restrictions of orthodox community life.

Dov Zeev began to come in touch with the Jewish Renaissance Movement of East European Jewry. Even though he was steeped in Jewish communal traditions, he slowly emerged as a Zionist. But although he became more secular, he did not abandon traditional community life. Thus he became a political rival to the reigning orthodox party in Brisk. In 1904, when the rabbi of the Great Synagogue of Brisk tried to prevent a memorial service for Theodor Herzl, the spiritual father of Zionism who had just died, Dov Zeev took an axe and broke down the synagogue door to hold a sparsely attended memorial service.

With exceptions like the Herzl incident and the abortive bid to run away from home, Dov Zeev strove for conventionality and success in his life. He remained in Brisk, whereas his friend Mordecai Shienerman, father of Ariel Sharon, emigrated to Palestine.

In Brisk, Dov Zeev met Hasia Kosovsky, Begin's mother, who came from a rabbinical family in Vohlin, Lithuania, the center of Talmudic learning. Upon his marriage to Hasia Kosovsky, the granddaughter of a moderately wealthy wood merchant, Dov Zeev settled down to a life as a clerk in the local bank in Brisk. But, his preoccupations continued to be public ones.

Dov and Hasia were married in 1906 in Kurtiz, and the union produced three children—Rachel, the eldest, Menachem, and Herzl (now dead). Hasia was Dov's second wife. There was a first wife, from whom he was divorced, about whom there is no record. None of the Begin children ever spoke publicly of their father's first marriage.

Begin hardly ever spoke of his own mother. His first son, Benyamin Zeev is named after his father. His second child, a girl, was named after his mother. We can only speculate that Hasia must have been a traditional Jewish wife, one subservient to her husband. At any rate, there is no noticeable attachment to his mother on the part of Menachem. Until the coming of Zeev Jabotinsky, his father was always his model.

To this day, Begin likes to portray his early youth as being lived partly in abject poverty, a picture that is not strictly true. There was no water or electricity in the Begin home, but this was not uncommon for most Jews living in Brisk and, in fact, for the majority of Poles. The truth of the matter is that Begin's youth was a typically middle-class existence for the time, affected as they were by the turbulence of the war and its immediate aftermath.

In 1915, the eastern front of the war came down on Brisk. The Russians moved in looting, murdering, and mutilating Jews in their wake. (Eventually the town was destroyed in the war.) Not surprisingly, many of the Jews of Brisk, Dov Begin among them, were actively pro-German, because at that time German rule was much more tolerant and benevolent to Jews than Russian or Polish rule.

My own father received his only real education in Bialystok under the aegis of the German conqueror in 1917. He never stopped reminding me throughout his life of the image of the well-dressed, correct German principal to whom he owed his fluency in German and the gift of a "Western education." Dov Zeev Begin was very likely no different.

Dov Zeev was arrested by the returning Russians on suspicion, a correct one, of being pro-German. The Russians packed Dov Zeev off to Siberia. The family dispersed toward Kovno and Vilna, with Dov Zeev feared dead. The family at first found refuge with a cousin in Drohiczyn. Meanwhile, the elder Begin, Menachem's grandfather, made do in his own way, having found an abandoned house in the forest off the River Bug. Dov Zeev somehow escaped the Russians and found his way to Warsaw. From there, he trudged to Drohiczyn, where, like some figure out of a fairy tale, he happened upon his daughter Rachel. The family was reunited and eventually moved in with their grandfather.

Until the coming of Jabotinsky, Begin's father had been his primary influence. His father's way of life was his way of life—meaning both adventuresome and highly traditional. Thus, the family was at the center of Begin's life—he revered, respected, and emulated his father and saw his mother—he told me but never wrote—was nothing less than the Jewish equivalent of a saint. Often, in his later life, when Begin talked about Revisionism and his early political career, it sounded as if he were a highly active, innovative, and rebellious leader. The truth is he followed his father wherever his father led him. Begin's youth was an act of respect and emulation played out against the background of Polish nationalism and Jewish factionalism.

Begin was a leader only in the reflected glory of his father's position in the community. In education, in politics, in culture, he followed his father. Begin today is well known for his prowess at and passion for chess; it was a game learned at his father's knee. His early life was laid out and planned by his father.

One need only to look at Dov Zeev to know how Begin's was forged. Dov Zeev had many vocations and preoccupations: He was secretary of the Kehilah in Brisk; he was a Zionist; he was a lover of literature; he was a linguist, a social conservative and something of an ardent Zionist, which was considered radical in his time.

Technically speaking, he was not a professional, since he held no degree even though he undoubtedly possessed the skills required to earn one.

He remained active in the Zionist movement and the Jewish self-defense movement. Dov Zeev developed Menachem's desire for secular learning, for languages, for a career as a lawyer and Zionist. As a way of fulfilling his own aspirations, Dov Zeev wanted to make certain his son acquired a degree.

Disciplined by his father, Begin was never thought to rebel, as several of the Socialist-Zionist leaders did. He accepted his father's authority, his lifestyle, and his politics. He grew up as the proverbial good son, well mannered, well dressed, disciplined, and professionally oriented. Reflecting his father's ambition and bringing an aura of professional pride into the household, Begin became a lawyer.

When Dov Zeev returned to war-ravaged Brisk, he assumed the role of a nonlicensed notary public and negotiator, using his language skills and fulfilling his hunger to be involved in public community activities. He organized Jewish holidays in schools and negotiated with the authorities to allow Jewish festivities and education. He was active in the furthering of Jewish education and in restoring Jewish life in Brisk, and he even persuaded the occupying German authorities to repair the roof of the local synagogue. In addition he restored the Jewish archives and organized a Jewish census.

One can get a sense of the man from a period photograph: with a distinguished beard, wearing a high necktie and black tuxedo, he appeared a formal, traditional and ambitious man, a man at ease and imposing in public. His father was an ideal to which Begin would forever aspire, and no doubt Begin inherited some of his negotiating skills from him.

Thus, Begin's formative years were spent in a traditional Jewish community. In this he was markedly different from both Jabotinsky, whose background was urban and secular, and Ben Gurion, who was formed in the wilderness of Palestine. Begin could best be described as a typical, middle-class Zionist youth. As a child he was taught to respect family, tradition, success and property.

The young men and women of Begin's generation were seeking a

synthesis which would blend activism and nationalism with traditional Jewish aspirations, whereas Zionism, as practiced by the Socialists in Palestine,
was steeped in revolt against traditional values. Jabotinsky would develop
that synthesis for them.

Jabotinsky doubted the sincerity of the post–World War I Polish regime. He admired the aspirations of Pilsudski's nationalism, but he feared
that the new nation's inherent Catholic base was linked to anti-Semitism,
and he was right, but he also hoped against hope that the new regime would
be liberal and tolerant of diversity.

There were some similarities between Zionism and Polish nationalism,
two movements that were antagonistic but also attracted to each other.

The Revisionist Zionists were inspired by Polish nationalism. Non-
Zionist Jews, too, looked at Polish nationalism as a vehicle which would
hopefully achieve Jewish equality within Poland. This was the attitude of
Jewish assimilationists, who rejected Zionism because it might interfere
with their aspiration to be assimilated Poles.

The Poles, however, looked at Zionism with a jaundiced eye. There
was no denying the rampant anti-Semitism in Poland. It was something a
Jew could feel in his everyday life. Jews could not mix with Poles in school;
at the university they had to sit in the back of the lecture halls. Cafes and
theaters were restricted.

To be a Jew in independent Poland, to quote Professor Richard Pipes,
the Harvard historian, was "like being black in America."

Like many other nationalist Jews, Begin was ambivalent about Poland,
admiring the spirit of nationalism, but hating the anti-Semitism and the
suffering it entailed for the Jews.

The test of Polish intentions in the post–World War I period was how
faithfully the newly independent nation would deliver on Jewish civil rights.
The Jews at first saw nothing but hope in the new nation, in the very fact of
independence. As Norman Davies wrote, "The rebirth of Poland seemed to
many Jews to herald the crossing of the Jordan."

As a result, many Jews volunteered for the Polish Army, even though
extreme Polish nationalists had tried to intern all Jews during the battle for
Warsaw. The majority of Jews decided, with some misgivings, to cooperate
with the government.

The Zionists were caught in a dilemma. They were captured by the
romanticism of nationalism, with its colorful and proud Polish legions. They
were also attracted to the momentous events which were beginning to shape
Jewish history, such as the implications of the Balfour Declaration. All of
these new winds gave rise to activism and brought a surge in the creation of
Jewish youth movements. One of these was Hashomer Hatzair, the Young
Scout Movement, of which young Menachem Begin eventually became a
member.

A lot of mythology surrounds Begin's membership in this organization, especially the manner of his leaving. The story, as Begin and his followers tell it, amounts to that of a man seeing a vision, seeing the specter of Marxism and Communism, seeing, so to speak, the light of conversion. Begin, chagrined that his record shows his membership, tells everyone he left because the group began to show Marxist and radical leanings. This is not even close to the truth.

Hashomer Hatzair was a movement named after heroic Jewish guards who protected pioneer settlements against Arab marauders. The image of armed Jewish cowboys of Galilee on horseback appealed to Jewish youth in Eastern Europe. The thematic appeal was romantic and a little militant. Its appeal was that it was one of the first youth movements begun by youth, without links to old political and ideological parties.

But in Brisk, the movement was essentially harmless, a boy scout club with few political overtones. Most of Hashomer Hatzair's members came from the Jewish middle class, sons and daughters of merchants, professionals, and semiwealthy artisans. In Brisk, the group was a glorified boy scout movement. Begin joined at the recommendation of his father, one of the adult sponsors of Hashomer Hatzair in Brisk, where it was clearly nonpolitical, nonideological and "safe." When Begin joined Hashomer Hatzair, it was not an activist, Palestine-oriented group. It gave lip service to "Next Year in Jerusalem," in a vague way which had nothing to do with uprooting the everyday life of its members.

Certainly Dov Zeev Begin thought it was a suitable club for his children, since he sent all three of them there. Hashomer in Brisk was committed to scoutism and to very traditional Jewish traditions and concepts of education.

Begin joined in 1925, at the age of twelve. After his bar mitzvah at thirteen, he left. His tenure was very inauspicious and quiet, contrary to the mythology, which had Begin writing stirring essays and speechifying at great length. It was very much a family affair—Begin's father was on the governing board and Begin's first instructor in Hashomer Hatzair was his sister Rachel.

Begin did leave in 1926 but not because Hashomer was veering leftward. Dov Zeev was behind his son's withdrawal. He did not feel that Hashomer Hatzair was politically suspect as much as he wanted Menachem to pursue a more traditional career, and he could not do it with Hashomer Hatzair as a base. He wanted his son to join the Polish state gymnasium, and his parents feared that if Menachem belonged to Hashomer Hatzair, he might not be admitted.

Begin's father wanted him to be a lawyer, not a pioneer in Palestine as Hashomer Hatzair required, and Menachem acquiesced. Except in his romantic rhetoric, Palestine was the furthest thing from his mind. In the Polish gymnasium, no matter what hardships, slurs and taunts he endured, he could at least work toward a professional career that would be played out in Poland. He wanted to become a lawyer.[7]

In Poland, Begin learned to appreciate not pioneer values, but nationalistic and patriotic ideology. Although Polish nationalism was steeped in anti-Semitism, its substance was full of heroism, romanticism, militarism, and political action, all of which appealed to the somewhat dreamy and impressionable middle-class Jewish youth of Poland.

Betar, Jabotinsky's youth movement, was established between 1924 and 1925. Unlike the socialist youth movements, Betar drew on the middle-class Jewish population. It was a nationalistic and educational movement to support Jabotinsky's new Zionism.

Betar fit perfectly with Dov Zeev Begin's aspirations and Menachem's romanticism. Betar espoused political and military action while upholding traditional values. Betar would be a Zionist solution without the added pain of emigration, romance without reality. Going to Palestine would have meant Begin's giving up his legal career, since Polish degrees were not recognized in Palestine.

Begin, in short, did not revolt or even struggle over the choice. He was moved into Betar by his father. Others did choose the Zionist youth as a revolt against their elders. Ben Gurion told me of one such case, that of his friend Shlomo Zemach, from Plonsk, Poland. According to Ben Gurion, Zemach Senior was a "respectable and notable [member of] our community who was enamored of Socialist Zionism. On his way to Palestine in 1903, Ben Gurion stayed in Warsaw to help with a Socialist-Zionist paper. Zemach looked him up. He had run away from home and was looking for a place to hide from his father. Zemach's father showed up in the editorial room looking for his son. Ben Gurion pleaded ignorance. He felt that he could not convince the father that pioneer work in Palestine would be better "than becoming a lawyer in Poland."[8]

Menachem Begin, it is safe to say, never gave the matter a second thought. Until his rise in Betar, Begin was essentially under Dov Zeev's shadow. Now, as the late 1920s and 1930s dawned, another, equally large star emerged in Begin's firmament.

That star was Jabotinsky and the movement he created.

When Begin started out in Betar, it was a time of mass movements all over Europe, within Poland, in Germany, Russia, and Italy, and among the ranks of the Jews. Polish nationalism flourished, as did Communism and Fascism, as well as a variety of Jewish Zionist movements.

The late 1920s and the early and mid 1930s constituted a golden age for Zionism within Poland. It was the beginning of a tremendous Jewish political awakening in the Diaspora. But, as usual, it was marked by fratricidal arguments; Zionist parties were divided among the Left, Right and Center.

Initially, while history and great movements swirled around him, Begin, like many others, operated on the margins. The image one gets is of a slight, dogged individual. There are really no detailed records of deeds, speeches or activities, but one can presume that Begin was very much like any rising young Betarim. Most young Jewish men who became involved in Zionist parties were working as volunteers, fueled mainly by idealism. Very few of them became full-time party employees. Jabotinsky himself earned his living as a journalist, translator, poet and lecturer.

Party functionaries like Begin usually had another career, or were supported by their parents. Begin most likely earned money as a legal aide, and was later helped by his wife's better-off parents; the couple never seemed to have enough money.

The initial activities of Betar functionaries like Begin were most likely centered around recruitment and propaganda. Thus, Begin went from door to door among the homes of friends in Brisk, trying to get parental approval for their children to join Betar. As a functionary, he was also involved in writing propaganda and educational material. He distributed literature and led discussion and indoctrination groups.

Betar was created primarily to be a youth group, a preparatory and recruitment school whose graduates would eventually evolve into the adult ranks of Revisionism, or Zohar. The function of Betar was to recruit youths just past bar mitzvah age from Jewish and Polish schools. It was an arduous task, because competition among the various Zionist groups was fierce. Thus, Betar started out as a movement that was a combination of boy scouts, active nationalists and a cradle ground for future Revisionists.

Graduation from Betar meant becoming a dedicated Revisionist—for some the movement would become a life's work. In any case, it meant following the concepts and precepts of one man—Zeev Jabotinsky, who became the shining ideological and political light in the life of Begin.

4

Jabotinsky's Legions[1]

Even in his muted retirement, the popular conception of Menachem Begin is that of a leader, a man in the vanguard of nation, movements, ideologies and armies. Much of this conception stems from his seven years as Israel's Prime Minister, as well as from the mythology that surrounds his years as leader of the underground Etzel before and during the War of Independence.

Obviously, Begin prefers to think of himself as an important historical figure, and so do his followers, sycophants and biographers. He sees himself as both leader and disciple, a propagator of Revisionist Zionism and faithful student of its founder, Vladimir (Zeev) Jabotinsky.

Begin's rhetoric and flamboyant gestures propagate a picture that is muddled and misleading, a picture of Begin and Jabotinsky as almost twins —one older, the other younger; one the founder, the other the heir apparent. A portrait emerges that feels warm, intimate and close

There is no questioning one aspect of this picture, and that is Begin's loyalty to Jabotinsky—if not to his basic tenets, then certainly to the man. But it is also misleading: Begin was not yet a leader and firebrand but was still being molded by strong figures like his father or Jabotinsky. He does not come into his own until he takes command of Etzel. Moreover, even late in his career he was admiring military leaders like Moshe Dayan and Ariel Sharon.

U. Z. Gruenberg, the poet-laureate of romantic and radical Zionism, described Jabotinsky as the would-be hero of the great Zionist romantic novel, ". . . writer and politician, leader and orator, beloved and scorned, the playboy and the bad boy of the Hebrew national movement, the founder of the Jewish legions, the conqueror of Palestine . . . in spite of

Zionism . . . the most stubborn believer among the few of our national renaissance."[2] For Gruenberg, Jabotinsky was "the richest in spiritual properties of all Zionists since Herzl and Nordau."[3] Begin echoed Gruenberg, seeing Jabotinsky as an anointed messiah of Zionism, when he wrote that "no other leader of Zion was bestowed with the oil and perfume of kings, no leader of Zion spoke more eloquently, in more languages and in more places, than Jabotinsky. No leader represented the idea of *Mamlach-tiout* [kingdom, etatism] better than Jabotinsky."[4]

Begin called Jabotinsky "the exalted, a father and a rabbi." As late as 1950, Begin wrote in a special issue on Jabotinsky in *Herut* that Jabotinsky was a man who lived his ideology and his doctrine, who left us, his disciples, guided in his deeds and beliefs as our ways.[5] Twenty-five years after he first met his mentor, Begin's admiration for Jabotinsky had not diminished.

For the young Begin, Jabotinsky's aura, his immense charisma, were impressive and dazzling. Early in his career, as a junior political operator in the fledgling Betar movement, he could only admire Jabotinsky from afar, a situation that in fact, never changed in all of the following years.

Begin would reminisce about what the young could still learn from Jabotinsky: "The idea of a state, of a Jewish statehood fired me and my generation's imagination."[6] If Marxism and world revolution inspired young Socialist Zionists, then Jabotinsky's call for *Hadar,* or Jewish majesty, turned Begin from a middle-class would-be lawyer into a Betari, a Jewish nationalist and future revolutionary.

Jabotinsky could inspire in a multitude of ways. Already an accomplished intellectual, poet, writer and speechifier, he assured himself a place in legend when in 1920 he organized a Jewish defense group which became the Haganah created to fight Arab rioters. In 1920 he was arrested and imprisoned in Jerusalem by the British for organizing a strike. Eventually he was forced to leave Palestine by a British order in 1929. By the time Begin first heard of the Jabotinsky legend, Jabotinsky, along with Trumpeldor, was already the founding father of the Jewish legions. Now, he was more than an orator and rhetorician. He was a hero, and that impressed the impressionables—Begin among them.

For the Socialist Zionists, the new Jew was a pioneer spirit, imbued with the idea of reclaiming the land; for the Betarim he was a fighter standing tall and proud. That idea must have been especially appealing to a bookish young law student like Begin. The philosopher would somehow transform him, if not outwardly then inwardly. Begin was never more proud than when friends and foes alike would call him a "gentleman," like Jabotinsky. He would wear suits no matter how hot the weather to reinforce the image.

Jabotinsky instilled Hadar in Begin, a quality that the Polish life of the 1920s and 1930s failed to offer him. Hadar, as Jabotinsky described it in a work of fiction, was majesty, an act of magic, the magic of self-defense, resistance, military preparedness, even terror—and liberation.

In his novel *Samson*, Jabotinsky's fictional Samson calls for iron to fight the Philistines. What the Jews needed was a king to lead them, and iron to fight to be free. That was Samson's legacy; that was Jabotinsky's legacy to Begin, which he would nurture all of his life.

"What else did we learn from Jabotinsky?", Begin wrote in *Herut*. "He simply taught us to shoot, no more, no less than to shoot".[7] Then he would write, "The key is in war, that's what Jabotinsky taught us, not begging. Our policy is not diplomacy. A war of liberation is the most glorious of all revolutions."[8]

He further described how Jabotinsky taught them, "to love the land, the nation, Eretz Israel. If my country is poor, it is mine nevertheless . . . Character above all . . . Belief, a mighty one. One that cannot be described in simple language. A superior belief that our nation, despite all, will deliver its own freedom and independence."[9]

Jabotinsky instilled character into Begin; his influence would become a kind of dogma, an altar at which he worshiped and to which he would always return.

However, this was no master-disciple relationship with the disciple in close proximity to the master, dutifully gathering in every word. Nor was Begin's rise in the ranks of Betar and Etzel inevitable or prodded and pushed by Jabotinsky. When Begin takes on the mantle of Jabotinsky, he is toying with history, hoping to take on the aura of his master's greatness.

Jabotinsky, in all his activities with Betar, was never close to Begin and exchanged mainly formal notes with him. Their age difference and Betar's hierarchical structure had much to do with their rather formal relationship, however cordial. Theirs was not a relationship of comrades but one in which Begin worshiped the master from afar and remained loyal to him, even when the ranks of Betar were jolted with dissension and acrimony.

Begin may have tried to emulate Jabotinsky, and he cleaved to the master's ideas, but the two men could hardly have been more different.

Begin, when all is said and done, is a prosaic man, an ascetic who cares little for the finer pleasures of life, a mundane man whose upbringing and much of his life in Poland was a study in the blandness of traditional middle-class life. Far from being a leader, young Begin was a classic movement and party *apparatchik*, an operator—steady, patient, a man with few original ideas of his own. He was to develop his skills as an orator late in the 1930s. Begin wrote, but he wrote badly—the proof lies in his two published works, *White Nights* and *The Revolt*—which, while of historical value, are a tortuous chore to read, full of self-proclamation and polemic.

He had however, a gift for politics and an even greater gift for oratory. A different Begin emerges when he stands up to speak; the rhetoric flows as naturally and as passionately as a windstorm. It is this gift, as well as his patient work within the Revisionist Movement, which accounts for his rise in the ranks, his painfully slow elevation toward the top.

Begin, as Israel's Prime Minister, would change the map of the Middle East and the whole nature of Arab-Israeli relations. The irony is that Jabotinsky, who was a genuinely great man, never had the opportunity to see his ideas take fruit in such a strange way, in the hands of what must have seemed to him one of his not so outstanding but loyal disciples.

Jabotinsky was a man of huge, variable and far-reaching gifts, a man who seemed comfortable from the start in striding the stage of history; he seemed made for it. In the age of the common man, he was, as his biographer and chief aide, Joseph B. Schechtman, says of him, "an uncommon man."

He had the sensibilities of both a poet and a leader. As a writer, he transcended genres and moved smoothly from fiction to poetry, pamphleteering, essays, speeches, even to rhymes. He was an original thinker, a passionate Zionist, a soldier, an organizer, a man of great humor, a world traveler, a superb linguist.

"While Jabotinsky lived," Schechtman writes, "no man in Jewry or any other Western nation surpassed him in the range and intensity of his activities, in the fertility of his thinking and multiplicity of his interests. Here is a man of vision and action, who pursued truth where he saw it, a fighter who never admitted defeat; here is a political leader and a poet, an orator and a soldier, a publicist, diplomat and linguist. Starting out as a noted Russian journalist, he became a man of letters who wrote in seven languages and whose writings were published in at least twice as many tongues. Here is a man who repeatedly was arrested by the Czarist police; a man who translated Dante into Hebrew, and the poet Bialik into Russian; the man who created the first Jewish Legion in World War I and who was sentenced to fifteen years of hard labor by a British military court in Palestine for defending the Jews of Jerusalem against Arab attack. Here is a man who with his battalion helped to cross the Jordan and was rewarded with the Medal of the British Empire—and twelve years later was permanently barred by the British from re-entering Palestine. This man, reared in the best traditions of nineteenth-century liberalism, was later decried as a Fascist and militarist . . . No other political leader in modern Jewry has been so passionately revered and so fiercely hated, followed so enthusiastically and attacked so bitterly. To many he was a prophet, to others, an irresponsible adventurer. His life was tense, stormy, controversial—the life of a man who may be described as a political poet in action, always far ahead of his contemporaries."

It is not my purpose here to give a detailed account of Jabotinsky's life, although some salient moments are worth noting. More important are Jabotinsky's effect on Begin's thinking and life, and the essense of Jabotinsky's ideas as they are reflected in Revisionist Zionism. Most important of all is Jabotinsky's evolution toward the idea of Jewish Legions, an idea which would form the core of Betar, in which Begin began his political life.

Jabotinsky came from a fairly well-off middle-class family in Odessa, where he was born on October 5, 1880. The Jewish community in Odessa was very much a part of the entire city and existed, in poverty and in wealth, among all the social strata. In this bustling, heterogeneous seaport, everyone was a newcomer, so the Jews did not feel as if they were outsiders. Nothing in Jabotinsky's schooling awakened him to Zionism or political activities.

Zionism was latent in him, and as he began to travel, it began to emerge—where he worked as a correspondent for Odessa papers in Rome, and in Berne, perhaps even earlier. But what most awakened Jabotinsky's fire and his Zionism were the Russian pogroms.

In 1903, rumors of pogroms began to stir in Odessa. With amazing prescience, Jabotinsky, then a journalist and something of a budding Zionist, set about to organize a Jewish defense, even though at heart he knew that it was a hopeless project.

Nevertheless, his immediate efforts proved effective. Perhaps because of the prospect of an active Jewish defense, Odessa was spared the bloody pogroms suffered by nearby villages and towns.

One can see the beginning of his passionate Zionism in his activities in Odessa, from his organizational abilities to his pamphleteering against the pogroms. Here, too, may have stirred in his mind the first glimmer of Jewish armed forces as an effective tool toward gaining statehood.

Predictably, Jabotinsky's ideas and goals sparked conflict with the political forces of the Yishuv, led by David Ben Gurion; with the World Zionist Organization, led by Chaim Weizmann; with radical splinters in his own movement; and with the British. But Jabotinsky was used to controversy and opposition. At the core of the controversy was his practical ideal of Jewish Legions.

It is worth looking in some detail at the creation of the first Jewish Legions, where they came from, and where they led. They would become the model for Betar, a movement that would have the appearance of Jewish Legions, but that would end as both a political and a guerrilla force, with a character entirely different from Jabotinsky's original conception.

Jabotinsky had begun thinking about Jewish defense—meaning a form of militarism—at an early age. To him this notion was not necessarily revolutionary, but rather legal, and absolutely necessary in order to achieve statehood.

Jabotinsky had inspiration close at hand—Józef Pilsudski and his legions, who helped establish the postwar state of Poland. The future Jewish

Legions would be patterned after Pilsudski's. In him, Jabotinsky saw a man who had wedded nationalism to militarism and who had succeeded in achieving independence with military power and influence.

In January 1915, Jabotinsky met Yoseph Trumpeldor, who, like himself, thought of "forming a Jewish contingent which would play a key role in the future politics and diplomacy of Zionism." The two men, not surprisingly, hit it off immediately. With the backing of a number of prominent Jews, the two prepared to petition the British for the right "to form a Jewish Legion and to propose to England to make use of it in Palestine." For Jabotinsky, the idea of a fighting Jewish force, the idea of Jewish legions, contained the essence of statist Zionism. Without arms and an army, there could be no Jewish state. To that end, he nearly exhausted himself, negotiating with the British, the Zionists, the military, and with other Jews to try to bring his concept to practical fruition.

World War I, however, was the practical laboratory for Jabotinsky and the Jewish Legions. Throughout his efforts to create Jewish units to fight the Turks, Jabotinsky faced furious opposition, not only from the British but from within Zionist ranks. Still, starting from small beginnings, he persisted.

Once Jabotinsky had found out that Turkey had entered the fray on the side of Germany and Austria, he began working toward Jewish participation, of "the establishment of a fighting Jewish contingent."[10]

In Alexandria, Egypt, a battalion of Jewish refugees and volunteers from the Ottoman Empire was established to be put at the disposal of the British army and government. In Jabotinsky's view, they would participate "in the fight for Eretz Israel."[11]

Now protracted negotiations began with the British. Jabotinsky and Trumpeldor, the latter wearing his old Czarist officer's uniform complete with medals won at Port Arthur, stood before General Maxwell, the commander of British troops in Egypt, and Ronald Graham, the adviser to Egypt's "interior minister." Maxwell was impressed with the martial bearing of Trumpeldor. Although the British were not overwhelmed by the idea, Maxwell was in favor of volunteers. He wanted to use the Jews in a noncombatant capacity and suggested the formation of a Jewish mule corps. Jabotinsky remained firm. "Absolutely not," he said. "We want a fighting force, not a donkey force."[12] For Jabotinsky, it was not only a matter of fighting Turks; it was a matter of recognition by the British. But Trumpeldor, the professional soldier, was enthusiastic about the idea. His logic, militarily speaking, was impeccable: "To get the Turks out of Palestine," he said, "we've got to smash the Turks. Which side you begin smashing, north or south is just technique. Any front leads to Zion."

Jabotinsky refused to join, but when the British actually made an offer to create a mule detachment, Trumpeldor accepted.

They were about to make history. On April 17, 1915, they were sent to

Gallipoli as part of Winston Churchill's ill-fated attack on the Turks. They were inexperienced and had never been given a clear role to play, but they nevertheless tasted combat and fought well under fire, suffering few casualties in the process. The Zionist Mule Corps performed well. "Our legion will serve Zionist political aims," wrote Trumpeldor, "even if we are only 'mules'."

Under Trumpeldor, the Jewish soldiers finally proved to the British that they were indeed courageous, real soldiers. As one of them, Nissan Rosenberg, wrote in his diary, "If it be necessary to die, then one must. I will meet death with laughter, even though going to war is not like going to a wedding."[13] Jabotinsky, in retrospect, saw his mistake and gave full credit to Trumpeldor: "I was wrong. Trumpeldor was right. Those six hundred muleteers actually opened up a new avenue in the development of Zionist possibilities . . . Though it was not in the Jordan Valley that we were victorious, the way through Gallipoli was the right way."[14]

Eventually, the legions were disbanded. However, in Jabotinsky's mind, the idea of Jewish Legions—Jewish armed might—as a basis for the creation of the state of Israel never dimmed. Jabotinsky's concept of Revisionist Zionism, not born until 1923–25, whose central tenet was an armed Jewish Legion, was fervently clasped as an article of faith by Jabotinsky.

By the early 1920s, Jabotinsky had gathered around him a group of young intellectuals, the nucleus of a budding Zionist political movement, an alternative to the Socialist Zionists who were creating a political and practical entity in Palestine.

Revisionist Zionism was the brainchild and the handiwork of one man, and that man was Jabotinsky. Revisionism grew during a time of high crisis in the 1920s, when, in the wake of the whittling down of the Balfour Declaration, the British tilt toward the Arabs and the Arab riots, Jewish immigration to Palestine was on the decline and Zionist groups were scrambling for funds. Revisionist Zionism's main strength lay in Diaspora Jews, especially in Poland.

Jabotinsky called for the organization in the Jewish Diaspora (meaning Poland), of Jewish legions and paramilitary organizations with the goal of eventually taking over the Mandatory by force. Despite this program, Jabotinsky looked to the British, and sought to uphold and defend the principles of the Balfour Declaration. He believed in the concepts of political and diplomatic statism, and he wanted the British to defend and protect the Jews in the Yishuv. He called for mass evacuation of the Diaspora to Palestine and asked the British to facilitate that process even as they were doing everything in their power to impede it. For Jabotinsky, Palestine was both sides of the Jordan, hence Eretz Israel (The Land of Israel, or All of Israel), and so it is with Begin. "Since we know Jews have higher ideals than Arabs," he wrote, "we want to create a new Hebrew culture, therefore we must dominate all of Eretz Israel. Only when that happens can we normalize our relations with Arabs. We must have an immigration of forty thousand Jews a year to become the majority in all of Eretz Israel. We must therefore create the political and economic conditions to become the majority. We must evacuate the Jews of the Diaspora and place them in Eretz Israel . . . The Annexation of Trans-Jordan is imperative."[15]

Whatever else can be said about Betar, its beginnings are found in the Jewish Legions. Betar and its offshoots were all permeated by militarism, and that militarism was ignited by Jabotinsky. Eventually, it would find its way to Etzel and Lehi, in a form that Jabotinsky surely would have disowned, but that, in a sense, would have been like disowning a son one had sired.

Betar would be Jabotinsky's next political and military child. Its history would be turbulent, its schisms and political battles complicated and far-reaching. Betar would also forge and make Begin, and in the end break Jabotinsky.

5

Betar in the 1920s:
The Arrival of Begin[1]

The real story of the life and times of Begin begins with the creation and evolution of Betar, which is really the story of the whole generation of young Polish Jews caught up in Polish nationalism and in the mysticism and romanticism of the form of Zionism espoused by Theodor Herzl.

Begin did not join Betar until 1926, when he was thirteen, fairly young even for the ranks of a movement that was geared toward youth. For years, he would be a rising but not a central figure in the movement, although his hagiographers will later try to paint a different picture.

Still, Begin was captured by the air of romanticism and redemption that was to draw so many other young Jews. The choices available were several. Instead of opting for Revisionist Zionism, for example, Begin could have ended up with Hashomer Hatzair, which he joined briefly, or in the ranks of the Socialist Zionists, directly at the opposite end of the Zionist political spectrum.

In the era which followed the Lovers of Zion (1880s), in the era of fighting Zionism, Socialist Zionism was geared toward practical action and work, unlike the almost visionary romanticism of Revisionism. Action meant pioneer agricultural collective work in Palestine. For the Socialist Zionists, redemption or self-realization *(Hagshamah)* meant both personal and collective therapy. The real Zionist work, they felt, was in conquering one dunam (about a third of an acre), one after another, for the fulfillment of personal and national goals. Immigration to Palestine along with building a better society for Jews in the traditional Jewish homeland, was the primary goal.

An even more radical option was presented by Hashomer Hatzair, which evolved into a militant Kibbutzim experiment, a Marxist Collective whose aim was to settle the land through the formation of independent Jewish farmer communities in Palestine. The two groups—Socialist and Marxist—aimed to dry the marshes, irrigate the desert, and make the mountains habitable, and thus create the foundation for a future Jewish agricultural homeland in Palestine. These were serious and practical options for young Zionists everywhere, and for the Zionist movement in general.

Revisionism eschewed those goals for ones that appeared and sounded militaristic and action-oriented, but which actually took to the high road of idealism and romanticism. Betar was molded in the tradition of East European nationalist youth movements. Its political culture rejected pioneerism and any form of Socialist thinking.

In essence, the difference between Diaspora Jewry and Palestine pioneers was a conflict between utopian Socialists and utopian Nationalists. Most of those flocking toward the banners of Socialist Zionism and the more leftist orientations would appear in Palestine in three large waves of Jewish immigrations in 1904-5, 1919-25, and 1931-35, among them most of them men and women, like David Ben Gurion, Levi Eshkol, Golda Meir and the commanders of the Haganah, who would make up the leadership of Mapai and eventually Labor.

Begin was not among those who emigrated to Palestine, preferring to stay with Jabotinsky and Revisionism in the Polish Diaspora. His cultural, economic and class background drove him to stay rooted there until 1940, when he was uprooted by the Nazi occupation of Poland. Begin had no sympathy with the concept of agricultural socialism and would develop a heated antipathy toward the Left. Like Jabotinsky, he was not excited about Jewish farmers cleaning horse manure in the kibbutzim and milking cows in the greened desert. An educated, budding lawyer and bourgeois to the core, Begin, as befitted his training, became a radical nationalist, which is to say he took an intellectual and political route that was remarkably similar to that of the Polish nationalists. For Begin and Pilsudski's Polish disciples, the solution for the motherland was political independence now, statehood now, freedom now.

Thus Jabotinsky and his protégé took a military route for the Jews, emulating the concept of legions while seeking a more militant solution for the fulfillment of the Balfour Declaration. There was a basic difference, of course, which Begin never quite grasped until late in his career: the post-Pilsudski generation was already living in a basically independent Poland, whereas Begin's approach was to attempt to liberate the Jews far from their Palestinian homeland.

There was a strain of idealism and downright unrealism in much of Jabotinsky's thinking that was constantly being challenged by events, by his own followers and by the political realities in Palestine.

In the politics of the Wall of Iron for instance (the Arabs being the wall), Jabotinsky correctly envisioned, a long inescapable struggle between Arabs and Jews, a struggle he saw the Jews as winning. He reasoned that there would always be an Anglo-Zionist cooperation, that the British would protect the Jews and be steadfast in their support of the Balfour Declaration. He foresaw prolonged antagonism, not open warfare, which would be prevented by the British.

This kind of optimism, to which Jabotinsky clung almost beyond reason, was openly challenged by the more radical element in Betar, and later Etzel and Lehi. They sneered at his belief that once Jewish sovereignty was achieved, an Arab-Jewish compromise was in the realm of possibility. They thought it a naive prognosis at best, impossibly utopian at worst. The youth movement that he inspired—Betar—never embraced the idea that Jewish independence would deter Arab wars.

Jabotinsky did not actually found Betar. It sprang up in Poland and Lithuania among other places, prompted by the romantic myth of the martyr killed by the Arabs in Tel-Hai in 1920, Yoseph Trumpeldor. Its birthplace was actually Latvia, one of the three Baltic republics which enjoyed a short-lived independence between the two great wars. The occupation of Vilna by the Poles left a strong, fertile, and anti-Bolshevik legacy which would influence Betar and especially the impressionable middle-class Zionist students and the movements that sprang from them. "For us," Jabotinsky wrote, "Latvia was a desert oasis amid the anti-Semitic Russian and East European wolves." "A liberal paradise," he called it on another occasion.

Jabotinsky gave his formal blessing to a Betar cell in Riga, but at first he did not really pay much attention to the fledgling movement. Once he did, he immediately set about turning Betar into a recruitment tool for the Revisionist Zionist Movement, a potential minilegion that would be the forerunner of future Jewish legions, whose hard core would be composed of Zionist student intelligensia influenced by Herzl.

From the start, one can see Jabotinsky's basic visionary approach—calling for legions and spouting militaristic rhetoric with no practical means of genuinely creating a real military force. For him, Betar would be purely nationalistic, untainted by any foreign doctrine except Revisionism, untouched by either Marxism or Fascism—although by the 1930s the more radical elements of Betar, with their uniforms and parades and military posturing, would in fact be accused by the Socialist Zionists of being "Fascist."

To Jabotinsky, it did not initially matter what the Socialist Zionists thought of the Revisionist forces. Betar's success would come not in Palestine, but in Poland in the twenties and thirties, where it would grow into a truly nationalistic youth movement that would become the Zionist alternative to the Socialists, and that Betar would diminish their recruiting efforts in Poland and eventually challenge them in the Yishuv itself.

Officially, one can say that Zionist Revisionism was born between 1923 and 1925 as a result of a meeting between Jabotinsky and a group of Russian Zionist activists who were followers of Herzl's statism.

By 1925 the Zionist Activist League led by Jabotinsky joined the Zionist activist student movement in Riga, Latvia. They established the Zionist Revisionist Union (Zohar)—a new party that was represented in the Zionist Congress, the Zionist parliament established by Herzl. At the outset, Betar grew autonomously from Revisionism, but soon was amalgamated with it under the leadership of Jabotinsky, who headed both Zohar and Betar. Jabotinsky was a rising new force in the ranks of Zionism, and he went about conquering and consolidating various nationalist Zionist organizations and establishing his own new Zionist Revisionist Union *(Zohar)* faction of the Zionist movement.

Revisionism was something of a subculture within Zionism, interpreting Jewish history in a unique way. It had an almost radical, romantic view of ancient, biblical times, as well as of the condition of Jews in the Diaspora, the meaning of Zionism and the concept of Eretz Israel. In this, as we have said, Revisionism clashed violently with the Zionist pragmatists led by Weizmann and the left-of-center socialists and agricultural collectivist movement.

Revisionism's strong nationalist bent appealed to the romantic and activist feelings of young Jews in Poland and the Baltic states. "The aim of Zionism," wrote Jabotinsky in *Razviet,* in which the first Revisionist platform was published, "is the gradual *transformation* of Palestine (including Trans-Jordan) into a Jewish commonwealth—that is, into a *self-governing commonwealth* under the auspices of an established Jewish majority."[2] Revisionism literally meant to revise the truncation of Trans-Jordan by the Palestine Mandate and the Balfour Declaration.

There were five tenets of Revisionism:

1. Mass immigration to Eretz Israel.
2. The end of the separation between Trans-Jordan and Palestine. (The British had separated Trans-Jordan from Palestine in 1922.)
3. The establishment of a colonial British regime in Palestine, which meant confiscation of the land of Eretz Israel and Trans-Jordan to open them for Jewish settlement, while paying reparation money to their original owners.
4. The formation of a Jewish legion in Eretz Israel.
5. Jewish immigration to an Eretz Israel dominated by Zionists, as opposed to Mandatory authorities, meaning free and unrestrained immigration as opposed to restricted immigration.

For Jabotinsky, Revisionist Zionism must be single-minded, meaning monistic, as opposed to the Marxist-collectivist type of Zionism espoused by the Socialist Zionists. There was no role for "foreign" (read Marxist) influence—only Jewish nationalism and statehood counted. Monism meant the integration of a national consciousness with a political plan for the liberation of Jews and conquest of the land, Eretz Israel.

Jabotinsky envisioned the gradual transference of Jewish sovereignty over Eretz Israel and the formation of a Jewish majority which would, ipso facto, lead to the eventual formation of a Jewish state. Zionist Revisionism called for acquiring the political tools for the fulfillment of Jewish purposes in Eretz Israel, including a Jewish military force, customs agencies, land acquisition, and immigration.

Not unlike many Central European boy scout movements, Betar grew from the middle-class Zionist milieu. Betar, the Revisionist youth corps, grew around Jabotinsky's charismatic personality and basked in his heroic and legendary status. Jewish youth were spurred on by a general storm of nationalism that swept over Poland and Europe. But Revisionism was not touched by the kind of brutal nationalism that prevailed in Germany and Italy. It was grounded in serious, philosophical writings of the *risorgimento* that heavily influenced Jabotinsky.

Jabotinsky was influenced by the writings of Professor Yoseph Klausner, the Jewish historian who wrote in 1905 about "Judaism and Humanitarianism," suggesting a synthesis between them, a synthesis of Jewish history and nationalist ideas that were positive. All nationalist movements choose a heroic era in their nation's past with which to identify. Here Professor Klausner inspired Betar and contributed a most significant historical symbol to be emulated—the heroic era of the Jewish revolt against Rome—the era of the Second Temple (100–200 A.D.). Like the zealots of that era, the Betarim in our own time would continue the tradition of revolt.[3]

The Betar and the Zohar party movements, which were totally dominated by Jabotinsky and his Zohar officers, were semi-independent structurally and organizationally. This setup was inherently weak, since Betar and its more radical elements never considered themselves dependent on or subservient to the parent organization, only to Jabotinsky, personally.

Jabotinsky turned Betar into an instrument to mobilize youth and create the potential Zionist legions. By 1923 Jabotinsky, moving tirelessly like a ferocious, rhetoric-filled lone wolf all over the Eastern European Diaspora, had begun to propagate his legionistic, political Zionist philosophy. He was turning into a fervent missionary, a Jewish Saint Paul delivering Revisionist gospel. All of his attention began to focus on those intellectual, middle-class Jewish youths untainted by Marxism, not in the thrall of Socialist Zionism. Here, he saw, was a source to fill up the ranks of Jewish legions. Jabotinsky, through Betar, was emphasizing a different road for Zionism:

"We must end the Jewish anarchic life in Diaspora," he said. "Betar must serve as the model for Jewish youth and Zionism. The goal of Betar is the return to Eretz Israel on both sides of the Jordan River and the establishment of a Jewish state over all of Palestine's territory. We must inculcate into the Jews the idea that without a state there is no survival."[4]

Yet at heart, however "active" Jabotinsky's rhetoric might sound, Jabotinsky's and Betar's brand of Revisionism dealt mainly in symbols. They were trying, primarily, to create a new and different Jewish social and cultural orientation.

Jabotinsky envisioned Betar as the political arm of his newly founded Zohar; it would become the most active force within the ranks of Revisionism. Jabotinsky would now draw Zionist youth from the world Zionist movement. Because of Jabotinsky's unique faith in himself, the force of his personality and willpower, he believed wholeheartedly that he would change the course of Zionism, and the World Zionist Organization took him at face value. Jabotinsky's policies and his creation of Zohar, while ineffectual in reality, were enough to precipitate a split from WZO in 1931 which had the practical effect of depriving his movement of organizational and financial resources.

In 1925, Jabotinsky was preaching new principles of behavior, not a new ideology. He sought to create a new mentality, not a new Weltanschauung. Speaking before the Hashmonaim group in Latvia, he preached legionnairism and activism, but he was not advocating militarism or even the politics of power. He was trying to fight pacifism among Jews and within the ranks of Zionism.

The legions, to Jabotinsky, were actually a *political*, not a military instrument, to which he would add other important components of a Jewish renaissance. Militarism and legionnairism would aid Jewish renaissance but would not be its base. For Jabotinsky political struggle was the key. Without it, national fulfillment was doomed.

Jabotinsky was talking about armies: "The agricultural settlements in Palestine would not bring political results," he preached. "In a ruthless world, Jewish legions are more impressive than agricultural settlements. The legion must also educate and form a new Jewish generation and a new Jewish race."[5]

It was a matter of concepts and principles, of symbols. But the radicals infiltrating Betar and the future members of Etzel would disabuse Jabotinsky sharply of his notions—there was a literalness in their approach that was harsh, bloody and real.

Meanwhile, Jabotinsky continued to preach his gospel of the legions. But he wanted no one to mistake his ideas: the function of Betar and the minilegions was not merely to train youth in military tactics but to form a new kind of Jewish youth. Militarism, as defined by Jabotinsky and Betar, meant discipline, ceremony, and pride. It was, in the end, an act of symbolism.[6]

He was not only looking for thousands of Betarim skilled in rifle marksmanship. He was after bigger game. He was attempting to create a Jewish-Hebrew treasury, a storehouse of symbols so that romanticism would wear a Hebrew garb, dressed in the trappings of Jewish authenticity, in Hebrew patriotism. "Let our enemies know," he told them, "that we can sing, dance, and drink a lot of wine. But we must sing and dance and drink in Hebrew."[7]

Just as Polish nationalism was replete with symbols, so Betar was full of Jewish nationalist symbols, old ghosts from an ancient and glorious past. Betar literature was filled with Hebrew historical heroes—Bar Kokhva, Shimon Bar Yochai, the Kanaim, or Zealots, Juda Maccabeus. All of these were part of the maturing Begin's literary diet, as well as the awesome stories of Jewish suffering and disasters—the destruction of the temple, the exiles, the pogroms and massacres, and the heroes who emerged from disaster. Burning at the center of this mythology was the image of the glorious Jewish King David and other great Old Testament kings like Saul and Solomon.

By 1926, Betar underwent some serious changes, transforming from a basically student movement that went about singing patriotic songs to a Zionist, nationalistic, radical, political mass movement.

The Arab riots of 1920–21, the growing pro-Arab stance of Great Britain, and the first partition plan in 1930, along with the rise of anti-Semitism in Poland and the rise of Fascism in Europe, all combined to change the character of Betar, in Poland as well as in Palestine.

In Poland, Jabotinsky, through his tireless efforts and his charisma, had finally succeeded in turning Betar into a mass movement that inspired large rallies and demonstrations. As he looked ahead to setting the Betar program for 1935, Jabotinsky said that "Betar's organization would become a mixture of school and army."

It was precisely the mass appeal of Betar, as well as the changing times and the fresh radical wind blowing from Palestine that made Betar in Poland vulnerable to increasing penetration and infiltration, of which Jabotinsky became aware too late. This is when Menachem Begin arrived.

The penetration of Betar into the ranks and life of Jewish youth was a latent development in Zionism, linked indelibly, as we have seen, to the romantic and utopian spirit of Polish nationalism, utopianism, which was heavily influenced by the spirit of Adam Mickiewicz, Poland's messianic and romantic poet. Listening to some lines of Mickiewicz from his lyric drama "Forefathers Eve," one might hear the voice of Betar: "My fatherland and I are one great whole, my name is million, for I love millions."

Although the two movements were basically antagonistic at heart, the divergent spirits of Polish nationalism and Zionism seemed to come together in Betar. The two somehow related to each other, so much so that in the late 1930s, they would attempt a military alliance of sorts.

Betar's apparent orientation toward the military impressed the young Begin, as it did thousands of other Jewish youths. The curricula called for pomp and circumstance, military training, parades, order, spectacle and sports. Betar recruited athletic types wherever possible and organized for competition.

Like other young Betarim, Begin was meticulous about wearing his brown uniform with the Two-Sides-of-the-Jordan emblem at the top of his pentagonal hat, which, not surprisingly, resembled the regulation Polish Army hat. The Polish Betar sometimes seemed totally enamored of uniforms, and of aggressive military symbolism.

Begin would help write about the military training and propaganda for Betar. *Masuot* (the Beacon), the organization's first biweekly newspaper, opened in 1927 with the following: "Hebrews, we are and aspiring to be a Hebrew state. Young we are—and aspiring for life, freedom, free and fresh, on fire."[8]

Begin became involved in Betar during its most promising, growing years, just about the time Jabotinsky's presence was becoming felt in a real way. Its first World Congress was held in Warsaw in 1929. By that time, Betar already had branches in Romania, Czechoslovakia, Latvia, Brazil, Bulgaria, Germany, South Africa, Greece, the United States and Palestine. In 1930, there were nine hundred cells comprising close to five thousand members in some twenty-one countries. Over 40 percent of the Betarim were students.

The early 1930s involved mobilization and recruitment activities with the most intense centers of activity, of course, Poland and Palestine.

Begin was beginning to play a conspicuous and active role. He was leader of the Brisk cell and would later move to Warsaw where he became a leading activist. He concentrated on helping with manpower, training and propaganda, and was involved in the illegal traffic of weapons from Poland to Palestine.

In the early 1930s, Betar reorganized itself in Warsaw, whose cell was formed as Betar's High Commission under the leadership of Aaron Propes —whom Begin replaced in 1939. It was at this time that both the movement and Jabotinsky would increase their emphasis on legitimate militarization and try to get the help of the Polish government for training purposes.

The 1929 convention, for instance, brought thousands of Betarim to Warsaw to commemorate Herzl's death. Never was there such a splendid show of Jewish militarism. Begin was among the Betarim who showed up, all dressed in shining military uniforms. Even the Poles were impressed. With pomp and ceremony, the Jews marched to the accompaniment of martial music through the streets of Warsaw to Pilsudski square and laid a wreath on the Tomb of the Unknown Soldier.

As early as 1930, the Second World Congress in Danzig was already taking up the issue of how to fight the Mandatory in Palestine. In Poland Betar may have talked about resistance, but it was in Palestine that the issue really flourished, and where rebellion within the ranks of Revisionism would emerge and spread.

6

The Radicalization of Betar:
The Rise of Etzel in Palestine[1]
1931–35

In the 1920s Betar was still an essentially lay scout movement. The late twenties and thirties would turn it into a mature political movement of growing significance among young, middle-class Zionists in Poland and in Baltic states. Concurrently, the movement would become more than young Betarim graduating into Revisionism. It would become the spearhead of Jabotinsky's Zionist Revisionism, in fact of radical Jewish nationalism. Betar, and not Revisionism, became *the* radical nationalist Jewish movement. The ideology of the movement was directed toward two militant goals—the cancellation of the 1922 truncation of Palestine and warfare against Zionist Marxism and Socialism. This pitted the movement against the Mandatory and Yishur leadership in Palestine.

Thus it must be examined from two different perspectives, Palestine and Poland. In Palestine, the organization would turn radical and terrorist, while in Poland, it would become a mass movement and finally split and turn against Jabotinsky under the aegis of the Palestinian radicals then dominating Etzel.

Begin will climb in the hierarchy of the movement in Poland during the 1930s, and he will also be influenced by its Palestinian spell. Thus, although he remains totally loyal to Jabotinsky, the Palestinian Betar and Etzel will eventually turn the young Begin from a party apparatchik into an Etzel revolutionary. To capture this development, one must next turn to the crucial change in the life of Begin, and of Betar, to the Palestinian context, the ideology of the *Biryonim* (the zealots), and to the rise of Etzel and the challenge to Jabotinsky.

From the late twenties and thirties, political life in Palestine was dominated by the pioneer Socialist-Zionist movement and its parties and appendages, the Kibbutzim, the Histadrut, and other structures which served as the political and social foundations of Eretz Israel.

Until 1927, the Betar hardly existed in Palestine. Its roots and its structures existed as a purely Diaspora phenomenon. Whereas the Socialist Zionists saw the Diaspora as a reservoir for pioneers to Palestine, the Revisionists did not look upon immigration to Palestine as mandatory. There was a small (and basically insignificant) Revisionist party in Palestine, but the real center of Revisionism was wherever Jabotinsky happened to be at the moment. Since he was barred by the British after 1929 from entering Palestine, the movement suffered accordingly. Thus, it was no surprise that the Revisionist movement in Palestine would end up being captured by a small group of Betar ultraradicals whose impact on the movement would be enduring.

In the 1920s, the Revisionist movement could not compete with the Socialist Zionists. It was plagued with problems of finance and recruitment. By 1929, Mapai and the Socialist Zionists constituted the major political force in Palestine.

While Socialist Zionist parties were able to firmly embed themselves in Palestine with a highly effective system of organizational apparatus, Zohar was never able to match that kind of effort, certainly not in Palestine. What tenuously united Zohar and Betar was not a carefully thought-out organizational system, but the lone, charismatic figure of Jabotinsky.

If anything, the potentially rich soil of Palestine would stimulate in Zohar, Betar and Revisionist Zionism a growth of differences and radicalization which would all but tear the movement apart and lead it in a direction that Jabotinsky, its founder, had never envisioned.

In Palestine, in contrast to Poland, Betar faced the open hostility of the Mandatory and of the Socialists. Here, Betarim were no longer in the rejected Diaspora, but what would be their course? Jabotinsky's political ideology of cooperation with Britain could no longer be defended. Betar intellectuals in Palestine called for revolutionary action, for a revival of the deeds of the Zealots and for a revolt against the Mandatory. Jabotinsky and the Revisionist movement were not ready for so many changes—the splintering from world Zionism, recruitment of new Betarim, and also the open revolt called for by the militants in Palestine, some even defying the Rosh Betar himself.

Zohar, especially after its split from the World Zionist Organization in June 1931, was never able to establish effective organizational control over Betar in Palestine.

One might think that Jabotinsky's ideology would have been enough to form a cohesive bond between Zohar and Betar, one serving as the organization and the other as a recruitment system. Yet both Zohar and Betar in Poland were remarkably old-fashioned in ideology. Jabotinsky clung to old and familiar Herzlian ideals, however much he tried to introduce to his movement new socioeconomic and political concepts. While Socialist Zionism gave its adherents and followers a wide range of solutions and ideas to choose from, Jabotinsky and even radical Betar could only offer a narrower variety of doctrines. Their only original offerings were the ideas of Eretz Israel (both sides of the Jordan) and legionnairism.

As originally envisioned, the division of labor between Zohar and Betar seemed simple. Zohar was the political arm of Jabotinsky. Betar was the educational, cultural and propaganda instrument of Jabotinsky and Revisionist Zionism.

Betar's propagandists, including the ideally suited Begin, were publishing literature and journalism in Yiddish, Hebrew and Polish. Begin, who would rise to become Betar's chief of propaganda, would travel year in and year out throughout Poland, Lithuania, and Latvia to speak, recruit, and propagandize for the movement. Betar, in essence, functioned both as a propaganda and a recruiting organization. In this, it resembled Socialist Zionism, and here the comparison ended.

Since the 1930s, Socialist Zionism, the dominant political ideology of the pioneers, was and would remain basically cohesive and centralistic. Mapai, the leading party, and its leaders, especially Ben Gurion, abhorred factionalism of any sort. In Palestine, its socioeconomic organizations, the Histadrut and the Kibbutz-collective movement, were large-scale bureaucratic organizations, modeled after Socialist and Marxist parties in Eastern Europe, designed to function smoothly and cohesively and to minimize internal strife.

A fresh wind of ideology would soon blow from Palestine, a radical wind led by a group of Betarim who would become known as the Biryonim, led by Aba Achimeir and the radical Hebraist-Canaanite ideology inspired by A. G. Horon and Yonatan Ratosh (Halperin).

However unrestrained the political structures of Revisionist Zionism, Zohar and Betar seemed created almost to guarantee strife. There was a continuous struggle for power between the parent movement, Zohar, and its youth movement, Betar, especially when the latter became heavily infiltrated by the radical forces spawned in Palestine.

In terms of issues, the struggle centered on active and terrorist struggle against the Mandatory and the Socialists.

Socialist Zionism had its own military organization, the Haganah. The Haganah was the military instrument of Mapai, the Histadrut, and later the Yishuv and Zionism. It was true that some Haganah activities were clandestine such as illegal immigration. But Socialist Zionism preferred legitimate, open military activities, a policy which Betar's eventual military arms, Etzel and Lehi, would reject.

Betar and its military underground would eventually impose on Jabotinsky, almost against his will, a military-underground organization. Throughout his life, Jabotinsky would remain dedicated to a legal military formation.

Unfortunately, however, he was absent from Palestine and he failed to establish anything there similar to the Betar in Poland. Thus it was possible for more militant elements to penetrate the movement in Palestine.

Zohar never achieved any real political hegemony, especially after Jabotinsky pulled out of the WZO in 1931 and although the geographical center of both Zohar and Betar was in Poland, the Palestine faction, through its militancy and infiltration, would achieve primacy, if not autonomy.

Jabotinsky on his last trip to Palestine in 1928 (he was banned from going there by the British in 1929), had hoped to build the movement there, to wed the activists to his cause and recruit "outsiders," non-Marxist workers, members of the middle class, and non-Ashkenazi ethnics. According to Yaacov Shavit, the nonpartisan historian of Revisionism, Jabotinsky wanted to create "a large center of liberal bourgeoisie nationalists in Eretz Israel."

By 1931, with Jabotinsky no longer in Palestine, the activists led by Abrasha Weinstein and Dr. Wolfgang von Weisel, had become highly prominent. Jabotinsky acquiesced. "If I am to choose between activists and nonactivists, I choose the first group," he said.

Several factors—Jabotinsky's exile from Palestine, a lack of organizational, social and economic structure, the pressure of the Mandatory, the furor and controversy surrounding the assassination of Dr. Chaim Arlazaroff —would combine to turn Betar into a pariah organization in Palestine, with the active complicity of Mapai. All these factors fueled the great struggle for power within Revisionist Zionism.

With Revisionism withdrawn from WZO, the political struggle between Zohar and Betar between 1929 and 1935 centered around the structure and nature of Revisionism. The radical Biryonim called for a party and national dictatorship and for terrorist operations against the Mandatory. Jabotinsky rejected this, preferring instead a form of centralization for the movement, with himself, naturally, as the focus. In this, indeed, Zohar-Betar was no more centralist or nondemocratic than Socialist Zionism, which mixed Marxist traditions with some type of social-democratic party centralism.

The radicals were calling for conspiratorial and authoritarian approaches, which ill-suited Jabotinsky or, for that matter, Begin. They were turning Betar toward an ideology which was nationalistic, terrorist, and tainted with the trappings of Fascism. Events in both Palestine and the Diaspora had fueled this change. Its impact was profound. From Trumpeldor's pioneerism and the almost innocent Betar youth movement, Betar turned into a militaristic laboratory for clandestine legionnairism. By the mid-1930s, its dominance had become clear.

The rise of political anti-Semitism in Poland and fascism in Europe, combined with the bloody Arab revolt in Palestine and Britain's gradual tilt toward the Arabs and away from the Balfour Declaration, all nourished the new Betar radicalism. But the real mobilizing force of the movement was basically negative—a ferocious and fanatic anti-Marxism, focused on a political battle within Palestine against Mapai and the forces of Socialist Zionism.

The struggle was fierce. Betar would be smeared with the taint of "fascism" while Betarim tried to accuse Socialist Zionism of "Stalinism."

The shift within Betar toward paramilitary and terrorist underground activities was sparked by the radical Biryonim in Palestine. The influence, history, and impact of the Biryonim remain to this day a matter of considerable controversy in Israel, periodically prompting debates among the reigning political parties.

Their influence should not be measured in deeds but rather in intellectual and literary terms, because this is the base from which they operated. They were fiercely radical intellectuals and writers whose words were warlike.

The Biryonim movement was an outgrowth of the attitudes of Polish-born and Palestinian Socialists who had become increasingly impatient with and disappointed in the leadership of the Yishuv and Zionism. When they looked at Revisionism in its present state, they saw a weak imitation of Weizmann Zionism, a tepid and ineffective movement not to their more activist tastes.

They called for the overthrow of the Mandatory, the elimination of the Left, cessation from WZO, and the establishment of a Jewish state to be conquered from the British with the help of a vast number of Jewish legionnaires trained in Poland with the help of the Polish military. They called for immediate mass evacuation of Jews from Poland and, if necessary, the assistance of Italian Fascists under Mussolini or any other foe of the British Empire.

The leaders—Achimeir, Yeyvin and Gruenberg—were all young, highly educated members of the right-wing, nationalist-inclined part of Mapai, which had originally seceded from the left and turned toward militarism, Hebrew style. From the vantage point of history, the Biryonim constituted a romantic, radical, university youth movement, similar to movements in Germany in the 1840s and Russia in the 1860s. It was fueled by the powerful, passionate poetry of Gruenberg, the acerbic, satiric, and belligerent pen of the scholar-journalist Achimeir, and the romantic, almost monarchical novels of Yeyvin. Begin was greatly impressed by Aba Achimeir, and although he remained loyal to Jabotinsky, his rhetoric was sprinkled with the literature of the Biryonim. His letters from Vilna in 1940–41 clearly demonstrated his Biryonim orientation. A devotee of Jabotinsky's etatism and patriotism, he was nevertheless more deeply influenced by the intellectual and social philosophy of the Biryonim.

Although Begin was never a bona fide member of the movement (it was purely Palestinian in origin), their ideas on Britain, fascism, Marxism and the Arabs became a steady intellectual treasure for Begin.

THE BIRYONIM

In a three year period (1930–33), a group of young Biryonim intellectuals organized for the first time the nucleus of a resistance movement against the Mandatory.

It is important to understand that their radicalism was much more than a bent for violence and a hatred of the Mandatory. As much as it smacked of an impatient, passionate, and reckless drive to create a Jewish state, it was a revolt, pure and simple, against the legalistic and static leadership of traditional Revisionist Zionism. What distinguished this radical, nationalistic movement is its acceptance of political terror as a tactic and its willingness to use it against the Mandatory.

In spite of Jabotinsky's sometimes strident rhetoric, Betar in Poland remained a legal, slow-moving movement expressing its ideology, its yearning for Eretz Israel, in legalistic terms. This was true of Jabotinsky as well as his disciple Begin, who would also find himself in the moderate, legalistic camp of Revisionism throughout the 1930s. Yet the influence of the Biryonim on Begin will grow as he advances in Betar ranks. Like Jabotinsky, he would not reject the Biryonim; in fact, he embraced them as long as they did not personally challenge the leader. And what did Begin write?

As a true disciple of Jabotinsky, Begin's writings of the time, meager as they are, are moderate and legalistic in tone, calling for legal armies and democratic political action. In a Betar pamphlet from 1934, he wrote to concerned Jewish parents, "We seek a Jewish State on the two sides of the Jordan . . . we seek a Jewish government. Betar's actions are nonrevolutionary."

This may have reassured parents, but it no doubt left the radicals cold. Jabotinsky's plea, after all, remains Herzelian, "an end to Jewish misery." Following in the tradition of Trumpeldor, he urged Jews to fight legitimately for their national rights.[2]

In Begin's pamphlet nothing could be found that was truly revolutionary or incinerating. Jabotinsky himself, however, was activist-oriented, but in a very specific way. His activism was directed against Socialist Zionists. Jabotinsky's platform, which Begin would follow, called for "a political offensive," but it would be an offensive directed against Socialist Zionists in Palestine.[3]

"We must prepare in Eretz Israel cadres of young, organized, and disciplined youth," he wrote, "who will study the military sciences and be ready for battle."[4]

Within Poland, Jabotinsky's movement was basically gradualist and middle class. Most of its leaders were well-educated, intellectual Zionists and university graduates, in marked contrast to the more down-to-earth lower-middle-class Socialist Zionist leaders. The majority of Betar leaders were graduates of Jewish-Hebrew and Polish-Russian schools. Revisionism in Poland was not a shtetl movement but a movement of urban professionals and middle class Jews. Thus it comes as no surprise that Begin and other senior Betar leaders would develop an anti-Socialist, and populist nationalism of the type prevalent in Poland at large.

In Eretz Israel, similar, university-trained types carried this to its logical conclusion. Radical intellectuals, frustrated with Socialist Zionism, impatient with Zohar, Jabotinsky, and the Diaspora Revisionists, would finally come to advocate the theory and practice of terror. Betar ideology and doctrine laid the groundwork for the Biryonim, the modern Jewish zealots who would eventually try to take over the movement, and even oust Jabotinsky.

Oddly enough, the Biryonim did not start out as an anti-socialist underground movement, but had their roots firmly planted in the Left—oddly enough, in the pacifist Hapoel Hatzair party.

The party's ideological gurus were the non-Marxist Socialist Zionists A. D. Gordon and Y. C. Brenner, who influenced the three leading Biryonim with their doctrines of Hebraic supremacy and anti-Marxism. Their impact on Begin was indelible.

The role of each of the three major Biryonim would depend on each man's particular intellectual and ideological bent, as well as his talents and abilities.

Achimeir was born in Bobryosk in 1889 and was a graduate of the Russian gymnasium. He went to the University of Kiev to study history and literature and fled to Vienna in 1918 with the coming of the Bolsheviks. In 1924, he received his Ph.D., writing a dissertation on Spengler and Nietzche. At the same time, he joined Hapoel Hatzair in Palestine and began a journalistic career, writing for Socialist-Zionist papers.

He soon became disenchanted with what he saw as that movement's pacifist tendencies. In 1928 he joined the Revisionist movement and began writing a column in Hebrew called "From a Fascist Notebook" for *Doar Hayom,* a nationalist-oriented daily.

Achimeir, who was emotionally and intellectually seared by the Russian Revolution, saw in fascism the perfect antidote and bulwark against Marxism and Bolshevism. By 1929 he was a leader in the Palestinian Betar, and by 1930 he established the first anti-British underground, the *Brit Habiry-onim*—the Pact of the Zealots. ("Zealots" approximates "Biryonim." There is no literal translation of "Biryonim.") By this time, his activities had taken on a frenzied aspect and became immediately noticeable. In 1930, he called for resistance to Marxism (meaning Socialist Zionism) in Palestine and to the British Mandatory. In 1931, he organized resistance to a census being conducted by the Mandatory, a census which Achimeir thought discriminated against the Jews and was a retreat by the Mandatory from its responsibilities toward the Jews.

In 1932, he organized a violent demonstration against the activities of Professor Norman Bentwitch, an Anglo-Jewish Zionist and senior officer in the Mandatory in charge of the census. In 1932, he and Yeyvin were editing the militant nationalist paper *Hazit Haam,* a paper which would help instigate riots and the assassination of Jewish "collaborators" and British officials and politicians. In 1933, he removed the swastika from the German consulate in Jerusalem.

Achimeir was a brilliant, resourceful, energetic and acerbic journalist. In focusing his attacks on Socialist Zionism, on Mapai and on the "collaborationism" of Ben Gurion and Weizmann, Achimeir saw himself as an educator, propagandist, soldier and terrorist:

"One must debunk the old Zionist Weltanschauungen," he wrote. "Fighting nature is not its primary goal; dying in the marshes and fighting malaria (references to Kibbutzim building in the 1920s) is wrong. It's wrong to move the nation from urban to rural environments. Zionism is the last movement of utopian liberal nationalism which is fading in the aggressive world of postwar nationalism."[5]

There was more.

"Zionism is an immoral movement—a movement of amateurs who never called for real sacrifices," he wrote. Achimeir called for militarism. "There is no nation without an army," he wrote. Zionism, he argued, which should have set the tone and direction for Jewish youth, which should have become the Shin Fein of the Jews, had betrayed its mission. "We in Betar must set the example," he said. "We need a leader like Mussolini."[6]

In truth, Achimeir and the Biryonim were fascinated by fascism in a romantic way, entranced by the trappings but not the substance. They were no more Fascists than Ben Gurion—who admired Lenin and adopted some of his tactics—was a Bolshevik.

The Biryonim contributed to the growth of the radical right and were the forerunners of Etzel and Lehi, but they did not lay the groundwork for fascism. However, they did influence those who would later form Etzel and Lehi, their spiritual descendants, who took their advocacy of terrorist techniques against the Mandatory at face value and put them into practice.

The second member of the Biryonim was the novelist Dr. Yehoshua

Heshel Yeyvin, born in 1891 in the Ukraine. He received a traditional religious education and graduated from the Hebrew gymnasium. He also had a degree in medicine from the University of Moscow. He served as a front-line physician during World War I, but gave up the medical profession for literature, traveling to Moscow, Odessa and Berlin. In 1925, he emigrated to Palestine and joined Hapoel Hatzair, leaving it in 1928 to join Revisionism. All along, his literary career flourished. He was an editor, poet, and writer, first in Warsaw and later in Berlin, joining a center of Yiddish writers in 1923.

Yeyvin's major contribution to the Biryonim was impassioned fiction that extolled Jewish heroism and glory, often to an improbable degree. His rousing novels would draw considerable admiration, especially from U. Z. Gruenberg, probably the most original, fiery, and prophetic of all modern Hebrew writers, whose sentiments and symbols would reverberate through the years, to be taken up like a blazing torch by Betar and Etzel-Lehi.

Gruenberg was the scion of an influential Hasidic family. He too was a World War I veteran, serving with the Austro-Hungarian army. By 1928, he had, like Achimeir and Yeyvin, joined Revisionism and become a fiery, unrelenting poet of Jewish heroics and violence. His poetry absolutely rang with pugnacity, defiance, and symbolism. In his Hebrew poetry, the language itself became a tool of nationalism and daring. Long before Gruenberg actually joined the Revisionist movement, he was identified as a Revisionist poet.

The impact of the Biryonim was in their ideology, for the beginning of their influence marked the end of optimistic liberalism everywhere. For mainstream Zionists and the Mandatory, that damage would prove to be irreparable. Their cry was heard throughout Palestine and would spread to the Revisionist forces in the Diaspora: "In blood and fire Judea will be restored," wrote Yaacov Cohen, a poet and Biryonim follower. It was a prophetic motto.

Blood would also undo the Biryonim themselves, and would create a major fissure among all the forces of Zionism. The Arlazaroff assassination of 1933 would seem to turn the rhetoric of the Biryonim into a bloody reality.

THE ARLAZAROFF AFFAIR

On June 16, 1933, Chaim Arlazaroff, the head of the political department of the Jewish Agency in Palestine and a Mapai stalwart, was shot by an unidentified assailant while walking with his wife Sima on the Tel Aviv beach near the Hotel Keta Dan.

Three days later, on June 19, Avraham Stavsky, a protegé of Biryonim stalwart Achimeir and a friend of Begin's from Brisk, was arrested, arraigned, and accused of participating in the assassination.

Three months later, Stavsky was released, principally because the main witness against him was Arlazaroff's wife. Although English law required only one witness, the colonial Mandatory law required two. Achimeir, as a suspected collaborator, was arrested and imprisoned for twenty-one months.

The assassination and the subsequent arrest, trial, and release of Stavsky convulsed and shocked the entire Jewish community of Palestine, as well as the Zionist Diaspora. For Zionism, the assassination and trial were its Dreyfus, its Sacco-Vanzetti. When it was all over, the division between Socialist Zionism and Revisionism was complete and unbridgeable. All elements of the Zionist movement became embroiled in the affair. Fifty years after the event, the actual killers have never been identified, although Ben Gurion went to his grave believing that Stavsky was the murderer.

The affair shook Revisionism to its foundations, tarnished it with the brush of murder and irresponsibility, and took it out of the mainstream of Zionism, a position from which it did not recover until the rise of Begin in the wake of the 1967 war. In effect, Revisionism turned into a political pariah within the Yishuv.

In the wake of the assassination, a frightened and startled Revisionist movement tried to distance itself from the Biryonim and their hot-blooded rhetoric. The Socialists, shocked by the loss of their outstanding leader, immediately pointed a finger at the Revisionists, and especially at the Biryonim, whose verbal violence they blamed for the assassination.

Some case could be made for this accusation, for the Biryonim had indeed put teeth and fire into their writings, and may have created an explosive atmosphere.

It was no secret that the Revisionists, and especially the Biryonim, condemned Arlazaroff's personal brand of diplomacy, and the Jewish Agency's efforts to negotiate a deal for the transfer of Jewish money from Nazi Germany to Palestine in 1933. Arlazaroff became a key target for Achimeir's acid pen.

While Gruenberg and other radical Palestinian Betarim were traveling in Poland, the Biryonim paper, *Hazit Haam,* (the *National Front)* was full of indirect allusions to Arlazaroff, pointing to him as a symbol of collaboration, referring to him as "The Red Wonder Boy," or "The Red Diplomat." The Histadrut was called the "Red Rug," Ben Gurion "Stalin" and "Hitler." None of this was subtle,[7] and all of it was inflammatory, but then so were the Socialist attacks on Betar and Revisionists, whom they called "fascists, assassins, terrorists, and Hitlerites who were helping Mussolini and Hitler."

The air was full of venom. In 1932, with Ben Gurion slated for a visit to Poland, the Polish Betarim warned that he would never leave alive.

Yeyvin, writing in the *National Front* warned that Arlazaroff was "willing to make peace with Hitler." The Socialists were fearful of potential violence, so much so that Arlazaroff was issued a pistol to protect himself.

Years later, Gruenberg dismissed the rhetoric he had helped to generate. "The call for violence was for literary reasons," he said.

When violence came with the assassination of Arlazaroff, Ben Gurion and Mapai manipulated the whole affair into a hugely successful political weapon against Revisionism.

While the Mandatory and the Palestinian police prepared for a trial at which many witnesses would be called, both political camps immediately and independently established their own investigation commissions into the assassination.

The Socialist-Zionist Commission on the Arlazaroff assassination led by Berl Katznelson and Haganah leaders Eliahu Golomb, as well as Dov Hoz, Moshe Shertok and Shaul Meirov, could not come up with any hard conclusions, but the thrust and intent of their report was that the assassination was the work of radical Betarim, a stigma that Revisionism could never quite shed.

The Revisionists, frightened by the possibility that Arlazaroff's death could have been instigated and stimulated by their own extremists, lashed out right and left, blaming the Jewish Communists, the Comintern, and finally the Arabs. Their charges had about as much, and perhaps less, foundation in truth than those of the Socialist Zionists.

But it was Jabotinsky who saw more clearly than anyone else what was happening. Jabotinsky realized that the trial and the investigations were really not about truth and justice. The whole affair was a political battle royal.

Knowing this, realizing the tremendous political implications of the affair, he took charge of the Revisionist's private investigation commission. He set out his strategy to clear his movement in two key articles. First, in an article in Yiddish, he flatly denied that Stavsky was a Comintern agent, a plant in his movement. Stavsky, he said, was a patriot accused falsely and politically by his enemies, the Socialists.

Jabotinsky staked out the political issues more clearly in another article, thus contributing to the politicization of the affair. The second article was called "Blood Libel," and he invoked the 1913 Mendel Belis trial in Russia, in which a Russian Jew was accused of conducting blood rites. For Jabotinsky, Stavsky was the blood victim and the whole case was a blood libel committed against Revisionism.

Jabotinsky appealed to his friend Oscar Gruzenberg, a Russian Jewish trial lawyer to be the defense attorney. But it was Horace Samuel, an assimilated Jew, a former judge in the Mandate and one of the finest British legal defenders, who took the appeal to a higher court after a lower court had found Stavsky guilty. Samuel's defense was apolitical, technical, and in the end simple. He succeeded in getting the prosecution's chief witness, Arlazaroff's wife Sima, to contradict her earlier testimony on numerous occasions.

Although Samuel succeeded in obtaining Stavsky's release, Jabotinsky continually pounded the theme of blood libel, exacerbating the political climate. He refused to disavow the Biryonim, even though they attacked him in the pages of the *National Front*. Between the pariah pejoratives and the blood libel charges, the balance of power in Palestine was shifting inevitably toward Socialist Zionism.

The Arlazaroff affair ended the brief career of the Biryonim. Achimeir was arrested and jailed. The *National Front* stopped publication. Athough the Biryonim continued to write and propagandize, their immediate influence waned. But their real effect was felt in the Diaspora in Poland, especially among the ranks of the Betarim.

Although legacy of the affair left wounds in both major movements, it probably hurt Revisionism the most. In fact, by 1935 Mapai and Ben Gurion had consolidated their predominance. Mapai and Histadrut captured the majority in the Yishuv, the Jewish Agency and the World Zionist Congress.

Curiously enough, although the Biryonim themselves began to fade in terms of individual influence, their doctrines flourished, helped by the 1936 Arab Revolt, the Royal Commission Report on Partition in July 1937, and the whittling by the Mandate by 1938–39 to the commitments of the Balfour Declaration of 1917. Betar was driven to its extremist fringes.

The Revisionists in Poland, especially the Brisk nest led by Begin, was not left untouched by the affair. Brisk became a hotbed of opposition and passion, as Jabotinsky went all over Poland railing against Ben Gurion, yelling "blood libel." Brisk became the center of riots and pitched battles between Betarim and members of the leftist Hashomer Hatzair.

Part of the reason for the strong reaction was that Stavsky was a Brisk native, a member of Begin's nest who had emigrated to Palestine. Begin himself was touched by what had happened to his old friend, so much so that when Jabotinsky proposed a reconciliation with Ben Gurion and Socialist Zionism in 1935, Begin opposed it. "One does not believe in shaking the hand of those who hate," he cautioned. Jabotinsky, as usual, ignored his advice.

Begin's attitude throughout the controversy and later is revealing. At the time, he was an avowed enthusiast of the Biryonim, especially Achimeir. Later, he would claim a kind of spiritual kinship and closeness to Achimeir, seeing him as the forerunner of the Revolt, its champion and seer.

For example, in 1962, when Begin was Herut's political leader but nevertheless a politician still without power, he made Achimeir the subject of a speech to his party faithful. Reviewing the dangerous and controversial events of the 1920s and 1930s, Begin praised Achimeir, "who called for the beginnings of the Revolt." Not coincidentally, he was establishing a direct link between himself and Achimeir.

Listening to Begin, you would think he was right in the thick of the battle, as he recalled the sufferings of the Biryonim in the midst of the Arlazaroff affair. "The hatred [emanating from the Left] was unbearable," he said. "The ridicule of our efforts to overthrow the British colonial rule was even harder."[8]

Of course, the Herut followers would not overlook the fact that Begin himself had proclaimed a revolt more than a decade after Achimeir. He praised Achimeir for taking on the mighty, awesome British Empire. "To stand against today's Rome, the British Empire, that was about as revolutionary as one could get. Changing of values and attitudes and preparing the heart for the greatest of deeds, as Ahad Haam has written, the king's road toward a Jewish war of liberation."[9]

"Of Aba Achimeir," Begin proclaimed, "the teacher of the generation of the revolt and liberation, we can say he belongs to the pantheon of the greats of all time of our nation and so he will remain forever and ever." That was in 1962. He was also enthusiastic in 1935, but in a more radical way.

In 1935, he wrote in Betar's Yiddish paper *Our World* that Achimeir "is a pioneer of the idea to delegitimize the British Mandate for Palestine . . . Achimeir's cry will not be silenced."

Coming from Begin, this was strong stuff. It was a cry for the Revolt, which was a heresy in traditional Revisionist circles.

"The message of Achimeir will demonstrate to the nation," Begin wrote, "that we can no longer sit and wait. Words are not sufficient."[10]

Stavsky, upon his release returned to Poland to live with Begin for a while. Both of them wrote to Achimeir.

"Dear Aba," Begin wrote, "I don't know if I have the right to begin a letter like that, but I couldn't otherwise . . . But what shall I write? To congratulate that you won your freedom? All the Polish Betar movement and its branches and nests send you hearty congratulations but I also want to shake your hand and call you *Tel-Hai, Tel-Hai* (the Betar salute). All I want is for you to come to our Vienna conference. I don't have to add words to demonstrate to you why you must come. Your arrival is most necessary. How happy we shall be with you amongst us, and we shall never forget you, never, nor your actions. Come, come, come."[11]

Begin obviously didn't know his man. He might have been surprised to learn that none of the Biryonim expected much more Betar activity in Poland. And Achimeir himself did not show up for the congress, which was a living rebuke to both Jabotinsky and Begin.

As was the case with the Dreyfus affair in France, the Arlazaroff affair would haunt a generation of Israeli political leaders; the searing passions it ignited would never quite cool. This was true for Begin, and it was true for the old Laborites.

I was struck by the immediacy of the Arlazaroff affair once again in the 1980s. In 1981, all the old debates, differences and hatreds surfaced with the publication of a book called *The Arlazaroff Trial,* by Shabtai Tevet, a Ben Gurion biographer who had come across old documents from the 1930s which seemed to prove that Arlazaroff was a victim of the Biryonim. Once again, the debate raged across the nation in speeches, editorials, and pamphlets.

In the summer of 1983, on the fiftieth anniversary of Arlazaroff's assassination, Shimon Peres led a delegation of old Laborites, Histadrut stalwarts, and Kibbutzim leaders from the 1930s on a pilgrimage to Arlazaroff's grave in the old Tel Aviv cemetery.

It was an impressive moment at a site that reeked of old memories, old glory. Here lay the old founding fathers of Israel; here lay Max Nordau, Menachem Ussishkin; here lay the poets, the soldiers, the builders—all in fact, except Ben Gurion, finally quiet in his grave at Sdeh Boker, and Herzl, buried on the mountain named after him outside of Jerusalem which also held the remains of Jabotinsky.

The cemetery was packed with the living Laborites. Peres led the eulogy, while Rabin stood by, stoic and grim-faced. It was an eerie spectacle, giving one the feeling of having been transported back to the 1930s, when the passions were still fresh.

I saw an old uncle of mine whom I had not seen in decades. He was a Labor zealot, a friend of Ben Gurion's, and a true believer of Socialist Zionism. He saw me and began to talk about the occasion. "My dear Amos," he said, "every year I pay my respects to Arlazaroff's grave. Only a few of us old-timers remember what the Fascists did, and go to his grave. But these phony young leaders (he meant, I suppose, Peres and Rabin), our 'leaders,' are using this anniversary because Tevet reminded them that Arlazaroff is a good electoral issue against Menachem Begin and his ilk."

Listening to him, you could feel the contempt and passion in this man's voice, whom I always remembered as a considerate, cultivated Russian Zionist. You could hear the voice of the zealot and realize the power of the Arlazaroff affair fifty years later.

Begin, too, was still impassioned. Even as he was planning the Lebanese incursion, he found time to personally attack Tevet and his book, and the whole spectrum of the political Left. He was still basking in the achievements of Camp David and his political star. He was at his zenith, yet he loudly made the case for his old ally and friend Stavsky, for to defend Stavsky was to defend the legacy and the inheritance.

Perhaps long after Begin and my uncle and his like, and after Peres and Rabin, are gone, the Arlazaroff affair may finally be put into historical perspective. Today, as in the thirties, as in 1983, the issue still has the power to stir political passions, it has the power to bare long-dead political scars to public view.

THE RISE OF THE FIRST ETZEL: 1931–33

In Europe, Betar, Jabotinsky and the Sternists were all engaged in a furious struggle about the future. Etzel, however, preceded that struggle.

The National Military Organization (Irgun Zvai Leumi or Etzel) was not the creation of Jabotinsky, Begin, or even Stern. It was born in the bosom of the Haganah and the Histadrut, and was sparked by the 1929 Arab riots against the Jewish communities of Hebron and Jerusalem. It would eventually be captured by Betarim and, in the years 1937–40, by the Sternists. It is indeed interesting that when the nineteen Haganah commanders seceded in the spring of 1931, they announced the name of the organization as National Military Organization, or Etzel—a name inspired by Pilsudski's P.O.W. *(Polska Organizacja Wojskowa).*

It was this activist group of young Palestinian militants who saw the need for some kind of autonomous, apolitical, organized Jewish defense, that became Haganah B or Etzel.

The first cadres of Haganah B or Etzel were not particularly military or political in nature. They were volunteers—anti-Marxists, not strongly attached to Mapai or Socialist Zionism. Neither did they have close ties with Revisionism or to Jabotinsky, although they were sympathetic to both.

Avraham Tehomi, the Haganah commander in Jerusalem, was attached to neither Labor or Betar. By 1929, he commanded a force in Jerusalem of some one thousand, a considerable size for what was basically an ad hoc defensive unit.

Tehomi organized additional forces and trained a whole new cadre of leaders, including a very young Avraham Stern, his lieutenant. Tehomi was committed to the idea that Haganah should be divorced from political parties and should be an autonomous professional force. This met with stolid disapproval from Mapai leaders. The then Mapai head Yitzhak Ben Zvi hotly recommended that Tehomi be reprimanded for "anti-Socialist and militaristic orientations." The official Haganah commander Eliahu Golomb went so far as to have Histadrut loyalists spy on Tehomi.

Meanwhile, the heads of the Haganah moved against Tehomi. Histadrut officials tried to paint Tehomi and his men as "terrorists." Tehomi tried to quell the furor by offering his Jerusalem arms cache to the National Committee, the executive arm of the Yishuv, hoping to stem the influence of the Left, but to no avail. Tehomi then approached Jabotinsky about the formation of an independent national military organization. In 1932, he met with Jabotinsky and offered to organize an underground military unit loyal to the principles of Revisionism, i.e. working within the legal framework.

Tehomi stayed clear of Betar after Jabotinsky demanded to subordinate NMO to Betar. Nevertheless, Betar responded to Tehomi's call for volunteers, and soon NMO was joined by protégés of Biryonim. A Hebrew University nationalist club, El-Al, consisting of Betarim and radicals who would later play a key role in Etzel—Raziel, Kook, Stern, and others—joined Tehomi's Etzel.

After 1931, Etzel would undergo several splits and upheavals, its ranks swelled by both apolitical militants and revisionists. It would become the harbinger and the academy for the Betarim. In 1933 Tehomi was persuaded to return to the Haganah and surrendered his cache, and Etzel was practically moribund. But the seed for Etzel was planted.

7

The 1930s: Betar, Jabotinsky
and the Rise of Begin[1]

In the middle 1930s, after the Arlazaroff affair and before the onset of serious encroachments by the Stern group, Betar in Poland made an imprecise but noticeable effort to cast itself as a mass movement. This meant defining itself almost as a reflection of Polish nationalism, which had achieved independence for Poland without shedding its innate if sometimes benign anti-Semitism.

Józef Pilsudski was the major figure, the historical giant, who sparked this yearning in Betar to emulate Polish nationalism and to forge closer ties with Polish universities and the military.

The culmination of this effort is nowhere better illustrated than the occasion in 1936 when a monument for Pilsudski was erected in Cracow. All the Poles came out in droves to honor their dead hero. Pilsudski had left an enormous leadership vacuum at his death. But what was sharply noticeable was the number and breadth of Jewish representation at the memorial ceremonies.

The entire range of Jewish political movements was represented, from *Agudas Yisroel* to the anti-Zionist Marxist Bund and all the various Zionist parties and groups. Most impressive and startling of all, however, was Betar, its members all decked out in their brown shirts, splashy lapels and Polish military hats.

Their appearance so impressed the colonels, Pilsudski's military heirs now running Poland, that they gave Betar a place of honor in the marching formations, right behind the veterans of Pilsudski's Legion #1, the Colonels and assorted Polish dignitaries.

There is something almost unreal in the scene, of Betar's shiny uniform. Here was Jabotinsky, solemn, dressed in his best civilian mufti, marching at the head of the Betar, followed not too far behind by Begin in full uniform, stern and imposing, leading a Betar phalanx.

Jabotinsky, as perhaps befitted a friend of the regime, was given the honor of participating in the eulogies for the late marshall. He rose to the occasion, eloquently throwing a sack of sand from the grave of Trumpeldor onto the grave of Pilsudski.

Jabotinsky hailed Pilsudski as the great Polish liberator. "I proudly salute Józef Pilsudski as well as all of our heroes, including Yoseph Trumpeldor, the father of fighting Zionism," he said, thus linking Polish nationalism with the cause of fighting Zionism.[2] Afterward, the Betarim marched in a triumphant and stirring torchlight procession through the streets of the city.

What would happen to Jews now that the tolerant marshall was gone?

Jabotinsky was always optimistic. Speaking before a club of Jewish physicians and engineers in Warsaw early in 1936, he said that "the group representing Marshall Pilsudski will continue in his policies. For you, the Pilsudski group represents the best allies and the only honest allies for the Jews.

"As a nomad amongst the nations of the world going from one country to another seeking allies to our cause, I can categorically say I don't see better allies than in this group of colonels, the disciples of Pilsudski. I have no doubt that the disciples now standing at the head of the Polish Republic wish to stand against the noises of the anti-Semites who are listed among their rivals. I know they aim to help plan and advise a solution for the Jewish problem in Poland."[3]

Jabotinsky was suggesting that Polish help would be forthcoming for his scheme of massive Jewish evacuation and emigration from Poland to Palestine, to which, admittedly, the colonels were somewhat sympathetic, if only as a means of getting rid of the Jews in Poland.

The problem with the scheme was not so much one of convincing the Poles per se, but how to overcome British hostility. Jabotinsky tried to appeal to Polish nationalism and romanticism, calling for the Poles to demonstrate "against treacherous Britain." Jabotinsky hoped that the Polish government would pressure Britain to change its increasingly harsh Palestine policies. But the new Polish government was leery and not ready to upset London, even though Foreign Minister Jozef Beck was skeptical about Britain's and France's willingness to give real assistance to Poland in case of war with Germany.

Through all this activity, the rise of Betar as a mass movement and the changes which it was undergoing, Begin moved slowly up the ranks.

All the rhetoric and language and Betar concerns of the time still seem strangely divorced from any genuine ideological doctrine, or any relationship to the Jewish past and present. The major concerns and topics were organizational and internal in nature. They talked about recruitment and military training.

In contrast to the highly organized and highly ideological Socialist-Zionist movement, Betar was downright meager in both organization and ideology. Revisionism, after all, was a one-man show, and that show was Jabotinsky.

The Polish authorities, at least, were benign in their feelings toward Betar, and were sympathetic to its militarism. On the occasion of yet another symbolic laying of wreaths on the grave of the Unknown Soldier, the Polish press sympathetically described the "image of a new Jewish soldier, tall, blond, and strong." Thus, Betar borrowed its image of strength from those who were ruling Poland.

While Jabotinsky and the movement concentrated its efforts on Polish assistance, Begin's life in the gymnasium and the university was unremarkable, not at all different from the lives being led by other Jewish Zionists and Betarim.

Early on, long after coming under Jabotinsky's spell, Begin had always been impressed by the pomp and ceremony of Betar. Surely, nothing must have pleased him more than the gigantic, large-scale Betar congress held in Warsaw in July 1929, when literally thousands of Betarim from all over Poland and Eastern Europe traveled to Warsaw in full regalia, and camped out in Praga, the city's largest suburb. This was a demonstration of the Jewish Army. A host of Jews wearing military uniforms, marching to military music, stepped into Pilsudski Square to give homage to the Unknown Soldier. The parade ended with a huge sports competition, in which the Brisk nest, headed by Begin at the time, won most of the prizes.

When Begin moved to Warsaw in 1930, he appeared already embarked on a future career as political leader and organizer. But the move to Warsaw was not primarily an opportunity to further his political career but rather a way to advance his legal studies at the University of Warsaw. In Brisk, he had been a Betar cell leader, but in Warsaw he became a national party organizer, earning a meager 100 slotzy a month (as compared to, say, the wages earned by a common laborer, 116 slotzy). But the money did help him through law school.

It is in Warsaw where Begin's real political career began. By 1931, he was appointed chief of Betar's organizational department, although he had wanted a propaganda-education position, for which he felt better suited. Not much is known of Begin, when he was chief of Betar's organizational department, but in August 1930, he took part in the conference of district commanders that met in Warsaw, where he spoke on the need to reorganize the movement, to move toward a true spirit of legionnairism.

As a newcomer in the big city, it could not be expected that Begin would be a conduit for fresh ideas or a rising ideological orator. In fact, there are no records of his oratory from that time. But his writings in the Betar press and his letters to friends reveal something of the budding functionary.

In a Betar publication of 1934, he writes in Yiddish about the purposes of Betar: "Defending the territory on two sides of the Jordan is imperative"; and, "We will demonstrate a different way for Zionism."

This is not particularly fresh or startling and echoes the party line. His main theme in the mid-1930s is anti-Socialist and anti-Communist, echoing Jabotinsky's call for a struggle against Socialist Zionism. He writes in an effort to wean Jewish youth away from the radicalism of Socialist Zionism. "Judenstadt [a Jewish state] is our aim," he wrote. "Betar struggles for a Jewish state, for our two-thousand-year exiled nation, for a kingdom, for a piece of the land." These exhortations are in the tradition of all Zionist youth movements, except for a call for military strength as a way of regaining the land.

In Begin's early writing, there is an obvious lack of political and social theory, an absence of dialectic and programmatic challenges. This is especially glaring when one peruses the literature of the left of the period, a literature that was erudite, specific, and dealt with the whole spectrum of politics, economics and social theory. By comparison, Begin's writings are limited indeed.

In this, Begin reflected Betar as a whole. Dr. Israel Shayeb-Eldad, who stayed with Begin in his exile in Vilna, recalls Betar of the 1930s in this way: "In Betar, all that we cared for was military education, parades and ceremonies." Eldad saw Betar as a movement of the middle class, intellectually and philosophically starved, with the exception of its leader, Jabotinsky.

For Begin, the early and middle 1930s are years of preparation and learning, of finding himself and his role within the ranks of Betar. In practical terms, he was also trying to make his way in the world, living as a law student in Warsaw on Grantiz Road next to Betar's High Commisariat.

In 1937, he graduated, and had the option of going to Palestine, as Socialist-Zionists almost invariably did. But this was not the declared policy of the Revisionists. Betarim, as a rule, were not required to emigrate to Palestine. The Diaspora was still the focus of Revisionist activities, although that would change. In fact, at the time, Palestinian leaders came to Warsaw, as did U. Z. Gruenberg, who came to edit the leading Betar weekly Hamedinah (The State), and Aba Achimeir, whose motives were to radicalize Polish Betar.

Begin was turning into a superb, vehement and vindictive orator. Oratory was the crucial skill for mobilization and organization of Zionist movements and was the impetus of Begin's rise in Betar. He would rail against anti-Semitism, promote the rights of Jews forming their nation state, and espouse freedom and the end of the Diaspora, while attacking Ben Gurion, Weizmann, and the stalwarts of mainstream Socialist Zionism. In many respects only the Biryonim in Palestine were more virulent in their propaganda and oratory efforts.

Jabotinsky had a good deal to do with Begin's rise, for in the late 1920s to the late 1930s he was Betar. Yet Jabotinsky barely acknowledged Begin's existence. Begin is never mentioned in his writings, and much as Begin champions like to portray Begin as his mentor's natural heir, Jabotinsky never intended him to be.

Whenever the leader was challenged by the radicals, Begin's loyalty to Jabotinsky was steady, even though later, as head of Etzel, Begin would embrace some ideas and actions that would have been objectionable to Jabotinsky. This happened, however, four years after Jabotinsky's death.

In 1935, the next Betar convention was held in Cracow. It was not like the first in 1931. It now represented Betar as a mass movement. Thousands arrived, including Jabotinsky, who was a very agitated leader at this point. The crucial battle, he contended, was over immigration and certificates, new issues for Jabotinsky. "We have to create a new Jewish fighter. We must set up naval and marine training to organize illegal immigration." Ousted from WZO Zohar-Betar they were denied certificates needed for immigration to Palestine, controlled by WZO. Thus Betar now started an illegal immigration movement to Palestine. This was to become Betar's first *major* conference, which would crystallize and define its ultimate principles.

With Begin sitting at the executive table, Jabotinsky, weary and tired, outlined for the last time the fundamental and historical mission of Betar:

1. To create the " 'model Jewish citizen,' . . . Betar must climb uphill," he said, "and only disciplined, uniformed and dedicated Jews would do that."
2. "The Jewish state is the central mission of Betar. The state would be the laboratory for the model Jewish citizen. Freedom means living in a free, democratic and parliamentary democracy, for which we can emulate the British and their system."
3. "We must achieve a Jewish majority in Palestine through the return of all Jews to Zion. A Jewish democratic nationalist state must be established on the two sides of the Jordan."
4. "Betar is a rock that must stand on the concept of legion. We need to train military activists who are ready for the campaign over an independent state. We must create the nucleus of a legal, professional Jewish army."

"We are not a reform movement," he told the gathered Betarim, "we are a nationalist movement. Our function is not reform but to build a state on the basis of the old and the new. Reality will dictate to us what is holy.

We have no time or space to design international or Socialist ideas. Our only goal, like the hedgehog, is the creation of a Jewish state."[4]

Begin had the honor at the convention of announcing the formal ritual of the election of Jabotinsky as Rosh Betar, and it was Begin who proposed the notion that one of the functions of Betar should be to "duplicate young Betarim," not to create mature Zoharim. As a true Jabotinsky loyalist, Begin could never do away with the political movement Zohar, and he could never surrender Betar to pure militarism, now demanded by the Sternists in Etzel. Jabotinsky insisted that Betar was the incubator for future Zohar members, for future Revisionists. Thus spoke Jabotinsky, and Begin loyally followed, saying that all branches of the movement must be linked together. "What fits a youth movement doesn't fit a military cell," Begin said, reiterating Jabotinsky.

What was happening, of course, was that the movement that Jabotinsky created was coming apart at the seams, and being infiltrated from inside. Betar opted for military Zionism. Jabotinsky was not yet ready for this revolution, or his movement. It is in this conference that the relationship between Zohar and Betar was turned around. Not only did the latter achieve autonomy, it now claimed ideological seniority and purpose. Begin and Betar, Commanders in fact, set the new rules separating Betar from Zohar in the Betar Commanders' meeting in Prague in 1930. Jabotinsky reluctantly accepted Betar's new role. From then on, Betar set the direction of the movement.

From 1935 on, the struggle for power within Betar reached intense and dangerous proportions, and Begin would find himself walking a tightrope between conflicting positions, between loyalty to Jabotinsky or to military Zionism.

For the next three years, Begin adhered to the Jabotinsky line, at least in public speeches. He conducted an energetic recruiting campaign to Betar, railing against Socialist Zionists, moving from place to place, from city to city. He spoke from any platform available to him—from boxes in market squares to stages in the cinemas, to street corners, to cafes, always honing his gifts for rhetoric and demagoguery. But in the inner struggle within Betar, he moved closer to Jabotinsky's rivals' positions.

In 1937, he was sent to replace the high commissioner of Betar in Czechoslovakia and began a hurried campaign of recruitment and organization. His eye, however, never left the future. He returned to Poland and secured a position with a law firm in Borslav, Galicia, allowing him to combine work with political activity. It also allowed him time to get engaged to seventeen-year-old Aliza Arnold, whom he had met two years earlier. Jabotinsky himself married the couple.

In 1937, however, Begin's concerns remained rooted in Poland. He talked of emigration, of legionnairism and regaining Palestine, but he also had obtained his license to practice law in Poland, still not seriously considering emigrating to Palestine himself.

Stern and his Etzel followers had already given up hope that Great Britain would ever respect the terms of the Balfour Declaration and assume its responsibilities toward the Yishuv and Zionism. It was clear to Stern that Jewish aspirations toward immigration, independence, and statehood were no longer compatible with British goals in Palestine and, in fact, that the British were openly hostile to these goals. Stern's declaration of war against the British Empire rang loudly, even as Jabotinsky vainly clung to the Mandatory.

Even Ben Gurion despaired of the British. "The era we live in," he wrote in 1938, "is the era of power politics. Moral arguments are void. Right and justice are unrealistic demands. The ears of the powers are deaf. The power will only listen to guns, but the Jews have none."[5]

Ben Gurion saw a crisis coming. "I see a situation," he wrote, "when we may fight against England—a political warfare—but the war's target must be to capture the help of England."

Stern further challenged Jabotinsky regarding the nature of the movement itself. Stern saw Betar as a reservoir of military talent for Etzel. This could not be tolerated by Jabotinsky and was unacceptable to Begin. Both Jabotinsky and Begin fought fiercely to maintain the integrity of Betar, even though they could not eliminate or dominate the Stern radicals.

Begin hostility to Britain expresses itself in an article in the Revisionist newspaper *Hamedinah,* warned Britain against treachery and the price it would pay for it.

"We cannot tailor the Zionist problem in diplomatic cloth," he wrote. "Eretz Israel is not bought with money or with diplomacy. We need to demonstrate our frustrations, the hopelessness of our heroism. This is our mission, the mission of heroic desperation."[6] His stance espoused militancy, as when in February 1938, talking to Czech Betarim, he called for Betar to educate, for the Betar in Eretz Israel to fight. "We must become ready to assume a military-revolutionary position. Only Betar can do that," he said. Faced with the prospect of action, Begin retreated to protect his leader and the integrity of Zohar-Betar. Begin speaks of military Zionism, but the action was Stern's, who did more than talk and incite. In December 1937 he arrived in Warsaw to organize clandestine Etzel cells among Betar nests. Stern on his own negotiated with Polish military leaders for training and weapons supply. Neither Jabotinsky nor Begin was aware of his activities or else tried gamely to ignore them. Yet it was clear to many Revisionists that Stern was trying to increase the power of Etzel in Betar.

Stern was mustering recruits and trainees, garnering close to two hundred in his brief stay, and managing to smuggle Polish and French small arms to Palestine. Jabotinsky knew about the training and gave it tacit approval, since it seemed to fit into his concept of "creating a professional Hebrew military." But he was not ushered by Stern into specific Etzel-Polish military cooperation. In reality, Stern was creating terrorist cells, aimed not at persuading Britain but at fighting it, turning Jabotinsky's entire concept of legionnairism upside down. Stern's direct ideas fell on fertile ground, capturing the enthusiasms of numerous young Betarim itching for some kind of action. Now, Etzel's illegal immigration became linked to training fighters against the Mandatory in Palestine.

Stern, who studied in Italy in 1933–34, was influenced by Garibaldi and had translated *Garibaldi and the Thousand,* by George Macaulay Trevelyan into action. In the summer of 1937, Stern planned the training of forty thousand Betarim and others for an invasion of Palestine like Garibaldi's 1860 invasion and conquest of Sicily (with eleven hundred volunteers). To do that, Stern exploited Jabotinsky's good offices with the Polish Foreign Minister, Jozef Beck, the Prime Minister, and the head of the minorities department in the interior ministry. Jabotinsky started negotiating with the highest Polish officials. Although the tacit understanding was that the Poles welcomed the exodus of Jews since 1936 and that the Etzelites needed weapons and training, Marshal Symygly-Rydz, a Pilsudski follower, sought for political purposes, not solely because of tacit anti-Semitic considerations, to guide the Polish-Etzel emigration policy. Jabotinsky signed a secret agreement in October 1937 with the Polish authorities, promising to support "Polish border rectifications." Jabotinsky, unaware of Stern's clandestine deals, opposed the recruitment of Betar to Etzel. When Jabotinsky was congratulated by the Polish Count Lubiansky on the many Zionist military camps and training in Poland, the embarrassed Jabotinsky asked Begin, who was present, "Are they ours?" [i.e., not Haganah camps].[7]

Etzel commanders, under Stern's directorship, expanded their training under Polish officers with the open support of the military authorities. Through Gdansk, weapons for Etzel were shipped to Palestine with the help of Polish authorities.

Betar's reorganization efforts kept everyone busy in 1938, while Stern feverishly continued his recruitment activities. His most conspicuous successes came in the organization of illegal immigration and naval training, which would eventually become almost an exclusive Etzel domain. As war clouds rose, a whole new wind of action was stirring in the ranks of Betar.

In all this Begin was not heard from. And Jabotinsky seemed irresolute, trapped within conflicting feelings. At first he looked with favor upon the military training as a necessary means. At other times, he scolded the "underground" and "immigration zealots." Few of these zealots were listening to him. Hillel Kook, now Stern's man, was conducting immigration activities. The activist tide had swung to Etzel.

The recurring struggle within Betar carried Jabotinsky far away from his own ideas. Often, he accepted some of Etzel's new ideas—Etzel in Palestine, the Betar platoons, and military training, even while he loathed the idea of an independent Etzel. Slowly but surely, even as he remained an enduring symbol of the movement, he became a leader who was being left behind.

By this time, the Betar youth movement had almost totally succumbed to Etzel's fiery influence. It was an Etzel fortress, for all intents and purposes. They disdained the humdrum process of young Betarim becoming staid Zoharim, a process which had about as much appeal for them as the pursuit of Hebrew language and culture did to an earlier generation of Zionist firebrands and revolutionaries. For a highly militaristic movement such as Etzel, Betar was no alternative.

Begin, meanwhile, was operating in the dark, while becoming the focus of the drama within Betar. He continued to fight the creation of illegal cells, but he also became the head of an emerging opposition within the mainstream sectors of Betar, an opposition that was now out in the open and tolerated by an increasingly weary Jabotinsky.

Actually, Begin's move toward military Zionism was meant as a challenge to Stern, not to Jabotinsky. Begin's group published an open letter calling for Etzel to disengage itself from domination of the Betar and to change its political orientation and goals, a rather ambitious program. Begin's aim in this was to defend the autonomy and integrity of Betar.

Begin continued to advocate active resistance in Eretz Israel, using the same methods that had resulted in victorious liberation movements in other countries, using Garibaldi's Italy as an example. Begin also continued to advocate political warfare against the anti-Zionist Agudas and the "salon Communists" in Socialist Zionism.

Begin tried to bridge loyalty to Jabotinsky's concept of legionnairism, and fidelity to military Zionism by calling for the creation of a nucleus of legions in Palestine. He was vague, however, as to whether the military means employed by Betar and Etzel were legal or illegal.

The Begin position was instantly recognized for what it was, a direct challenge to Stern's call for the overthrow of the Mandatory, the conquest of power and the establishment of a Hebrew state. Begin, like Jabotinsky, was aware in 1937 that direct confrontation with the Mandatory would lead to disaster.

Begin continued to equivocate. He was attacked by the radicals but continued to publically support Jabotinsky's legal militarism against Etzel's especially stern call for illegal militarism.

Begin opposed the polarization of Betar as well as the concept of an illegal army. In an article entitled "Our Gift," published in 1934, he wrote of the need to train Betar militarily but not at the expense of Betar itself. "Betar," he wrote, "must be the root from which our movement must nurture itself and its manpower, but not a political movement engaged in politics."[8] Like Jabotinsky, Begin rightly was concerned with an Etzel take-over of Betar.

Thus, it would seem that Begin was thrusting himself in the forefront, carrying the new ideological torch of Revisionism. He did not quite do so, being unwilling or unable to cut the cord with Jabotinsky. Instead, he created a dilemma for himself. He could not bring himself to desert his leader, and by not doing so, he offended the militants. Begin never spells what would be the practical consequences of military Zionism to Betar and Jabotinsky.

When it came to the political struggle against the Left in Palestine, Begin harnessed himself to Jabotinsky with all his might. Here there are no dilemmas. He stepped to the forefront of the ideological-propaganda warfare. In several articles in Yiddish and Polish in Betar's mass papers, Begin blasted the Socialists with unmitigated fervor, unleashing his scathing rhetoric, calling the Socialist Zionists traitors, falsifiers of Jewish nationalism, betrayers of the Zionist cause and even lackeys of the USSR. He called Socialist-Zionism a movement that "would lead Zionism into the abyss."

The idea was to create more favorable conditions for Zohar's workers unions within Palestine. One of the major differences between Jabotinsky and Ben Gurion concerned the right to organize and work in Palestine, which the Left and its tool, Histadrut, monopolized. Jabotinsky wanted neutral labor boards and equal treatment for Revisionist workers.

This amounted to a class struggle. The Left, for political and organizational reasons, did not want to give workers a role in arbitration, whereas the Revisionists felt that arbitration was a national right for workers.

Jabotinsky, in the middle 1930s, had become desperate for an agreement, with the head of the Jewish Agency, his rival David Ben Gurion. Since Zohar had split from the World Organization in 1931, it lacked funds and had no control over the precious certificates of immigration, which the Jewish Agency controlled. Ben Gurion appeared ready for an accommodation also, and the two men came together to sign the London limited-labor agreement of 1935, which gave Revisionist workers equal treatment. To Jabotinsky, this agreement was crucial. Ben Gurion, however, was out of step with his own party, Mapai, which defeated and nullified the treaty that was clandestinely negotiated between Jabotinsky and Ben Gurion. On the Revisionists' side, a minority had opposed the agreement, including, significantly, Begin.

Events, however, were rapidly coming to a head. By 1937, Stern had organized clandestine Etzel cells among Betar organizations in White Russia, in Lodz and in eight other Polish cities, with the help of no less than Avraham Amper, deputy to Propes, the high commissioner of Betar in Poland.

Etzel was beginning to make serious inroads. It was becoming obvious that Stern and his followers were beginning to try to take over. He would try and recruit followers and take over Betar from within. Stern, a man supremely confident of his own views, was contemptuous of Zohar, calling it "too political." His ire was also aimed at Jabotinsky, whom he accused of not fulfilling his duties.[9]

Begin was also openly admiring of the Biryonim and spoke in support of them. He spoke on the unstoppable national spirit of the Jews, and favored breaking the Jewish Agency's policy of containment with Britain, calling for a forceful challenge to the Mandatory. At one point, Begin organized a Betar demonstration in front of the British consulate in Warsaw, resulting in his arrest and imprisonment for six weeks. His prose from jail was passionate—"our Youth is ready for the greatest sacrifice of all for Eretz Israel." In February 1938, at the Zohar convention, only Begin supported Ratosh's (Stern's Canaanite mentor) proposal, opposed by Jabotinsky, to proclaim a Hebrew state.

Matters came to a head in October 1938, at the Third Betar Conference in Warsaw. It was, to say the least, a dramatic moment. Outside, thousands of Betarim in full regalia marched and paraded. Inside, some 130 delegates from 16 countries took their places along with hundreds of Betarim from all over Poland, who had been invited as special guests of the conference.

There was an almost ominous, overtly dramatic tone to the last and most fateful meeting of the Betar faithful in Warsaw in the week of October 11–16.

The meeting, with a host of the Betarim, old and new, in attendance, was held in what was an entirely appropriate place, the Novoszchi theater in Warsaw. One hundred thirty delegates from Betar around the world and hundreds of Betar's youth in Polish cities and villages attended. One could almost hear the ghostly, loud voices of the teeming Polish youth of the past. The large, imposing building overlooking Warsaw was a perfect place for this gathering, which was dominated by voices from the past and voices of the future.

On stage, a menorah two meters high overlooked the table where the officers of the Betar governing body were seated. They included Yirmiahu Halperin, Commander of Betar's Naval School and organizer of illegal immigration; Isaac Remba, editor of the Revisionist newspaper *Hamashkif* (The Observer); Aaron Propes, the current High Commissioner of Betar; Eliahu Glazer; Dr. Arieh Koppel; Rafael Rozov; Yehzkel Dillion; and Yoseph Thrust, the secretary of the Betar governing body. They were all waiting for a legend to make his appearance.

And where was Begin? In 1938, he was now the center of action. On the rostrum, he stood off to the side, a third from Jabotinsky, looking very disciplined in his Betar uniform, his glasses dominating his face, giving it a peculiar imbalance, his hair long and combed back. He was still a middle-level operative but rising in rank. All of his instincts tugged him toward the call for military Zionism, but he could not bring himself to completely desert Jabotinsky, who was his personal idol.

Jabotinsky, representing the past, dominated the meeting, which was held even as the shadows of war encroached upon Europe. It was not the same fiery Jabotinsky. He was markedly older now, and considerably frailer, ailing, his heart a time bomb. But sneaking through the meeting like some silent wraith was Avraham Stern, cool, quiet, a ghostly figure who was much admired by the younger Betarim for his connections with the Polish Army, for his call to action, for his growing inroads into Betar, organizing clandestine Etzel cells within the main body. Discreetly, but in a growing fashion, he stood more and more in defiance of Jabotinsky, who was being seen by many as an elder statesman of waning power.

Jabotinsky by this time was becoming increasingly disillusioned and indecisive. "He is aging," writes Stern to his girlfriend (later his wife), Roni. "He is no longer the man that the masses will follow."[10] He knew in his heart that legal militarism would not work, but he was not ready to countenance illegal militarism and terror, the kind of action that was being advocated by Stern.

Stern spoke softly, so softly that often he could not be heard. He was like a shadow, moving from delegate to delegate. He had the face of a priest, angular, cold, determined and purposeful. Stern represented the future of Etzel and its revolutionary fervor. The conference was attended by young radical and militant Betarim—Stern, Amper, Shayeb and Begin.

The curtain rose and Zeev Jabotinsky, the Rosh Betar, emerged, followed by thunderous applause as young Betar girls showered him with flowers. The conference opened with the singing of "Hatikva," the Jewish national anthem, and with Jabotinsky once again restating the two major aims of Betar.

"We need to create the new citizen of Israel's *Mamlacha* [kingdom]," he said. "Second, we must inculcate into the life of Israel a set of ideas without which there could be no Jewish state."

For Jabotinsky, this meant citizen education as well as military preparedness. Even to Jabotinsky, this must have sounded a little hollow, since he was well aware of the growing separation between the two, and the growing and successful infiltration of Betar by Etzel forces. He felt impotent to unite the two, or to halt the growing influence of Etzel radicalism, which was threatening to destroy his movement. Nevertheless, he felt compelled to try. He had to defend his movement and Betar against growing Etzel radicals who challenged his authority. He told Betar members: "Eight years ago in our conference in Danzig the role of Betar was relegated to that of a youth movement, a step toward Revisionism. Today, it has become a mass movement of grown individuals. Thus the weight of this Herzlian movement must change and shift. We no longer demand that Betar's attitude toward Zohar be merely a respectful recognition of their elders. A gentleman's agreement must prevail between Betar and Zohar. Betar is no longer a youth movement. In Betar, there has emerged a broad elite of major leaders."

Jabotinsky tried to assuage the concern of Betar graduates who might think that joining Zohar would be a step towards aging and irrelevancy. "Betar graduates are the keepers of Betar's treasures and symbols," he said. "They must graduate into the movement (Zohar) and continuously replenish it. The school of Betar, the unity of its soldiers, must be preserved. The treasure of Betar must become . . . the backbone of the Jewish liberation movement."[11]

Obviously, this was a clear call to head off the efforts of Etzel, and to bring an end to radical penetration of Betar. Betar's philosophy was, in a rambling way, charted by Isaac Remba, who called for a synthetic education of civilization *and* militarism for Betar. "Culture," Remba said, "is not only book culture, it is all-inclusive. We who seek the expansion of Zionism must find a balance of the book and the gun. We must inculcate in Betar children aged twelve to twenty-three the other half, the education of the gun, which is more important than cultural schooling."

Stern and his followers apparently recognized that there would be no major changes emerging from this conference. He and Etzel were already operating without concern for the leaders' pleas. But those attending were still expecting some rhetorical fireworks. They came, not surprisingly, from Begin, in a discussion over the uses of the movement's fund *Keren Tel-Hai.* Begin began by offering the money to help Etzel in Palestine.

The conflict reached crescendo proportions on September 13 at 9 A.M. when the conference was thrown open to general public debate. Verbal knives which had been sharpened for years appeared in all their ugly forms. And at the focus of the conference there suddenly appeared Begin, who opened the proceedings and came as close to challenging Jabotinsky as he would ever do in a life devoted to hero worship.

Rising to speak in the debate over means and ends in Palestine, Begin seemed to strike out on his own. "The problem today," he stated, "is not one of what but how. In the last fifteen years of our existence, we in Betar thought ourselves and others out of the first question: Betar wants a large Hebrew state, Betar aspires for a complete solution of the Jewish problem. No one will deny that recent events could do nothing but strengthen our statist orientation. But precisely because of recent developments [Nazi anti-Semitism], the second question arises: How? What will be the means by which we will fulfill our life?"[12]

Begin now called for the startling step of pulling the movement away from politics toward "military Zionism." "We now stand on the threshold of military Zionism," he proclaimed, "and the integration of political and military Zionism will eventually take place. The symbols that accompanied us were Cavour and Garibaldi. Cavour would not have achieved the liberation of Italy without Garibaldi."[13]

Jabotinsky, beginning to bristle, intervened, "I hope," he said acidly, "that Mr. Begin remembers the percentage of Italians and non-Italians in Italy."[14]

Begin all but ignored him and went doggedly ahead.

"Let me bring you some examples from the Irish War of Liberation," he said. "You can fight in another country for your patrimony." "But please," retorted Jabotinsky, "Mr. Begin, sir, tell me how you would move the soldiers of Betar to Eretz Israel without the help of foreigners? [meaning support of the Polish army for Etzel]"

"I say we stand on the threshold," Begin continued, "but we are not yet within the era of military Zionism. I want us to start preparing our military force so that it will not be dependent on the good will of others. When the force is established, the Diaspora will come to help."[15]

"How would that be accomplished?" asked officer Levenberg.

"I only propose an idea," Begin said defensively. "To accomplish it, we must consult the experts."[16]

Jabotinsky challenged him again.

"Sir," he said, "did you pay attention to the disproportion of Jewish and Arab military forces in Eretz Israel?"[17]

Begin remained adamant and quite disrespectful, for him.

"We will win by our moral force," he insisted.[18]

This was too much for Jabotinsky, who, as Rosh Betar, was not about to be told how to set the goals of Betar by an officer member of his movement. He tried to openly embarrass Begin. Jabotinsky was the undisputed leader, and he would have the last word on the debate:

"You must allow me, members and officers, to tell you some harsh words. As your teacher, it is my duty. Forgive me if I speak with some harshness. There are all sorts of noises. There is the whistle and there is the whistle. My attitude toward a whistle differs from others. We tolerate the whistle of a machine, of a car. We clearly do not tolerate the whistle of a door because it has no purpose . . . In Betar there is no place for chatterings."[19]

"The words of Mr. Begin are such chatterings, such whistles. We brutally must suppress such whistles [meaning the Etzel underground]. Truly there is need of Garibaldi's spirit and there is a place for it in Betar. But if we want to adopt Garibaldi's way, this is the whistle of the door. Garibaldi died waiting for the Italian spirit to follow. It was only a hope. Garibaldi didn't face another nation in Italy. In Ireland, the Catholic Irish also live on their land.[20]

We began Zionism out of shame. The shame is that we are not in Eretz Israel. And even if we try to become heroes, against whom shall we revolt? The question of entry into Eretz Israel precedes the eruption of heroics. To Eretz Israel we come with the force of the conscience of humanity, and thanks to that, few of us today dare to speak such talk [as Begin].[21]

"No strategist anywhere will tell you that we can emulate the deeds of Garibaldi and de Valera. This is sheer chatter. Our conditions are far apart from those of the Irish and the Italians, and if you think there is no other way except the one proposed by Mr. Begin, and you have weapons, then you commit suicide."[22]

Few supported Begin in his one and only challenge to his mentor. As Stern coolly predicted, nothing was changed. The only result to come from the convention was a change in Betar's vow from "I will turn my hand only in defense" to "I will prepare my hand to defend my nation and to conquer my land," sponsored by officer Begin.[23]

Yet, Shimshon Unitchman, Betar's High Commissioner in Palestine, who went along with Jabotinsky at the convention, nevertheless was prophetic in analyzing Begin's minirevolt:

"When one speaks of conquest of the future," he said at the time, "let me make some points in Rosh Betar's reply to officer Begin. I don't hear in the words of Begin the whistle of a door. I hear only early voices humming the Hebrew revolt and revolution that is to come . . . But as to the question is the time ripe to hear such things . . . however great the pain, we must guard our nationality even if the heart is torn. But God forbid if we put all the future of our movement on one card."[24]

The tension within the movement remained, but as a result of his brief, heartfelt rebellion, Begin appeared to be shunted aside. Instead of being elected to the security committee of Betar, he was relegated to the ideological propaganda committee. Yoseph Katznelson became Betar's commander in Warsaw and deputy chief to Eri Jabotinsky, the founder's son, who was head of Betar's illegal immigration department, a position which Begin had coveted.

Although Begin had voiced his approval of Zionist militarism not to Jabotinsky's liking, he remained loyal to Jabotinsky, but he was especially hurt and stung when his mentor publicly rebuked him, in front of everybody.

In any case, early in 1938, Begin for the first time contemplated emigrating to Palestine, probably because he was feeling increasingly caught between the movement's warring factions, especially after Jabotinsky excluded him from negotiations with the rebels. He felt alienated, frustrated; choices beckoned, but they seemed rooted in politics and ambition.

After years of loyal Betar service, he still felt left out, kept from knowing what was happening in Etzel, unfulfilled in the hierarchy of Betar. It might have seemed at this time that it was practical to start the journey toward Palestine, as many Betarim were doing now. In Palestine after all, military Zionism and Etzel flourished.

Yet, Begin was probably not yet ready to go to Palestine. He was freshly married; he had just attained his law degree. Begin wondered what his father and father-in-law would think.

There was also the fact that he had put in years of loyal service in the ranks of Betar, and while his name was not exactly a household word, he had managed to find a place on its executive committee.

Begin dreamed of becoming Betar commander in Poland, and then perhaps he could show Jabotinsky and everyone else how he would handle the rebels, the upstart Etzelites. He saw no future in Palestine for himself. David Raziel, Jabotinsky's choice, was Etzel's chief, and Unitchman and Yirmiahu Halperin were commanders of Betar platoons, while Eri Jabotinsky had become the Betar High Commissioner in Palestine.

Begin dreamed, but he was not optimistic. He was frustrated because he had to contend with the powers that be in Betar and in Zohar, the doctors—Dr. Altman, Dr. Unitchman, Dr. Shofman, Dr. Bader and the Weinshalls, and Etzel's favorite young men, Hillel Kook, Shmuel Merlin, David Raziel and Avraham Stern, of course. But still, staying in Poland was the more promising option, competition or no competition. Here, he could achieve the goals of his father, Dov-Zeev, of Vladimir-Zeev. He could become a lawyer, and perhaps the Betar high commissioner.

Jabotinsky's way of dealing with Etzel and the radicals was not to mount a direct challenge. After the conference, he sent a memorandum to all Etzel leaders, saying: "Even today, I really don't believe there are secret cells which are not subordinated to Betar's command . . . I don't believe your aim is to destroy Betar, my creation and my favorite . . . you must bring an end to all these doings."[25]

The note seemed almost desperate and pleading, a wail from a leader witnessing the slow destruction of his movement. In any case, it was to no avail. The radicals stepped up their work of encroachment, and recruitment.

Betar did dole most of its meager funds out for military training, but Begin did not participate in that decision, even later in 1939 as high commissioner. He still held his law office job and thus needed no salary to finance his trips around Poland, where he would lecture, orate and rhetorize at will—with little effect on the movement's direction.

Jabotinsky, meanwhile, continued to precipitate his own downfall, which would in later years be romanticized and turned into a different kind of myth by Begin.

Even at this late date, with the Anschluss and the partition of Czechoslovakia, with which Great Britain acquiesced Jabotinsky's faith in the British was unwavering, not to mention unrealistic.

Jabotinsky once believed that Great Britain never would turn its back on the Balfour Declaration. Jabotinsky's hopes that Great Britain would uphold its promise to Zionism waned, in spite of the White Paper, which was a thinly disguised desertion of the Balfour Declaration and a decided shift toward the Arab cause in Palestine. It woke up even Weizmann, all but radicalized Ben Gurion, and made a mockery of Jabotinsky's position, as well as boosting the cause of Etzel. Cries of armed revolt were everywhere, and in the forefront were Etzel stalwarts like Stern (Yair) and Natan Friedman-Yellin.

Yellin was Stern's second-in-command, and he recalls how Etzel vigorously called for open revolt.

"We want a free Hebrew state," Yair told Yellin. "It is true that we see in Eretz Israel our fatherland. Without it we have no home. It is true that only in Eretz Israel can Jews live as free men. We must recognize the fact that the non-Hebrew government in Eretz Israel prevents the nation from becoming free, which is our right. In our case, the government in Eretz Israel is British and it is a foreign government."

"We must fight this foreign power until it withdraws," he continued. "We must establish a Hebrew government instead. In order to accomplish this, no petition, no demonstration will suffice. Only war, using guns, will bring about a Jewish state."

"We are lucky that the Hebrew nation is not confined within the boundaries of Eretz Israel. Millions of Jews live in Diaspora. Many are attached to the land in which they live but many are also craving for Eretz Israel, especially the youth."[26]

Yellin explained that he came to Warsaw to recruit youth and organize them as secret Etzel cells. Avraham (Yair) Stern hoped now to recruit and train and arm youth all over Eastern Europe, and with them, to invade Palestine. Yair thought that to suppress a revolt of this magnitude, the British would need all their resources in Palestine, and perhaps more. In view of the international situation, the British would not be able to reinforce their troops in Palestine and, as a result, the Jews would win.

In the wake of the last Betar party conference in Warsaw in 1938, Jabotinsky was beginning to feel desperate, as his grip on the movement he created began to loosen and as the rift between the activist Etzel cells and Betar itself widened.

"Midsummer, 1939, was for Jabotinsky a period of ever-deepening inner conflict over his personal position in the *Irgun's* struggle. One day, after a tense discussion with a strongly pro-*Irgun* couple, he exclaimed: 'Well, so what do you want me to do? If you can explain to me exactly how you visualize the struggle, if you have a real plan for proceeding from now on—an all-embracing plan which can only fail because of insufficiency of forces but not because of faulty conception—if you convince me, I swear: I am all yours! I will drop everything; I will not touch my pen except for what the *Irgun* will ask me to write; I will not speak at meetings except at the *Irgun's* request and in accordance with their views. I am ready the moment I am convinced, and your people consider it right, to go illegally to Palestine on the day they tell me to do so, and to do there any job I am told to do.' "27

Clearly, the wind of revolt was blowing from non-Revisionist sources. Stern was not a Betari, and about this time, a rumor spread that it was Jabotinsky himself who had contrived a farfetched plan to send armed Betarim to invade Palestine.

Jabotinsky, dejected and fast retreating into depression, never crossed the border into fantasy. It was true he told Betar youth in June 1939 that "we unfortunately have discovered that the only way to liberate our country was by way of the sword."28 But there is a note of desperation and resignation in that statement, not a full-scale call to action or the development of a practical plan. Jabotinsky was doing his best to keep his movement together.

It was at this time that Jabotinsky, in a flight of desperation, began to formulate and voice a plan for the invasion of Palestine. When Etzel representatives visited Jabotinsky in Vals-les-Bain in early August, 1939, they were startled to hear Jabotinsky ask, "Do you think that the Irgun [Etzel] is in a position to launch an armed revolt in Palestine and, at least for several hours, occupy the Government House in Jerusalem?"29

The Etzelites, rather imprudently, replied in the affirmative, which was enough for Jabotinsky. Far from Palestine, he had no idea of the real conditions there, or of the meager capabilities of the Etzel cells as they existed then.

He went as far as to write a complete outline of a military rebellion in Palestine, to be staged and sparked by Etzel force. The plan called for the transporting of a force of "illegal" immigrants, who would disembark somewhere in Palestine, probably in Tel Aviv. Jabotinsky was planning to come to Jerusalem with the invading force. The landing would be secured by Etzel forces in Palestine. There would be a call for an armed uprising, which would be followed by the takeover of the Government House in Jerusalem, the seat of the Mandatory government in Palestine. During the takeover and occupation, however brief, a provisional government of the Jewish state would be established and announced, with Jabotinsky at its head, simultaneously with the proclamation in Europe and America of a government in exile, as the symbolic embodiment of Jewish sovereignty.30

The plan was grand, unrealistic, probably impossible, and mainly symbolic. It was intended rather as an event that would be highly useful as a propaganda tool. For Jabotinsky, it was highly uncharacteristic, an act of desperation by a man who was losing his grip on the movement he created, a movement that was slipping into the hands of activist Zionists, Etzelites, and Sternites. Yet in only eight years, this plan will become the blueprint for the *Altalena.*

Stern angrily called the plan "quixotic," which it was, and suspected that Jabotinsky was plotting to undermine Etzel radicals, that he was probably placating Etzel with a dream of invasion. More than likely, the plan was the last act of a lost figure who was drifting into grandiose, unrealistic thinking. He was a rapidly aging man, tired, desperate, deprived of his life's creation.

In the end, Etzel's cause was torn asunder when most of its leaders were arrested by the British. But a myth was born and would later make its reappearance when Begin finally came to Palestine to take over Etzel, by then floundering and splintered. The myth was that Jabotinsky was the father of the Revolt and Begin was its heir and implementer.

In reality, armed revolt was always a basic principle and tenet of the Etzel radicals, not of Jabotinsky, Begin and mainstream Revisionism. Begin would turn Jabotinsky's last desperate fantasy into the foundation of the Revolt. History was transformed in retrospect—not for the first time.

Jabotinsky, in a bind without great enthusiasm turned to Begin and appointed him Betar's high commissioner in Poland in March 1939. The appointment came about almost out of default and can be traced directly to a stormy Paris meeting among Zohar, Betar, and Etzel representatives, between January 27 and February 1, 1939, which convened to end schism in the movement which led to the resignation of the high commissioner for Poland.

Zohar was represented by Jabotinsky, Shlomo Yaacobi, Dr. Arieh Altman and Dr. Shimshon Klinger. Mordecai Katz, Eri Jabotinsky, Isaac Remba, Aaron Propes the high commissioner and Yirmiahu Halperin represented Betar while David Raziel, Hillel Kook, Chaim Lubiansky and Chaim Shalom Levy represented Etzel in Palestine. Conspicuous by their absence were Stern and Begin.

The meeting produced some sparks when Etzel was asked to disband its illegal cells. Kook furiously attacked Betar for not supporting illegal immigration. This upset Jabotinsky, who suddenly saw one of his favorite disciples, Kook, turning against him. Etzel refused to call for dissolution of the cells. What finally emerged from the meeting was a rather pristine resolution calling for David Raziel, who was both an activist and a Jabotinsky loyalist, to head Etzel *and* Betar in Palestine. Stern who purposefully didn't attend the Paris meeting refused to accept its resolutions. Behind the back of the new commissioner in Poland, Begin and Stern continued organizing his clandestine Etzel military cells within Betar.

Almost as an afterthought, Propes, realizing he could not work with a denuded Betar and unable to harness Etzel, asked for a leave of absence, which left the position of high commissioner of Betar in Poland open and led to the elevation of Begin.

The meeting left Jabotinsky deep in depression. He had been hovering on the edge of despair for a long time. "I have had it," he wrote a long-time colleague as far back as 1938. "My soul suffers as in death. I am not ready to suffer any longer. Poland is our pivotal center. If Revisionism cannot secure the movement in Poland, then we must leave the stage . . . If we must go down, we shall. I cannot tolerate it anymore. They act like infants, they endanger all that is their dearest and with no reason."[31] Thus Etzel and Stern were winning the day. The British White Paper policy in 1939 turned the scales on Jabotinsky (and certainly on Weizmann). The activists in Etzel, Haganah and Palmach were on the ascendancy. When confronted by loyalists (Propes), Jabotinsky replied, "Don't worry too much. Remember as much as Etzel is important it is an *ad hoc*, temporary instrument, while Betar is forever and ever."[32]

The tragedy and irony of Jabotinsky's career as a leader is that in spite of his obvious charisma and eloquent genius, he lacked the practical political skills and management to keep his movement from falling apart or being taken over by radical forces. It must have frustrated him to know that his movement, which he saw through the prism of his own idealism and romanticism, was being dismissed as a form of "gangsterism" in the mainstream Yishuv, or to hear reports of Stern describing him as "a Hindenburg."[33]

Faced with the potential takeover by Etzel, Jabotinsky tried to harness and control Betar, both in Poland and in Palestine. He appointed Raziel to head both Betar and Etzel in Palestine to head off the increasingly radical influence of Stern. In Poland, he would eventually come to Begin, but in a haphazard, off-handed way that was a far cry from Begin's own description of his rise to the Betar high commissionership.

Begin was not Jabotinsky's first choice. Jabotinsky first offered the job to Dr. Shimshon Unitchman, a Palestine Betar leader and commander of Betar platoons. Unitchman, perhaps recognizing the futility of the job, refused.

Finally, as a last resort, Jabotinsky turned to Begin and appointed him high commissioner in Poland in March 1939, but even that cannot be construed as a show of respect for Begin's merits. In fact, he did not even bother to write Begin a personal letter congratulating him on his appointment.

Even though the faithful Begin supported "military Zionism" at the last party conference, he remained a Betari, unable to control infiltration into Betar by the radicals, his friends. Yet the idea for Begin's Revolt had its origins in Jabotinsky's plan for a Palestine invasion. It was ironic that it would be Begin who would fulfill Jabotinsky's last, desperate dream.

And what was happening in Palestine? Etzel grew by leaps and bounds over Betar and declared war on the Arabs as a response to the 1936 Arab revolt. Etzel called for a war also against the British and the Jewish Agency. The shift from Betar to Etzel in Palestine was rapid.

Etzel's challenge to the Arabs was pushed by young Betar leader David Raziel, an Etzel commander in Jerusalem who, on his own, led attacks on Arab quarters in Jerusalem. The British, with enough trouble from Arab riots, retaliated by arresting Etzel leaders.

The atmosphere for radicalism became more favorable after the hanging of Shlomo Ben Yoseph, in June 1938, one of three young Betarim who attacked an Arab bus in the Galilee Heights. He was captured, brought to trial and condemned to death. The sentence and execution created a storm of outrage among the sympathizers of international Zionism and revitalized the fortunes of Etzel, whose members had all along argued against the Yishuv's policy of containment and cooperation.

At this time, Raziel replaced Moshe Rosenberg as commander of Etzel. Raziel would end up as almost a transition figure, personally loyal to Jabotinsky and Betar, trained by the Haganah, but a firm believer in military activism.

Raziel was born in 1910, in a small village next to Vilna, son of a rabbinical family. He emigrated to Palestine in 1923 and received his early education in the Tachkimoni Religious Gymnasium, then studied literature at the Hebrew University before joining the Nationalist Student Organization El-Al whose most prominent member was Stern and which had become subject to Betar influence. Closely trained by Tehomi, he was part of Etzel and Haganah B, and was opposed to the offshoot reuniting with the Haganah, now firmly under control of the Yishuv and Mapai.

The hanging of Ben Yoseph galvanized Raziel. "Ben Yoseph," he wrote, "was the first victim of a Jewish National Liberation Front, a sacrificial lamb to the foreign Molech [God of Babylon]." Raziel said that terror was the answer to British action in Palestine.

It was Stern who caused giant schisms within the movement in Betar in Poland and precipitated the split of Etzel from Betar in Palestine. "A warfighting organization," he said, "must be totally autonomous. Only a national liberation force can dictate political goals and only it can achieve national liberation by means it sees fit."[34]

Stern had finally thrown down the gauntlet to Jabotinsky. From now on, Etzel would ride the radical, activist storm.

In Palestine, Etzel, disregarding all efforts at reconciliation, launched a three-month spree of terrorist activities just before the outbreak of World War II. Led by Raziel, the outburst was specifically designed to derail all efforts at moderate containment. It resulted in sharp British retaliation and Raziel's arrest in May 1939, along with several other members of Etzel.

Even Jabotinsky's apprentice betrayed the leader. We must remember that Raziel's deputy was no other than Stern, whose influence on the Etzel, at this time was considerable.

When the war broke out, Jabotinsky ended up in exile in New York, where he died in August 1940. He called for the support of Britain against the Nazis. The Haganah cooperated with the beleaguered British in the Middle East. Raziel, instructed by Jabotinsky in defiance of his deputy, Stern, led a mission for the British in Iraq after "mysteriously" being released from a British prison, and was killed in May 1941. At the time of his death, Raziel was respected, but he was no longer popular with senior Etzel commanders. His relations with Raziel were severely strained.

The vacuum in leadership of the radical forces was soon filled by Raziel's deputy, Avraham Stern. Stern, neither a Revisionist nor merely a terrorist, finally split in August 1940 to form Etzel in Eretz Israel. It became *his* organization and was the only active organization representing the radical nationalists of Betar deeply removed from the principles of its founders. Stern's Etzel was an entirely new organization. The old Etzel lingered on under the ineffective leadership of Yaacov Meridor. Not until Begin's takeover in February 1944 would the pre-Stern Etzel be restored to its previous glory.

Stern set forth his own mystical, and messianic philosophy, his own principles of Renaissance—including eighteen points announcing the most extreme, ideological and radical platform in the history of Zionism. Among them were statements like: "the Jewish nation is unique"; "the patrimony of Eretz Israel, of the Torah, borders from the Nile in the South to the Euphrates in the North"; "Jewish proprietorship *(adnut)* over all of Eretz Israel"; and "alliances will be formed with *anyone* who is interested in helping Eretz Israel." The last was a tactical consideration that would lead Stern into strange territory indeed.

For Stern there was always a clear distinction between enemies and how to deal with them, a distinction between *oyev* and *tsorer*.

The *oyev* (enemy) were the British, the Mandatory forces—a transient enemy of the moment. The *tsorer* (oppressors) were the traditional oppressors of Jews everywhere and throughout history, the racists, the anti-Semites of Poland and the mass-murdering Nazis of Germany. They were traditional and permanent foes.

Perversely, Stern had no qualms about forming a tactical alliance with the Jews' historical foes in order to better fight for future independence, which required evicting the British forces from Palestine. A former Lehi commander explained it. "After all," he argued, "didn't Herzl negotiate with the Russian Interior Minister Plehve, who was responsible for the pogroms? Didn't Arlazaroff conduct negotiations with Hitler to transfer Jews and property to Palestine?"[35]

Stern was of course vehemently opposed to any sort of cooperation with the British, but he went further. He considered himself and his group an enemy of the British Empire. He went as far as to attempt to contact the Nazis via the Vichy authorities in Syria. His idea was to organize Jewish youth in the Balkan states to help fight the British as they did with the help of Polish officers in Poland in 1938–39. Obviously Stern never really considered the true meaning, the dark underside of Nazism. Stern, in his fanatical naivety, thought that the Nazis merely wanted to get rid of the Jews, which, to him did not mean a Holocaust. Like so many in 1940–41, he had no inkling of what was to come at the end of 1941.

The negotiations never amounted to anything. Even putting aside the fact that the Nazis had very different plans for the Jews, any contact with the Zionists would strain German-Arab relations, which were counting the Arabs as Rommel made one victorious inroad after another in North Africa. More than anything, the scheme was a reflection of Stern's passionate hatred of Great Britain.

Stern was now building an organization in Palestine and recruiting Betarim who arrived from occupied Europe on illegal ships. They included Natan Friedman-Yellin, Dr. Israel Shayeb and, Yitzhak (Shamir) Yizernitsky all future leaders of Lehi. But as the level of Etzel's activities stepped up —assassination, murder, bank robberies—its fortunes declined.

By the end of 1941, some forty of its leaders and functionaries were imprisoned in the Mizra camp in the valley of Jerusalem. The failure to establish contact with the Axis, the public image of Etzel as "the Stern Gang," a group of unruly, murderous killers in the Yishuv, all combined to tarnish and undermine the movement's effectiveness.

Increasingly, Stern was becoming isolated. His aides were gradually imprisoned and killed in terrorist actions. He was being hunted by the CID and the Haganah, and he found himself wandering from city to city, village to village, often sleeping in streets and alleys. The writing was on the wall.

The situation broke open in January 1942. Two Etzel leaders were killed in a botched bank robbery, which resulted in the death of three other Jewish officers. The Yishuv was up in arms. "The gangsters are once more in action," a moderate paper complained in Jerusalem. Stern was running for his life, and this time he was caught. When the British surrounded the house he was hiding in, he was found unarmed in a closet and shot to death on the spot by British CID officer Geoffrey Morton.

In spite of the death of Stern, which turned him into an even more mythic figure, Etzel refused to die. Instead, it went into another transmutation. The Stern Gang—what was left of it—now became Lehi, leaving behind a badly disorganized and shattered Etzel group. Forty of Stern's followers escaped from Mizra. They were now led by Yellin, Eldad and Shamir.

The years 1938–40 were transitional ones for Betar and Etzel as new commanders radicalized the movement. All the squabbles, the bitter fratricidal warfare, the verbal onslaught against Jabotinsky were drowned out as Hitler's terrible war on the Jews began in Europe. Still, Zionist leaders' rhetoric, Zionist Left-Right warfare did not come to an end; nor did Stern bring an end to clandestine activities within Etzel. Did Begin have any new ideas in response to the war? Hardly. The debates within the movement continued in an atmosphere of unreality—all while the Polish state was destroyed and occupied and Zionist leaders, including Begin, escaped eastward toward Soviet-occupied territories. The 1939–40 debates went on in Vilna and Palestine as if the war would be over in a matter of months. The war ravaged Polish Jewry but not the Jabotinsky-Stern fratricide. This was true of other Zionist leaders in Diaspora and in Palestine.

Let us join the exiled Betarim in Vilna to find out how they thought and acted.

8

Warsaw–Vilna: 1940–41[1]

The outbreak of World War II and the systematic destruction of European, and especially Polish, Jewry by the Nazis marks a watershed in the life of Menachem Begin and also represents a mystery, an imposing mountain of unanswered questions.

The mature Begin, who became Israel's Prime Minister, invoked the Holocaust whenever possible. The Holocaust, for Begin, was an experience and a symbol as well as an effective rhetorical device. Obviously, his experiences in defeated Poland and subsequently in the Russian Gulag marked him vividly. When Begin detected signs of criticism, especially from abroad, he would wrap himself in the mantle of the Holocaust. To criticize or oppose Begin's policies was to become instantly anti-Semitic, to give lip service to the Holocaust. In the terrorist attacks of the PLO, he saw the ghost of resurgent Nazism, an enemy as implacable as the Germans in its determination to destroy Israel. In the Iraqi nuclear reactor, he saw the specter of genocide.

The Holocaust was Begin's justification for aggressive actions like the bombing of the nuclear reactor, the air strike against PLO headquarters in Beirut and the invasion of Lebanon itself. He was, after all, a survivor, a man who had suffered great losses, who had lived through the horrors of the early years (1939–41) of World War II directly, as few political leaders in Israel had.

Yet few historians and contemporary observers have concerned themselves with the question surrounding Begin's survival. Why did Begin, unlike many of his contemporaries in Betar and others in the Jewish and Zionist movements, remain in Poland? Why did he go to Vilna? Why did he not arrive in Eretz Israel until the early 1940s? What exactly happened to Begin at the outset of the war?

There are probably no clear-cut answers to those questions, but some suggestive hints arise, not the least of which is that Begin, in the fall of 1939 and afterward, began to show those signs of emotional and psychic paralysis which would surface again and again during his later career—in the 1950s, in the election of 1981 and in the wake of the Lebanese invasion. This paralysis, or indecisiveness mixed with stubbornness and ambition, was then and would be later accompanied by a strange unawareness to what was going on around him; the leader was being led, oblivious to what was happening in the movement that he was theoretically and nominally heading.

The Holocaust was the greatest single tragedy and disaster ever experienced by a people that had experienced tragedy throughout their long history.

The Jews had experienced the Roman destruction of Judea, the Spanish Inquisition, the ouster of the Spanish Jews, Khmelnitsky's annihilation of 65 percent of Polish-Ukrainian Jews in 1648–49, and the anti-Semitism of every nation of Europe. Yet even the most enlightened and farsighted could not and did not foresee the systematic destruction that was coming at the hands of the Nazis. It was true, the Poles had often been blatantly anti-Semitic, the Ukrainians had a history of running pogroms, and there was the evidence of the Nazis, their *Krystallnacht,* their concentration camps, and their systematic expulsion of Jews from public and economic life. Yet there was probably no way one could envision the highly organized, determined plan of destruction conceived and executed by Hitler and his minions. No one could see the determination latent in the SS, the SD, the Einsatzgruppen. No one could foresee the idea and execution of total annihilation, of the Final Solution.

The Holocaust—as a reality—was something beyond the human imagination. What Walter Laqueur called "the terrible secret," started in all its intensity in late 1941 and continued right up until the last days of the war. It was in the nature of a surprise attack, in that the victims, the Jews, knew something was coming, but they did not know its exact nature, its vastness or extent, its timing. The Jews of Europe, on the whole, preferred to underestimate the true horror of Hitlerism. They saw in the Nazis another, perhaps more virulent, act in the long line of tragedies that the Jewish people have endured throughout history, a terrible burden to live through and somehow survive.

After all, Jews in Germany still survived the war. The Jews of Eastern Europe, which made up the bulk of European Jewry (some six to seven million), remained intact in 1939. Even when Hitler invaded Poland, many Jews remembered the days of the German occupation in the Great War, an occupation that had been basically benevolent. Once this invasion began, however, the Polish Jews of the western part of the country fled to the Soviet-occupied zone.

Even here, few could imagine the possibility of gas chambers—better a sterile life of slavery than death. Disaster seemed predictable, but in no sense did anyone foresee the disaster as taking the shape of the Holocaust.

Thus life for occupied Jews constituted an effort to create stable situations, making the best of dreadful circumstances, exercising a form of damage control. The whole political spectrum of Jewry reacted in similar fashion, from Betar to Hashomer Hatzair to the Left and Right, along with their ideologues and leaders. None believed the dimensions of the coming disaster.

The Final Solution was a horrible secret, one not to be believed, and in this the Jews were no different from the gentiles, the neutralists, the active foes of the Nazis in Europe, Great Britain, and America. The Jews in America had no more of an inkling than the militant Zionists in Palestine, no more than the officials of the Jewish Agency. Jabotinsky, Weizmann, Ben Gurion and Begin all were equal in their ignorance. As late as 1942, they seemed unconsciously preoccupied in their internal politics, in dealing with the British Mandatory, in fighting among themselves.

Begin, who has perhaps had more direct experience on the threshold of the Holocaust than any other Jewish leader, fleeing in its wake to be imprisoned by the Soviets, cannot be singled out for his ignorance. Etzel, Betar, Revisionism, Ben Gurion, Socialist Zionism, Weizmann, the Jewish Agency —all share in the blame, or rather all are devoid of blame for not conjuring up in their imaginations the ultimate tragedy.

Begin, in this context, was no different from anyone else. At the time of the invasion Begin was concerned with the possible Bolshevik suppression of Betar. Mapai, in Palestine, still carried the Arlazaroff torch and worried about the danger of Sternism and the splits in the Kibbutz movement. Stern himself, supremely cynical, advocated some type of cooperation with the Nazis in order to rid Palestine of the British. The Holocaust had not taken place yet, not in 1939–41.

There is no blame to lay here. The Jews of Palestine were no different from those who made up the *Judenrats,* the so-called Jewish self-governments. They were men acting to preserve and save what could be saved, ordinary men acting under the most extreme conditions.

Begin did not see the scope of the tragedy, but he carries it with him more than most, and remembers it more vividly than any Jewish political leader surviving today. There is no mystery in what happened. It is, one suspects, a matter of being the victim of an enormous inferno. You feel the heat, without sensing its size and scope. And you suffer the suffering of millions individually.

In the short-lived but most significant correspondence between Begin and Unitchman in the crucial year of 1941, there are some clues as to why Begin left Warsaw and why he didn't try once more to immigrate to Palestine.

In answer to Unitchman's queries, Begin writes: "We left the capital [Warsaw] and I did it out of simple arithmetic, however ambivalent. After all, all of us believed that Poland could withstand [the struggle] for a month or so and that you could be safe being a hundred kilometers east of Warsaw so that you could wait and think about your next move. Thus we decided on advancing—going eastward so that we could be amidst Betar's masses [in the east] and continue from one of the country seats our limited activities. But we were all disappointed, all of us, including U. Z. Gruenberg, [who did not believe] that the state [Poland] would be ruined in a matter of a month's time, and no one among us could guess that the Russians would come from the east. Thus we were trapped. Thanks to this complication, we remained in the Diaspora . . . I realized that from here there would be no chance for *action,* from here we could not leave. I knew that very limited activities could be possible—thus in view of the conditions here and in Eretz Israel, [what conditions?], it is not possible but to wait with our friends. That's the best possible solution [for now] . . . [as to going to Eretz Israel] there is a very special reason why I cannot accomplish this plan [he doesn't tell Unitchman what it is], but with God's help we shall meet in our time, and then I will relate to you the tragedy and all the complications . . . the main thing is that fate's judgment is that I stay here and—suffer of course, spiritually—since I am not asked to suffer [physically] . . . and only you know how painful is that suffering, nor am I among the last to suffer. But this is the situation, which I cannot change."[2]

Before the war, many visitors and what may be charitably described as Polonophiles called Poland God's playground, but, as the Revisionist radical poet U. Z. Gruenberg wrote, for the Jews it would become the "greatest Jewish cemetery."

For the Revisionist movement, for Begin, for all the factions of Zionism, the invasion of Poland and the bombing of Warsaw came as a deep and profound shock. It represented an awakening from a bad dream and a general, as well as personal and individual, tragedy.

The tragedy was not, of course, a peculiarly Revisionist one, but affected all Jews and Zionists, of whatever political orientation. But it was Jabotinsky and the Revisionists and the Polish Jews who were more affected than most. Poland, after all, was their political homeland, and for the Revisionists, independent Poland, which was now disappearing faster than a quick dream, had provided them with a political example. There is a peculiar unwillingness to recognize reality in the Revisionist's approach to Poland, the war, and the Nazis, even though all the signs were there on the international scene, just outside the borders. Thus Jabotinsky, Begin and company, aware of German rearmament, the rape of Czechoslovakia, the Anschluss and the Nazi regime's strident persecution of its Jewish population, continued blithely with their political activities, activities that would be swallowed up by the tidal wave of the invasion.

On May 29, 1939, Menachem Begin married Aliza (Ola) Arnold, in a ceremony in Trotskowicz, Poland. The nuptials were attended by no less a personage than Jabotinsky himself, a singular honor for the rising Betari.

Aliza would remain steadfastly at Begin's side throughout his career, through the good and bad times, the trials of his escape from Poland, his imprisonment, his days as the leader of the Revolt, the years in the political desert, and his triumph as Prime Minister, right up until the disaster in Lebanon. Aliza died at the time of the Sabra-Shatila massacre, and there were some who speculated that Aliza's death, more than the political fallout from Lebanon, contributed largely to his subsequent resignation, retirement and silence.

Begin himself would tell friends that Aliza was more than a wife and helpmate to him, that she was his best friend, the one person in the world he could talk with. But when one pursues the story of Begin, she seems more often than not to disappear altogether; she becomes a shadow in the background.

The only political activity that appeared to be left to the Betarim in Poland, with Begin as high commissioner, was illegal immigration. Escape from Nazi-occupied Poland to the Soviet zone or to Palestine was on everyone's mind.

Betar's strength was that it had already established some escape routes from Poland via Romania, Yugoslavia and Italy. Its illegal immigration efforts had actually started as long ago as 1936. After 1937, and certainly by 1939, these efforts intensified. Begin and his Betar executives now became totally engaged in escape or *bricha*. Gdansk (Danzig) now became a center of Betar escape attempts, along with Rumanian, Yugoslavian, and Italian ports of safety.

Throughout 1939, one ship or another headed for Palestine, 300 here, 175 there, 350 there. The efforts were usually financed by individuals, since by now Zohar as an organization was all but bankrupt and in disarray. Haganah's escape attempts were called Aliya B; the Betar-Etzel attempts were called Aliya C. In Paris, Jabotinsky, unrealistic as usual, called for a massive five thousand-man escape attempt.

In August 1939, Begin, as high commissioner of Betar, was among the many organizers of a large convoy of Betarim slated for clandestine immigration to Palestine via a tortuous route across the borders of Romania.

He accompanied it to the Polish-Romanian border. The convoy, consisting of close to fourteen hundred—perhaps as many as two thousand—trained Betarim, was scheduled to cross the border on August 31, 1939, and eventually to leave for Palestine in five ships. It was a monumental plan by any standards. Had it arrived in Palestine, it might have seriously disrupted the balance of power in the Yishuv.

The convoy left for southern Poland from the Praga Station in Warsaw as both Poles and Betarim cheered lustily. U. Z. Gruenberg recalls hearing the Polish train engineers singing happily, "The Yids are leaving Poland." The Betarim didn't mind. Yoseph Katznelson, head of Betar's illegal immigration organization and a protégé of Aba Achimeir, happily proclaimed that "We were lucky to obtain trains, and we shall be lucky if the ships come."

The train, however, never reached its scheduled destination, the Polish village of Schiniatyn, just opposite the Romanian border and the village of Grigora-Gika-Vera. The trains were separated en route, with the sections carrying the Betarim separated from the main train, which continued on into Romania.

The eventual destination was to be the port town of Solina in Romania, which lies on the shores of the river, where the illegal ship, *Naomi Julia,* lay waiting. Solina was totally isolated. No roads led to Solina. The only way it could be reached was by man-driven carts in the winter or by small boats in the summer. Nevertheless it was the major illegal immigration port for travelers to Palestine.

The *Naomi Julia* was a four-thousand-ton ship slated to go across the Black Sea into the gates of Palestine. It had once transported Spanish Civil War fighters; now it served a similar purpose, transporting Jewish liberation fighters.

The British consul in Bucharest looked askance at such activities, as the English were tilting heavily toward the Arab cause in Palestine. He called the sea captains engaging in immigration transportation "slave merchants," and the British government put an extreme amount of pressure on Romanian officials. As a result, most of the Romanian visas issued in Poland were canceled. After three weeks of negotiations, the *Naomi Julia* left port, carrying over 1,130 immigrants. But only 300 of them were Betarim, and none were Begin's men. They were not granted visas.

The Betarim were stunned and clung to the hope that it was all some kind of technical misunderstanding. No one was more surprised than Begin, upon whose shoulders rested the decision of what to do next. Begin was stricken with indecision. War had broken out on September 1, 1939, and he told the remaining Betarim to return to their homes if they could. Most volunteered to return home.

It was not an easy decision for any of them to make. Most had already liquidated their businesses in Poland, said farewell to their families and friends, and were psychologically prepared to go to Eretz Israel. The return must have been bitter, painful and frustrating.

Yet, even with war raging furiously in Poland, most of the Betarim, like so many other Jews in Poland, still clung to the hope that the war would be over soon and that the Polish Army could stop the invasion. None of them, not even Begin, could quite perceive what was in store for the Jewish masses in Poland.

What happened? Clearly, Begin and his followers had made a major error. It would seem, from this distance, that even without the train, Begin and his semimilitary organization might have infiltrated across the Romanian border, with the highly corruptible Romanian border guards hardly posing a serious challenge. Yet there was no follow-up plan in case some kind of disaster struck the planned immigration.

For Begin and his movement, the convoy debacle was unforgettable and devastating. No honest or penetrating explanation to it is found in any writings by or about Begin. Conveniently, Begin's autobiographical *The Revolt* starts in 1941 in the Soviet Gulag.

Some of Begin's biographers have suggested that he returned to Warsaw and went to Polish military headquarters with the offer to organize Jews to fight under the Polish flag. There is almost no way this could have happened, because Begin, even though he was the leader of Betar, was not responsible for establishing contact with the Polish authorities. He was never seconded to take part in Polish-Betar negotiations, let alone the secret Etzel-Polish military contacts. There is no evidence whatsoever which suggests that Begin or anyone else toyed with the idea of Jewish legions in the Polish army, not until the end of 1941.

What is more likely is that Begin returned to Warsaw with the idea of going on as usual, as if the war were a temporary intrusion. So many people felt that Britain and France would negotiate for peace. Even though by this time Warsaw was being bombed regularly by the Germans, Begin continued to publish *Der Moment,* while attempting fitfully to organize a joint Jewish effort to escape.

The imminent arrival of the Germans posed a problem for the politically active Jews and their various movements and presented a historically significant moment of decision—whether to flee or to stay with the flock. What is known is that a large proportion of the major leaders of Jewish political parties and youth movements, including Begin, eventually left Warsaw.

"There can be no doubt that the departure of the elite leadership of Polish Jewry," writes ghetto historian Professor Yisrael Guttman, "which included communal leaders and representatives of the Jewish public in Polish institutions, left its mark on the image and bearing of the Polish Jewish community throughout this period. In the course of time, political activists in the underground and the heads of youth movements were to cite this retreat as the cause of confusion and weakness."

Yet those Betarim that remained stayed to fight. Some of them were now in the retreating and disintegrating Polish army. This was an immense undertaking, since Betar and all the Jewish groups were in disarray after the war began and especially after the Poles surrendered. While Jabotinsky was in New York with the organization dispersed, there was no single policy to follow within Poland, even though Begin was acting now as a temporary high commissioner. (He resigned to leave for Palestine.) The refugees, bombings, exiles, and flight of Jewish leaders left Betar impoverished.

Betar had military caches which had been slated for shipment to Palestine but which could be used against the Nazis. The group of Betarim who had joined the Polish army were now itching to continue the fight. Begin himself knew nothing of their plans and did not join them, and never furnished a substantial reason why. Within the Warsaw Ghetto, the Youth of the Revisionist Movement was led and organized by David Wdowinski, the leader of Betar in Warsaw and later head of the Jewish Military Union, Zydowski Zwiazek Wojskowy (ZZW), that was formed in the walls of the ghetto sometime between the end of 1942 and early 1943. They would later play a key role in the abortive and tragic but heroic Jewish ghetto revolt of 1944.

While the battle of Warsaw raged, Begin was still suffering from indecision, still waiting hopefully for the expected Polish counteroffensive which never came. But when a bomb fell on the building where he was staying, he saw the light of necessity. "Let's go," he said to Dr. Israel Shayeb. "Everything is over here."

Unitchman scolded him for leaving, for failing to stay and fight. "You cannot simply relinquish your watch on Betar's High Commission, the highest Betar position in Poland," he wrote Begin. "The captain doesn't desert his ship. Jabotinsky joined the Jewish Legion in World War I to fight." Begin, touchy, turned to hair-splitting, his conscience apparently pricked. "More can be done outside the Nazi zone of occupation than within it," he replied. "A leader doesn't necessarily have to stay. There is no need to sacrifice leaders and men for the sake of symbols."[3] This from a man who followed Jabotinsky and the symbols of Revisionism almost blindly. Begin, however, was not staying. A host of Jews now began to leave Warsaw, heading wherever they could, to Romania, Russia, back to Palestine, or to the United States, if they could secure a visa, and Begin was among the departures. A good many Betar officials, including Begin, would make their way east, into what would prove to be the Russian-occupied part of Poland —something close to going from the frying pan into the fire.

In a perilous journey, Begin headed toward Vilna. Still, the question remains. Why, for a man who later would be so dedicated to resistance, did he not stay in Warsaw or attempt to return? Looking back, Begin saw his actions, as he wrote to Unitchman, and his fortunes, as an act of God, and believed that he was "preserved" by the Supreme Protector so that he could initiate and lead the Revolt. What is just as likely is that he was suffering from physical and mental exhaustion and depression, which would plague him intermittently throughout his life.

Escaping from the invading Nazi and Soviet forces was drama, but it was not the apocalyptic one experienced later by Jews faced with the actuality of the Holocaust. Basically, Jews were forced to decide between the Soviets and the Nazis. At least under Soviet occupation the chances of physical survival were much better. By train, wagons, bicycle, and on foot, thousands of refugees, most of them Jews, Belorussians and Ukrainians, flocked into Soviet-occupied Poland, away from the Nazis. Begin and his family, Aliza, Dr. Arnold and his brother-in-law packed their belongings, and, joined by Dr. Shayeb and Friedman-Yellin, who would become the Commander of Lehi in 1942, started on their journey. The train in which they were traveling was constantly being harassed and bombed by Nazi Stukas and was stopped in Lvov after forty kilometers. The entourage decided to make the rest of the journey by foot. For a week they walked on roads from village to village, and on September 17, 1939, they finally reached the village of Machov.

Begin never wrote about that journey, perhaps because it was not nearly as dramatic as his sufferings in Soviet captivity. His autobiography picks up in Vilna, with his arrest by the Bolsheviks.

His autobiography also does not take up the question of the numerous options still available to him at this late date. He could have, instead of waiting to be arrested in Vilna, journeyed south as so many other Jews did. He had access to money through his father-in-law, a well-to-do lawyer. In fact, the Lithuanian government was encouraging Jews to leave until 1941, following a government policy that the refugees [Jews] did not "fit with the Sovietization of Lithuania." Some of the refugees, under the auspices of the NKVD, were given certificates of good conduct as well as visas, although many Jews saw the visas as a plot by the Soviets to obtain information for future use.

Begin, unlike so many others, fled neither to the United States nor to Palestine. He and Yellin made the slow forty-kilometer journey, walking the last part of the trip, to the village of Machov. On September 17, they found out that Russia had invaded eastern Poland. The choice now was whether to continue east or to return to Nazi-occupied Poland. Begin decided to go to his wife's home city of Drohiczyn. Then when the Soviets returned Vilna to the nominal control of Lithuania, that city suddenly attracted hundreds of Betarim and thousands of exiled Jews, including the Begins, who saw it as an island of relative safety in a deadly and stormy sea.

In the early days at Vilna, the Begins stayed with the Rabinowitz family. While Begin busied himself with organizing the Polish refugee Betarim, Vilna's Betar leader Yoseph Glazman tried to find ways of escape. There were several ways out. There was the possibility, at least for males, to join the Lithuanian army, not a terribly realistic option. Another was to buy exit visas using dollars, which the Russians desperately needed. There was also the option of joining the Polish underground, hardly an attractive alternative, since the Soviet NKVD was also busy squashing the nationalistic tendencies of the Poles and Lithuanians. By this time, Zionism had become a political crime.

The Betarim refugees opted to hide in the outskirts of Vilna, in a summer resort called Fabiliona, populated mostly by Polish government bureaucrats and apparently safe from Soviet intelligence authorities. Menachem, Aliza, Israel and Batia Shayeb, and Dr. Leon Arnold, Aliza's brother, all camped out at the resort.

Small wonder that Vilna, in spite of the tragic situations and harrowing dangers now confronting Jews, would seem so attractive a haven. Ever since the sixteenth century, Vilna was known as one of the most glorious cultural centers of East European Jewry. Founded in the twelfth century, it was there that many of the intellectual and cultural changes which rocked East European Jewry would find their focus. It was in Vilna that the first signs of the Haskala or Enlightenment were detected. The father of the Jewish romantic novelist, Avraham Mapu, lived there. The most famous Jewish publisher *Dfus Ha-Almana Ve-hachim Reem* was in Vilna. Vilna was also the storm center for the great international cultural conflict between the *Hasidim* (orthodox) and their opposition the *Misnagdim* (secular), the two major schools of Jewish orthodoxies.

The Treaty of Versailles had established the Polish frontiers in the west, and the Allied Supreme Council laid down the so-called Curzon Line for Poland's eastern frontier, which deprived Poland of Vilna. In April 1919, the Polish troops entered Vilna after defeating the Red Army. In 1920, the Poles overran the Ukraine, but a Soviet counteroffensive drove the Poles out of Kiev and Vilna. Once again, Vilna became a Lithuanian capital, but only for a short time. On January 8, 1922, an enforced plebiscite showed a majority of Vilna's citizens favoring incorporation into Poland, which duly occurred in April. Although the Lithuanians never gave up their claim to Vilna, and the Soviets supported them, Vilna remained a part of Poland until the Nazi-Soviet Pact of August 1939.

In the wake of the Russian invasion in 1939, Lithuania was forced to sign a mutual-aid treaty with the Soviets that gave Russia the right to fortify the Lithuanian-Soviet border. In return, Lithuania got Vilna back.

By early 1940, Vilna was bulging with Jewish refugees, most of them from western Poland. It was a polyglot city with an already huge Jewish population now made larger. Arriving in the wake of German victories were some 2,200 Pioneer Zionist Youth Movement members, another 2,000 Yeshiva Orthodox Jews, some 400 rabbis and their entourage, some 100 Bundists, 300 Poale Zionists, and 700 Revisionist Betarim, including Begin and his wife.

The city was bristling with diverse, passionate and conflicting Jewish and Zionist activities. It began to fill with Zionist and non-Zionist leaders, writers, students and professionals of all sorts. Lithuanian Jewry came to the aid of the refugees with open arms and great warmth.

Soon, the refugees were organized back into their old political forms, although with considerably less effectiveness. They established a Palestine office, made contact with other Polish-Jewish organizations in London and New York, and received help and money from Jewish organizations abroad.

The question is that although danger from both the Russians and Germans was approaching steadily, could Begin have made his escape from Vilna? We know that he did not, but did conditions exist to allow such an escape? The answer is yes; hundreds and thousands did make their way out of Poland, and Begin was in better shape to do so than most. During the Soviet rule in Vilna, some twelve hundred Polish-Jewish refugees left between June 1940 and July 1941 for Palestine via the Odessa-Constantinople-Syria-Palestine route. Their departure was made possible through the purchase of NKVD visas paid in dollars to Soviet controllers.

Obviously the Soviets were trying to do something about foreign refugees. They did not allow Lithuanian Jews to emigrate, since that meant a rejection of Bolshevism. Sometimes they resorted to exile, and, in fact, some one thousand Lithuanian Jews were exiled to Siberia in June 1940.

The Soviets resorted either to allowing Polish emigration or exiling local Jews because the presence of so many diverse Polish-Jewish political groups threatened Soviet interests in Lithuania.

Another possibility was emigration to the United States, although this was a difficult route. The Lithuanian delegation in the United States was attempting to enlarge the quota of Lithuanian emigration, to no avail. In fact, the U.S. State Department throughout the war went to great lengths to block Jewish immigration from occupied Europe.

Finally, in November 1939, the Jewish Agency appealed to the Soviet Government to permit the transfer of Polish Jews in Lithuania to Palestine via the USSR. Some four thousand Jews left Vilna in 1940. Yet Begin did not take advantage of this route, even though he and his wife possessed a visa which allowed departure.

And what was he doing in Vilna? He wrote letters and appealed for help in the United States, sending reports to Jabotinsky in New York about the situation in Vilna:

"Thus," he wrote to Jabotinsky, "despite the great tension . . . we were lucky not to fall to the forward authorities. We can wait here and look ahead . . . Our plan is provisional, of course, and we won't know if we can succeed when the time of crisis really arrives, but it would be possible to save [the remaining Jews] through certain measures to delay the threat of arrests. For this purpose, we need means [money], . . . There are now great opportunities for real help; we can transfer groceries [weapons] to the occupied territories where we have close contacts . . ."[4]

Begin ends the letter in a respectful, almost apologetic tone: "Mr. Rosh Betar, please forgive us that we make now these requests. We are aware that it will be a most difficult task and that money is necessary for a thousand other purposes. But recognizing our responsibilities to our friends who face real danger on one hand and poverty on the other, we hereby honorably request immediate help."[5]

Begin's biographers and apologists suggest that during his stay in Vilna, Begin was busy organizing, or was active in Betar politics. The truth is that Begin seemed to be passive, spending a good deal of his time writing letters and being unaware of what was happening in his own movement. Escape plans and operations were organized not by Begin, but by Yoseph Glassman, the Betar commissioner in Vilna who later became a famous Partisan. It was Glassman who organized the refugees in Vilna, not Begin. In the new Betar hierarchy, Glassman was appointed Gondar (the next highest rank under Jabotinsky, exiled in the United States) while Natan Friedman-Yellin was his deputy. Begin's only role was to participate mildly in a Betar conference organized once again by Glassman.

Begin seemed unaware of what was actually happening in Betar, and especially with Jabotinsky. In Vilna, removed from the mainstream of Revisionist policy and activities, Begin was unaware that Jabotinsky had declared Betar's support for the British declaration of war against Germany; nor was he aware that secret cells of radical Etzel members continued to thrive, even among the Betarim in Vilna.

Moving closer to Etzel policy, he wrote to Shimshon Unitchman, Betar leader in Palestine, that Betar must not become petrified, that it must conform to "the true flow of life." In his letters, he is categorically certain that Great Britain will never fulfill the promise of the Balfour Declaration, that it would attempt to prevent the establishment of "the kingdom of Israel." While Jabotinsky was calling for support of Britain's war against Germany, Begin wrote that "Zionist support of Great Britain is unrealistic."

"This has been the source of our woe for the last twenty-three years [since 1917]," he wrote to Unitchman. "We were hit by lightning, and the movement cannot be struck in times of crisis."[6]

Exile from Warsaw to Vilna didn't end the internal debate among Betarim, which came to a clash with Rosh Betar himself at the party conference in Warsaw in 1938. The issues of relations with Britain, and military Zionism (i.e. Etzel) were now complicated by the war. What should Betar's policy be? No guidance had been given by Jabotinsky since the 1938 conference, where he reiterated his policy of legal and political above-board struggle against Britain. Writing a long letter from Vilna to his comrade, Betar platoons commander Dr. Shimshon Unitchman, Begin continued the debate. It is interesting to read what a former Betar chief in Poland, now a refugee in Vilna, thought about Britain, and especially what he thought about the new world war, now that he had become its victim.

Begin is certainly consistent. He writes of his distrust for Britain and his faith in the Jewish people and in Betar. He scolds Dr. Unitchman for "believing faithfully that those who now fulfill the White Paper policy [Britain] will tomorrow establish the Jewish state." He writes: "It was our affliction in all the centuries to believe, to trust. . . . To believe is to believe only in oneself [and that self is] my poor Jewish nation, but I believe in it. I may succeed and, if not, there will be those who come after me . . . The key is: this is the way that I know, and I faithfully believe in it!"[7]

Begin, unlike the Revisionist party in Eretz Israel and the rest of the Yishuv leadership and parties, is certainly not reconciled to cooperation with Britain in its war with Germany.

Now comes the Begin crescendo, the rise of the true Etzel ideologue four years before he became its chief in Palestine. You may recall that Begin challenged Jabotinsky on military Zionism in 1938 in the Third Betar Party Conference in Warsaw. And Jabotinsky rebuked him without mercy. From Vilna, the refugee who started his first sojourn in the era of the Holocaust to come, continued the debate of 1938. After relating to Unitchman his innermost yearnings and considerations, he writes that he is not really sure whether the "storm," i.e. the war in Europe, will last and for how long it will change everything. "On the matter of Garibaldi [military Zionism] I am sorry I cannot add much [whether it's a matter of formulas or principle]. As you may recall, I debated the issue with Rosh Betar not only in the conference but personally as well. I have had very long private conversations with Rosh Betar in Warsaw, and I have a clear position in this matter [opposing Jabotinsky's formula for legal military Zionism]."[8] We now come to one of the most interesting of Begin's thoughts in 1940. From the letter he seemed much closer to Stern, Shayeb, and Etzel radicals than to Betar and Jabotinsky. Stern and Lehi clearly distinguished *tsorer* (oppressor), the *haman*—Hitler, from *oyev* (foe)—the British.[9] You can cooperate with the oppressor temporarily against a foe.

Begin, in the same letter to Unitchman, now advocates a Sternist argument: "Concerning my attitude toward the war . . . *I confess today this war is not our war. . . .* 'Our war' is probably a most positive concept, but I, a Zionist, have searched for its reasons [its purposes] and I haven't yet found them. In what way is the war 'ours'? Because the other side hates Jews? and the coalition [the Allies] is its foe?

"May I remind you that several previous [historical] cases prove me right [no examples] . . . one of our Lithuanian friends [a Betari] told me, 'We call ourselves partners [with Britain].' But what sort of 'partnership' is it? We only *hate** [together with Britain, Germany], but our common hatred in itself doesn't create a political partnership. . . . *This is not our war.* Of course it would be most awful if the Germans won the war. [He doesn't call them Nazis!] Bad for not only us Jews but for all humanity."[10]

Those words, in view of the Holocaust and Begin's late oft-repeated invocation of it, now sound soft and ingenuous, as if Begin was operating in an atmosphere of unreality. In many ways he was.

These letters to Unitchman seem not so much a description of reality as a list of ideological arguments.

Unitchman scolded Begin for leaving Warsaw, reiterating that he realized Begin did not flee merely to save his own skin. Unitchman was writing from the relative safety of Palestine, and advised Begin to first stay in Vilna, then flee, or join the Soviet legions, at least until the political situation changed.

The correspondence between the two men reveals a doctrinal, ideological and perceptual difference, perhaps only natural, between the Betarim of Poland and Palestine.

Thus, Begin writes that "the nests in occupied Poland must not be abandoned. But you are wrong in your judgment that the leaders must remain . . . it would be of no value. It would only be symbolic. What we could not have done [from the occupied territory] we can do here. . . . We are renewing the publication of *Hamedinah* for all Betar in Poland, which we couldn't have done from occupied Poland."[11]

Begin justifies his continued presence in Vilna as a way of carrying on with the publication of *Hamedinah,* which seems a curiously lame explanation. The two men continued to engage in long-distance ideological arguments.

"Dear Begin," Unitchman writes, "I have received from you a detailed letter but I cannot accept your assumptions. I have a feeling that you now are further from reality than you have ever been. You make judgments and cupboard decisions as if nothing had changed in the world. As if we were back in Warsaw [1938], peacefully discussing matters in Betar's High Commission, making decisions on what we would have done in 1914. Times

* Begin's emphasis.

have radically changed. I will try to explain in a most fundamental way so that we don't get lost in phraseology. I was always realistic in my idealism, and thus I never believed and always opposed such chatter as 'England the *occupant'* [occupier] or a 'Revolt against England.' I always demanded the practical arithmetic, and I never believed we could get anything from England in that manner. I completely believe that the Jewish question will also be resolved in a Hebrew state with the help of England and within the framework of the British Commonwealth . . . I never conceived that we would force England, but I was also convinced that England would treat us as a nation and not as 'rogues.' "[12]

It is this Unitchman who defended Begin in the 1938 Warsaw Conference against Rosh Betar. "Permit me to note Rosh Betar's reply to Officer Begin: I do not hear in his words the whistle of a door, I hear in them the voice of the promise of the revolution, the Hebrew revolt that is going to come."[13]

Unitchman thus represents mainstream Revisionist Zionism, which Begin, when he leads the revolt, would desert. But then, Etzel and their beliefs represented an extreme form of Jewish romanticism, which Unitchman rejected.

The morale of the endangered Betarim in Vilna and elsewhere was further jolted in August 1940, when they found out that their Rosh Betar, Jabotinsky, had died suddenly in New York. The shock was monumental since the attachment of the Betarim to their leader, no matter what the schismatic differences within their ranks, was total and filled with reverence and affection.

Already harassed by the watchful Nazis, the Betarim in Warsaw could not conduct a funeral parade for their beloved leader. Still, *Hamedinah* published the news in Warsaw, proclaiming Betar's grief and its inability to mourn in public. In Vilna, they mourned openly, conducting a memorial for Jabotinsky in the Jewish cemetery and raising the blue and white flag of Betar.

All along, Begin seemed aware of the danger from both the Germans and the Soviets, yet he seemed unable to move, as if he had gone into a sudden emotional and political retirement.

In a letter written to Shalom Rosenfeld, a Betar leader in Palestine, he writes as early as November 1939: "We hear awful news from the German-occupied territory, concerning Betarim. The German governors . . . threaten Betar members with death. . . . I have been sent here, and I am miserable. I have no information on the movement. Every little detail will interest us here. Don't save on information."[14]

The tone is helpless, like a man resigned to his fate, which was coming soon. He was unaware of Etzel activities. He seemed to have little to do with the actual workings of the Betar units in Vilna. He could have escaped and chose not to. It was as if he turned to stone.

Eventually Begin went underground as pressure from the Soviets increased. The newspaper *Hamedinah* was destroyed, along with its printing press. The Soviets were hunting Betar-Zohar operatives who were seeking refuge in the underground.

To the very end, Begin made no attempt to leave. Warned that the Soviets were searching for him, he left for refuge in a small village near Vilna, where he was easily found and captured.

It is not my intent to judge Begin, but rather to present the mystery of his passiveness, which will occur again and again at moments of crisis. No one can judge Begin's predicament in World War II Poland, nor say what he should or should not have done. His behavior, however, was symptomatic. It would lead him to the Gulag, out of which would come *White Nights.*

The calm did not last long. On July 15, 1940, the Red Army entered Vilna, and soon its NKVD agents were rounding up refugees. The Betar group immediately went underground, along with its newspaper as the NKVD, with the help of some Jewish informers, began searching for politically active Jews, and that included Begin, who was, after all, a nominal Zionist leader.

Begin's hesitant freedom and inactivity lasted for only three months. In the first week of September, Begin, then twenty-seven years old, received an "invitation" to present himself at Room 23 of the Vilna municipal office between nine and ten A.M., ostensibly to "arrange for your papers."[15]

Begin must have had no illusions about what the summons meant. He was to be interrogated by the NKVD. Begin ignored the so-called "invitation." "I had nothing to do with it," he would say later. "If the Vilna authorities wanted to arrest me, they could. Their agents knew how."[16]

Now the NKVD took over. Begin later said they wanted "live meat," in the person of one Menachem Begin, and soon their agents came after him, couching their actions in diplomatic doubletalk.

Begin would have none of it. He bluntly protested to his interrogators that he had been arrested, even as they insisted for the longest time that he had been merely "invited" or "summoned." "Who told you that you were arrested?" they asked, relentlessly keeping up the charade. "We have only a few honest questions to ask you, and if you'll answer them honestly, you could be back home soon."[17]

Begin, characteristically, saw through the charade. It was the first step toward the Gulag, toward the ordeal that he recounted in his *White Nights,* a work on the Gulag predating Alexander Solzhenitsyn.

Begin's book and his experience do not by any means constitute as moving a human and moral document as that produced by Solzhenitsyn, but they do present us with a glimpse of the man, his capacity for courage and defiance, and his pride in being a Revisionist Zionist and loyal follower of Jabotinsky. There is suffering here, certainly, but there is also humor and patience and a cool, realistic logic, a willingness to be a martyr. He was not thrown into a genuine, forgotten and miserable Gulag, but he was on the precipice. He was close enough to the edge to see the system for what it was.

From his first summons, to his arrest, through his interrogation, through the journey to the camp, he was a man prepared to be humiliated, harassed, and deprived. This readiness made him strong. All along, ironically, this was an experience he could have avoided: he could have escaped after his first "invitation," or he could have joined partisans, or returned to Warsaw. He chose to stay and suffer what was to come.

Through the interrogation, through the entire experience, he never lost the sense of who and what he was in his mind: a Jew, a Zionist, a Revisionist, a Betari, a man of Jabotinsky. He took a proud and uncompromising stand against the darkest machinery of Stalin's Soviet system. His style in *White Nights* may be dry, but the message is moving. He all but cried out his activist message to his interrogators, proud to be a leader, a follower, and a Betari. In this instance, at least, his self-image as a romantic figure stood him in good stead. His view of himself as a new, activist Jew and his abilities as a hairsplitter and rhetorician helped him survive right from the beginning.

His initial stance of defiance remained. His refusal to respond to the first invitation was typical. "Let them seek me, why should I volunteer?" he asked. "Why should I respond to this 'polite' invitation?" He saw through the charade of questions and answers and said so. "I will not be a witness testifying for you. I will not be a turncoat."[18]

The most crushing development was not his arrest, but the news of Jabotinsky's death. "I nearly died," he recalled. "The bearer of hope was gone." But when they came to arrest him, he reacted with humor. He had been playing a game of chess with Dr. Arnold. "I concede the last game," he said. "You were ahead anyway."

The NKVD, assisted by Lithuanian informers, soon found Begin and arrested him for his Zionist activities. David Yotan, a Betari who lived not far from the resort, remembers how the NKVD officers came for Begin, how Begin resolutely and with great, simple dignity said goodbye to Aliza and Dr. Sayeb. Aliza stood by with quiet courage. There were no tears, no overt signs of fear, although Aliza obviously must have feared for her husband. Aliza visited Yotan's home frequently when Begin was being interrogated by the NKVD. Her main concern centered around being able to send Begin packages, which were enormously expensive, since food, like anything else during that time, could only be bought on the black market.

All of Begin's friends stood by Aliza while she waited near the Lukishki prison to deliver her packages. The packages were rifled by the Soviet and Lithuanian guards to the point that Begin never got more than half of their contents.

The Yotans were trying to persuade Aliza to leave Vilna and, as a prisoner's wife, she could have gotten permission from the NKVD to do so. But she refused to involve herself in the negotiations over her departure. She wanted to stand by Begin, to be near him.

In many ways, her behavior was remarkable. She was, after all, only twenty years old. In a short, whirlwind period of time, she had become a refugee and exile, had watched her husband imprisoned and now heard even worse news: her husband was being sent to northern Siberia. There appeared to be no possibility of his release.

Finally she broke down and accepted her fate. She would leave with the Yotans. "I don't know if I should bless or curse you for the rest of my life," she told Yotan.

Begin would learn of her departure for Palestine in a curious manner. One of her last packages contained a handkerchief, engraved with the monogram OLA. It was meant to designate the Hebrew word *Olah*, which stood for immigration to Palestine.

Not until March of 1942 did Aliza know with any certainty where her husband was and that was after Begin had been released into the ranks of the Anders army. They renewed communications after his release from Siberia. Before that, all had been silence.

His interrogators kept insisting that he "better tell us the truth." Begin was quite willing, and he engaged a succession of questioners in debate about Zionism, politics, and Communism. This infuriated them. "How dare you compare Jabotinsky with Lenin?" one of them screamed. He was accused of active crimes against the state because he was a Zionist activist.

Begin would not deny his activism. He was quite proud of it. "When God handed out ten degrees of pride," he said, "the Poles took nine of them," but he could have been talking about himself.

The interrogators tried to break that pride by insulting Zionism, calling Jabotinsky a "Fascist," depriving Begin of sleep, tantalizing him with the possibility of seeing loved ones. "We have ways of making you talk," they said, echoing movie villains.

Begin countered with legalities, even as he was accused of fifty-eight antirevolutionary activities. "Why do you keep wanting to play the hero?" his interrogators asked him, as their frustration rose. Begin *did* want to be a hero, but he was not playing. His idealism held up. "Happy is the man who believes in the world that rejects tyranny," he said to himself. "I am ready to give up my life for my ideals."[19]

He told them what they already knew, and quite readily and proudly admitted to being the Warsaw head of Betar. He went on a hunger strike. In the questioning, he continued to split hairs, to debate, to set forth the ideas and ideals of Revisionism.

To no avail. He was convicted in one of those eerie, almost unreal Soviet-style court proceedings where everything is cut and dry, by the numbers, where people become numbers. So began the journey north toward the camps, which Begin describes vividly but with also a curious detachment, spending time to tell stories about other prisoners.

Begin might have disappeared into his own dark night in the Gulag, but history and politics intervened with the Nazi invasion of Russia, which changed the Soviet stance toward the thousands of Polish refugees within its borders. Begin, of course, was one of them.

9

The Polish Anders Army, The Jews, and Begin[1]

In all of Begin's career, writings and speechifying, there is a deafening silence about his experience and feelings about serving in the Polish army, an organization that was notoriously anti-Semitic.

The Polish army laid every imaginable obstacle in the path of the Jews wanting to serve in its ranks. It discriminated against them, and so strongly discouraged Jewish recruitment that Polish political representatives in the USSR and in London were embarrassed.

Yet there was never a word from Begin on the subject of the Polish government in exile. Ambassador to the USSR Stanislaw Kot wrote that "several times, I called to the attention of the military authorities the danger to Polish interests if the army, due to its bitter feelings or the behavior of the minorities—i.e. the Jews—during the Soviet occupation, or due to nationalist irritation (by Jews and Poles) were to let itself fall into the Machiavellian political trap laid by the Soviets . . . Unfortunately, the army command didn't demonstrate serious understanding of the situation."[2] "The command continued its anti-Semitic and discriminatory policy, now arguing that the policy of restricting Jewish recruitment was due to the fact that the Soviet administration with vindictiveness directs the Jewish masses to the army *in order to distort its national character.*" [italics mine.][3]

But we do not hear the usually strident voice of Begin defending Jewish pride, condemning Polish racism or the Polish Army's notorious anti-Semitism. Begin remains silent in *The Revolt* and elsewhere, while railing against basically liberal England.

Begin joined the Anders Polish Army after his release from his imprisonment in the Gulag, what he called his "white nights" in Siberia. He served in the army as a corporal until the end of 1943, when he finally emerged in Palestine to become Etzel's fourth commander. The story of Anders is important for two reasons: First, because Begin served there; and second, because he played a role in the abortive effort to establish a Jewish legion in the Anders army.

The Polish Army in the USSR, better known as the Anders army, was organized after the Germans invaded Russia in the latter part of 1941. It was created after a Polish-Soviet agreement which provided the formation of a Polish Army on Soviet territory. Up until that time, there existed nothing but open hostility between the Poles and the Soviet Union, which had ruthlessly joined in still another dismemberment of Poland after Germany ignited World War II by invading it. Prior to the latter part of 1941, the Polish government-in-exile in London had no official contacts with Soviet Russia whatsoever.

Although the German invasion of Russia did not immediately ignite a thaw, Polish General Wladyslaw Sikorski, a pragmatist, changed the rules. He favored negotiations with the USSR, echoing Polish poet Adam Mickiewicz, who wrote, "Measure your power by your purpose, not your purpose by your power."

It was a realistic approach, considering the actual, as opposed to mythical, situation of Poland. Sikorski opted for an eastern solution to Poland's drastic problems and precarious geographical situation. "Emotions pass," he said, "but territory remains."

The situation was simply that Poland was sandwiched between the Soviet Union and Germany, between Hitler and Stalin. "We wish to cooperate closely with the Soviet Union," Sikorski wrote. "Nevertheless we shall oppose vehemently the transplanting of Communistic ideas on our homeland." What Sikorski had in mind was an eventual broader Central European union, a Polish-Czechoslovakian federation at the expense of Germany. His thinking was innovative and iconoclastic, but highly pragmatic at heart. It took into consideration the Poland that existed, not the Poland that was, cutting right through the cherished dreams of between-the-wars Poland, which envisioned that country as a great power, one that could somehow retain its integrity against the onslaught of its two powerful neighbors.

Sikorski's policy and outlook served the Soviet Union well. Stalin sought to divide the West from Poland, and when Sikorski promoted Anglo-Soviet rapprochement, Stalin was sympathetic. On July 20, 1941, an agreement was reached between the forces in Poland and the Soviet Union, which stipulated the creation of an autonomous Polish armed forces within the army of the USSR. Sikorski conceived of the army primarily as *political* rather than merely a military instrument.

The Polish-Soviet Treaty of July 1941 more or less guaranteed a brief era of good feeling and mutual, if wary, cooperation between the Soviet Union and Poland. The Soviet Union was in no position to antagonize its allies, and with the Germans launching their massive invasion of Russia, Operation Barbarossa, its very survival was at stake.

On August 14, 1941, a military agreement and a series of protocols were signed between General Wladyslaw Anders, appointed to head the Polish Army by General Sikorski, and General Panfilov of the USSR. The treaty provided for the creation of two infantry divisions consisting of ten thousand men and a reserve regiment.

The Soviets now released thousands of prisoners, who would provide a source for an army that would grow. The number of Polish refugees was close to 1.5 million, some 400,000 of whom or about one third the total, were Jews. In fact, in some of the early units of the Polish army, according to a complaining Anders, 60 percent of the soldiers were Jews.

Recruitment for the Anders army took place among those refugees from the formerly Soviet-occupied zone of Poland. The agreement stipulated that the commander of the Polish forces would be Polish, appointed by the Polish Government, but subordinate to Soviet authorities. The Soviet Union agreed to pardon all Polish citizens whose civil rights had been abrogated under the Germans. Begin was among the refugees, one of those 400,000 Jews for whom this constituted a golden opportunity to regain their civil rights, to fight as equals to the Poles and to obtain their release from detention.

Relations between the Jews and the Polish Army were complex and reflected very old antagonisms. Inevitably, Polish anti-Semitism, especially among the officer corps, reared its ugly and familiar head. Dr. Stanislaw Kot, the Polish ambassador to the USSR, complained that the Polish army was being "overwhelmed with Jews."[4] Anders himself questioned Jewish patriotism. Writes Jewish historian Yisrael Guttman: "The dominant factor motivating the attitudes of Anders' High Command toward the Jews was a deeply embedded anti-Semitism among the Poles."[5]

Thus the Anders Polish High Command was determined to curtail the number and role of the Jews in their fledgling army. Their spurious rationale was that the Jews had betrayed their citizenship when the Soviets invaded by collaborating with the invaders. Yet they failed to mention that the Soviets had actually come as "liberators," liberating their portion of Poland from the Nazis. Many Poles as well as Jews had hoped that their lives would be more tolerable under the Soviets than under the Nazi regime.

Now the Jews were trapped in the struggle between the Soviet occupiers and the Polish authorities. The Soviets reluctantly and grudgingly tolerated the Polish authorities within the Soviet Union. The early, devastating defeats of 1940–41, the dependence on Anglo-American aid and good will, forced Stalin to temporarily compromise. Yet Stalin never intended for the Anders army to become a base for postwar Poland, as history clearly showed.

The legal relationship between the Soviet Union and the Polish government-in-exile was extremely tenuous and vague. All along, the Soviets tried to destroy any vestige of Polish nationalism. Thus the citizens of occupied eastern Poland clung to their Polish citizenship even as refugees in Soviet territories, while the Soviets exerted pressure to force them to become Soviet citizens. The Polish Jews, whom the Soviets did not want as citizens, steadfastly claimed Polish citizenship (and the right to join the Anders army). The Jews would make up close to 30 percent of the Anders army, a development which Polish authorities viewed with xenophobic alarm.

The Polish army command would find numerous excuses to reject Jews, questioning their citizenship, loyalty, health and so on. The Soviets, to make matters worse, were interested in widening the gap between Poles and Jews, and the Polish High Command, spurred by its blind anti-Semitism, played into their hands.

Many Polish officers tried their utmost to curtail the flow of Jews into the army, demoting Jewish officers, and eliminating other Jewish candidates on the basis of stringent health regulations or other technicalities.

Kot was in charge of the Polish-Soviet negotiations and took his "Jewish problem" to Stalin, who was already questioning Polish willingness to fight for the Russians. "Poles won't fight," Stalin said in a meeting with Kot, Panfilov, Sikorski and Anders. Said Anders:

"I reckon on 150,000 men, i.e. eight divisions, together with auxiliary services. There may be even more of our people, but this includes a strong Jewish element which does not want to serve in the army . . . Many of the Jews who have applied to join are speculators or people who have been punished for smuggling; they will never make good soldiers. The Polish Army doesn't need these. Two hundred and fifty Jews deserted from Buzuluk on the false report that Kuibishev had been bombed. Over sixty deserted from the fifth division on the eve of an anticipated distribution of arms to the soldiers." Kot quotes Stalin as saying, "The Jews are rotten soldiers . . . Yes, the Jews are poor soldiers." At least on this issue of Jews, Sikorski and Anders, both fervid anti-Communist Polish patriots, nevertheless found it easy to agree with their arch-enemy, Stalin.[6]

The Poles remained lukewarm about recruiting Jews. In spite of the military debacle which struck Poland at the hands of the Nazis, Polish anti-Semitism had not abated.

Nevertheless, thousands of Jews flocked to the banners of the Anders army for a variety of reasons and motivations. Certainly most non-Communist Jews had a keen desire to get out of the Soviet Union and out from under the thumb of Soviet rule and persecution. There were patriotic Polish Jews who joined to fight against the Nazis. There were also Zionists trying to eventually make their way toward Palestine. Begin signed up to fight for the duration of the war. But nowhere does he explain why he joined.

There were reasons and options in the air. The old dream of a Jewish legion was reborn, although only briefly and with no basis in reality. It seemed to have originated with two Warsaw Revisionists, Dr. Mark Kahan and Miron Szeskin, who appealed to Anders, Kot, and Sikorski for the creation of a separate Jewish legion. Kot and company may have given the idea lip service, but they never intended to carry it through. As historian Kalman Nussbaum suggests, "It [a Jewish legion] was a mirage lifted up by the Poles so that it would be easier to get rid of the Jews."[7]

Kahan himself thinks the idea was discussed in the Stalin-Sikorski talks and killed then and there, although this could not be corroborated. It seems likely, however, that the rabid Polish officers corps was vehemently opposed to the idea.

Another idea—the creation of a small Jewish battalion—actually came to fruition with the help of a Polish officer Colonel Jan Galadyk, who was a Sternist-trained Revisionist. But it quickly came to nothing, as Kot indicated when he wrote that "Both our anti-Semites and the Jewish Nationalists [the followers of Jabotinsky] are putting forward the idea of a purely Jewish detachment under Polish command. Politically, this is very undesirable and it would be good if London did not encourage the idea."[8] Obviously London did just that.

Meanwhile in Koltubanka, the Anders army barracks in Tosk in the Soviet Union, Kahan and Szeskin were making an abortive effort to create a Jewish Legion, the prospect of which gave Polish authorities fits. Kot believed the creation of a Jewish Legion would only abet the Soviet's efforts to divide the Poles, but he was also concerned that observers in the West might see it as a Polish attempt to "discriminate against the Jews." He wrote that the whole idea was engineered by the "Jabotinsky Revisionist lawyer Kahan and the engineer Szeskin."[9] It's quite likely that Begin, considering his past Betar status, was involved, but it was the brainchild of Kahan and Szeskin. At any rate, the whole idea died a slow death in Koltubanka, although its memory lingered on.

By 1942 Anders was under Soviet rule and worried about how his army would be put to use. He was eager to leave the Soviet Union. Sikorski finally persuaded Stalin that some five thousand Polish officers and men, including a corporal named Begin, could leave for the Middle East via Iran.

The departure of the Jews in the Anders army became a problem, especially for the Jews themselves, who were once more caught between Soviet-Polish antagonisms and the anti-Semitism prevalent in the Anders command. As Guttman writes, "There is no doubt that to look for the dominant motive for the Polish High Command's attitude toward the Jews, one must search for anti-Semitism, which is so deeply rooted in so many Poles and was thus representative in the Anders army."[10]

In December 1941, the Soviets themselves restricted the recruitment of Jews, Ukrainians, and Belorussians who resided in the Polish zone occupied by the Soviets, regarding them as Soviet citizens under their occupation laws. This, it would appear, permitted the Poles to happily exclude Jewish-Soviet "citizens" from admission into the Polish Army.

The Soviet purpose in all this was not anti-Semitic. "The Soviet initiative," Guttman writes, "was thus to keep from a considerable number of Jewish citizens of Poland (now proclaimed Soviet "citizens" or non-ethnic Poles), the right to join the army which could have helped Polish aspirations to claim Eastern Poland by plebiscite with the help of Jewish citizens."[11]

The Polish government blinded as it was by its own anti-Semitism, accepted the Soviet design. Thus, when the Anders army prepared to leave the USSR in April 1942, controversy raged within its ranks. Kot and Anders appeared to play the Soviet game, but suddenly Anders contradicted himself and called the Jews in his army "Polish patriots."

Now that the Anders army was beginning to evacuate, the Jewish problem resurfaced with a vengeance. Some 114,000 Polish soldiers and civilians were leaving the USSR, in two phases. Among them were some 6,000 Jews, 3,500 soldiers, and 2,500 civilians—and corporal Menachem Begin.

While the Soviets officially refused to allow Jewish-Soviet "citizens" to leave, thus forcing many Jews to remain in the USSR, the NKVD, on the other hand, was insisting that its Jews leave, hence forcing the Poles to evacuate some seven hundred Jews to Iran. This particular group suffered a host of insults and abuses from the Polish army authorities, so much so that United Press reported the story and it was picked up in London and New York.

The Poles became anxious about Western opinion and in a second cable emanating from the Soviet Union, this one mentioning Begin, Kot apologized and naturally, blamed the Soviets. "While forbidding us to accept Jews," he complained, "the Soviets simultaneously spread through their agents among the Jews the story that they were doing this at the demand of the Polish authorities."[12] It would appear that Begin, helping out Kahan and Szeskin, must have negotiated with the Poles for the release of additional Jews, thus defying Soviet rule. Kot cabled Jerusalem, "Let the [Zionist] Revisionists get the information from Beigin (sic) and Szeskin, who have reached Teheran," meaning that Begin could testify to the good will of the Poles.[13]

Part Two

THE ETZEL YEARS
1943–48

With the onset of the revolt, Menachem Begin steps onto center stage, a transformed man.

The man who had been an often indecisive Betar functionary and pamphleteer, always operating in the huge shadow of his hero and mentor Jabotinsky, would now become a true leader and commander of a notorious, ruthless group of terrorists and freedom fighters.

If the transformation seems startling to observers, it must have also seemed that way to Begin. Begin explains the metamorphosis as stemming from "the climate in the homeland," a cursory explanation at best, and yet it might have just been a case of a man and occasion coming together at the perfect time. The passion was always there, at least in his rhetoric, and now he would become a man of action.

Begin inherited an Etzel that was in disarray—ineffectual, schismatic and unfocused, lacking in the kind of leaders that had turned Mapai into such a powerful force within the Yishuv. Begin, in many ways, was ideally suited for the job—he was an embodiment of the ideas and passions of Jabotinsky. If not Jabotinsky's acknowledged heir, he was a natural teacher and guide. And, in his own eyes he personified all the virtues and ideals of Revisionist Zionism. More importantly, he convinced his followers.

It was not that Etzel lacked fighters or spirit, they simply lacked direction. Etzel as well as Lehi was motivated by the spirit of action and rebellion, so it is only natural to assume that they did not easily accept outsider authority and discipline. The young men of Etzel were ready to fight to the bitter end, and they were prepared to die. At the outset, they were indeed suspicious of him and his abilities, even disrespectful, but Begin managed to win them over with his leadership ability, his spirit and his own passion.

Thus what emerges is almost a totally new Begin, a reinvented man. Opportunity and accident managed to propel him into history's focus at a crucial time. From now on, the myth of Menachem Begin begins in earnest.

10

Etzel in Palestine: New Commander in Chief[1]

The Soviets and the Polish government-in-exile reached an understanding that the Anders army should leave Poland. The Soviets had the Polish Peoples (Red) Army in mind to replace the nationalistic and disloyal Anders Army. Thus the Anders Army and Corporal Begin left for the Middle East, through Iran and Iraq to Palestine. Anders was happy his army could make a contribution to the war fighting with the British. For the Zionists in the Anders Army and several Jews, it was a golden opportunity to depart from Russia and Anders at the same time.

Begin was happy, of course, to go to Palestine, where unhappily the British were still in power. After all, he had not changed his mind on perfidious Albion since 1938. Nevertheless, he was going home to Eretz Israel finally and meeting once again with his Betarim and Etzel friends. Unaware as yet of what had transpired in Palestine since 1940, Begin was soon caught up. His friends told him of their troubles and of Etzel tribulations, of the deepening chasm between Betar and Zohar and the rise of Lehi, the deadly struggle of the dead heroes Raziel and Stern.

Palestine, Eretz Israel, the Yishuv, the *Moledet (Patrie)* had figured strongly in Begin's mind and in the way he looked at the world. But only now, in the latter part of 1942, does Palestine actually come into view as a reality, as Begin arrives at last, if somewhat dubiously, as a corporal and clerk in the Polish Army. Begin has come "home."

One can only imagine what went through Begin's mind as he first set foot on Eretz Israel. In a way, he was following in the footsteps of thousands of others before him, although not in the traditional fashion.

One remembers what Rabbi Yehudah Halevy, the great Spanish-Jewish philosopher and poet of the eleventh century did when he first arrived. He fell to his knees and kissed the ground beneath him, crying out, "Shalom to Zion, bestow peace on your prisoners," harkening back to the millions of Jews in the Diaspora.

It is not likely that the stoic Begin dropped to his knees, as Rabbi Halevy did. At any rate, we do not know, since he never referred to the occasion in any of his written works.

We do know that Begin's arrival in Palestine was a markedly different experience from that of his predecessors, like Ben Gurion and the Socialist-Zionist leaders, who came to a barren land and nurtured it, made a thriving community out of a desolate land, of some 150,000 Jews plus a few thousand pioneers. Begin was arriving to a Yishuv that already had a population of 600,000 people. A city-sized Tel Aviv did not exist in Ben Gurion's time. Haifa was a bustling port used by the British as a major naval installation. The land was crisscrossed with roads and transportation networks, and had turned from a bleak brown to green Kibbutzim and Moshavim all over. Begin was a latecomer, not a pioneer coming to work the land.

It is likely that Begin first sought out his old Betar compatriots, with whom he had corresponded continuously. Although his life as a corporal and clerk was no doubt gray in its aspects, Begin nevertheless must have been brimming with joy upon his arrival. And it is likely that the first person he sought was his wife Aliza, whom he had not seen since his arrest by the Soviets. Although it is known that the meeting took place in Ramat-Gan near Tel Aviv, where Aliza lived, it is not described in any of Begin's writing—a haunting omission by any standards except Begin's.

Aliza Begin herself was also a member in good standing of Revisionist Zionism, an old Betari who had studiously kept abreast of events in the movement. Sitting in their new one-room apartment in Rehavia in Jerusalem, she now had to tell him some disturbing news: the movement, Etzel and the other organizations were in disarray; the underground was paralyzed and leaderless, and activities were almost at a standstill. The news must have seemed grim to Begin.

Unitchman, Altman and others were likely the first Revisionists to meet with Begin, and later Etzel commander Meridor, Ben Eliezer, and Dr. Lubotsky all came to consult with him and discuss the common plight of the movement.

It should come as no surprise that Begin was welcomed by old Betarim and Revisionists when he arrived in Palestine, rather than by the new breed of Etzel commanders and activists, several devotees of Stern and Raziel.

Who, after all, was Begin? What did they know or think of him?

For the Betarim who had participated in the 1938 Warsaw Conference, he was the man who had been reprimanded by Jabotinsky himself. For some in Betar, he was the one who had defied their leader, a military Zionist.

For Sternists, he was part of the faded past they associated with Jabotinsky. For Shayeb-Eldad and Friedman Yellin, both now Lehi commanders, he was the man who had refused to leave Vilna. For Shayeb, he was part of "Betar of the uniforms and the big talk." Eri Jabotinsky was more sympathetic, but as far as he was concerned, Betar was Raziel and Kook, meaning pristine pre-Stern Etzel.

The Zohar leaders, more conservative in their outlook, were uncomfortable with the Etzel renegades and welcomed Begin, in spite of his military Zionism. To them, he was still part of the mainstream.

Jabotinsky had left no clue about the practical aspects of running a movement. He left no heirs, only a legacy. Begin at this time had become fully aware of what had happened to the Jews of Europe. He saw the danger in the ongoing split between Etzel and Lehi. He was, to Betar officials, a leader untouched by the schism that had fractured the movement during the war years. It must have seemed to Begin that it was time to take the lead. The movement as a whole was in disarray. The war had decimated its ranks. There was no effective day-to-day leadership, no ideological guidance.

Etzel was ineffective and Lehi was operating wildly on its own. The moribund movement was failing to attract the young. The only real leadership, such as it was, resided in the United States under the Committee (Vaad) headed by Kook and Merlin.

The acrimonious battle between Etzel and Lehi over control of the underground had been brewing for a long time, and had contributed to Etzel's decline. Etzel, along with Lehi, was the sole surviving organizational remnant of Jabotinsky's movement; some of Etzel's best commanders had defected to Lehi. All during the war, the movement had been split in two: Betar, and especially Jabotinsky in New York, came out strongly in support of the Allies. Zohar, the mainstream organizational arm of Revisionism, supported the Yishuv's policy of tacit cooperation with Great Britain. Etzel was advocating neutrality, and Stern had gone so far as to seek the help of the Nazis against the British Empire. Etzel was now without an authoritative leader. Meridor, the commander, was never respected as a leader, only as an imaginative terrorist. Thus the position was open for Begin.

The painful fact of Jabotinsky's recent death still hung in the air, and to the old-timers, Begin was the right man, even if he was not an heir apparent and did seem to spout the rhetoric of the new Etzelites. Raziel, the obvious heir, was dead. Stern, the most effective and determined rival, had been assassinated. A leader for Etzel was now urgently needed. Who should it be? Menachem Begin was out of the Raziel-Stern squabbles, out of the Zohar-Etzel battle. He was remembered as both a Jabotinsky loyalist and a military Zionist.

His reception, however, was by no means extraordinary, nor was there great enthusiasm among the Etzel commanders about his appointment as head of Etzel. Many of them opposed it.

But in the end, he seemed a logical choice because the situation demanded a decision. Etzel was in desperate straits, immersed in fratricide, beset by the Haganah, short of money and weapons. It had been reduced to robbing British banks and weapons caches to support its activities, a course that further blemished its already tarnished image. Etzel, in short, needed a leader, almost any leader—a commander, a political strategist, someone who could give it strength and cohesiveness.

Begin, a corporal in the Polish Army, a political operative with no military experience, a newcomer to Palestine, would turn out to be the right man in the right place.

By 1943, it seemed, Begin was already a part of the Palestine Betar inner circle. His main interest was to be the future of the movement after Jabotinsky. Ben Eliezer, who, along with Hillel Kook and Shmuel Merlin, were with the leader in his last days in New York, was in Palestine, and it was to Begin that Ben Eliezer turned. After Jabotinsky's death following a heart attack Ben Eliezer had stood guard at his grave in the cemetery in New York. To the end, it appeared, Jabotinsky was haunted about the fate that might overtake the Jews in the Diaspora, about the fate of the movement, and the need to arm the forces of Revisionist Zionism. There was no mention of successors, of heirs, and least of all, there was no mention of Begin, which must have disappointed him greatly. The road to command was sown with hurdles: first, how to get Begin out of the Army; second, whether he would be accepted by the Etzel commanders in Palestine. How to get Begin out of the Polish Army was the Betar-Etzel leaders' next task.

The story of how Begin came to finally leave the Anders Army is an unlikely one, and is an Etzel-Herut legend. It was Arieh Ben Eliezer, a Revisionist just returned from the United States, who finally persuaded Polish officials to release Begin from his obligations to the Polish Army. Ben Eliezer and Dr. Mark Kahan called for the immediate appointment of Begin as Etzel's High Commissioner, and Begin, still in the Army, tentatively accepted the appointment. Or so the story, or legend, goes.

Ben Eliezer describes a "legendary Begin, who like the captain of a ship unwilling to abandon it to a storm, remained in Vilna with thousands of Betar soldiers to defend the Betar fort."[2] This is, as we have seen, from Unitchman-Begin letters, pure nonsense.

Ben Eliezer said that Begin would be willing to serve in a task which he considered "the greatest honor friends and fighters could bestow on me."[3] But there was a hitch.

"I consulted with Meridor, inquiring what the problem was," said Ben Eliezer. "The problem was that he [Begin] served with the Polish Army in Palestine, but refused to desert the Army as so many Jews did. Meridor told me Begin absolutely refused to do so. Begin said, 'A deserter is a deserter, it makes no difference from what military organization.' "[4]

For over six months, Ben Eliezer and other Revisionists argued and tried to persuade the Poles or Begin, to no avail. "I decided to consult our elders—Unitchman, Shoffman, Wienshal, Mark Kahan, and Yohanan Bader," Ben Eliezer recalls. "Only after the loss of General Sikorski [killed in a plane crash in 1943], and the creation of the pro-Soviet Polish National Committee for Liberation, did the Poles become interested in legitimizing the London government, and for that they needed good public relations."[5]

Now Ben Eliezer was a Vaad leader with excellent connections in Washington. "They knew of our success in the press, Congress and among American statesmen. They were interested that we might work on their behalf in the United States. Since they seemed to think of the Vaad as a special force of pressure in the United States, I decided to appeal to them on behalf of Begin's release."[6] "Will you agree, Menachem?" asked Ben Eliezer. "Yes, but will you succeed? And how? There is no chance," answered Begin.[7]

For six weeks, writes Ben Eliezer, there were meetings between Etzel representatives and a Captain Swiencicki to discuss Polish-Etzel relations and the release of Begin, among other issues. "I had given up hope," he writes. "Then one morning Unitchman came to him excitedly saying, 'We must go to Polish headquarters in Rehovot. Captain Swiencicki wants you to meet the Polish commander in Palestine, General Okulicki.' "[8]

Ben Eliezer and Unitchman went to Rehovot for the meeting. Here they met Kahan and General Leopold Okulicki. The general promised to release five soldiers, Begin among them, in exchange for a promise that the Etzel leaders would lead a delegation to the United States supporting the London Polish cause.

This was and remains the official version of how Begin was finally released. We have to take Ben Eliezer's word for all this, a convoluted tale about an event that might have been much simpler.

In 1944 there were some efforts being made toward the creation of a Jewish joint command among the various undergrounds, including Etzel, Lehi and the Haganah. Dr. Lubotsky was working tenaciously to establish contact with some of the younger Haganah commanders in order to establish a common national front. The Etzel leaders were trying to overlap the usual chain of command in the Yishuv, which led from the Haganah, to the Histadrut and Mapai and its leadership to the Jewish Agency. On the Haganah side, leaders like Eliahu Golomb and Dr. Moshe Sneh were also trying to establish contact with Etzel and Lehi. A new commander for Etzel became imperative.

I find it difficult to accept that the Poles would put up so much resistance to the release of one Jewish corporal while hundreds of Jews were deserting with little or no opposition or recrimination. The Poles were anxious to get rid of the Jews within their ranks, because as long as they remained they represented a potential public relations problem.

According to Dr. Leopold Labedz, a Polish-Jewish officer who served in the same Anders Army that Begin served in, when he, Labedz, became sick and was sent to Tel-Litvinsky Hospital near Tel Aviv, and was gone for a number of weeks, his Polish colleagues assumed that he had simply deserted. They were astonished that a Jewish officer was absent but came back and had not deserted.[9]

The fact remains that Begin refused to budge or desert. He was not exactly being held prisoner. It was common knowledge that the Polish authorities were looking the other way when it came to Jewish deserters and that they were quite happy to get rid of them. Begin's supporters suggest that he wanted to dispel the image of Jewish deserters and cowards. Perhaps he was grateful that the Poles had allowed him to finally arrive in Palestine.

There is still another and the most plausible version, which links Begin's honorable release from the Anders Army to Revisionist-Etzel-Polish relationships in 1943–44.

According to this version by way of Ben Eliezer and the Polish government-in-exile's documents,[10] the Polish Government played a key role in the history of Israel by outright releasing the man who would take over Etzel.

How was this accomplished? Begin's release, according to this version, was to serve as a cornerstone of the relationship between the Polish government-in-exile and the Revisionists, serving to spark renewed contact. The Polish Government, trying to shore up its tarnished image in the world of Zionism, fighting charges of anti-Semitism in the Anders Army, could improve its relations with Zionism and in London and New York. Etzel, on the other hand, hoped to receive military training, and Polish arms for Etzel.[11] All of this once again smacked of a renewal of the old Polish-Revisionist romance, Polish-Etzel style, of the late 1930s.

It's quite possible that the Anders Army, like any other army, was full of romantics, but it's not likely that the Polish government-in-exile would enter into such an implausible enterprise. Etzel and the Polish governments were hardly ever that close, and whatever relations existed then and in the past were mere opportunistic spasms. The Polish Government in Exile could ill afford to antagonize the British by endearing Etzel and its relations with the Yishuv would also be damaged by such a move. Such a rationale, used, I feel, mainly to establish the validity of Begin's *honorable* release from the Anders Army, does not hold up. No Polish documents exist attesting to the importance of Begin. We have only Ben Eliezer's version to substantiate such a claim.[12]

In my opinion, the confusion over whether Begin defected from the Anders Army, as many Jews actually did,[13] or was honorably released is at the heart of the creation of the Begin legend, commander of Etzel.

In the Ben Eliezer-Mark Kahan version, Begin received a complete, honorable release from the Anders Army. The truth is that he only received a one-year leave of absence, a kind of extended furlough, in order to enable him to join an Anders Army Jewish delegation which would go to the United States seeking help for the Polish government-in-exile.[14] The delegation never materialized, mainly due to British opposition.

Begin, however, *never* received an order to return to the ranks of the Army. Yet according to a Polish document, Begin "was the object of a search by the Polish and the British authorities for terroristic activities." There exists also an Anders Army claim that Begin was a deserter, since he never received a formal and fully honorable release from the Army.[15]

The Begin version, which had the future Prime Minister receiving a full and honorable dismissal, which he proudly passed on to friends over the years, is the one that has somehow stuck to history (see Korbonski's post-hoc testimony in 1977).[16] What we have is the making of a myth and a Ben-Eliezer "official history." After all, how could a Betar Hadar graduate desert, even from an unfriendly, and hostile to Jews, Anders Army.

The story of Begin's departure from the Anders Army turned into full-blown legend when Begin became commander of Etzel. What was the attitude of Etzel's commanders toward the new leader?

In 1943, Etzel was nominally under the control of Meridor, and heading slowly toward disaster. Shlomo Lev-Ami, today a scholar and historian, served as a senior Etzel officer and for two months acted as a bridge between Meridor and Begin. He contends that Meridor was a "dreamer" with little organizational ability or military knowledge and that many of Meridor's Etzel operations were disasters.[17] Etzel commanders had no confidence in Meridor's leadership.

Meridor, Lev-Ami says, was "inconsistent and untrustworthy."[18] It was under Meridor's leadership that Etzel all but collapsed. Many of the Etzel commanders flatly refused to serve under him.

Early in 1943, Lev-Ami recalls, Meridor suggested that Etzel be dissolved and that it sell its arms caches to the Haganah, with the proceeds going toward strengthening Betar. "I was terrified," Lev-Ami said. "We had vowed that only death would separate us from Etzel. That's what I had told Raziel when he split from Stern. We could never accept such a proposal. Thus, we realized that Meridor was not fit for command."[19] Clearly, with Etzel engaged in guerrilla warfare, a new kind of leadership was called for.

When the Etzel leadership finally went to Begin, they said the only way that Meridor could remain was as a member without portfolio. Meridor, far from graciously accepting Begin's authority, was furious. He refused to leave. But numerous senior Etzel commanders insisted he do so.

Initially, Meridor seemed very impressed by Begin. "Begin," he said, "is the man we're looking for. He's admired by thousands of Betarim."

Meridor, at least outwardly, seemed willing to work with him. Years after the fact, Meridor, who is still close to Begin, recalled the changeover as relatively mild and his own attitude as accepting. He recalled being impressed by Begin's oratory and by the fact that Jabotinsky had spoken highly of Begin, a tale passed on by Meridor's father. He recalled being "shy and respectful" of Begin and suggesting to Begin that he, Begin, was the only legitimate commander of Etzel now that Jabotinsky was dead.[20] The truth is much more shrill. Meridor did not step down gracefully, head bowed in respect. He was forced out, not by Begin but by other Etzel commanders.

Clearly, Etzel lacked leadership. Meridor was floundering. Six Etzel commanders registered a vote of no confidence in Meridor. Lehi leaders contemptuously accused Etzel of being lax with intelligence and blamed Meridor. "It's an agency of the British CID," one Lehi fighter said.

Begin may thus have seemed like a logical choice, although Etzel's field commanders in Palestine suspected his politics and ideology. Ostensibly, he was still loyal to the principles of his mentor Jabotinsky. He had stated his declared opposition to the White Paper—although he had failed to say how he might go about opposing it. His perception in 1943 of international and Jewish conditions was at best murky. In 1943, he still talked of "pressuring the British" and called for a Jewish struggle—without presenting an operational plan. He still clung to Jewish legionnairism—"We need a Jewish army; without one there is no hope," he wrote. He discussed a Betar propaganda campaign similar to the one used by the American Committee for a Hebrew Army. Yet most of what he said and wrote at the time consisted mostly of half-baked rhetoric. Events conspired to change the loquacious, passive Begin into a man of action.

For Etzel officials at the time that, it was to be Begin. "He was from Poland," one Etzel veteran told me. "He had a good record as a Jabotinsky loyalist. He was intelligent and had not been part of the endless Etzel-Lehi struggles in Palestine. So why not Begin?"[21]

"Menachem Begin was a loyal Betari," said Mrs. Ben Eliezer. "He was not Jabotinsky's choice. But Arieh was known to the CID and Zohar was in disarray."[22]

Mrs. Ben Eliezer also told me, "Menachem was not considered by the Palestinian Etzel members to be a military professional. They respected the man who had been Betar's Poland chief. But they were military guerrillas, warriors, not Diaspora ideologues. They needed a pamphleteer, a revolutionary and nationalist philosopher. They were in need of a writer, one that could write with a great deal of passion. Above all they actually needed somebody who knew next to nothing about military matters. Begin was the ideal answer."[23]

Etzel leaders in Palestine were ready to settle on Begin, not so much from conviction, but because there seemed to be no other alternative. The fact that Begin had not been very active in the Etzel underground in Palestine also proved to be a boon for him and the movement. It gave Begin what every revolutionary leader needs to survive: anonymity.

The British CID had no previous record on Begin and knew little if anything about him. There was no British follow-up in 1943, when Begin was still wearing a Polish uniform. From the very start, he was an unknown quantity to the British, who allowed him to operate in relative safety right up until the War for Independence.

In 1943, Etzel's conspiratorial structure was incomplete and rather poor, a condition which allowed Begin to establish open, nonclandestine meetings with his friends.

Begin was, of course, well known among his Betar Polish friends in Eretz Israel, and whatever reputation he had among the forces of Revisionism stemmed from his activities in Poland. But to the Betarim and Etzel members born in Palestine, he was much less familiar.

In 1943, he met with several high-ranking Etzel senior commanders, including Meridor, Lankin, and Ben Eliezer, to discuss the future of Etzel. According to the former Etzel Chief of Operations, Eitan Livny, Begin met only once with Etzel senior commanders, and even then he spoke to them from behind a screen to prevent his identity from becoming known and to minimize chances of betrayal to the British.[24]

Even though there were probably only a handful of people within the ranks of Etzel who knew what Begin looked like, which was a key factor in avoiding detection and capture by the British, his reputation and prestige among the ranks of the Etzel fighters was soon established, and with good reason.

Begin's chief asset as a leader was that he could inspire, and this he did through his writings, pamphleteering and speeches. Begin's writings and billboard proclamations held a great appeal to Jewish youth, both in the ranks of Revisionism and among the Betar youth thirsting for action since the death of Stern. The writing was full of bombast, boasting, passion, and sloganizing, but it was highly effective.

Here for instance is an order of the day, emanating from Etzel headquarters and written by Commander of Etzel Menachem Begin for a combined operation and attack on the CID center in Jerusalem on September 3, 1944.

"On the 22nd of Adar, 5534(8/23/44), between 2200 and 2300 hours, our soldiers in a direct battle attacked the centers of terror in Jerusalem, Jaffa and Haifa. The Palestinian intelligence officers, the instruments of oppression of the treacherous government, were bombed and destroyed . . . We fight for the opening of the gates for our dying nation. The traitorous government erected, with the help of its policemen, spies, and bayonets, a fortress that separates between the truncated and a secure land in the

Moledet . . . We fight to liberate our *Moledet*. We fight like men, like soldiers against soldiers."[25]

Note the language and how it uses symbolism that is direct and revealing and how it could appeal to an impatient youth. He held out the possibility of striking against a Mandatory that was closing the gates of Eretz Israel to the Jews. He always described his men as soldiers and members of an army, insisting that they be regarded as fighting soldiers, not as terrorists.

The phrasing of his rhetoric was passionate, angry, full of contempt and a love of glory. It evoked the strongest sort of images, vivid and harsh, calling the British "treacherous Albion" and "Hitlerites." Jewish moderates were "cowards" and "synagogue clerks," "slaves and Yahood." Begin bridled at the moderates and the Yishuv establishment: "The leader, the leaders, these leaders of Yishuv, they and only they lead the nation astray, endlessly, compromising, [talking] of peace and appeasement with the foreigners."[26]

The junior Etzel fighters who never met Begin were now in awe of him through his writings: "The terrorist government in Eretz Israel conducts an unheard of terror campaign. This terror is hidden behind laws, statutes, regulations, and "books" [a reference to the White Paper]. Great Britain conquered the land with the help of the Jews [the Yishuv]. With their help it has received legitimacy . . . They are worse than the Czars. The Czars oppressed their nation, but the British help to annihilate the nation."[27]

Begin's orders and declarations were indeed masterpieces of strident propaganda, a tool for inciting frustrated and idealistic youth. They were speeches and pronouncements against specific targets, such as individual Zionists—Ben Gurion, Weizmann, Goldmann, the high commissioners, not to mention Churchill and Eden.

He attacked institutions like that "traitorous government," "the Nazi CID," the "government of the clerks," meaning the Jewish agency. Here was a different Zionist writer, lacking eloquence but making up for it in stridency. Near the end of 1944, he wrote: "The Yishuv are not just crazy, but one large madhouse, and in this madhouse the Jew that is *not* satisfied selling merchandise and silence is considered crazy . . . We do not know who has persuaded the British that we are crazy . . . but is it not the Whole Jewish Existence that's crazy." "There is," Begin suggests, "always somebody ready to annihilate and oppress the Jew, either in a totalitarian society or a democratic one. Given that state of existence, Zionism," Begin mocks, "is 'a moral madness.' "[28]

From the outset, Begin attacked the Mandatory, but he also was willing to cooperate with left-wing Jewish politicians. "We don't want Etzel rule," Begin insisted. "We want a Jewish government, even one led by Ben Gurion, but one that is ours."[29]

The propaganda was effective as Etzel swung into action. In 1944, there were at least eight major Etzel operations, including attacks on the CID, on immigration offices, the internal revenue, broadcast stations, police stations and ammunition dumps, all symbols of the Mandatory. As one of Etzel's senior commanders said, "We at first doubted Menachem's rhetoric, but he surprised us to the good."[30]

He gave Etzel action which legitimized his leadership that earlier was in doubt.

If Begin's rhetoric was harsh and violent, the man himself led a life that seemed remarkable for its ordinariness.

Certainly his existence hardly resembles what one might expect of the life of a feared, hunted and sought-after revolutionary leader. His daily life was that of a petit bourgeois. No ammunition belt and rakish hat for Begin. He always dressed properly, wearing a tie even when he met with high-ranking members of the underground at his own home. He looked like a lawyer.

He conducted what appeared to be a regular middle-class life with his wife Aliza, his son Benyamin Zeev, and his young daughter Hasia. He spent much of his time reading the Palestinian Jewish press, listening to the BBC, where he managed to learn English, and reading the daily British papers. Every day, he carefully pageproofed and reread his pamphlets and billboard writings. So much did he insist on accuracy and correctness that he would return an unproofed galley to the underground press, risking the lives of messengers for a typographical error.

To protect him from the British, and from the Haganah for that matter, a special hiding place was built for him in the attic of his apartment house, which he never really had to use except for three days in the wake of the King David Hotel bombing. He was never in any real danger, in spite of the constant searches and hunting parties that set after him. Most of his contact with Etzelites consisted of planning talks with senior commanders like Ben Eliezer and Meridor, until their arrest in 1945, as well as with Dr. Mark Kahan of the Anders Army and Eitan Livny, his chief of operations until 1947.

Early on, through the latter part of 1943 and early part of 1944, he traveled in Eretz Israel, which he had, after all, never seen before, but most of his activities were confined to Jerusalem, Tel Aviv and Haifa. Once he traveled to Ramat Gan to meet Lehi leaders. But command meetings usually took place in homes near the center of Tel Aviv, usually close to his own residence.

All along, there were no real efforts made to deceive the CID. Begin held no deceptive day-to-day job. He was never isolated or left alone.

What was then Begin's concept of the Revolt? What did he intend to do with Etzel under his command and, above all, how did he change the course of Etzel? Begin provided Etzel with a powerful idea, a desired goal, a strategy for action, and that was what Etzel most needed. As it became moribund and lost its luster to Lehi, Begin recreated Etzel as a vigorous, dynamic, aggressive, and goal oriented movement. The goal was no less than revolt against the Mandatory, against England. What more could be offered to Betar and Etzel youth crying out for action? Henceforth there would be a new Etzel, and a new Begin.

11

The Logic of the Revolt[1]

In the annals of Zionist history, the years 1944–48 are the years of the great struggle *(Maavak)*, the years when the Haganah, Palmach, Etzel and Lehi all forged their energy into what was termed by Begin the Revolt *(Hamered)*. For Etzel and Lehi, the struggle had been raging intermittently since 1940, and for Begin it began in 1944, with the Revolt.

They were the Zionist years of heroism, 1944–46, culminating in the bloody 1947–49 War for Independence against the Arabs. The literature from and about Haganah is large, but the Etzel-Lehi literature is relatively meager; what little there is is replete with myth, tales of heroism that offer little in the way of perspective and meaning.

This much is certain, however—without the emergence and participation of Etzel, and to a much lesser degree, Lehi, the story of that struggle would have almost totally focused on the Yishuv, and on the political and diplomatic warfare conducted all over the world; it would have been the story of the American Zionist Emergency Committee, only the Palmach and Haganah, Ben Gurion, Rabbi Abba Hillel, Silver, about votes in the United Nations.

The results of new research and documentation serve the twofold purpose of toning down the self-serving heroism permeating much of the literature of Etzel and Lehi, and also of placing them in the perspective of their time. Thus, Etzel's and Begin's Revolt, even as, in some ways, it has shrunk in political importance with time, has gained stature in terms of the repercussions of the events of those times.

Etzel demanded a considerable share of the attention of the Yishuv, and of Great Britain, from 1944 to 1947, much more than the protracted diplomatic dealings that were also occurring at that time.

Of course, for Begin and his followers the Revolt, over the years, has taken on the aspects of a myth, its importance and glory exaggerated. The Revolt was a time when both Etzel and Revisionism emerged from their pariah status to become respectable institutions. The process would echo down the years, and would eventually allow Begin and Likud to capture Israel's seat of power.

The Revolt also vaulted Begin into a place in history, and remains a remarkable achievement, through which a basically obscure former Betar party operative from Poland rose to the status of revolutionary hero and mythical figure. Commanding a force of only 250 fighters in 1944, in 1948 he led over 2,000, of whom 800 were fighters. (The numbers are always suspect.) It is in Palestine that Begin's talents and gifts come into focus, a singular irony, since Begin had never set foot in Palestine, knew little about it except what he had learned second-hand, and knew even less about the British. He barely knew the major figures in Etzel whom he commanded and had never had experience in leading military operations.

Begin's leadership stemmed from his authoritativeness, his will, and his drive, and those qualities enabled him to turn a moribund and fading organization into an effective unit. Begin surprised many by superbly commanding, maintaining, and organizing an underground organization. By his rhetoric and personal force, he kept together for four years a group that would otherwise have probably fallen apart.

Begin emerges as a militant figure but, unlike Stern, he was not a fanatic. He believed in the establishment of Zionist power and in terrorizing the Mandatory to achieve that goal, but he was not totally uncompromising. With few other means at his disposal, he saw Etzel and the Revolt as a catalyst for a general uprising.

In order to understand Begin and the effect the Revolt had had, it is important to understand the political context of the years 1944–1948.

By 1943, in the aftermath of El Alamein and Stalingrad, the British revived their anti-Zionist policy, restricting immigration and land purchase. They had basically returned to the hated White Paper policy of 1939. The short honeymoon that had existed out of necessity between the Zionists and the Mandatory (1941–42) due to the war against Nazism began to ebb. Mutual cooperation between the forces of the Yishuv and the British Army ceased. The military cooperation, the semi-legalization of the Haganah, the Haganah-British joint operations against Syria and Fascist Iraq were all but forgotten.

The British, in fact, had never really intended to abandon the White Paper, but rather had temporarily shelved it between 1940 and 1943.

The Yishuv's frustration with the Mandatory policy was growing by leaps and bounds. The younger members of the Palmach and the Haganah, as well as the youth of the Yishuv, wanted an end to the White Paper policy and British rule in Palestine. They were growing impatient.

The Zionist leadership, especially Weizmann, still clung to its faint loyalty to Great Britain. But Ben Gurion had grown increasingly skeptical of British intentions. He and his followers set about forging and honing the new Jewish military arm, the Haganah. Thus, Etzel, although its activities were more direct and violent than other groups, was nevertheless part of a growing spirit of Jewish activism and impatience with Great Britain.

For Ben Gurion, the crucial issue was the rescue and gathering of the Jews of Europe. For this massive project of basically illegal immigration he would use the Haganah. The gathering of the remnants of Europe was a typically mainstream Zionist activity. It was an activity aimed at the abolition of the White Paper policy, not at the British Empire itself.

Begin and Etzel fell somewhere in between, and here Begin showed his true talents, his genius and political vision. He called for a Revolt against the British Mandatory, not the British Empire. He aimed to oust the British from Palestine, not merely to conduct a limited war against the White Paper.

His singular success would turn a floundering Etzel into a genuine movement, rescue Revisionism from obscurity, and put it back in the forefront of the Yishuv. Had not Begin arrived at the right time, it's quite likely that Etzel might have disappeared altogether, its remnants being either absorbed by the Haganah or drifting off to Lehi and similar organizations. Before Begin arrived, Etzel had no real leadership; it was splintered, disorganized and ineffectual. It is quite likely that without him there would have been no Etzel by 1944, and certainly no organization that could make the British withdraw from Palestine.

The Haganah, for instance, never took Etzel seriously until Begin took over; it recognized Begin's leadership qualities and his tendency to negotiate. Begin's challenge, while openly directed against the British, was also a challenge to the dominant powers of the Yishuv. Even Ben Gurion, although he treated Begin with contempt, grudgingly recognized that Begin was more than just a political nuisance. Begin and Etzel were a force to be reckoned with.

THE REVOLT[2]

The Revolt began in February 1944. Etzel launched the war against the Mandatory in late 1944 against what seemed impossible odds and with no general backing in the Yishuv. Begin's aim was to shake the Mandatory and its 100,000 troops, which was certainly a legitimate and large target. Begin had only some 250 fighters under his control. With those odds, the Revolt had become symbolic of the whole history of the Jews.

Begin's singular achievement prior to becoming Prime Minister of Israel is that he kept Revisionism-Betar alive, brought it back from the dead and personally moved it from one mutation to another with great skill and political acumen. If not for him, the legend of Jabotinsky and Betar would have long since faded, perhaps remaining as an obscure historical footnote.

Begin's medicine was much stronger than Jabotinsky's. The principles of his "Revolt" consisted of a "doctrine of pressure," meaning the establishment of a Jewish army within the legal framework of the Mandatory, and the use of it as an instrument of struggle to achieve statehood and independence.

Jabotinsky *never* called for a revolt. Etzel radicals and Begin did. Neither did the Yishuv, which used the Haganah as an instrument for political resistance and military struggle. Military means were sanctioned *only* if they were tied to the political struggle.

The Revolt was to be a purely military action, whose goal was to oust Britain from Palestine. Begin, of course, saw the Revolt as a process linked to the achievement of Jewish independence. The Revolt was an act of liberation, not an act of statehood. It was metaphysical as much as it was a call for action. The Revolt could be won only if its Yishuv mobilized to its call. Begin also flatly rejected Weizmann's call for an international commitment to Jewish independence. Begin thought this futile, a false hope. The Revolt would be against the Mandatory, not against the Empire.

The means of struggle employed by Begin were different from those of the Haganah and Lehi. He meant to use urban guerrillas extensively, but with a purpose, as "pressure" on Great Britain.

Nevertheless, in spite of the grandiose title of "Revolt," Begin's underground urban guerrilla warfare should not be confused with a real revolt. If anything, the Yishuv and Haganah were the essence of a nationalist revolution—the all-inclusive use of political, diplomatic, and military means and structures in order to gain independence, and statehood employing each according to the need. Begin's Revolt was a war specifically limited to terrorizing the British in Palestine.

In actual fact, the Revolt was a proclamation of revolt couched in classical Zionist language, a declaration of war against Perfidious Albion. We must clearly distinguish between a proclamation and a real war to take over Palestine. Etzel never tried to overthrow the Mandatory by force or to supplant the Jewish Agency and the Yishuv leadership and authorities—those were Stern's aims, not Begin's.

Where did Begin now differ from Jabotinsky? One of the principal differences between Begin and Jabotinsky had been their cultural outlooks and backgrounds. Jabotinsky was and always remained a child of the West, an Anglophile, living in an Anglo-American political culture and remaining sympathetic to it.

Begin, on the other hand, was totally unfamiliar with Anglo-American political culture. His English, such as it was, was learned from BBC news broadcasts. Begin, and the Poles he grew up with, perceived England as a treacherous and unreliable ally. His outlook, already hostile to the British in 1940, was further honed in the days of the Revolt, when he encountered CID agents, spies, policemen and narrow-minded and intolerant colonial officials. He saw England's ugly tail. In fact, Begin and his Etzel cohorts were more like radical anticolonial natives struggling against imperialism than they were mainstream Zionists.

Despite Begin's respect for British parliamentary traditions, which he retained throughout his political career, on the whole he remained anti-British, a feeling deeply implanted by the Holocaust, which he felt was aided and abetted by British White Paper policies.

This was Begin's outlook when he published the Proclamation of the Revolt on all the walls and information kiosks of the Yishuv. It was pure Begin.

He was careful about timing, and waited until he had reorganized the Etzel High Command. He had also, out of necessity, urged rearmament, to assure Etzel an adequate supply of weapons. Thus, we see Etzel regrouping and rearming in 1943, training new recruits, getting additional sources of financing.

The main objective of the Revolt clearly was not to determine the nature of the Jewish state that would emerge after the departure of the British; rather, it was to discover the specific methods by which the ouster of the British could be achieved.[3]

Begin split the Revolt into two stages:

First, a military underground would battle the Mandatory until it was forced to evacuate Palestine. Second, this goal must be accomplished with the passive cooperation of the Yishuv, which, hopefully, would conduct massive acts of civil disobedience, such as refusing to pay taxes and engaging in general strikes. With news of the ongoing Holocaust slowly emerging from Europe, Begin felt he could expect to receive support from the Yishuv, especially since the war was coming to an end and the fight for Jewish refugees and the creation of the state was looming large.

Begin did not seriously believe, nor ever claim, that he could oust the British with his puny forces. Rather, he saw the Revolt as a catalyst that would awaken the Yishuv and spur it into action. It was clear to Begin, though not to Etzel radicals, that an open military confrontation with Britain would lead to a fiasco. He opted instead for urban guerrilla warfare.

On the surface, Begin's chances for success must have appeared slim. There was the example of the 1936 Arab revolt, which the British had put down ruthlessly. Now Begin, a party operative, out of action for years, only recently a non-com in the Polish army, was proposing to lead an underground army in Palestine, where he had only lately arrived. The ground was not even fertile for recruiting, since most of the Palestinian Jewish youth were firmly attached to the Haganah-Palmach Socialist-Zionist organizations and groups. The Proclamation of the Revolt was abstract. Its fulfillment was more prosaic, an ideological shield for Etzel military operations. He knew that Etzel would be working almost entirely in isolation at first. He saw his 250 Etzel soldiers as a national task force, a forward army of shock troops. There was nothing martyrological in the Revolt.

In this, he was very different from Lehi. Begin saw the Revolt as permanent and ongoing. Morally and practically, he disapproved of Lehi's style of personal assassination and brute terror. He envisioned the Revolt as a nuisance for the British, a gigantic toothache from which there would be no relief. Fundamentally, Begin knew that while the British would never leave on their own, they were also weakened by and tired of the war and that a continuous underground action could possibly pressure them into a decision they did not want to make.

Begin saw that Great Britain, unless prodded, had all the incentive in the world to stay. Palestine figured importantly in Great Britain's strategic considerations because of treaties with the Hashemites, because of Arab interests, and because of oil.

The only choice, Begin argued, was the gun and the hand grenade. "We have no right not to use it," he said, evoking recent European ghetto revolts. Indeed, the symbol of Etzel was a gun across the land of Eretz Israel, copied from an old national Polish slogan, *Rak Kach* in Hebrew, *Tilko Tak* in Polish ("only thus").

And what of the Arabs? Well, to Begin they were murderers. This was always Begin's way, and it has persisted over the years. There was mention of cooperation between the two peoples in the Proclamation, but it was a statement without specifics or focus. The Arabs, Begin said, echoing his mentor, are not serious rivals. The Revolt would frighten the Arabs away from the main battle, which would be between Etzel and the Mandatory. The Arabs of Palestine were not independent players in his eyes.

Initially, the Yishuv's various groups and factions thought the ideas of the Revolt "foreign, crazy and strange." Ben Gurion and others like him never believed in the underground by itself. They believed and continued to believe in political action supported by the Haganah, an instrument of political power, illegal immigration, and diplomacy. They saw the Revolt as a nuisance that would bring down British wrath on the entire Yishuv.

Begin, it appears, was not very concerned with British repression, and may have even welcomed it. Etzel's losses were never very great, and its members could often successfully disappear like shadows into the Yishuv, for the British never really learned to distinguish among Lehi, Etzel and Haganah members. Begin felt that if the British did retaliate in an oppressive manner, it might spark a general revolt, and thus he welcomed a British reaction.

One of the many contradictions inherent in the Revolt was that on one hand, it portrayed the British as oppressive and imperialistic, and even hoped to exploit this quality, while on the other hand, it hoped that Britain's parliamentary, democratic traditions would prevent repression and would force the British to ease off.

Certainly, the British never came down full force on the Yishuv, and rejected any such recommendations from its military staff. There was no serious collective punishment, no real destruction of Jewish property and mass exile of Jewish leaders as there was with the Arab revolt. No innocent people were systematically executed, and no economic sanctions were applied against the Yishuv. Even at the height of the Revolt, when several Etzel members were publicly executed, the Jews in the Yishuv were never perceived as or treated as "natives" by the British, who saw them as a civilized, if hostile, people.

Begin and his Etzel members saw themselves as the only forces taking on the British. The British saw Etzel—as opposed to the majority of Jews in the Yishuv—as a pack of murderers, as Jewish Fascists. Both perceptions were wrong, products of frustration and ignorance. Begin always inflated the importance and effectiveness of Etzel, which, he contended, frightened the British by its mere presence. The British, however, were much more worried about the more nebulous and larger Haganah.

Neither did Etzel activities or British reaction, such as it was, spark a Yishuv uprising. Quite the contrary, it spurred the organized Yishuv and Ben Gurion into attempting to destroy Etzel in a long Sezon. Obviously, there were periods of cooperation and unity, periods that did not last very long. In the end, the politics of the Revolt and the politics of the three major Jewish forces in the Yishuv seemed almost to preclude unity.

12

Politics of the Revolt[1]

Begin's decision to initiate the Revolt, and its consequences, are perhaps one of the more well-documented series of events in the history of Etzel.

An almost complete set of protocols and records survived long after the events, in spite of the conspiratorial nature of the various organizations involved, especially Etzel. Surviving records of five months in 1944 give us a haphazard but incisive picture of Etzel, and especially of Begin and his often contradictory attitudes.

For some reason, these records were preserved, and we have Begin and the Etzel High Command to thank for them. They are uneven but rich; some were highly selective, some obviously judgmental. They were never intended for publication and were typed on thin paper, recorded by the chief of staff, Eliahu Lankin, and edited and submitted for publication by Shlomo Lev-Ami several years later.

All the handwritten records were usually immediately destroyed, but the typed materials were hidden in milk cans buried in the orchards next to Etzel headquarters in Petach Tikva. They were eventually unearthed and brought to the Jabotinsky Institute by Yaacov Amrami, former Etzel chief of intelligence and today a Tel Aviv publisher. The protocols cover a time span between July and November of 1944, and include meetings of the High Command, meetings with local commanders, Etzel military court proceedings, and meetings between Haganah and Etzel representatives, as well as a key letter between Begin and Friedman-Yellin of Lehi.

The materials clearly demonstrate Begin's domination of Etzel, showing his roles as chief strategist, propagandist, political analyst and negotiator. Perhaps surprisingly, considering his reputation, his function as an initiator of military operations appears small. He was, first and foremost, a political personage—wordy, self-assured, and contradictory. In other words, he had by this time become the quintessential Begin, and has remained basically unchanged.

Here, for example, are some vintage Beginisms from a meeting on October 27, 1944. While expounding on and analyzing the internal and international situation as seen from the viewpoint of Zionism and Etzel. On the Holocaust, he has this to say:

"There appears to be a good chance to save the remnants of Jews surviving in Europe since the war is going to end soon. We can save a considerable number of Jews still alive.

"We shall be without restraint in our struggle since the war effort is now nonexistent. Haganah will no longer be an obstacle." For Begin, the Revolt is to become the apatheosis of military Zionism.

"We are facing now the crucial battle which will decide the fate of our nation."

And what about his rivals on the left?

"Our attitude toward Haganah is that there is nothing to talk about. They are mentally not ready for war." And on Revisionism?

"The leadership of Revisionism (Altman) is not our kind of Revisionism. We still believe in Revisionism as the only movement which in the end will see eye to eye with us and in the moment of crisis will support us. After all, it's Jabotinsky's movement.

"Their [Lehi] slogans are empty, but in fact, there is less distance between us concerning ultimate goals."[2]

Obviously, his attitudes and feelings waver wildly, but when he is talking about the Revolt, he is unwavering. On August 8, 1944, he sees himself and his movement standing on the threshold of a historic moment: "We must persuade the nation to our cause . . . we do not believe the British government . . . We need to have the Yishuv behind us . . . the call for legitimacy is the major task of the Revolt . . . in my view, legitimacy will only be established when Etzel restores its image and at least receives tacit or silent support from the Yishuv."[3]

He was both urgent and overly optimistic about the unity of support he would receive from the Yishuv and about the possibility of unity among Etzel, Lehi and Haganah. This was a nationalistic Revisionist dream he had inherited from Jabotinsky. It was a pipe dream, unity with the Haganah never really was or could be fulfilled—except, of course, at the expense of the Revisionist camp.

Begin believed that "We have convinced the Yishuv no longer to think in terms of containment. We have convinced the Yishuv that the Jews can be restrained only up to a point, hence they are capable of revolting."

He was imagining a majority in the Yishuv that did not exist. None of the writings and actions of Mapai, Histadrut, Palmach, Haganah or even the mainstream Revisionists demonstrate any preparedness or willingness to revolt, certainly not without any linkage to political action—always the crucial departure point between Haganah and Etzel.

Meetings between Begin and Haganah leaders Moshe Sneh and Eliahu Golomb should have convinced Begin of the difficulty of final reconciliation between the two forces. Golomb, while appearing sympathetic, reiterated forcefully the Haganah attitude: "I presume," he told Begin, "that there is no future or security for political Zionism if it will not lead to an armed force showdown . . . We never gave up this power nor intended to surrender it . . . From the beginning, we developed and encouraged Jewish forces, we knew in the end they would serve as a basis for our existence and lead toward the final fulfillment of our goals."[4]

This was all well and good, but then Golomb added, just as forcefully, that "military force must be anchored in political power . . . No revolutionary movement ever achieved its goals just with terror."[5]

The negotiations which began in October of 1944 would eventually end in failure. Here is Sneh, Haganah's chief of staff reporting on a lengthy five-hour meeting with Begin on October 9:

"We wanted to suggest that they end their operations, and we wanted to find out what they really wanted. I challenged his [Begin's] failure to link military operations with political aims."[6]

Sneh continued to push the point that the Haganah would go right on dealing in illegal immigration and illegal settlements as a way of fighting the White Paper and as a way of tying action to politics. He was tentative about any further steps. Cautiously, he told Begin that "it is possible that we would call for a general revolt against a hostile authority if most of the people in the Yishuv were keen on that." He knew that they were not, even if Begin did not.[7]

Sneh says he tried to caution Begin on international repercussions stemming from Etzel operations. "Churchill," he said, "is favoring a partition favorable to us, and Etzel actions could torpedo that." He was also trying to placate Begin, saying that "I am trying my best to enter into your thoughts and to feel that your actions are essentially positive efforts proving that the Yishuv can fight, that the youth is ready and willing. But Etzel actions encourage negative forces in Great Britain and around the world."[8]

Sneh emphasized how much the Yishuv depended on international factors. As far as the Arabs were concerned, Sneh told Begin: "I realize that your challenge to Great Britain impresses the Arabs and make them fear the Jews. I understand this gives you a great deal of pride, but you must understand that your actions may also bring them [the Arabs] to revolt against us."[9]

Sneh recalls that Begin's reply was lengthy (and terribly boring). He defended vehemently Etzel's operations against the Mandatory.

"These actions are fully justified," Begin said. "Look what they have done—they have closed the gates against us, there is no rescue of Jews, they left us to be slaughtered . . . They deserve our whip."[10]

On Arabs, Begin reiterated an old theme. "One of Zionism's most fatal errors has been to think that our conflict was with the Arabs. You [the Yishuv] have imposed on us the British lie. Our struggle is with Britain."[11]

Begin dismissed almost defensively, as well as heatedly, Etzel's influence on the Yishuv.

"The Yishuv suffered very little in this war," he argued. "It was merely a little disturbed about the slaughter in Europe, no more. They did little. Our actions create sympathy for resistance among the youth. We redeem their feelings and prepare them for war."[12]

"Our axiom is that we *must* act," Begin repeated. But, Sneh asked, "Can you separate military actions from political leadership?"[13]

Begin seemed torn.

"I confess, you are right. Military action must be subordinated to political leadership and serve it. I am no ignoramus. But our Rosh Betar is dead. We have no political leadership, no political inspiration. We have no desire to rule. We are ready to share in power, part of it, we are also ready to accept Yishuv authority. But when? When it will head a national liberation committee, when it will proclaim a Jewish Prime Minister, when it will start waging war against the government, when it moves from Rehavia Street [headquarters of the Jewish Agency in Jerusalem] to the Mountains of the Galilee."[14]

Nevertheless, Begin expressed a willingness to cooperate, an ability to be realistic.

"We know that our war has no chance to succeed, not unless it is a total war, and we know we are not capable of doing that. You are. You have the leader of the Yishuv to lead this war. You have all the political, economic and military potential, and you will succeed."[15] "After the death of Rosh Betar . . . we see David Ben Gurion as the only person heading the political warfare of Zionism."[16]

"We would accept your authority," he said. "But of course, only if the Haganah will accept the principles of the Revolt."

According to Sneh, Begin began to explain his thinking. "There are three underground groups operating now," Begin said. "One [Lehi] engages in individual terror; another in sporadic military operations [Etzel], and another can throw its large weight into the final battle [Haganah]."

"Yes," Sneh said, "but this division of labor can only succeed if it comes from one disposition."[17]

Begin, according to Sneh, was becoming increasingly angry. "I refuse to accept the Yishuv authority unless it turns to the Revolt," he said. "I didn't think we have to kill every Tommy or British boy because he is a goy. We have to be selective, we must discriminate."[18]

Sneh insisted that the Yishuv was the only legitimate authority. At this, all of Begin's old frustration, bitterness, and feelings of inferiority broke out, all the old battles between Revisionism and Socialist Zionism surfaced.

"Rosh Betar [Jabotinsky] already challenged your monopoly over everything. You are the princes of this land, you are its builders, you are the fighters, you are the saviors of us all. I am a small man for you."[19]

Sneh noted the sarcasm and anger and said that "these outbursts were typical, they reveal much of their mentality."[20]

Begin, writing thirteen years later, recalls things somewhat differently, in a much more benign manner. He remembers that his view of Etzel's role paralleled Sneh's, and, in retrospect, appears omniscient, in that he recalls saying that "others will reap the fruits of the war we fought." Begin, in fact, saw a good deal of comradery and agreement where none existed: "with a smile, the emissary told me that he was convinced that there was a need for a united Hebrew Military Force."[21]

Actually, there was little for the Haganah and Etzel to negotiate unless both were to give up their most cherished orientations and commitments. For the moment, neither was prepared to do so.

As the protocols and writings show, things were not much better between Etzel and Lehi, who, on the surface, at least, seemed much more alike.

The schism, which was wide and bitter, was based on tactics and misperceptions, and rooted in long-standing enmity as well as terminology. The struggle is once again between Stern's successors and Begin; however rebellion before 1940 came from Betar, Raziel, and Etzel.

For example, the Yishuv representatives referred to Etzel and Begin as the renegades *(Porshim)*, while Begin, harkening back to the days when Stern dominated the radicals in Etzel, called Lehi members "The Stars," those who think they are the self-appointed princes of military Zionism. For the Yishuv, the Lehi assassins were deviants (horgim). There was more to this than mere name-calling, however.[22]

Although Begin clearly understood the difference between Etzel and Lehi, he could not understand why the two groups could not work together. In a letter to his Vilna comrade now Lehi leader Nathan Friedman-Yellin after the Moyne assassination (see later) in 1944, we can see the essence of the conflict between the two groups and the problems Lehi caused for Etzel and Begin: "I believe," Begin wrote, "that we must end our differences and immediately unite objectively. Now is the time . . . Your attitude is that there is no historical or objective need for a joined fighting group. You have failed to accept our minimal suggestion, that of a joint command, yet Stern and Raziel worked together in spite of their differences."[23] Of course, Begin didn't add that Raziel was killed in 1940, and undoubtedly Raziel's policy supporting Britain would have condemned him if not split Begin from Raziel's Etzel. In the end, in fact, Raziel and Stern's relationship was bitter and only Raziel's death brought an end to the rivalry.

Did Begin still believe that Lehi was a slightly different group of Betarim who had somehow gone slightly astray? He could not accept that, while Lehi was an outgrowth of Betar, it was an organization that was distinctly anti-Jabotinsky in nature. Its harsh and uncompromising principles of Renaissance were a direct challenge to all of Jabotinsky's and Begin's major premises, not to mention those of the Yishuv. Lehi did not merely represent a splinter, but a chasm of enormous proportions that could not be bridged.

Lehi hostility grew with the emergence of Begin and the proclamation of the Revolt. Lehi spokesmen violently attacked the ideas and principles of the Revolt, ridiculing the strategy behind Etzel operations of attempting to avoid killing British soldiers. Friedman-Yellin wrote sarcastically that "this kind of Polish knightly gentlemenhood stems from the discredited theories of Jabotinsky."

Nevertheless, Begin wanted some sort of accommodation, initially almost desperately. Begin thought it absurd that two underground organizations should be at odds over old and seemingly dead political issues from the past.

Yet that was exactly where Lehi's vehement opposition came from—the sins of the past. Friedman-Yellin acerbicly reminded Begin that Stern's Etzelites were the only Jewish military people fighting during the Arab rebellion [untrue] while the Haganah stood by uselessly as Jabotinsky "collaborated" with the British. Friedman-Yellin called "legionnairism" ridiculous; he talked about Jabotinsky with contempt. Friedman-Yellin and Lehi refused to accept the concept of military action linked to political action. They were loners, wild cards in the Jewish underground.

The assassination of Lord Moyne, a Lehi operation, was typical and it shocked Etzel to the core.

Begin had no particular compassion for Lord Moyne, but he knew there would be repercussions, and prophetically he saw that they would fall, not on Lehi, but on Etzel.

"The deed," he said, "was untimely and would bring serious political consequences. Etzel may pay the double price of both Yishuv and British antagonism."[24]

He was angry.

"We cannot forgive them," he said of Lehi, "for permitting such an act without consulting us." For Begin, it meant that either Lehi stopped acting as an independent organization or all negotiations between Etzel and Lehi would be over. The negotiations, it turned out, were over.[25]

Other Etzel members were even sharper in their reaction to the Lord Moyne assassination. Yaacov Meridor, Shlomo Lev-Ami, Eitan Livny and others called it "irresponsible, despicable, a deed soiled in treachery." Like Begin, they knew it would work like a thunderbolt against Etzel.

The assassination had violated the very precepts of the Revolt, of the continuing revolution. It would also spark the Sezon and give birth to Etzel's most tragic and, oddly, Begin's finest hour as Etzel's supreme commander.

13

The Sezon[1]

The Sezon, "the hunting season" was an operation by David Ben Gurion designed to eliminate the Etzel by assisting and informing the British and torturing Etzel members.

The assassination of Lord Moyne in 1944, perpetrated by Lehi, brought on one of the most fratricidal episodes in the history of the Yishuv, a time when Jew turned against Jew. It also became, against all the designs of its originators, Menachem Begin's finest hour, elevating him to the status of a legitimate leader of a legitimate movement, and secured his place in history.

Moyne's killing brought an end to the hesitations of the Haganah and the Socialist-Zionist leadership about moving against Etzel. The assassination provided the opportunity. "The time has come to finally strike at the heart of terrorism," wrote Israel Galilee, one of the leaders of the Haganah. Ben Gurion was slowly developing an alternative to partition and feared Etzel's activities would wreck his plans.

Begin's rejection of the Golomb-Sneh ultimatum of November 1944 to end Etzel activities, as well as the Moyne assassination, on November 6, 1944, triggered the Haganah into action. Already in mid-1944, the Jewish Agency decided "to prevent by Jewish force and Jewish means the deeds of the gangsters and gangs [Etzel and Lehi]." Reluctantly, Ben Gurion said, "We will have to use force."[2]

The only problem remaining was to persuade the leaders of the Histadrut and Labor. The decision to use force was made by the Left. In their propaganda, they made no distinction between Etzel and Lehi. Although the Moyne assassination was a Lehi operation, Etzel would bear the brunt of the Haganah's attention. In Socialist-Zionist circles, the battle was described as a class struggle between the workers, representing the Zionists, and the right wing, represented as irresponsible Fascists.

After a final decision was made in an Executive Committee meeting of the Histadrut, the Haganah's High Command was ordered to begin Operation Hot Hunting Season *(Sezon),* or "Operation Against Terror."

By way of preparation, about 170 members of the Palmach were given a special course in anti-terrorist tactics. The battle officially opened with a formal declaration of "a struggle against Etzel and Lehi." This statement had already existed in written form fourteen days *prior* to the assassination.

Instructions for the operation came in military and political terms. Haganah Intelligence (Shai) collected information it had in its files on "renegades" and their activities, such as training, arms caches, and hiding places. Shai, fearing too close a contact with British Intelligence (CID), appointed special Sezon liaison officers to work with CID. Their function was to inform the British about Etzel personnel—where to find them and how to capture them—as well as to provide them with updated general information. At the same time, the Haganah had to protect itself, lest any of its own members fall into the hands of the British during the course of the hunt.

The headquarters of the Sezon was situated in the home of Haganah Chief of the General Staff Yaàcov Dostrovski (Dori) in Haifa. Both Shai and Palmach were under the overall authority of Jewish Agency liaison officer Teddy Kollek, now mayor of Jerusalem. The Shai officer was Reuven Zaslany (Shiloah), a leading Arab expert and intelligence officer while the Palmach liaison officer was Shimon Avidan of UKM (Commander of Palmach troops in the 1948–49 War for Independence in the Negev Front).

Avidan's deputy was Palmach Commander Yigal Allon, who found the whole operation deeply distasteful, to the point where he refused to collaborate with the British—although the whole operation was designed for that purpose. Allon and other Palmach officers who refused to join in were never forced to volunteer. Allon complained that the operation violated the integrity of Palmach, as well as the Haganah. Begin in later years would remember Allon's deeds in the Sezon.

Nevertheless, some 250 Palmach officers became involved in the hunt. Their duties were to protect the homes of Mapai and Haganah officers, to follow up on the movements of Etzel's members, and to disturb the distribution of underground Etzel literature. The objective was to intimidate and to cripple Etzel as an effective military force.[3]

Approximately three to five hundred Etzel members were supposed to be captured and interned in makeshift Haganah prisons and kibbutzim for interrogation, but the operation was simply beyond the Haganah's capabilities. Finally, the Haganah tried to merely pin Etzel down to limit its operations. Sneh at last offered Begin an opportunity to call for cessation of Etzel's terror, but Begin irate refused and Etzel continued to operate in spite of the temporary paralysis. In 1945, a series of Etzel hijackings commenced.

The Sezon did enjoy some limited successes. Meridor, Lankin, and Shlomo Lev-Ami all surrendered or were captured. By 1945, a Haganah historian claimed that some seven hundred Etzel members were caught in the Sezon, which would have left some five hundred active Etzel members still at large. (Etzel members and fighters almost tripled since Begin's proclamation.) In addition, the Moyne assassination widened the already large rift between Lehi and Etzel. It was Etzel which bore the brunt of the Sezon. Lehi was largely ignored or left alone.

In the end, the Sezon was a sharp failure for Ben Gurion. None of the stated goals—to crush Etzel and to convince the Mandatory to adopt a more moderate stance toward the Haganah and the *Yishuv* itself—materialized. All the efforts of the Haganah and the British failed to capture Begin. Moreover, in the ranks of the Left, there were serious splits. Not all of the Palmach could be disciplined into joining the hunt.

Finally, both Sneh and Allon, exasperated and tired, called for an end to the Sezon. Even Ben Gurion finally concluded that the politics of the Sezon had failed miserably. He realized that the British had not changed their stance toward the Yishuv and that the energies of the Yishuv, the Haganah, Palmach, and Shai had been wasted. Ben Gurion, however, never gave up the fight against Etzel, a fight that he would successfully pursue in 1948 by destroying the *Altalena* and dissolving Etzel.

In retrospect, the Sezon looms as one of Ben Gurion's major political mistakes. He tried to placate Churchill, who failed to change the cabinet's White Paper policy; he demonstrated to the British that the Yishuv would not tolerate terrorism, and he tried to isolate Etzel and the Revolt—all at considerable cost, and he did not succeed. In the process, he was forced to ally himself with his lifelong foes, the binationalists, not to mention the United Kibbutz Movement and his radical opposition, groups like the Hashomer Hatzair. He used UKM to destroy Etzel, by using the Left to club the Right.

In the end, nothing really changed, except for one thing. Begin, by evading capture and by acting for once like a genuine Zionist statesman, saved Etzel and himself. Without a doubt, the Sezon provided Begin with his finest hour. Furious, angry, hunted all over Palestine, Begin nevertheless refused to retaliate. "Under no condition will I give my hand to a Jewish Civil War," he said. "My reply [to Sezon preparations] to trustworthy Jews of the Yishuv, that there will be no war of Jews against Jews in this land."[4]

Begin's statement, made while the Palmach and Haganah were hunting Etzel members side by side with the British, impressed the whole Yishuv with its statesmanlike, reasonable, and quite noble attitude. Begin, it was felt, was not fanatical like Stern; he was no Lehi killer. He demonstrated in the Sezon that there is a statesman and a leader among the "renegades." Even the Sezon leaders reluctantly admitted that they had handed Begin a large degree of legitimacy.

Under pressure to retaliate by his own harassed and hunted Etzelites, Begin never gave in. With that stand, he was elevated above party and political interest. To him, the Sezon was a Jewish betrayal of the essence of Zionism, and he said so. The Sezon gave this slight, bespectacled Polish Betari unparalleled power in Etzel and, if anything, strengthened Etzel as an organization and movement.

In spite of the Sezon, his small, tough organization was still an effective, resilient urban guerrilla operation. In the end of 1944, he had 800 pounds sterling in the treasury, some 500 fighters armed with four submachine guns, 60 pistols, 40 guns of various types and 2,000 kilos of explosives. By itself, this did not constitute a force for large-scale operations, but when the British and the Haganah never quite managed to break Etzel, they raised Etzel's expectations far beyond its actual capabilities.

There has been considerable speculation over the years over why Begin was not among those captured during the height of the Sezon. No real evidence has emerged, either from those conducting the Sezon or from Begin and his cohorts.

Some of the Sezon people, like Shimon Avidan, claimed Begin was not that important. The late Yigal Allon blamed the British Central Intelligence Department. He said their files were woefully inadequate. In spite of the fact that at the time of the Sezon Begin had been Etzel's leader for over a year, there was no real file on him.

Sneh of the Haganah offered a more intriguing argument. The Haganah, and perhaps Ben Gurion, knew that Begin was important as a negotiator and they saw Begin as more moderate than his followers, which he was. For these reasons, their search for Begin may have been lukewarm and in any case, most of the Haganah and Palmach Sezon hunters viewed their overall task with little enthusiasm.

Ben Gurion never supported this argument, but he was vague about the details. In 1971, when I asked him about the Sezon, he said that he had given a personal order to capture Begin. "Whose fault was it that he wasn't captured?" I asked. Ben Gurion shrugged his shoulders. "Some Haganah leader or another, I don't remember who."[5]

Begin on the other hand saw the Sezon's and the Haganah's inability to capture him as a victory for "our efficient intelligence methods." There is some truth in this, since during Begin's tenure, Etzel's capacity for clandestine activity improved considerably.

Whatever the reason, the Sezon and its results did count as a Begin victory, not just because he eluded capture, but because he managed to rise above the battle and thus gain what he had always craved, a legitimacy within the Yishuv as a whole. This outcome was due to Begin's restraint, a quality Ben Gurion did not display on this occasion. If Begin had given in to the urgings of his commanders, who advised retaliation, there is no doubt that a bloody Jewish civil war would have ensued.

After a heated debate in which he threatened to resign several times, Begin prevailed, his viewpoint winning out by a bare five to three vote in the Etzel High Command. In the process, he cemented his authority within Etzel, gained respectability and showed his statesmanlike qualities, while preventing serious bloodshed. He had much to be proud of, and he still boasts about it. As it turned out, Begin was no formidable, bloodthirsty warrior, but rather a very able political leader and a superb propagandist.

Although through the years, Begin has become known as a leader of an underground terrorist group, he was not a true terrorist, either by inclination or talent. He never really mastered the art of guerrilla warfare, either in tactical or operational terms, nor did he know very much about military planning or strategy. His only real contact with anything remotely military prior to taking over Etzel was his service as a corporal in the Anders Army, where he actually worked as a clerk, not as a combat soldier. In this, he was very much like his mentor, Jabotinsky. He had no training in the Etzel camps, where Raziel, Stern, Meridor and other Etzel-Lehi leaders all distinguished themselves. Unlike Ben Gurion, he did not bother to study military tactics and history.

What about Lehi and Sezon? Lehi in this period played an ugly double game. Ben Gurion's Sezon targeted only on Etzel. The Haganah leaders perceived Lehi as confused romantics, and perhaps for this reason left Lehi alone despite the Moyne assassination. My speculation is that since Stern was neither in Betar nor a Revisionist, he did not threaten the ideologues of Mapai. The argument that Ben Gurion intended to split Etzel and Lehi is historically incorrect. For Ben Gurion, Etzel was *never* a serious challenge. He considered the Ahdut Haavoda-Palmach renegades a more serious rival. To Ben Gurion and the Haganah leaders, Begin was a Revisionist, a historical rival. Stern and his people were misguided patriots.

Begin's rise to the leadership of Etzel met with some opposition and considerable surprise. Shlomo Lev-Ami, for one, thought little of him as a military tactician and opposed his appointment. The senior Etzel commanders in the big cities were closer to Stern. The Sezon changed all that. From now on Begin became the undisputed leader of Etzel. Shmuel Katz, now bitterly opposed to Begin, a chief Etzel ideologue, told me years later that "Begin was and still is an excellent propagandist and competent leader [but] his knowledge of military affairs is minuscule . . . If you put Begin in a room by himself, he is very good. The outside atmosphere, Jewish or Gentile, has a bad influence on him."[6] The Sezon changed all that, and certainly during the Camp David negotiations, Begin behaved as a states-man.

Begin served a distinct purpose as Etzel chief. Here his own peculiar talents could shine and turn him into a leader. He was a born political leader, and propagandist, and a charismatic, fiery orator who could show the way as long as the road was not too detailed. In military affairs, this made him susceptible to the sway of other, more capable men.

After the Sezon the division of labor within Etzel was both clear-cut and confusing. That is, Begin was the leader, the political chief, the propa-gandist and pamphleteer. The rest of the command specialized in urban guerrilla operations and tactics. Even if Begin was the symbol of authority for any and all Etzel operations, the operations themselves depended on the military skills of its commanders.

This organizational setup left Begin literally at the mercy of his lieuten-ants, a pattern that would resurface later in his career. The chief operations officers and the heads of small units thus had considerable discretion in terms of how they carried out their tasks, and they often took full advantage of it—especially Amichai Paglin. This process would be repeated again and again in the King David Hotel operation, the *Altalena* affair, Dir Yassin and, years later, with Sharon and the invasion of Lebanon.

In military affairs, Begin had, in Amichai or "Gidi" Paglin, a brilliant if erratic alter ego during the Etzel days much as he later did with Sharon when he became prime minister. Although Begin personally abhorred ter-ror for its own sake, he was frequently associated with Paglin operations like the bombing of the King David Hotel and the hanging of the British ser-geants, acts closer in substance to Lehi's than Etzel's philosophy. It was also Paglin who stimulated Begin to take provocative actions.

Begin was overly enamored of Paglin, who had a strange history. Born into a Labor family, he had all the earmarks of becoming a Socialist-Zionist stalwart. His uncle and aunt were Mapai-UKM leaders. His brother Nurel was Galilee's personal secretary and was a Shai intelligence officer. Why did he join Begin and Etzel? Paglin wanted action.

Paglin had become frustrated and bored with Haganah's apparent inac-tivity, and soon found himself all but driven into the arms of Etzel, where he thrived. He started as an operative but soon emerged as chief of operations. Begin doted on Paglin, who was an imaginative, tactical genius uncon-cerned with moral considerations. Begin called him a "wunderkind," whose military talents burdened him with genius. Between 1946 and 1948, he commanded over two hundred Etzel operations, many of them wildly spec-tacular.

Begin's own leadership solidified, not because of the flair of Etzel's military operations, but because of his own ability to radiate authority. He was frugal, living modestly, concerned with the life of his fighters, taking it hard when they were captured or killed. He protected his men, was loyal to them, trusted them, and they trusted him in return. One of his major achievements, especially during the dark times of the Sezon, was to create and maintain a strong feeling of esprit de corps.

The Sezon also solidified Begin's position with Palestinian Revisionism. Zohar had stood aside when the Haganah went after Etzel, and now they were isolated. This only helped Begin to distance himself. He had never accepted their authority or their advice. Now he ignored them. As a result, Zohar became an anachronism with no effective leader or purpose. Etzel under Begin had become truly autonomous and independent. Zohar was clearly orphaned by Jabotinsky's death.

The Yishuv leadership continued to mistrust Etzel. To Ben Gurion, Etzel represented not so much a rival for leadership in the Yishuv as a potential problem in the Yishuv's relationship with the British. Correctly, they perceived that Begin was attempting to use the Yishuv as a shield for his own political purposes. The goals of the Yishuv were exactly opposite those of Begin and Etzel. The Yishuv would not countenance any political or military action not directly harnessed to its strategy.

The purposes of Etzel and its operations frightened the Yishuv, which was waiting to reap political fruits at the end of the war. Etzel represented a bothersome nuisance, an obstacle to its goals. The Yishuv wanted to continue to focus on illegal immigration and opposition to the White Paper policies. They were concerned about how the British would react to open resistance.

Although the British had already drawn up and approved a plan to meet Jewish resistance, the Mandatory authorities in Palestine were aware of Jewish concerns. Brigadier General K. William of the CID wrote that "there is reason to believe that the Jewish Agency is not interested now in imposing a confrontation with us before the end of the war. It seems that they are concerned that unforeseen acts of the extremists would create a crisis before the time they have chosen for it to happen."[7]

The Sezon, from the Yishuv standpoint, at least managed to postpone until the "Black Sabbath" of 1946 a serious British bid to cripple the Yishuv's power. So, if anything, Sezon had bought some precious time.

All along, the Yishuv's goal had been to train soldiers and to accumulate military power that could be used against the Arabs in the coming war.

What is most interesting to observe during the Sezon is the relationships of Etzel, the Haganah, Lehi and the British. Their perceptions of each other were often misleading and highly colored by ideology or personality. This was especially true of how Begin was viewed.

The Haganah and the leadership of Mapai-Histadrut hated Begin passionately, because to them he represented everything that was unbridled, half-baked, and unruly about the forces of Revisionism unleashed by Jabotinsky.

Toward Jabotinsky himself, long dead, the attitude was one of respect. He had, after all, been a Haganah leader in 1920, and he was the founder of the Jewish legions and the idea of Jewish militarism. Revisionism and Socialist Zionism were natural rivals, and the ideological and political battle between them was intense. Even though they failed to come to a mutual agreement in spite of repeated efforts, Ben Gurion and Jabotinsky always maintained a stance of mutual respect. Jabotinsky was always considered a giant of Zionism, equal to Weizmann, and Ben Gurion, even though his ideology and goals clashed with those of Socialist Zionism.

For Begin, this was not the case. His image was that of a bespectacled, unremarkable, political operator of Betar. His rhetoric—anti-Marxist, anti-Socialist, militant, and flowery—was despised. The Socialist Zionists bridled at Begin's contemptuous references to the "builders" of agricultural collectives, and his contempt for the achievements of the kibbutzim. They saw him as a neo-Fascist, and relegated him to the political no-man's-land.

The pragmatic, hard-nosed activists of Mapai-Histadrut, especially those on the Left, perceived Begin incorrectly as a clown, a street agitator and bombastic rhetorician.

The Haganah leaders and members saw Begin as both a dreamer and a potential threat and Etzel as a desperate, ineffective military force, unrealistic in its goal of ousting the British Mandatory. The more outrageously violent Etzel actions were also dangerous to Haganah, because they provoked severe British reactions that affected to Haganah's own activities.

Begin also represented an internal threat to the Haganah because he spoke of direct and violent action against the British, an approach that appealed to the young Palmachites and Labor activists who were thirsting for action, a group that included people like Amichai Paglin, who eventually defected to Etzel and led some of its most famous—and notorious—operations.

The Haganah never really appreciated Begin's potential for leadership and political survival, evident in the restraint he showed during the Sezon. They continued to see him as a romantic lawyer in charge of a group of undisciplined thugs. They saw Etzel operations as unrealistic, imbued with fantasy, conceived in a military never-never land.

Ben Gurion never let go of his feeling of contempt for Begin. In a meeting in his home in Tel Aviv in the early 1970s, he told me that Begin was "a romantic lawyer who was responsible for the assassination of innocent Jews, Arabs, and British" (a reference to the King David Hotel bombing).

The British were also vehement in their hatred of Begin and Etzel. They felt more strongly about them than they did about Lehi, which had led an operation that resulted in the assassination of Lord Moyne. Haganah, likewise, did not have strong feelings about Lehi maybe because they failed to distinguish between the two. In fact, in many ways, some Ahdut Haavoda-Palmach leaders secretly sympathized with Lehi and admired the fallen Stern, its proto-leader. That was certainly true of the founder of Palmach, Yitzhak Sadeh, an avid reader of the poetry of U. Z. Gruenberg. Lehi's leadership was not "contaminated" by a Revisionist-Betar strain, even if the successors of Stern—Lehi leaders Friedman-Yellin, Yitzhak Yizernitsky (Shamir) and Dr. Israel Shayeb (Eldad)—were Betarim. (Remember, Yellin and Shayeb stayed with Begin in Vilna.) Lehi subscribed to Hebrew government and culture. It was imbued with authentic cultural aspiration. It was a Hebrew, not a diaspora, oriented movement.

To the various groups in the Yishuv, Lehi, in spite of its radical, fanatic nature, seemed more an authentic product of Eretz Israel than did Etzel, which had its roots in Diaspora Europe. Lehi moved to the Left after 1948 and always remained a bloodily violent organization. Even Ben Gurion entertained a secret admiration for it, to the point where, in 1953, he actually joined a Lehi Kibbutz, Sedeh Boker in the Negev, where Yehoshua Cohen, who was involved in the murder of Count Bernadotte, was a member, and who became a lifelong friend of retired Ben Gurion. He had a great affection for Geula Cohen, a Lehi fighter, now leader of the radical Nationalist-Renaissance party.

It is less puzzling that the British authorities should so passionately hate Etzel and Begin. And this is because of the hanging of the British sergeants and the bombing of the King David Hotel, yet Begin always distinguished between the British people and the Palestinian administration. If anything, he wanted, perhaps naively, the sympathy of the British people against its colonial policies and officers. In the end what he had was a lifelong hatred of both the British people and British governments. In 1970, when he visited London, official Britain ignored and shunned Begin.

Of course, we don't really know what Begin thought of Begin during this time. In the four years during which he led Etzel (1944–48), we have no firsthand record, although there are dramatic, if unrevealing, pamphlets, speeches and pronouncements. There is no diary; there is no personal, immediate Begin.

Unquestionably, Begin was no military genius, nor was he a great administrator or operational commander. Yet he had vision and leadership qualities, and a sense of the greater good, as he demonstrated during the Sezon.

14

The Hebrew Resistance Movement,[1] *1945–46: A Pragmatic, Short Honeymoon*

For a moment, it seemed as if the Jewish underground's fratricide and struggle would end.

There was an air of optimism all around. The war ended in Europe on May 8, 1945. Roosevelt, who had refused to take direct action to rescue the Jews of Europe, died, his place taken by Harry Truman, who was more sympathetic to their plight. In England, the Labor party, whose party conference had supported the abandonment of the White Paper policy, won a stunning upset political victory. The World Zionist Congress had met and called for active and passive resistance to the White Paper policy. It demanded an unconditional, immediate immigration of some 100,000 Jews, now in former Nazi concentration camps controlled by the British. Begin, who had never trusted Britain, had no cause for optimism, as other parties in the Yishuv did.

Etzel, in fact, never stopped its war against the British Mandatory. Begin's Revolt, his armed resistance, continued. The Sezon was petering out, flickering only here and there. The Haganah was off and on at war with Etzel. But the effort to bring the undergrounds together did not cease. Meanwhile, Begin went on his own.

On May 9, Etzel fighters attacked police headquarters in Jaffa and Sarona, the Templar colony near Tel-Aviv. An abortive effort was made to attack British Army headquarters in the King David Hotel in Jerusalem. On May 17 and 22, Etzel attacked the oil pipeline in Haifa. Benyamin Lubotsky, the leader of the National Movement, a Revisionist front group, called for the formation of a broad national liberation front whose aim would be to turn Eretz Israel into a Hebrew state.

On July 23, a combined Lehi-Etzel operation destroyed the main link of the Cairo-Haifa railroad near Yavneh. Etzel robbed the Agrobank in Tel Aviv of three thousand pounds of sterling, a considerable sum at that time. In Bergen-Belsen, the first Jewish refugee and displaced persons conference called for the immediate opening of the gates of Palestine for the remnants of European Jews.

But the optimism that the British would abandon the White Paper policy at the end of the war was to wither away quickly. There was deep frustration within the Yishuv over the continued stringent treatment of Zionists by the British.

Those Zionists who still believed in Weizmann's ability to impress his good friend Winston Churchill, or those who believed that a British Labor government would somehow have a special affinity for Israel's Laborites, were sadly disillusioned. Professor Yoseph Gorni, writing with great devotion to Israeli Socialists, tries to explain Labor's attitude toward their British counterparts:

"The development of relations between British Labour and Zionism can be viewed from several angles. From the purely moralistic aspect, which deplores the divorce of political interests from moral values, the policy of the Labour Government appears to be a clear example of deliberately heartless Machiavellian politics. The more cynical view is that Labour's constantly shifting policy towards Zionism stemmed neither from moral hypocrisy nor from political malice, but rather from the essential nature of politics as such, and parliamentary politics in particular. According to this view, interests and values should be kept apart, and interests should always prevail. In parliamentary regimes it is customary for the opposition to object to government policy, and to proclaim the importance of values. Yet when the opposition party comes to power, it is not expected to keep all its former promises, and interests dictate policies. The policy of the Labour Government on Zionism from 1929 to 1931 and from 1945 to 1948, can be cited in support of this viewpoint. Hence, it could be said, that policy should not be regarded as a betrayal of values and commitments, but as part of the 'game' of democratic parliamentarianism and of the power struggle between conflicting national interests which are of the essence of politics."[2] This was the attitude of Mapai leaders, written by their house historians.

Sezon had not deterred England's new Labor government from continuing the White Paper policies, nor had it diminished Etzel's capacity for resistance. On the other hand, it had enhanced Begin's chance to acquire more recognition and respectability. In response to the rigid British policy, an agreement was reached on October 25 among the Haganah, Etzel and Lehi establishing a joint Hebrew Resistance Movement (HRM). From the start, no integrated command structure was established for the HRM. It was to meet once every two weeks to coordinate operations. The Haganah was represented by Moshe Sneh and Israel Galilee; Etzel by Menachem Begin and Chaim Landau; and Lehi by Friedman-Yellin and Dr. Israel Shayeb. The political oversight over the HRM, the "X" Committee, was a body that knew or understood little of HRM's operation and timing. Several times it approved operations retroactively. On the whole, the chief of Haganah *(Rama)* and its chief of staff *(Ramatkal)* were to be in charge of operations. Most of the HRM command structure was that of the Haganah. But in the case of the King David Hotel bombing—Operation Chick—political and operational authority went wrong, and the Hebrew Resistance Movement officially created on November 1, 1945, came to an end on October 31, 1946, after the Etzel operation against the King David.

The Hebrew Resistance Movement was an umbrella organization covering all three active resistance movements—the Haganah, Etzel, Lehi—formed at the end of the Sezon, as it became clear that the British would not moderate their stance toward the Zionists and the White Paper. It was the Yishuv's first successful effort to bring about the cooperation of all the undergrounds. HRM had, overall, no tight control, nor were its policies comprehensive or clear. Military coordination demanded similar political goals. HRM had no such goals nor political structures to reinforce them.

The Hebrew Resistance Movement was intensified when the Yishuv leaders were thrown into prison (the Black Sabbath) and Kibbutzim were destroyed in arms searches; There was no authority in Palestine. David Ben Gurion, the Yishuv's leader, was in Paris; Dr. Weizmann was lying on a sick bed, almost blind, in London; the Zionist movement faced the abyss. "The possibility [existed]," writes Zvi Ganin, "that the Yishuv built by the toil and blood of three generations, would be destroyed by the British."[3] Neither the British Left nor Right were to be trusted.

Although HRM activities were under the supposed umbrella of the organized Yishuv, the initiative to form the HRM came from Sneh in the Haganah and Sadeh of the Palmach. Begin was to help in the act of creation and to play an important role. Ben Gurion was always opposed to any deals with Etzel. Ben Gurion clearly indicated that HRM will legitimize Begin, who was now cooperating with the Haganah. He reluctantly went along with the idea of including the Etzel in HRM. The Haganah had become a considerable instrument of power in the hands of the Yishuv. The Palmach was a force of some 2,000 full-time professional soldiers, with an added force of 4,500 part-time urban forces and reserves of 4,000 as well as an additional force of some 12,000 youths ages fourteen through seventeen and a reserve of some 30,000 to 35,000 men. In addition, it sported a large small-weapons industry. Its aim, however, wrote the Haganah paper *Bamachane,* was political—the ouster of the British from Palestine.

Begin's interpretation of the formation of HRM was single-minded and myopic. Ben Gurion looked to America to eventually deter the British and wanted to use the Haganah to enhance Zionist diplomacy and HRM as a deterrent to British policy. But Begin felt that he now had license to go full steam ahead against the British. Ben Gurion knew that the real war would be with the Arabs. Ben Gurion was not ready to enhance Etzel and Begin's reputation. For Begin, the real war was against the Mandatory.

Begin had "great" plans. He envisioned a combined large-scale operation of all the resistance movements, including Palmach, Etzel, Lehi, and Haganah's reserves. It took Sneh, Galilee, and Friedman-Yellin a whole night to dissuade him from such folly.

Thus, Haganah, which was also trying to steal some of the thunder from Etzel, still maintained that the "real" enemy was the British White Paper policy, not the British soldiers themselves. "We don't see the British soldier or policeman as the enemy," Sneh said. "Strategically, we want to avoid open confrontation with the British armed forces and police. We will determine the time and place of armed confrontation . . ."[4]

Their idea centered around linking military actions to all the phases of the struggle against the Mandatory, a strategy that involved securing the new settlements, illegal immigration and retaliation against such targets as radar stations used against illegal immigration and the new communications systems for the freshly-arrived army of 100,000 British soldiers, to fight the rise of Jewish terror. The target was Britain's anti-immigration policy, a strategy that did not necessarily dovetail with Etzel's.

The HRM divided its activities into three levels of operations. Level one was linked to the phrase "securing our constructive institutions," meaning illegal immigration. Level two was designed to start large-scale passive and active operations against "persons and institutions designed to implement anti-Jewish policies." It was presumed that the British would make a systematic effort to destroy the Haganah, the Palmach and their weapons caches. Passive and active operations meant an attempt to paralyze the administration and police structures of the Mandatory. Level three was an all-out declaration of war against the Mandatory, which, Begin hoped, would include the full-scale participation of Etzel.

HRM could become political dynamite, destroy the structures of Zionist diplomacy, and turn Jewish resistance into the hands of the Porshim. Clearly, the creation of the HRM was a godsend for Begin and Etzel; it was for this reason Ben Gurion was apprehensive about the eventual consequences of HRM activities. Nevertheless, it was Ben Gurion who initiated the new activist line of Zionism in defiance of Weizmann and the moderates of the Jewish Agency.

The new policy of activism was in danger from two directions, however. One was the chaotic state of Zionist diplomacy in general, which was apprehensive about a direct military confrontation with Great Britain. The other was Ben Gurion's genuine concern that the extremes of either Left or

Right—Ahdut Haavoda-UKM and Palmach on the Left; Etzel and Lehi on the Right—would capture and take control of the HRM.

Ben Gurion was shrewd and manipulative enough to be ahead of both his lieutenants and the Jewish Agency. He sensed the new mood of activism within the ranks of Zionism, especially among the young, and acted accordingly; very much in character, he seemed to follow one course while pursuing another.

The success and failure of the HRM depended almost entirely on the attitude of Ben Gurion, not of Begin on the Haganah, not Etzel. What was happening was that the "X" Committee was approving HRM's operations retroactively. Ben Gurion realized that HRM seriously lacked political clout and could upset Zionist diplomacy. He thus was going to bring an end to HRM. But not right away.

Meanwhile, Ben Gurion, without technically saying so, was nevertheless approving the new activist policy, only as a means of restraining Etzel. In a letter to Sneh, written from Paris on October 1, 1945, he wrote: "The Stern group is ready for full cooperation with us. This time it seems serious. If we accomplish such a unity, it would be possible to prevent Etzel's independent action."

Ben Gurion was looking ahead, hoping to harness Lehi and split it from Etzel.

"I don't think," he also wrote, "that we could accomplish much with the [British] Labour government, if we depend only on our demands. In addition to political pressure, we must add the resistance force of the Yishuv. If England were forced to use terror measures on us, then the Yishuv would receive from World Jewry and World Zionism the okay to break the White Paper policy with deeds."[5]

Although this obviously signaled a tendency toward action on the part of Ben Gurion, he had not been delegated by the Jewish Agency to initiate or approve Jewish resistance activities without its approval. Ben Gurion was aware that his constitutional role prevented him from taking action without prior consultations. The Jewish Agency had refused to approve the new activist policy. Even as he negotiated with Weizmann and the Jewish Agency, he appeared to be "ordering" Sneh to proceed with the new policy in Palestine.

To the moderates, Ben Gurion acted as if his letter to Sneh was merely a recommendation, when in reality it was a realistic prodding that recognized the state of affairs in Palestine. Weizmann was not entirely unaware of Ben Gurion's activist, independent mood.

Ben Gurion, with Sneh right behind him, was now in control of the HRM and was riding the growing activist mood of the youth in Eretz Israel.

In short, it was Ben Gurion and his prodding that tamed the HRM. Years later, Begin would have us believe that he had "swayed" the Yishuv leader toward activism. This is simply not true. Both Ben Gurion and Weizmann considered Begin a latecomer, a petty intruder who needed to be restrained.

It is true that the creation of the HRM, and the Sezon, catapulted Begin into a major role and gave him respectability. Begin benefited; but he did not lead.

With Ben Gurion giving reluctant approval and with Sneh and Sadeh leading the way, coordination was established with Etzel. Etzel and Lehi hit police stations in Tel Aviv while the Haganah struck against railroads, bridges and coastal radar stations. Although there was never formal approval of Etzel actions, there was coordination with Haganah. Begin welcomed the coordination, even though it was with the same people he had sneered at and called "British collaborators."

Etzel and Lehi soon saw in the cooperation a license to increase the tempo of their activities. For instance, when the Anglo-American Commission arrived in Palestine in March 1946, Haganah wanted to temper HRM activities. Instead, Etzel felt that highly visible terrorist activities would influence the Commission even more. Perhaps they were right, for the Commission ended by giving a favorable report and recommending the immediate importation of one hundred thousand Jews to Palestine.

The British reaction to the HRM was not unexpected. Incensed, they all but ignored the Commission's nonbinding recommendations. The HRM retaliated by increasing the level of terror. This time the British response was Operation Agatha, a wholesale, but basically ineffective military action against the entire infrastructure of the Jewish underground. The war on illegal immigration went into high gear; the British brutality against the remnant of European Jewry antagonized even the most moderate members in the Yishuv.

Between 1946 and 1947, until the United Nations General Assembly recommended the partition of Palestine, terror was on the upswing on an unheard of scale, with most of the actual operations conducted by Etzel and Lehi. Illegal immigration increased. Between October 1946 and April 1947, eighty British personnel were killed, as well as forty-two Jews and numerous Arabs. In one sense, Etzel was attaining its goal. Palestine was beginning to become ungovernable for the British.

The British generals in Palestine were at Bay and they complained loudly. Montgomery shot off a sharp note, accusing the Colonial Office of "appeasement." He called for harsh, unilateral action against Jewish terrorists. He wanted new and harsher search-and-destroy operations. In this he was supported by almost all of the top military brass in Palestine. But the government and high commissioner vetoed the proposition. "In view of the major political factors involved and the extreme difficulty of hitting the sections of the community involved, we cannot approve your recommendation."

By June 1946, the British cabinet approved Montgomery's recommendations, but paradoxically it also approved the High Commissioner's position. In retrospect, Montgomery was probably tactically correct in the sense that his methods may have been the only way to effectively suppress resistance. He was recommending unrestrained occupation, but in the wake of the Holocaust and world opinion, a British cabinet simply could not go along with it. His recommendation to assassinate the fifty leaders of the Yishuv was certainly cruel and politically callous.

By March, conditions in Palestine really did resemble a war. On one day, March 1, Etzel carried out sixteen major operations, including the bombing of the British Officers Club in Tel Aviv and the hijacking and kidnapping of officers in Jerusalem. On March 2, the British retaliated, and the high commissioner imposed a military curfew on Tel Aviv and its surroundings—as well as on a part of Jerusalem. For fifteen days, the army searched for terrorists and arms caches. It did not work. On March 7, Etzel struck against military camps and equipment in Jerusalem, Haifa, and Tel Aviv. Etzel's unrestrained activities were beginning to worry the Haganah, which was hurt more than Etzel, and in May 1947, it decided to initiate a mini-Sezon in order to prevent terror from getting out of hand.

In June, to its horror, the Haganah discovered a large Etzel tunnel running under the Citrus House in Tel Aviv, headquarters of a British security compound. Etzel operatives had intended to lay a huge quantity of explosives under the Citrus House and warn the British to evacuate before detonating the explosives. It was a classic Etzel strategy to undermine British prestige and morale. The Haganah averted the plan, but some of its members were killed when a charge left by Etzel was accidentally set off. The British praised the Haganah for having prevented a great tragedy and marched alongside Haganah officers at the funeral of one of the Haganah men.

Clearly, life was becoming intolerable for the British—which was after all the aim of the Revolt. The only hope for the British was the United States, which would not help, or the UN, which the British hoped would vote against partition. They turned out to be wrong, as they had been about many things during their rule in Palestine.

The Haganah and Socialist Zionism, Etzel and Revisionism, Lehi and Sternism, all held different political views and ideologies, but all held to the policy that military action followed policy. And all of them wanted to take the major share of the credit for the creation of the state of Israel—except that in the case of Etzel, it was primarily a military not a political organization. Haganah and Mapai-UKM were identical. Etzel stayed autonomous from Revisionism.

In a debate over the HRM some twenty years later carried on in the pages of *Maariv* by representatives of the Haganah, Etzel and Lehi, Begin had this to say: "Only during the era of the HRM did the Haganah fulfill one of its three goals [illegal immigration, illegal settlement, armed resistance], and that was armed resistance when we were part of it."

"I think," said Begin, "that this period was one of the most glorious epochs in the history of our nation. For us, the Etzel, HRM symbolized the end of the darkest era (the Sezon), the era of oppression. For us, HRM meant a political struggle using military means."[6]

Begin was replying to Sneh, former commander (Rama) of the Haganah, who had claimed that the Haganah was the military arm of the Yishuv subject to "the responsible authorities," meaning the Jewish Agency and the Zionist Executive. "Etzel," Sneh said, "was free to do what it did unrestrained by political forces."[7] It was not subject to the Zionist authorities, and therefore it could engage unrestricted in armed resistance.

"We conducted a political war all the way by military means," Begin replied. "We never conducted a war for strictly military purposes. We, after all, knew we were the few against the many. Could we have prevailed by the use of force? . . . Each operation followed a political purpose, the continuous armed struggle against Britain."[8]

Begin was aware of the weaknesses of the combined Jewish military forces. "Although Ben Gurion told us that the British would not dare to use weapons against the forces of Eretz Israel, Galilee told me that 'our force is limited,'" referring to the Haganah, and thus the British would dare use force against the undergrounds if "the idea of blowing up all British installations out of the HRM agenda was adopted. We of Etzel, however, did offer to use all our forces."[9] At the time, Begin advocated policy of total war against Britain in the agenda of the HRM, which was rejected at the Haganah.

Natan Friedman-Yellin, former head of Lehi, recalled that it was impossible for the components of the HRM to work together except to coordinate, recommend and logistically help in operations, since there was no political unity of purpose. Haganah's goals were immigration, settlement, and protection of its weapons. Etzel aimed at armed resistance and urban warfare in order to call worldwide attention to the effects of British rule. Lehi pursued personal assassination and robbery, its targets personnel involved in the implementation of the White Paper policy.[10]

Sneh challenged Begin. "I remember from conversations I had with Mr. Begin at the time," he said, "that when it came to differences between Haganah and Etzel concerning Britain Begin paraphrased a remark made by Field Marshal Jan Smuts, the South African Premier, 'We fight you so that you can become our friends.'" Begin did not reply to Sneh, but his deputy, Chaim Landau, said that according to Begin, "The alliance with Britain is secondary." To which Shalom Rosenfeld, the *Maariv* editor and a Betar-Etzel friend of Begin's added, "This idea is a Jabotinsky concept anyway."[11]

Looking at it from the vantage point of forty years, how are we to judge the importance of events and deeds? Who was responsible for Jewish independence?

Hewing to one viewpoint, one might agree with Begin and Etzel that armed resistance helped to force on the British the decision to depart Palestine, that continued Etzel pressure finally made them drop the situation into the hands of the Anglo-American Commission and the United Nations. There is little doubt that Etzel actions and operations certainly stimulated if not caused the British departure. Yet, Etzel's importance diminishes when thrown into the larger arena.

We know now that the United States policy in the Middle East, the Holocaust, and the destruction of the British Empire were all huge factors in the British departure from Palestine, along with its dogged insistence to keep the White Paper policy that enraged not only the Yishuv but the world at large. Above all, its Arab allies refused to heed British advice to at least end restricted immigration. Thus, the Bevin policy paralyzed a British policy already thwarted by Arab unwillingness to compromise.

When the British failed to persuade the Americans joining them as partners in the Middle East in the fight against Communism, they relinquished their hold on Palestine.

Begin said that "without Jewish undergrounds, the British would not have left in the time that they did and the state would not have been established."[12] This is certainly a myopic viewpoint, one that Begin still clings to.

The answer lies elsewhere. Bevin's closest advisor, John Martins, has this to tell professor Gavriel Cohen: "What influenced the government and decision makers were the combined operations of the Haganah and the decisions of the Jewish Agency on *maavak* (struggle) . . . To the extent that *public opinion* weighed in British policy decisions, the latter was mainly influenced by the actions of Etzel and Lehi. Terror influenced public opinion in two directions. At first it aroused the public *against* the Zionist struggle. But in later phases, disgust had its *accumulative effect, which brought public opinion pressure to evacuate Palestine.* The public now was tired of loss of soldiers." [Italics are Martins'.]

Kenneth Younger, one of Bevin's deputies, had this to say: "Personal assassination influences *public opinion;* here, undoubtedly, Etzel-Lehi operations were decisive . . . but the demonstration of restrained military power [Haganah] *did not influence public opinion.* The operations of the Haganah influenced the experts . . . Haganah's major effect was on official circles." Yet the judgment of the Imperial General staff was, "that all policy options could have been exercised if the government had decided to stay there [in Palestine]." However, American lack of cooperation with the British Government prevented such a decision.[13]

Etzel and Lehi and, to a degree, the Haganah, may have been catalysts and a source of frustration for the British, but they are not responsible for the victory in the war of independence. One should leave that honor to Ben Gurion and Haganah leaders, who wisely withheld the Haganah from a large scale confrontation with the British. Had the Haganah, and the Palmach, which formed the major forces fighting against the Arab invasion and for liberation, actively battled the British, they would have been decimated and exhausted by the time of partition and probably been defeated by the Arabs in that desperate war of 1947–48.

15

Black Sabbath and the King David Bombing[1]

The HRM undoubtedly was the most comprehensive exercise by the Yishuv of the military resistance option. The three undergrounds, together and separately, hit the British quite hard.

By mid-1946, the British had almost had enough. They decided to move forcefully and en masse against all strains of the Jewish underground.

On the Sabbath—Friday night, June 29, 1946—some seventeen thousand British troops of the Sixth Paratroop Division, backed by tanks, heavy guns, and armor commenced Operation Broadside, a bold sweep against the Hebrew Resistance Movement.

The Mandatory announced a total blockade of the country. Borders were closed, telephone service stopped altogether, and a night curfew was imposed on the Yishuv. By Saturday morning, almost all of the Yishuv leaders, of whatever political persuasion, were surprised to find themselves under arrest. They were taken to Latrun prison near Jerusalem for internment. Arms searches in Kibbutzim inflicted heavy damage to Kibbutz Yagur. The British offensive was brutal. Yet it was nothing compared to its offensive on Arab terror in 1937–39.

Jerusalem bore the brunt of the operation. The Jewish Agency's headquarters in Rehavia was surrounded by a large force of troopers and police, some of whom forcefully entered into the home of the National Religious Party leader Rabbi Y. L. Fishman, the head of the "X" Committee. Meanwhile, nearly thirty Jewish settlements underwent searches by British soldiers looking for Haganah arms caches. The Histadrut, the newspaper *Davar*, and numerous Yishuv institutions were surrounded and searched. For a week, soldiers roamed in Kibbutz Yagur searching for weapons and harassing Kibbutz members. The British clearly held Haganah and the Jewish authorities in the Yishuv responsible for anti-British terror.

Ben Gurion happened to be in Paris at the time, and Golda Meirson (Meir), much to her shame (she said), also escaped detention. Few others did.

At the Kibbutz Yagur, where a small cache of arms was discovered, search and occupation went on for a week. Numerous Haganah and Palmach leaders were detained.

Moderate Jewish leaders like Weizmann were thoroughly alarmed. But those Haganah leaders who had managed to evade capture continued in their work. In retaliation, HRM units attacked British arsenals near Bat-Galim in Haifa and Etzel, and Lehi units were given the go-ahead to attack British military installations, something the X Committee had disallowed previously. The Etzel-Haganah-Lehi HRM machine went to work.

Meir Weisgal, a Weizmann representative, was appalled. He demanded that Sneh put a stop to the anti-British HRM terror activities. When the X Committee capitulated to the demand, Sneh resigned in disgust as Haganah Commander (Rama). The ineffective X Committee was disbanded—even a hint of moderation was abandoned.

In reality, the X Committee was impotent to stop HRM activities. The Yishuv leadership were in jail or abroad. Only Yitzhak Sadeh, the Palmach commander and deputy chief of staff of the Haganah, was left. Ben Gurion was in Paris, Sneh had resigned just before the operation and Galilee and Golomb had been arrested.

Events were rapidly coming to a head, events which would put an end to the Hebrew Resistance Movement. By this time, plans were actively under way for one of the most spectacular and in many ways disastrous operations of the Revolt, the bombing of the King David Hotel.

When Begin became Prime Minister, the casual observer of the international scene was hardly familiar with his name or his politics. Most people did not know the significance of Revisionism, Betar, Etzel, Herut, the *Altalena,* or the Sezon, but they had heard of Begin in association with terrorism.

That reputation, for non-Israelis, probably rested solely on the bombing of the King David Hotel. The bombing had widespread results, and not just as an act of terrorism. Although it succeeded in tarnishing the names of Begin and Etzel (or the Irgun, as it became popularly known worldwide), it also dramatized the Jewish struggle against Great Britain more than any combined operation of the Haganah, Etzel, or Lehi, and had a considerable impact on British and world public opinion. The King David Hotel bombing was symbolic as well as horrific, for the hotel housed the headquarters of the British Army in Palestine, whose commander in chief, Field Marshall Sir

Bernard Montgomery, had seriously suggested the assassination of all Jew-ish leaders, no matter what their politics.

The year was 1946, one year after the war in Europe had ended. By this time, the whole world knew the extent of the horror of the Holocaust, but few had heard of the White Paper, of the British policy of keeping Jewish refugees in camps in Europe in order to prevent them from immi-grating to Palestine. It was not until the early 1960s that this perfidious British policy was dramatized with the publication of Leon Uris' *Exodus,* which also became a highly popular film.

For the first time, millions saw the ugly side of British policy—how the British, a democratic society, held the Jews prisoners in camps; how the whole British political establishment, Labor and Conservative, supported the policy of brutally repressing illegal Jewish immigration; how the British hunted illegal immigrants with warships. Here was a genuine David vs. Goliath battle, and the bombing of the King David Hotel, however terrible its results, helped to dramatize that battle. According to the historian of Israel's struggle against the British in the years 1946–47, out of four outlets for Jewish anti-British resistance—political, military, settlements, and illegal immigration—the latter was singled out by former Mandatory and military high officials as the most effective and hurtful to the British image in Amer-ica. It was, in fact, the *instrument* that created Jewish, Zionist consensus and American support behind it.[2]

There was no Jewish consensus on partition, binationalism, common-wealth status, or use of terror except in relation to the Jewish European remnant. Bevin's folly and insensitivity, his war against the refugees, finally alienated his only hopeful source of support—the United States. The Zion-ists brilliantly exploited this indifference to the Jewish refugee plight, and this conducted by a Socialist government. Begin clearly understood the political weapon that illegal immigration provided Etzel, but he relin-quished it to the Haganah, whose resources he argued were superior, to run Zionist rescue *(bricha)* operations certainly an insensitive and politically blind position on his part.

As we know now from recently surfaced documents, the real heroes of illegal immigration were members of the Haganah, the Haganah's counter-intelligence network—the Mosad—which ran illegal immigration from the camps in Palestine. This particular chapter of heroism was written by David Ben Gurion, by the Ahdut Haavoda men, the pragmatic militants of the Mosad. Begin and Etzel had no part in it. Begin was totally preoccupied with anti-British terrorist activities. Now he turned to Etzel's most famous operation, under the auspices of HRM.

The King David operation (Operation Chick) was not just one act in the struggle to overthrow British rule, but rather the incident focused worldwide attention on the plight of the Yishuv. The attention of the world and, more importantly, of the United States suddenly focused on the cause of Jewish statehood, the suffering of Jewish immigrants and refugees, and the policy of the British, as well as on the terrorist activities of Etzel and Lehi—which were perceived as a reaction to the British war against illegal immigration. Operation Chick was also to be a major symbolic act of resistance to British rule and a demonstration to the planners of Broadside how ineffective they really were. The HRM counteroffensive was to demonstrate to the British the following:

1. They tried to confiscate our weapons; we shall confiscate theirs.
2. They tried to paralyze our national institutions; we shall paralyze theirs.
3. They tried to demonstrate their superiority; we shall demonstrate our national will over theirs.[3]

Thus the first targets were the King David Hotel, the high commissioner's Secretariat offices, and the David Brothers Building, another Mandatory government center.

Although the Haganah originally suggested Operation Chick, it was Begin, Paglin and Etzel who actually executed the operation.

The idea was the brainchild of Paglin, Etzel's brilliant and ruthless young chief of operations. For once, after Black Sabbath, the Haganah was beginning to march in step with Etzel, at least in terms of language. In a radio broadcast, the Haganah declared that "the British Nazi government, under the so-called Labor Party, has declared war on the Jewish people." The voice was Haganah, but the language and rhetoric were pure Etzel.

The Haganah, under Sneh, approved Paglin's operation, which came to be called Operation Chick. He gave his approval without the knowledge or approval of the X Committee, nor that of any of the Yishuv bigwigs, some of whom were in hiding, most of whom had been detained. In this, Sneh seemed to be following normal HRM practices.

The operation was to be a three-pronged affair in which the Haganah would attack British arsenals, Lehi would take on the offices of the Palestine Information Office, and Etzel would blow up the government and military headquarters in the King David Hotel.

Sneh argued that the operation fell within the range of the doctrine of *Havlagah,* or containment, or "Defense of Defense." "They attacked our government body and sought to paralyze it; we will attack and paralyze their government bodies."[4]

The premise, especially coming from a Haganah official, seemed odd, but not in terms of an HRM contingency plan. Nevertheless, the High Command gave its approval. So did the impotent X Committee, although Sneh failed to tell its members the actual target or the date for its execution.

The X Committee had no executive or administrative capability to check HRM's military initiatives and plans. The HRM was an umbrella for the three undergrounds but never acted as its executive committee. Operations were initiated by individual underground commands, which coordinated with the HRM committee on a rather loose basis. Operation Chick was a classic example of the actual powerlessness of the HRM when confronted by an actual Etzel operation.

On July 1, Sneh asked permission to go ahead with an operation called "Return of the Lost Items," which was to ostensibly return both Haganah arms but especially the highly secret papers captured in the British raids and hidden in the King David Hotel.

On that same day, Begin received a letter from a Haganah courier. It read: "You are to carry out as soon as possible the Malonchick [code name for King David Hotel] . . . Inform us of the date. The identity of the organization which carries out the operation should not be made public, either implicitly or explicitly."[5]

Even Begin was puzzled. There were no details. Begin was concerned about casualties, both Etzel and civilian. He expressed his concerns to Paglin. Paglin tried to mollify Begin by telling him that the British were known to evacuate buildings when they were forewarned about a bomb threat. The British indeed had done this, but lately there had been so many bomb threats that the British stopped taking them seriously. That piece of information Paglin kept from Begin.

Meanwhile, serious negotiations involving Weizmann and Weisgal were going on with the British for the release of the Haganah's detainees. Weizmann had counseled caution and restraint. Now Sneh, without telling Begin of the negotiations, began to ask for several postponements of Operation Chick in a bid to buy time.

On July 15, the X Committee reversed its earlier decision and went along with Weizmann's ultimatum to resign if HRM continued its antigovernment operations. Sneh neglected to pass along that information to Etzel and decided to string Begin along with another series of postponements. He canceled the attack on the Bat Galim arsenal while telling Begin and Lehi that their operations had been postponed.

Begin agreed, but he was worried. "These postponements are becoming increasingly dangerous," he told Galilee, Sadeh's superior, "especially because so many people know about the operation."[6] Meanwhile, the overall crisis seemed to be easing. The Mandatory had ended its occupation of the Jewish Agency, stopped arms searches, and slowly began to release some of the detainees.

Unaware of or indifferent to what was going on, Begin and Etzel went ahead with their plans, assuming approval from Sadeh and Haganah's command.

On July 22, the charges were set. Adina Hay-Nissan, a teenaged Etzel courier, made three phone calls—to the British Command, the French Consulate, and the *Palestine Post*—warning about the bombs. She remembered her precise words to the British: "This is the Hebrew Resistance uprising. We have placed bombs in the hotel. The building is going to blow up. You must evacuate it immediately. You have been warned."[7]

Apparently none of the warnings were taken seriously or they were ignored. The charges went off, and the explosion all but leveled the hotel, killing ninety-one people, British, Jewish and Arab.

It did more than that. The Yishuv, the Jewish Agency and world opinion were up in arms, so much so that the Hebrew Resistance Movement was no longer workable. Etzel and Begin were blamed, and once again they were labeled "terrorists and bandits," while Sneh's and Haganah's part in the operation was ignored for years.

The largest share of the blame was heaped on Begin, perhaps wrongly, because history suggests that his deputy Paglin, along with Sneh, were at least as if not more responsible.

It was claimed later that the warning time had not been sufficient, and Begin was blamed for this. Yet Sir John Shaw, chief secretary (the chief administrator of the Mandatory), ordered that no one should leave the hotel.

The question remains: Why was Begin blamed?

Thurston Clarke, in his book, *By Blood and Fire,* which is, on the whole, sympathetic to Etzel, tries to answer that question.

"Begin," he writes, "was a political, not a military tactician, an amateur in questions of fuses, blast effects, and evacuation times. The highest military rank he had achieved was corporal, a filing clerk in the Free Polish Army. He believed in armed revolt but had never fought a battle, fired a gun in anger, or planted a bomb. He had risked arrest, imprisonment, and execution, but not death in combat."[8]

Paglin's disrespect for authority stunned both Palmach commanders and his cohort in the operation, Sadeh. Arrogantly Paglin had only asked for 350 kilos of explosives, not enough to blow up the hotel.

Sadeh asked about a warning.

"But you promised to give a warning?" he asked Paglin.

"I devised a bomb that cannot be dismantled," was Paglin's answer.

"But can you assure us the operation will result in absolutely no loss of life?" Sadeh asked.

"It is our experience that the British abandon a building quickly once they've been given a warning," Paglin said.

Sneh was skeptical. "Are you sure?" he asked.

"Of course," Paglin said.[9]

This is Paglin's version, and Clarke in his book accepts it. Paglin was wrong.

Paglin was cocky and supremely confident, and he wanted more than anything else to go ahead with the operation. He lied about the degree of precaution exercised by the British, who lately had begun ignoring the frequent warnings. Paglin was contemptuous of the Haganah and their worries. He considered them cowards.

Paglin told Sadeh that a forty-five-minute warning would be given. "That's too long," Sadeh said. The Haganah's main concern about the King David Hotel was that it housed captured Haganah documents and that forty-five minutes would give the British time to secure the documents. "It will give the British time to save the documents as well as people," Sadeh said. He asked for a fifteen-minute warning. They finally compromised on thirty minutes.

Begin, meanwhile, had made a political decision on the warning. He wanted to warn the Jewish civil servants working in the hotel. "The Irgun must not be responsible for the mass murder of the Jews,"[10] he said. So he approved Paglin's thirty minutes' notice.

Yet the fact remains that the warning was given for 12:15 P.M., and the operation begun around noon. Another warning was given at 12:21. The hotel blew between 12:32–12:35 P.M. Paglin claimed ignorance as to why that happened and Begin steadfastly defended him, much to his own harm.

"I understand that the casualties were out of your control," he told Paglin. "You should not blame yourself; we all share the responsibility."[11]

The bombing brought an abrupt end to the HRM. But Paglin continued to go around Begin, to do him vast political harm, to go beyond his responsibility. In this, he would presage another ruthless Begin subordinate, Ariel Sharon.

Once again, Begin and Etzel were outcasts. But time was running out for the Mandatory in Palestine.

Above, the leader and the officer.
Reviewing the troops.
(The Jabotinsky Institute)

Right, the young officer
that challenged Rosh Betar.
Warsaw, October 1938.
(The Jabotinsky Institute)

Above, coming as close to
Rosh Betar as ever.
The Warsaw Conference, 1938.
Between Begin and Jabotinsky
is Aaron Propess, Betar's
High Commissioner for Poland.

Right, just married,
Menachem and Aliza, June 1939.
Drohovitz, Poland.
(The Jabotinsky Institute)

"Rabi" Israel Sassover.
Wanted by the British Mandatory government.
Price 10,000 sterling.
Year c. 1943. (The Jabotinsky Institute)

The "Rabi," Aliza, and
Benyamin-Zeev, 1943–44.
(The Jabotinsky Institute)

Not a Holiday Inn,
but "Rabi" Sassover's hideout
(not always used).
(Private Collection)

Above, training on the ship Altalena.
(The Jabotinsky Institute)

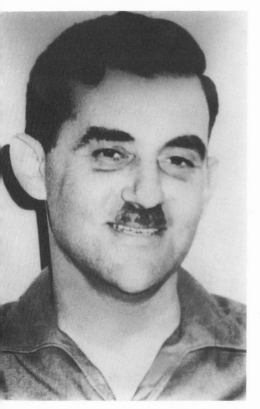

Altalena's *Chief of Operations,
Begin's Amichai Paglin, who
blew up the King David Hotel
in Jerusalem, July 22, 1946.
(The Jabotinsky Institute)*

The Altalena *is burning. Tel Aviv, 1948. (The Jabotinsky Institute)*

The commander, one of the Altalena *fighters, 1948. (The Jabotinsky Institute)*

Etzel's underground is alive in the state of Israel. The commander and his troops. Etzel Camp, Kfar Yona, June 1948. (The Jabotinsky Institute)

The last march of Etzel. Tel Aviv, 1948. Front, from left to right, Eitan Livny and Amichai Paglin, Chief of Operations, Etzel Yaacov Meridor, Begin's deputy, Begin. (The Jabotinsky Institute)

First American visit, a guest of the Vaad. Begin is flanked by future challengers: to the left is Hillel Kook (Peter Bergson, head of Vaad) and to the right is Shmuel Tamir.

The gallant Begin kissing the hand of the leader's widow, Johanna Jabotinsky. To the left of Mrs. Jabotinsky is the Vaad activist and playwright Ben Hecht. (The Jabotinsky Institute)

run. They all pursued a strategy limited to fighting Britain and the local Arabs of Palestine.[3]

Etzel's actions were designed to gain headlines and sympathy and to harass the British. But there were larger forces at work. The British Empire's days in the sun were diminishing, not just in Palestine, but all over the world. In addition, the legitimate forces of Zionism were hard at work gathering the remnants of Europe's Jews. The VaaD in America, the Haganah, the Mosad, the Jewish Agency (which Begin had dubbed the "traitor" government), the Palmach, and formidable figures like Weizmann and Ben Gurion fought on a world stage, each in their own way. All of them, in their own way, proved to be successful. The battle over Palestine and the fate of the state to be was being decided in the international arena, especially with the arrival of the Anglo-American Commission of Inquiry on Palestine in 1946, which drew world attention to England's treatment of the Yishuv.

This was a perfect setting for Begin and Etzel, who now wanted to demonstrate to the Yishuv and the world that they were a part of the struggle, that they were making an important contribution to the impending liberation of Israel.

Etzel's targets were British personnel and military installations in Palestine. The Haganah fought British efforts to stymie massive Jewish immigration to Palestine. Etzel sought to paralyze and outrage the Mandatory's police and military efforts in Palestine. "We must get them out of Palestine," Begin said time and time again. The departure of the British was Begin's chief goal, even as the authorities of the Yishuv sought to gather the Jews into Palestine. That spelled an end to the Hebrew Resistance Movement and to joint efforts, because the goals of Etzel and Lehi no longer ran parallel to the goals of the Haganah and the Yishuv.

Etzel's fight against the British reached new heights—or depths—of terror. In January of 1946, Etzel attacked railroads, airfields, and military installations alongside Lehi fighters. The British reacted ruthlessly. Captured Etzel members were tortured by the CID. By the middle of 1946, several Etzelites had been tried and were awaiting execution by hanging. When Etzel fighters Michael Eshbal and Yoseph Simhon were condemned to be executed, Etzel struck back by capturing five British officers and holding them as hostages for the captured Etzelites. Initially, the tactics worked. The high commissioner commuted the verdicts to life imprisonment.

The tempo picked up. When Etzel fighters were flogged, Etzel retaliated by flogging captured British soldiers. The British resorted to a strong hand. On April 10, the British executed three Etzel fighters—Yehiel Drezner, Eliezer Kashany, and Mordechai Elkoshy—on the gallows of Acre prison near Haifa. All international and Jewish efforts to commute their sentence were in vain.

The Yishuv was outraged. Sympathy for Etzel grew again, especially among Palmach and United Kibbutz movement (Ahdut Haavodah) members. Some joined Etzel in protest to organize Yishuv efforts to respond with force to the Mandatory and Britain. In America the Vaad and Etzel aroused the American Congress, media, and public against British policy in Palestine.

Two actions bespoke both the courage and brilliance and the potential ruthlessness inherent in Etzel operations: Etzel's raid on Acre prison and the execution of two British sergeants. These events were the bright and dark sides of the Etzel coin.

Early in 1947, the British government and the CID in Palestine had become more aggressive. On April 21, 1947, two teenaged Etzel fighters, Moshe Barazani and Meir Feinstein, were to be hanged, and Dov Gruener, an Etzel commander, was sentenced to suffer the same fate. As an act of revenge, Etzel smuggled hand grenades to the two condemned fighters to kill their executors, but instead they only committed suicide due to the unexpected appearance of Rabbi Goldman.

The prison authorities invited Rabbi Yaacov Goldman to pray for the two prisoners at the time of execution even though the British had been secretive as to the exact timing. He came despite the efforts of Barazani and Feinstein to dissuade the Rabbi from coming. Since they did not want to also kill the Rabbi, their plan for revenge was abandoned; they committed suicide by blowing the grenades into their own bodies, hence avoiding execution by the hated British.

Etzel decided to launch an ambitious and brilliant operation to break into Acre prison and release its fighters. The prison, which once had housed no less an inmate than Jabotinsky, was guarded by 150 policemen and held some 600 prisoners, mostly Arabs, some of whom had been incarcerated since the Arab Revolt of the 1930s.

The operation was planned by Amichai Paglin, an Etzel convert and chief of Operation Chick. Etzel's command managed to smuggle explosives to the Etzel and Lehi fighters held in the prison. The prisoners, some eighty in all, would lead the charge.

The commander of the operation was Dov Cohen, a veteran soldier who had served as a British commando in the just-ended war.

The unit from the outside cut the road to the prison, and entered disguised as a British convoy of soldiers supposedly on their way to Beirut. In Acre, they broke up into small units which were to cover the breakout. Eitan Livny, a former Etzel chief of operations, coordinated the activities inside and outside of the prison. The unit reached the prison walls undetected and planted explosives, blowing the walls. Inside, the prisoners exploded the heavy doors and chains of their cells and rushed out into the open streets of Acre, bringing with them a hundred Arab prisoners as well.

The prisoners boarded waiting trucks and everyone seemed well on their way to freedom.

Unfortunately for the operation and its planners, the escapees ran into a platoon of British soldiers who had been swimming nearby. A fierce firefight developed and Cohen was killed. Nine of the thirty-nine prisoners were also killed, and six of the attackers were captured.

The raid on Acre, brilliantly planned and staged, created a rush of optimism within the Yishuv and boosted morale for Etzel. Yet in it lay the seeds of tragedy to come.

On June 16, 1947, the day UNESCOP held its first hearing in Jerusalem, Avshalom Habib, Yaacov Weis, and Meir Necker, three of the Etzel fighters captured in the raid, were condemned to death. During the course of their trial, Etzel hijacked two British policemen to be used as hostages. But, partly because of the presence of the Anglo-American Commission in Palestine, the policemen were released in an isolated part of Tel Aviv.

The results of the trial, with three Etzel fighters now awaiting hanging, toughened Begin. On July 12, 1947, Etzel captured two British sergeants, Clifford Martin and Marvin Paice, in the city of Natanya between Tel Aviv and Haifa. They were obviously hostages for the lives of Habib, Weis and Necker.

The Haganah again cooperated with the British, helping CID to search for the missing sergeants, even though their hearts were obviously not in the job.

Yet the kidnapping of the sergeants and legitimate efforts by Jewish authorities failed to result in the commutation of the sentences against the Etzel fighters. The Commander of Acre prison, although fearing for his life, stood firm. After another Etzel officer was added to the list, four Etzel members were duly executed.

The execution of the Etzel fighters sealed the fate of the sergeants, who were hanged in a bunker in a factory near Natanya. Their bodies were carried in bags and strung up in a wood near Natanya, surrounded by mines. The mine blew the bodies to pieces and injured a British officer. The action was so unnecessarily brutal that all factions in the Yishuv and the Jewish Agency condemned it in the strongest terms.

For Begin, the execution of the sergeants was the carrying out of a formal sentence, not a ruthless lynching. He issued a declaration:

"The two British spies, Martin and Paice, who were under custody of the underground since July 12, 1947, were put to trial at the end of the investigation of their anti-Hebrew crimes. Martin and Paice were found guilty of the following crimes:

"*a*. Illegal entry to our land.

"*b*. Belonging to a British criminal and terrorist organization also know as 'The British Occupation Forces in Eretz Israel,' which is responsible for denying the rights of nation and life, deeds of oppression and torture, murder of men, women, and children, the murder of war wounded, the murder of war prisoners, and the exile of Hebrew citizens from their nation and land.

"*c.* Illegal carrying of weapons intended to establish the regime of tyranny and oppression.

"*d.* Anti-Hebrew spying under the guise of innocent civilians.

"*e.* Organized efforts against the Jewish underground, its soldiers, bases, and weapons of freedom.

"The court found the two guilty in all of the above accusations and sentenced them to die by hanging until they can no longer breathe.

"The request of the accused for commutation of sentence was turned down.

"The verdict has been executed.

"The hanging of the two British spies is an act of retaliation for the murder of Hebrew underground prisoners of war. We have tried and will continue to try the criminals that belong to the British-Nazi criminal army of occupation. The blood of our prisoners of war who were assassinated in the actions against the enemy will be revenged in strikes over its head.

"Signed Irgun Zvai Leumi"[4]

If Begin thought he could create a basis of legitimacy and legality for the hangings by comparing the British to the Nazis, he was resoundingly mistaken. His rhetoric, sounding like the pronouncements of those European resistance movements who fought against Hitler, failed to convince the Yishuv or to deter unanimous reaction of outrage.

The reaction in the Yishuv as well as abroad was immediate and angry. "We were never more ashamed," Golda Meir told the High Commissioner on the day that the bodies were discovered.[5]

"[Their motive was] not the honor of the nation but the prestige of the gang and their deed—there was no political coordination which guided them; It was, rather, doing the work of the enemy." So editorialized DAVAR, the Mapai-Histadrut paper. "The terrorists know no boundary, no moral, humanitarian or political boundary. They have not honored the Yishuv or even the movement itself."[6]

The immediate reaction among the British was a wave of violence against Jews in Tel Aviv by British soldiers, resulting in the death of five Jews and the serious wounding of twenty-four others on July 31.

Begin had sought legitimacy and had gained glory with the Acre raid and Yishuv's sympathy for the martyrdom of its hanged fighters. But now he and Etzel were showered with outrage and disdain. One immediate result was a decline in terrorist activities. Only some ten Etzel actions were executed near the end of 1947, as international diplomacy among the British and Americans began to take center stage with the appearance of a UN Resolution on the partition of Palestine in November.

The latter part of 1947 marked a decline in Etzel, which was being hunted by the British and harassed by the Haganah, and was suffering financial strain to the point where it resorted again to robbing banks.

Begin's Revolt, as it stood at the end of 1947, was a mixed success, its declaration unfulfilled. The Revolt carried the flag of military Zionism proudly and sustained Jabotinsky's ideology of Revisionism, with Begin as heir apparent. Although its actual deeds often seemed reckless and brutal, it prevented the memory of Jabotinsky and Revisionism from fading into irrelevance. It contributed to the British ouster from Palestine, but it was not the single and exclusive catalyst.

17

The Revolt: An Assessment

Over the years, Menachem Begin and his followers have insisted that the Revolt was the decisive factor in the eventual departure of the British from Palestine.

This claim is simply not true and actually disguises the Revolt's achievements, which were considerable and complex.

From February 1944 until after the actual departure of the British from Palestine on May 15, 1948, Etzel and Lehi conducted scores of quasi-military, terrorist, and urban guerrilla operations that resulted in the deaths of numerous British soldiers, officials, and policemen, as well as Jews, Arabs and civilians, and bystanders. These operations destroyed villages, blew up arms depots, and disrupted communication lines, sometimes in tandem and sometimes in direct coordination with the Haganah. The means and the targets varied. Often, the operations and the strategies behind them seemed to make little sense militarily. Some were spectacular failures. They did their best not to hit the innocent, but they did, unavoidably. Urban guerrilla warfare routinely meant the death of bystanders.

In the end, the success or failure of individual military operations was almost beside the point. One of the key objectives of the Revolt was to create a myth as well as a reality, a sharp and bloody history of a movement and a perception among the Yishuv, the world, and the British that Etzel was a real and legitimate entity and that it was here to stay. The message from Begin to the British was that Etzel would fight British rule to the end, during the war and after.

Over and over again, Begin sought to separate Etzel from its old image and history as a movement of renegades, killers, radicals, and political deviants, to separate it from the "irrational" and "irresponsible" Lehi and to give it a legitimate place in the struggle for Jewish independence and in the political fabric of Israel after statehood. In this, more than anything, he succeeded.

Although Ben Gurion saw Begin and Etzel as rivals, Begin never really sought to challenge the Yishuv per se, or the Haganah. He understood its power and the fact that it was part and parcel of the Yishuv. He never challenged the Haganah's legitimacy, in spite of the periodic insults he hurled at it. In fact, he sought cooperation and negotiation as another way to legitimize Etzel. The Haganah contributed to the struggle, but his Revolt, he believed, was the decisive factor in the ouster of the British from Palestine.

The Revolt was a Begin creation. Without Begin, there would be no Revolt. It catapulted the Betar leader, the recluse from Vilna, the exile from the Gulag, into a legitimate—almost mythical—Zionist leader who commanded the attention of the Yishuv, the British, and the world.

The Revolt was also a challenge to Jewish Zionist practices of the Diaspora, and to the idea of Jewish meekness. It was a call for action, for liberty, for a war of national liberation and independence, a war that would end the faltering spirit of the Diaspora, exactly opposite of the seemingly plodding Zionist diplomatic process. It boldly called for fighting anti-Semites amongst them, the Goyem, the oppressive British. There would be no deals, no negotiations, no compromise. The Revolt represented Jewish defiance.

Begin understood better than did many of the Yishuv leaders—and much sooner—that the British were securely and doggedly wedded to their White Paper policy and would not budge from it. They had decided long ago to play the Arab, not the Balfour Declaration card. None of the mainstream efforts of Zionism, of diplomacy, of moderation and negotiation, really deterred them from this policy.

Certainly, the years of bloodshed, raids, casualties and destruction of property had an effect on the British, not to mention on world opinion. Certainly they helped prod them toward their decision to leave and made them realize that the effort to continue governing an increasingly chaotic Palestine might not be worth the price in blood and money. But Etzel was not crucial in the ouster. If there was a decisive factor, it was probably U.S. rivalry with Great Britain over influence in the Middle East coupled with the exhaustion of British power at the end of World War II. The United States refused to act as Britain's partner in dominating the Middle East or resuscitating the Empire's waning power.

In any event, Etzel and Begin could not have operated independently or in a vacuum. In spite of the hostility of Ben Gurion and much of the Yishuv, Etzel operated behind the protective infrastructure of the Yishuv and even more, behind the military infrastructure of the Haganah. This was why Begin was so enthusiastic about the HRM. He successfully sought to end Etzel's isolation in the Yishuv.

In the end Begin's singular achievement was a political one. Like Ben Gurion, he wanted a free Eretz Israel and an ingathering of the Jews. The Revolt's first article called for "the formation of a Hebrew army." For Begin this was the principal and *only* instrument of politics. For Ben Gurion, however, the Haganah was only *one* of the instruments—along with immigration and settlement—and was always subject to the total discipline of the state-to-be or the so-called "organized institutions" of the Yishuv, to use Begin's term.

Begin separated himself and Etzel from Lehi squabbles, tamed the renegades, and established Etzel as a legitimate movement that restored Revisionism and the ideology of Jabotinsky. Ben Gurion accused him of instigating Jewish civil war, but this was simply not the case. If anything, it was Ben Gurion who sparked a mini–civil war with the Sezon. Begin steadfastly refused to fight other Jews in military terms.

Begin, like Jabotinsky, wanted to achieve political power through the use of force. He took the militants under his wing and wrapped himself in the mantle of Jabotinsky, although Jabotinsky had always rejected the use of illegal force. Ben Gurion all along understood what was happening, which may account for the bitter battle he waged against Revisionism and Begin, a battle waged in a manner the more gentlemanly Begin might never have considered adopting.

In short, however romantic the Revolt might sound, Begin was not a radical revolutionary. Begin was pursuing Jabotinsky's old doctrine of pressure, but through illegal means which Jabotinsky would have abhorred. It might not seem unusual to use guerrilla warfare as an extension of politics, but this did not make Etzel's Revolt a revolution.

He didn't change the British regime by force, or alter the political structure of Zionism, the Yishuv.

Begin's rhetoric can be traced faithfully to the doctrine of Jabotinsky, and while his actions were tactical deviations from Jabotinsky's aims, the Revolt was, nevertheless, what Jabotinsky, the father of the legions, might have done had he lived and led his troops into Eretz Israel. In that sense Begin was Jabotinsky's true heir.

In fact, Begin remained politically and philosophically loyal to Jabotinsky. Like his mentor, he remained steadfast to the idea of Eretz Israel, only reluctantly accepting Jordan as Palestine. Unlike his mentor, he did not particularly care about the Arabs, never studied them and knew nothing about their culture or their priorities. In this, he represented Revisionism's blind side perfectly, for the Arabs continue to be Israel's principle problem. Lehi was not much different, although its members claimed to confront the

Arab issue, which is to say they saw the Arabs as an instrument of British policy.

The Socialist Zionists had their own problems, and one of the chief ones was how to deal with the British. Throughout the war, they were still tied to the British, if only because of the Nazis. Ben Gurion had already charted a difficult course. "We shall fight with British against Hitlerism as if the White Paper did not exist," he said, "and we shall fight the White Paper as if there were no Nazism."

The Zionist moderates, Weizmann, Goldmann and others clung longer than might be expected to the hope that somewhere down the line the British would soften their White Paper policy. Begin never even entertained the thought, a position that derived from Begin's direct experience of the Nazi onslaught on Europe. The Palestinian Zionist had no such experiences—he never believed the British.

The Holocaust hit Begin personally—he lost many members of his family to the Nazis, including his parents and older brother. He suffered displacement early in the war and imprisonment at the hands of the Russians. To a great degree this experience was critical in forging Begin's character, in giving him a mind-set from which he would never waiver. It added fury and anger to his commitment to fighting the Mandatory and England, whom he accused of colluding with the Nazis. The White Paper policy indeed ended the hope of East European Zionist immigration to Eretz Israel. More than a homegrown Palestinian leader could be, Begin was genuinely touched by and conscious of the Holocaust and would remain so, even though he left Europe before it started. Born and bred in authoritarian and anti-Semitic Poland, he was not a pioneer Zionist, not a stranger to Britain and its traditions and values. He saw the ugly Albion, represented by the anti-Zionist Mandatory administration and intelligence forces.

Until he became Etzel commander, Begin was often militant and certainly he was a dynamic orator and propagandist. But the Holocaust may be said to have given him that added touch of hardness and determination which made him prevail as Etzel's commander through victory, disaster, and humiliation, while being hunted by both the Haganah and the British. He was a survivor.

Looking at the Revolt itself, it does not seem quite as fantastic or amazing as Begin seems to have wanted to paint it. It operated against the background of the Yishuv and this made it a practical effort. Begin's expectations were much higher than the reality in Palestine warranted. However, he certainly provided Etzel's members with action, without which they would have left it for Lehi.

Nevertheless, it was the Haganah which represented the Yishuv consensus that military and diplomatic action and illegal immigration were linked to political action. Begin never quite understood or accepted this. The Yishuv was not ready for or didn't seek heroes.

Let us for a moment disregard Etzel's operations but consider their results. Begin was entirely correct when he said that our actions will "influence British opinion through the important press, *The Times* of London . . . What we have is serious public opinion support for our cause," Begin said.[1] This was also true in the United States, where Etzel was aided by the Kook-Merlin Committee (the Vaad), which lobbied Congress and liberal progressive public opinion. The Yishuv itself was never quite convinced of Etzel's legitimacy, but nevertheless reluctantly accorded it recognition, Etzel protocols reveal that acceptance within the Yishuv, using the leverage of British and world opinion, was one of the major aims of the Revolt—in fact, it was its essence. Looked at in these terms, terror and guerrilla tactics, although its trademark, were merely tools.

It must be emphasized that the Revolt was successful only in the context of the wider Jewish struggle for independence. If Etzel had ended up actually leading that struggle, there is no doubt that it would have failed disastrously and that the British, or the Arabs for that matter, would have destroyed them.

The Revolt did not singlehandedly oust the British from Palestine. What it did was to legitimize Etzel's war against Britain and pave the way for Begin's political legitimacy and, in the end, his political power. And what did the Revolt do for the Jews trapped in Nazi Europe? No more than the Haganah, the Yishuv, Weizmann, or Ben Gurion could do.

The years 1944–48 were years of feverish political activity in Palestine but not in the Diaspora.

There was tremendous ideological intensity; huge political battles took place, all spurred by the realization that after two thousand years the Jews were on their way toward creating a state of their own, struggling to dominate their own land. Some of the activists involved in all this feverish activity appeared nearsighted, concentrating all their efforts on evicting the "occupiers" while ignoring the ferocity of the Arabs. This was clearly true of Begin's Etzel and Stern's Lehi.

But these years were also the years when close to half of the world's Jewish population was being exterminated in Europe. All the Zionists—Begin and Etzel not excluded—failed to recognize the proportions of the disaster or were unable to do anything about it. Eliezer Livneh, a Mapai renegade and Haganah publicist, summed it up for everyone. "All of us," he wrote, "erred."

"Why," he asked harshly, "when the undergrounds were engaged in battling the British and Arabs, didn't they send demolition teams to the railroads between Auschwitz and Treblinka? We erred. The Nazi exterminators and their unwilling collaborators, FDR and Anthony Eden, refused to rescue the Jews lest they upset the Arabs or the isolationists."

Certainly Dr. Wyman demonstrated in his book *The Abandonment of the Jews* (1984), that FDR, the media, and the churches, all were INDIFFERENT to the Holocaust.

But, Livneh continued, "We erred . . . In 1939, we failed to save Jews, in 1941–42 we didn't believe . . . We sent paratroopers to Europe, supposedly to organize a Jewish resistance, but they only served the British, not our war interests."[2]

Livneh was harsh, and not always accurate. He even questioned Begin's survival. "We did all we could, Mr. Livneh," Begin replied. "No one knew when the war would end . . . In those days, Mr. Livneh, we couldn't send even one man to Europe. Not Etzel, not Lehi. We could not even send one man to partly liberated Europe in 1944. There was no way. The sadness knows no boundaries. We thus said: The Germans exterminate our people, the British steal our country, and the two are indeed linked. We demanded a Hebrew government [the Vaad] which would handle the rescue of the Jews to Eretz Israel. The main obstacle to rescue was the British rule that was, from the point of view of the destruction of the Jews, an ally of Hitler. All that has been documented since . . . So one could say in fact we failed to establish this Jewish government in 1944–45 and the Jews were not rescued. But was it right then not to try to fight for this goal? Didn't we in the Etzel call upon the organized Yishuv, saying, 'If you can't fight with weapons, call for a civic resistance, go to Jerusalem in your masses, surround the high commissioner's palace, bombard world public opinion'?"[3]

This was typical of Begin—a call arousing public opinion. It was the essence of the Revolt, which was not a full-blown armed resistance, but rather a series of brilliant and devastating urban guerrilla operations designed to mobilize world opinion in order to oust Britain from Palestine. The Vaad in the United States, took more seriously the campaign for the rescue of European Jewry under Hitler.

Begin, Ben Gurion, Weizmann, all indeed did what they could. If there is to be any judgment of them in the matter of the Holocaust, then all are equally guilty.

Part Three

ETZEL'S LAST HURRAH
1948

The years leading up to 1948, partition and the formation of the state of Israel were years of military struggle for the various underground and above-ground Jewish forces in Palestine, specifically, the Haganah, Etzel and Lehi. The years 1946 and 1947 were the years of the Revolt, Maavak, and terror actions against the British reached their apex.

The British, meanwhile, clung even more tightly to their White Paper policy, clamping down on Jewish military activities, tightening the noose around Jewish refugee immigrants, clinging desperately to their dwindling foothold in the Middle East.

Near the end of 1947, with partition a logical outcome of the struggle, Etzel reorganized its forces with a view to participation in the War of Independence. At the time, Etzel claimed to have a total of six battalions composed of 750 men, the equivalent of two normal-sized battalions. Even with these basically meager forces, Etzel divided Israel into six "military" districts.

Begin and Etzel wanted military autonomy for themselves, without control or supervision from the Haganah. At the end of 1948, neither Etzel or Lehi sent its men to be inducted into Haganah units, although in Jerusalem they cooperated with the Haganah in 1947 and 1948.

Etzel directed its own particular campaign in two specific arenas—Jerusalem and Tel Aviv and their environs. These operations were mostly small, but Etzel quite seriously intended to occupy Jaffa, the largest single Arab city adjacent to Tel Aviv.

Jerusalem was the prize, however. Etzel openly defied the United Nations plan to make Jerusalem a divided city. "We are sad," proclaimed Etzel headquarters, "the Moledet (Patrie) was not liberated. Our historical task is still ahead of us." Lehi was *more blunt. It said it believed that the partition of Jerusalem was a "historical crime, that it was intolerable that the historic geography of Eretz Israel be ripped from the Hebrew nation."*

By the start of 1948, it was clear that both underground organizations, not to mention the Haganah, would concentrate on Jerusalem. Etzel had a force of some four hundred in the vicinity, only about a hundred of whom were actually experienced in any sort of military action. They tried an offensive in the old quarter of the city that failed miserably, but they did succeed in raiding British installations and arsenals. Lehi did its usual bit by blowing up an Arab irregulars center in the city.

At the start of the War of Liberation, 1947, against the Arabs; Haganah and Etzel cooperated on a Haganah-IDF offensive on Jerusalem. The result was almost predictably disastrous. There was a singular lack of coordination between the groups and a harsh variance in methods of operation. The underground units of Etzel and Lehi were not regular military units and had no experience acting professionally. It was King David all over again, and the result this time was the infamous attack on the Arab village of Dir Yassin, in which Etzel and Lehi irregulars ended up slaughtering a number of civilians in the heat of battle. Dir Yassin was one of those tragedies which would blot the reputations of Etzel and Lehi, but especially of Begin, who would be tagged with the label of terrorist for years to come.

In Jaffa, the cooperation between Haganah and Etzel proved more successful, and would eventually end with the conquest of that city.

More important, in terms of the story of Begin and Etzel, were the political undercurrents of the time.

In a way, the times represented both the defeat and triumph of Begin, defeat at the hands of David Ben Gurion, triumph within his own movement—as he emerged the true heir of Jabotinsky.

There was more than one war being fought at the time, it was more than just a matter of the Jewish nation battling the Arabs. Underneath that ferocious struggle, a different war was being waged from within, a war that was mostly political in nature, but one that was just as crucial and vehement. It was fought on two levels: within the various structures of Revisionism—the Vaad, Etzel, Lehi and Zohar; and between the two Jewish leaders of the time, Begin and Ben Gurion, the leaders of the Yishuv and nationalist camps.

The symbolic centerpiece of both of these struggles was the Altalena *affair, for it would involve, in one way or another, all of the various factions and leaders.*

Let us first take a look at Etzel and Begin as they faced the end of the British Mandate.

18

Etzel at the End of the Mandate[1]

Partition in Palestine had become a reality. The Jews were fighting five invading Arab armies. The State of Israel beckoned on the horizon as the British retreated from Palestine, while the IDF formed up. But not until a decisive war against the Arabs ends in Israeli victory.

And where is Begin and Etzel? Still fighting the retreating British, not the invading Arabs. Etzel in Europe speaks of a government in exile. Etzel in Jerusalem seeks to liberate the city without the help of the IDF, in defiance of the UN. And Etzel, ironically, goes underground just as the new State of Israel is announced.

Begin, it appears, still hoped against hope that Etzel would somehow prevail, that Etzel in Europe would organize an invasion force, division-strength, which would hit the beaches of Palestine, liberate Israel, and win the war against the Arabs. Begin and the more radical Etzel commanders unrealistically hoped that they could do the job themselves and, failing that, that they would play a major role in the Israeli War of Independence. Thus, Begin rejected partition outright along with integration of Etzel into the IDF. It would take six months before Etzel would finally be forced to dissolve; its members joined the IDF not as an underground, but as individuals.

With the coming of partition, the leadership of Etzel faced a crucial decision. Nothing less than its future was at stake.

The immediate questions concerned what form the movement would take in the future Jewish state and what role Etzel would play in the War of Independence, which would surely be conducted against the invading Arab armies. Would Etzel be able to retain its autonomy or would it submerge itself into the military and political structures of the mainstream Yishuv?

The immediate reaction from Etzel to partition was unequivocal and gives no real clue as to what would eventually happen. Begin announced his total rejection of partition. "The division of the Moledet [Patrie] is unlawful," he said uncategorically. "Partition will not obligate us. Partition will not guarantee peace or the Land of Israel." He thus loudly and clearly stated his strategic conception and political aspirations. "Our nation," he announced over the shrill Etzel underground radio, "will fight to liberate the territory that is bounded between the Mediterranean and the desert, that extends east of the Jordan River and from Dan to Beersheba.[2]

The difference between Begin and Ben Gurion couldn't have been more clear, strategy being declared in ideological terms by Begin, and on cold, pragmatic and military grounds by Ben Gurion. It seemed from listening to Begin's rhetoric that he would in effect forfeit the southern Negev as unclaimed territory, since Beersheba, his southernmost border, was in the northern Negev. For Ben Gurion, the capture of the Negev was politically crucial and strategically vital. Here was the difference between Revisionism and Pioneerism. The Revisionists, blinded by their dedication to the east of Jordan, totally misunderstood the strategic importance of the Negev. Nor could they see that the territory east of the Jordan, then the Kingdom of Trans-Jordan, would become a bloody battleground. A struggle for territory east of the Jordan would mean the kind of war that Israel, and certainly not Etzel, was in no position to fight.

On the eve of partition, Etzel faced a dilemma and a three-fold task: to continue the political struggle against Partition, as it had done since 1937; to continue the Revolt against the British in order to assure that the British fulfilled their promise of leaving "occupied" Eretz Israel; and to prepare militarily against the almost certain Arab invasion.

For a moment, let us survey the international and political situation which led to the coming of partition.

The years 1946–47 witnessed a tripartite struggle over Palestine among Zionists, Arabs and British, a struggle that would soon involve the United States, the emerging world power in the free world.

Exhausted economically in the wake of World War II, militarily weakened, the British were nevertheless not quite ready to relinquish their empire, certainly not in the Middle East. In the Middle East, the British faced the challenge of both mainstream and radical Zionism in Palestine, and emerging varieties of nationalism in Egypt, Iraq and Palestine. All of the actors—whether radical or moderate Zionists, Arab nationalists, radical Arabs or conservative monarchs—pulled against the British with their various aspirations.

The British could see the waning of their empire over the horizon and realized that a different strategy and approach were required. New ideas were also coming from a new British government, Clement Attlee's Labor party which had wrested power from the exhausted Tories and Winston Churchill.

Without a doubt, the key figure in the Labor government was the dynamic Foreign Minister, Ernest Bevin, the ambitious son of a mining family who had risen to become a seasoned foreign diplomat. Roger William Louis, writing in his *British Empire in the Middle East, 1945–1951: Arab Nationalism, The United States and Post War Imperialism,* said of Bevin:

> In all of the complexity of Middle Eastern issues facing the British Labour government in the postwar era, there is one individual and one theme of paramount significance: Ernest Bevin and his policy of non-intervention. Otherwise all might have been different. During his tenure as Foreign Secretary from July 1945 until March 1951, Bevin, when confronted with the choice, refrained from toppling kings and unseating prime ministers. What has not been revealed until the opening of the archives is that the policy of non-intervention was a matter of principle espoused in secret discussions above all by Bevin and endorsed by his colleagues. . . . What distinguished the postwar Labour government was the conscious affirmation of the belief that intervention would ultimately undermine rather than sustain British influence in the Middle East.[3]

Bevin dominated the cabinet and restrained the interventionists of the permanent officials. He presided over foreign and "Imperial" affairs with a grasp of detail as well as a command of general policy in a manner unparalleled since Lord Curzon at the end of the First World War.

Bevin had already played a key role in Great Britain's war effort. Throughout the war, he was in charge of mobilization and domestic front matters. Bevin's role in preparing Great Britain for war at home, maintaining an imposed industrial peace and harnessing the working classes to the war effort was one of the great achievements of British statesmanship.

The role of Foreign Minister would, on the surface, not have seemed an appropriate one for Bevin. His international credentials were sketchy, and his experience in trade union politics certainly did not prepare him for the role of foreign policy expert. Nevertheless, as a Labor negotiator and as an international strategist, Bevin could and did become a consummate diplomat and statesman, one of Britain's outstanding Foreign Ministers of the twentieth century. The Middle East, and especially Palestine, would stretch his gifts to the utmost—and he would utterly fail.

On the Middle East as a whole, Bevin's policy was guided by the following principles:

1. The feudal and ancient regimes of the Arab world would have to find a way to end corruption, mismanagement and self-indulgence, and move effectively toward reforms. Bevin was a heated anti-Communist, and he believed firmly that the old monarchs of the Middle East would have to

act quickly, in order to stave off the threat and appeal to their people of radical Arab nationalist movements which might turn to the Soviets.

2. The independence of Arab regimes was a historical and imminent inevitability which would require a new type of British-Arab partnership. Bevin's thinking on Palestine was tilted toward achieving a new relationship with the Arabs. To the Foreign Office and Begin, the Palestine problem must be treated in the context of British Arab policy. His answer to Zionism was that the problem of Jewish refugees and displaced persons lay in Europe, not in Palestine, that the refugee question be indelibly separated from the Palestinian question. He looked on Palestine as being predominantly an Arab country, and for the British to maintain influence in the Middle East, they would have to maintain the goodwill of the Arabs.

3. The solution for the Jews in Palestine was some type of confederated autonomy in a British-dominated Palestine. He avidly and dogmatically opposed partition.

Bevin based his policy on three pillars, each irreconcilable with the others:

1. Arab support for his Palestine policy.
2. Heavy pressure on Zionist diplomacy, to abandon partition, i.e. statehood and suppression of Jewish resistance.
3. Cooperation in British policy from the United States.

He didn't succeed in neutralizing Zionist diplomatic activities, especially in the United States where their insistence on statehood throve; he failed to break Jewish resistance; he failed in his war against Jewish refugees and in separating the issue of the Holocaust's remnants from Jewish statehood; he didn't succeed in gaining support from the Arab League to become more flexible on its Zionist policies; and above all, he failed, beginning in September 1945, to neutralize U.S. action in the Middle East by seeking its cooperation. In fact, it was the United States that refused to separate the refugee question from the Palestine question. It was the policy toward the refugees that lost Bevin American support and his harsh war against illegal immigration that turned public opinion in the U.S. and liberated Europe against Britain.[4]

How did all this happen in the short period between the spring of 1947 and the spring of 1948?

Obviously, the violent contradiction between Zionist and Arab nationalism seriously impaired British influence in the Middle East. Bevin realized that the British could not impose a pro-Arab settlement in Palestine that would be acceptable to the United States. In order for Great Britain to remain the dominant regional power in the Middle East, it needed both Arab cooperation and the goodwill of the United States. Writes Rogers:

"Without their [Arab and U.S.] goodwill, Britain's influence would decline, and not only in the Middle East. Britain would sink into the status of a second-class European power like the Netherlands."

What Bevin very quickly discovered was, according to his biographer Lord Bullock, "the inability to isolate the problems he had to deal with and prevent them from complicating each other."

"The Balfour Declaration is dead," Bevin announced in 1947 in a comprehensive review of the Palestinian question to the House of Commons. Henceforth, Bevin would use a strategy that aimed toward dismantling the *idea* of a Jewish state, i.e., partition, an approach that found a great deal of favor with the Arabs and with the U.S. bureaucracy (the military, state, intelligence, and defense establishments). Thus, Bevin charted his course, always aiming toward the connivance and collaboration of the United States. He would be sorely disappointed.

His first step was to create the Anglo-American Commission of Inquiry (on Palestine), composed of six British and six American members. Bevin hoped that the commission would recommend a halt to Zionist illegal immigration, thus undermining the idea of a Jewish state.

The tactic backfired in a big way. Not only did the commission recommend the admission of one hundred thousand Jewish refugees into Palestine, thus shortcircuiting Bevin's European answer to the refugee problem, but it focused public attention on the plight of the refugees. It also moved President Truman a step closer in the direction of the Zionists.

Truman was not yet ready to endorse the idea of a Jewish state, but he was sympathetic to the plight of displaced European Jews. Bevin now tried a different tactic. In order to soften the effects of the committee recommendations, he devised the Anglo-American Morrison-Grady Commission, to undo the former commission's recommendations which favored the cantonization of Palestine for a period of five years, with the British controlling an autonomous Jewish and Arab canton.

Both the Zionists and the Arabs flatly rejected the idea. Members of the American bureaucracy favored the formation of a binational state, which was after all the essence of the Morrison-Grady Commission Report. But Truman himself was being pulled in a variety of different directions.

Truman was strongly anti-imperialist by nature. He was also affected as a human being by the situation of the refugees. Politically, he was also being pulled by a strong Jewish electoral constituency and a strong Jewish lobbying effort. There was, after all, an election coming up, and Truman's prospects looked chancy at best. He was slowly warming up to the idea of a Jewish state. But what most determined Truman's decision was the plight of the refugees, not electoral consideration.[5]

Against the background of increasing Jewish terrorism in Palestine, which he supremely ignored,[6] a frustrated Bevin, anticipating the failure of his policy, turned to the United Nations on February 18, 1947. He hoped the UN option would save him from his own cul-de-sac.

Bevin and his Foreign Office had little reason to think the outcome in the United Nations would be favorable toward their cause. The United States, whose support was crucial, would not change its attitude—although they assumed that U.S. and Soviet antagonism would result in polarization and a veto in the Security Council. Bevin also hoped that the strong Catholicism of the Latin American nations would result in an anti-Zionist resolution. He still hoped the United Nations would not support partition. He was not *ready* to evacuate Palestine, and the U.K. Joint Chiefs were firmly in favor of staying in Palestine.

The results came as a shock to Bevin and perhaps the world. The U.S.S.R. came out strongly for partition, even as the United States was gravitating in that direction. Jewish influence and anti-British attitudes also tilted Latin American countries toward partition. The U.S. bureaucrats who tended toward binationalism, were overruled by Truman. The United Nations, on November 29, 1947, voted for partition, thirty-three to eleven. It was a triumph for the traditional diplomacy of the mainstream leadership of Weizmann, Ben Gurion, and Sharett, although it was more the doing of Truman—and the undoing of Bevin.

Begin and Etzel viewed the result with dismay. They saw Zionist diplomacy as bankrupt. Partition was a betrayal of the Jabotinsky solution that only Jewish military power could bring about Jewish liberation. International Revisionism, as represented by the Vaad (American Committee for a Hebrew Army), would raise even more of an outcry against partition and would propose even more radical reactions to it, contradicting Begin's plans.

Thus, the Revolt in 1947, before the creation of Israel, was directed against partition, against the UN decision. Begin didn't trust that the British would ever evacuate Palestine, and therefore the policy of the Revolt was to continue the struggle against the British to the end—a war against partition that he would wage to the end of his political life.

Nevertheless, although he often sounded radical, Begin needed to answer a crucial question: What would Etzel's role be in the emerging nation of Israel? Begin was forced to alter the strategy of the Revolt. It offered no answer to the new and radical circumstances of partition.

The strategy contained the following propositions:

To initiate the establishment of a government by Etzel that would ostensibly dominate all of Eretz Israel, i.e., an anti-Partition government, which would include the construction of an underground in "partitioned Israel." Etzel's major military effort would be the capture of Jerusalem. It would also attempt to establish a new political party (Herut-Freedom), that would contend electorally for a role in Israeli politics and government. The

International Etzel movement would be maintained as a reserve that will continue the struggle for liberation. Etzel would act to abolish the "ghetto Israel," Etzel's contemptuous term for the partitioned state.

Etzel now asked for a response from the Etzel in Europe and the United States, who called for a policy of a "conquering offensive"—i.e., a war against the expected Arab invasion. But the Revolt never prepared Etzel for this mission. For this Begin needed money and arms and people. At the moment, his forces consisted of some 800 fighters and some 1,200 auxiliaries—not enough for a battle royal against the British. Like Ben Gurion, he was now struggling to enlarge his forces, but Ben Gurion and the Yishuv forces had at their disposal close to forty thousand fighting men, a force which would later grow to one hundred thousand men. The Revolt did not militarily or politically prepare Begin for the war against the Arabs and for independence. He hurriedly changed course while continuing the Revolt against Britain.

Begin was looking for practical help in the Diaspora. What he got from Etzel's Paris headquarters was a strong, radical, harsh response. The Paris headquarters advocated the formation of a National Committee for Liberation, an Etzel government-in-exile since the Jewish Agency and the Yishuv authorities were "traitors" and untrustworthy. It advocated that Etzel in Europe would continue to terrorize the British, while Etzel within Israel would concentrate on the conquest of political power, mighty fantasies indeed.

These were revolutionary ideas that Begin could not accept; they contained the potential for Jewish civil war. "I don't see any reason to maintain the underground in the area of [official] Jewish jurisdiction or even in part of the country," he said, aware of the meagerness of his fighting forces. "If partition is executed, and a Jewish government is formed, we will need new structures to handle it, so that we can continue our struggle for Eretz Israel."[7]

Begin was heading for a political turnabout contradicting his new war against partition. "We will establish a new political movement," he said, "whose purpose will be to prepare the ground and educate the nation on the principles of Eretz Israel."[8]

Begin vehemently rejected the idea of a National Committee for Liberation as impractical. "Any attempt to capture power," he said, "means not only a bloody civil war but defeat for Etzel and a catastrophe for the nation."[9] But how else did he intend to fight partition? He could do so only if Etzel in Europe could send Begin the troops necessary for the war.

But Paris headquarters, or more accurately, the Vaad group headed by Hillel Kook, was adamant. Kook wanted Begin, in his position as head of Etzel, to proclaim the formation of a Hebrew government in exile. The politics of Etzel in Europe was as unrealistic as Begin's hope that the Betar "division" in Europe would soon be shipped to Palestine.

Begin realized that Vaad's radical ideas were dangerous for Etzel in the War of Independence, but he was determined to establish an effective military force using European Etzel volunteers, which the ship *Altalena* would provide.

The idea of men and weapons for Etzel were Begin's, but the idea for *Altalena* originated, not with Begin, or Palestinian Etzel but with Vaad and the European-American Etzel members. It is worth examining Vaad and Begin before going on to the *Altalena* affair. But we must return to Etzel in Jerusalem first.

19

Etzel in Jerusalem[1]

The war against partition, now that the British Mandatory had decided to officially evacuate Palestine on May 15, 1948, suddenly put Etzel in a state of crisis. They did not have enough troops to fight against partition while IDF, the army of the state, was fighting the invading Arab armies. As a result, IDF fought the present danger—the Arabs, while Begin fought the ghost of partition.

All of Begin's and Etzel's energies over the previous three to four years had been devoted to the Revolt, actions and rhetoric that tied them securely to the image of an underground organization. Now the future beckoned as the Yishuv prepared itself to battle invading Arab armies and to establish a Jewish state under chaotic conditions. Etzel's problem would be how to fit into the general framework of an emerging state, how to create a role for itself in the coming war, and how to eventually forge a new political role for itself.

From the day the State of Israel was declared by David Ben Gurion before the National Provisional Assembly on May 15, 1948, and Haganah became the IDF, Begin and Etzel were not clear about the future and role of Etzel in Israel. Who is the enemy, against whom to fight—and with whom? There is nothing in Begin's or other Etzel writings on their role once Israel became independent. Begin and Etzel had concentrated on "ousting the British from Palestine." There was no Jabotinsky to formulate the role of Revisionism and Etzel after independence. Begin is not a political philosopher and, unlike Jabotinsky, failed to prepare intellectually, politically, and militarily—as Labor and the Yishuv did—for the day after independence. Thus, in a way, Etzel and Begin were overwhelmed by the event of the creation of the state. They were never state builders. Only Jabotinsky could have been ready intellectually where Ben Gurion was. All of Etzel's actions, since 1947 and after May 1948, were reactions to events, while Ben Gurion, and the organized Yishuv, were riding, not ridden, by events. Begin had clearly stated that Etzel would dissolve only *within* the state of Israel, yet Etzel forces in West Jerusalem, which were completely within the territory of Israel that was liberated, refused to dissolve the organization. Etzel was to be dissolved after June 1948 by various agreements first with the Haganah and IDF and was later to be integrated gradually into the IDF. Even after May 1948 Etzel maintained a military command in Tel Aviv that was supposed to coordinate Etzel operations and integration into the IDF. However, it really served as an autonomous command for Etzel's operation. Some Etzel operations, in fact, were requests from the Haganah and IDF. Thus, unclarity prevailed. In Jerusalem and in Europe, Etzel remained intact and totally independent of the IDF.

Almost immediately, the hot point of attention for Etzel as well as the Yishuv, would become the city of Jerusalem. Yet, initially, Begin and Etzel were slow to react, as if they were still paralyzed by the struggle against the Mandatory, a struggle that for all intents and purposes had been won. All of Begin's tendencies toward indecision, lack of control and military and political myopia would come into the forefront, would rise to the surface in the struggle over Jerusalem.

In July 1948, Etzel in Jerusalem was composed of one thousand men of which seven hundred were combatants. Its function was to protect Jewish neighborhoods and to help liberate the old city. Etzel autonomy in Jerusalem clearly disturbed Israel's authorities. Etzel sent to Jerusalem one of its most articulate and intelligent but also militant leaders, Shmuel Katz, to run the political affairs of Etzel in Jerusalem. In a ceremony in Jerusalem in August, Begin transferred Etzel's flag to Jerusalem. Etzel in Jerusalem was replete with symbols and contradictions; for Etzel in Diaspora Europe, Etzel in Jerusalem was a fortress, a promise. But as an autonomous military group, it undermined the IDF's authority over the city, and gave rise to a short but troublesome chapter in the history of Etzel, IDF and Israel.

By agreement with the Israeli government on June 11, 1948, Etzel's command was established to help integrate its men in Jerusalem with the IDF. Etzel was given a list of names of commanders to be drafted into the IDF, but it didn't always comply. Certainly not in Jerusalem.

Jerusalem was a logical choice for Etzel as the focus point for its military attentions. Militarily, it made sense to concentrate its meager military efforts in one spot, especially one so symbolic. As a military force, it could not effectively compete with the Haganah, which was well on its way to transforming itself into an official, better organized, and better-armed Israeli army (IDF). Even Begin realized this. For him, Jerusalem would become Etzel's focus of attention, since the UN Resolution on partition had turned it into a divided city. Etzel would try and capture the whole city, thus turning the resolution into a dead issue.

Yet, the obvious fact that the time for a political and military underground had passed should have been immediately clear to Begin and the Etzel leadership. Begin should have been aware that Etzel was facing dissolution and radical change, but he could not accept this outcome. An entirely different orientation and organization was called for. Partition, no matter how much Begin railed against it, was an established fact. The Yishuv accepted partition. The Yishuv now had an army, the IDF, and the military reality was that the new nation would have to face an invasion by the Arab states set to destroy it. Yet Begin remained in his underground shell and continued to fight the fading ghost of the Mandatory.

As late as November 27, 1947, on Radio Etzel, Begin remained defiant. "Etzel will never accept the division of Eretz-Israel," he proclaimed. "The United Nations decision does not obligate the Israeli nation. Partition will not guarantee the peace in the land. Our nation will fight to liberate the territory that extends from the Mediterranean to the desert and from Dan to Beersheba."[2]

This was a combination of downright foolhardy military strategy (the strategically critical Negev desert was totally overlooked), and a restatement of classic Jabotinsky Revisionist ideology, waving the banner of Two Sides of the Jordan.

Many of Etzel's leaders, including Begin himself, still wanted to focus their attention on the British. They could not quite believe that their old foe would really leave the scene. Two of Etzel's intelligence commanders, Aaron Rousseau and Azriel Gershuny, tried, in a long letter to Begin, to explain the situation. The letter shows Etzel's continued and late obsession with the old occupier.

The two commanders wrote Begin that they feared the British still had the military initiative and that a form of paralysis in the UN Security Council might persuade the British to attempt to "establish order." Even after they evacuate, they may return. The British, they said, could also use the excuse that they were needed in Palestine to prevent a potential Soviet penetration in the ensuing chaos caused by evacuation. Therefore, they advised, the Jews, meaning Etzel, must continue to destabilize the British and strongly discourage them from trying to play a continued role in the affairs of Palestine.

"Confrontation with the British may lead to efforts to disarm the Jews," Begin wrote. "Nevertheless the daily situation is that *we must prevent Arab murderers.* We must destroy their centers at Abu Kabir, Abu Salema, all near Tel Aviv. Therefore the movement must enter the war all over again against the occupiers. It may become impossible. Thus, Zero Hour means the beginning of Jewish Conquest."[3] [Italics mine.]

This document and Begin's later rhetoric reflect the continued confusion and paralysis within Etzel. On the one hand, Begin remained obsessed by the occupier, on the other, he knew Etzel must join in the struggle against the Arabs who now threatened Jewish lives and territory. Ben Gurion and the Haganah had understood this all along, yet Begin was incredibly slow to react.

Begin remained stubbornly wedded to the idea that the Mandatory was Israel's chief enemy, and that the Arabs are merely instruments of British imperialism—a dangerous idea to hold at this late date. Begin, reflecting one of Revisionism's biggest weaknesses, believed the Arabs were merely terrorists acting as agents of the British. He could never conceive of or understand the force and threat of Arab nationalism.

"Zero Hour," he wrote, "is not connected with the general attitude of the Arabs, even if we might expect such an attack once British rule will be terminated. For us, Zero Hour means the annihilation of British rule. We must concentrate on our Zero Hour."[4]

"Our Zero Hour must thwart theirs (meaning the British)," he writes. Yet he does not know what the British will do next, and so, in between the critical months of November 1947 (UN Declaration of Partition) and May 1948 (Israeli Declaration of Independence), he presents a vague and vacillating picture to his followers.

"In this transition period," he writes, "we must regret that we have done less than we should have. Too bad. But we should not lose perspective. We must not be trapped into asking curious questions on the role of the Class [the underground name for Etzel]. The role of the Movement is not judged by one action or another. For someone not caught in impressionistic visions, the role of the Class is not a thing of the past now. Hence the last word has not yet been said in this land. I am not vouching that we will be saying it, but we aspire with all our hearts to achieve it."[5]

This is a most curious, unrealistic pronouncement, even with its slightly ominous threat to have the last word. Consider the setting: It is the most critical hour in the history of Zionism and Israel; the entire Yishuv is preparing for a major war; Ben Gurion is even now raising the budget for the Haganah from a minuscule 175,000 pounds sterling to three million pounds; he has totally reorganized the Haganah. When the emerging IDF is already fighting the foe in the north, when Israel is bracing itself against an onslaught by several Arab armies, what is Begin ruminating about? The nature of the Class, underground name for Etzel, and of the old foe—the British.

Still ambivalent, he continues, "It is clear that at this stage flogging the British will not change the UN resolution . . . The outcome will be determined in the battlefield by blood and weapons, but all I have said so far . . . does not mean we will not flog the British for their despicable actions here. However, even if we flog the British, we will not argue before the people of Israel that this would change the decision in UN headquarters."[6]

The secretive nature of Etzel's organization did not help matters. Begin, the nominal and spiritual leader, always on the run, moving about, often lacked real control over the immediate decisions of his local commanders, especially in Jerusalem. Jerusalem was encircled by the Jordanian Arab Legion. There was no access to Jerusalem except through the Haganah-IDF.

Events were ahead of Begin's vision, and it became clear to everyone that Jerusalem would be a critical factor. Unfortunately, Begin had little if any control over Etzel commanders in Jerusalem, the most volatile, eclectic of all cities in Palestine. Etzel cells and groups within Jerusalem represented its most extreme faction heavily influenced by the old Biryonim and Sternites.

Foreign embassies, especially the pro-Arab American consulate in Jerusalem, were aware of Etzel-Lehi activities in Jerusalem. William C. Burdette, American vice-consul in Jerusalem, cabled to Secretary of State George C. Marshall, "During past few days increased activity of Irgun Zvai Leumi and Stern gang [Lehi] in Jerusalem has become extremely apparent. Both groups have succeeded in bringing into city reinforcements, arms, and supplies from Tel Aviv and have taken over strategic areas in Jerusalem what are being turned into fortified enclaves. Haganah authorities here admit that IZL and Stern gang do not submit to Haganah discipline and it is known that Haganah has considerable difficulty in dealing with two groups. It also appears that IZL and Stern enjoy preferred positions regarding food and wartime restrictions. Since unification agreement signed by IZL and Stern with Haganah are only valid within Israel, former consider themselves free to act as they wish in Jerusalem. Reliable Jewish source indicates that two groups are augmenting their forces here to serve as threat and reminder to Israel Government that IZL and Stern will not tolerate any concession on immigration or status of Jerusalem. Regarding latter it is possible that IZL and Stern will reject international status for city believing that Jerusalem should be capital of Jewish State which they regard as ultimately including all of Palestine. Dr. Bernard Joseph, Chairman of Jewish Jerusalem Emergency Committee, has stated to Truce Commission his inability be responsible for acts IZL and Stern in Jerusalem. Moreover as proven in recent failure by Haganah to dislodge Stern members from enclave in Talbieh quarter of Jerusalem, Haganah unable cope with situation. It is also known that Haganah commander in Jerusalem, David Shaltiel, is under severe censure by Stern for what they consider his conciliatory attitude in present truce negotiations."[7]

In Jerusalem, control would have been impossible even without the everpresent Etzel factionalism. Jerusalem, after all, was an international, cosmopolitan city, a symbol for all of its citizens. The Hebrew University, from which many extreme Lehi intellectuals emerged, was located in Jerusalem. It was the headquarters of the Mandatory, Etzel and Lehi's major preoccupation during the Revolt. A large number of Lehi and Etzel fighters came from Jerusalem, including the Strelitz family, a group of notorious Lehi fighters. The Arab extremes were also well represented in the confines of Jerusalem. It was from Jerusalem that Hadj Amin al-Husayni, that most virulent of Arab nationalists and extremists, emerged and directed repeated Arab revolts and massacres of Jews. For decades, as the mufti of Jerusalem, he had dominated a particularly hostile strain of Palestinian nationalism, and now he was directing the Arab attack against the Jews. The most fanatic of urban nationalist Arab youth could be found in the streets and back alleys of Jerusalem. Jerusalem was also the headquarters of CID, the British Palestinian intelligence organization, the Jewish underground's most implacable foe. David Raziel, an icon and martyr for Etzel and Revisionism, was also from Jerusalem. That city, so divided, so reflective of three of the world's major religions, was a tinderbox of political and racial division and hatreds, a city that would be continually bathed in blood.

So strongly entrenched was Etzel in Jerusalem, and so independent from mainstream Revisionism were the Etzel groups there, that it was agreed in February 1948 that Etzel in Jerusalem would remain autonomous. The agreement with the Haganah stipulated that Etzel units in Jerusalem, if integrated within the IDF, would nevertheless enter as autonomous Etzel units. When Etzel units were dissolved all over Israel, many of its members joined up with the autonomous Jerusalem units. Etzel in Jerusalem was more radical than Begin, who had no control over Jerusalem. In fact, many Etzelites left Tel Aviv for the fight over Jerusalem, which was crucial to both Etzel and Lehi.

By the end of 1947, Etzel units in Jerusalem were conducting hit-and-run terrorist warfare against both the British and Arabs within the confines of the city. In spite of the April 12, 1948, agreement with Haganah, which strictly forbade independent action against the Arabs, Etzel continued in its own old ways, assassinating, for example, a British officer in the center of the city.

The controversy over the autonomy of Etzel as a military force would come to a head in the tragic, controversial Etzel attack on the small Arab village of Dir Yassin, just outside Jerusalem.

20

Dir Yassin

Dir Yassin, a military fiasco and a great and unwarranted tragedy, is another black mark on Etzel and the Revolt. It has become a stark symbol of Jewish terror, an example of Zionist perfidy for Arabs all over the world. It would taint Begin's name forever, even though, as with the *Altalena* affair and later the Sabra-Shatila massacres, he had little to do with it, except in terms of reaction.

Although I will try to delineate what happened at Dir Yassin, it is not my purpose here to place blame or pass moral judgment. Dir Yassin must be understood in terms of Begin and his attitude toward Arabs, and in terms of the military and political background of the times. It must also be understood in terms of attitudes he inherited from his mentor Jabotinsky and the more virulent offshoots of the Biryonim and Sternists.

Jabotinsky recognized the Arab nationalist movement but did not appreciate its military capability or acknowledge its claim to be a modernizing force. The Revisionist attitude toward the Arabs of Palestine was to reject any Arab territorial or political claim over Eretz Israel, and any Zionist effort to compromise with the Arabs over Palestinian territory.

In Revisionism, one finds a certain amount of pragmatism, but not on the issue of Arabs, especially in regard to Eretz Israel. Revisionists, for example, did not recognize Palestinian nationalism on either side of the Jordan River, but did recognize Arab nationalist rights over Syria and elsewhere in the Arab world, as long as it was not in Eretz Israel proper.

But when it comes to the East, and the Arabs in general, there were marked differences in the ranks of the Revisionists. For Jabotinsky, it meant deromanticizing the East. "The East is my stranger," he wrote. "We Jews, thank God, have nothing to do with the East . . . the Islamic soul must be broomed out of Eretz Israel."[1]

The Orient, and pan-Arabism were products of British colonialism, but basically unreal. For the Revisionists, pan-Arabism was not a viable entity, although the Arab *Vatan (patrie)* was. Jabotinsky recognized only the authenticity of Syrian and Egyptian, not Palestinian nationalism. The Arab Revolt, according to Jabotinsky challenged the whole concept of Jewish proprietorship (Adnut), over Eretz Israel.

The more radical Biryonim and Stern, for that matter, saw the Arabs with even less subtlety. To them, the Arabs were murderers, beasts of the desert, not a legitimate people. It was primarily this concept that Etzel inherited, not the more intellectual viewpoint of Jabotinsky.

Jabotinsky, who had hoped that British-Zionist cooperation (which ended in the late 1930s) would impose on the Arabs a Zionist solution, was no longer a guide for Begin. Begin arrived in Palestine when Jabotinsky's ideas on the Arabs were obsolete. Thus, Begin became heir to the Lehi-Stern concept of the Arabs as primitive murderers and beasts. It is no small coincidence that the majority of Jewish fighters at Dir Yassin were composed of the heirs of Stern, the members of Lehi. It was Stern, after all who wrote in 1940 that "Arabs are not a nation but a mole that grew in the wilderness of the eternal desert. They are nothing but murderers."[2]

Stern advocated terror against the Arabs as well as the British. Thus Dir Yassin was the outcome of an entrenched Etzel-Lehi ideology as much as it demonstrated Etzel-Lehi's military incompetence.

Dir Yassin was a typical medium-sized Arab village just west of Jerusalem, one of a chain of such villages, which included Jewish Bet-Hakerem and Givat Shaul. There was nothing very distinguished or singular about it. Strategically, however, these villages tended to be important because they were the bases from which Arab irregulars would sporadically launch raids against the Jewish sections of Jerusalem. They were also situated along the roads leading into Jerusalem, roads that would come to represent Jewish Jerusalem's lifeline. In fact, the period between November of 1947 and May of 1948 was marked by increasing Arab terrorist and marauding activities against settlements, Jewish munitions and supply convoys to Jerusalem.

Initially, Dir Yassin was not considered very significant by the Haganah. In fact, some of the Arab villagers, afraid of being caught in a crossfire, had sought to make peace. Haganah intelligence had gone as far as to say that the inhabitants of Dir Yassin were "loyal to the peace arrangement." This situation lasted until the Haganah launched its major offensive to open the road to Jerusalem in late April of 1948.

As the battle for Jerusalem was beginning to take on crucial importance for Ben Gurion and the Haganah, Dir Yassin became strategically significant. This battle was, above all, political. The military strategy of Ben Gurion was not unlike Etzel's—total Jewish domination over all of Jerusalem. Although the United Nations had approved partition, it was by no means an unalterable, established fact. The United States, at one point, appeared to be wavering, retreating from partition and inclining toward a British-sponsored plan for a United Nations trusteeship. There were many officials in the United States who were afraid of becoming embroiled in the struggle. They were fearful that the Jews would be so weak as to require U.S. intervention and assistance. A trusteeship plan would have meant Jewish autonomy, under British patronage, but not independence.

What was needed was a display of the Israeli mailed fist; a show that it was capable of staying the course, no matter what the cost in lives and material.

On March 20, 1948, Ben Gurion defiantly proclaimed, "We are the force that will decide our fate here. We established the foundation of the Jewish state and we will build it. We shall not accept any trusteeship, not a short, transitional one, not even for the shortest period. . . . We shall never again accept any sort of foreign rule."[3]

For any display of Jewish force, Jerusalem was crucial, and so was the continued, intense diplomacy of the Jewish Agency and Weizmann in the United States, which resulted in getting the Americans back into the fold. Ben Gurion and the IDF High Command had already prepared a military contingency plan to meet the Arab invasion. The plan called for the creation of 22 battalions and a force of 22,500 men, the capture of Jerusalem and the conquest of the Negev Desert.

The battle of Dir Yassin represented for Etzel the battle over Jerusalem —the battle royal against partition.

Etzel was planning a vigorous campaign and was waiting for an excuse to break its independent action agreement with the Haganah. Etzel-Lehi forces in Jerusalem were sitting with the trigger ready.

Commander Mordechai Ra'anan, leader of the Jerusalem Etzel-Lehi unit, informed General David Shaltiel, the Haganah IDF commander in Jerusalem, that Etzel-Lehi planned to attack the village of Dir Yassin.

Shaltiel's reply to Ra'anan was cautious and provisory. He indicated that Dir Yassin was one of the targets in a planned Haganah offensive. "But I see no reason that you cannot do the job," he wrote, "on the condition that you have enough force to hold the village until Haganah forces arrive. But if you intend to blow up the village in order to make the villagers run away, thus making its ruins vulnerable to capture by foreign forces [meaning the formidable Arab Legion as well as Arab volunteers], the situation would only be a burden on the general campaign if we have to conquer it once again. This would be costly."[4]

There is obviously a tacit approval of a *military* operation in this communication, but nothing that would indicate an assault on the village population. On the contrary, the letter cautioned against such an approach, not necessarily from a humanitarian standpoint, but from a tactical one.

Shortly after dawn on April 9, 1948, three platoons (2 Etzel, 1 Lehi) totaling 120 men assaulted the village, charging up the hills outside of Jerusalem. From the start, the attack was a fiasco—uncoordinated, wild, with many mistakes. The Etzel commanders, while being experienced urban guerrilla fighters, had no experience running a field operation or dealing with a genuine military battle, nor did their men have any regular army field training. From the start the operation was a divided effort, with Etzel units attacking from Givat Shaul and Lehi units attacking from the direction of Bet Hakerem. There was no effective coordination and communication between them. The new submachine guns which had just arrived from Europe did not operate efficiently, and Etzel's own weapons were homemade and primitive.

The Etzel units did make a small effort to warn the general populace of Dir Yassin that an attack was imminent. A truck equipped with a loudspeaker warned the civilians to clear the area, but in the night, the truck ran into a ditch, so that this feeble effort to alert the villagers was heard by only a small number of them.

When the two forces finally fought their way into the village, the situation had already become unglued. They were met by a thin field of fire from the schoolhouse at the top of the village, which was occupied by a volunteer Iraqi force. Several Etzel soldiers were killed and wounded, including some officers.

By 11 A.M., the attack was faltering, although a Palmach unit had arrived at the bottom of the hill to help evacuate the wounded. Etzel leaders considered a retreat, but their forces were spread out all over the village. Their units, by this time undisciplined with rage and frustration and fearing attack from the houses, were running wild through the village, firing at random into the village and throwing hand grenades into the homes as they ran by. At 4 P.M. all of the firing had ceased. Five Etzel-Lehi soldiers had been killed and another thirty-one wounded, an appalling 33 percent casualty rate. Worse, although some of the villagers had managed to run away and avoided capture, Etzel and the Haganah were about to make a shocking discovery. When they returned, and when the Haganah arrived, they found the bodies of 254 villagers, many of them women and children. Not a single home had escaped death or harm. Not only were Arab homes but their occupants blown up.

Dr. Goronshik, a doctor on the scene, admitted in unpublished testimony that the massacre began in earnest after several Etzel men had been killed and wounded, including one "who had helped the wounded . . . We decided to kill them [the wounded Arab fighters] before our withdrawal because we couldn't carry them back."

Ra'anan, the Etzel commander, became frightened and panicked. In a hurried, immediate press conference, the Etzel commanders on the scene admitted the massacre and apologized for the deed.

In the Yishuv, the reaction was immediate—shock and outrage. Ben Gurion sent a hurried apology to King Abdalla of Jordan, with whom he had been negotiating for peace over Jerusalem. General David Shaltiel, who had given his tacit approval of the operation, condemned the Etzel-Lehi massacre in the strongest terms, while explaining that the operation itself was a combined Etzel-Lehi effort. The British threatened to bomb the village if Etzel did not evacuate it.

For the Arabs, the massacre would become seared into their collective memory, and indeed, although they needed no encouragement, the level of ferocity that followed throughout the war stemmed at least in part from what happened at Dir Yassin. Dir Yassin would become a major propaganda tool to use against the "civilized" Jews. They made no distinction between Haganah or Etzel-Lehi—all, after all, were Zionists.

Initially, although the deed and name would become part and parcel of Etzel's historical burden, the official reaction, especially from Begin, was slow in coming, and when it did it seemed out of touch with what actually happened. In fact, it sounded like defiance. It was another case of Begin, unaware and not in control of a particular action, defending it, rising to the bait and trying to whitewash it with glory, as he had already done in the King David Hotel operation.

Begin, in his book *The Revolt,* written in 1951, had an equally specious rationale: "I am convinced that our fighters and commanders wanted to spare any unnecessary casualties among us in the battle of Dir Yassin."[5] The whole affair is discussed in less than two pages. Dir Yassin is described as just another Etzel battle.

Yet, in his initial reaction, Begin was full of vainglory and bluster. He called Dir Yassin "an *'Esseg Gadol,'* a great achievement." Chaim Landau, Begin's deputy, issued the following pronouncement from Etzel to the commander of the operation: "Accept my congratulations for this wonderful conquest. Tell all the men, the fighters and commanders, that we shake their hands. We all are proud of your magnificent command, your spirit of battle and conquest, your magnificent offensive . . . Tell the soldiers that you have made history in Israel by your offensive and act of conquest. Until victory, as in Dir Yassin and elsewhere, we shall storm and annihilate the enemy. God, God, to conquest you have chosen us."[6]

What really happened at Dir Yassin from the standpoint of Etzel? On January 19, 1983, *Koteret Rashit,* an Israeli weekly, published one of the documents which are stored in the Jabotinsky Institute in Tel Aviv, relating to the Dir Yassin operation. The documents are by one of the commanders of the operation, Ben Zion Cohen.

"The commanders were divided over what to do in Dir Yassin," Cohen wrote. "A majority were in favor of destroying all the males or whoever would resist, including women and children."

Yehoshua Goronshik testified that his men shot women and prisoners. And Cohen adds that "in view of Dir Yassin's resistance, [we] felt a desire for revenge, especially after the enemy hit us hard in Gush Etzion and Atarot [referring to a March operation in which the highly professional Arab Legion had conquered the Etzion bloc around Jerusalem]." Cohen tells of snipers which hit his ill-organized fighters from the houses of Dir Yassin. "Thus we eliminated every Arab that came our way for fear of the battle starting behind our backs."[7] Lehi proposed to destroy all the villagers to show them what could happen if they again met Etzel-Lehi combined forces. In the aftermath of the action, instead of apologizing for and admitting to the massacre, Etzel officials and especially Begin, tried to find all manner of excuses for it. The most popular rationale was that the massacre would somehow or another break Arab morale and lead to Arab evacuation of the Israeli partitioned Palestine.

On April 11, Begin, who had earlier cautioned his command against massacres of any kind, now argued that "in spite of the vicious instigation of the hypocrites, the attack on Dir Yassin saved Jerusalem's environs from the terrorists' fire. Our forces were faced with a serious and dangerous confrontation with the foe, which was better fortified and equipped. Our forces acted *unlike any other fighting force,* giving up the advantage of surprise so as not to injure innocent civilians. Before the battle, they warned the villagers . . . and in fact, most of the women and children were saved this way. The rest, who failed to obey our warning, were hit in the battle [italics mine]."[8]

Begin, warming to his task, called Dir Yassin "a mighty battle where Etzel, Lehi and Palmach fought together shoulder to shoulder."

It was nothing of the sort. As a military operation, it was a fiasco, and the resulting civilian deaths amounted to an out-of-control massacre and a blot on the record of Etzel and Israeli fighters.

Once again Begin correctly admits he knew nothing of the operation when it was being planned since it was carried out by the Etzel in Jerusalem under the conditions of the blockaded city. Communications with Tel Aviv were poor. Once again Begin rose to defend an action about which he had less than complete information. More accurately, however, Begin had no control over his subordinates in Jerusalem. His habit as commander was never to intervene in military planning but to dictate and support politically the operations. Dir Yassin was a political operation—it was meant to liberate Jerusalem, to defy partition. Responding much in the manner that he would respond in the wake of Sabra-Shatila (when he said that Israel had been tarnished by a "blood libel"), he lacked the courage, after he found out its results, to admit the tragic error and instead tried to pass it off as an act of heroism.

Others knew better, including one former Etzel official who wrote in 1982: "I learned that Begin's rhetoric was once again at work. The Shaltiel letter okaying the operation was his alibi, although it was obvious that the Jerusalem commander had clearly warned against the massacre."[9]

And Natan Friedman-Yellin, a Lehi commander and hardly a man who shrank from terror, wrote thirty years later in highly condemnatory tones about Dir Yassin. "I am and was repelled," he wrote, "by the fact that the Dir Yassin massacre was a turning point in the history of the 1948 war."[10] But he was Lehi's chief at the time and his postmortem condemnation is little more than hypocrisy. Dr. Shayeb was indeed honest, he defended Dir Yassin.

The Yishuv, and especially Ben Gurion, would use Dir Yassin to tag Begin with the label of terrorist. The only result of Dir Yassin, for Begin, was that it greased the process by which Etzel would fade from Israel as an autonomous and independent force.

It is logical to ask why Begin defended Dir Yassin and does so to this day, even though at the time he already knew the dimensions and nature of the massacre.

The explanation must relate once again to the context of the times and Begin's stubborn personality. To admit to the massacre was tantamount to admitting that he had no control over Etzel's forces in Jerusalem, or that he was not an informed military commander.

Politically, it would have been a harsh admission, especially at a time when the transition from Mandatory to statehood threatened to blot Begin's role in Israel's War for Independence. He was aware of the historical importance of the moment, and he wanted his share in it duly noted for future generations. It would not do for history to record that Etzel's major role in the war was the perpetration of a massacre.

As in the case of the *Altalena,* and later in Lebanon, Begin had no control over and lacked the military know-how to direct the actions of his underlings. He was loyal to his men, a trait which reflects credit on him personally, but it was a loyalty that was never returned by ambitious and ruthless men like Paglin and Sharon.

Throughout his career, Begin would pay a high price for shielding his men—a high personal, political and moral price.

What is perhaps especially perplexing and painful is that Begin, so sensitive and attuned to the woes and sufferings of the Jewish people, could never extend that empathy to the Arabs, his foes. But he is probably not unique in this, perhaps no different than some other Zionist leaders, whatever their political persuasion.

21

Two Etzels for One Ship:
The Altalena[1]

Crisis followed crisis. The Dir Yassin massacre was just over, but the political trauma for Begin was not. Like a sailor in a stormy ocean, Begin was carried from one coast to another by waves of uncharted events.

Next came the *Altalena* affair, Begin's albatross. In this supreme test of will and force, Begin proved to be a terrible crisis manager. Another chance for legitimacy was once again literally thrown away on the rocks of Tel Aviv.

The drama of the *Altalena* is better understood if set in the context of the times—the Israeli War for Independence against the Arabs and Begin's failure to take part in it.

The ship *Altalena,* named after Jabotinsky's pseudonym, would become a watershed in the life of Begin, in his career, in Israel's history, and in Etzel.

The ship was bought in 1946 through the combined efforts of Etzel in Europe. It would eventually land in Natanya in Israel in June of 1948, during the height of Israel's War for Independence.

The shortage of men and experience was at the heart of the Dir Yassin fiasco. The reservoir for Etzel was in America and in Europe. In the United States the Etzel committee, composed of Jabotinsky's self-appointed heirs Hillel Kook and Shmuel Merlin, known as the *Vaad* or the American Committee for a Hebrew Army, sought to fulfill Jabotinsky's moribund dream of 1939—an invasion of Palestine—this time not to oust Britain, which was withdrawing, but to establish Etzel's role in Israel's War for Independence, indeed to challenge the government of Israel, an ambition that was not shared by Begin. The rivalry between Etzel in the United States—the Vaad —and Begin's Etzel was not yet in the open but was brewing underneath seemingly peaceful waters. The death of Jabotinsky, with no heir appointed, left Begin in Palestine, and Kook and Merlin in the United States to contend over his legacy. In Europe, the Etzel command was composed of Eliahu Lankin and Yaacov Tavin, both Begin's men. In the United States the Vaad was led by Hillel Kook (alias Peter Bergson) and Shmuel Merlin. The rivalry was both ideological and personal. Ideologically, the Vaad was influenced by Sternist ideas of a Hebrew nation and army, while Begin was still a pre-1939 Jabotinsky Revisionist—even if his tactics against Britain were closer to Stern's than to his leader's. Personally it was a struggle between two successful Etzel leaders. Begin's Revolt catapulted him into the role of the heroic guerrilla fighter who ousted the British from Palestine.

Kook-Bergson and the Vaad established their reputation in the United States as champions of Jewish independence who challenged the American Zionist leadership's pusillanimity in failing to save European Jewry from the Holocaust. In the tradition of Jabotinsky, Kook-Bergson and his colleagues employed the best public relations techniques to arouse Jewish and Christian leaders against FDR's unwillingness to become aggressive in saving the Jews of Europe from genocide. Drunk with its public relations success in America, the Vaad was now to set the stage for the invasion of Palestine by a Hebrew army consisting of American and European remnants, Betarim, and other forces. An Etzel command and network were established in Paris to train Betarim and purchase weapons for the fight in Palestine. Desperate for men and weapons, Etzel in Palestine and Begin found their source in Europe, and Begin sent his best men—Eliahu Lankin, Shmuel Katz, Yoel Amrami, Yaacov Tavin and others—to organize a division that would become the Etzel task force, and hopefully play a significant role in the Israeli War for Liberation. The battle between Etzel factions about Etzel's role in the war took place over the *Altalena,* the ship of men and weapons sent from Europe to replenish Etzel and win it an honorable place in the history of the liberation of Eretz Israel. *Altalena* combined the dreams of Jabotinsky, the ambitions of the Revolt, and the aspirations of the Vaad.

For Ben Gurion, there was only one Etzel. Busy commanding the War for Independence, now at its peak (May 1948), he was unaware that there were actually two Etzels seemingly acting as one. For Begin, the *Altalena* meant more weapons for his troops; for the Vaad (Kook-Merlin), it meant a military action in the context of a Hebrew government; for Ben Gurion, it was exactly what the Vaad meant it to be. The price for what the ship meant to the Vaad would be paid by Begin's Etzel and the Vaad. Once again, Begin, politically not ready for the kaleidoscopic events of 1948, is caught between dreams and reality.

When the *Altalena* set sail from Marseilles for Palestine on May 29, 1948, the former Panamanian freighter carried a cargo of 800 men, 130 women and children, some 500 guns, four to five million rounds of ammunition, 250 Bren submachine guns, 50 to 150 Spandau submachine guns, two antitank guns, 250 Sten handguns and 50 bazookas.

Two years previously, in 1946, Vaad had set up a fictitious shipping company called the Three Stars Lines, which was registered in New York. The *Altalena* was originally a Panamanian boat, bought in 1946 and registered in Houston by Armando Carlos, the Panamanian Consul General, for 175,000 pounds sterling. It arrived in Marseilles in the spring of 1948. For Kook and the Vaad, the arrival of the *Altalena* and Etzel's urgent demand for weapons and money converged in his mind, signaling that the time was ripe for an Etzel invasion of Palestine. He envisioned an expedition force formed, trained and equipped in Europe becoming a main landing force in the invasion.

That expectation made the ship's presence alone something of a powderkeg. It carried more than its human cargo, more than an impressive array of weaponry needed by all the Jewish fighting forces preparing to meet the Arab invasion that would come in the wake of partition. Politically, ideologically, historically, and mythologically, it was weighted down with significance. The origin of the *Altalena,* and what happened to the ship and its cargo, would be the subject of debate for decades to come. Across the years, it would fester like an open wound in Israeli society, still raw to the touch, shifting, still open to interpretation by history's survivors.

Originally, the ship was meant to spearhead an invasion force, at least in the minds of the Vaad and Hillel Kook and those last, diehard, romantic Etzel radicals who, for a brief moment, very seriously entertained a fragment of Jabotinsky's most ill-conceived dream. The ship was, after all, the Vaad's brainchild, and it was the Vaad that bought and equipped it.[2]

Very quickly, however, the *Altalena* would pass from the Vaad's control and into the Begin mythology. Almost by accident, it became the centerpiece of the struggle between the Etzel-Begin camp and the Yishuv-Labor-Ben Gurion interests. Depending on who is viewing the event, the *Altalena* was Begin's folly and shame or a mark of bravery and political courage. The affair allowed Ben Gurion, on the other hand, to crush Etzel, to solidify his control over the fledgling state, and to shape the fate of Israeli history for years to come. From the *Altalena* would emerge the end of Etzel's organized existence as a military underground in independent Israel, but it would also mark the birth of Herut, a new political movement and party.

The *Altalena*'s inception stemmed from yet another Etzel internecine struggle, the battle between Europe and Palestine, between Kook's Vaad and Begin's representatives in Europe, Etzel's European command headed by Eliahu Lankin—this despite an official memorandum of cooperation between the Vaad and Etzel's command in Europe signed in Rome on May 1, 1948,[3] coordinated by Arieh Ben Eliezer, a Begin loyalist and Vaad member. But the tensions were always high, as was to be expected from individuals like Kook and Begin. Some operational parts of the agreement were not approved. For instance, the Vaad, influenced by Stern and the Canaanites preferred terms like "Hebrew" not "Jewish government," and Eretz Israel, not the Palestine government. These semantics represented a growing ideological divide between the Vaad and Etzel.

In 1948, there emerged in formerly Nazi-occupied Europe a new kind of Etzel, composed of old Betarim, radical Revisionists, and, most importantly, a transplanted Vaad, still fresh from its successes in America and led by Kook and company. It would attempt to mount a serious challenge against the authority of the new government of Israel and, indirectly, of Begin in Palestine Israel.

The Vaad wanted to become Revisionism's version of the Jewish Agency, a proto-government in exile, with the Etzel being relegated to a military arm, very similar to the function the Haganah served for the Yishuv and the Jewish Agency. This was, of course, viewed with dismay by Begin, who had already all but anointed himself as Jabotinsky's heir.

Situated in Europe, the Vaad saw itself as a government in exile. As such it was conducting affairs of state, dealing in rescue attempts and arms acquisition and engaging in diplomatic efforts, including the establishment of diplomatic relations with the Vatican and France.

In 1948, the Vaad in Paris was prepared to announce, very much as it did in America, the Hebrew government-in-exile. The Vaad had connections with Lehi, and went as far as to help plan the blowing up of the British Embassy in Rome as part of a general Lehi wave of terror in Europe. All of this was viewed with disquiet by Begin, but finally a formal but not very intimate relationship began to be established between the two groups.

In 1948, the Etzel in Europe was in no way subordinate to Etzel, meaning Begin, in Palestine, at least not in any formal way, and that created tensions with the Vaad and other Betarim in Europe.

In order to coordinate Etzel efforts in Europe under the authority if not the supervision of Etzel in Palestine, a negotiator was needed. That turned out to be Eliahu Lankin, a respectable member of Etzel's High Command and a close friend of Kook and Merlin, who was designated to become Etzel's European commander.

Begin was aware of Kook's and Vaad's importance and wrote to them, suggesting the establishment of an Etzel headquarters in Europe, or a headquarters for the countries in Diaspora. This did not mollify Kook and the Vaad, which remained independent and defiant.

Kook and company proved to be more radical. He called for the formation of a supreme national authority to "unite all the revolutionary forces and give them political expression as understood by its fighters." This meant autonomy for the Vaad in Europe. The debate between Kook and Begin was over the aspiration of Etzel in Europe to establish an exile government and its denunciation of the "Palestine government of the Jewish Agency." It also called for the immediate conquest of Jerusalem.[4]

Begin's attitude was deceptive, and his response was noncommittal. "Your idea is attractive," he wrote. "We will accept only a complete Eretz Israel. The British must be ousted and the Arabs repelled. But for that we need soldiers, weapons and money."[5] Begin was strongly suggesting that the Vaad, not Etzel, serve a Haganah-like function—to become the weapons supplier for Etzel. But he remained strongly opposed to an exile government in Europe. Begin suggested that the Vaad and Etzel should show opposition to partition, that Etzel should concentrate on conquering Jerusalem and that it should end its underground form of existence in Palestine.

"We must avoid a civil war and bloodshed," he wrote, "and a government-in-exile opposing Israel's new government means assessing our forces realistically and building political power in Israel proper, accepting the legitimacy of the government of Israel, yet seeking a special role for Etzel in Jerusalem."[6] Begin cautioned against an underground in Israel. "We will not establish an underground to fight against partition in the jurisdiction of a Hebrew rule on any part of the country . . . An underground in Israel would be pursued by Jewish intelligence. In a period of immigration and absorption [the task of the new state] . . . This is not the way to reach the masses."[7] At the same time, Begin sought autonomy for Etzel in the newly established state, not a war against the newly established government of Israel or the IDF.

By this time, Lankin, the Etzel commander in Europe, had become an advocate for the Vaad in Europe, which had established its headquarters in Paris in the luxurious Hotel Luticia.

Kook appeared to convey his loyalty to Etzel in Palestine, but in reality he and the Vaad were acting autonomously. "I know they sometimes act independently," Lankin wrote to Begin, "but we need their services and experience . . . Their work is tremendous. In my view they are the only serious political group which behaves in a statesmanlike fashion."[8]

Begin was not in the least convinced, especially after Kook charged that Etzel had become a part of the Israeli establishment, especially the Jewish Agency. "We are Israel's liberation army," he wrote Kook. "We are independent of any other Jewish group. We never accepted the authority of the Jewish Agency." Again, he angrily and emphatically rejected Kook's idea of a government in exile:

"A government in exile," he wrote, "is a death blow to our movement. Such a government will never be recognized by the United Nations. We may have to establish some type of political institution which will handle the territorial status of the state . . . We must continue to fight for *Shlemut Hamoledet* [The Integrity of the Land]. But a state declared before we accomplish our struggle for the integrity of our land is doomed to fail . . . The UN partition of Eretz Israel is partial and temporary. We shall have to fight for the Land."[9]

These are consistent with Begin's ideological positions. He could not have been more precise or clear. But in early 1948, the idea of an invasion of Palestine raised blood in the minds of Kook and his followers. It would be a resurrection of Jabotinsky's dream. They rejected Begin's positions and continued their autonomous actions.

For the dream to become a reality, the *Altalena* was needed.

Begin envisioned some ten thousand soldiers invading Palestine, a considerable force, but this plan soon collapsed. The volunteers, who did not know the difference between the Haganah and Etzel, soon diminished in numbers, so that at the end only about one hundred men showed up for the invasion. They were sent to Etzel centers in Italy and Germany for training. The intent, however, was made clear by Begin: "If we would have had a supply of ten thousand men . . . we could have fought partition . . ."[10] Begin would later write that "five thousand soldiers of Etzel will invade, exciting the soul . . . Their addition could determine the battle."[11]

One wonders which battle he was referring to. In any case, it can be surmised that, in spite of his later protestations, Begin supported in mind and soul the idea that would become the *Altalena*.

It indeed could be that Begin did not intend the *Altalena* as a vehicle for acquiring power. There were Etzel members who did entertain this pure dream. But clearly the *Altalena*'s weapons were not an innocent cargo. *Altalena* was part of an overall effort of the Etzel organizations in Europe and in America to establish their claim on Israel's War for Liberation, and thus increase their political power in Israel.

Begin scoffed at the idea of a coup. He simply wanted guns and money. He clearly understood that an Etzel "invasion" would be harshly foiled by the Haganah and the IDF, not to mention Great Britain.

Nevertheless, the Vaad hatched its plan, a move that was clearly a sign of the lack of communication, not to mention a divergence in ideology, between Paris and Palestine, and aims of the two forces.

In March, the invasion preoccupied the minds of the Vaad in Paris. The idea grew and bloomed like the spring flowers that year and enraptured a variety of people.

The invasion was planned to occur in the middle of May to coincide with the British departure from Palestine. The leadership of the Yishuv, with more practical plans such as the conquest of the Negev and the liberation of Jerusalem, was already aware of the invasion talk emanating from Paris. Kook suspected (wrongly) that they would make catastrophic compromises in order to establish its fledgling Jewish state. He thought that

Etzel could pre-empt the Yishuv and the world by planting a Jewish flag on the coast of Palestine.

That spring, not only Kook but a number of other Etzel members were caught up in the invasion plan. Lankin thought it was a great idea. Eitan Livny, the Etzel chief of staff sent from Palestine, now conceived of a grand encirclement strategy, in which an Etzel force from Palestine would meet the invading force from the sea and capture the land, pushing the Arab armies out along with its population. "We need to stab the Arabs at their heartland in the Western Galilee," Livny said. Lankin agreed. Yaacov Meridor, who had escaped from exile in East Africa, was also excited about the idea and proposed a direct air link between Israel and France, where a radio station would coordinate the invasion offensive.

As hotly and quickly as it had bloomed, the invasion plans collapsed on May 15, 1948, when Etzel headquarters in Palestine announced an agreement with the IDF.

Now the Paris headquarters was being restricted in its use of the *Altalena.* Its mission, as now understood by the Etzel command in Europe, was restricted to serving the military purposes of Etzel in Palestine with weapons and men; no other political motives were discussed. Dutifully, for once, the command went to work, recruiting an Etzel force for the ship, purchasing its store of weapons, and negotiating with the French government for permission to allow the *Altalena* to sail.

Meanwhile, Etzel in Palestine was becoming edgy. It was also at a crossroad. Ben Gurion had proclaimed the establishment of the State of Israel. What would Etzel's role now be—a quick decision, a decisive one had to be made—and how would it fit into the overall War for Independence?

The answer was the agreement between Etzel and the Haganah on May 15 that would spell the end of Etzel. Of course, the Haganah knew about the *Altalena,* had known about it as early as April, and was concerned. But first, the disposition of Etzel and Lehi had to be considered.

All along, the Haganah High Command had maintained a stern attitude about the underground movements, as stated in one of its proclamations: "The renegade organizations have only one way to cooperate with the Jewish nation in the struggle for liberation—to dissolve their organizations and submit their weapons to the Haganah."

This Etzel was not ready to do, much less Lehi. For over two months, the Haganah had negotiated over Lehi-Etzel dissolution. The negotiations were played out against the background of the murderous Dir Yassin operation. The negotiations were becoming especially critical, with Haganah facing an expected Arab invasion. Ben Gurion was now the master of the Yishuv, Secretary General of the Jewish Agency and its Defense department, and the boss of Haganah, with Israel Galilee and Levy Eshkol as his deputies.

By May 15, an agreement that was supposed to go into effect by June 1 was ready to be hammered out between representatives of Etzel and the Haganah, although all along Ben Gurion had refused to meet face to face with Begin.

The major provisions of the agreements were as follows:

1. Etzel would be dissolved as a military organization as soon as a Jewish government was established.

2. Etzel would not attack British or Arab targets and forces without prior consultation with Yishuv authorities.

3. Etzel would acquire and requisition weapons only with permission.[12]

Etzel, to say the least, appeared not to be negotiating in good faith. Very soon, it was violating all the requirements of the agreement. Almost immediately, it demanded weapons the Haganah had sequestered earlier. It dragged its feet on the process of dissolution and it continued to attack Arab and British targets without permission. It was the agreement itself which appealed to Etzel, not its provisions. Signing it gave Etzel some legitimacy in the new nation, but Etzel nevertheless continued to exist as an underground in Israel until it was dissolved after the *Altalena* affair, which ended in September 1948.

On May 29, after the Haganah had turned down an offer to buy the weapons on board the *Altalena,* the ship embarked from Marseilles. The following day, a grand party was held at Etzel headquarters in Paris, attended by Lankin, Ben Eliezer, and Shmuel Katz, who was Begin's deputy and emissary. Yet the party was conducted in a disquieting atmosphere. The situation in Palestine was anything but sanguine.

Ben Gurion, now Prime Minister and Defense Minister, was reluctant to renew negotiations with Etzel now that the Etzel-Haganah agreement had expired. Although Begin must have steered his Etzel group in the direction of legal political action, Ben Gurion and others in the Haganah and later the IDF intelligence establishment continued to suspect his and Etzel-Lehi's real motives. Even though Ben Gurion reluctantly approved Etzel's "autonomous" role in Jerusalem and the Etzel-IDF agreement of June 1, 1948, Y. Gruenbaum, Minister of the Interior, brought fresh Etzel pronouncements, which Gruenbaum supported, that there could be no negotiation over Jerusalem and that "in Jerusalem an Etzel command has been established and only it can decide Etzel's standing in Jerusalem." Ben Gurion replied: "I am only interested in Jerusalem and noninterference in the war until I know the situation in Jerusalem—I have no interest in negotiating."[13] Ben Gurion continued to receive negative information on Etzel. On July 20, 1948, he recorded in his *War Diary* that Iser Arel, Chief of Counterintelligence (the *Shin Bet)*, reported that Etzel was prepared to establish an underground in the IDF; that Etzel refused recruitment of its commanders to the IDF; and that Arel recommended that they break Etzel apparatus in Tel Aviv [Etzel's headquarters in the Freund hospital in southern Tel Aviv] and take over their finances. "One must be vigilant about their transfer of weapons from overseas. There are importers who help them. They could also steal weapons from the IDF and the mayors of Tel Aviv, Israel Rokach and Avraham Krinitzy of Ramat-Gan are helping. One must prevent their clandestine purchases as well."[14]

In the period after the May agreement, Etzel operated under the Haganah's general plan without serious coordination. Yet Etzel was militarily weak and incompetent to fight a nonurban guerrilla war. Etzel began to disintegrate, and several of its members operated as part of the Haganah force, ceasing to take orders from Etzel's command.

Fifteen days after the state was officially proclaimed by the government of Israel, Begin reluctantly signed with Galilee, now an official of the government of Israel (Deputy Defense Minister) an agreement on the dissolution of Etzel. This was a more stringent and demanding agreement than the one signed two weeks earlier. What was agreed was to become crucial in the *Altalena*-IDF conflict.

It was agreed:

1. Etzel members will join the IDF and swear allegiance to the government of Israel.

2. Etzel recruits will operate as independent battalions under the IDF command.

3. All Etzel equipment will be surrendered to the IDF.

4. All its war production will be surrendered to the IDF.

5. A temporary Etzel command will operate under the IDF until the battalion is in order.

6. "On its own free will Etzel ceases to exist as a military command and division within the jurisdiction of the Government and the State of Israel."[15]

The agreement was signed by Menachem Begin for Etzel and Israel Galilee for the Israeli government. There was no dispute over Etzel's dissolution as an autonomous military command, but as to its role in IDF, paragraph 2 is rather vague. As a result, a battle would rage over where the weapons of the *Altalena* would go, to Etzel units in the IDF or to the IDF. Once again the majority of Etzel commanders—certainly those in Jerusalem and Paris— were neither privy to or in favor of the agreement. Begin was now caught between the radicals in Israel and Europe and his better instincts to make a deal with the official government of Israel.

However, he was still concerned that the leadership now in Israel would modify the partition boundaries. Begin still believed that if Etzel acted as an army and was unrestrained by the Yishuv, it could liberate all of Palestine. This is what Begin meant by continuing to support an independent Etzel in Jerusalem—Independent from the IDF! Events caught up with Begin as he made a deal with the Haganah-IDF.

The *Altalena* sailed, on the decision of the Vaad and Etzel members in Paris, even though they were unaware of conditions in Israel or of the Begin-Galilee deal. (If they did know about the agreement, they ignored it.) Agents of Shai (Haganah's intelligence) already knew of the ship's departure and had cabled the Prime Minister. Thus Ben Gurion knew of the ship and its contents, and this, to Ben Gurion, meant a serious violation of the arms requisition stipulation of the agreement and only further exacerbated his hostility toward Etzel.

Communications between Begin and the Etzel command in Europe were also practically nonexistent or at best were extremely poor. The *Altalena* was at sea, its exact destination unknown, its purpose, mysterious and provocative. Begin was in the dark.

On June 12, Begin became concerned about the *Altalena* and sought to stop its arrival. It was too late. The ship sailed on, clearly in defiance of the Israeli government. Certainly its arrival would defy a UN administered cease-fire.

The IDF leadership now wanted details about the *Altalena,* and on June 16, Galilee and Eshkol traveled to southern Tel Aviv's Etzel headquarters to ask Begin about the ship. A nervous and reluctant Begin told them the whole story, beginning in New York and ending with its departure from France.

What he didn't tell and perhaps didn't know then was that the weapons were stored in crates. That they were not intended for an invasion. The weapons were to be distributed to Etzel's fronts, especially Jerusalem, thus strengthening Etzel's bargaining and political power.

Begin asked permission to have the ship put into Tel Aviv. The IDF leaders pressed for information about the weapons on board. He was also becoming more nervous and suspicious and continued to try to stop the ship for fear the IDF would seize it. Earlier, on June 14, Shmuel Katz, Begin's representative on board the *Altalena,* tried to divert it to Yugoslavia, to no avail.

In Paris, the whole operation had dribbled through Kook's hands. Begin was beginning to see the potential for disaster.

On June 16, Galilee and Eshkol arrived at Etzel headquarters in southern Tel Aviv to meet with Begin, Meridor, Ben Eliezer, Landau and Paglin, Begin's masterful and radical chief of operations.

Begin asked, since there was a semblance of a ceasefire, if the government would give permission for the *Altalena* to disembark. But the former Haganah men, now IDF and Defense Ministry representatives, seemed to be interested only in the weapons. Ben Eliezer reluctantly gave the information, but years later, he insisted that "I never trusted them. I had a premonition they were there to deceive us."

Distrust was deepened between the negotiators. Begin, in a radio speech on June 22, 1948, claimed he was ready to deliver *Altalena*'s cache to the IDF. Galilee said that Begin charged $250,000 for the weapons.

Kook, in retrospect, concurred. "Begin was a naive man," he said. "He was deceived by Galilee and his master, David Ben Gurion."[16]

Eshkol was astounded by the very presence of the *Altalena*. "How do you do such things, now that there is no way for [the ship] to return?" he asked incredulously.

Begin, now deeply suspicious, disturbed and confronted by the deeds of his European colleagues, and his own as well, had no answers. He could not admit that he was not in control; nor was he ready to surrender the weapons now that they were on their way. He felt the IDF was devouring the weapons, and would not deliver parts to Etzel units. This was true, but the real issue was the age-old struggle between Begin and Ben Gurion. Now that Begin had the authority over the state, the issue had to be decided with the *Altalena*. This incident only emboldened Begin to become more defiant.

In the midst of the negotiations, the *Altalena,* like a political beacon, arrived on the horizon on July 19, looking for all the world like a real challenge to the now established order in Israel. It reached the northern coast of Tel Aviv, at Kfar Vitkin, at 9 P.M. Paglin, who masterminded the King David Hotel bombing, was there to take charge of unloading the weapons.

With the emergence of Paglin, Begin began to slowly lose control of the situation in a manner that would predate the Begin-Sharon relationship in the Lebanon war. Things began to get out of hand. Begin was never distinguished as a crisis manager.

On July 20, the government of Israel met in Tel Aviv. Foreign Minister Moshe Sharett solemnly announced that "it is possible we are facing a violation of the ceasefire [UN ceasefire established on June 13, 1948]. It is going to be another Etzel bombast." The issue was becoming clear, even if the proceedings were rapidly becoming more confusing by the minute: Etzel must surrender the weapons as stipulated by its agreement with the Haganah, and later the Government of Israel, otherwise a dangerous military confrontation between the IDF and Etzel was very much in the offing. In response, the IDF ordered a military alert and surrounded Kfar Vitkin.

Galilee, now Deputy Defense Minister, and IDF Deputy Chief of Staff Yigael Yadin, had already informed the cabinet of the arrival of the ship at

Kfar Vitkin. The cabinet to a man agreed that the ship represented a challenge to the legitimacy of the government, but they were fearful of the possibility of a civil war. Still, they could see that the use of force might become necessary. They ordered that "the local commander must try his best not to use force but if his orders are disobeyed, he can resist with force." The government voted to "delegate authority to IDF for a counterattack *if* Etzel accumulates force" (italics mine).

Ben Gurion was decisive where the Cabinet was not. "Mr. Begin will not do as he pleases. We must decide if we shall relinquish power to Begin —or tell him to end his isolationist activities. If he will not surrender, we will open fire."[17]

Orders went out, although the exact nature of the weapons on board the ship were unknown. However the weapons were clearly not ready to deploy for an invasion. Galilee deployed the Alexandroni Division, commanded by General Dan Even, around Kfar Vitkin. The latter was not aware of the cabinet and IDF command decision.

Foreign Minister Sharett was clearly upset. "I am at a loss," he said. "What should we do? We didn't deserve this terror, for all our patience and reasonableness in the past. The fact is that Etzel maintains its organization in spite of our agreements." Ben Gurion, however, had no time for hand wringing. He notes briskly in his diary that "on June 11, 1948, Begin accepted and signed [an agreement] that all independent purchasing of weapons by Etzel in Palestine and abroad must end." After hearing the details of the negotiations from Eshkol, he wrote: "On the eighteenth, as soon as Begin was informed of the ship's arrival, I insisted that all the weapons must be surrendered on the beach to the government of Israel."[18]

Begin seemed amenable at first, striving for accommodation in the face of surrender. After he consulted with his colleagues, he replied that the weapons would be surrendered in a double ceremony, with Etzel and IDF units present. The surrender of weapons would be on the basis that twenty percent of the weapons be allocated for Etzel in Jerusalem with a vague promise that Etzel members now in IDF units would receive some of them.

Ben Gurion accepted the twenty percent condition but did not accept distribution to any Etzel units other than those in Jerusalem; he insisted that Etzel must surrender the weapons on the beach to the IDF and that the IDF must distribute the weapons according to the agreement. At first Begin seemed to agree to these conditions. But then he wavered, as the presence of Paglin began to loom larger. Had he accepted the conditions then and there, the affair would have never ballooned to the dimensions of a tragedy and a legend.

The sticking point was the distribution of the weapons to Etzel units in the IDF in Jerusalem. Like a devil's advocate, Paglin warned Begin that Ben

Gurion couldn't be trusted and that the weapons would go to IDF units, not Etzel units. He reminded Begin of Sezon, always a sore point.

Finally, Galilee told Paglin that the issue was moot, that there would be no Etzel military units in the end. The two sides began to escalate their demands. Then Paglin advised Begin to insist that the weapons be stored in Etzel caches and that Etzel decide what to do with them.

Influenced by the insistent whispering of Paglin, Begin demanded that only Etzel units unload the weapons. Galilee bluntly said only the IDF would unload them. Galilee could clearly see that Paglin was now in charge, but he tried one more time; he called Begin in the middle of the night. Begin was adamant; only Etzel could unload the weapons. Galilee broke off contact. Now the decision lay with the government. It was a tense situation. There were Etzel units in the area and Etzel fighters among the Alexandroni division. Some five hundred Etzel men were set to square off with the IDF units. Even as Etzel men unloaded troops and weapons, Galilee tried again, but Begin, by now worried that he might be detained, refused to meet him.

Galilee and Yadin gave Begin an ultimatum on June 21 that Etzel surrender the weapons within ten minutes; otherwise the IDF would use all means at its disposal to enforce the order. Begin not only rejected the ultimatum, he ridiculed it. The situation was coming close to an explosion as both Israeli naval forces and more Etzel forces began to move toward Kfar Vitkin.

At this point, Oved Ben-Ami, a man acceptable to both sides, was asked to help in negotiating. Ben-Ami, although nominally a Haganah man, was also mayor of Natanaya, an Etzel stronghold. Ben-Ami hoped to persuade Begin to give up the struggle, but he was frightened by the volatility of the situation as he watched armed Etzel men facing soldiers of the IDF. Although Ben-Ami wrote a report to Ben Gurion suggesting Begin and Etzel surrender the weapons, he could not prevent what now appeared to be the inevitable from happening.

In the midst of continued negotiations, Etzel and IDF soldiers, operating at close quarters in an intolerably tense situation, opened fire on each other. Several soldiers were killed and more were wounded. Jews were killing Jews; Begin's and Ben Gurion's nightmare was unfolding.

Begin remained defiant, but the actual bloodshed stirred him. Like a man emerging from a dream, he began trying to avoid further violence by ordering most of his men aboard the *Altalena*. He himself went on board the ship as it disembarked on the night of July 22.

The *Altalena* headed for Tel Aviv, turned toward the rocks to avoid the suggestion of any aggressive intention. Nevertheless, Ben Gurion had had enough. He ordered the Palmach (still autonomous within the IDF) to finish the ship off with a field canon.

Ben Gurion was cryptic about the events in his diary: "July 22, 1948,

Etzel Day. What was finally inevitable happened. In Kfar Vitkin, they surrendered today, but at night they moved the ship to Tel Aviv. The government met early in the morning and a two-thirds majority demanded surrender. One of our guns hit the ship and she blew up and began to burn. Etzel
people requested help. We sent them a rescue Palmach team to aid the
wounded. The ship is burning."

Defiant about the ship, Begin was already talking about "the great
betrayal" and honing his image as martyr and hero. Nevertheless, he had
avoided further disaster by moving the ship out, by finally not giving into
the activist, radical voice of Paglin. In Kfar Vitkin, Meridor was surrender-
ing Etzel forces to the IDF. Etzel didn't gracefully dissolve, it was destroyed
and, as a force of the Revolt, was already beginning to fade into history.
Now the myth-making and the controversy would begin.

The controversy that raged over the *Altalena* affair would, in many
ways, surpass the controversy which had surrounded the Arlazaroff affair.
Mention it even today among certain people in Israel, and you are certain to
start a heated argument. At the time, the debate went on for weeks, in the
highest reaches of government and down to the lowest levels of Israeli
society. While the action raged, it involved underground and mainstream,
soldiers and diplomats.

To this day, Begin believes that the whole affair was some sort of dark
plot concocted by Ben Gurion, that the *Altalena* all along was designed to be
destroyed.

The truth is far less subtle, and perhaps even more tragic. Its singular
element is not design, but a lack of design. None of the actors—the Vaad,
who wanted to use the ship as an invasion force; the Etzel leaders, who did
not quite know what to do with it (surrender the weapons or preserve them
for Etzel units), or Ben Gurion and IDF—were ever in full and complete
control of the situation. They were carried away by events and prejudices
that had a momentum of their own.

But Defense Minister Ben Gurion prevailed in establishing the authority of the fledgling state, and Begin, as in the Sezon, claimed he averted a
Jewish civil war.

In the end, Begin managed to restrain the radical forces under his
command, especially Paglin. But his repeated claim that he bore no responsibility for what happened in the *Altalena* affair, that he was, in fact, a conciliatory martyr to the greater cause, does not bear close scrutiny. As he had in
the past, and as he would in the future, he showed definite flaws in his
leadership ability, a tendency to wilt under the pressure of a volatile situation and the influence of a more forceful personality—in this case Paglin.
Until the climax of the affair, he was indecisive and irresolute.

Begin, however, with his submission to Ben Gurion at the end of the
Altalena affair, could also be said to be the man who prevented the real

tragedy from occurring. Paglin, more than anyone else, was the man who almost made it happen. There were radical forces at work at the time which would have liked nothing better than a civil war.

Paglin was the man who planned the King David Hotel bombing, who urged violence upon Begin time and time again, and who repeatedly chided him for not going far enough. Paglin's political vision, crude and often ignorant of the British and the Arab mentalities, was basically romantic, and he saw violence as a tool to achieve his romantic goals.

When Paglin talks about the *Altalena,* he talks about decisions *he* made: "I rejected Haganah's offer . . . We decided to act as Begin would have, had he had a free course to follow at the time." He went further. He left the *Altalena* in Kfar Vitkin because "Begin refused to accept my advice on how to deal with the IDF encirclement on the beaches." Paglin's advice was extreme, to say the least. He wanted to go to IDF headquarters and take over the government. In effect, he was pushing for a revolt and a putsch. "In my view it was possible," he said. He had some equally extremist support in Lehi quarters.[19]

Natan Friedman-Yellin, after Stern the leader of Lehi, told me in 1966 that Lehi had prepared a list of some fifty Yishuv leaders "to be eliminated." "I went to Yitzhak Sadeh of the Palmach, Commanding General of the 8th Division, which integrated Lehi fighters," Yellin told me, "and I suggested that we have a coup. He turned me down. He said a coup was 'silly.' What do soldiers understand about politics?"[20]

Perhaps that was exactly what made Begin draw back from Paglin. Assassination was not Begin's style. He was not a revolutionary but a politician who wanted to win with respectability and gain a foothold in the new Israel.

In the end, Begin proved indecisive and too susceptible to the whispering of Paglin. Had Begin agreed initially to Ben Gurion's demand—and it was a legitimate demand—that he agree to the stipulations of the cease-fire, the violence that occurred would have been avoided.

Begin's efforts to prolong Etzel's autonomous survival and influence cost him considerably. After all, how much longer could Ben Gurion and IDF tolerate an independent military underground in Israel—certainly not after IDF's decisive victory against the Egyptian forces at the end of 1948. Sooner, rather than later, Etzel was bound to dissolve. But Begin was not emotionally ready for its absorption into the IDF.

For that matter, Ben Gurion and his negotiators were not exactly decisive either, and did not take advantage of opportunities to put an end to the whole problem at an early stage. They failed to establish order and authority even while having the military means to do so. Often, the negotiations took on the appearance of a drawn-out squabble, with farcical rounds of nitpicking in which the actors seemed unaware of the looming tragedy.

Years later, Ben Gurion claimed he had no idea of the real intentions of the *Altalena* and thus saw it as a threat to his authority and the legitimacy of the new government. Also, years later, Begin would claim innocence, that he had negotiated in good faith. Both were probably right in general terms —i.e., both sides seemed not to be operating in a haze of ignorance, but were fighting over fundamental issues of military and politics in the newly established State of Israel.

The real results could not have been clearer: the dismantling of Etzel began in earnest at the insistence of Ben Gurion and with the basic compliance of Begin. On September 29, 1948, Etzel was officially dissolved. Its members joined the IDF as individuals. Although Etzel would remain in force in the Battle of Jerusalem and although Lehi would not disappear until its assassination of Count Bernadotte, the *Altalena* marked the end of Etzel and the emergence of Herut.

POST-*Altalena*

It was clear, in the wake of the *Altalena* affair, that Etzel was in no way ready to put its weight into the War of Independence. Dir Yassin had already marred its image as an operational and disciplined military force, among other things.

Altalena, Etzel's last effort to influence the course of the war ended tragically for Begin, although in his own mind it would remain an hour of triumph. Even if Etzel had turned in the appropriate direction, toward battling the Arabs, it is highly doubtful that it could have fought successfully against regular Arab units.

What if Etzel's political ambitions had met with success? From hindsight, it is interesting to speculate on what might have happened if the *Altalena* affair had turned out successfully for Etzel. The thoughts and questions are disquieting.

Had the government of Israel been forced into a negotiated settlement over *Altalena,* Etzel might have created a formidable political alternative in the new State of Israel. Etzel's reputation, instead of being irreparably damaged, might have grown. Etzel units might have been able to successfully compete for more weapons and men. Etzel, in fact, and Palmach for that matter, might not have been dissolved, and the United Nations resolution on Jerusalem might have ended up being violated. A Jewish civil war might have erupted and the United States might have abandoned Israel.

The *Altalena* affair was a direct challenge to the authority and viability of the new Israeli government. Ben Gurion, under the circumstances, did the necessary and politically astute thing, for he recognized the challenge implicit in the presence of the ship. He was aware that partition was hanging precariously in the balance and that he had to terminate Etzel's continued revolt as soon as possible. He ended up dissolving both Etzel and Palmach and establishing the authority of the IDF over all Israeli military forces. Even so, he waited almost too long to dissolve Etzel.

The *Altalena* affair represented the newly formed democracy's first major trial. It ended in victory for the pragmatic nationalist oriented forces. History has, after all, vindicated Ben Gurion. But what of Begin? Begin did not originate, organize, plan, or launch the *Altalena* on course. It was a brainchild and product of U.S.-European Etzel. Yet, ironically, his involvement in the affair catapulted him into the position of being the single major political actor in the affair. He had adopted the cause of the *Altalena* as his own, until it became the epitome of a great deed of injustice. Begin wrapped himself in the flag of the *Altalena*'s failure and tragedy, and in an act of political alchemy, turned it into a heroic, personal act of triumph.

Altalena, like the Sezon, the Revolt itself, would become a part of Begin's legacy, a glowing myth of defiance. Begin never ceased to remind his own lieutenants, not to mention the Israeli people of the *Altalena*. It would become a running, heated dialogue between Begin and Ben Gurion. It became a symbol of the past, a heroic symbol of the remnants of the Revolt.

Part Four

THE DESERT YEARS
1949–77

Menachem Begin's political career between 1949 and 1977, when he seemed to ascend out of political cul-de-sac to the Prime Ministership of Israel, amounted to a kind of parched, prickly desert, where he labored loudly but to little effect, sometimes in obscurity, often beset by forces within his own Herut party, always attacked and belittled by his giant rival David Ben Gurion.

There is something almost dutiful and despairing about this period for Begin. It is as if he had set himself upon a political course without confidence or conviction, knowing full well that the days of the underground were over, that the only recourse for him was to enter in party and parliamentary politics, because the former was all he knew outside of the Revolt.

That his efforts seemed to bear little or often bitter fruit can be traced immediately to two factors: the very raw, unformed nature of the political arena itself and of the Knesset; and the almost total dominance of Mapai-Histadrut, as, under the leadership of Ben Gurion, it shaped the nature of the fledgling state.

The first two Knessets, which emerged in the wake of independence, were an uphill battle for Begin and his electorally minority Herut party, for the new institution had its roots squarely in the Yishuv. It was also a haphazard process for the Knesset itself.

Knesset procedures took a long time becoming institutionalized. By and large, they still followed the rules of a provisional government, not a firmly-grounded one. Those rules at first proved to be highly inadequate for the conduct of a parliament with a truly free-wheeling kind of party politics. The tradition which guided the Knesset in its early stages was not political professionalism but the Mapai kind of centralism which had pervaded the Yishuv for decades.

True, there had been Jewish Congress assemblies in the past as well as Yishuv assemblies, but they were conducted all too infrequently. They were not legislative bodies. The first Knessets thus amounted to a continuation of old Zionist Congresses and Palestinian Yishuv politics, with Mapai decidedly in control. The government coalition was the current form of the Jewish Agency's coalition. The state itself was all but synonymous with Socialist Zionist, Mapai, Histadrut-Kibbutzim traditions, touched heavily with elitism and centralism. The institutions of Socialist Zionism were not ideally suited for parliamentary, democratic politics, but were rather tools to inculcate Zionist ideology into the fabric of Israeli society.

Thus, the Knesset, for over a decade and a half, never functioned as a genuinely effective parliamentary organization. It was an institution dominated by one party— Mapai—and effectively closed off in an important way to opposition parties like Mapam or Herut. It would not be until 1967 that a Herut member would gain membership in a Foreign Affairs and Defense committee. For Herut members, promotion within the IDF would be slow and access to senior civil service positions would be tightly controlled, at least until the early 1960s.

It did not help Begin or the fledgling Herut party that Revisionism and its various forces had not played a very large role in the life of the Yishuv. As a potential —but not very viable—alternative, whatever life they had derived mainly from the stature of Jabotinsky, who was now dead. Betar had been a highly hierarchical organization and Etzel and Lehi had been underground guerrilla organizations, not political parties; the Revolt had not exactly been an ideal background for debates or parliamentary processes. Thus Herut entered into politics with the additional handicap of having no political experience.

Begin labored under a variety of difficulties, not the least of which was the giant shadow cast by Ben Gurion, the state's founder and dominant political figure— Begin's chief antagonist. Begin could only helplessly flail against Ben Gurion in a welter of abrasive rhetorics, which Ben Gurion deflected easily and with scorn. Ben Gurion was after all the leader, the Founder, the father of the state and the army, the Defense Minister and maker and shaper of Israel's security and foreign policy, to which Begin had no access and no recourse. Ben Gurion's only serious challengers came from within his own party and movement, but primarily his animosity seemed to be directed against Begin and Herut. His iron law was: "A government coalition without Herut and without Communists."

Ben Gurion's idea of government was not necessarily participatory. He had no intention of sharing power or forging a coalition with either the left or the right. Scathingly, he would refer to Begin in the Knesset as "that member of the Knesset sitting next to Knesset member Dr. Bader." He was intent almost throughout his political life in carrying on a political war against the forces of Revisionism.

If the scorn and ire of Ben Gurion and Mapai were not enough of a burden to bear, there were additional problems within Herut. As we have already seen, Begin, in order to form Herut as a political party, had to effectively destroy the opposition of the conservative, established Zohar and almost immediately found himself dousing a revolt led by the Vaad-American forces of Hillel Kook, Shmuel Merlin and Eri Jabotinsky. It was a process that would continue throughout the desert years, as if Begin, the founder of the party, were sitting on a perpetually shaky throne, sometimes captured by the most radical forces of Revisionism, sometimes fending them off after bitter political struggles.

Herut never became an electorally viable alternative. In the 1949 elections, the first, it managed to obtain only fourteen seats, compared to forty-six for Mapai and twenty for the left-wing Mapam party, partly an off-shoot from Mapai. Herut did even worse in 1951, and Begin, beset by recalcitrant members of his party and by a despair and paralysis which would return again and again throughout his career, almost resigned.

From the beginning, Begin was a staunch believer in parliamentary, democratic government, along the style of the Polish Sejm, which he still remembered vividly. He knew in his soul that Etzel could survive only as a political party within the framework of the Knesset and parliamentary politics. He had hoped that Herut would be a way to reach the masses and he had designed Herut's constitution as the framework of a mass party, but his efforts at seeking political alliances with the organized Sephardim and the then liberal General Zionist party failed.

Begin, the once-daring terrorist, had turned into a parliamentarian. He had not listened to the advice of Dr. Azriel Carlibach, the Editor-in-Chief and columnist of Maariv, who in 1947 had written: "Dear Mr. Begin, you have done great deeds for the nation. Now you must serve the nation as never before. Get out of politics."

Begin did not get out of politics, although he often stepped on the threshold of such a decision, going so far as to seek resignation after the stunningly disappointing 1951 election results.

That he remained in politics at the helm of Herut was due a great deal to the efforts of his principal aide and follower, Dr. Yohanan Bader, who supported Begin, egged him on, and proved to be his most important mainstay and ally. Bader, a Pole, twelve years older than Begin, was a staunch Revisionist and proved to be Begin's lynchpin in the Knesset. Like Begin, he had suffered in the Gulag, and he had been one of Begin's principal supporters within Etzel. In time, he would become one of Israel's most outstanding parliamentarians. It was Bader who would do most of the tedious legislative work grudgingly apportioned to Herut, while Begin took front and center with his often wild and impassioned rhetoric.

The first two Knessets proved to be trying times for Begin and he became an extremely unhappy, almost miserable, sort of politician who would rise from his torpor only to deliver another salvo of rhetoric. Not until 1955, when Herut became the second-largest, but still a small, party in the Knesset, did Begin begin to assert himself and regain some of his old fire and enthusiasm. During all that time, Begin's real contribution would be not his legislative work in the Knesset, which was negligible, but rather his role as protector and espouser of parliamentary politics itself.

22

From Underground to Political Party: The Emergence of Herut[1]

The *Altalena* affair left the Revisionist movement in a certain amount of disarray, as well as at a crucial crossroad. It would now enter into a phase that amounted to a battle for political control among Begin's Etzel, the established but decaying Zohar, and the aggressive Vaad veterans. In the immediate future, Kook-Merlin's Vaad, for tactical reasons, would join with Etzel in the battle against Zohar.

The initial alliance seemed logical, and the battle itself seemed a generational one, the Vaad and Etzel, both young, vigorous outgrowths of Jabotinsky's movement, opposing the establishment as personified by Zohar. The battle was not only ideological, but practical and symbolic. It was a political battle over who would inherit the mantle of Jabotinsky.

World War II had separated Vaad from Eretz Israel physically, and Begin's Revolt had estranged Etzel from Zohar. Etzel and the Vaad had emerged as groups with significant successes behind them, the Vaad with its efforts to rescue the Jews from the Holocaust, Etzel with its largely successful Revolt against the Mandatory.

Zohar, on the other hand, had been quiescent; its leaders, ordinary, uncharismatic politicians, had for the most part opposed the efforts of both the Vaad and Etzel. Both movements, while giving lip service to Zohar's authority, largely ignored what was supposed to be Revisionism's Palestinian headquarters. The questions involved were not questions of ideology but of politics and personalities.

Yohanan Bader, a leading Betari and Herut politician who would later become Herut's Knesset chief, wrote, "There is no contradiction between what the people of Zohar and Etzel perceived. On the one hand, a large segment of Etzel were, after all, Zohar and Betar activists and members. On the other hand, almost all the Betarim were Etzel men and admirers. The dual role played by members of the underground and the formal movements is only a natural consequence of conditions that existed during the British occupation, and there is no reason now to continue the duality, for its purpose has disappeared and doesn't exist now."[2]

Actually, relations between Zohar and Begin became genuinely strained during the Revolt. The Zohar looked at Etzel's unrelenting guerrilla and military actions with great concern and disapproval. Zohar felt a legal army was perfectly all right, but an illegal underground went against the grain, certainly when the Yishuv supported the British in the war.

With the coming of partition, Etzel and Begin needed to take a hard look at the future. There were really to reiterate only four options left open to Begin: one, for Etzel to proclaim itself as the formal government of all Western Eretz Israel, a position espoused by the Vaad; two, for Etzel to concentrate on conquering Jerusalem; three, for Etzel to establish a political party in Israel; four, for Etzel to continue to operate in the new state within the framework of the UN partition borders and to work to erase those borders.

The *Altalena* affair, the dismantling of Etzel as a military force along with Lehi, robbed Begin of the first two choices, although there is doubt that he had seriously considered them.

Accepting the last two options also meant challenging the established power of Zohar, which would turn Begin away from the classic roots of Revisionism. This did not mean abandoning the concept of the Revolt or its continued warfare against partition, but it did mean opting for an evolutionary, parliamentary form of struggle, as had Jabotinsky in the past—this time to achieve the abolition of partition by legal means.

Begin had hoped and believed that Etzel, in its new guise as the political party Herut, would gain a respectable and important place in Israel's political system and that the people of Israel would be grateful for Etzel's role in the War for Independence. After all, "hadn't Etzel ousted the British?" Begin seriously hoped that Israel's new-found political momentum would result in the end of partition and in the creation of "Complete Eretz Israel," his most cherished dream.

Yet what he found wounded him deeply. The Revisionists were split, fighting among themselves and against Begin. Lehi had gone its own way to create the independent Freedom Fighters Party led by Natan Friedman-Yellin. Several Etzel commanders, who had joined the IDF, turned to civilian life and shunned politics altogether. In fact, most former Etzel fighters, except those close to Begin like Meridor, Landau, and Ben Eliezer had turned their backs on political life. They echoed another time and place. As one of the senior comrades told me: "Pilsudski said that when Poland became independent, he left the Socialist train (to which he belonged) and proclaimed that he had arrived at his final destination—'Poland is free.' "[3]

There was a similar, although less ebullient feeling, among the disbanded Etzelites. The mood was one of remorse, frustration and disappointment. Those who had not joined or volunteered the IDF—like Begin, Meridor, Shamir, Yellin-Mor, Shayeb-Eldad—were adrift. They were not required to join, and they were never asked to explain why they had not. Begin was thirty-five in 1948 and still eligible for the draft. All were exempt from the draft to organize their undergrounds into political parties.

In 1951, Begin was almost ready to give up politics. The post-*Altalena* period was probably one of the most difficult periods of his life. All the drama, action, underground heroics, and romanticism of the Revolt was over and a mundane—by comparison—atmosphere set in. Begin found it difficult to cope.

Nevertheless, right after the war, he decided to enter politics. There weren't many other choices, since he had no license to practice law in Palestine and there was no longer any role for underground leaders. With the persuasive Dr. Bader prodding him, and with the support of Unitchman of Zohar and Etzel, Begin jumped into the politics of emerging Israel. Etzel leaders, with the exception of Begin, had no political experience, and Begin's rhetorical and electoral power was crucial if Herut was to be a serious political contender for power in the new state.

And what about the future of Etzel in Europe? After the sinking of *Altalena* and the arrest of several Etzel members, including Hillel Kook, who was aboard the ship, Eli Tavin suggested that Etzel in Europe be Herut's military arm. Begin categorically ordered Etzel in Europe to dissolve.[4] Yet Tavin reports 150 *Altalena* Etzel were "smuggled" to Jerusalem and that Etzel in Europe was reorganized by Etzel members released from their East African exile (after the Sezon). Ben Eliezer, Begin's lieutenant, was in charge of the reorganization. All depended on Etzel's future in Jerusalem. If it ceased to exist, Etzel's European command would be threatened. Ben Eliezer wrote to Begin on September 4, 1948, that "in order to pressure for the widening of borders [sic] the *Ma'amad* [Etzel's underground name] should be sustained."[5] To extricate himself, Begin informed a press conference in Tel Aviv on September 20, 1948 after the assassination of UN mediator Count Folke Bernadotte by Lehi, that Etzel cells in Europe were no longer under his command.[6]

Finally, on his return from New York, he stopped in Paris for a week (December 20–26) and after a long debate and the use of personal persuasion to detail his story of the *Altalena* and after stating again that Etzel in Jerusalem was dissolved, Begin categorically stated: "The political reality in Eretz Israel dictates the dissolution of Etzel in the Diaspora and turning Etzel in Europe into agencies of Herut—and there is no other way."[7]

The lessons of *Altalena* were deeply embedded in Begin's mind. He was, after all, a leader, a politician and a propagandist, and it was almost perfectly natural for him to come to the idea of forming a political mass movement and party.

Better than most of his Etzel colleagues, Begin understood that Etzel could no longer move simultaneously in two directions, both legal and illegal. He probably realized that the time of the underground was past. Now was the time to strive for a political role in Israel. Begin was already concerned that Zohar, which was about as established as an organization could get, would pre-empt Etzel as the legitimate heir to Jabotinsky and would muffle any future role for Etzel.

Being a politician, Begin made a decision at once daring and eminently practical: form a political party in the guise of the continuation of a movement.

In order to form a party and movement, which he would call Herut (Freedom), he faced some formidable tasks:

1. Establishing an *apparat*, a full-time organization and administration.
2. Formulating a party platform that could meet new conditions and hopefully appeal to a mass electorate.
3. Operating within the open parliamentary political system of Israel.
4. Cultivating a new, unknown electorate which would go beyond the established loyalists of Revisionism.
5. Formulating a new relationship with the established Zohar movement and leaders.

When one looks at this agenda, the tasks seem almost impossible, in light of Etzel's condition at the time. It had no experience in the business of organized, open democratic, electoral politics. The Herut administration and organization would depend on the established Etzel staff, most of them experienced as underground activists, not politicians.

Etzel did have one tremendous asset, and that was Menachem Begin himself. He was a seasoned politician, an electoral asset, a former Betar High Commissioner well-versed in Zionist politics from first-hand experience, a powerful orator, and a cunning propagandist—and soon an expert in parliamentary procedure. More than that, he had charisma. As a leader of the Revolt, he had become more than a fighter, more than a politician. He was a symbol. It would become clear from the start that without Begin there could be no Herut. Begin was Herut and Herut was Begin. The two were one and the same and would remain so to the bitter end in 1983, in spite of challenges from within and without.

On June 2, 1948, Menachem Begin proclaimed the birth of a new party "to be composed of all political and national forces of the people. The basic ideas of Etzel are to be identical to the Zohar principles and ideas,"[8] hoping to conciliate Zohar, now that he had become a politician.

On August 1, 1948, Yitchak Gruenbaum, the Minister of Interior of the new government of Israel, formally approved the formation of a new political party to be called Herut. Begin was immediately appointed interim chairman of the new party, and his Etzel loyalist Chaim Landau was appointed his deputy. He was joined by two Vaad leaders, Shmuel Merlin, appointed Chief of Propaganda, and Arieh Ben Eliezer, appointed financial chairman. Dr. Yohanan Bader was appointed Chief Parliamentarian and would play an important role in the institutionalization of the new party in the Knesset. There was also a special department formed to deal with Jews who had arrived from Muslim countries such as Morocco, Libya and Iraq, a group which would eventually form a formidable part of Israel's electorate.

The first offices of Herut were opened in July 1948 in 15 Rothschild Boulevard in Tel Aviv. The temporary staff went into action, all of it Etzel personnel. It then moved to Tchernichovsky 15, Tel Aviv. Branches were opened and run by Etzel men in Tel Aviv, Ramat Gat, Jerusalem, Haifa, Patach Tikva, Bnai Brak, Hedera, Rishon Lezion, and Rehovot. All were established Yishuv cities and villages. Meetings took place all over the country. The main and most sought-after speaker was Menachem Begin, now out of the underground and capturing his audience as he did in Betar in Poland. The challenge to Zohar was clear—the movement appealed to Sephardic Jews and to old Betarim. Registration was spread throughout the nation—all under war conditions, of course.

Herut had the advantage of being composed of young men. Thus Etzel's command and regional officers turned immediately into Herut's party staffers and electoral group. No other group in the history of Zionism succeeded so quickly in turning an underground movement into an electoral party. All this, of course, is to Begin's credit. His dilemmas were real: To fight partition he had to maintain the underground as Kook suggested, but he was clearly opposed to illegal acts in the new state, which would be contrary to his own beliefs and to those of Jabotinsky.

The reaction was not long in coming from Zohar, which had not been consulted at all about so stunning a development in the Revisionist movement. Zohar leaders—Arieh Altman, Meir Grossman, Yaacov Weinstein, and Elizer Shostack, the powerful head of the Nationalist Workers (Revisionist) labor union *Histadrut Ovdim Leumit* (Nationalist Federation of Labor)—all saw the formation of Herut for what it was—a direct challenge to Zohar.

The reaction was one of hurt, outrage and betrayal. Altman and Grossman immediately began dashing off a series of letters to Begin in the form of pamphlets. One of them said: "To the sons of Betar and Zohar and the Sons of Zeev Jabotinsky, wherever you might be. We, a group of Jabotinsky patriots met in Europe to meet the crisis created in the Revisionists Movement by the formation of a new movement, Herut. The purpose is clear: to annihilate the movement of Rosh Betar. There is no purpose in such a movement. There is no reason to divide our forces. There is no new ideology to justify it, nor to challenge the established forms."[9]

The pamphlet attacked both the Vaad and Etzel as co-conspirators, challenging the legacy of Jabotinsky. "Some of them (meaning Vaad), were well known to make the life of our leader miserable when he was still alive. Nor did the new movement even once mention the name of Jabotinsky, except in passing."[10]

Zohar seemed determined to fight. Another pamphlet read: "The answer is *NO*. We will not let it happen. Herut is no heir to Jabotinsky's movement. We shall fight like sons of the wolves (referring to Zeev, which means Wolf). It is clear to us what the purpose of the new movement is—to exploit the heroic dead of Etzel when they were only acting as Jabotinsky's soldiers."

Basically, the struggle was one of seniority, the elders facing a challenge from their offspring. Zohar, perhaps rightfully, claimed seniority. In a meeting on June 2, 1948, between members of the two groups, Begin tried to persuade Zohar that Herut was a "completely new movement." "We," he asserted, "are the only movement which was born in the *Moledet* (the Patrie). The movement had no inspiration from the Diaspora. The movement was established because the Revolt took place in Eretz Israel." Zohar wanted to know if the Herut would accept the authority of World Zohar. Begin rejected the plea. Thus Begin, the Diaspora Betari, is transformed by the Revolt into a Hebrew in Eretz Israel, guarding its territorial integrity.

Now the battle lines were drawn. In a letter to Begin, Meir Grossman, the President of World Zohar, bluntly rejected the idea of Herut. "This is an effort to obliterate Zohar," he wrote. "Herut only duplicates Zohar's doctrines and aims to topple Zohar . . . We cannot accept the formation of two rival nationalist parties."[11]

Begin turned a deaf ear to pleas from loyalists not to challenge Zohar. Shmuel Katz, Begin's chief negotiator with Zohar, challenged Zohar in a letter that let its leadership know that Herut intended boldly to become an international movement, to establish branches and cells in Europe and America.

Zohar now knew that it was on shaky ground. It tried a conciliatory approach, praising the efforts of Begin and Etzel in the revolt but insisting on its right to remain the major political instrument on the nationalistic front.

The pain lay at the core of what was happening. Zohar did not merely feel offended by the presence of Herut, but felt, rightfully, threatened by

Herut's efforts to devour Zohar. Herut was a sword aimed at Zohar's existence.

"Who are you, new recruits of Herut?," a Zohar pamphlet asked, then pleaded, "Return to your home in the World Zohar."

Begin's intent was all too clear. He intended to obliterate Zohar from the political map, even though years later, in a 1974 lecture before the Tel Aviv Institute for Zionist Research, he would say that "Herut was to be the movement in Eretz Israel and Zohar in Diaspora."

It was clear from the 11th Zohar Conference, which met in Tel Aviv in the latter part of 1948, that the Herut takeover was all but complete. There were sixty-three Herut delegates and thirty-two Zohar delegates, which came as a complete shock to the Zohar members. At the conference, it was resolved that "The Zohar Movement in Eretz Israel will unite with the Herut movement founded in Eretz Israel." All the arrangements and constitutional and institutional details were voted on, but this was certainly no unity conference. It represented Herut's takeover of the old-guard Zohar party. Grossman complained loudly and tried to have the union dissolved, but Begin was triumphant and rebuffed a motion that the new movement be subordinate to World Zohar.

Grossman tried one more desperate move. He appealed to the World Zohar High Court to have the union abolished. The court ruled against him. This last-ditch effort further isolated the Zohar, making its members seem like some disgruntled group of old men trying desperately to hang on to power. The only support shown to Zohar was by the independent Nationalist (Revisionist) Workers Union (NWU) whose leadership was hostile to Begin and would remain so in years to come.

The death blow for Zohar came in the 1949 Knesset elections—the first.

For Begin and Herut, the challenge was not to topple Mapai, an unlikely proposition, but rather to prevail against the rival Zohar as well as the Lehi's Fighters Party, which was formed with much less fanfare in 1948. Herut was ready. It had won eighty percent of the delegates in Zohar's 11th Conference, and it had been buttressed by new recruits, including illustrious Revisionists like Shmuel Katz, Eri Jabotinsky, Esther Raziel (David Raziel's sister) and the Biryonim poet laureate Uri Zvi Gruenberg.

For Zohar, the 1949 elections were disastrous. While Herut garnered a not inconsiderable 13 percent of the national vote, making it the third-largest political party in the nation, Zohar failed to get the mandatory 2 percent threshold for Knesset representation, winning only 2,892 votes or 0.66 percent. Zohar as a political movement and organization was finished.

Herut effectively managed to broaden its appeal. It drew its strength from the anti-Socialists of the urban Moshavot areas, from the newly emergent and political conservative Sephardim, as well as from most of the old

Revisionists and Etzel loyalists. After 1949, Zohar all but disappeared; most of its members would end up merging with Herut. The old guard could not defeat the man they described as "power-hungry." They joined in an uncomfortable alliance with Herut in the position of very junior partners. They had been hampered all along by their quiescence, by their lack of leadership and political instincts.

Herut, the parliamentary party in the first Knesset, was led by Begin, and he was joined by Meridor, Bader, Ben Eliezer, Landau Katz, Kook, Merlin and Eri Jabotinsky, along with Chaim Magouri-Cohen and U. Z. Gruenbaum, Unitchman, Altman and Rachel Raziel-Naor.

It was obvious that Herut had become not only Begin's creation and brainchild, but also his political barony and fiefdom. But now, in a challenge that seemed eerily reminiscent of Begin's own challenge to Zohar, he was attacked from within, by the Vaad Leaders who had never given up in their battle with Begin. Now that Zohar was finished, Kook-Merlin still refused to accept Begin's leadership.

In a letter to Begin on April 18, 1950, Eri Jabotinsky attacked him sharply. "Herut lacks clarity and purpose," young Jabotinsky wrote: "The ideology of the movement is frozen. It doesn't serve as an alternative to the government . . . The party was no longer a party of principle . . . it does not fight for the fulfillment of the two sides of the Jordan principle, it has accepted the partitioned state."[12]

He further challenged Begin's unwillingness to integrate with the Nationalist Workers Union, which Begin saw as representing old-style Zohar Revisionism. "Who speaks for Herut's social causes?" asked Jabotinsky, "We *are* the Nationalist Workers Union."[13]

Begin was coming under attack from all sides as political blood spilled. It was noted by Ben Gurion in his diary, cryptically as usual: "In Herut, there is chaos—even after Kook and Eri Jabotinsky were ousted." (They were not ousted. They resigned from the Herut Parliamentary Party in 1951.) Begin was being attacked as an ineffectual leader and financial manager from all directions. Etatists like Merlin and Shmuel Tamir, along with Altman and Zohar, as well as old Lehi fighters like Friedman-Yellin, all challenged Begin; they charged that Begin had lost his messianic zeal.

Worse for Begin, he and Herut had lost some of their punch at the polls. In the September 1951 elections, for the second Knesset, Herut dropped from fourteen to eight seats, losing some five thousand votes.

Faced by the challenge from within, depressed over the 1951 election results, which he had hoped would solidify his position and institutionalize his party, Begin despaired. He was struck by one of those periodic bouts of depression that arose in his career (when the Nazis invaded Poland, in the *Altalena* affair) and would do so again (during the 1981 elections, in the wake of the Lebanon invasion). For Begin, these are moments of total darkness and despair, fits of indecisiveness. At this low point, he wanted to quit. He tendered his resignation as Herut party chairman, handed it to Ben Eliezer, resigned from the Knesset, and went off on a tour of the Herut movement abroad. He announced his decision to resume the career he had been trained for: the law.

As in the past, and in the future, Begin could not quite be counted out, although many knowledgeable observers at the time did so, either decrying or gloating over a political career that seemed to be over.

As we shall see, Begin once again emerged from the shadows to tame his internal opposition and to rise again as a force in Israeli politics.

23

The Parliamentarian[1]

Now there was no Etzel—no British, no *Altalena,* no war with Arabs. Begin's party, Herut, had been ostracized by the mainstream political coalition led by Prime Minister David Ben Gurion. Herut was out in the opposition. None of its men were recruited or promoted in Israel's emerging bureaucracy and military. No former Etzel officer had a chance to go beyond major or lieutenant colonel in the IDF. The taste of exclusion, of isolation, of insult by Ben Gurion in Parliament directed at Begin, was indeed bitter. What was left for Begin and his party but the Knesset? In the Knesset it found a home, a base for action, although even here its members were never assigned positions in senior and key parliamentary committees. For Begin, the Knesset was not a legislative body. It was a platform for speeches on Eretz Israel.

To see Menachem Begin at work in the formative years of the Knesset is to see a lonely figure, the lone champion of parliamentary politics. Not a distinguished legislator, he became one of the Knesset's best and most vocal orators. The Knesset was Begin's theater.

This may seem like a strange, contradictory idea when one thinks in terms of popularly held clichés. Israeli institutions, as built by the Mapai Party, are as firmly democratic as one would care to find. And Begin, in many ways, is perceived as authoritarian, a wild figure of the right.

This is not to suggest that Begin was a hard-working legislator, purposefully building the web of democratic structures like a patient spider. Begin, in fact, had little patience for the actual legislative workings of the Knesset. Rather, he embodied the idea of parliamentary politics itself, defended it, insisted on it in a way that the centralized forces of Mapai and the huge political figure of David Ben Gurion did not. For Mapai, the Knesset was only one arena, like the Cabinet, not a major one. For Begin, the Knesset was his single arena of expression, of political influence.

To get some idea of how Begin fit into this brand new parliament, and how the institution itself functioned against the background of the new state, it is necessary to examine at some length the roots of what constitutes politics, electioneering, and political institutions in what was to become the state of Israel.

The state of Israel emerged from the Yishuv, another institution entirely. From the Yishuv, the new state inherited the traditions of a democratic society, and a tradition of state-building and party-state relations whose history extended back to 1905, against the backdrop of Socialist-Zionist pioneering.

It is important to realize the contradiction that lies at the heart of the Socialist-Zionist state builders. They espoused and believed in a parliamentary-democratic form of government, but all their efforts at state-building, almost of necessity, took the form of a very centralized, elitist structure.

The legacy of the Socialist Zionists was imprinted on all socio-economic and political institutions and structures of the Yishuv and of the new state. Yet, ironically, it would seem to the outside observer, the one area which was badly neglected in the political development of the Yishuv and Zionism was the building and operation of a legislative assembly. The Zionist movement—and this is one reason why it was successful—was composed of strong, charismatic, powerful leaders—elitists and authoritarian personalities. This was as true of Herzl, Weizmann, Ben Gurion and Jabotinsky as it was of the second and third echelon of Yishuv and Zionist leadership. In a contradictory way, Zionism and the Yishuv, both of which were imbued with a voluntaristic quality, managed to establish highly personalist forms of administration and central rule. This sprang from the very nature of these movements, none of which had a political base, homeland, or state to call their own. It was run by powerful individuals and centralists who operated within the confines of an executive, not a legislative structure.

True, there were the Zionist Congresses, the early Jewish parliaments, and elections to a variety of assemblies of one sort or another. But the Zionist Congresses met infrequently, at best once every four years. They were more a demonstration of Zionist unity and purpose than they were actual working parliaments. The Jewish Agency, which continued to operate between one congress or another was actually the Zionist executive arm. Elections to the congresses were democratic, but haphazard. By paying a shekel (an appropriate amount), one could vote for the Zionist Congress.

Yet representation was dominated by Zionist political parties, in which the iron law of oligarchy was predominant. This was, ironically, the only way they could effectively accomplish their gargantuan and historic task of organizing immigration to Palestine, purchasing land, conducting diplomacy and building an army—which would lead to the eventual formation of the Jewish state.

In Palestine, both the Arabs and the Jews were vehemently opposed to the formation of mutual national assemblies. Therefore, the Yishuv would vote for its own assemblies, again mobilized by the principal Jewish political parties. Beginning with 1917, for over thirty years, there were only five elections held to the national assembly of the Jewish Agency. By 1935, Mapai, the party of the Socialist-Zionists, had become the dominant political party operating in the Yishuv and within Zionism itself. It was conducting the affairs of the Yishuv and the Jewish Agency in an authoritative fashion. Mapai managed to penetrate into every area of the life of the Yishuv. Its impact was felt in economics, in labor, culture, in social organizations, as well as in military decisions and the conduct of diplomacy, and, of course, within politics itself. The Socialist Zionists created the Histadrut, the settlement system of big industrial and agricultural cooperatives. It dominated the Haganah, illegal immigration, the intelligence services, and diplomacy.

The career of Ben Gurion is in many ways highly representative of the dominance of Mapai-Histadrut. Between 1922 and 1930, he was secretary-general of the Histadrut and from 1930's onward he headed Mapai and the Jewish Agency for Palestine and in 1947 head of its Defense Department. When the new state that he had helped to forge was created, he became head of the government, head of Mapai and held the defense portfolio. He used his leadership in the Yishuv in Mapai and in Zionism to catapult himself into the role of chief architect of Jewish and Zionist diplomacy, although at one time or another, he had to share this responsibility with Weizmann and the American Jewish leaders. In the position of Defense Chief from 1947 on, he would set the strategy and structure for the future of the first Israeli Army, the IDF. He was the true father of the IDF. Mapai, with Ben Gurion at its head, set the tone and strategy of every aspect of Israeli statehood in the first decade of Israeli politics. Ben Gurion was the Israeli George Washington, the father of Jewish statehood, and the founder of Israel. Mapai treated Israeli society as a private fiefdom over which it had almost absolute control. Its pioneer, elitist ideology permeated every aspect of society. Mapai as a political party derived its power not from the parliamentary or electoral process but from the institutions it had created: Histadrut, Kibbutz, the economic enterprises and the largest institution of all, the state.

Although Ben Gurion and the Mapai party were dedicated to the *idea* of parliamentary institutions, they did little to make the legislature an important institution. In their domination and development of Israeli pioneer society, they established the socioeconomic, not the political-legislative, foundation of the state. They established the state bureaucracy and military and they dominated the Cabinet. Their party penetrated all the state's activities, but the Knesset was not a significant instrument of power for Mapai and Ben Gurion.

The Knesset, however, would turn out to be a natural arena for Begin, and even more so for his lieutenant, Dr. Bader. If Begin was not a legislative activist, he was nevertheless a believer in parliamentarianism. In theory and in practice, he was dedicated to the concept of parliamentary democracy. He was raised on the workings of the Polish Sejm, where the Jewish delegates had the rights of a minority, and he came to see the Knesset as a combination of the British Parliament and the Sejm. Although the Sejm was, historically, not the most democratic of institutions, especially under the rule of the authoritarian Pilsudski and the colonels, it still often gave lip service to the idea of minority representation, as minorities comprised 46 percent of the Polish population.

Begin himself was familiar with the work of Jewish delegates to the Sejm, and he brought this knowledge with him to the Knesset, perhaps appropriately since Herut was so decidedly a minority political party. For Begin, a besieged minority, the Knesset must become a political fortress within whose walls the rights of minorities would be protected.

The transformation of the underground leader of the Revolt into Menachem Begin, Member of Parliament, leader of a political party—into a politician, as he was in Betar Poland—was not his most desired goal. Without a doubt, his emergence from the shadow world of the legendary underground must have come as a great surprise to many, above all to Begin himself. Part of the problem was that he simply did not look the part of a charismatic leader, and the general populace had a lot of faces and personages with whom they could compare him. There were the dashing, military heroes of Palmach and the Haganah like Dayan with his rakish eyepatch; there were Allon and Rabin. There were more startling examples within his own party, forceful men like Shimshon Unitchman and Hillel Kook, who was always manicured and dressed in well-tailored clothes.

By contrast Begin was frail, unassuming, looking at best like a middle-class Histadrut-Mapai operator, at worst like a middle-class Polish Jew emerging from a time machine, a season or two spent out of the sun. He still sported a weak mustache, but he was dressed in ill-fitting old Warsaw clothes, suits that seemed as if they were tailored decades ago. He looked neither like a revolutionary hero nor like a charismatic political leader, but rather like someone's poor relation.

For a moment, I must digress to a personal memory that is pertinent. On February 19, 1949, when the first Knesset opened for business, I was a junior officer in the newly formed IDF, assigned as a Knesset guard, and I happened to get my first glimpse of Begin upon his arrival. At the time, the Knesset met in the main hall of the Jewish Agency in the Rehavia section of Jerusalem.

The bourgeois lawyer, head of Herut. The only pain is the political desert. 1951. (The Jabotinsky Institute)

מולדה

The crator: Moledet and Herut (Patrie and Freedom) speaking before party audience. Israel, c. 1952. (The Jabotinsky Institute)

Minister without portfolio flanked by Generals Ariel Sharon and Avraham Yoffe, victors of the 1967 Sinai War. June 14, 1967. (Government of Israel, Press Office Photo Department)

Retired Prime Minister Ben Gurion sits with "Knesset member who sits next to Dr. Bader"—minister without portfolio. Begin, General Ezer Weizman, and David Ben Gurion. Knesset, Jerusalem, December 11, 1967. (Government of Israel, Press Office Photo Department)

Prime Minister designate
Menachem Begin kisses the hand
of Mrs. Katzir.
Between the two,
President Ephraim Katzir.
June 7, 1977.
(Government of Israel,
Press Office Photo Department)

"What kind of nonsense
is written in Davar?"
Yehiel Kadishai is unusually serene.
Jerusalem, June 21, 1977.
(Government of Israel,
Press Office Photo Department)

Mrs. Prime Minister, June 7, 1977.
(Government of Israel,
Press Office Photo Department)

Anwar al-Sadat and the Israeli team in Camp David. Seated from left to right are: Professor Barak, Begin, Kadishai, an aide, General Poran, Sadat, standing behind Sadat, General Tamir. September 17, 1978. (Government of Israel, Press Office Photo Department)

"Oh, really, Anwar!" and "What about it, Menachem?"—an intense Carter sits in the corner. Camp David, September 6, 1978. (Government of Israel, Press Office Photo Department)

The Camp David Trio in the White House. Only Jimmy touches his heart. September 1978. (Government of Israel, Press Office Photo Department)

"And what do you think, Ben Gurion?" Speaking in a meeting to commemorate Ben Gurion. Jerusalem, September 30, 1980.

The conqueror of Lebanon pointing already to a line far above the forty-kilometer war. Ariel Sharon and his favorite maps. June 1982. (Government of Israel, Press Office Photo Department)

The day the Lebanese lifted an Israeli flag, "Welcome, liberators," in Lebanon. They produce several flags for multiple welcomes. June 8, 1982, South Lebanon. (Government of Israel, Press Office Photo Department)

"So the price of Israel's leaders is in the next world, according to the Talmud?" queries the Prime Minister. Begin's last photo as head of the Cabinet. June 15, 1983. (Government of Israel, Press Office Photo Department)

Now, Begin's face was familiar to me from the old CID wanted posters, but I was not quite prepared for the man in the flesh, and not only because of the way he looked. All the cabinet members, and Ben Gurion himself had arrived in a wave of formal limousines, but suddenly I heard cries of "Begin, Begin." From my stand near the top of the fence surrounding the building, I looked around and here came Begin, *walking* to the first formal opening of the Knesset. He was passing the old Synagogue Yeshurun just across from the Knesset building. There was pushing and shoving as the police tried to maintain some kind of order. Begin was waving his hand over his head, a gesture that would become a trademark. He looked as if he were holding a Torah over his head in a traditional sign of respect and victory.

For me, as for many of my generation, Begin had become a symbol of Jews fighting against the Mandatory, and yet, watching him stride up the steps to the Knesset, myself standing next to Yigal Allon, in my youth one of my personal heroes, Begin looked oddly unimpressive, almost quiescent.

I heard Begin give his maiden speech in the Knesset, and I was struck by the Polish accent and the meticulous Hebrew, which struck a familiar chord in me. I realized that Begin reminded me very much of my old grammar school Hebrew teacher. So close was the resemblance, and so strong was the feeling that I almost expected Begin to point his finger at me and say, "Perlmutter, you, of course, did not memorize Bialik by heart." Which is to say that Begin seemed somehow very pedantic, heavy-handed and preachy in his manner.

It must be remembered that while Begin was, in thought and spirit, the very champion of parliamentary democracy, he had no patience for the actual legislative workings of government. He spent most of his time making speeches and traveling in Europe, even in Argentina, where he met Perón, and in a variety of countries where he was sure to be received warmly. The Jabotinsky photo archives have more pictures of Begin's 1951 tour of Latin America than I found of him in Israel between 1949 and 1959.

Begin had no time for the tedious work of committees, deal-making and legislation. Here, Dr. Bader proved to an invaluable workhorse, and he would be a significant influence in helping to establish the rules and behavior of Israel's new parliament. Not in vain did Bader call his autobiography *The Knesset and I.* It was Bader who would be active on committees, including such basically inglorious, but essential committees as Procedure, Justice and Finance, where he would play a key role in setting and processing legislation—the bare bones work of any parliament.

Begin and Herut obviously had high hopes for the first Knesset, but Begin nevertheless failed to distinguish himself. Nor was Herut much of a political force, with good reason. The policy of contempt, isolation, and denigration effectively orchestrated by Ben Gurion hurt Begin. On the floor of the chamber Ben Gurion either ignored him or effectively insulted him. Ben Gurion also made sure that Herut would have no access to the genuinely crucial committee of Foreign Affairs and Defense. To this day, Bader resents the exclusion. "Each one of our fourteen members would have certainly preferred to become a member of the Foreign Affairs or Defense committees. We saw in them an opportunity to continue Etzel's political fight for a sovereign Jewish state in Complete Israel . . . But as Jabotinsky taught us, where there is no man, try to be one. So I agreed to become a member of the justice, law and finance committees."[2]

The next fight for Begin and Herut in the Knesset would be over Jerusalem and its identity. It was the second round fought by Herut against partition, the fight over the Bernadotte Plan, which called for a second partition of Palestine—dividing Jerusalem while internationalizing it as well.

The Swedish Count Bernadotte initially proposed the plan on June 11, 1948, during the first truce between the Arabs and Jews, which Bernadotte had negotiated. He had been negotiating with Dr. Goldmann, Weizmann, and Moshe Shertok (Sharett) and he was of the conviction (like the U.S. State Department and the British Foreign Service) that a binational entity was preferable to a partitioned state. At first, Bernadotte had called for Arab domination of Jerusalem, and the exchange of the Galilee for the Negev, a concept which was angrily rejected by Ben Gurion. Later he would reverse himself in favor of making Jerusalem an international city, but both sides, Jews and Arabs, found the idea intolerable. In any case, his plan was derailed by events when the war resumed, and later, he himself would be assassinated by Lehi terrorists. When hostilities resumed, Israeli forces ended up occupying the Negev and the Galilee, which were territories in the November 1948 UN partition, by force, not by negotiation. It was the IDF, not the UN or Begin that selected the division.

At the time, Bernadotte's plan smacked of conspiracy, but in any event, the Arab resumption of war made the plan obsolete. In addition, there was no Bernadotte to impose it. But the status of Jerusalem would remain a volatile issue, and Begin and his Herut party would make it a rallying cry in the Knesset in the years to come.

"Our responsibility is high, and we will do the best we can," he said in his first Knesset speech, and basically Begin would remain faithful to that tenet, through thick and thin, through opposition from within and without, and through scathing, open attacks from his biggest enemy and rival, David Ben Gurion.

24

The Ideology of Menachem Begin—
The Ideology of Herut[1]

What was Herut? Did it have a different ideology than the old Revisionism? Was it once more a one-man party, this time Begin's? The answer is simple: Herut is Begin's party more than Zohar was ever Jabotinsky's, and if Herut's ideology is Begin's, what, then, is Begin's ideology?

Even though he often toiled in the shadows of great men like Jabotinsky and Ben Gurion, Begin was never a minor political figure in Israel. What is remarkable about him are his relatively brief spurts of vivid achievement—the years of the Revolt and Etzel, and his ascension to the Prime Ministership of Israel decades later.

The paradoxes in the man, and his ideas and ideology, remained constant through triumph and relative obscurity. As he shrank politically, however, he became more of a Jabotinsky purist. A biographer seeking to discover something of the inner person would normally turn to a man's writings and speeches to find the sources and inspiration of his deeds. With Begin, this represents a difficult and tremendously tedious task. Yet a theme emerges, and it is, in the end, something of a tragic one. What one discovers is that somewhere in his life, Begin became impervious to change, remained wedded to the concepts of his mentor Jabotinsky and struck a stubborn, constant tone to the end of his political life. Because he could not change, Herut, his party, could not change either, until electoral conditions, the decline of Labor and domestic and regional and international events made it ripe for acceptance, but only under the cloak of Likud.

But first, let us, in order to penetrate Begin's rhetoric, try to distill some of his ideas from his speeches and pamphlets, his writings. This represents a tedious chore; although Begin is an interesting writer, his syntax is complex, rhetorical and repetitive. Up to 1944, Begin's writings were sporadic and meager. He became more prolific and ideologically mature with the Revolt. By the time he formed the Herut, the ideologies of Begin and Herut were synonymous; Herut's ideology is found in his writing beginning in 1949.

Begin's articles and essays are replete with legalistic, Latin phrases. He spoke and read in Hebrew, Polish, Russian, Yiddish, English, and German. He also knew some Latin. As a literary person, he is remarkably similar to Ben Gurion, and in this, he is a genuine rival of Ben Gurion. Both men were, to be frank, terrible writers. Begin never comes quickly to a point; he exhausts the reader with long, meandering opening paragraphs. Reading Begin, you can hear him talking, because for Begin, writing is another form of speechmaking.

Like Ben Gurion, Begin hid his personality in his writing, including his letters. Both men had pretensions to be sage political philosophers. Ben Gurion's *forte* was to present himself as a biblical scholar, archeologist and historian. Begin paraded his knowledge of law, his concern with legality and his Latin.

Here is a rather lengthy example of just how pedantic and simplistic Begin could actually get. In a Herut pamphlet, *World and National View* (1952) and *Leftism, Nationalism, Nationhood* (1965) Begin set his world outlook. In fact, it is in this fifty-page pamphlet that the Herut ideology is established, not to be changed until his retirement in 1983.

First, in a dangerously naive analysis of Marxism, he attacked it as a false prophecy and castigated the errors of international Socialism (including social democracy). Analyzing in a rather rudimentary way "socialism" in its varieties—Marxism, Revisionism, Communism and the assorted left— Begin ridicules " 'scientific socialism' (i.e. Marxism) as a false prophecy." Marx's notion that the accumulation of wealth in highly industrial societies is accompanied by an endless process of poverty has not been proven. "On the contrary, the process of poverty has deepened in underdeveloped nations"—i.e. Marxism is a false prophecy.[2]

The socialist camp (including various Social Democrats) are fighting each other "not in debates or conferences but with tanks, guns and planes". Socialism is not cosmopolitanism. It is now used in the pejorative in Lenin's land. And what do all socialist groups and parties have in common? Internecine warfare and fratricide. "In our era a new left has emerged" he writes in 1965, "of course pretending to raise the flag of the most progressive progress. Therefore the new left issues itself license to do."[3] This is the legacy of the Biryonim, but short of the Hebrew-Canaanite ideology. Then he moved to Revisionism's Herut, middle-class, liberal policies.

From there, Begin focuses on a discussion of personal freedom, societal reform, and the supremacy of law. His discussion resembles the testimony of a nineteenth century liberal, as freely ranging over the French Declaration of Rights, the American Constitution, and an exhaustive explanation of the concept of Herut (Freedom), including the spiritual, political, and economic freedoms. Liberty, Freedom in Begin's writings are abstract and fundamental concepts. They do not relate to the reality of zionism in the newly established Israel.

Then Begin's prose is weighed down by an overconfidence of Latin, talking about *fabricae adsciptus* (tied to the factory), *glebae adsciptus* (tied to the land), *cuius regio lius relegio* (the one who rules dictates your religion), and so forth, all in order to explain the separation of the ruler from the ruled, his point being that no party, certainly Herut, must be separated from the people.

Begin's use of Latin in the essay is redundant and unnecessary. It is used to impress the reader with his sagacity, a technique he often used in Knesset speeches, never quite realizing that he often put his listeners to sleep. There is snobbism in the use of Latin, a way of declaring that he, Begin, was better educated than the Socialist-Zionist ruffians and the small shtetl boys.

Later in the essay he comes to his concern with supremacy of law. "According to the Weltanschauung of true freedom lovers . . . the law and judge must be autonomous of the ruler . . . we have chosen the emblem of our flag of freedom *(Herut)* and the supremacy of the law."[4] He launches into a review of the Montesquean separation of powers, which amounts to no more than a high school civics lesson in the basic division of power within government. Begin's concept of the Revolt and of politics was fundamentalist. As a nineteenth-century Liberal, he was unconcerned with the social and political aspects of the state-to-be. Once again, he cites Marxism as a false doctrine (while ignoring the influence of nationalism). From there, the quintessential Herut ideology: the Liberation of the Moledet or Patrie. "Our national outlook," he wrote, "is set in the liberation of the Moledet and the territorial concentration, reuniting the old Herzlian concept of the ingathering of the Jewish nation in the Jewish land." Where it differs from the old Herzlian conception is its embracing Jabotinsky's refrain of the liberation of *all* the land of Israel. Here is the essence of Beginism in our times—complete Jewish sovereignty over Eretz Israel, liberty or death. In the Herut platform, written and edited by Begin, special sections were devoted to opposing the deprivation of the newcomers of ethnic origin (e.g., Sephardim), to rescuing Jews in the Arab countries, and to planning to help make them citizens and loyalists. The appeal to a traditional, nationalist, nonsocialist, non-Ashkenazi constituency was Herut's focus as early as October 1948. This constituency became Begin's most loyal group of supporters, and their votes helped to place him into power in 1977 and in 1981. This policy was deliberate in the tradition of Betar and Etzel in Palestine whose number of Sephardim fighters was high.

Begin was not a creator of ideas but a messenger bearing a message from the word of Zeev Jabotinsky into a romantic future. Throughout his life, Begin has believed that he never wavered from his mentor's ideology even when, in practical political terms, he needed to do so the most. He never doubted Jabotinsky, and he was hostile to change. For Begin, Jabotinsky was the irreplaceable Rosh Betar, and for all of his life he would remain Jabotinsky's praetorian guard, the keeper of the flame. Thus he doomed himself and Herut to the symbols and rhetoric of old-line Revisionism, including a heavy reverence for militarism and martyrdom. The movement often seemed to survive only on pain. Again and again, the old images, the old wounds, are raised up for adoration—Shlomo Ben Yoseph, the Etzel soldier executed by the British, the Sezon, *Altalena*, the Revolt, the Etzel terrorists that were executed by perfidious Albion. Herut became the depository of Etzel's glorious past. The Revolt was the step that Jabotinsky aspired to and Begin has fulfilled.

For the Hebrew resistance movement, martyrdom was of course a powerful symbol and source of motivation, as well as a powerful moral force. The ideology of Begin, even as leader of Herut, remained the ideology of the Revolt of defiance and death, and is anchored in the postulates of Jabotinsky. The watchwords of Jabotinsky—*Hadar* (majesty), *Gaon* (genius), *Adiv* (polite) and *Achzar* (ruthlessness)—become, for Begin, Revolt-Herut symbols and would remain so. But Begin carries the Revolt into martyrdom.

Symbols were, after all, Jabotinsky's way to spread the flame of Revisionism. Begin inherited those symbols and remained frozen at their level.

Begin's major achievement was to mold a party against great insurmountable odds, attacked and beset as he was not only by Ben Gurion, but by rivals from within. His success was to swallow Zohar and establish Herut, to convert a political underground into a funtioning political party, a remarkable feat in Socialist-controlled Israeli politics.

Without a break, Begin emulated Jabotinsky, waving the banner of Two Sides of the Jordan confident of eventual success. Ben Gurion and Mapai so dominated the nation that Begin and Herut remained ineffectual, in the prison of the more or less loyal opposition.

Actually, Begin had already lost the battle with Ben Gurion upon the dissolution of Etzel and the burning of the *Altalena*. It would take years of fighting over the political role of the opposition before Begin would fulfill his potential and meet his old foe on somewhat of an equal footing.

25

The Holy Canon: Begin Versus Ben Gurion[1]

The early years of Begin's parliamentary life were dominated by the shadow of his chief antagonist, David Ben Gurion. In Parliament Begin was constantly subjected to Ben Gurion's wrath and insults.

When you think about the endless struggle between David Ben Gurion and Menachem Begin, you notice two things almost immediately. The first is the ferocity that went into it, especially on the part of Ben Gurion. The second is its one-sidedness. From the outset, it was a David vs. Goliath battle (with "David" being Goliath, in this case). The battle between the little giant of Zionism and the frail heir of Jabotinsky was grossly unequal.

Ben Gurion, the Lion of Judea, a small, striking man, brought the weight of his stature and position in history to the struggle, as well as an undying enmity—not entirely toward Begin, but toward what he stood for—the forces of Revisionism. Ben Gurion was not politically generous. In the path of his political life, there were several, important casualties—among them, Chaim Weizmann, whom he pushed into the obscure office of President of Israel.

Ben Gurion had always fought Revisionism, even though he personally respected Jabotinsky. Revisionism for Ben Gurion represented the opposite of Socialist Zionism; its romanticism, militarism and mass appeal threatened his own movement. He would go to any lengths to destabilize Revisionism, eradicate it, discredit it, turn it into a pariah movement in the ranks of Zionism and in Israel. He had shown this during the Arlazaroff affair, he had shown it during the Sezon and during the seizure of the *Altalena* and he would show it again throughout in the way he treated Begin and Herut in the early decades of the life of the State of Israel.

In retrospect, the hostile struggle, especially as conducted by Ben Gurion, seems almost not worth the effort, especially when you compare the stature of the two men at the time.

Ben Gurion was an authentic statesman and Zionist leader, an ideologue and commander without peer who had been a major figure within the Yishuv and Zionism since the beginning in the 1930's and would remain so for the first two decades of Israel's existence. He established the IDF and through it would set military, security and foreign policy. He was the author and embodiment of the doctrine of *Mamlachtiout,* the dominance of the state over society, economics, and politics. He had set the norm for Israel's coalition government and molded the IDF, the tool with which Israel would keep the Arabs at bay. He helped make the IDF the leading military force in the Middle East, an achievement that would place him squarely in the history books.

Ben Gurion had come to power as the new state's leader in 1948 after years of leading Israel's trade unions and its major political party, after being its chief diplomat and its leader during the war of liberation. By 1948, Ben Gurion was already celebrating forty-three years of active participation in Zionist history.

By contrast, Begin was neither a statesman, nor a Zionist philosopher. He was a pale replica of Jabotinsky. While Ben Gurion was forging ahead as the unchallenged leader of Mapai, Begin was only a struggling functionary among the Betar ranks in Poland, where even Jabotinsky treated him with some scorn. He never set foot in Palestine until 1943, where, still in the Polish uniform of the Anders Army, he would be tapped to lead Etzel and to lead the Revolt, his first major achievement for the Zionist movement. Until then he had been an excellent propagandist and speechifier as a regional Betar leader. When Ben Gurion became head of the state, Begin was struggling to make the transition from underground leader to head of a small and indecisive political party.

When the new state of Israel emerged, Mapai was already a firmly entrenched, powerful political party which dominated the state, the instrument of state-making. Its ranks included pioneers, ideologues, military leaders, diplomats, bureaucrats and statesmen. Begin's Herut party, by contrast, was replete with ex-terrorists, radical ideologues (Kook, Merlin) and leftover Revisionists who had played only a small role within the Yishuv and Zionism.

While Mapai ruled the state, Herut, as a new party in transition, was busy trying to legitimize itself and decide if it was the true heir of Jabotinsky's moderate Revisionism or more a party along the lines of its motto— "Herut, founded by Etzel." In 1949 Herut was peculiarly uncomfortable within the ranks of politics and unprepared to participate in parliamentary politics.

It was in the Knesset that the battle between Ben Gurion and Begin was fought and where Ben Gurion unleashed his contempt. It was a vicious battle. At best, Begin was a leader of the right-wing opposition, although Ben Gurion never gave him that much recognition or respect. He used a strategy of personal character assassination, insult and naked contempt in dealing with Begin, with the goal of delegitimizing both the history of Etzel and the standing of Herut as a political party. As far back as the 1930s, Ben Gurion had called the Revisionists "Fascists and Nazis," and he did not change his tactics in dealing with Begin.

He called Begin that "bespectacled petty Polish solicitor," and a "clown." Begin, less prone to reply in kind, was always on the defensive, unable to deal with Ben Gurion's sarcasm and insults. Sometimes the insults would run a colorful, bilingual gamut.

In their rivalry, both men were trying to set their version of history for posterity, especially when recording the *Altalena,* or "holy cannon" affair.

One of the most famous exchanges between the two occurred in 1955, when Begin was still trying to exonerate both himself and Etzel over whether or not he had violated state laws and called for insurrection leading to a civil war between the Jews.

Debating in the 5th Knesset, Begin spoke with a plaintive note, pointing at Ben Gurion, "He had ordered to shoot at me with a cannon," referring to Ben Gurion's order to have the ship destroyed while Begin was still on it.

Ben Gurion was not the least bit ashamed; he sounded proud. "I was the man," he said, "who issued the order for a holy cannon to fire on the ship."

"You will be called to justice for it," Begin yelled.

"We voted to destroy the *Altalena* and our decision came to fruition," Ben Gurion replied.

Begin saw it more passionately. "The words, the deed, is that you spilled innocent blood."[2]

It's quite clear from Ben Gurion's war diary that he would brook no opposition. He meant to destroy Etzel and show that he was pleased with the outcome of the *Altalena* affair. "If Etzel revolts, it will be suppressed. Etzel is mistaken if it thinks it is confronted with liberal vegetarians. I helped Gruenbaum [the Interior Minister] arrange for peace even if I didn't believe I could achieve an amicable arrangement. But it will be necessary for Etzel to be mercilessly suppressed and be unable to raise their hands again . . . Etzel and Lehi are trying to walk over the state and murder it. Blessed be the cannon that blew up this ship. If the Temple were built again, there could be no better place for it."[3]

Begin saw things differently.

"It was our force that won against the British," he wrote Dr. Bader, asserting what he saw as Etzel's rightful importance and legitimacy. "We have always been in the right. After all, no one has served our nation more loyally than we have."[4]

Begin tried to rise to the level of a statesman. He shaved his mustache to look more respectable. He traveled abroad, where he was received warmly by old Betar and Etzel veterans. "Everywhere I am treated better than in Israel" he wrote when he visited Juan Perón in Argentina. This was true of his many trips to the United States. In 1948 he was celebrated as a luminary in New York City.

In the Knesset, he cultivated the image of being above the battle, while seeking controversial issues with which to flail Ben Gurion and the government. His goal was to be viewed by the Israeli electorate as an alternative to Ben Gurion and Mapai. He was uncompromising on such issues as the territories.

In the streets and during elections, he attacked the armistice agreements, which he said would "bring about the loss of half of the territory (the West Bank). They (Mapai) must be tried for this terrible disaster that they have brought on the nation,"[5] he accused.

Years after the fact, Begin reminisced about his debates with Ben Gurion in the Knesset seeing them as titanic, oratorical battles. Perhaps that's the way he remembers them; perhaps that's the way they seemed to him at the time.

But Begin's main battles occurred when, within the ranks of his own followers, repeated attempts to depose him were mounted.

In the early 1950s, after the War of Independence, when Israel was preoccupied with establishing political and military viability, Begin was not yet seen as a leader of the loyal opposition. In the hierarchy of Israel's coalition politics, Herut was on the fringe, out of the mainstream. Herut appealed to the old diehard Etzel stalwarts, and it thus acquired the status of an oracle not a party.

It would remain an outsider for a long time to come, until the late sixties and seventies, when the influx of Sephardic Jewish immigrants in the 1950s reached political maturity and saw themselves reflected in Begin. Both were outsiders, on the way inside.

26

The Underground Against Herut:
The Challenge of the Militants[1]

THE CHALLENGE OF SULAM

The birth of Herut emerging as it did from the ruins of Zohar, the dissolution of Etzel, and the trauma of the *Altalena* affair, was extremely painful.

As the new party struggled to assume a role in the state of Israel, resentment arising from the pain of confusion grew within its ranks. Much of it was directed against Begin, who had dropped the image of underground leader to become a Knesset politician. Many of the radical ex-Etzelites felt betrayed. They had worn their heroism proudly, and now that heroic spirit, sustained throughout the Revolt, was being systematically dismantled for the mundane political world of the Knesset.

Already, the Vaad militants in Jerusalem were intriguing against Begin's leadership. As a new sort of underground, more vehement, more dangerous in some sense, was beginning to make itself felt, the threat came from the right, from the remnants of Lehi and Stern disciples.

The legacy of the Biryonim was resurrected, now in the person of Israel Shayeb-Eldad, who as Stern's former cohort and the former Lehi chief of ideology, had established a club and a nationalist messianic historical magazine called *Sulam* (The Ladder) which sought to take on the character of a new underground movement. Shayeb was joined by the old guard of the Biryonim, poet U. Z. Gruenberg, and novelists, pamphleteers, poets and ideologues like Aba Achimeir, and Y. Yeyvin. Eldad worked in the style of Stern and Lehi; it was responsible for the assassinations of Lord Moyne and Bernadotte. It now contemplated the assassination of Ben Gurion. For Eldad, the government of Ben Gurion was a cabal of traitors that had forsaken the ideals of messianic Zionism. "Essentially," wrote Shayeb, "there is no difference between the government of Israel and the Mandatory."[2] They called for the overthrow of the government of Israel.[3]

Sulam and Shayeb advocated the restoration of the old historical kingdom of Israel. The Ladder, quite literally, meant ascending toward the fulfillment of greater Israel. Sulam claimed borders stretching from the Nile to the Euphrates. In their writings, they advocated that "the Nation of Israel could achieve its potential only when the Kingdom of Israel is restored." So wrote one of the Sulamites, Yaacov Heruti: "The type of government and life that form that nation and the Torah—give us both belief and action . . . The Torah laws are the nation's foundation. The state of Israel violates these rules, separating religion from the state. The direct consequences of this separation is the total loss of the national character."[4] In and of itself, this seems like an old, preaching, radical form of the messianic dream of a Jewish Kingdom in its historical boundaries. The approach is by no means democratic, since kingdoms tend to be run by kings, not Knessets or parliaments or political parties.

Sulam's third target was Zionism's primary foe—the Soviet Union and international Communism. Sulam called for a war against the USSR as a response to Stalinist anti-Semitism and the anti-Semitic trials in Czechoslovakia in 1953.

The challenge of Sulam was not only to the government but to Begin's control of Herut. Their attacks included a renewed, if futile war against the British Empire, which Sulam and Shayeb considered Israel's and the Kingdom of Israel's principal enemy. The British, they complained, had been ousted from Palestine, but were making new inroads in the Middle East against Israel with their maneuverings with Iraq and Jordan, which resulted in the Baghdad Pact in 1954. Sulam had declared a second war against the British Empire. Sulam defied the laws of the state by advocating a continuation of revolutionary activities.

The Shayeb group was a fanatic group of hard-core, antidemocrats. While Begin and Herut hoped to topple the Ben Gurion government by legitimate, electoral means, the new Sternists of the 1950s quite openly advocated violent overthrow of the government. Yellin and Shamir veteran Sternists split from Eldad. Sulam called Begin a "traitor" and heaped abuse on Friedman-Yellin and Yitzchak Shamir, who were quietly moving to the "left" advocating the "neutralization" of the Middle East. The latter writings were typical of Third World anti-imperialism, seeing the Arabs as victims of the reactionary classes. Shayeb and his group were slowly and painfully tunneling into the heart of Herut, creating havoc and arousing opposition to Begin.

For Begin the struggle with Sulam was the continuation of his old battle against the left and right Sternists, who had challenged his leadership in the past. Begin, according to Eldad, "betrayed" Herut. Sulam penetrated into Herut by reaching old Etzel radicals who were unhappy with Begin's preference for parliamentary life. For them the time had not arrived for the end of the Revolt.

Sulam translated its beliefs into action with terrorist activities that roused all Israel against it, and indirectly, against Begin. In a fit of anti-Communism, members of Sulam tried to sabotage the Soviet Embassy in Tel Aviv and threatened to send letter bombs to Moscow, all the while resurrecting the image of Stern and the old renegades.

The victims of this internecine, underground and violent activity were Begin and Herut. Forever trying to legitimize himself and his party by demarcating Herut from Lehi and Stern, Begin was being tarnished by association with terrorists.

When some of the Sulam activists were apprehended and jailed, Begin had to disown them. "This underground," he proclaimed, "insults the name of the underground in Israel."

The more Begin sought legitimacy, the more it seemed to elude him. This was because Israel in the 1950s, was not a country of political extremes.

This was never more true than in the furor over German Reparations, and Begin reveled in the whirlwind. It was an issue that touched the entire body politic.

GERMAN REPARATION AND THE CHALLENGE OF UNDERGROUND

In 1952, Dr. Nahum Goldmann, acting on behalf of the Jewish Agency, negotiated a treaty of reparations with West German Chancellor Konrad Adenauer. The West German Government, recognizing its moral debt to world Jewry, was prepared to pay reparations to Jewish victims and their relatives in Israel and in the Diaspora for the losses suffered under the Nazi regime.

The treaty, which, on the surface, had little to do with the complicated politics of Israel, and was humane in nature, nevertheless sparked a political battle of the highest order.

Begin turned German reparations into a target against the government. The emerging underground of Sulam also played out its endgame against the background of the reparations controversy, and Begin found himself facing a new and most volatile force within his own movement in the person of Shmuel Tamir, a follower of Sulam.

Begin's initial reaction to German reparations was verbally extreme as he took to the streets with violent rhetoric, drawing huge crowds and igniting parades and demonstrations. His speeches, directed against the government, amounted to a near insurrection. His attacks on Ben Gurion and the government were more emotionally charged than they had been in the days of the Revolt and the *Altalena* affair. The reparations issue became another opportunity to declare the legitimacy of both the Revolt and Herut. He fulfilled what he failed to do in Vilna or in the Revolt—turn the Holocaust into a new political weapon, one that he would use for many years hence.

Begin shrilly attacked the authority and very legitimacy of a Jewish government that would exchange the martyrs of the Jewish Holocaust for blood money. In an article in his *Herut* daily newspaper, typically crowned with a Latin title, *"Vindicea Contra Tyrannos"* ("The Monster of Treachery and Abomination"), Begin asked, "Who is the great criminal, the German who will arrive in Israel or Israel's leader?"[5]

After three years of frustrating political activity, Begin had found a new outlet. "Nothing can convince Etzel veterans that it was their surrender of terror which made democracy possible in Israel," he wrote on January 8, 1953. "Why do you, the government, awaken some to acts of the underground [a reference to the rising tide of Sulam activities]. The traitor is Ben Gurion, who signed the treaty of reparations with the heirs of Hitler."[6]

But Begin would not be alone in the war against reparations. There emerged on the crest of the reparations controversy a figure who haunted Israeli politics and Begin throughout the 1950s. He was a young, former junior Etzel leader in Jerusalem and flamboyant lawyer named Shmuel Tamir.

Tamir was the scion of a Rabbinical-Hasidic family from Bobriosk, Poland, a nephew of Berl Katznelson, Mapai's chief ideologue. Another uncle was Yitzhak Katznelson, a senior diplomat and ambassador to Scandinavia. Tamir was educated in the Jerusalem Gymnasium, and a graduate of the London School of Law, a Mandatory correspondence school. He was ambitious and articulate, commanding several languages, a gifted politician who never really became a successful leader as he had hoped to be in the 1950s. He was a disciple of Stern and the Betar radicals, and time and time again he would lead the opposition to Begin within Herut. He had been imprisoned several times by the British during the Revolt, so his radical credentials were nearly impeccable. In the Kook revolt against Begin, he sided with the rebels. "The making of a Hebrew nation surpasses border-territorial disputes," he had said. "We must most certainly fight—not the foreign oppressor who is already gone—but the oppressor from the Diaspora. The time is now for a revolt within the state."[7]

Like the turnabout Friedman-Yellin of Lehi, Tamir advocated an end to ignoring the Arabs, a practice which was one of Revisionism's most crucial weaknesses. "We must turn the Arabs of Israel into a bridge to other Arabs,"[8] he challenged. Of course neither he nor Yellin ever confronted the contradiction of how their concept of Eretz Israel could serve as a "bridge" to the Arabs. He was antigovernment to the extreme, calling for the liquidation of the Jewish Agency, and basically the dismantling of the Histadrut and the corporate agricultural cooperatives to bring an end to Socialist "anti-democratic" and anti-populist centralism. He attacked Begin for his lack of original thinking and his unwillingness to change.

Yet, Tamir preferred to conduct his challenges and his battles in the courtroom rather than the halls of the Knesset. He was a brilliant, contrary, and dramatically gifted attorney, and he used the courtroom to attack the government and all of his foes. He knew how to stage a political battle royal within the confines of a courtroom.

In his youth he was influenced by the Biryonim, of which his uncle was a member. He was also a commander in an Etzel officers' school and a political prisoner under the British—he was interned in Kenya. When he returned to Israel, he refused to enter parliamentary life and politics.

Tamir made the courtroom the showcase for his campaign against the government and against reparations. He distinguished himself as a defender of the anti-Nazi, underground which began its activity on April 24, 1952, when a letter bomb was sent, probably by some of Shayeb's Sulam forces to Chancellor Adenauer. That letter was intercepted by Israeli intelligence officers. The previous month, two men had given some children a bomb package to be delivered to a German post office. The bomb exploded in a police cellar, killing one German policeman and wounding two. In April of 1952, a letter bomb was sent to an anti-Nazi friend of Israel who happened to be a member of the Reparation Committee. For the people of Israel, this seemed like an organized campaign of terror that had nothing to do with sane politics.

On May 12, Dov Shilansky, a Betar-Etzel activist who had come to Israel on the *Altalena,* was arrested after being discovered carrying a time-bomb in his attaché case. Shilansky asked Tamir to defend him, and Tamir did so gladly, using the case to attack the government and reparations.

Herut and Begin saw in Shilansky's arrest a government "provocation" against Herut, and Begin came to Shilansky's defense, calling the police testimony a "pack of lies." "The ashes of the martyrs have now become a form of exchange," Begin charged bitterly.

Years later, Shilansky, a deputy minister in Begin's 1981 government, would remember Begin's vigorous support. When I saw him in 1983, he pointed to Begin's office. "This was the man who defended the innocents and challenged the provocateurs,"[9] he said emphatically, as if it had all happened only weeks before.

Provocation was Tamir's defense. Tamir charged the government with using police power to quell revolutionary forces. Faced with the Shilansky trial and the reparations issue, Begin was reluctantly drifting into the extreme camps of Tamir and his forces. Tamir and then Dr. Bader attacked the government. On September 10, 1952, Bader wrote that "A government without majority in the Knesset, dependent on Arab votes, is once again engaged in shenanigans." Bader pointed to Shilansky's Etzel record and as an *Altalena* immigrant and Herut loyalist with high standards. "In your camps there are Quislings," he accused, pointing at the government. "In your camps there are the collaborators of CID, the Sezon Petainists. Seek in your camp the provocateurs."[10]

With all, the old wounds seemed to be bleeding. Shayeb-Eldad waged underground warfare. All the old grievances emerged and spilled over into the new battle.

The Israeli public did not accept the provocation charge and, moreover, the government defended itself strongly. The Israeli press also challenged the provocation charge and strongly condemned the underground terror that the controversy had brought out into the open. Now the press and the populace were becoming alerted to a new form of terror: "The tension between Etzel and Lehi [Sulam] is a real national civil war," writes the independent *Haaretz*. "The name Shilansky is a warning to the forces of order."[11]

The underground war, forced into the open by the Shilansky trial, was becoming a real cause of fear throughout the nation. "The Etzel-Lehi versus Haganah struggle of the past could not have turned into a real civil war," wrote Herzl Rosenblum, Editor in Chief of *Yediot Aharonot*, "since all of us were united against Great Britain and the British could impose law and order. But the situation is different today. There is no power to stop terror."[12] Shilansky's antireparations acts were being interpreted as the rebirth of the old Etzel-Lehi struggle.

The Herut establishment denied the provocation charge. A Nationalist editorial said: "There was no provocation. No police planted the bomb in Shilansky's attaché case. They are too sophisticated to instigate the terrorists. We must be sure that this sort of crime does not spread . . . We must mobilize the nation to attend to the dangers that stem from this new terror, which has its roots in the old underground that was dissolved and broken but not completely annihilated."[13]

The accusation of provocation, while stated wildly, was not altogether off the mark. Certainly the police and intelligence services played some sort of role, although their having actually planted the bomb cannot be proven. Iser Arel, the head of the Mosad at the time and a Ben Gurion loyalist, was instructed to spy on the Left and the Right at the time. During the period of the spread of the new terror, Arel devoted himself to hunting the radicals and amassed a considerable amount of information about the inner workings of the various schismatic groups within Herut.[14]

Lost in the shuffle was the fact that Shilansky was convicted and that there was no real public support for the argument against reparations—as Begin found out to his regret.

Reparations and Shilansky became political footballs, used by everyone —from Begin and Tamir, from the underground to the establishment. Begin ended up being the loser once again, for in his shrill defense of Shilansky and opposition to reparations, he became once again a target for Ben Gurion and was forced into defending Herut against the most extreme renegades from his movement, the old Sternists. On May 15, 1953, Dov Shilansky was found guilty and sentenced to three years in prison.

In a sense, what actually happened to Shilansky or to reparations did not seem to matter. In all the tumult and the shouting, you could hear the bitter cries of outrage of the Sezon. You could hear the thunder of the holy cannon of the *Altalena* affair.

TAMIR'S ABORTIVE REVOLT: THE ATTACK FROM INSIDE, 1955–59[15]

One by one over the years, Begin's challengers rose and fell, and faded. The old Vaad militants had taken their leave from politics, Merlin returning to New York to become active in North African revolutionary activities, Kook returned to a business career, to which he was well suited. Eri Jabotinsky quietly returned to academic life as a professor of mathematics at Israel's Technion in Haifa. Shayeb and his ill-fated Sulam underground had been stifled.

Yet in 1959 a new challenge arose, this time from within Herut, from Shmuel Tamir, who had been a key attorney for the defense in 1952 in the Kastner libel suit against Malkiel Gruenewald, a journalist. Kastner, a Jewish Agency officer in Europe, was involved in the rescue of Hungarian Jews, in his capacity as head of the Hungarian Zionist rescue committee. He was in contact with SS officers in his official capacity. The trial was the first to expose to the Israelis the role of Jewish collaboration. Kastner was assassinated by the underground in March 1957, according to Iser Arel, who singled him out as the symbol of Yishuv-Nazi "cooperation" in 1944–45.

The ensuing ideological battle would once again challenge Begin and represented almost a new wind in the ranks of Revisionism. Begin was now again exposed, by Tamir, dooming him to remain for longer than necessary the ineffectual leader of an ineffectual opposition party, which further isolated him from the mainstream of Israeli politics.

By 1955, Begin was almost entirely surrounded by old cronies from the Etzel days, people like Meridor, Landau and Bader.

In 1955, Tamir formed the *Haolam Hazeh* (This World) movement, which originated from the Canaanite-Hebraic strain connected to the old

Biryonim Stern and Lehi. Tamir called for the establishment of a political bloc composed of journalists, dissidents and malcontents drawn from both Mapai and traditional Revisionist ranks. Together with the publisher of *Haolam Hazeh*, Uri Avnery Tamir joined the ranks of a neo-Semitic movement founded by Yonatan Ratosh (whose great disciple was Stern himself). They eventually joined forces to become the New Order–*Hamishtar Hehadash* movement whose function was to expose the complicity of the Jewish and Israeli leadership in the silence of the Holocaust and Israeli government neglect of the Arabs in Israel.

The New Order represented the most original, militant and intellectual group to come out of the radical wing of Revisionism. It echoed Stern, the Weinshall brothers, the old ranks of the Biryonim, and the old Renaissance–Stern ideologues who themselves were anti-Marxists.

The New Order–Hamishtar Hehadash sought to locate Israel's origins in the Hebrews of the ancient Near East. Its neo-cultural ideology was based on Semitic historiography—nineteenth-century writings seeking the origin of the Hebrews in antiquity. They claimed that the Hebrews descended from the Canaanites and must be separate from the Jews now of mixed races.

Searching for an atavistic past, the poet Yonatan Ratosh, Stern's mentor and the Semitic scholar Yohanan Horon, founders of the Canaanite movement, argued that the Jews of European civilization were not the same race as the Hebrews of the ancient Near East. Horon and Ratosh substituted the word "Hebrew" for "Semite." The Canaanites, they claimed, were part of the ancient land of Canaan, which had been overrun and conquered by the invading Hebrews, who soon began to share their culture. Politically, this implied that all the Land of Canaan, which once extended from the Sinai to the Euphrates, at one time constituted the empire of the Hebrews. There are obvious similarities to Stern's old Renaissance viewpoint here, inspired by Ratosh, and a link to Revisionism's territorial aims, except that they were extended to a wild extreme. This was not the old doctrine of Two Sides of the Jordan, it was nothing less than messianic empire making. The nature of this new ideology represented a direct challenge to Jabotinsky's classical Revisionism.

Tamir's movement reflected the Hebraic ideology espoused by Ratosh. Tamir, personally abhorring Begin, sought to challenge him. For Tamir, Begin represented the old order; he was a classic Diaspora Jew. Tamir, the Sabra educated in Jerusalem, the Etzel fighter, could not tolerate the old-line group of sycophants who hovered around Begin like spiders building a protective web of old ideology and faded ideas.

The New Order hoped to run a slate of candidates in the 1959 elections but the party lacked unity, and in the end, disunity would dissolve its effectiveness. Tamir was concerned about the effect of radical progressives

like Uri Avnery and Dr. Yehoshua Leibovits, who were the Philo-Arab
ideological strain of the New Order. He was also extremely unhappy about
Avnery's proclamation calling for the establishment of a Palestinian Arab
state bordering on Israel. Dejected, he returned to Begin's Herut party, but
not without delivering a parting shot. "God save the state of Israel if you
come to power," he warned Begin just before the elections.

Although it had floundered, the New Order had demonstrated the
possibility of change. It had exposed Begin's and Herut's basic tragedy—
they could not accommodate new ideas. Herut was a Begin-Etzel shrine for
old-style Etzel and for the words and ideology of Jabotinsky. The myth of
Jabotinsky resurrected a protective shield for Begin from Sternists,
Hebraists and Zionist messianists who would certainly wreck Herut and its
political future. Herut and Begin survived. The revolt was ten years old and
its charisma was spent.

Certainly some of the ideas of Tamir and his movement may have been
misguided, radical and impossible to ingest. But the challengers represented
an intellectual freshness, a new and energetic generation of imaginative
men, armed with new ways of looking at the past and the future. Had Begin
and Herut taken them seriously, they might have injected the party with a
new energy, but they might also have changed Herut's character for good.
Yet, as it was, Herut did not present a serious political challenger to Mapai,
which itself was in the process of ossification, a state party spending its
pioneer political capital without paying attention to the need for new men
and ideas. All of the challenges conducted from within his ranks, the ideas
of Kook, Merlin, Shayeb and Tamir, left Begin basically unchanged. Except
for the fact that he had subdued Zohar, he seemed almost indistinguishable
from the Grossmans and Unitchmans.

Young men like Kook and Tamir never really felt comfortable with the
old guard, and they would rise again and again only to be subdued by the
iron wall around Begin and his party. Ironically, Begin's unresponsiveness
left him even more vulnerable to attack by Ben Gurion. He was never taken
seriously because he had nothing to offer in the way of a new and serious
challenge.

The 1950s was a graveyard of new ideas that were never adopted and
challengers who never succeeded, as a wealth of Etzel political talent died
by the wayside. Although such talent was sometimes incorporated into
Herut, and helped the party maintain the kind of energy it needed to survive politically, it was never able to turn Herut into an attractive alternative
that might have appealed to a younger Israeli neo-Revisionist generation.

27

1955–66: Time of Routine, Time of Crisis[1]

By 1966, Menachem Begin's political and personal life had settled into a deceptively calm routine. Begin, along with Herut, had become an icon, a persistent presence that nevertheless failed to make itself deeply felt on the Israeli political scene. The underground was moribund. The opposition was out.

A portrait of Begin's routine, in the early part of 1966, his day-to-day political and social life, seems serene and comfortable, imbued with a great deal of pleasantry and warmth. That serenity is about to be cracked by a serious political challenge from within against Begin, and by the shattering events of 1967, which would change the map of the Middle East, as well as the political face of Israel, forever.

In 1966, when he was not gesticulating and bombarding the Knesset with impassioned rhetoric, Began lived a routine life. Most of it centered around Tel Aviv, either at the Herut headquarters at 14 King David Avenue (better known as Jabotinsky's Castle), or at his three-room ground-floor residence at 1 Rosenbaum Street, on the corner of Ben-Nun, a quiet street hidden between the bustling Dizenghoff and Ibn Gabirol Boulevards in central northern Tel Aviv.

No. 1 Rosenbaum Street was an inconspicuous condominium, a four-floor structure, part of three buildings built during the late 1930s and early 1940s. It was more modern than most buildings to be found in Tel Aviv, but lacked the charm of the old Ottoman, Arab and Mediterranean architecture which characterized much of the old city. The Rosenbaum Street structure was white and brown, its paint beginning to chip away with age. It had no elevator, and sported only a small garden.

To get to Begin's "portier" or ground-floor apartment, one enters from a small cement path into a dark staircase which leads to the first floor. One pushes a little square bell to announce one's arrival. In 1977, and this was true a decade or more earlier as well, the Begins, Menachem and Aliza, would usually entertain on Saturdays beginning around 5 P.M. It was the end of Sabbath and Begin would be there, unshaven, tieless, to greet a coterie of old comrades, Etzel fighters, friends, politicians, and just so-called "ordinary Jews." Begin is dressed simply, an open white shirt, black pants and black shoes, but his greeting is, as always, effusive and physical, full of hugs and hand-kissing.

One notes, upon entering, that the apartment is small, and seems even more crowded than it really is. The five- by four-meter living room is dominated by an old, heavy dining table on which are placed the Sabbath candles. To the left is a hall, with some room for furniture and a rack for clothing. To the left of the hall is a bedroom, and next to that an old, outmoded kitchen from which emerge tea and cochin for the invited guests. There is a homey, bustling atmosphere, accentuated by the presence of some twenty-five guests.

I went to one of these gatherings in the first week of June 1977, when Begin had become Prime Minister, but in many ways, the place and the man and the nature of the gathering had not changed in over ten years. Any visit to the Begin residence began to take on a déjà vu quality—the place and the people often seemed like memorials to the Revolt. On the dining table, you could see photos of several incarnations of Begin in the 1940s, on the run from the British, in disguise. Proudly, Begin said that here at No. 1 Rosenbaum, Jewish Etzel and Lehi revolutionaries who were being sought for a reward of ten thousand pounds sterling by the British, hid for five years, hardly ever seeing the light of day.

Here, Begin said, is where he listened constantly to an underground radio, tuning into BBC to find out what was going on outside the confines of Palestine. Listening to the radio is also how he acquired his curious, Polish-accented English, which, in 1977, seemed stilted, from another time, very much like the man himself.

Out on the balcony, you could see the wild, unkempt Rosenbaum garden and the trashcans, and the steady stream of new arrivals, veterans of political and military battles, all of whom Begin described as "simple Jews." In Begin's house, everyone became, simply by virtue of being there, a "simple Jew." There were no introductions, no formalities. Here was a veteran from the *Altalena,* now working as a carpenter in Tel Aviv, here a blind man who lost his sight training Etzel fighters in the dangerous art of throwing hand grenades. Accompanied by his wife, he was a friendly man who did not inquire after my name, but instead told me several good jokes I had not heard before.

Begin pulls up a chair for me, which I refuse. "We are all simple men and women," he tells me. He has been Prime Minister for only a week, and he is nothing if not egalitarian in the surroundings of his own home. Everyone is equal here. There is some politicking, but most of the talk is warm, friendly, chatty, "unimportant," as Begin described it.

The seeming serenity that marked his life and that seemed typical of Herut was misleading. Herut seemed almost comfortable in its constant defeat and in the continued survival of Begin, its first and only leader. Thus it came as a surprise when Herut was rocked by an internal challenge at its 1966 conference.

It was at the Eighth Herut Party Conference at Kfar Ha-Yarok in 1966 in a suburb of Tel Aviv the challenge to Begin came from Shmuel Tamir, who had already led an abortive political revolt against Begin in 1959. This time Tamir made a much more serious challenge, so much more serious that liberal Israeli media observers at one point were describing it as Begin's political funeral. In the end, however, the challenge and the ensuing battle once again would demonstrate Begin's resilience, especially when cornered.

Herut, as a party, was certainly ripe for challenge; indeed, it was rife with frustration. Not everyone was complacent and few were pleased with Herut's electoral progress, which, statistically, was insignificant. In 1955, Herut had received 12.6 percent of the vote, a figure which rose to only 13.5 percent in the 1959 elections to the fifth Knesset. Meanwhile, Mapai, Ben Gurion's party, had kept a steady one-third dominance of the Knesset. Not much had changed as the 1960s emerged. It seemed more and more a party of prematurely old men who tended to look backward. Much of its talent had either disappeared or become paralyzed.

Although the candidate selection process for Herut was not the rubber-stamp kind, like Mapai's, by the middle 1960s its central committee was still composed almost entirely of Begin sycophants like Chaim Landau, Yaacov Meridor, and Yohanan Bader.

If Mapai and the Socialist Zionists were not exactly humming with new ideas, they at least controlled the apparatus of the state—the army, the bureaucracy and the political tools of control and power. Begin and Herut, on the other hand, could offer nothing new or practical to a fresh generation of Ashkenazy and Sephardim, neither a new ideology nor political power.

Although the political significance of a new generation of Sephardic voters loomed on the horizon, he continued to live from one national, municipal and Histadrut election to the next, and all of the campaigns tended to look alike, full of pomp and circumstances, phalanxes of motorcycles, impassioned but empty rhetoric. Begin had settled into the role of party sage, of Etzel elder statesman. He helped to publish a history of Betar and fought to create a Jabotinsky Institute. All his political battles were rooted in the past. He fought a rearguard action to rewrite history, to enlarge the importance of Etzel and the Revolt. He fought with the national and Defense Department publishing house and successfully demanded that its official history of the Haganah include chapters on the Etzel and Lehi undergrounds and the importance of their contributions.

As in the Herut Conferences in 1956, 1960, 1962, and 1964 Begin stood at the podium in 1966 and his voice was, as usual, filled with nostalgia. It seemed that this party meeting would be like all the rest, not a meeting to set an agenda for the future, but a meeting to celebrate the small glories of the past.

Begin talked and shouted about the time when Herut would take over political power in Israel, but no one really believed him. He had become too mellow. He spoke in giant, dramatic gestures, his arms reached out as if to embrace the world, he invoked all the magical old words—"The Movement," "Shlemut Hamolodet," the "Biryonim," and slowly, the conference began to sound like a funeral, a memorial service for Etzel and its fallen leaders.

The most critical for Begin was Herut's eighth party conference in July 1966 in Kfar Hayarok, near Tel Aviv. The speeches never ended, but this time, there was some added excitement, which also attested to the changing and softening of Begin. Begin, too, was elated. In spite of the Arlazaroff affair, in spite of the Sezon and decades of implacable opposition from Ben Gurion, this Herut conference will have as one of its principal speakers an Israeli Socialist-Zionist prime minister.

Speaking in front of a map of Complete Eretz Israel, Levi Eshkol of Mapai, the political party that for decades had branded the forces of Revisionism as thugs and fascists, now came to praise Herut and Begin. He blessed the party with long life, and called it and its leader the "loyal opposition."

Begin began his speech, drumming his one old, giant formula: Eretz Israel. He flailed at great length while managing to display his nontalent for predicting the future. "The question," Begin told his audience, "is [not] what will we do if the Arab offers peace today . . . It [this question] is not even flying in space. It is radical even to think that the Arabs would entertain the idea of making peace. The only truth is our right over the land of Eretz Israel. This is the truth that sustained us in the past and will for the future of Israel." Prophetically, he adds, "we cannot achieve Complete Israel without war." No one knew just how soon that war would come.

The attack on Begin did not come from an unexpected corner. The familiar and still youthful figure of Shmuel Tamir once again rose to challenge Begin, as he did in 1959. Tamir, back in the folds of Herut, was as recalcitrant as ever. Ever since his return, he had insisted that Herut seek an alternative to Begin and his petrified ideology. Tamir would not accept Begin's leadership in the 1950s, and he did not do so now.

This time a little more subdued, in the sense that he did not go to the press with his challenge, Tamir called for the election of a new Herut executive committee, through which he hoped to change the party platform. The old platform called for the Jabotinsky staples: Two Sides of the Jordan, the liberation of Palestine, but "only if the Arabs attack first," and so forth.

Tamir, calling for a new Herut constructivism, this time had formidable help from Eliezer Shostak, the head of the National Workers Union, a Revisionist answer to Mapai's Histadrut (Histadrut Ovdim Leumit). Shostak had always seen the National Workers Union as an independent organization and, more than likely, as a personal political vehicle.

Begin had seen also the political potential in the National Workers Union. At the seventh World National Workers Union Conference held in Tel-Aviv Begin, sounding statesmanlike, but probably being politically shrewd, had devised a "Blue-and-White" scheme in which NWU would infiltrate the Histadrut. This was done under guise of what Begin called "addressing the role of the worker in our movement." Begin's argument was that the base of the nationalist movement's rank and file must be widened, principally by infiltrating labor's traditional barony and stronghold, the Histadrut.

Shostak took a more ominous view of what was happening. He saw Begin's move as a way to circumvent his own movement's independence and autonomy. The National Workers Union was a huge financial fundraiser for both Herut and the Revisionist movement as a whole, an achievement which gave Shostak and his movement considerable political clout, which Begin wanted very much to circumvent. Shrewdly, he argued that the Histadrut was not monolithic, and that the Blue-and-White's NWU entrance into the Histadrut would not in fact threaten NWU independence.

Begin brought out the hallowed name of Jabotinsky, reminding conference delegates that Jabotinsky had tried to reach an agreement with Ben Gurion back in 1935. Histadrut members, the staunchly anti-Communist Begin told the conference, were no longer real Marxists, but were rather working Jews. The NWU he suggested, was established because, before the creation of the state of Israel, Revisionist workers could not join the Histadrut. Things were different now, he suggested. "What about the Red Flag?" he asked rhetorically. "You know there is quite a difference today. Once it was a red flag in their [Socialist] heart, today it flies only above the Histadrut building."

The vote on the Blue-and-White issue created a deep fissure and ended in a pyrrhic victory for Begin. NWU members reluctantly agreed to join Blue-and-White. The final result was 324 in favor of Blue-and-White, 257 opposed and 12 illegal votes. It was a hollow victory, and a vote that Shostak did not forget. But this was Begin's first step toward a coalition with the General Zionists.

Since 1956 Begin had been searching for electoral and parliamentary coalitions to take Herut out of its political isolation. Even at the eighth party conference, Begin was busy searching for electoral partners. The natural partners for Begin were the General Zionist Party (to become, in 1964, the Liberal Party), a bourgeois party run by Tel Aviv merchants, industrialists, and public relations agents, formerly the party of Chaim Weizmann and Nahum Goldmann. When Begin found in December 1955 that the General Zionist Party, having been defeated in the 1955 elections, was seeking to negotiate a possible electoral coalition with Herut, he (in opposition to Herut Central Committee members) made an offer which was not accepted by the General Zionist Party leadership. But Begin did not give up. In the fifth Herut party conference in November 1958, the idea of an electoral coalition with the General Zionists was raised and again dismissed. The election of 1959 persuaded the General Zionist Party, declining from twenty-one seats in 1951 to eight in 1959, that a coalition or even unity with Herut would be a political lifesaver which it has. It has saved him from political oblivion. In Herut's seventh party conference in 1964, Begin pushed hard for negotiating such an electoral alliance. The first move toward Gahal (Herut-Liberal bloc) was to join the Herut Histadrut in an alliance with the General Zionist Histadrut delegation and in opposition to NWU. The days of parliamentary and coalitional building blocs had begun. The straw that broke the camel's back, i.e., the General Zionist Party, was a split of the Progressive Party from the General Zionists. Thus, the Liberal Party was established (1964), ousting the true progressives from the party left along with the nationalists and the economic conservatives, and making possible an electoral merger with Begin's Herut. As a result, for the 1965 election there emerged the most serious right-wing party thus far in Israeli politics, the Gahal (Electoral Bloc Herut-Liberal) party. Thus in the election of November 1966, Gahal garnered twenty-six seats (fifteen for Herut, eleven for the Liberals), not a spectacular electoral face-lift.

Begin told me in 1973: "In the electoral-parliamentary alliance, in the formation of the Gahal bloc, I see the jumping off point for our movement's replacing Labor in power."[2] Thus the notion of Herut as the political alternative was beginning to grow roots in the wider Israeli public. Begin's efforts to widen his electoral base in the electoral coalition, the Gahal, but above all, the 1966 victory against NWU and Shostak, now left Begin open to challenge from two directions, Tamir and Shostak.

The crisis came at the eighth Herut Conference in 1966. Shostak teamed up with the rebellious Tamir. Before the conference began, Shostak told the press that he was not leading a revolt. "The press reports made us out to be some sort of serious opposition to Mr. Begin. We do not intend to hurt Mr. Begin, nor do we want to replace him. What we want is for the conference to cancel the decision concerning the Revisionist Nationalist Workers Union."

Yet, the battle ran deeper than that. The younger forces, led by Tamir, saw Begin as a fading light. The son of an old Herut man said, "Begin, until now, led the opposition to the government. But he has not succeeded in leading the party to power. He must conclude that his own resignation, along with that of the leadership of Herut, is imperative."[3]

Begin was still wily, and emotional enough, to triumph in this kind of battle. On June 27, in the wake of attacks by Tamir and others, Begin abruptly resigned from the Herut chairmanship. "I am returning my Knesset membership to the movement that elected me," he said in typically dramatic fashion. The gesture, and it was no more than that, shocked the conference. Ben Eliezer, as always, tried to act as conciliator, but in truth, the political battle had already been won by Begin, because the majority and the hierarchy were not prepared to accept his resignation. Responding emotionally to the attacks on him, Begin ignored the more realistic challenge from the NWU, which had organization and financial backing behind it.

Begin concentrated on Tamir—in a battle over the cult of personality, Begin was bound to win. Even as he was loudly calling for Herut to free itself from Begin's spell, Tamir underestimated the strength of Begin's support. Begin won the battle in the committee meetings while his supporters took to the streets and to writing pamphlets, praising and hailing him with propaganda slogans such as "Begin, Begin, the power must stay with Begin, no one can fill his chair. He saved the nation from a holocaust; he transfused the nation with pride. Without Begin we would go to our grave."

To some, however, the movement was already going to its grave. This latest defeat of the radicals, especially Tamir, meant that the party was losing even more fresh, new blood, leaving behind a rank and file that was badly split and confused and a leader who was shaken.

To a liberal and an anti-Begin reporter covering the conference it seemed "like the twilight of the Gods. Begin, the last of the memorable politicians of Israel, the last party dictator, was frightened by a challenge and resigned."[4] During the course of the battle, even as devoted a loyalist as Paglin attacked Begin and his leadership qualities. Although Tamir and his followers were noisily rebuked and booed at the conference, Begin showed some bruises.

The reporter wrote: "I will not comment on Tamir's political future, but I think a new phase has emerged in Begin's career. Outsiders who participated in the conference thought Begin deep within his complex personality, was breaking up."[5]

Begin rose to defend himself in a rousing, *Altalena*-like three-hour speech. "I cannot tolerate this cold attitude," he said. He was disturbed that the press continued to describe him as having cold eyes, as a Fascist and fanatic. "Aren't my eyes warm?" he asked friends.[6]

"The Jabotinsky movement gave birth to Begin," the reporter wrote, "but to whom will the Begin movement give birth? With the absence of Begin, perhaps voters will no longer give their support to those advocating the Two-Sides-of-the-Jordan approach."[7] This, like many predictions floating loosely just before the 1967 war, proved to be wretchedly off the mark.

Nothing was ever the same after 1967, a year that yielded watershed events for all of Israel's politicians, military leaders and strategists, including Begin. The quick and devastating six-day war ended Egyptian hegemony over the Arab world and changed Israel's borders in dramatic fashion. For Israel, the results of the war meant an end to insecure borders, but it also put a crack in the national consensus.

The war was the beginning of a temporary new role for Begin. For Herut, it meant the start of the fulfillment of Eretz Israel—although the party would now find itself, ironically, lagging behind the new political forces that were striving for that goal.

28

No Inch of Territory—The Watchdog: A Brief Encounter with Power, 1967–70[1]

The Egyptian dictator and pan-Arabist Nasser was indirectly responsible for infusing new life to Begin and Herut. He destroyed the boundaries of 1949 with his reckless military challenge to Israel in 1967. The opportunities for establishing Eretz Israel were now in Israeli hands in the form of a fully occupied east Palestine, the Golan Heights and Sinai. The undoing of the UN partition was the result not of Zionist expansionism, but of Arab adventurism. Certainly neither Begin nor his Herut party had had anything to do with achieving what seemed to be the dream of Eretz Israel taking on substance.

Since 1949, the Arab states surrounding Israel had remained unreconciled to its borders. Each challenge to Israel was expressed in military invasion, once in 1948–49, intermittently with terrorist excursions from Egypt's occupied Gaza between 1953 and 1956, and finally with an attempted full war in 1967. Each time Arab efforts were repulsed, the Arab armies suffered bloody defeats and disasters, and Israel occupied Arab territories.

The 1967 war was unique in the annals of modern warfare for swiftness and results. In only six days, three Arab armies—those of Egypt, Syria and Jordan—were either repulsed or destroyed. Israeli armies occupied Arab territories four times the size of Israel itself.

This decisive and strategically brilliant military victory was the accomplishment of David Ben Gurion and his political and military heirs. It was not just a victory for the Israeli nation, but a victory for Mapai, Labor and Socialist Zionism. Begin and his Etzel-Herut cohorts had always complained bitterly that it was "their state, their government, but our army" (Begin never calls the army IDF, for "D" stands for Haganah, defense. He will always refer to the army or armies of Israel). The IDF was a creation of

Socialist Zionism, nurtured and formed in the bosom of Mapai and the Left. Most of the IDF elite and High Command came from the ranks of the Palmach or were British-trained. Only a handful of senior officers came from the ranks of Etzel or Lehi, and their influence was minimal. The traditions of IDF were the traditions of the Haganah, of Palmach, of Ben Gurion and the Labor elite. Although Jabotinsky, and later Begin, had always dreamed of a Jewish legion, the IDF was not the realization of their dream. The Left and Ben Gurion created the army.

One might have expected that the decisive victory of 1967 would have resulted in Mapai overwhelming the Herut-Gahal coalition at the polls and perhaps even bringing about their political extinction. Had it not been for Begin's political tenacity it might have happened that way.

Begin played a significant role in the 1967 victory, a role which came about from his innate political instincts and deep patriotic spirit.

On June 6, 1967, Begin, Israel's political pariah, excluded for over twenty years of his political life from real power, joined the coalition government as Minister Without Portfolio; it was for him a political quantum leap. To understand this startling development, one must examine the inner political struggles within the coalition government, the ruling Mapai party, the behavior and motivations of the Prime Minister and Defense Minister Levi Eshkol and, above all, the critical role played by Ben Gurion's splinter party Rafi and its Secretary-General Shimon Peres.

Between May 15 and June 2, 1967, the government, the IDF and the Israeli intelligence services had been engaged in one of the most dramatic internal and diplomatic struggles since the days of the War of Independence. In the forefront of the struggle were two extremely cautious men— Prime Minister Eshkol and IDF Chief of Staff Yitzhak Rabin. From the moment intelligence reports reached the government that Egyptian President Gamal Nasser was proclaiming the state of emergency that would later lead to the ouster of UN forces from the Sinai and the closing of the Straits of Aqaba, the IDF, the government, and the political system of Israel were split over what the official Israeli reaction should be. Should there be a political-diplomatic reaction, a military-diplomatic reaction, or a purely military response?

Eshkol was no Ben Gurion. He lacked the weight, the respect, and the charisma of Israel's Founding Father, nor did he have the will to dominate that Ben Gurion had. Eshkol was by nature conciliatory, a founder of Israel's agricultural cooperative Degania, with its tradition of consensus and coalition. He sought consensus among the cabinet, the IDF and the nation as a whole for the decision to go to war. On the international front, Eshkol would certainly not move without first exploring the American position. He behaved in an international crisis very much as he would in a union crisis, treating it as something that could be handled through collective bargaining. The internal debate on going to war that was being waged in Eshkol's cabinet spilled over into the nation, and soon enveloped the political opposition as well, not to mention public opinion.

The cabinet, given the nature of Eshkol's leadership, was openly split into two camps, one opting for a cautious, diplomatic approach, the other wanting to take pre-emptive, offensive military action. Not surprisingly, the IDF was favored of the military offensive option.

The most vocal opposition, other than the expected one from the Communists and the Arab parties, came from the Center Right of Labor and from Gahal, led by Begin. The tacit coalition that would emerge between Peres, who had split from Labor in 1963, and Begin would eventually cause critical changes, including Eshkol's surrender of the defense portfolio to retired General Moshe Dayan, also of the Ben Gurion faction. And last but not least, the entry of Begin and two other Gahal party members into an extended coalition government.

One day after Nasser closed the Gulf of Aqaba on May 23, Eshkol invited members of Gahal and Rafi to join the Knesset Foreign Affairs and Defense Committee, which were headed by Mapai veteran David Hacohen. A special invitation was also extended to General Dayan by Prime Minister Eshkol, acting under his authority as Defense Minister. Dayan would review the troops in the Negev, accompanied by two other former chiefs of staff.

The three Herut members of Gahal—Begin, Arieh Ben Eliezer, and Chaim Landau—and the two liberals—Yoseph Serlin and Dr. Elimelech Rimalt—were flown by helicopter from Jerusalem to Tel Aviv, along with Rafi members Peres and Yoseph Almogi, the former Mapai Haifa baron.

Before boarding the helicopter, Begin tapped Peres on the shoulder and asked him for a moment of private conversation. Begin, dressed in a dark summer suit and long-sleeved white shirt, seemed intense and what he had to say startled Peres. "Is Mr. Ben Gurion [then nearing eighty] ready to assume the responsibility of running the affairs of state?" he asked abruptly. "Would he be able to do so as head of a national unity government?" Ben Gurion had resigned in 1963 after a most bitter controversy with Mapai— the party executives *ousted* Ben Gurion from the party. It was then that he formed with Peres and a reluctant Dayan the Rafi party that won seven seats in the 1965 Knesset election. By 1967 Ben Gurion was no longer in politics.[2]

Peres was stunned. Although these were astonishing times, it was incredible to hear Begin promote the return to power of his old, bitter rival. "I have no doubt that Ben Gurion is physically capable of doing the job," Peres answered, "but he is retired and has vowed not to return." But in this invitation the seeds for a coalition government were sewn.

Begin's historical and patriotic sentiments were stirring. "Each day since May 15," he told his colleagues, "I believe more and more that the hour of decision, the confrontation between Israel and its enemies, is coming."[3]

Begin may have been ready to participate, but there was a great deal of opposition to and furor over the possibility of a coalition government. The left-wing Mapam party challenged Eshkol's suggestion on May 24 that Gahal and Rafi parties join the coalition. Golda Meir, one of the most influential cabinet members, adamantly opposed both Gahal and participation in the central decision that lay ahead. The animosity to Ben Gurion after he split from Mapai in 1963 was still fresh and the opposition and contempt felt toward Begin was as firm as ever.

Events moved rapidly. Nasser mobilized several divisions in the Sinai even as American attempts to open the straits with an international flotilla were failing to draw support. The momentum for a national unity government picked up speed, almost on its own, its source being the general lack of confidence in Eshkol's capabilities as Defense Minister.

Doubts about Eshkol had been growing. The man most often mentioned as a possible candidate for the job by Gahal and by the press and public was former Chief of Staff (1953–57) Moshe Dayan. Israel Galilee of Ahdut Haavodah suggested Yigal Allon, the former commander of Palmach and of the southern front in Israel's war for liberation as an alternative to Dayan. But Galilee and his Ahdut Haavodah colleagues in the cabinet were not insistent enough in the debate to make Allon Defense Minister.

At this point, Peres, Dayan's colleague, launched a serious campaign to appoint Dayan. Peres recruited the National Religious Party and arranged a meeting at the office of M. C. Shapira, Minister of Interior. The meeting constituted what became known as the Club of Three—Begin, Shapira and Peres.

Begin was highly vocal at the meeting. "There must be serious changes in the political leadership," he argued. "We need an event that will shake the system."

Begin's idea of an event was to bring Ben Gurion back, and he once again suggested this to Peres, asking him to "officially relate to Ben Gurion my offer from yesterday . . . If Ben Gurion is ready, you can tell him I will support him publicly." Peres repeated that Ben Gurion had been informed of the suggestion and had rejected it. "I will not work with that man (Eshkol),"[4] Ben Gurion had said. Begin then suggested that perhaps Ben Gurion would serve if Eshkol were merely his deputy.

This time, Ben Gurion was apparently more receptive. Peres informed Begin that Ben Gurion was ready to serve as head of a national unity government with Eshkol as his deputy. Begin, now totally caught up in the idea, offered to mediate with Eshkol. Only longtime parliamentarian Dr. Bader seemed to realize that such an arrangement was politically unrealistic. "The balance of power is in the Knesset," he told Begin, "and the Knesset is against Ben Gurion."[5]

Ben Gurion or no Ben Gurion, the idea of a national unity government was catching on. Gahal members were holding constant meetings to push it and public opinion in the growing crisis was beginning to catch up with the concept. What was being demanded or thought of on May 24—an attempt to put Ben Gurion back in the government, the call for Dayan to take over the defense portfolio—amounted to a political coup, because neither Eshkol nor Mapai would have accepted the suggestion at that moment. This is basically what the informal coalition between Peres and Begin was attempting to accomplish although neither man would admit to it.

On May 24, Begin had a meeting with a harassed and worried Eshkol, who had already sat through a meeting with senior officers of the IDF who were pressuring to go to war. Eshkol, aware of the organized opposition that was emerging, was trying to stem the momentum of the entry of the NRP into the political battle.

Begin started the meeting on a conciliatory, almost social note, complimenting Eshkol on his assistance in helping to arrange the reinterment in Jerusalem of the remains of Jabotinsky. Then, Begin swung into a full-blown patriotic tone, trying to persuade Eshkol that Ben Gurion should join the government. "I have not forgotten the times of my humiliation at the hands of Ben Gurion," he told Eshkol, "but this is no time for division." Not unexpectedly, Eshkol categorically refused to consider Ben Gurion. "What if he served as Defense Minister?," suggested Begin. Eshkol remained firm. "No," he said bluntly, "these two horses will not pull the cart together."

At this meeting, it was Begin who showed his political acumen and stature, not Eshkol, who delivered a petty aside by suggesting to Begin that the IDF had no faith in Ben Gurion's capabilities as Defense Minister. "In the past," Eshkol hinted, "he [Ben Gurion] made several errors which had to be covered up."[6]

What Eshkol did not realize was the crisis of national security had given the opposition to his government a golden opportunity. The idea of bringing back Ben Gurion was basically unsellable and unrealistic, but coming from Begin, Ben Gurion's old enemy, it had a basic, patriotic appeal and it showed that Begin's political instincts and his patriotism were eminently sound. Just as in the time of the Hebrew Resistance Movement and the dark days of the Sezon, Begin refused to play partisan politics during times of national crisis. In May of 1967, Begin the Jewish patriot showed his dedication to Jewish unity and safety, and foreswore party and ideological rivalries.

While no one may have seriously considered Ben Gurion as Prime Minister or Defense Minister, except Begin and the old lion himself, the cry mounted for the taking of Dayan into the cabinet. Now the Kibbutzim members of Mapai were calling for Dayan's appointment to the Defense Ministry.

The catalyst was Peres, who in promoting Dayan, was also working to widen the base of the coalition. In this, there was fierce opposition from Golda Meir. A veteran of many political wars within Mapai, Meir saw the threat from Peres and she momentarily managed to hold Mapai together in resistance against it.

Events were combining to pave the way toward a national unity government. Diplomacy was failing and the United States had not succeeded in opening the straits. Foreign Minister Abba Eban's trips to Paris and the United States did not yield tangible results and convinced the hawks in the cabinet that he was merely trying to by time to defuse the crisis diplomatically.

On May 26, the idea of a national unity government was raised at the cabinet meeting; Eshkol suggested a compromise, the participation of Gahal and Rafi members in a cabinet-ministerial Committee on Defense. Begin seriously considered the proposal, but members pressured him to reject what they saw was a "political tactic to save the government." Meanwhile, left-wing Mapai members of the current coalition threatened resistance to the "right-wing war-mongering efforts."

Offstage, outside the cabinet meetings, the crusty voice of Ben Gurion was heard. He had become a center for consultation, being visited by old defense hands, retired IDF generals and party stalwarts. He pushed the idea of Dayan as Prime Minister. "If Eshkol offers Dayan only the Defense Ministry, the answer should be negative and stubborn."[7]

Peres knew this was also unrealistic and he continued to push Dayan for Defense Minister, because he knew this would mean a broadening of the coalition government.

Events came to a head on May 28. The IDF High Command, increasingly anxious, now confronted the politicians. Time was running out, they told the government. Diplomacy had produced no solution, no miracle, it was time for a decision. Eshkol and the leader of the hawkish wing of the Israel Air Force (IAF), General Ezer Weizman, were not ready. "Wait for a while," he told the generals. Meanwhile, Ben Gurion was explaining his view of the situation to the religious bloc in the style of an expert elder statesman. Diplomacy was not working, he said. And it was useless to rely on the great powers, who could not perceive the growing challenge to Israel the way Israel did.

Peres increased the pressure on the Mapai leaders as public clamor for a national unity government and for national unity increased. The IDF furiously prepared for war. The Knesset rocked with ferocious debate. There was already a consensus, even if not for a wide coalition government, on the question of going to war. Public opinion, as well as political maneuvering, had put the Eshkol-led Mapai-Maarach coalition government into the corner.

Eshkol and Mapai might have defused the pressure by appointing Allon to the Defense Ministry, but they did not. In an effort to protect the integrity of the government, the coalition, the party and Eshkol sought to form a war council that would include Dayan—although not as Defense Minister.

The consensus growing within the party that a place must be found for Dayan in the cabinet automatically implied a broadly based coalition government that would include Gahal and Rafi. Through all this, Begin feebly hoped for Ben Gurion, but he knew this was a lost cause. "We were persuaded to accept Eshkol as Prime Minister without Ben Gurion but with Dayan," he said, somewhat disappointed. "We can work with Rafi. But Mapai is proving to be stubborn."[8]

It was obvious that the opposition was gaining strength moment by moment. The religious bloc had come out firmly for the establishment of a national unity government. In a meeting, Ben Gurion and Peres agreed: a national unity government with Dayan as Defense Minister. There was no talk of Gahal or Begin.

The Left made one futile, last-minute attempt to stop "Dayanism" and offered up Allon again. The question now was, What would Dayan do? Dayan told Eshkol he was not interested in the Defense Ministry, that he preferred to command the southern front in the Sinai. Eshkol was relieved, but his relief was only temporary.

On June 1, which came to be known as the Longest Day, matters coalesced. Gahal increased the tempo of its campaign for a national unity government campaign. Rumors were rife. Eshkol was backed into a corner.

On that day leaders, including Peres, Yitzhak Navon, and another former chief of staff, Zvi Tzur, came to Begin's home to persuade him to help push Dayan's appointment. After all, who could reject Begin's offer of this key post to his political opponent. Begin's apartment, small to begin with, was more crowded than usual. In addition to the Rafi delegation, there were Begin, Ben Eliezer, Dr. Bader and several Liberals from Gahal, along with a special delegation from the NRP. They all opted to see Eshkol in his office.

Eshkol knew that his own party wanted Allon, but his visitors did not. Begin told Eshkol firmly that there would be no national unity government, no coalition, without Dayan as Defense Minister. Ben Eliezer insisted on knowing who the nominee to the Defense Ministry was. Eshkol remained noncommittal. "Tomorrow, you will all find out," he said cryptically.

Begin, however, had judged the moment more accurately than Eshkol. He now rose from his seat and implored Eshkol in dramatic fashion. "Mr. Prime Minister," he said, "you could unite the whole nation around you in half an hour if you would only agree to the appointment of Dayan as Defense Minister. You will then have a national unity government and the nation will rejoice."9

So the Club of Three challenged Eshkol, they were in the forefront in the clamor for national unity and Dayan's appointment. Public opinion was solidly in favor of it. The nation was united in spirit, even if the Government itself was not. The NRP, during the middle of the day threatened, "No Dayan, no national government."10 Golda Meir tried vainly to hold the fort, but she, too, knew it was a lost cause. At the end of a Mapai conference, she glumly called Galilee and informed him, "Sorry, Israel, the party secretariat supports Dayan instead of Allon to the post of Defense."11

The mood swept the nation. A group of women demonstrators outside Mapai headquarters called for national unity. *Haaretz* editorialized for national unity and so did much of the rest of the press except Davar Labor's paper. The Progressives, members of Eshkol's current coalition, bluntly told Eshkol to appoint Dayan. Rabin, the Chief of Staff, did not care (who knows), but he wanted a decision, and quickly. "I don't take opposition," he said. "I don't care who—Eshkol, Allon or Dayan, I will cooperate with each—but let's make up your mind and soon."12

Finally, at 10:35 A.M., Eshkol invited Dayan to his office. "I invite you to join the Government as Defense Minister," Eshkol said formally. "Is it a private invitation or am I invited as a Rafi member?" Dayan asked. "I don't have a need for another minister in my government," Eshkol said. "I invite you as a member of Rafi unless Rafi rejects my proposal. Then, I'll invite you anyway, personally."13 Coming from Eshkol, this meant that he was now ready to accept a National Unity Government. "There is no Rafi without Dayan," he told his colleagues, "and no Gahal without Rafi."14

There was probably only one person not entirely happy about it all and that was Ben Gurion, who was opposed to Dayan's entry into the government. In spite of Peres's arguments, Ben Gurion had lost faith in the government of the party he had helped to establish.

When the great decision was made, Eshkol's secretary called Begin's home, only to find that Begin was not there. Aliza was told that a national unity government was in the making.

At that moment, perhaps appropriately, with war looming on the horizon, Begin was at Mount Herzl, paying homage to David Raziel, delivering his own eulogy on the eve of war. "When the hour of decision arrives, we shall destroy the enemy with the help of Almighty God," he intoned over the grave of Raziel, "and the nation of Israel will be free in the land of his forefathers."15

When he returned to the Tel Aviv Hilton with his assistant, he called home and Aliza told him of the message from Eshkol. Begin listened to news of Dayan's appointment and said, "Great news indeed, my son." Soon thereafter, Shapira of the NRP called and said, "Mazel tov, we have a national unity government."

At 7:45 that evening, members of the Gahal Executive met to assess the result of their success, certainly with the help of Rafi, in imposing on Eshkol and Mapai a national unity government. The Herut faction had already decided that Begin would be their representative in the government. Begin became a Minister Without Portfolio in the national unity government on June 2 and remained so until July of 1970.

After twenty years in the political wilderness, he was finally a member of the Israeli government. Speaking to the executive committee, he tried to sound modest. "You know very well I am not excited to enter this government," he said ". . . I do not join it in order to become a minister of Israel. Gahal has a purpose in joining the government. I have a suspicion that something critical will be decided by the government."[16]

It did not take much of a talent for prophesying that great events were about to happen. On June 2, the day Begin joined the cabinet, the government did indeed make a critical decision, deciding to pre-empt and go to war against the combined armies of Egypt, Jordan and Syria.

Begin was optimistic about the war from the start. Meeting Rabin in Jerusalem, he patted the chief of staff on the back. "We're proud of you," he said. "This will be victory for Israel."[17]

At 5 A.M. on June 6, the Israeli Air Force rose up to all but destroy on the ground the air forces of the three Arab states. Later, IDF armored divisions roared triumphantly into the Sinai, and took Jerusalem, the West Bank and the Golan Heights. Six days later, by June 12, the war was over. Israel, in the words of Dayan, had reached "perfect borders."

Begin basked like every Israeli in the unprecedented triumph. He made clear what his function in the government would be: to preserve the victory, the borders, and the physical reality of Eretz Israel. "Now, that we possess all of it," he proclaimed, "we shall not surrender another inch of territory." From now on, Begin was fixed on the goal of annexation. He would not relent until the day of his retirement.

We saw Begin in the wake of the Israeli triumph. For the first time in his long political life, he was part of the power elite. Begin had come into his own, he was now something more than the vocal leader of a party forever in the minority, the loyal opposition. Surely now, Begin emerged from the shadows, one might think.

Almost the exact opposite happened. Instead of emerging, Begin, for the first eighteen months of his tenureship as Minister Without Portfolio, actually *receded;* he all but disappeared. During all that time, he made a single speech in the Knesset. In fact, for a long time, Begin almost became a recluse, a stage he had gone through before in Vilna, and would again later —after the Lebanese war. He stopped attending Herut party functions. He isolated himself from the public. He refused to give interviews to reporters. The only official record of his political and governmental existence is that one speech in the Knesset.

The new job, instead of appearing to rejuvenate him, seems to have neutralized him. His sharp tongue was strangely silent, his opposition muted, his former active, peripatetic routine broken.

Years later, Begin would explain his absence of oratory by saying that he did not want to steal time from his fellow Herut members in the Knesset, that he muted his criticism because he did not want to spark schisms in the government. Yoel Markus, writing in *Haaretz* in November of 1968, called Begin's tame behavior a gift from heaven for the government. Begin himself preferred to think of it as the behavior of a loyal member of Israel's government.

Begin, the fierce rebel and oppositionist, was at war with the man who wanted more than anything else to gain legitimacy and political respectability. He preferred to see his good behavior, his silence, as a form of above-the-battle statesmanship. He had, after all, played a decisive part in the creation of the national unity government, and he wanted to reap the benefits of belonging to a victory cabinet.

Begin told me years later that he saw his role in the years 1967–70 as that of a watchdog, the preserver of *Shlemut Hamoledet,* of Eretz Israel. He would guard against the possibility of any withdrawal from the occupied territories. For Begin, the "victory cabinet" must also be unregenerate in its attitude toward withdrawal. His voice would always be ready to come to the defense of Eretz Israel.

But what did Begin actually do in the cabinet for such a long time? Not much. His position was nebulous. As Minister Without Portfolio, he was relegated to a second-floor office in a building which also housed the Prime Minister in Jerusalem. The Prime Minister was on the first floor, while the second floor was occupied by the Deputy Prime Minister and the Ministers Without Portfolio, the only ministers who did not run departments of their own and who were therefore not entitled to a building of their own.

Begin's office at the time displayed large portraits of Herzl and of Jabotinsky. Begin was tremendously proud of that portrait. "Think of it," he would say. "For the first time a Jabotinsky portrait hangs in the office of a cabinet minister of Israel." It was not a flashy, ministerial existence. A Minister Without Portfolio was allowed only one secretary, a driver and an office manager.

Eshkol deliberately never defined Begin's duties for him. Begin often served as an arbiter of disputes, except when someone like Finance Minister Sapir would ask him to go overseas to raise money. Once, in 1968, Begin tried to mediate a heated dispute between Eshkol and Dayan, during which

Dayan became so angry that he called for Eshkol's replacement. Eshkol in turn demanded that the government publish a rebuke to Dayan, and it took all of Begin's skills to calm both men down.

Begin served on six permanent ministerial committees: the Committee to Supervise Jerusalem; the Legislative Committee; the Committee for Holy Places; the Fundamental Laws and Ceremonies Committees and some ad hoc committees, including one which supervised the writing of a book on the twentieth anniversary of Israel. One cynic of the time said that Begin's lack of assignments gave him "time to think."

Yet Begin did not see himself as killing time. Everyone in the cabinet knew what he stood for and what his purpose was: to guard against IDF withdrawal from the occupied territories. Begin himself argues that his presence strengthened Eshkol against pressure from the Leftists.

Begin also spent a great deal of time learning about the area, its history, geography, and politics, gleaning information that would be useful years later during the Camp David talks. He would call the Foreign Office for information on legal and diplomatic issues connected with the occupation. Curiously, for a man of his politics, Begin had a great deal of respect for Abba Eban, the Foreign Minister, upon whom he relied for professional judgment, in spite of Eban's "concessionist" stances. Often during this time, Begin seemed to be in training, examining every detail connected with foreign affairs. It is not as if he were sleeping during cabinet meetings, where he raised questions and arguments over every foreign and security issue which was discussed.

Quite simply, he seemed to be happy in his new role and status, in the knowledge that his vote and that of Gahal could become crucial and balancing. For instance, in a government letter to UN Mediator Gunnar Jarring, Begin made sure that the line "withdrawal of forces would be conditioned by direct negotiations" was deleted.

The Gahal bloc rarely voted against the government, and Begin and Gahal appeared to have been neutralized. But the very presence of Begin assured that the government would for the time being remain inflexible on the question of withdrawal, whether it was Eshkol's government or that of Golda Meir, who succeeded him after his death in 1969. Thus, it can be said that Begin deprived the nation of an opposition, but its absence meant a more unified cabinet.

As time passed, however, Begin's almost passive stance became increasingly impossible to maintain. Events, especially the actions of the Arabs, made sure of that.

In spite of their devastating defeat, the Arab states refused to accept the results of the war. Defiantly, the architect of the Arab disaster, Nassar, proclaimed in Khartoum in 1968 "No peace, no negotiations, no recognition of Israel." The Arabs—like Begin—were not ready for any formula of territory for peace. Syria and the Palestinian Liberation Organization opposed UN Resolution 242, which had been adopted in June of 1967 as a basis for future negotiations. Begin would also continue his legal war against Resolution 242.

Nasser decided to continue Egypt's war against Israel in another form. Since a direct military assault against Israel had failed spectacularly, he began a war of attrition in the middle of 1968 over the Suez Canal, a war which in a matter of two years resulted in close to six hundred Israeli casualties. It would appear that the territories conquered in 1967 no longer constituted "ideal" borders, as Dayan had so confidently declared in 1967.

The war spilled over into the big power arena as Soviet SAM missiles in Egypt moved closer and closer to the Suez Canal. Israel retaliated by long-range bombardment.

The United States and the rest of the international community became alarmed. They were not ready for another major Middle East war, especially one that had the built-in danger of big-power confrontation. In that sense, Nasser's war of attrition amounted to a political duel that led to some unpleasant results for Israel.

Three factors finally combined to bring Begin out from under his shroud of silence, into the forefront of his self-appointed role as protector of Eretz Israel, and out of the national unity government.

In August of 1970, the government of Golda Meir, after long U.S.–Israeli negotiations, accepted a cease-fire along the Suez Canal, together with a partial Israeli withdrawal from the canal. The cease-fire took effect on August 7, 1970.

American policy toward the Middle East was proclaimed on December 9, 1969, hence known as the Rogers Plan, which was followed by the American-Soviet negotiations over an Israeli-Egyptian settlement.

The Rogers Plan was as much of a milestone in American Middle Eastern policy as UN Resolution 242, whose essence is "the inadmissibility of the acquisition of territory by war." U.S. Secretary of State William Rogers had been instructed by President Richard Nixon to determine whether the Soviets would be ready to cooperate with the United States in bringing an end to the conflict in the Middle East. Toward that purpose, Rogers issued a paper which outlined a plan calling for all parties to recognize UN Resolution 242, which had as its basis the security of all nations in the area.

What shocked Israelis about the plan, however, was that it called for the return of all the occupied territories conquered in 1967 with only minor border rectifications, or "insubstantial" boundary alternatives, mainly in and around Jerusalem. Above all it called for consideration of the status of Jerusalem, once more rejecting Israel's unilateral occupation of east Jerusalem. Luckily, the Soviets, acting on the advice of their Arab clients, rejected the plan, but for Begin the intent was enough.

For Begin, Gahal, and Herut, not to mention the Labor Party hawks, the Rogers Plan became a symbol of an American-imposed solution to an Israeli problem. Now Begin roused himself with all the rhetorical and political skills at his command. The Rogers Plan became Begin's personal bête noir. Washington added to Begin's fury by encouraging the Swedish Ambassador Gunnar Jarring's mission, a UN-sponsored mediation effort, to find a verbal agreement between Israel and Arab states on UN Resolution 242 which also had Soviet and Egyptian backing.

Begin whipped up and mobilized all the rejectionist forces in Israel as he led the opposition to the Rogers Plan and the Jarring mission. All of his energies, which had lain dormant for the last two years, were now stirred up with a vengeance—in speeches and in writings in the nationalist evening newspaper *Maariv,* which, at the time was probably the most widely read publication in Israel.

For Begin, the cease-fire, the Jarring mission, the Rogers Plan and the Soviet-American meetings were all links in a chain which could lead to the surrender of Eretz Israel by the Meir government. He was willing to risk the end of the national unity government in order to fulfill his role as watchdog of Eretz Israel, calling for the resignation of the Gahal members in a special Gahal executive session.

The day after the signing of the cease-fire, Begin and five Gahal members of the national unity government resigned, including Chaim Landau and Ezer Weizman of Herut and Elimelech Rimalt, Arieh Dolzin, and Yoseph Sapir of the Liberals.

On August 12, in a special Knesset debate on the Jarring letter, Begin attacked the government for accepting this mediation effort, which was, he said, backed by Moscow and Cairo in order to impose on Israel unacceptable territorial solutions. "The government announcement of the Jarring letter," Begin charged, "clearly demonstrates that once again it is ready for a new partition of Western Eretz Israel . . . This," he said, "is why we of Gahal resigned."[18] Begin asked, "What happened to the government of Israel? What happened to the Jewish state? Has this turned once again into a game in the hands of foreigners?"[19]

"I was a member of a government that was resolved that Israel would not become an object of superpower politics," he continued. "Washington and others have deceived us."[20]

Fortunately for Begin, the Egyptians violated the cease-fire almost immediately by bringing the Soviet missiles even closer to the canal the following day, which gave Begin's rhetoric added power. "Let us remember the days of Bevin," he said. "Let us remember when the British tried to establish a Palestinian state in the midst of the Mandatory." He reminded his audience that Israel would no longer be secure if the West Bank were returned, deftly turning from ideological concerns to concerns of security. He painted a frightening picture of Russian Katyushas pointed at the heart of Israel from the West Bank. "All Jerusalem will be under Fatah's cross-fire," he warned grimly. "The surrender of territory could mean another bloody and ruthless war unlike any known in human history."[21]

Begin called for Jewish leaders in the United States to put pressure on Nixon to seek an end to the Rogers Plan. "No one will play checkers on a Jewish board," he said ominously." "Israel," he said, "must remind the United States that the Rogers Plan is in the interest of the Soviet Union."[22]

In an August 28 article in *Maariv*, Begin elaborated on the reasons for his resignation and that of the Gahal members. "The victors are sad," he wrote. But he went on to attack those who were "friends of withdrawal," meaning the peace elements of the Labor Party. "Gahal," he wrote, "could no longer remain in a government oriented toward the Rogers Plan." In typically legalistic fashion, Begin enumerated the painstaking arrangements on Gahal's entry he had made with the Eshkol government since 1967. He charged that the government, not Gahal, had strayed and betrayed the principles of the national unity government.

Though he had bolted from the government, Begin wanted to reassure the electorate that he was a statesman and a law-abiding, loyal minister who had resigned only after the government had changed the original rules. "I fought all along so that the government would never use the word 'withdrawal,' " he wrote.[23]

Begin espoused an argument he used almost verbatim in the August 25 Knesset debate on the United States attitude toward the cease-fire. Mrs. Meir had sent the Israeli Chief of Intelligence to the United States with a report to the Pentagon on the results of Israeli reconnaissance, which showed Egyptian violations of the cease-fire. The U.S. response to the breakdown of the cease-fire was very slow and not very forthcoming.

Begin started his speech in the Knesset by attacking the Rogers Plan, reminding the government of its responsibility to protect the cease-fire regions, which it had obviously failed to do. He ranged all over the diplomatic map of the twentieth century, quoting Bethmann-Hollweg (the German chancellor who in 1914 said that agreements are "nothing but pieces of paper" according to Begin); referring to the Versailles Treaty and the Kristalnacht (crystal night) in Berlin of 1934, Buchenwald and Senator Fullbright and Dr. Nahum Goldmann, President of the World Jewish Congress, who had called for a return of all the territories conquered in 1967. He invoked all of his personal devils and peppered his language with legalisms and Latin phrases, to make them sound more authoritative and less shrill.

He argued that fear of the anti-Israeli Senator Fullbright and a U.S.-imposed solution were nothing but the products of "a Jewish inferiority complex which has no place in Israel. This cowardice leads to Buchenwald," he said.[24] Begin began to conduct a debate with his old ally, Defense Minister Moshe Dayan, with whom he had collaborated in the national unity government. Dayan had opposed Gahal's departure from the government. Begin needed a basis of legitimacy for his resignation, and this time he needed it from Dayan, his 1967 partner.

In a *Maariv* article entitled "Mr. Dayan Asked for an Answer," Begin tried to supply one by continuing the debate. Dayan at this time was immensely popular. In the article, Begin attacked Dayan for accepting the Jarring mission, which he had told Begin was "like jumping into cold water." "Let's talk eye to eye," Begin wrote. "If we are driven into the Jarring talks, violating the government's cease-fire agreement with Egypt, the next thing we would have to submit to is a map of withdrawal." Begin implied that Israel would have to surrender territory without a quid pro quo, and scoffed at the idea that the Arabs "would talk to us."

Begin adopted in public the same role he had played in the cabinet— the protector of Eretz Israel, pursuing a policy of confrontation over the "surrender" of territory. "Since the Arabs reject Jewish sovereignty over Eretz Israel," he wrote, "the conclusion must be this: the opposition to partition must deny any diplomatic moves [such as the Jarring effort and the Rogers Plan]."[25]

Begin had charted a course of opposition to the partition of Palestine or Eretz Israel. "The partition of Palestine leads to war, not peace," he said in the Knesset. "Does Sadat really seek peace?" he asked rhetorically. "Is he the first Arab in our generation who wants peace? Hitler and Stalin also spoke of peace."[26]

In a June 9, 1971, Knesset debate, Begin attacked the new Egyptian President Sadat as a phony peace seeker, untrustworthy in negotiations over the opening of the Canal. "If the Canal is opened, then the Soviets will dominate both of its banks." Begin was prepared to fight against any compromise: "We cannot withdraw from the Canal without a peace treaty with Egypt."[27]

In a debate with the left-wing party Mapam in the Knesset, Begin staked out his political stance: "We know by now that the choice between Complete Israel without peace and partitioned Israel with peace is no choice at all. It just doesn't exist. What is the difference between a policy of complete and divided Israel? The former guarantees our future, while the peace treaty is very remote. [It is] only in undivided Israel that the peace will grow."[28] What are the alternatives to the Labor party policy, he asked: (1) the principle of direct negotiations; (2) the borders would be established in the context of peace treaties; (3) as long as there is no peace treaty, Israel must protect the 1967 cease-fire boundaries, meaning Eretz Israel. Of course, this was proposed by Begin because he, like most Israelis, felt that no Arab state would *ever* make peace.

Begin challenged the opposition on the role of an Arab minority within the boundaries of annexed Palestine, and he did it boldly. He said, "We have now some eight hundred thousand Arabs in Eretz Israel—i.e. the West Bank and Gaza. Yes, they will live under Jewish rule. We believe in civil rights, in the rights of a national minority. What kind of crime is it to believe in annexation?"[29]

Begin never relented in fighting the Dayan-Sisco efforts to open the Canal in the middle of 1970 and to indirectly arrange a Sadat-Israeli deal. He argued that Egypt had no right over the Sinai, that there was no need to have a confrontation with the United States. His activities were feverish, but he was not, as he would later like to think, alone in his passion for the new Eretz Israel movement. He was not even among its leaders.

The organization, ideology, ideas, writings, lectures and recruitment for the Eretz Israel movement came, not from Revisionism, Herut or Begin, but from The Land of Israel Movement *(Lim—Hatnua Le-Maan Eretz Israel Hashlema)*.

LIM was organized by young dissidents from the Labor movement. It had its roots in Ahdut Haavodah (the United Labor Party) and the United Kibbutz movement, a nationalistic movement of the 1920s led by Kibbutz ideologue and sage Yitzhak Tabenkin, one of Ben Gurion's greatest rivals. Tabenkin believed that the empty spaces, deserts and territories must be settled to become the Republic of Kibbutzim.

Like Revisionism, LIM was anchored in Herzlian Zionism contending that a territorial solution to the Jewish problem meant a return and occupation of all the *historical* Jewish homeland. Its manifesto stated the matter clearly:

Zahal's victory in the Six-Day War placed the people and the state within a new and fateful period. The whole of Eretz Yisrael is now in the hands of the Jewish people, and just as we are not allowed to give up the "State of Israel" so we are ordered to keep what we received there from "Eretz Yisrael."

We are bound to be loyal to the entirety of our country—for the sake of the people's past as well as its future, and no government in Israel is entitled to give up this entirety, which represents the inherent and inalienable right of our people from the beginnings of its history.

Our present boundaries are a guarantee of security and peace, and open up unprecedented vistas of national material and spiritual consolidation. Within these boundaries, equality and freedom, the fundamental tenets of the State of Israel, shall be the share of all citizens without discrimination.

The two prime endeavors on which our future existence depends are immigration and settlement. Only by means of a great influx of new immigrants from all parts of the Diaspora can we hope to build up and establish the Land of Israel as a unified national entity. Let us regard the tasks and responsibilities of this hour as a challenge to us all, and as a call to a new awakening of endeavor on behalf of the people of Israel and its land.[30]

LIM, although small, embraced all manner of dissidents, intellectuals, poets and renegades from the Left and the Right, including Rafi, Hashomer Hatzair, Labor, Ahdut Haavodah and Herut. It was a movement that sparked with the ideals to which Begin and Herut were wedded.

LIM succeeded where Begin failed—by penetrating, mobilizing and enhancing the maximalist territorialism of the pre-state, prepartition nationalist ideologies and forms. It combined secularism with security concerns and tied them to a scriptural heritage and an offensive security doctrine. It was not Revisionism, but a Biblical territorialism.

LIM's emotional appeal, as opposed to its electoral appeal, was broad. It penetrated the government, the IDF and the educational system. The Friday editions of *Maariv* and *Yediot Aharonot* regularly carried articles by LIM writers. They published their own paper, *Zot Ha'aretz,* which soon outdrew the smaller publications of the Left and of the peace movement.

From the outset, LIM tried to create a new consensus, attacking the Labor concept of "territories for peace." Although only marginally effective at the polls, LIM was nevertheless representative of an ideology on the rise. Its influence over the Israeli political establishment was steadily growing. One could say, looking backward, that LIM legitimized the very concept of Eretz Israel even as the journalist Amos Elon was writing in 1966 that the Eretz Israel concept had no constituency in Israel, and was nothing but a fading dream.

The 1967 war and its results, the frustration with the ensuing "peace," Nasser's bloody rejectionism, the rise of the PLO, the Rogers Plan all were factors paving the way for the eventual acceptance of LIM, as well as the Begin-Herut brand of Complete Israel ideology.

Yet Begin and Herut never took the initiative, nor did they have the kind of appeal that LIM commanded. Herut's and Begin's dilemma was an old one—all of the party's young, innovative and radical members had been driven away through disgust and impatience and the party had become petrified around Begin and his cronies. Before 1967 the party's appeal had been on a steep decline, and only the alignment with Gahal, the 1967 war and Begin's entry into the national unity government saved it from further decline.

Herut, for example, had no appeal for the Ashkenazi generation of state builders or the pragmatists of Rafi and Ahdut Haavodah. Ideologically, the party had offered a dream that, in the years between 1949 and 1967, had become obsolete and withered. Begin's style, politics, and methods had become repugnant to a younger generation. Begin, who believed in supernationalism and Jewish heroics was seen by a younger generation as a Diaspora-style old Jewish politician, an old-time Zionist rhetorician out of step with the times, even more trapped in the past than the Palestine-Yishuv generation of the 1930s.

LIM was a movement of dissidents who belonged, who sprang from the political and intellectual establishment.[31] Even when he became Prime Minister, Begin would never be a part of the real establishment. The only Revisionist and Etzel members of LIM were dissidents who had broken away from Begin and Herut, people like Shmuel Katz, Eri Jabotinsky, Lehi ideologues Dr. Israel Shayeb-Eldad, Uri Zvi Gruenberg, all of whom had rejected Begin's style and dogmatism, Herut's unwillingness to entertain new ideas and its growing irrelevancy.

In many ways, Begin became a transition figure for the forces of Complete Eretz Israel. LIM was a movement of Canaanites, scripturalists, and left territorialists in whose ranks Begin could find no comfort. It would have been impossible for Begin to forge a political alliance with LIM, nor did he try until after the 1973 war, after which emerged Likud, another incarnation of Revisionism with Begin, almost unaccountably, at its head.

Part Five

THE YEARS OF POWER
AND DECLINE
1977–83

29

The Rise of Neo-Revisionism—Likud, 1970–77¹

Etzel was the radical product of Jabotinsky's Revisionism. Herut was Etzel's heir, its political and parliamentary movement. Likud, which emerged in the 1970s, is a more radical version of Herut. Likud revived and made effective the idea of complete Eretz Israel that Begin—without fulfillment—evoked in his rhetoric before 1967. Likud became a mass movement beginning in 1973. It is still growing. Begin's Herut (Herut never polled more than fifteen percent of the vote) could never have accomplished the colonization of all of Eretz Israel without the Likud. The Likud became Labor's alternative for rule.

Likud became the first Israeli political coalition which would fiercely adopt and implement the ideology of the Land of Israel Movement, incorporating some of its members, steadfastly seeking to fulfill its goals. Strangely enough, some of its members and some of its leaders included people from Ahdut Haavodah, Rafi and Hashomer Hatzair, traditional rivals of both Begin and Jabotinsky and Revisionism, and Etzel.

As we have seen, LIM's ideology arose, not from the right but from the left from Labor, and it forged a new ideology for Likud. Ideologically, LIM all but overwhelmed Begin and Herut, circumventing them from the left. The LIM ideology, which had been growing in popularity for a decade, helped legitimize Likud in a way that Begin had never managed to do in all his years in politics.

If LIM's major contribution to the emerging Likud was its ideology, Gahal and Begin would provide the organization, the parliamentary structure, and the political and electoral know-how and masses. LIM, dominated as it was by dissident but nevertheless elitist Ashkenazim, was a trifling electoral force. Historically whenever its members ran for office, they met with resounding failure. LIM, in fact, was never really intended to be an electoral party. It was an ideological force, not an organization. It would remain for Likud to provide the electoral clout.

Likud as an electoral coalition of the radical nationalists, was created in July 1973, combining the Free Center party (headed by Begin's old nemesis Tamir), La'am party (Ben Gurionites and renegade Rafi members who refused to return to the Labor fold) and diverse nationalists.

The leader that organized the coalition, the man who dreamed up the name *Likud* (Unity) was then retired General Ariel Sharon, who, after an unsuccessful bid to become chief of staff, had quit his command of the Sinai Southern Front in July 1973. Always eager for power, he set about organizing a nationalist electoral coalition, the first such in Israeli history.

Begin and Herut lagged behind. They had little to do with the origin of Likud, but Likud could not have existed without them, since they provided Likud's electoral base. Without Begin's approval, the Liberal members of Gahal would never have accepted Sharon's entry, because Sharon's had a reputation for brutality and opportunism.

Let us, for a moment, step back in time and look at the conditions that helped to create the climate in which a coalition like Likud could thrive.

Herut, like Mapai, was running out of ideas that were relevant to the dynamics of politics and society in the Israel of the 1970s. Its effectiveness remained electoral, but only if Begin stood at its helm. Now, more than ever, without Begin Herut would end as Revisionism did in 1948.

The Labor party was slowly, like Herut, becoming ossified, but in 1968 and 1969, it was at the height of its power. Labor was then made up of Mapai, Rafi, and Ahdut Haavodah, as well as an electoral coalition with Mapam called Maarach, a coalition that was a major political victory for the late Prime Minister Eshkol and his successor Golda Meir.

When Eshkol died in 1969, Labor commanded fifty-six seats in the Knesset. Gahal, in the 1969 elections, had not improved its standing, remaining with twenty-six seats, the same number it had received in 1965.

The year 1969 began Labor's slow but steady decline. Labor's decline was caused by many factors, chief among them the traumatic 1973 Yom Kippur War. But the party was aging noticeably. It had lost its ideological elan—it could no longer capture the imagination of the nation as it once did. Labor continued to be sustained by holding the reigns of power, and the money, offices, and influence that go with control of the state machinery. It subsisted on the achievements of the past, along with its organizational and institutional riches. It dominated the economy, the military, and the defense industries, all in the name of collectivism and etatism. Its elite remained a select club of aging East European Ashkenazies and their sons.

Begin deserves credit for keeping Herut together during the hard years from 1969–1973. In spite of the immobile state of Gahal, Begin never gave up, and through his rhetorical skills, as well as his constant use of the media, through *Maariv,* he managed to widen, if not enlarge, his electoral base. Through it all, Begin remained dogmatically dedicated to the preservation of Eretz Israel and to the principle of the annexation of Western Palestine.

Begin, when the time came, would provide the ideological and political alternative constantly sought by the 1967 militants, by the Ben Gurionites, and by the NRP radicals and assorted radical nationalists in the labor movement. As a watchdog of Eretz Israel, through his columns in *Maariv,* in countless Knesset debates and public forums, Begin became the figurehead, the charismatic flashpoint for the alternative to Labor's long rule.

Begin was always willing to build a broad political base. He built his electoral alliances block by block, step by step, carefully and systematically. In seeking a coalition with Gahal in the 1960s, he compromised by being flexible on the entry of liberals into his coalition. Likud, of course, would represent the influx of militant nationalists, and here too, Begin would bend —but in a radical direction, just as he did by joining the Labor national unity government in 1967. That willingness to compromise kept Begin afloat. To resuscitate moribund Herut, Begin moved to court the ambitious and politically frustrated IDF's 1967 heroes. He was after two generals, Ezer Weizman and Ariel Sharon. Weizman, realizing that his chances to become chief of staff of the IDF were fading, in 1969 joined Gahal and the government in a most speedy change. The negotiations and Weizman's entry took place in less than a week. Begin, behind the scenes, was elated. Negotiations between the Liberals and Ariel Sharon, another candidate for the position to which Weizman aspired, fell.

With the advent of Likud, Begin's gift for political coalition building came to the forefront; he was proud of the fact that Likud included "Socialists and members of the organized working classes of Israel," a clear indication that he had finally, in some small way, penetrated the political fortress of Socialist Zionism. More than his radical new allies from the right and left, Begin was the one who proved himself politically resilient, a quality that would eventually lead to his electoral victory in 1977.

Nevertheless, it would take something like a political earthquake to radically alter the political climate of Israel. That earthquake was the October 1973 Yom Kippur War, which proved to be the launching pad for Likud potency and legitimacy. After the October war, nothing remained the same, as was proven in the November, 1973 election, a turning point in the electoral history of Israel—the beginning of the serious decline of Labor and the rise of Likud.

The new Likud alignment had improved Gahal's previous electoral showing of 26 seats in 1969 to 39 seats in 1973 and 43 in 1977, while

Labor declined from 56 in 1969 to 51 in 1973 and 32 in 1977. The war had quite a bit to do with these remarkable changes.

The Yom Kippur War shook the foundations of Israel, in particular the political foundations of the Labor Alignment Maarach. The surprise Egyptian-Syrian attack of October 6 caught the IDF by surprise on the Suez Canal and in the Golan Heights, with the Egyptians crossing the Canal and the Syrians in the Golan Heights. The IDF eventually went on the counteroffensive, but it took two weeks for the offensive to bear fruit. By October 21, the IDF dominated Egyptian territory west of the Canal, had surrounded an entire Egyptian army, and was into Syrian territory only twenty miles from Damascus.

In the end, the war amounted to an Israeli tactical victory, but it was also a strategic Arab victory. The Egyptians had managed to cross "the canal of shame," as described by Sadat. If the results of the war did not exactly wipe out memories of the 1967 disaster, it did provide Sadat, Egypt and the Arabs with a measure of pride and a basis for future negotiations.

In Israel, the war broke the back of the Meir coalition. In a short time, Meir and her Labor coalition lost its preponderance in the the Israeli electorate, as the November 1973 elections would show in a startling way. If there had been no October war, it is highly doubtful that Likud could have made such a dramatic showing at the polls. The electorate "punished" Labor for the 1973 *Mehdal* (misdeed).

The war further divided a nation which was already beginning to show the strains of the ideological battles between Land of Israel Movement followers, the annexationists and those who clung to the idea of historical partition. The vote in November showed the rise in popularity of the more radical political factions, mirrored in the surprising strength of Likud.

"You see," Begin told me at the time, "we will be the alternative to the Socialists in the next election," and he proved to be correct. Labor won the 1973 elections, but it was a wounding victory, and the aftermath of the war only exacerbated the process.

The troop separation agreements of 1974–75 with Egypt and Syria were negotiated by Meir's successors, Rabin, Peres, and Allon, who sought accommodation with Egypt and Syria through the Kissinger negotiations. For the first time, the borders of the 1967 war were compromised. Israel returned a strip of land in the southwestern Sinai and the Egyptians now dominated two banks of the Suez Canal. The capital of the Golan Heights, Kuneitra, and a great part of the northeastern part of the Heights were returned to Syria. In exchange, Syria recognized the validity of UN Resolution 242. In addition, the Americans guaranteed Arab nonbelligerency and the protection of the neutrality of the territories surrendered by Israel.

For Begin, Likud and the LIM, the troop separation, IDF withdrawal and territorial surrender meant only one thing: a change in Israeli international politics—territorial withdrawal in exchange for security. This was totally unacceptable for the growing camp of annexationists and religious and secular militants and would delineate the future political battleground.

Labor leaders Meir, Dayan and Israel Galilee pursued a policy of Dynamic Zionism, meaning a policy that favored the establishment of a security zone populated by Israelis along the Jordan River, in the environs of Jerusalem and the mountains of Samaria. Strangely enough, this was very much a part of LIM ideology. Dayan conceived of the West Bank and Jordan River as a security zone, while Galilee had a concept of security settlements and Mrs. Meir steadfastly proclaimed her refusal to return to the 1967 borders. All of this demonstrated that LIM's ideology had seeped into Labor thinking and pragmatism, although not in its ultimate biblical or Revisionist sense.

Labor Party leaders refused to draw maps, but came up with something called "oral maps," as Dayan described them. Stripped of detail, "oral maps" meant basically a pragmatic military-security policy oriented toward partial annexation. It certainly left no room for Palestinian self-rule, self-determination or self-government. However grudgingly, the Labor party, Maarach, electoral alignment, and the government were moving toward adoption of some of LIM's practical demands without embracing its ideology.

Although the war sparked Labor's decline and the creation of Likud hastened the process, Likud did not grow in stature merely at the expense of its political opponents in Labor. Begin himself had helped lay the groundwork for the rise of Likud, which was, after all, a *major* electoral alignment, by undermining the effectiveness of Israel's myriad small parties.

As early as 1972, Begin and Gahal entered into a parliamentary alliance with Labor-Maarach to bring an end to the power of the smaller parties. The Bader-Offer Law, which both Labor and Gahal supported in the Knesset, in effect restricted the smaller parties. The law provided that the two major voting blocks would share the votes of the smaller parties that had not succeeded in gaining Knesset seats. The law was designed to discourage small parties from running independently, while at the same time encouraging them to join large coalition blocks like Maarach, Gahal, and later Likud.

Begin fiercely defended the law. Writing in *Maariv*, he said, "We must become indifferent to the small parties in the Knesset. The small parties are not the rivals of Gahal. Maarach is our rival." Begin said he supported the law in order that the debate over Eretz Israel would be sharply focused between Gahal and Maarach. In an article entitled "Let Us Debate On Issues, Not On Blockages," Begin wrote that it "behooves us that the public debate over Eretz Israel be conducted between Maarach and Gahal."[2]

Begin attacked the small parties in no uncertain terms. "You are responsible for the rule of the Socialists," he said. The law, which came to be known as the blockage law, would "end the fog over the debate about whether Eretz Israel can be partitioned again." The law, he wrote, "was the national mission assigned to Gahal."[3]

There was more to the law and Begin's support than the question of Eretz Israel. It was also practical politics, because Begin wanted to be able to widen and broaden Gahal's base of power by eliminating the small, liberal, center parties that competed with Gahal over Eretz Israel. He saw that a greater Gahal coalition was needed and the smaller parties were partially preventing that from happening. He sought to swallow the electorate of these parties.

The war and the troop withdrawals, and the ensuing heated national debate, had strengthened the smaller center and right parties. Tamir's Free Center party had gained two seats in the 1969 election and the Rafi dissidents had managed to gain three seats as the La'am party. Begin's strategy worked and both of these minuscule right parties ended up joining Likud in 1973, which was well on its way to becoming a genuine national party.

The origin of Likud itself had almost nothing to do with Begin. Begin did not create it, conceive it or even give it its name, but his role in its formation and durability was critical. Likud's origin lay with General Ariel Sharon, one of Israel's greatest political chameleons.

Sharon is a curious political figure, even for Israel. He was no newcomer to Gahal. In 1969, frustrated and contemplating retirement, he approached the Liberals of Gahal who were interested in having him in a prominent place on their ticket. Sharon was not politically affiliated at the time, but that didn't bother Gahal. Sharon's appeal lay in the fact that he was a soldier—a general—and one of the heroes of the 1967 war.

Sharon's political career, which conformed more to his ravenous ambition than to any political principle, started rather late, even for an officer, although Labor almost claimed him. Back in 1956, when Sharon was an aggressive major, then Foreign Minister Moshe Sharett wrote in his diary that "Major Sharon is one of Israel's emerging officers and he is one of ours," meaning Mapai. Sharon always denied the claim.

Initially, Sharon's ambition lay with the military, where he dreamed of becoming IDF chief of staff. But so ruthless and radical was his behavior and so naked was his ambition that none of the Labor stalwarts liked or trusted him and they blocked him at every turn. Ben Gurion, who pampered him as a fighter, never contemplated inviting Sharon to join Mapai. Golda Meir detested him for his brashness and ruthlessness, and his rivals within the IDF did their best to keep him from power. She told Sharon that he would never become chief of staff as long as she was Prime Minister.

After the 1967 war, all of the major political parties engaged in an orgy of political head-hunting among the ranks of the IDF officers, looking for those who were now salable political commodities. The Herut-Gahal coalition sorely lacked charismatic officers within its ranks. Sharon, as a divisional commander in the Sinai, was a hot political commodity. Getting Sharon was the prize, and they managed to get two when Ezer Weizman, retiring chief of staff of the air force, joined Herut. He was, after all, an old Etzel fighter.

Sharon planned on joining the Gahal coalition through the Liberal Party door, not because he was attracted to the party's ideas, but because the chances for advancement were better among the Liberals, who lacked charismatic and powerful leaders like Begin. Clearly, one of his aims, as he suggested to me in 1973, was not merely to join Gahal, but to take over its leadership.

Labor party stalwarts were not unaware of what was happening or of Sharon's electoral appeal. Through the auspices of Pinchas Sapir, Mapai-Maarach's chief electoral strategist and Minister of Finance, Sharon was offered a Southern Front command to assure that he would stay in the IDF and out of politics, and particularly out of the ranks of Gahal.

Sharon returned to the IDF, but he still did not get a shot at the top spot. In July of 1973, he demanded that he be made chief of staff. Golda Meir was adamant in her refusal. Angry and frustrated, Sharon resigned again. His eyes were on a political career and particularly in the 1973 November elections.

Leaving his options open, and showing that ideology did not particularly matter, Sharon first approached a group that later became the Dash party in the 1977 elections. He realized quickly that this group of retired senior officers, diplomats and professionals was not fruitful political ground for him, because it was stuffed with what he contemptuously called "Admorim" (or, in English, Hasidic rabbis) his term for the retired super elite of the state who were not great fans of his. Sharon went so far as to flirt with the peace movement, while simultaneously negotiating with Dayan's close adviser, hawkish Professor Yuval Neeman.

Sharon told me that he finally decided on Gahal, but with a condition. The condition was that Sharon would help to organize a wall-to-wall coalition of right-wing and nationalist parties. "I'll call it Likud," he told me in August of 1973. "Don't you agree that Likud is a good name?"

Sharon then told me his strategy. To enter via Herut was futile because Begin blocked the way. The Liberals, he said, "were impotent" and therefore represented the best route to power and the best way to organize and mobilize the coalition en route to a takeover. Typically, Sharon aimed high. Less than the top or even near it was simply not good enough.

First, Sharon still in uniform negotiated with his friends in Tamir's Free Center party and in La'am, led by Mapai renegade Yigal Horowitz. Sharon then turned to Gahal and talked with Begin and his deputy Simcha Ehrlich.

Now, a frantic series of negotiations, maneuvers, talks and manipulations began which would culminate in the official creation of Likud. Much of the stumbling blocks and controversy centered around the negotiations. As the process began, Tamir had attacked Begin in the Knesset for his support of the Bader-Offer law, charging that the law was a ploy to crush his Free Center party. This was not far from the truth, but the newspapers carried a bigger headline—"Arik Leaves IDF," heavier with import. Sharon, the great aggrandizer, helped the news travel fast, when all of the right-wing parties were abuzz.

A rash of meetings resulted from the news. Horowitz and his La'am followers met. Tamir conferred with his lieutenants in the Free Center Party. Gahal faced now a political blitz by Sharon, a tactic he would use throughout his political career, very much the soldier-tactician in the arena of politics. Sharon was demanding a new coalition whose base would be Gahal, with the inclusion of Tamir and La'am. Without consulting Gahal, he catapulted Tamir's candidates to the top of the Gahal electoral list.

Begin was defiantly opposed to any deal with his archenemy Tamir. Gahal was inclined toward La'am, but Herut would not put up with Tamir.

Sharon needed to outmaneuver Begin, and so he conducted a political flirtation with Ehrlich. On July 16, Sharon and Horowitz met. Horowitz agreed to join Gahal as a parliamentary unit. In a press conference the following day, Sharon was coy. He refused to say which Gahal party he would join but presented himself as a politician above the battle of internal strife. All he wanted, he says, was to present an alternative to Maarach, meaning that Israel needed a large electoral alignment to challenge Labor.

Now, Sharon was reassuring Tamir that Begin would not reject the idea. Sharon was also busy recruiting Weizman who resigned from the Meir cabinet in August 1970 along with Gahal. On the telephone, Sharon stated his case to Weizman. "Going together means that we will have a wide front," he said. As he hung up, he told me that "Begin is encircled," a smug, somewhat premature analysis, to say the least. The Weizman-Sharon ultimatum, imposing Tamir on Gahal, was that the two generals would withdraw from Gahal if the latter was not properly integrated.

Even as Weizman denied that he had made a deal with Sharon, Sharon was running to the Liberals. The stumbling block was Tamir. The Liberals had had no love for him, and Herut was strongly opposed to him. He was seen as a maverick, a potential disturbing force. Tamir's many challenges to Begin were coming back to haunt him, and his most recent attack on Begin in the Knesset didn't help matters. The Liberals now lobbied Begin—"Give Arik a chance," they argued.

On July 19, Begin began to enter the picture. He "consulted" with Herut's executive committee on how to deal with Sharon. Begin appeared inclined to favor the idea of a broad coalition. Dov Shilansky, who was defended by Tamir in a sensational trial in the 1950s, reminded everyone of Tamir's credentials. But he was not trusted by Begin. "Tamir," tells a Begin advisor, "is a time bomb." Begin pressured his Herut colleagues to decide. "What if," he suggested, "Sharon should come to us via the Liberals?"[4] Begin already perceived Sharon's intentions and he was now trying to evade them. As a Liberal, Sharon would have no claim on Herut, certainly not on its leadership.

Meeting with Gahal, Begin in effect evaded the responsibility for the final decision and for both Sharon and Tamir's expected irresponsible behavior. Begin and Sharon then met over the Weizman-Sharon "ultimatum," Begin spoke to Sharon in the style of a father scolding his wrong-headed son: "I have great affection for you Arik. I was among those who waited for you [to join Gahal]. I never advised you to retire from the IDF, as I have never advised Ezer. But now that you have decided to retire, I shall embrace you two. The decision to establish Likud was for me as tortuous as those days when I got out of the underground [1948]. The [Tamir entry] is not a question of how many mandates Gahal is to gain but of the future of the whole enterprise."[5]

On July 20, there was a meeting with Sharon, Begin, Dr. Benyamin Halevy of the Liberals, Landau and Eitan Livny, Herut's Secretary-General. Begin tried to persuade Sharon to join the Liberals, but Sharon remained noncommittal. Sharon's conditions for joining, or rather his approach and manner, upset everyone. They could smell his naked ambition. They suggested he present his demands to an all-Gahal forum. Sharon was demanding that Likud be an all-nationalistic alignment against the Labor alignment. Begin was put off by the nature of the offer, which was in the way of a diktat. Both the Liberals and Herut were worried about the protection and defense of their internal party integrity, which superseded the basic attractiveness of Sharon's idea. They were all wary of Sharon and his ambition. Ehrlich insisted that Sharon accept their terms.

But now Begin "melts." In a special June 22 Herut meeting, Begin calls "for a rehabilitation of Gahal to meet the challenge of Maarach . . . To save democracy in Israel, Gahal must achieve numerical parity with the Left."

Sharon now met with Begin on June 23. Begin, obviously warming to the idea, told Sharon about the numerous cables and letters he had received favoring the idea of Likud. "My only concern," he said, "is Eretz Israel's integrity. There is always a chance that a majority in the Knesset would turn the scales against the idea. We must narrow the gap between the two."[6] On June 24, Herut met again. Begin surprised everyone by announcing his readiness to propose Sharon's idea before an all-Gahal forum on June 26. There was still some opposition to Tamir, but without Tamir, there was no Sharon.

On June 26, at Begin's home, Begin told Sharon he was ready to accept the idea of the proposed national bloc, meaning Likud. On his way back from Begin, Sharon, elated, stopped by my house. "Now we [Likud] shall take over the government," he said, without explaining how he would manage that particular feat.

On July 31, after five hours of heated debate over the status of Tamir, Herut, following Begin's recommendation, votes for the formation of Likud. Sharon, as expected, joins the Liberals. La'am, as well as Tamir's party, are firmly within the fold that includes Herut.

Begin is rejuvenated in his heart. He sees a new, fresh, and larger Gahal, revitalized by two new parties and three generals—Sharon, Weizman, and Avraham Yoffe of La'am. The specter of Sharon, reflects the wise politician and Liberal leader Simcha Ehrlich, is haunting Gahal. In an interview with Avnery Ehrlich says: "Arik is not a team person. He is not a man who adheres to principles . . . For Arik the operational tactics supersede the principles of the operation . . . All his life he has been in the habit of planning and executing orders. His world is far removed from the public political one. He will want to introduce the habits of the military into civilian political procedures . . . He sees people hierarchically and sees public men as petty and decadent politicians."[7]

Likud was ready for its first electoral campaign, slated for November. In his *Maariv* column, Begin summarized the Principles of Likud:

1. The right of the Jewish people to settle in all Eretz Israel is inviolate.

2. No further partition of Eretz Israel is acceptable.

3. Begin the necessary legal procedures to establish Israeli sovereignty over the liberated territories.

4. Aspire and search for a formal peace with the Arab states. But peace is to be achieved only by direct negotiations.

5. Large-scale Jewish settlements in urban and rural Judea, Samaria, Gaza, the Golan Heights and Sinai. This settlement project should receive first-priority over all other state activities.

6. In Eretz Israel, all citizens will enjoy civil rights regardless of origin, race, nationality, religion, sex, or ethnic group.[8]

With the creation of Likud, which Sharon had so flamboyantly helped to accomplish in a flurry of media attention, many observers felt that Begin was losing his political grip on the coalition to Sharon and Tamir. This was simply not so. In many ways, Begin emerged stronger than ever.

"We are not at an end," Begin said, just nine days before the Yom Kippur War. "We, all, are just beginning a new year and, who knows, perhaps our redemption. . . . Likud is only a continuation of our service. There is much to do for the nation of Israel, for Eretz Israel, and with God's help we shall do so. You may get rid of me, or any individual, but you can never force me from the principles I have dedicated my life to."[9]

As the election neared, Begin imposed his own leadership on the new coalition, his own authority over the assorted nationalists and liberals who made up Likud.

The campaign was abruptly interrupted—and eventually altered—by the Yom Kippur War. The war also managed to accomplish what Likud could not—it strengthened the militant constituency while creating a huge chasm and division among the Israeli electorate.

Labor's inner circle, the cabinet of Golda Meir, was implicated in what came to be called the misdeed *(mehdal)* of 1973. Dayan was the chief villain and victim in the aftermath of the *mehdal.* Although a court of inquiry exonerated Dayan and the government of the intelligence disaster that led to the surprise attack, Dayan's reputation took a severe beating. After the war, he became noticeably estranged from his own party.

The misdeed became great political fodder for Sharon, who led the attack on the Labor government. Sharon attacked what he called "the faulty command of the Southern Front before the war" and attacked General Bar-Lev, his personal enemy and a proponent of the static defense policy along the Canal, which was known as the Bar-Lev line. Sharon gleefully challenged the old Left, the Palmach commanders who had participated in the Sezon and made life miserable for Begin's Etzel.

As the campaign progressed, Begin and Sharon seemed cordial to each other in public, but Begin was rightfully wary of Sharon and his ambition. The relationship was strictly correct without ever becoming intimate. Sharon would always remain lukewarm to Begin's old-style Revisionism. Sharon, and Tamir, with their fiery nationalism, presented a startling contrast to Begin's old version of the new music.

Surprisingly, Tamir, considering his animosity toward Begin, did not join forces with Sharon. Instead, Sharon and Tamir began to attack each other. Tamir accused Sharon of "shooting at each one of us separately in order to achieve his goals." "Not me," cried Sharon. "I am ready for a battle with Tamir if he wants one." Tamir still reserved some of his attacks for Begin. "What the movement needs is new blood and new young men," he cried, echoing an old theme, fighting a battle he had fought twice before. "The movement could not be but a confederation. We must protect our organizational and stylistic difference."[10]

Begin, of course, resented these statements, but he kept his silence and remained above the battle.

Likud had not won the 1973 elections, now, with 39 Knesset members, it represented a potentially formidable opposition to Labor.

Yet, between 1973 and the onset of the 1977 election campaign, Begin and Likud failed to sustain the momentum they had gained in the 1973 elections. To some extent this was due in part to the defection of Sharon and to the effective political maneuvering of Rabin.

Sharon lost patience with the slow, tiresome life of the Knesset, which was not an ideal arena for a man who yearned for action. He resigned from the Knesset. Now, as quick to change sides as ever, he accepted Rabin's offer to become his military adviser. On the surface, he seemed a strange choice indeed.

Yet, Rabin's choice was astute, at least for short-term purposes, because he wanted to outflank the Right and Likud and use the appointment of Sharon as a shield against the heavy political flak he expected to receive after the upcoming Kissinger troop-separation agreement.

Sharon "advised" Rabin during the troop separation negotiations, although his heart clearly was not in his job. As a member of a distinguished negotiating team, Sharon reined in his natural instincts and acted out the role of loyal lieutenant, so much so that he seemed to have left a deep impression on Rabin. Rabin writes that he was encouraged by Sharon's advice. Sharon told Rabin that "I dispute the concept of an interim agreement but as long as I am serving as your advisor, I will give you my advice within the framework of your policy."[11]

Rabin succeeded in using Sharon on two battlefronts: he isolated Sharon from Begin and used him as a wedge against his arch rival within Labor, Shimon Peres. Rabin favorably compared Sharon to Professor Yuval Neeman, a nationalist ideologue and Rabin advisor who organized radical attacks on the Prime Minister. "Comparing Sharon to Neeman is to compare civility with duplicity," wrote Rabin. "Not in vain did Neeman work with Peres and Sharon with me."[12] This may have been the first and last time that anyone set up Sharon as an example of loyalty, let alone civility.

Between 1973 and 1977, Sharon was muffled, operating, strangely enough, within the mainstream of Israeli politics. As 1977 approached, the nation girded itself for what promised to be yet another tedious election campaign, yet another defeat for Begin, who was facing what he thought was his last hurrah. It would turn out to be an entirely unique, watershed election for Israel.

30

The 1977 Elections: The Mahapach (Turnover)[1]

As the meandering, long 1977 Israeli election campaign got underway after the October 1973 war, there seemed to be no indications that the result would be a startling watershed in the political life of the nation.

One long-term result of the war was that it split the Labor party. Some of Labor's military, bureaucratic and intellectual elite bolted from the party and organized itself into a new movement-party called *Dash* (Democratic Party for Change). The movement was led by Professor Yigael Yadin, a war hero and acting chief of staff during the War for Independence and IDF's chief of staff 1949–52. Dash itself was a divided party, even though it was sometimes called Labor II. It was split between hawks and doves. It was an Ashkenazy, elitist party composed of the Bitzuists, the pragmatic doers, and included retired IDF generals, former intelligence and police officers, diplomats and professors. In addition, to give Dash an even stronger renegade flavor, a strong contingency of LIM members joined Dash along with a number of Labor hawks. Dash was essentially a hawkish party even if part of it was composed of liberal Tel Aviv University intellectuals. The formation of Dash hurt the Labor alignment at the polls, where *Dash* picked up fifteen seats. The 1973 war moved Israeli politics from left of center to right of center. Thus, a Likud-Dash combination could outvote Labor in the Knesset.

The Labor Party and movement, under one name or another, had ruled the Yishuv and the new nation since 1935, and there were no serious indications that it would not routinely win yet another election.

It was generally agreed that Labor appeared to be in a noticeable decline, but to its members and to the pollsters who gauged the pulse of the electorate, there was no reason to assume that its rule was in any serious danger.

Yet, Labor was extremely vulnerable and all the signs were there, if anybody had bothered to read them correctly. The movement, which had always been led by charismatic, powerful figures, was now startlingly impoverished of dominating personalities. Ben Gurion, Meir, Pinchas Sapir, the party politician and electoral tactician supreme, had all died or retired. Dayan was disillusioned with Labor. The two dominant political personalities of the movement—Prime Minister Rabin and Defense Minister Peres—suffered from a lack of perceived personality and, moreover, fought one another.

There was, in 1977, a feeling of Alice in Wonderland about the party. Its members seemed to be living in an air of assumed power, a belief that the rule of Labor was preordained and permanent. The Labor Party failed to realize that its pioneer and kibbutzim symbols were no longer as fresh and inspiring as they had been in the past. Far from being in the forefront of issues that galvanized the populace, Labor had become a storehouse of political and electoral power, static in nature, a transmitter of power and favors, of economic rewards and offices. It had become a party of functionaries and politicians, of bureaucrats and apparatchiks who spent their time wheeling and dealing for votes, for political office and for influence.

Prime Minister Rabin, and later Peres, could not command the respect or the adulation of even their own followers. Rabin was respected for his achievements as chief of staff of the IDF and as Israel's ambassador to the United States, where he was quite popular, but both he and Peres were perceived as essentially colorless, and rather dull. They could not inspire or dominate even their own political movements and parties.

By 1977, the Labor-Maarach coalition had been emptied of its political and ideological baggage. Simultaneously, a curious process of democratization had occurred within the party structure.

In the past, Prime Ministers and cabinet-level ministers had been chosen by the party hierarchy in a manner strongly reminiscent of older American-style smoke-filled back rooms. That is to say, party elites made top-level choices, bypassing the movement as a whole. As recently as 1974, Sapir could still use his guile and his tremendous political prestige in the selection of the nominee for Prime Minister, who turned out to be Rabin.

But in 1977 Sapir was dead, and with him died the closed-door style of doing business. There was no party machine, no elite, no inner cabinet—no kitchen cabinet—to dictate to the nation, the party and the coalition.

In April 1977, a thousand members of the Labor Central Committee dictated the choice for Prime Minister at a party conference. Their choice, over an embittered Peres, was Rabin, who, Rabin claimed in his memoirs, intrigued and plotted against him in an open display of the disarray of Labor.

According to Rabin, from the day of the acrimonious Labor Party conference at which Peres was defeated, Peres was determined to be, in his challenge to him, "unrelenting." All along, Peres, a veteran intriguer and political fighter, leaked innuendoes and information about Rabin to the press, for which Rabin, the straightforward IDF soldier, had no answer; nor had he any inclination to fight.

If Labor seemed to be thin at the center and at the edges, and indulging in public bloodletting, veteran political pollsters did not see this as a sign that it was on the way out. A spring poll indicated that 32 percent of the electorate still favored Labor, another 23 percent favored Likud, 15 percent were for Dash, 15 percent were undecided, and 15 percent refused to give any indication whatsoever. The latter two figures constituted a formidable number, but hardly any expert at the time saw its significance. Yet reflecting on those years, it would be correct to say that in 1974, for the first time in Labor's history, a leader of Mapai-Labor, Yitzhak Rabin, presided over a minority interim government stripped of its traditional allies and unable to pass legislation—not even the government's own budget, and unable to make the sharper decisions of the Ben Gurion, Eshkol and Golda Meir governments.

It would appear that with all of Labor's obvious problems, which were later compounded by Rabin's political blunders, the chances for the new Likud coalition should have been extremely promising at the start of the campaign. Yet even Begin, as the leader of Likud, was not all that optimistic about his and his party's chances. In 1977 Begin seemed to be facing his last political hurrah.

Many of the elements of Gahal-Herut in the Likud, after all, were almost as old and sterile as Labor, even though it was perceived as being an "outsider's" party. In 1977, Begin actually told me that he was preparing for his retirement, that he was ready to write his memoirs.

On the surface, nothing much had changed. Begin appeared tired and very much the same Begin. The Likud party platform had barely changed from the one presented to the electorate in 1973, and in fact contained strong echoes of the old Herut party dating back to 1951.

Yet a number of things were different, particularly the presence within Likud of fresh and invigorating political blood.

The most effective personality within Likud was Ezer Weizman, late of Herut and now returned to the fold. Although not a particularly deep political thinker, Weizman proved invaluable merely by his presence, and especially as a political campaign manager. He was an immensely popular man with a great deal of open, personal charm, and a war hero, of whom there were very few in the Likud ranks. He had been chief of staff of the air force when it delivered the rousing 1967 victory. Weizman was, politically, a fresh breath of air in the old Etzel ranks.

As campaign manager, he proved to be a thoroughly modern electoral technician, full of political savvy. He treated the election as if it were a series of American-style primaries, using American election techniques for all they were worth. He hired both Israeli and American electoral and public opinion specialists, who labored effectively to create a new, rational, streamlined image for Likud. He organized Likud headquarters in *Metzudat Zeev* (Zeev Jabotinsky Fortress), the Herut headquarters in Tel Aviv, and staffed it with young, nondogmatic, tough intellectuals.

Early in the campaign, in March 1977, Weizman was faced with what looked at first like a startling tragedy, but actually turned out to be something of a political boon. Begin was stricken with a serious heart attack and ended up in Tel Aviv's Yichilov hospital. The nature of his illness was kept from the public.

This obviously kept Begin off the campaign trail, but it also had the effect of softening Likud's usually strident campaign rhetoric which, originating with Begin, alienated many potential Likud adherents. Begin's absence contributed to a relaxed but professional atmosphere in Likud's campaign, one that was characterized, for the first time in Israel, by the extensive use of television. For three months, there were no noisy, bombastic, arm-waving speeches by Begin, nor were there any sarcastic, strident articles in *Maariv.* Instead, a sane campaign emerged, marked by the principal issue in Likud's platform—Eretz Israel, as well as by the usual Herut demands, this time calmly presented and stated.

Begin's illness also had another advantage. Begin would always remain a hero to the Herut-Etzel veterans, but in the past, he had been presented to the public as a buffoon, a clown, by Labor Party stalwarts. Now, bravely and stoically lying in the hospital, Begin suddenly commanded a great deal of general sympathy. No longer could Labor politicians mock him and deride him. Begin was sick, perhaps even dying, all the while bravely conducting a campaign.

This left Weizman time to concentrate on the issues without too much interference from Begin. Weizman was after that 30 percent electorate which had not made up its mind or refused to say which way it was leaning, not to mention rebel Labor voters and the new, as yet untapped, Sephardic generation of voters.

When Begin did return to the stump, he found himself a new target—the threat of the Palestine Liberation Organization's state-within-a-state in Lebanon. This time Begin's object of vilification was the PLO, and he went after it with a vengeance. In Begin's rhetoric, PLO members were characterized as Arab Nazis. He went passionately on the offensive. In the wake of the Ma'alot massacre, in which a number of Israeli children were killed after the PLO captured a school bus and were stormed by the IDF, Begin wrote a strong article in *Maariv*, entitled "Arab Nazism Against the Jewish Boy."

"We must renew the offensive against Arab Nazism," he wrote. "We are in the 1970s and we have a state. An enormous power is at our disposal. If the Jewish nation had had such a power in the 1940s, we could have hit hard at Hitler, Himmler, Eichmann and the Einsatzgruppen and the SS. We would have relentlessly hit them."

He said that Israel must organize a special kind of warfare to deal with "the cells of killers."[2] But what was going to determine the outcome of the campaign was not Begin's rhetoric. Not this time.

If Likud was now blossoming under the infusion of newer, young, politically professional campaigners, it was also being helped by an ideological trend that was apparently sweeping the country, although its political implications were not, this early in the campaign, being clearly understood.

Between 1967 and 1977, it was becoming increasingly clear that the electorate was moving toward a volatile nationalism, a shift that should have been observed as a warning sign by Labor. Clearly, the public mood was changing.

For example, when voters were asked about the question of returning or exchanging territories, the number who said *none* of the territories increased from 30 percent in 1969, to 41 percent in 1977. (It would rise to 50 percent by 1981.) The number of those saying "some of the territories" should be returned dropped from 59 percent in 1969 to 43 percent in 1977. Both sets of figures indicate a flow toward the idea of Eretz Israel, if only indirectly.

More interesting, and more ominous for Labor, was a distinct trend away from the Left of the political spectrum. In 1962, 31 percent of the voting populace had defined themselves as being "on the Left," but in 1977, only 4 percent identified themselves as such, while the momentum seemed to be turning toward the Right, whose supporters stood at 8 percent in 1962, went to 16 percent in 1969 and rose to 28 percent in 1977.

These findings might have given pollsters pause to think the time had come for Begin and Likud. But Begin and his hardcore Herut cohorts were, incorrectly, still perceived as being part of the political past.

What actually happened in the 1977 election is that it became a political free-for-all. The rise of Dash had something to do with that, but a grievous political mistake by Rabin did even more damage. Labor had carved its traditional coalition with the national religious parties as its natural allies, even though many of their members were in the forefront of the annexationist movements. The Rabin government, as a rule, tolerated this radical orientation as long as there was collective responsibility within the cabinet.

Rabin was essentially a military man, not an experienced politician. Ben Gurion's firm rule had been that the cornerstone of the Labor coalition must be the National Religious Party, that Labor would have trouble forging a government without it. Now Rabin made a fatal political mistake: he approved the arrival and acceptance of delivery of the much-needed American Phantom jets on a Sabbath, a traditional nonworking day, and the NRP, offended on religious grounds, protested strongly. Rabin ignored their protests and failed to mollify their members and they resigned from the government, leading to its fall. The coalition had been broken. In the past the NRP had made a coalitional arrangement with Mapai-Labor. In 1977, it was no longer bound by its historical tie to a Labor-dominated government. Begin immediately started to court the NRP.

Obviously, the election results stunned everybody. It was a turnabout of remarkable proportions. Perhaps most startled was Begin himself, who at the start of the campaign, had envisioned this to be his last charge, his last try. Certainly even his Herut party faithful might have turned away from him if he had failed again, and Begin was, by now, used to political failure. Certainly, the younger, new members of Likud would have moved to depose him, and if Likud had been defeated, the coalition probably would not have lasted a day after the election.

Obviously, it was the infusion of new blood in Likud that helped pave the way for a Begin victory. But people like Sharon, Horowitz from La'am, Tamir and Weizman would add diverse and badly needed new talent to the coalition government. On its own Herut could not have overcome even a weak, badly splintered Labor party.

The pollsters and experts had been wrong. They had overestimated the traditional power of Labor. They had misread Begin on the basis of his and Herut's poor electoral history. They had failed to see the changing demographic trends within Israel, and they underestimated the strength of Dash.

What had happened to a great degree was that the ideas and symbols of Labor, which for so long had captivated the nation and the electorate, had become passé—old and too familiar.

On July 15, 1977, with the help of Sharon's Peace of Zion party's two Knesset seats (for which Sharon would be rewarded with a membership in the cabinet), Begin presented his coalition government to President Ephraim Katzir.

It remained to be seen how Begin and Likud would form their government, and what the fall of Labor and the rise of Likud would mean for the nation and the world at large.

31

The Formation of the Likud Government: Begin and His New Associates[1]

Begin had often dreamed of following in the footsteps of his mentor Jabotinsky, of becoming a legitimate Zionist leader, of a great nationalist camp, but it is probably safe to say that after decades of electoral failure, of being treated as an outcast and political pariah, he may have been hard put to resist the temptation to pinch himself after presenting himself to Israel's President for the purpose of forming a new government.

Here, at last, was the grand opportunity, the bold task of implementing Revisionism's fondest hopes. Would this just be a flash in the pan, an isolated turnover *(Mahapach)*, or would Begin be able to fulfill Jabotinsky's old wishes?

In typical Begin fashion, his approach to forming a government was original and controversial, mixing his gift for political pragmatism, his unbending belief in Eretz Israel, and a streak of hero worship and military romanticism.

Although Likud had clearly emerged as a major mass movement party, spurred by LIM's Eretz Israel ideology and carried by Begin and Herut, the government that emerged was a mixed bag, a mongrel government, neither fish nor fowl, at least initially. It was not Herut, it was not LIM, it was not even Likud.

Clearly, the Herut party faithful, after waiting so long, wanted to be in the government, but their ranks were devoid of administrative talent, or national political experience, with the exception of Begin himself. In the end, only five Herutites would become part of the Likud coalition system.

The government as it began to emerge included Begin at the helm, Weizman as Defense Minister, Sharon, who joined Herut in 1977 after his own party gained only two seats in the elections, as Minister of Agriculture, and Simha Ehrlich of the Liberals as Minister of Finance. The rest of the cabinet was composed of National Religious Party members.

The crucial office, however, next to the Prime Minister and Defense Minister, was the Foreign Ministry, and here Begin showed his contradictory state of mind.

Much as he might have wanted to assume the office of Foreign Minister, he didn't see himself fitting comfortably in that role. Nor could he appoint a radical Likud or Herut annexationist to the post, lest he spark concern among Israel's allies in the U.S., who were startled enough by the election results and who knew very little about Begin.

Actually, there was only one person Begin really wanted, whom he thought he could work with, but it was on the surface an unlikely choice—Moshe Dayan, war hero, Labor's political outcast, the former IDF chief of staff and Defense Minister.

There is a noticeable element of hero worship in Begin's pursuit of Dayan and there are aspects of a courtship. It is like a picture of an elderly, oft-rejected suitor pursuing his goal wearing blinders. For Begin, Dayan represented everything that he himself was not, the best of his old enemies in the ranks of Mapai-Labor. But when one hitches Dayan to Weizman, and stranger yet, to Sharon, they seem very appropriate choices for a man enamored of armies, legions and militarism. One could dub Begin's first cabinet the cabinet of the generals.

To Begin, Dayan might have seemed an almost perfect choice. He was experienced in military matters and in diplomacy; he was, at one time, immensely popular with the Americans; he had flair and prestige, even if he was at one time a Mapai stalwart. Then, too, Begin must have remembered that Dayan was opposed to the Sezon, even though he took part in it as a loyal soldier. Dayan was famous for his anti-ideological pragmatic style. A man of purpose—a farsighted general. Begin respected and admired Dayan, who was not a ranting Labor ideologue, but a supreme pragmatist. Dedicated to improving military settlements, he was also in favor of improving relations with the Arabs. "I trust Dayan's hawkish pragmatism," Begin once told me.

Begin knew that Dayan was openly opposed to annexation, but between 1967 and 1970, when they were both part of the National Unity Government, they had begun to form a strange, not entirely uncomfortable alliance. Begin looked at Dayan and saw beyond politics, finding symbols. Dayan was a product of the agricultural settlements system, was raised on a moshav and came from the moshavim movement. Dayan, at his heart, was a settler, not an annexationist.

Begin, the Diaspora Jew, the latecomer to Palestine, looked at Dayan and saw the quintessential Israeli, raised on the land of Eretz Israel, the Sabra, open, free, courageous, tanned, a Bitzuist, or doer—in short, everything Begin was not. Begin was moderately ambivalent about Dayan's personal behavior because Dayan had a reputation as something of a hard liver and a rake. "Not exactly a model type," Ben Gurion once told me.

Begin's fascination with Dayan was certainly an outgrowth of Begin's general fascination with military heroes, a thread that runs all the way back to his Betar days, with their pomp and uniforms and parades. He would forever romanticize the IDF and the idea of Israeli fighters as he romanticized war, of which Dayan, the man with the black eye patch, was the example par excellence. Begin glorified his own Etzel fighters, clothing their acts of terrorism in heroism, he admired secretly the Palmach, which he detested politically, but above all he worshiped, like many Israelis, at the shrine of the IDF.

For Begin, the IDF was the symbol of Israel's liberation, its very existence, its security, and its unsullied ideals. For him, the IDF was the incarnation of Jabotinsky's revered legions, and Dayan epitomized the IDF, especially the IDF of the great 1967 lightning victory, during which Begin was part of the government. Small wonder that Dayan represented a political temptation that Begin could not pass by.

As for Dayan, his feelings about Begin must have been mixed indeed, although he never regarded Begin with the contempt and scorn of his Socialist-Zionist compatriots, who often stooped to calling him that "ghetto windbag."

There was a certain affinity between Dayan and Begin, at least as things stood in 1977. Like Begin before 1977, Dayan, the former hero and charismatic political figure, was now an outsider, a man apart from his lifelong political allies. An admired hero after the 1967 war, who might have achieved the Prime Ministership, he was blamed by the public for the initial failure of the 1973 war. In its aftermath, parents of sons killed in the war threw tomatoes at him in the streets, and booed and jeered him at public gatherings, where he often could not finish a speech. The years after 1973 were years of political decline for Dayan, although his charisma and reputation were still considerable. Small wonder the two might have felt some kinship when they talked. Begin, even more than Dayan, was used to political failure and vehement hostility. They were two patriots rejected by their nation. The year 1977 was fraught with the possibility of change for both of them.

When Begin offered the Foreign Ministry to Dayan, the choice startled many observers, including Begin's own Herut cohorts, who reacted angrily, especially the Etzel ancients. But this was no overnight decision. The negotiations and courtship between the two, with Weizman often acting as a kind of matchmaker, had been going on for some time.

Begin had begun the process, obviously intrigued by Dayan, with a number of articles in *Maariv* that either focused on Dayan or seemed to seek him out: "Where is Dayan?" or "What Is Dayan's Next Step?" or "A Controversy With Dayan," and so on.

Throughout the 1977 campaign, Begin and his campaign manager Weizman were constantly in touch with Dayan, either directly or through intermediaries. For them, Dayan, on the marginal fringes of his own party, indeed rejected by his party, loomed like a great political catch to be lured into the ranks of Likud—Begin saw it at times as a conquest, a luring away of Dayan from the party of Ben Gurion, Begin's lifelong nemesis.

On April 22, Begin, in a key *Maariv* article on Eretz Israel seemed to be sounding out Dayan. Under the title "Eretz Israel and Clarifications with Mr. Dayan," Begin began by denying rumors that Likud had made political approaches to Dayan. Nevertheless, he wanted to clarify where he and Dayan might agree or disagree on key issues, surely the beginnings of any political courtship.

Even in the midst of the campaign, and before that, Begin and Dayan had met often, either in Dayan's office or at Begin's home, to discuss political issues and especially the occupied territories and the concepts behind Eretz Israel. Sometime in April, Dayan visited Begin at home. "We met and spoke for several hours," Begin recalled. "Mr. Dayan related to me his great concern for the future of Judea and Samaria . . . He explained to me his opposition quite clearly: in the Labor Party Conference, he would demand that the conference must decide that before any action of withdrawal in Judea and Samaria there must be elections."[2] In other words, Dayan felt that the representatives of the government could negotiate only after there was a perceivable consensus to change policy.

Begin asked what was new about Dayan's proposal. Dayan replied that in this conference, he wanted to establish the rule that there could be no actual withdrawal from Judea and Samaria unless it was approved in elections that would be conducted for that purpose—in a special referendum.

"What if the conference failed to accept your demand?" Begin asked Dayan. Dayan told Begin that his friends had suggested that he start a party of his own. "But my intuition is," he told Begin, "that we should join Likud."[3] That was more than a broad hint, and it made Begin optimistic about his chances of landing the Labor star, even if this could have been a Dayan ploy to make Labor accept his proposals.

As it turned out, Labor did not adopt any of Dayan's demands. No referendum would be required for the government to initiate negotiations.

Begin and Dayan met again after the conference. Dayan had not changed his mind, but he said the majority of his party was not prepared to go along with him. Dayan asked Begin about *Sipuah*, or annexation, to which he was opposed. Begin said the concept of annexation did not apply to Judea or Samaria. "You don't annex what is yours," he said.

Much later in April, a proposal was brought to Begin for his signature late at night. It was from Dayan. If Begin accepted Dayan's principles, he would join up with Likud. The document stated that "as long as there are negotiations between Israel and Arab states, no Israeli sovereignty will be extended to the administered territories or parts of them. That includes the West Bank."[4]

Although this was not acceptable to Begin, he was pleased. "I had no doubt," he said, "that we could not sign that document. But Dayan is close to me in his concern for Judea and Samaria and that is commendable . . . But if we had signed what we were asked to that night, we would have lost the elections and above all *our world* (italics mine)."[5] Of course, in less than a year, Begin would ask Foreign Minister Dayan to do exactly what he had suggested in that document.

The negotiations were not over, however. Weizman, who also happened to be Dayan's former brother-in-law, now entered the picture. For Weizman, the possibility of Dayan entering Likud would have been a Godsend. With Dayan in the cabinet, Weizman would not feel so isolated among the dogmatist and hard-core radicals of Herut and Likud. Together, the two heroes of 1967 just might be able to pull off an electoral upset, and once in the government, buttress Begin against the extremists, save him from his own worst rhetorical instincts, and perhaps outmaneuver him.

On May 19, Dayan requested a meeting with Weizman at his home. Without fanfare, Dayan immediately told Weizman that Begin, prior to being hospitalized again, had offered Dayan the Foreign Minister's portfolio. This was news to Weizman, who had known absolutely nothing about the meetings between Begin and Dayan.

Dayan had come to tell Weizman that he had neither accepted nor rejected Begin's offer. He wanted some time to consider the proposal, but now that Begin was hospitalized, he was also concerned about Begin's health and political future. He wondered, he told Weizman, if Begin, assuming a Likud victory, could actually assume the duties of Prime Minister.[6]

According to Dayan, he asked Weizman: If Begin, for reasons of health could not assume the office, would Weizman do so? And if so, he was agreeable to serving under Weizman. For Weizman, this seemed like a political and electoral gift, for Weizman figured that Dayan was worth at least six seats in the Knesset.

Dayan had once said that he felt "closer to Begin than to Meir Ya'ari (the head of the leftist Mapam party, part of the Labor Alignment),"[7] but he reiterated that he was committed to territorial compromises over Judea and Samaria. He still firmly believed that there should be a national referendum over territorial issues. True to form, he remained firmly opposed to closed options.

On May 21, the announcement of Dayan's acceptance of the position of Foreign Minister fell like a bombshell across the political spectrum of

Israel. It shocked the Labor party and his former colleague Shimon Peres and it shook profoundly the Herut-Likud-LIM militants.

To them, Dayan was all but taboo, politically disloyal and unreliable. They argued hotly that Dayan would be unable to serve a Likud government because he did not believe in the concept of Eretz Israel or its ideology. Here was a man who had said, after all, that "Israelis are foreigners in the West Bank, and neither are they its masters." Dayan, like his master and mentor Ben Gurion was dedicated to strategy, security, and borders and believed that Jordan was Israel's natural partner. For Begin, for Herut, Jordan was a usurper on the West Bank.

Dayan's version of his appointment did not contradict Begin's. This is how Dayan describes his appointment in *Breakthrough:*

"On Saturday morning, 21 May 1977, Menachem Begin telephoned and offered me the post of Foreign Minister in the Cabinet he was in the process of forming. . . . My own Labour Party, which had been in office without interruption since the establishment of the State in 1948, had lost. I myself had been returned to the Knesset on the Labour list. For Begin to ask a member of the Opposition to assume a key post in his government was without precedent.

"I told the Prime Minister that if he could reassure me there and then on two policy issues, I would weigh his offer and give him my reply three days later, on the following Tuesday. The first concerned the limits of Israeli sovereignty—I was against extending it to the territories Israel had captured in the 1967 Six-Day War, which we now administered. Begin clarified this point to my satisfaction.

"The second concerned my parliamentary seat. If I accepted his offer, I might decide to give up my membership in the Knesset since I had been elected on the Labour Party ticket . . . With that our telephone conversation ended."[8]

Nevertheless, Dayan's appointment was thought to be crucial in the formation of a Likud government by both Begin and Weizman. Only a few hours after Begin presented the Likud government to Israeli President Ephraim Katzir, Dayan submitted a six-page memorandum to Begin outlining principles for peace and permanent borders between sovereign Arab governments and Israel.

Dayan began with the premise that "both Begin and I believed that the peace process must be launched in the near future."[9] Dayan's strategy in preparing the memorandum, in his own words, indicated that:

"While composing the memorandum, I weighed the alternatives— whether to formulate our position in ideal terms, expressing what we would really like or whether to present only the minimal conditions that Israel considered essential for a just and lasting peace. I decided to follow the second course: to give the Prime Minister my frank views, and not to make proposals which I believed the Arabs would not accept;"[10] and "I told Begin that to secure a permanent peace with the Arabs, we had first to reach agreement on a variety of complex subjects, notably, the permanent boundaries with the four neighbouring Arab States, special arrangements for Jerusalem, and the settlement of the Palestinian refugees. . . . I therefore proposed to the Prime Minister that we show willingness to deal separately with each item, and not hold up the settlement of some only because others still proved intractable."[11]

There was immediate and strong opposition to Dayan's appointment from the Herut party faithful, most notably from Shmuel Katz, probably the most militant of all the annexationists in Herut.

Katz was a brilliant, soft-spoken South African Zionist Revisionist, highly articulate, literate, a true intellectual, and a former member of the Etzel High Command, its chief ideologue and self-styled "foreign minister." Begin respected Katz partly out of loyalty, because Katz had played a key role in the *Altalena* affair and in Etzel in Jerusalem. Begin trusted Katz enough to send him to the United States immediately after the election to present the Begin government's policies to the Americans. The efforts of Katz did much to allay immediate U.S. fears about Begin. In spite of Katz's vehement opposition to Dayan, Begin stood by his decision. It marked a victory for Dayan over an old-line Etzel stalwart.

Obviously, Dayan was the most magnetic personality in the Likud cabinet, but he was not the only military veteran minister who carried weight in the new coalition. To a degree, he had to share the spotlight with two other war heroes, two men opposed in political outlook and style: Ezer Weizman, the new Minister of Defense and Ariel Sharon, the new Minister of Agriculture.

Weizman, in spite of the fact that he was generally considered a hawk, had much in common with Dayan. Both men made an indelible mark in the 1967 war, and Weizman, as Air Force chief of staff was considered to be the man most directly responsible for the destruction of the Arab air forces, a key to the lightning victory. Weizman was also the nephew of the venerable President Chaim Weizmann and a veteran of the National Unity Government, in which he served as Minister of Transportation.

Begin was not overjoyed to see Weizman return to the fold, since Ezer had attempted an abortive coup against him in the party after Begin had left the Meir government in 1970. But Weizman, upon his return to Herut, had masterminded a slick political campaign in 1977, which was at least in part responsible for the Likud electoral victory. Weizman, for the moment, remained a mystery man, generally considered to be hawkish.

There was not much mystery about the third general in the cabinet, Ariel Sharon. He was, pure and simple, conniving, manipulative, naked and brusque in his drive for power, a man whose politics were consistent only in their expediency.

As we have seen, Sharon's political trail since 1969 constituted a remarkable zig-zag. In 1973, with an eye toward deposing Begin as Herut and Likud leader, he became a member of the liberal Gahal wing of Likud. Shortly thereafter, he resigned to become Rabin's national security adviser. In 1977, this most ruthless of generals launched, ironically, a peace party called *Shlomtzion*. His party gained only two seats, but they turned out to be crucial to the Likud coalition.

Now Begin appointed Sharon Minister of Agriculture, an innocuous-sounding title indeed. Sharon was something of a farmer in private life, but in this case, as Minister of Agriculture, the only thing he planted was settlements. Begin might more honestly have appointed him Minister of Annexation, for that was exactly his function. Sharon would become Likud's "Bulldozer," symbolizing the bulldozer that prepares the land for settlement.

Under Sharon's ruthless leadership, Likud's true annexationist policy would emerge in the form of a massive settlement program, which planted some thirty thousand new Israeli settlers in the middle of Judea and Samaria, encircling urban Arab centers with Jewish military-agricultural settlements.

In spite of the appointment of Dayan, Begin could not conceal his true intent. Symbolically, in one of his first acts as Prime Minister, he joined the Gush Emunim (Bloc of the Faithful) settlers of Elon Moreh in a celebration, dancing for all the world to see with religious extremists, brandishing a Bible over his head.

As Begin assumed the mantle of the prime ministership, he was being pulled by two basically contradictory forces and goals. He wanted, of course, to fulfill the dream of Eretz Israel, a goal he would pursue sometimes openly, sometimes deceptively. He also wanted to demonstrate to his friends, to political enemies and to the world that he can start a peace initiative with an Arab state. Those two inclinations, which appeared to be so at odds with each other, were reflected in the makeup of his cabinet.

The purpose of achieving Eretz Israel was hardly a hidden goal—Begin had harped on it all of his political life. At sixty-three, he seemed finally ready to fulfill Jabotinsky's cherished dream, the annexation of Eretz Israel. However, never the starry-eyed idealist completely, he was aware, as a lawyer and politician, that outright, blatant annexation was totally unacceptable in Israel, not to mention the world at large.

His approach to the problem was at once simple and deceptive. Claiming that Judea and Samaria (he never called them the West Bank and Gaza) were ancient Jewish biblical lands (which they were), he challenged Jordan's claim to sovereignty over Western Palestine. "Only England and Pakistan recognized the annexation of Palestine by Jordan," he said. Thus, to Begin, the West Bank was "unsettled territory," an entity without political legitimacy. "Jordan is Palestine," he said flatly.

To further undermine Palestinian political legitimacy, and the Palestinian claim to nationhood and independence, he would embark on a campaign to annihilate the Palestinian Liberation Organization, an ongoing project that would eventually lead him into the quagmire of Lebanon. Begin, through repeated attacks on the PLO, through creeping annexationism, which began to change the physical and demographic nature of Western Palestine, wanted to kill the roots of Palestinian nationalism which grew strongly in the occupied territories.

Running side by side with his ambition to fulfill Eretz Israel was a strong passion to gain legitimacy. Begin, dedicated to the concept of *hadar* (majesty), shunned for much of his political life, now sought complete rehabilitation. Merely being elected Prime Minister was not enough.

In order to gain respectability he would have to curtail some of the more extreme and passionate Likud factions, a process that would eventually lead to schisms within the movement and make it difficult to govern.

Begin was faced with basically two different historical imperatives: first, to redeem the land of Israel, fulfilling the dream of a nation that stretched from the sea to the Jordan River, and second, to achieve peace with the Arabs. The question was how to achieve the two goals. How could Begin, the watchdog of Eretz Israel, the man of "not an inch of territory," also create the conditions for an Arab-Israeli peace?

Begin burned to achieve some sort of peace. Peace meant glory, a place in history, legitimacy. It would be the kind of peace achieved in the traditional Betar manner, a peace of formalities, ceremonies, spectacle. There would be parades, the comings and goings of superjets, limousines, all achieved under the klieg lights of the television age. It would be a peace that would not merely achieve tranquility for Israel, but would amount to a moral, political, and diplomatic victory over the Arabs. And belatedly, it would be a victory for Begin over Ben Gurion, who had, in spite of his momentous achievements, never managed anything of the sort.

32

Toward Accommodation:
Phase One of the Egyptian-Israeli Negotiations[1]

Menachem Begin was now Prime Minister of Israel, but he presided over a fractious, varied cabinet that resembled the biblical Joseph's coat of many colors.

His leadership of this new cabinet was as yet not solidified; nor was that surprising when one considers he was leading a coalition that included his old Herut followers, what was left of the Liberals, and Sharon's party, the National Religious Party.

Together, the coalition amounted to a steady, seemingly comfortable sixty-three seats in the Knesset, making Begin comfortable in the cabinet. It can be said with certainty that he had firm control over his old Herut comrades, but when it came to the others, he was not necessarily their favorite authoritative figure. But he was obeyed at least until 1979. Some of the Likud militants had other heroes to worship, like Ben Gurion and Tabenkin. In addition, Begin had to deal with old-style Etzelites, still infuriated about the appointment of Dayan, who were always on guard, protecting the right wing flank.

If Begin's hold on the cabinet seemed sometimes tenuous, the functioning of the cabinet itself differed markedly from the old Labor days, when friction, open, vocal and bitter, was the order of the day. The Mapai-Labor cabinets were characterized by tough and pragmatic trade union, collective and political leaders whose differences over personal and ideological matters sometimes carried over generations. There were labor leaders who did not speak to each other for decades, and even such notable figures as Pinhas Lavon and Ben Gurion himself were actually drummed out of the party in the aftermath of bitter struggles. No person, no leader, was so sacred that he escaped criticism or censure, and the only thread that often held the party together was the *Din Hatnua,* the Law of the Movement, a sort of democratic centralism which ostensibly forbade party factionalism.

The mood, the very style, of the Begin cabinet was different. There was only one authoritative figure, and it was Begin. While Labor coalitions were inclined towards the more liberal left centrists, Begin's 1977 cabinet was inclined toward the right. Given Begin's legalistic, sometimes rabbinical nature, the cabinet meetings often resembled seminars in which Begin took on the role of the teacher—wise, judicious, authoritative and often pedantic. He had after all been a propagandist, recruiter and teacher for Betar and Etzel, and at sixty-three he was not about to change his habits and ways of doing business.

While Labor leaders could never quite feel safe from the enmity of their own followers, such was not the case with Begin. Although there were repeated political challenges mounted against Begin from the Vaad to Tamir and on down the line, respect was maintained. Begin acted like a patriarch, a charismatic figure who deserved and was owed respect. In Begin's Herut party, the dignity of the leader was carefully observed, even under such trying conditions as the raucous party conference of 1966. Although Begin was challenged by Tamir, he emerged with his reputation intact, his leadership unquestioned. No Herut member, however senior, would even contemplate the ouster of Begin the way Mapai *officially* exiled Ben Gurion.

At the outset of Begin's government, with his old comrades solidly behind him, and newcomers Weizman and Sharon deceptively tame, it was becoming obvious that Begin and Dayan, at least initially, would be the dominant figures of the cabinet. This stung Weizman, who felt he deserved a larger role because of his work as campaign manager. Although he nominally ran the Defense Ministry, it was Begin who made the major decisions on security matters.

As the Begin cabinet looked at the work ahead, the two major issues become abundantly clear to them: settlements and peace with Egypt. The implementation of Israel's aggressive settlements policy was left in the hands of Sharon, who was now unofficial Minister of Settlements.

Foreign affairs, on the other hand, was a fiefdom shared between Begin and Dayan. The overall strategy would emanate from Begin, but Dayan would handle the tactics, the maneuverings and the diplomacy that would achieve Begin's strategy. Initially, it was an odd, but workable arrangement.

Begin approached problems from an ideological base, while Dayan was pragmatic, his eye toward short-run achievements and advantages. International observers, remembering only Begin's reputation, predicted an ideologically rigid government, a sort of last hurrah of the grand old Zionist generation born in the Diaspora. Yet working with Dayan, something different emerged from Begin: a rhetorical, ideological approach, tempered by a pragmatic style, the fusion of two Zionist traditions.

The key to the first Begin cabinet, in its early stages, especially when it came to opening the door to the possibility of a rapprochement with Egypt, was not rancor and division, but rather the relationship between Begin and Dayan.

If there was any hallmark to Begin's lifelong rhetoric, it was the question of Eretz Israel. As the Begin government began to work, this translated into settlements. For Likud, for Begin, for Revisionism, this had always been something in the nature of all the ten commandments rolled into one, the cornerstone of a political philosophy and rallying cry. Now Begin had the chance to begin working on that goal in a practical way by the immediate enlargement of the current settlement structure in order to ensure that Judea and Samaria would never become Palestinian entities of any sort. He also had the perfect instrument for the implementation of an aggressive settlements policy.

Although Ariel Sharon was an active political intriguer and a ruthless and effective military leader, he also had other talents. He was, as noted before, a *Bitzuist,* a doer of the first order. Begin had called for an open-door settlements policy, and Sharon was the ideal man to make the policy a settled fact. If Dayan seemed an ideal partner for Begin to initiate a peace process with, then Sharon, an activist with no compunctions about how to get a job done, was also a perfect partner for Begin in his settlements policy.

Sharon brought to the job his immense energy, which almost matched his huge appetite for food and his girth. He was imbued with the activism of the IDF and tackled the settling of Judea and Samaria with the energy of a field commander. He totally dedicated himself to drastically changing the demographics of Judea and Samaria.

He began by establishing Israeli settlements next to Arab rural and urban centers. Then he began work on an elaborate road system which would isolate major Arab cities on the West Bank, a system which would not only serve to speed settlers on the way but which would also serve as a military conduit. Officially, this was not annexation, but physically it had all of its appearances.

Sharon had the gift for encouraging settlement. Radical nationalist and religious groups flocked to the new lands with fervor, spurred on by their hero—for that is exactly what Sharon had become. In a matter of five years, Sharon changed the whole physical and demographic map of the West Bank, quadrupling the land occupied by Israeli settlers and doubling the Israeli population of the West Bank. Begin's rhetoric had found their perfect instrument in Sharon, who established himself as a Begin loyalist, dutifully and forcefully carrying out Begin's policies while waiting for a more important cabinet post.

The post which Sharon had his eyes on was occupied by Weizman, a not entirely happy man. Weizman felt isolated, away from the center of action, with nothing to do, apparently, except run the procurement department. There was, however, some consolation. As Defense Minister, he was charged with the occupied territories, which gave him an important voice in the treatment of the Palestinians.

However, as Defense Minister, Weizman had already made one important decision. He had appointed Rafael (Raful) Eitan to be Chief of Staff of the IDF, not quite realizing that he had a Sharonite on his hands. Eitan was considered one of Israel's outstanding fighting soldiers, a paratroop commander of uncommon bravery.

Weizman saw him as a nonpolitical general, politically unsophisticated, businesslike, a gruff soldier who would never stoop to meddling in politics or even to thinking on his own. "I have chosen a fighting horse," Weizman told me at one time, "Israel's soldier general, a Bradley, not a Patton, and not smart enough for politics or ideas." Weizman would be surprised later to find that he had chosen a man who was something of a closet LIM ideologue, as fervent as any radical in his espousal of Eretz Israel.

The Begin-Sharon partnership seems not at all unlikely, surely not as odd as the Begin-Dayan partnership. Yet Begin, the ideologue, and Dayan, the pragmatist, were remarkably similar in many ways.

Begin and Dayan shared three concepts. Dayan, like Begin, vehemently opposed the concept of negotiations with the Arabs through an intermediary, particularly the United States. For both men, the memories of the troop separation agreements engineered by Henry Kissinger—not to mention the abortive Rogers Plan of December 1969 that called for Israel to withdraw from the occupied territories with minor border modifications —still rankled. In 1966, Dayan had written in an article in *Haaretz* called "Negotiating Without Mediators," that once you negotiate indirectly with Americans, you end up making concessions to your American friends, not to the Arabs. Begin, not surprisingly, was also opposed to Kissinger-style negotiations. To Begin, the Kissinger policy meant the beginning of the end of Complete Eretz Israel.

Both Begin and Dayan were opposed to the establishment of a Palestinian independent state on the West Bank, as well as to negotiating with the Palestinian Liberation Organization on any matter. Dayan, however, was opposed to Israel's permanent occupation of the West Bank, not to mention annexation, both policies that Begin pursued.

Lastly, Dayan, an often brilliant military strategist, clearly understood the necessity of security imperatives for Israel on the Jordan River. He differed with Begin and Likud on the government's long-range goals of annexation, but Dayan preferred, as a pragmatist, to think in terms of short-term solutions and gains. Begin's policies tended to look toward the future, toward history itself.

Here, the two men dovetailed, because rapprochement with Egypt was both a matter for history and an attainable, long-term goal. The initial solution lay in the Sinai, which required Begin and Dayan to renounce territorial aspiration there. Begin, who believed in settling all conquered territories, had to give up Sinai, and Dayan, who had been the Defense Minister responsible for its settlement, had to bring about their destruction.

Dayan's approach to the West Bank was ambivalent and essentially strategic, but it was mixed with a romantic notion about the land itself. This seemed as contradictory as Dayan's policy on the West Bank since 1967. But on Egypt, the two men seemed to agree. There was, as they began to lay plans for initiating the peace process, a great deal of unspoken understanding between them. Dayan would be the chief negotiator for Israel, and Begin gave him tremendous flexibility to do things his own way—without violating Begin's basic plans, plans that ranged far into the future.

33

Sadat in Jerusalem, 1977:[1]
Sadat, Begin, and Carter

(It is not our intention in this chapter or the next to provide a day-by-day, blow-by-blow account of the peace diplomacy engaged in by Israel, Egypt and the United States during 1977–79, which culminated in the Camp David Agreements and the Israeli-Egyptian Peace Treaty. Our focus is on Menachem Begin, the person, Prime Minister and negotiator, and on how he related to and saw the major figures with whom he dealt—principally Anwar Sadat and President Jimmy Carter. We will also look at how they, in turn, saw and related to him. For those readers interested in following the highlights of the Egyptian-Israeli peace negotiations, a chronology is provided at the end of chapter 34.)

Before we begin examining what may yet be Menachem Begin's most enduring achievement, let us first look at the man as he stood at what was then the pinnacle of his career.

Long after many had thought Begin was finished politically, long after his closest friends and perhaps even Begin himself had thought it impossible, Begin had achieved the stunning political upset of 1977, attaining the Prime Ministership of Israel and ending for the moment the long rule of Labor.

We must remember, as Begin prepared to take on the duties of the highest office of Israel, that he had not changed. He was and remained a man of high moral standards and deep ideological commitments. Although he had been a political rhetorician all of his life, he was a man committed to justice. For Begin, justice was not an abstract, legalistic formula, but a tradition moored in centuries of history, written almost in stone in the books of law.

He was, almost self-consciously, aware that Arab leaders and outsiders in the western world who knew little about him until his ascension to the Prime Ministership, thought of him as something of a fundamentalist, a biblical, old-testament revanchist. Begin was determined to show the Arabs and the world that his concept of justice was indeed just, that it stemmed from a government of laws and from Israel's legal system, which was anchored in the traditions of the highly secular, not biblical, anglo-continental, democratic system of law. He would do justice to the Arabs as well as to the legal heritage of Israel.

Above all, Begin would do justice to himself, because his electoral triumph was, more than anything else, a personal triumph, a last, grand, and singular achievement whose principal effect would be to vindicate and legitimatize, not Revisionism, per se, but Begin himself.

His political history, as we have seen, had been full of more than the usual share of pain and abuse that politicians suffer. For Begin, thinking about his political past was a painful process. He had never really basked in glory or triumph except in those brief, violent passionate days when he led Etzel. But even that heady experience was marred by the *Altalena* affair, when the achievements of Etzel and the glory that went with them were, in Begin's mind, hijacked by the Socialists and by Ben Gurion—by his lifelong political foes.

Thus, Begin saw this somewhat unexpected political triumph so late in his career as a highly personal one as well. Begin and his newly won office would establish forever his legitimacy as well as the legacy, and the ideology of Revisionism and the deeds of Etzel. For Begin, the office would not be a political and statist tool to fulfill Zionist political purposes through statecraft, as it was for Ben Gurion. It would, first, be a means of vindication. Ben Gurion reached high office naturally so to speak, at the climax of his career. Begin reached office a tired man at the end of the road. His triumph meant an end to his long-standing pariah status, perhaps the end of pain.

It was unrealistic to think that all of the principles of the revered Jabotinsky would come to be realized and legitimized through a Begin electoral victory, that the spirit of annexationism and Eretz Israel would suddenly sweep the land. But the victory was a personal victory for Begin the man and Begin the political figure.

It is striking to note that when talking about the 1977 election, Begin never spoke or wrote of it as a victory for Likud, Herut or even Etzel, but rather as a victory for himself. In his mind, it was his own acomplishment, and he set about proving it in the way he formed his government, filling it not with members of his "fighting family," but with an eclectic group of men, some very far removed from both Revisionism's spirit and Begin's style, but people whose special talents Begin wanted and admired, and who would prove to be crucial to the peace process that was about to stir.

Begin needed a way to make his memories and bad dreams stop rankling and aching. He wanted to rise above the caricature of Menachem Begin first painted by Ben Gurion and embellished by his heirs. Now he would show his friends, but mostly his enemies, that he could be a statesman, a leader with high moral and legal standards, more than a man of vision who would launch Israel on a new era of peace and toward the fulfillment of an ancient dream.

From the moment Begin took office, the memories of the taunts of the now-dead Ben Gurion haunted him to the point where many of his subsequent actions and even the statesmanship, diplomacy and politics of the Israeli-Egyptian peace process seemed to arise out of this personal context.

Begin, upon taking office, sought to solidify his role as leader of an independent Israeli nation by pursuing two goals—peace and the fulfillment of Eretz Israel, goals which were squarely antagonistic and contradictory, and which repeatedly threatened to cancel each other out.

President Carter, frustrated when dealing with Begin, saw a stubborn, unreasonable man, slightly unhinged, while failing or unwilling to see the contradictory nature of Begin's aims.

Anwar Sadat saw Begin much more clearly, for in the two men's political history can be found tremendous similarities. Both were seeking the same thing—personal legitimacy. Sadat sought to escape the large, charismatic shadow of his predecessor, Nasser, who was practically worshipped in Egypt in spite of his numerous failures and flaws. Sadat, in pursuing peace in his own stylish and singular fashion, was carving out his own place in history in much the same way Begin sought a historical role beyond the reach of the ghost of David Ben Gurion.

Begin's domestic and international aspirations completely merged in his highly personal quest for respect, recognition and vindication. Ideological concerns were now secondary considerations when matched against these personal goals. To begin with, Begin was not a realpolitik sort of politician, and it is highly unlikely that he even understood the concept, certainly not in the way Ben Gurion, Israel's Bismarck, understood and practiced it.

Begin may have been an ideologist, but ideological considerations always integrated themselves in his private self, his idea of what he stood for. He saw Revisionism and its offspring—Betar and Etzel—as personal reflections of Jabotinsky. The Revolt and Herut were Begin's own creation and party, his private, personal and political platform. He was paterfamilias to his fighting family; it was a highly personal concept of leadership, as opposed to a political one. Herut existed as a monument to the glory of Etzel, and therefore Begin. He never bothered to try to institutionalize Herut politically, only himself, a fact that may explain Herut's long years in the electoral wilderness.

All of his political life, Begin thought and spoke in terms of abstractions and symbols, and he would not change as Prime Minister. The fulfillment of Eretz Israel and the achievement of peace were primarily abstractions to Begin, labels. They represented what psychologists have termed a *schemata* orientation, a commitment to the memories, feelings and cognitions that are part of a person's "scheme of things." All of the great issues in Begin's world—Jews, Christians, Israel, and Eretz Israel—were all thoroughly interwoven with Begin's personality stored in his memories. The concept of peace, for instance, now became a personal attribute for Begin, a part of his schemata. Peace was a category, not a deliberative side of human action.

For those who knew Begin, this was not unusual, but for Carter, it was totally incomprehensible. The result was a Begin "peace plan"—actually more a script than a plan—which he brought to his first face-to-face meeting with Carter, a plan which appalled Carter to such an extent that he set off on his own peace journey, a journey that would lead to Geneva and end nowhere, and which would rouse Sadat too, to take matters into his own hands.

The Carter administration abandoned Dr. Kissinger's prudent step-by-step approach toward peace in the Middle East. Kissinger, after all, succeeded in three troop-separation agreements—two between Israel and Egypt, one with Syria. The Carter administration, spearheaded by national security advisor Dr. Zbigniew Brzezinski, proposed a comprehensive settlement in the Middle East based on the bible of comprehensive settlement, the Brookings Institution Report of 1976. Carter, Brzezinski and Vance all were "comprehensivists" and all critical of Kissinger's step-by-step strategy for conflict resolution between Israel and the Arabs. The booby trap for the Carter-Brzezinski strategy lay in its utopian pipedream that the Palestinians had a leadership capable of and willing to make concessions. As Conor Cruise O'Brien has written, "The President and his advisors seem to have been quite sanguine about comprehensive prospects, as far as the Arabs were concerned."[2] But Menachem Begin was not a bystander to Carter's zeal. He was told in detail by former Prime Minister Yitzhak Rabin of the cold reception Carter gave Rabin's state visit of March 1976. Wrote a perceptive O'Brien: "Begin prepared his ground for the struggle with a coolness, shrewdness and pragmatism not widely attributed to him, either inside or outside Israel. He appeared adamant to Jimmy Carter, and adamant indeed he was on what mattered supremely to him: Judea, Samaria, Jerusalem. But he realized it would be folly to try to be adamant about everything. He was willing to 'trade territory for peace'—certain territory for a certain kind of peace."[3]

When Begin journeyed to Washington at the end of July 1977, he brought with him a "peace plan," or rather, the draft of a peace plan, a document legalistic in nature, and largely symbolic in content—bereft,

Carter believed, of any concessions, of any basis for negotiation. At its barest, it offered the Arabs "peace for peace." There were no suggestions of territorial compromises, no concrete proposals. There were no maps, no border realignments, no hint of a willingness, for instance, to withdraw from the Sinai or the Golan—both territories which were potential bargaining chips—not to mention Judea and Samaria, as Begin termed the West Bank and Gaza.

Begin, in fact, was blunt. There "would be no surrender of these territories to a foreign sovereign."

Begin was bringing, not the substance of peace, but the idea of peace. The document, as presented, was replete with the principles of complete peace and security arrangements, a plan that in its intent and generalities could easily have been drawn by any Laborite Prime Minister or stalwart.

Begin was attempting not so much to present a concrete, workable peace plan as to convince Carter of the sincerity of his desire for peace. More than that, he wanted Carter to submit his plan to Sadat, which, in retrospect, was as unlikely an idea as any ever invented by Begin, but one that also showed both his sincerity and his arrogance.

In that first meeting in Washington, both Carter and Begin had a chance to take a close look at each other, and oddly enough, it was Begin who judged his man better. Carter's response was highly negative to the point where Carter could barely conceal his feelings. He settled on a frosty, permanent dislike of Begin. To Begin, meanwhile, Carter seemed a mixture of Southern gentleman and shrewd politician, strained by a severe touch of moral self-righteousness, a not entirely inaccurate assessment.

The problem in this first meeting, however, was not just the clash of two dogmatic personalities, two moralists, but the content of Begin's peace plan, which struck Carter and others as a "peace of the victors." If anyone of lesser stature than Begin had offered such a plan, he might have been laughed out of the White House. But Begin, meeting for the first time with the American President, defended his case. As he saw it, it was very reasonable.

Although the document seemed couched in typically Begin-like legalistic terms, no lawyer would have presented such a brief—there were no concessions to the adversary; there was absolutely no incentive for negotiations. It was an ideological proclamation of the concept of Eretz Israel.

In the face of this proclamation, with no added details, one has to ask the question, and it surely must have crossed Carter's mind: Was Begin really dedicated to peace? The answer is yes, but he was dedicated to a peace on his own terms. Begin did not intend to present a realistic, detailed peace proposal to Carter. He was presenting a defense of his position, but his proposal was a nonstarter, and surely not a good beginning in initiating relations with an American President, who would come to doubt both Begin's intentions and sincerity, a feeling that would soon be reciprocated by Begin.

Carter felt obliged to present Begin's "peace plan" to Sadat, but he knew that the Egyptian President could in no way take the document seriously as a basis for negotiation.

Carter's negative reaction to Begin and his peace plan now set the president on the road to Geneva, i.e., to a comprehensive settlement, which was immediately and totally rejected by Begin. That ill-fated enterprise in turn stirred Sadat to action. But what about Begin? Did he sincerely seek accommodation with Sadat? Was he sincere in his search for peace?

The answer, it is clear, is both, although more yes than no. Begin was first and foremost, when it came to peace, thinking in symbolic, not operational terms. But, as was often the case with Begin, the symbol tended to run away from him and began to have operational consequences. Setting the highest goal for himself as a way of vindicating himself, Begin failed to realize that stating his *desire* for peace would almost automatically set the *process* in motion, although not in the way he had imagined. It was reminiscent of the way Begin failed to imagine the actual ramifications of events like *Altalena,* Dir Yassin, and the bombing of the King David Hotel, even as he imbued them with mythic and symbolic qualities. Thus, he enthusiastically and willingly embraced peace, like a fervent lover, without quite realizing that he would have to deal with reality, as represented by Carter and Sadat, once the process had gained a momentum of its own. Ideology cannot serve as a basis for foreign policy. Adversaries can always mold symbols for their own purposes and present the moralist with an unpleasant and unpromising agenda.

Begin's call for peace, however one-sided, nevertheless mobilized Carter and others, who in turn, by their action, galvanized Sadat. Once again, Begin was not quite prepared for the results of his abstract search for peace. Much of this had to do with the fact that in many ways, Begin had little experience in meeting this kind of challenge, that he was psychologically and emotionally ill-prepared to embrace complicated problems with broad international ramifications. Begin, used to thinking in the abstract, was inexperienced when it came to real statecraft and diplomacy.

It was Carter who first took matters in his own hands. Unhappy with Begin and his proposal, he now turned to his Brookings Institution–inspired plan for peace in the Middle East, a plan which was probably just as unrealistic as Begin's, pursuing as it did contrary goals. Carter's plan embraced the idea of Israeli security, Arab sovereignty, and the concept of an independent Palestinian entity. To Begin it was a plan that seemed heavily tilted toward the Arab cause.

Carter proceeded with his comprehensive Geneva approach, which would bring together several Arab delegations, Palestinians, and Israelis around a mythical table in Geneva. Even though Foreign Minister Moshe Dayan had haltingly accepted the idea of an All-Arab Palestinian delegation in September of 1977, Carter's plan was also as much of a nonstarter as Begin's. As far as Begin was concerned, Carter all but self-destructed when he and Secretary of State Cyrus Vance came up with the concept of a Comprehensive Settlement, an idea that Egypt approved heartily.[4] Carter, Vance and National Security Adviser Zbigniew Brzezinski now adopted a course that they knew would bring them into confrontation with Israel.

In effect, they had suggested that Egypt, Syria, Jordan and the Palestinians, along with the United States, the Soviet Union and Israel would somehow get together and negotiate a comprehensive settlement, a plan that even the most liberal of Israeli Labor governments would never have accepted.

Carter now stepped totally over the line, first with the idea of a "Palestinian Entity," which was totally unacceptable to Begin at this point, then by insisting on a joint U.S.-USSR chairmanship of the Geneva negotiations.

A communiqué on October 1, 1977, setting forth the joint chairmanship and inclusion of Soviet participation, something nobody had asked for except for the PLO, blew the Carter-Vance concept right out of the water, appalled the Israelis, who rejected it out of hand, predictably so, but, not so predictably, shocked Sadat, who wanted no part of a Geneva meeting dominated by the Russians and rival Arabs and Palestinians. Sadat had, after all, spent considerable political coin in ousting the Soviets from Egypt and was not about to slip under their thumb again. He now decided that the only way to circumvent Geneva was to act on his own, and in a highly dramatic fashion. "Israeli resistance has dented and deflected Carter comprehensivism," O'Brien wrote with much precision, "But it was from the Arab side that Carter comprehensivism received its death blow."[5] With the pressure of Carter on Begin growing, Yigael Yadin and Dashe's hawks decided to buttress his government and in October 1977 Yadin joined as Begin's deputy. Now the government was made of two former chiefs and two IDF generals.

Begin, by issuing his proclamation stating his desire for peace, had thrown down a symbolic challenge. Sadat now picked up the gauntlet in a very real way.

Sadat's decision to come to Jerusalem and circumvent Geneva was an act of political daring and courage but it also constituted the results of a shrewd assessment of Begin's character. Sadat saw beyond the caricature and cliché of Begin and saw a strong, quite stubborn man but nevertheless a man capable, in the end, of producing deeds to go with his rhetoric, if responded to in a dramatic way. Both Sadat and Begin were devotees of the grand theater of politics.

Sadat's arrival in Jerusalem was a historic occasion and also an opportunity for Begin to indulge his penchant for ready-made symbolism. It gave Begin a chance to give Sadat a royal welcome in the grandest tradition of Revisionism, Jabotinsky, and Pilsudski, all rolled into one. It would be a day for majesty *(hadar)* and honor *(kavod)*.

A phalanx of Israeli jets welcomed Sadat's plane and served as impressive escort, a veritable arsenal of an escort. Elite IDF units, infantry and armor, polished enough to blot out the sun, awaited Sadat on the ground. The ceremony at the airport, in fact, was strongly reminiscent of Pilsudski's funeral in 1935. Begin's welcome was effusive and warm, but his language on issues was euphemistic, evasive and broadly general.

Not so with Sadat, who seized the moment in an impressive speech to the Knesset on November 19, 1977. His language was clear, sharp, sometimes harsh, without ever skirting offense. There was to be no more war, no more belligerency, but there would also be an end of *all* Israeli occupation, a return to the 1967 borders, a recognition of Palestinian rights and grievances, a call for a Palestinian entity, and the Palestinian right to self-determination. Not once did Sadat mention the Palestinian Liberation Organization by name, but nevertheless, Sadat's speech was full of eloquence and free of euphemism. Clearly, he came as an Arab leader, calling for the surrender of all conquered territories, not just the Sinai or Egyptian territories. He did not, with sagacity, call for an independent Palestinian state, but he made it clear that the groundwork for such an eventuality must be laid.

Sadat came with no hand-written plan, no major points, no maps and no genuinely specific demands—no bill of particulars, but he did come with a clear vision, and spoke with words that were not empty, reminiscent of Begin's earlier, nonstarter peace plan. Sadat's speech was no more operational than Begin's "peace plan." But the significance of the speech is that it was made in the Knesset, not from the rostrum of the Egyptian majlis.

Perhaps more important, Sadat's visit to Jerusalem was the birth of an Arab superstar, for the Egyptian President made an indelible impression on Israelis and, through the eyes of the media, on the world. He proved to be both eloquent and human, accessible and statesmanlike. He joked with opposition leader Golda Meir, kidded his arch-foe Ariel Sharon in public. The media, the Israeli press included, sang his praises, marked his courage, his vision, his style and finesse, his charm and diplomacy.

Begin and Sadat met face to face privately, but nothing of substance emerged, nor was it expected to. The meetings were more of a way for the two men to get acquainted, to measure each other. Yet, it's entirely plausible that Begin, watching his people's response to Sadat, must have been seeing another shadow growing to blot out or threaten his own considerable charisma. The two would meet again in Ismailia in December.

Begin had to contend with his own self-made problems as well as the Carter administration. Carter and his advisers were nettled by Begin's seeming intransigence and his penchant for legalism. Carter continually held up to doubt Begin's compaign to persuade world opinion that he was no foe of the Palestinians, that all he sought was safety and security for Israel.

It was beginning to dawn on Begin that in his loud quest for peace, he had opened up the Pandora's Box of the Palestinian entity. It suddenly appeared that unless the Palestinian ogre were confronted, there could be no peace, but confronting the Palestinian issue meant endangering the cherished dream of Eretz Israel. Begin became aware that his two dearest and most symbolic goals—peace and Eretz Israel—could not coexist.

Once again, as he had before in his political life, Begin began to feel isolation, in fact, began to seek isolation. He trusted no one, feared that Dayan and Weizman would surrender parts of Eretz Israel, and actually opt for a separate peace with Egypt, freely giving up the Sinai, an idea he would not have entertained a year before. Feeling isolated and under attack when meeting with Carter, he began to feel bitter, moody, and irascible, so much so that Brzezinski privately told Rosalynn Carter that he felt Begin was "a psycho."

Begin once again went through a phase where he saw himself as the lone fighter, battling foes, allies, friends, and enemies, not to mention the media. Often, meeting with the Carter administration, he missed the presence of the likes of Shmuel Katz, Shamir or Sharon, who, at least, would have supported him, but, practically speaking, would also probably have caused a disaster in the Camp David negotiations.

Instead, he arrived in Ismailia for his meetings with Sadat with a great entourage, including Weizman and Dayan, but not the hard-line hawks of his cabinet. It was Begin's first visit to Egypt.

Begin's visit was not quite the triumph that Sadat's visit to Jerusalem was, probably purposefully so. Sadat did not accord Begin the pomp and circumstance that Begin so loved and cherished. Begin was not invited to Cairo. Sadat must have reasoned that nothing substantial had come of his trip to Jerusalem, and besides, he was not merely an Egyptian leader but an Arab leader, and he could not afford to give Begin, and, by inference, Israel, the kind of open legitimacy that he can or might want to give.

Begin, however, felt slighted and couched his talks with Sadat in his usual legalistic, thick-with-Latin language, even as the world media awaited some kind of solid breakthrough. But Begin was either unable or unwilling to rise to the moment. The great underground leader, the Etzel stalwart resembled a wheedling lawyer more than a statesman as he bombarded Sadat with euphemisms and generalities. He talks of the "Palestinians" or "Arabs of Eretz Israel," of "autonomy" or "withdrawals from territories," without ever stating specifics or searching for them. Sadat had been serious in Jerusalem. Begin was obviously not willing to grapple with the issues in Egypt, putting Sadat off with the vague air of a stalling attorney.

The meeting at Ismailia was not a success. Once again, the ball goes back to the Americans, and here, by now, Begin could expect no sympathy. Looking at the three main players in the peace negotiations, however, it's strange that this should be so. All three—Carter, Begin, Sadat—were perceived as political outsiders by the establishment, all had deep principles and to a degree all were deeply religious.

But Carter presented a special problem for Begin. He is a moralist who came to the White House obsessed with the idea of bringing peace to the Children of Abraham, as he put it in typically biblical fashion. He would become the first American President to lay his personal prestige on the line toward solving the Arab-Israeli impasse. As early as March of 1977, he had met with then Prime Minister Yitzhak Rabin and he had several meetings with Begin, all of which persuaded him that Israel was the stumbling block to peace, especially as personified by Begin.

Carter saw the Israelis as obsessed by "secure boundaries," a term they never clearly defined, that they constantly confused borders with security and that they had no intention of offering any compromises when it came to the Palestinians.

Carter seemed to the Israelis to be the coming Balfour of the Palestinians, whom he saw as an oppressed minority deserving of self-determination and an independent state, who had been ignored by the makers of American foreign policy for too long. Carter meant to rectify that state of affairs. To Carter, and he was not alone in thinking this way, there was no possibility of permanent peace in the Middle East without finding a solution to the Palestinian problem.

Perhaps it was inevitable that Begin and Carter should clash, and not just because of their political differences. The two men, in some ways, were very much alike in their political experience. Only a year before he became President, he was known as "Jimmy Who," an obscure, one-term Georgia governor who was quite suddenly and unexpectedly catapulted to the Presidency to deal with the highest international questions of war and peace. Like Sadat and Begin, he was a romantic and an idealist imbued with what some observers saw as an overly developed, self-righteous morality. Human rights was the Carter administration's flagship moral issue, dominating the making of foreign policy. Like Begin, he was something of a loner and zealot, stubborn and capable of meanness, which Begin was not.

Often he doubted Begin's sanity. Begin, in turn, called him that "fanatic Baptist preacher." Once they actually met, their antipathy toward each other deepened. Carter saw Begin as a petty legalist, unyielding, preachy and verbose. To Begin, Carter was a misguided American at best, insensitive to Jewish issues, to Israeli security, and at worst a champion of Israel's arch-enemy, the PLO. Carter hid his contempt in a show of good manners. Begin's essential disrespect was covered by his verbosity. Yet, like it or not, the two were chained together in the drawn-out peace process at the President's retreat at Camp David in 1978.

Carter was aware that the impasse between Sadat and Begin had become more than serious, so, in January of 1978, he traveled to Aswan enroute from Iran and Saudi Arabia to meet with Sadat at his winter resort and hopefully rescue the collapsing Sadat-Begin entente.

Out of that meeting came what was called the Aswan Formula for peace, which would become America's official formula for peace. It reiterated Sadat's demands for a serious, if inoffensive, Palestinian clause in any Israeli-Egyptian agreement. For Carter, the phrase "a Palestinian entity," acceptable to Sadat, became a kind of holy grail, writ in stone, as serious as the phrase "Eretz Israel" was to Begin. The Palestinians, he insisted, must have a future participation in the creation of their political destiny. The Palestinians' right to self-determination became Carter's cause celebre in his push for an Arab-Israel rapprochement.

Sadat still had no real plan of his own, but he appeared to have Carter's backing for all of his original demands in Jerusalem before the Knesset. Begin had no liking at all for the Aswan formula. Not only that, but he was beginning to feel pressured and cornered. After all, hadn't he presented a detailed, twenty-seven–paragraph autonomy plan to Washington in December? Hadn't he reiterated the principles of autonomy? His stand had been clear: No Israeli withdrawal from western Palestine, open-ended Israeli settlements, no sovereignty or self-determination for the Palestine Arabs, but a provisional autonomy, thus recognizing the population principle without territorial-political recognition.

In short, hadn't he been liberal and forthcoming throughout the process? Begin all but choked on the word self-determination, because for him, it represented a gross violation of the concept of Eretz Israel. Hadn't he made enough compromises, more than enough, by agreeing to return the Sinai to Egypt, along with the Israeli airfields and the oil fields, and a promise to dismantle Israeli Sinai settlements? And Carter had the nerve to push for *real* Palestinian self-determination?

Carter and his advisers had no sympathy for Begin. In fact, as Weizman told me, "Carter couldn't stand Begin." Dayan, never known to confide personal matters, also remarked on Carter's coldness toward Begin.

Dayan, on the other hand was respected by the Americans at Camp David. Vance told me that "without Moshe, there couldn't have been a successful resolution at Camp David." All Begin gleaned from Carter's attitude was Carter's "dedication to the Palestinian cause."[6]

If Begin's relations with Carter were caustic and bitter and somewhat hypocritical (in public, Begin called Carter a "friendly and understanding person"), his stance toward Sadat was formal and correct. There was no affection there obviously, but no animosity, either. For Begin, Sadat was, in the end, an Arab, and Begin had no time for or understanding of Arabs. He was simply not interested in Sadat's problems as an Arab, being preoccupied with the Jewish problem, Eretz Israel and the PLO. He treated Sadat as he would treat any adversary or outsider, with good manners, but with a firm and stubborn stance. He was immune to Sadat's vaunted charm, although this was not true of Weizman, of whom Begin was suspicious. Rightly, he suspected that neither man ascribed to his tough stance on the West Bank and both were willing to negotiate in private with Sadat, especially Weizman.

In fact, Sadat and Weizman met in Salzburg, Austria, in July of 1978 to try to patch up the strained relations between Begin and Sadat. Weizman did not trust Carter or his advisers. He hoped that by meeting with Sadat he could deter Sadat from his heavy dependence on Carter, and thus decrease American influence.

Carter now found it necessary to make one more trip to the Middle East in order to finalize the Camp David negotiations. After three months of negotiations, the accords had still not been signed. Begin, after a protracted negotiation, came to Washington and symbolically stayed away from Camp David. He resided at Blair House instead. He had four long talks with Carter and his advisors, during which a mild-mannered Carter explained that if the Israeli-Egyptian treaty were not ratified, Begin's quest for peace would be at an end, a total failure.

"What about settlements," Begin asked. He spoke of his good will, of Arab belligerency, of Israel's democracy, of the threat of communism to Arab regimes, of the defensive needs of Israel. They had, it appeared, reached an impasse, but the following morning, just as Begin was set to fly back to Jerusalem, he was called back to the White House. A compromise, "a minor modification" was offered to Begin, who accepted and jubilantly cabled his government that "Carter's new stand is an historical achievement for Israel."[7]

But Carter's final trip in March 1978 to Cairo and Jerusalem was still necessary. "The decision for Carter to go to the Middle East," wrote Brzezinski, "was precipitated by a message we received on March 4 from Sadat."[8] It was in line with the position that all must be done to save Sadat. "To overcome Begin's unwillingness to compromise."[9] Sadat wanted to come to Washington to denounce Begin's intransigence in Congress and the media. Sadat had begun to realize that Begin might not be afraid to fail after all, that he would not budge.

The drama finally came to an end in Jerusalem, even though Begin was livid that Egypt would not agree to an exchange of ambassadors. He remained angry at Carter through the next day when, at a dinner party before 360 Israeli dignitaries, he loudly lambasted Carter in a political speech.

It took Dayan, as usual, to break the impasse, not, as was claimed by the

Americans, Sadat, who reportedly said that he feels that the Americans represent his interest "as if it were my own." Dayan offered legalistic measures to circumvent the impasse. All serious points of disagreement between Sadat and Begin should be annexed to a treaty in personal letters written separately to Carter by Sadat and Begin as sort of a memorandum on points of dispute. Begin was agreeable, as was Carter. The President flew to Egypt with a big fanfare to accept this arrangement. What was left now was for the three to fly and meet in Washington to formally sign the agreement.

All that remained now was the formal ceremony, which was indeed impressive and a moment in history, as Carter, Begin and Sadat signed three copies of the treaty.

Begin could and would claim the treaty as a singular triumph, his own, but it was the product of many Israelis, Americans, and Egyptians. It would be a cold peace, after all, not a love match, a formal and correct process strained severely over the ensuing years.

The process itself did not make for friendly personal relationships among the Big Three. Long after leaving office, Carter continued to criticize Begin in the harshest terms. Begin was kinder, if not overly affectionate, speaking of his "friend, President Carter."

34
Camp David and the Big Three: 1978–79[1]

If one looks at the protracted negotiations and bickerings that constituted the Camp David talks, one is tempted to focus on issues and wordings, lines on paper and the detailed minutes that eventually go into making a formal agreement. Certainly the Palestinian issue, or rather how to approach it, burned like a hot ember at the center of the talks. This issue was the stumbling block, the lock to everything. It stuck in Begin's throat, it was like a holy grail to Carter and his aides, and it constituted Sadat's credentials as an Arab in good standing.

More important, however, in looking at the Camp David talks, are the personalities and how the issues, in particularly, the Palestinian issue, binds them, brings them together, tears them apart, isolates them and brings out the best and the worst in them.

From the outset, Sadat, for instance, was deeply suspicious of Begin's intentions and baleful about the prospect of agreement. He had, in effect, made his proposals in his speech to the Knesset and from there on essentially did not waver from them or compromise. In a sense, he was just as unyielding as Begin, if not as legalistic and pedantic.

He assumed, perhaps rightly, that Begin was firmly set in a concrete commitment to the slow but steady annexation of the West Bank, to which he, Sadat, could not agree.

Sadat already felt isolated from the rest of the Arab world, and felt that any further compromise with the Israelis on Palestine would all but exclude him from his Arab brethren in the future. Begin's somewhat detailed twenty-seven points presented at Ismailia seemed fairly clear to Sadat—and unacceptable: an administrative council for Palestine, no sovereignty, no political recognition and no curtailment or freeze of settlements.

Sadat, of course, should not have been surprised about Begin's stand. Instead, from the beginning of the talks he was relying on the Americans to help him, to pressure Begin to give up on his total commitment to Eretz Israel. He had every reason to expect the Americans to do just that because he sensed Carter's moral commitment to the Palestinian cause, which he took up with an almost crusading fervor.

He knew Begin would not accept his proposals, made so passionately and perhaps even rashly in Jerusalem. There would be no Israeli compromise on the West Bank, not even from the more flexible, moody Dayan, who, although no Eretz Israel fanatic, was nevertheless the son of early Zionist settlers. Dayan had advocated free Jewish settlement in the occupied territories, including the Sinai.

With the issues of Palestine, autonomy and settlements in the foreground, the negotiations inexorably started to grind to a halt. Now, only the United States could spark the momentum again, because by now the negotiations had reverted back to the traditional kind, the kind done through intermediaries.

Carter now took the lead, and his attention focused on the recalcitrant and isolated Begin. Carter was setting something of a precedent in his actions. No other previous American President had been so willing, in fact so eager, to become involved in direct negotiations in the Middle East. Until then, former Secretary of State Henry Kissinger had been the highest-ranking American official to become involved in direct negotiations, with his personal input in the troop separation agreements of 1973, 1974 and 1975 between Israel, Egypt and Syria. But Kissinger aspired to no such lofty goals as Carter's—the achievement of peace, a comprehensive settlement.

Between 1978 and 1979, Carter and his advisers had set for themselves, at the expense of Soviet-American relations, the goal of achieving peace in the Middle East. Perhaps only a born-again-Christian President such as Carter, enthralled by the Palestinian cause, could have entertained such high hopes for this enterprise. Now, he took off his political gloves and focused squarely on Begin.

Begin, the key decision-maker in the Israeli negotiating team, and its most difficult, stubborn and uncompromising member, began to feel the heat from Carter. Until the last day of negotiations, Carter never relented. Begin was Carter's target and he became the American media's target, suffering another kind of highly public pressure. The media, while fascinated, had no particular affection for this newcomer and latecomer to the international scene, this strange figure, part lawyer, part dogmatist, a former terrorist and now Prime Minister.

For Begin, the year 1978 was to be another trial by fire. It was as if the process which he had set in motion by loudly and symbolically calling for peace was now consuming him. Begin was under attack from all sides, but especially from the Americans. This was not like the glory days of Etzel. There was precious little glory here, only continuous pressure and a slowly emerging but quite evident attitude of hostility from the Americans, who were making it increasingly clear that no agreement would emerge without some sort of concrete progress on the Palestinian issue, which attacked the heart of Eretz Israel. Begin was under pressure from Carter, he was being pressured from his cabinet advisers, and he was being attacked from his own right wing. In April, when I saw him at a party at the home of Ambassador Dinitz, Begin seemed tired, subdued and despondent.

If Begin was beginning to have doubts about the forces he had unleashed, the Americans were going full steam ahead, their intentions becoming more clear with each meeting, with each *pronunciamiento*. "By early 1978," writes Brzezinski in his memoirs, "U.S. policy toward the Middle East had become less ambitious and more focused."[2] "We were determined to make certain that Sadat's peace initiative was translated into a tangible accommodation between Egypt and Israel, one that would generate also some progress on the broader, vaguer, and much more sensitive Palestinian issue."[3]

Clearly, the U.S. effort would build upon Sadat's early proposals to the Knesset. "Our effort to build on Sadat's initiative was to pass through many phases," Vance wrote in his memoirs.[4] Begin visited Washington in January, followed by Sadat, followed by a Dayan visit to Washington in February and another Begin trip in March. What was becoming clear with all these comings and goings was that the United States had become a full, working partner in the Middle East peace negotiations, perhaps the dominant negotiators.

Begin's trip in March and his talks with Carter were humiliating for the Israeli Prime Minister. Carter, as we have been told by both Vance and Brzezinski, made it clear to Begin in no uncertain terms that there would be no bilateral treaty between Israel and Egypt, that it "will include as little as possible on Palestinian-related issues." Obviously, the Americans wanted to shift Israel's position on the West Bank and Gaza and on UN Resolution 242. The Palestinian issue had come front and center.[5]

This is what Brzezinski had meant by American policy becoming "more focused." Now, Dayan and Weizman entered the fray. Dayan with the help of Aaron Barak, the government's legal advisor and Weizman with the help of General Avraham Tamir, his chief national security advisor, literally ganged up on Begin, even as Begin's supporters cried foul. Shmuel Katz, an old Etzel ideologue, had written a book entitled *No Majesty, No Honor,* charging that the Begin-Sadat negotiations were undermining Betar-Etzel's most cherished principles.

In any case, Dayan, prodded by the Americans, was entertaining the idea of changing the wording of Resolution 242 from Palestinian "sovereignty" to "Final Status."[6]

In the times leading up to Camp David, it became depressingly clear to Begin that the Carter Administration was operating from the Sadat initiative and that they intended to come down hard on Israel. In the chapter from Brzezinski's memoir entitled "Uphill to Camp David," he clearly shows that the administration had embraced Sadat's views and purposes and that it intended to lean on Israel and Begin. The U.S. was aware that "the starting point for Israeli policy had to be the preservation of the relationship with the United States," he writes.[7] He indicates that the United States was embarked on what he called a "secret strategy."

The "secret strategy" meant a policy of "toughness" toward Israel, which only worsened the deteriorating relationship between Carter and Begin. This was no more evident than in the March meetings between the two leaders. The issue in conflict was Begin's interpretation of 242, which Carter saw as meaning withdrawal on all fronts, while Begin interpreted it in the exact opposite way.

Carter, reports Brzezinski, spoke harshly. "My view," he said, "is that you are not willing to stop expansion or the creation of new settlements; you are not willing to give up the settlements in the Sinai; you will not accept the protection for the Sinai settlements; you will not politically withdraw from the West Bank; you are not willing to accept UN 242 on all its fronts; and you are not willing to let the Arabs choose between three different alternatives after the end of the five-year transition arrangements for the West Bank." "When Carter finished," writes Brzezinski, "the Israelis looked absolutely shaken. The President was particularly effective and dramatic."[8]

Carter's get-tough stance with Israel seems in retrospect a continuation of his natural inclinations, beginning with the frosty talks he had with Rabin in 1977. Carter was the first Democratic President to challenge the agenda of the traditional relationship between the United States and Israel, although it can be said that Carter, in many ways, was not a traditional Democratic President.

Begin, it was true, was rigid and unyielding in many ways, but Carter's embrace of the Palestinians certainly added to Begin's stubbornness and suspicions.

All in all, as the time for the Camp David talks neared, Begin had every reason to be depressed. He lapsed into one of his psychological and emotional withdrawals, reminiscent of the Vilna days of the 1940s and of the early 1950s. He was moody, indecisive, and felt the heat of the pressured peace process. His negotiations team was no less happy as they sensed Carter's hostile attitude. They knew that Carter meant to come out of Camp David with an Egyptian-Israeli agreement no matter how long it took.

As the Camp David talks opened, it quickly became clear that the three negotiations teams approached the process in highly differentiated ways. On the surface, at least, the Israeli team seemed to be both at a disadvantage and divided to boot. Brzezinski snidely speaks of the machinations within the Israeli delegation, of Dayan's "unspoken message" that the "Prime Minister was unnecessarily crude and rigid"; he writes that "Begin's attitude toward Weizman was patronizing," that Dayan saw Weizman as "a superficial person, excessively eager to please the Americans and the Egyptians," and that Weizman thought Dayan was "Machiavellian."9

Brzezinski's comments and assessment are basically correct, but also largely beside the point. They demonstrate both the virtues and weakness of the Israeli team. Brzezinski says the Israeli delegation "suffered from having the least cohesive negotiating team."10

That lack of cohesiveness reflects the tremendous differences between parliamentary and presidential political systems, the differences between the governments of the United States and Israel. Even such authoritative and dictatorial personalities as David Lloyd George, Winston Churchill and David Ben Gurion perennially had to contend with their parties, their ideological and political equals in the decision-making process. Begin's advisers, to his and their credit, never acted as yes-men, and if they had, there would not have been any Camp David agreements. Weizman and Dayan were not presidential advisers. They and Begin were collectively responsible to the Israeli people and acted accordingly. They were independent political figures, *not clerks appointed by the President.*

In spite of the personal, stylistic and even ideological differences, the Israeli team was never ready to surrender the West Bank to Sadat. This seeming division made the Israeli team seem an inviting target to Carter, to the extent that for many stretches of time the negotiations were almost limited to talks between the Americans and the Israelis, as if the Egyptians were never there.

The presidency of the United States, of course, operates in an entirely different manner. It is a powerful institution, with the President responsible to the Congress and to the people but not to his advisers. Carter was, in effect, the chief feudal lord of the office and all of his advisers were appointed bureaucrats. They were never his equals.

This was even more true in the Egyptian delegation, where Sadat was apt to get the kind of advice a dictator wanted to hear, which is to say soothing and flattering without being informative.

As the talks opened, it became clear that Carter would be his own diplomat, negotiator, and bargainer, leaving the full job of the Presidency to others at the White House. He was risking his reputation and his place in history on Camp David. He had been warned by his advisers that the best he could hope for at Camp David was an Israeli-Egyptian arrangement.

Carter, a zealot to the end, wanted more: He hoped to wring from the Israelis a realistic procedure for the recognition of Palestinian rights.

The Israeli delegation prepared its agenda, not in Israel, not even on the airplane enroute, but right at Camp David. The strategy session dealt mainly on how to deal with the United States, not Egypt. First Sadat met Carter, then Begin, and then all three were supposed to meet. The Israeli delegation immediately got into an argument. Both Dayan and Weizman insisted that there would be no reaching an agreement with Egypt without offering to withdraw settlements from the Sinai. Begin disagreed. No consensus was reached, which reflected the domestic political situation in Israel.

However, Begin, Weizman and Dayan all agreed on four basic principles relating to the West Bank. Dayan clearly summarized them: (1.) Jewish rights to settle anywhere; (2.) freedom of movement ("neither we nor the Arabs will be strangers to one another"); (3.) the IDF deployed on strategic lines but *not* interfering with the life of the population (withdrawal of military occupation); (4.) sovereignty for the West Bank to remain an open issue.

Thus split in style and personality, but not on basic issues, the delegation prepared to meet its American and Arab counterparts.

Sadat, meanwhile, had done his best to ignore or go over Begin's head. He related to Carter as his attorney, his intermediary, his defender, and constantly complained about Begin—first to Carter, then to Weizman and Dayan, bemoaning that he felt heavy in his heart about Begin.

When it came to bargaining issues, Sadat had not changed one iota from his first initiative back in November 1977 in Jerusalem. In fact, he had become even more rigid. His proposal was an exact copy of his November 19, 1977, speech to the Knesset—UN Resolution 242 in all of its parts to be adhered to; "substantial border rectifications," which meant withdrawal from all occupied territories and Palestinian self-determination. It was, almost to a tee, the Rogers Plan of December 1969.

Even Carter was a little uncomfortable with this proposal. "This was a rigid, tough stand that is not acceptable to Begin," he told his advisers, a mild understatement, to say the least.

When Begin met his team with Sadat's proposal in his hands he flatly told them that "when you meet the Americans tomorrow, tell them you are not even willing to discuss this document."[11]

Not only did the proposal demand reparations from Israel, there was no mention of normalization of relations at the end of the process. "This is retreat," shouted Begin. Dayan scoffed, "What chutzpa, to demand from us reparations. Are we or are they the defeated parties in the wars?"[12] Even Weizman was discomforted. "We are starting from scratch," Begin said. As a result of this rigid, almost insulting proposal, Begin would not personally meet with Sadat until nearly the end of the Camp David conference.

One might well wonder why Sadat, so often considered so reasonable, would come up with so uncompromising a proposal. The result was a reflection of the nature of the Egyptian entourage, for that was exactly what Egypt's delegation amounted to. Sadat was basically the pharaoh of delegation. While Begin's team worked hard to modify Begin's most rigid position, the Egyptian team did the opposite, feeding Sadat's rigidity.

The Egyptian proposal had no chance of succeeding. It seemed that Camp David was already doomed to failure. Of course, there was no press to oversee the impending failure. Carter and Brzezinski had made sure of that from the start, or, as Brzezinski wrote in a memo to Carter on August 31, 1978, "For the talks at Camp David to succeed you will have to control the proceedings from the outset and thereafter pursue a deliberate political strategy designed to bring about significant changes in both Egypt's and Israel's substantive positions." Brzezinski went further—"Sadat cannot afford a failure; both Sadat and Begin think you cannot afford a failure; but Begin probably believes that a failure at Camp David will hurt you and Sadat, but not him."[13]

This was a harsh miscalculation of the Israeli position. What dictated Begin and his team to modify their positions was precisely the fear that the United States and Carter would fail. All along, they were always more concerned with satisfying the American position than that of the Egyptians.

Brzezinski, at any rate, was something of a bête noir for the Israelis, perceived by several of its members as abrasive and antagonistic toward the delegation, "his approach was highly tendentious."[14] Luckily, for once, Carter chose the path of reason, by listening to the advice of the calmer and more reasoned Vance. Brzezinski, although he had kind words for Dayan— "I was struck by how relatively openminded Dayan and Weizman were"— nevertheless held Dayan in something less than admiration.

The truth of the matter was that the two men—Dayan and Brzezinski— did not get along very well privately. Dayan described him to an Israeli journalist as "a bull in a China shop." Dayan also described Brzezinski as "vain, closed-minded, using phrases, speaking as if he were the king of Poland." Dayan had total antipathy toward Brzezinski who, as one member of the delegation recalled, reminded Dayan of nothing less than, well, Begin. Brzezinski considered Dayan "rigid." "Dayan in effect was blackmailing the President," using Israeli influence in the country if Carter continued the pressure. If Brzezinski's memoirs and journals reflect his opinion he was unfriendly if not hostile to Dayan.

Dayan and Vance, however, worked beautifully together, and it was their relationship, and their influence, which finally produced a breakthrough and made such a contribution to the attainment of the agreement. Dayan and Vance were more forward looking than either Begin or Brzezinski. Both wanted badly to reach an agreement, and both succeeded in influencing their chiefs. The more cordial, relaxed atmosphere the two men succeeded in creating at Camp David broke the air of tension that had prevailed from the moment Sadat had made his rigid proposals.

The lessening of the tension and the steady advice of Dayan softened Begin and showed once again that given the right circumstances, Begin could rise to the status of statesman, that he was quite capable of compromising, much as he had at the end of the *Altalena* affair and during the days of the Sezon.

At Camp David, Begin demonstrated that, when surrounded by reasonable advisers, he could modify both his astringent behavior and his approach to policy making. There was still no satisfying Begin on the issue of settlements for the moment, but now Carter, Vance, Dayan and Begin reached a compromise on the wording of the Palestinian issue. Carter was persuaded to accept Vance's proposal, inspired in part by Dayan, to separate the difficult Palestinian paragraph from the final accords, in fact, having the parties "agreeing to disagree" on the issue. It was a Dayan-State Department solution which Sadat accepted also, although his staff was vehemently opposed to it. It was a purely technical, but nevertheless substantive solution which broke the ice.

All along, the Israeli and Egyptian delegations had been isolated from one another. In fact, it was the second-echelon U.S.-Israeli group of negotiators, below Begin and Sadat, and their technical advisers who were pushing hard for an agreement. Sadat took his cues from the American team. Carter, he calculated correctly, would negotiate honestly. Thus, the negotiations took place often without the actual participation of Begin. His team would make proposals, iron them out with their American counterparts, then reach a "compromise" with their chief.

Begin's legal advisers persuaded him to accept the linkage between Sinai and Judea-Samaria which was to be incorporated in the accords. Accord A dealt with the Sinai, Accord B with the Palestinian issue.

Begin finally caved in and his mood—dark, bitter and depressed until then—brightened. "He came back to himself," one member of the Israeli delegation said.

However, considerable modification on the issue of autonomy had been made—full autonomy, an administrative council, temporary abolition of military and civilian administration by the IDF, the transfer of authority from Israeli rule to an autonomous administrative council, recognition of the role of Jordan and the recognition of the fact that the Palestinians would have a role in their administration.

Surely, Begin must have seen that his own rhetoric, his penchant for symbols, had caught up with him again, had turned into a kind of reality. For Begin, autonomy had never been more than a word, a figleaf to satisfy

Carter that he had no intention of actually implementing. But at Camp David autonomy had grown, become fleshed out with detail.

His legal advisers tried to comfort Begin by telling him that there was "no real meaning in the phrase 'full autonomy.'" After all, it would not be achieved until after long and complicated negotiations with Israel. Israel would have the instrument of legitimacy at its disposal. For Begin, it was significant that the accord guaranteed the continuance of Israeli maintenance of Judea-Samaria, that all the legal armor could be used to preempt the creation of an independent Palestinian state or achieve ultimate Palestinian goals.

All of this seemed to satisfy Begin, in spite of such phrases as "the legitimate rights of the Palestinians," "the principle of self-determination" and "their rightful demands." The Palestinians, in their own way, had gained recognition, and some Israelis recognized what it might mean in the future. One member of the delegation laconically remarked that "At Camp David, we established the State of the Palestinians." Certainly that's what Carter had in mind all along.

Thus, after twenty-three drafts, on September 27, a general outline for an Egyptian-Israeli agreement was initialed triumphantly.

This, of course, did not occur without a snag, a major disagreement that was to grow bitterly in the ensuing weeks. This stemmed from a heavy misunderstanding between Carter and Begin over the issue of a settlements freeze. Begin understood that a "freezing of settlements" meant only for a period of three months between the end of Camp David and the signing of the final draft of the treaty. For Carter, it meant a freezing of settlements for the entire five-year period of negotiations over autonomy, a significant difference of interpretation.

To a great degree, this represented once again Carter's one-sided morality. Did he really expect Begin to, for all intents and purposes, stop settlements altogether? His sympathy for Palestinian nationalism indeed represented a moral commitment, but couldn't Carter see that a total settlement freeze meant the abandonment of Zionism "and its spirit" as understood by Begin and Likud?

To friends Begin said, "This is the end of Zionism. Who is he [Carter] to tell us what to do in our own country?" Carter, of course, did not consider Judea and Samaria as part of Israeli territory but rather as occupied Palestine. In spite of the euphoria in the wake of the signing of the accords, it was obvious that neither man understood the other and that neither man had changed or managed to see beyond their own dogma.

The differences between the Americans and the Israelis was clear in the way they viewed what happened at Camp David. Here is what Brzezinski wrote about Camp David: "The Camp David accords were not a settlement as such. Rather, they provided the needed framework for negotiations, a transitional agreement for the West Bank, as well as an agreement to sign a peace treaty between Egypt and Israel within a specified deadline." For Begin, however, Camp David was no such thing. It was first and foremost a peace treaty with Egypt. He had no inclination, nor did any other major Israeli political figure, to end Israel's rule over the West Bank in the immediate future or beyond. For Begin, there was nothing whatsoever "transitional" about Eretz Israel.

Brzezinski also saw the dangers in the incompleteness of Camp David: "The historic accomplishment of Camp David was to lay the groundwork for an Egyptian-Israeli peace treaty. Its worst failure lay in not obtaining Begin's clear-cut acquiescence to a freeze on settlements activity . . ."[15]

Begin had no intention of ending settlements activities, nor did the Likud party. None of them including Labor ever contemplated returning the land of the Palestinians or, for that matter, laying the groundwork for a future independent Palestinian state. The national Israeli consensus on this issue to this day is clear—no Arab sovereignty over the territory, of western Palestine or Eretz Israel.

Yet Brzezinski was correct in his assessment that "the outcome was a triumph of Carter's determined mastery of enormous detail and of his perseverance in sometimes angry and always complex negotiations."[16]

Begin, of course, felt differently. Camp David, to Begin's way of thinking, was his own personal triumph, just as his election to the Prime Ministership had been. He, not Ben Gurion, was the first Israeli statesman to make a peace with a major Arab nation. In his mind, he had managed to "save Judea and Samaria for Israel forever." That's the way Begin always described a crisis to which he was not always in command, even if it didn't conform with realities.

In a way, everyone left Camp David satisfied, at least in their own minds. Now the real strife and trouble began. Each would explain the Camp David accords in their own way to their own people and their own followers.

Begin, upon returning to Israel, faced the angry reaction of his own followers, the right-wingers of Herut, all of whom, with the odd exception of Sharon, were stridently opposed to the accords.

The political brawl which ensued in the Knesset was traumatic for Begin. It was led by old Etzel ancients like Shmuel Katz, Yaacov Meridor, Chaim Landau, Eitan Livney, Betar veterans Dov Shilansky, Yitzhak Shamir, Moshe Arens, and the young Betar-Herut leadership, with Yoram Aridor in the forefront. They, like Labor opposition leader Shimon Peres, saw the accords as "the Balfour Declaration of the Palestinians."

Begin defended himself in a cabinet meeting in October when he indirectly replied to his critics. "Peace," he said, "is very important, indeed. But Judea and Samaria are our forefather's inheritance and the importance of a solid Jewish settlement will not permit foreign statesmen to interfere"[17] —i.e. Begin did not give up Eretz Israel. Here, he continued the ongoing argument over settlements with Carter.

The accords were not by any means the end of the peace process. Begin's euphoria and optimism that his interpretation was correct proved ill-founded. Washington and Cairo saw things in a different vein. If Begin saw Camp David as a "great Israeli victory," Washington and Cairo were by no means ready to give him that victory.

Shmuel Katz, Begin's principal ideological antagonist and a former adviser, always had doubts that "Begin's 'peace proposal' would be acceptable to the world, and in fact Camp David buried Begin's 'peace plan.' "[18] For Katz, who articulated the old Etzel-Herut opposition, "the Camp David accords were a document written exclusively by Arab-inspired views and representing Arab political thinking, even if it was dressed in American garb. A careful examination sentence by sentence of this document, signed by an Israeli Prime Minister, a Jew and a Zionist, demonstrates the cosigner as one uprooted from his world, coerced by the use of a language foreign to himself, or he was hypnotized and is moving under the guidance of the person responsible for the hypnosis."[19]

In an interview, Katz told me that "Begin is good and faithful when he is among his Jews. But among the gentiles, he cannot be trusted. He has this 'legacy' of the Diaspora, [a tendency] to fear and respect the goy."[20] The battle in the Knesset, the opposition, all came from the Herut, from the adherents of Eretz Israel. Labor, with nowhere else to go, supported the accords, except Ahdut Haavodah members like Yigal Allon, who abstained. The Etzel-Herut core voted against the accords or abstained. Sharon was the only Herut member to vote for it.

Overall, the Knesset approved the accords in spite of Herut opposition.

On February 22, 1979, the principals returned to Washington to work on the final American draft for peace. It failed. Again, an eruption of bickering broke out and it seemed briefly that all of them would return to square one instead of finally nearing the end of the road to peace. On March 1, Begin arrived for a hard talk with Carter. Carter's trip on March 8 to Cairo and Jerusalem persuaded Sadat and Begin that "minor gaps" should not hamper peace. Returning to Washington with a sealed agreement, it was now left for all to sign the Camp David Accords in a historic ceremony in the White House on March 26, 1979.

The treaty was a crucial moment in the history of Israeli-Arab relations, and a triumph in the political life of Begin. Events, however, would overtake Begin as he embarked on ever more dangerous and more aggressive endeavors, actions that would in the end undermine his own quest to be known as a peacemaker.

CHRONOLOGY

1977

Nov. 19–21 Egyptian President Anwar Sadat visits Jerusalem, addresses Knesset, offers "peace with justice," calls for return of occupied territories; Sadat and Israeli Prime Minister Menachem Begin pledge "no more war."

Dec. 5 Arab rejectionist bloc opposing Sadat peace efforts is formed by Syria, Libya, Algeria, Southern Yemen, Iraq and Palestine Liberation Organization. Sadat vows to negotiate with Israel alone if other countries balk.

Dec. 13–16 Egyptian and Israeli representatives meet in Cairo.

Dec. 16 Begin tells President Carter in Washington that Israel would give Egypt the Sinai Peninsula and give Palestinians control over internal affairs in the West Bank and Gaza Strip, but the Israeli army would remain for security reasons.

Dec. 25–26 Begin and Sadat meet in Ismailia, Egypt.

Dec. 27 Sadat says that although Israel has offered to return occupied Sinai to Egypt, he will not back down from demands for full Israeli withdrawal and creation of a Palestinian state.

Dec. 28 Begin reveals twenty-six-point plan, which would set up an interim local Palestinian government on the West Bank for five years, while Israeli troops would continue to handle defense and security matters. Under the plan, Israel offers to review the situation after five years have passed. Begin says the next move is up to Egypt.

Dec. 31 Egypt reveals terms for negotiation on peace settlement; Israel must accept principle of full withdrawal from the West Bank and Gaza Strip, and must recognize the "inalienable rights" of Palestinians to self-determination.

1978

Jan. 5 Carter meets Sadat in Aswan. The determination of the Aswan formula. Solving the Palestinian problem in all of its aspects; recognition of the legitimate rights of the Palestinian nation; Palestinian rights to participate in deciding on its fate.

Jan. 15 Sadat personally attacks Begin in an interview in *October* magazine.

Jan. 17 Secretary of State Cyrus R. Vance, Israeli Foreign Minister Moshe Dayan and Egyptian Foreign Minister Mohammed Kamel meet for talks in Jerusalem on political aspects of a peace settlement.

Jan. 18 Sadat orders Kamel home, says talks will resume when Israel changes its position.

Jan. 22 Begin denounces Egypt's new "campaign of grave vilification against the state and government of Israel" and the Israeli cabinet agrees to postpone sending a delegation back to military talks in Cairo.

Jan. 31 Cairo military talks resume.

Feb. 3–8 Sadat visits Carter in Washington urging the United States to act as "the arbiter" in a Middle East settlement. Carter stresses U.S. intention to be mediator, not arbiter.

Feb. 10 Administration officials report administration has concluded that for peace talks to succeed, Israel must agree to dismantle Sinai settlements and give up control over West Bank and Gaza over a period of years. Dayan says Sadat broke off talks not because of an impasse but because both sides were near an agreement and Sadat couldn't sign without participation of other Arab countries, particularly Jordan.

March 11–14 Palestinian terrorists attack Israelis near Tel Aviv. Israel retaliates in southern Lebanon. Sadat denounces both attacks, says his peace efforts depend on what Israel does next in Lebanon.

March 21–23 Begin visits Washington. Talks with Carter end in cold exchange of statements. Carter tells Senate Foreign Relations Committee that "diplomatic process has come to a halt."

March 24 Vance reports that Begin rejected Carter's proposal that occupied areas be put under international auspices for five years after which the Palestinians could choose to affiliate with either Israel or Jordan.

May 15 Senate votes 54 to 44 to approve Carter's plan to sell warplanes to Egypt, Israel and Saudi Arabia.

June 18 Israeli government says it would negotiate "nature of future relations" after five years of limited Palestinian self-rule.

June 19 Knesset approves vaguely worded Israeli cabinet reply to U.S. questions about Israel's plans for the West Bank and Gaza Strip. Carter administration reports disappointment with cabinet's responses.

July 5 Egypt announces interim peace plan with five years for Gaza Strip and West Bank transition and eventual return of lands to Jordan and Egypt. Plan also offers specifics on security arrangements. Israeli spokesman calls plan inadequate but containing positive elements, parts of which may be negotiable.

July 18 Two-day conference of U.S., Israeli and Egyptian foreign ministers opens at Leeds Castle, England. Vance reports major differences remain, but U.S. officials say privately that some progress has been made. Vance indicates the three will meet again shortly.

July 24 Dayan tells Knesset that Israel will discuss sovereignty of West Bank and Gaza in five years if in the interim Arabs accept Israel peace plan granting Palestinians partial autonomy. Egypt's Kamel says no further negotiations will be held unless Israel presents new ideas or agrees to reconsider Cairo's peace plan.

July 30   Sadat calls Israel's plan "negative and backward" and says he will negotiate only with prior agreement excluding compromise on land and sovereign issues.

Aug. 5–8   Vance visits Jerusalem and Cairo, then announces Camp David summit.

Sept. 6–18   The Camp David Conference that concludes peace accords between Israel and Egypt.

Sept. 11   Blair House meeting. U.S. submits final draft for the peace treaty. Israel accepts. Egypt rejects seeking modifications.

1979

Feb. 2   Second Camp David Conference with foreign ministers Vance, Dayan and Khalil. It collapses.

March 1   Begin arrives in Washington. After hard talks with Carter, an understanding is achieved.

March 8   Carter travels to Cairo and Jerusalem to persuade Begin and Sadat to fill what Carter says are "minor gaps."

March 26   Sadat, Begin and Carter (as witness) sign a peace treaty between Israel and Egypt and prepare themselves for the autonomy talks.

35

Osirak:
Begin Bombs the Iraqi Nuclear Reactor—
and the 1981 Elections[1]

The election of 1981 was shaping up as an uneventful one, a period of quietude after the upheavals in the wake of the signing of the Egyptian-Israeli peace treaty. Herut had overcome its politically inadvisable opposition to the treaty. The economy was lulled into a false sense of optimism by the populist policies of Finance Minister Yoram Aridor, who was raising consumer expectations and good will.

Yet, in 1979, Begin, fresh from his triumph at Camp David, slipped into one of his periodic silences and depressions. Begin's inactivity and his long silence were beginning to become the source of rumors. There was talk that he was seriously ill, that he was frequenting a Japanese fortune teller, that he was barely in communication with the day-to-day workings of the government. He seemed exhausted, frayed and wan.

The end of 1979 was marked by a petit political coup against Begin headed by a strange trio, Weizman-Sharon-Levy. There was no secret among his close associates, members of the government and the press, that Begin was depressed. He had lost his feistiness; he was indifferent to friends and rivals. The fighting Begin became his own shadow. He sat lonely and brooding at the Knesset's Cabinet table. Once again, the "Vilna depression" moved in. The idea that Begin should "retire" was advanced by the trio, who prepared for a succession battle in the forthcoming Fourteenth Herut Party Conference scheduled for January 1979. Begin soon foiled the political coup. The trio's hope that Begin's unhealthy appearance would persuade the conference of the need for "new blood" was aborted. Begin, in conformity with his manic-depressive pattern, "awakened." He came to the conference with full vigor, demonstrating that he was "healthy." But after a few months, the depression returned. By now one of the "plotters" was out—Weizman resigned in 1979. The political conspirators gave up. Sharon, aspiring for the Defense Ministry, decided to stick with Begin. Weizman and Levy were joined by Yitzhak Shamir to establish a shadow cabinet in the party, ready to assume power on *approval* by the party when and *if* Begin continued to be incapacitated. This no longer was a conspiracy. Simha Ehrlich, the head of the Liberal party, became concerned. If Begin went, he felt, then the militants of Herut, especially Sharon, might be strengthened. He was going to defeat the idea of a "shadow cabinet." In fact, he negotiated with Labor to establish an alternative to the Herut-dominated coalition. The Liberals, he believed, would switch alliance only if Begin was replaced. All this took place without Begin's knowledge, even if some of his lieutenants got the drift of the coup makers and the Liberals' maneuverings. Ehrlich was hoping to establish a Liberal-Labor Coalition headed by the popular Ezer Weizman.[2]

All the above was contingent on a single event—that Begin would voluntarily retire. But none of it came from Begin or his camp. Ehrlich helped make a statement in a closed Liberal meeting that "when I met Begin on December 8, 1979, I could not help but be impressed that the Prime Minister is a *sick and broken man.* He is physically and mentally ill. Begin is a tragic figure. This poses a danger to the state."[3]

The immediate result of Ehrlich's maneuvers was clear—a Herut-Gahal demonstration of support for Begin. Begin pretended as if there was no coup, nor did he seek Liberal support. Thus ended another small-scale political coup to "retire" Begin. Clearly the concept and the men of 1979 were not as threatening as were the previous coups of Kook and Tamir. Begin was now the Prime Minister that brought peace to Israel. He was undefeated in Herut. But what about the electorate?

The 1979 polls clearly indicated Likud's, if not Begin's, unpopularity. Opposition leader Peres was confident. "We will win," he told me prior to the election. In a debate with Begin before the election of 1981, he clearly seemed the winner.

Begin clearly seemed like a candidate not for office, but for early retirement. Yet appearances, as they always were with Begin, were deceptive. Once again he recovered in a most dramatic fashion.

Begin was not ready to quit, not with his goal of attaining an Eretz Israel unfulfilled in reality. But first, he was going to settle a score with Iraqi president Saddam Hussein, whom Begin called "the Butcher of Baghdad."

Begin's target was the Iraqi nuclear reactor project at Osirak, a project that Begin saw as a weapon threatening the very life of the Israeli nation. Only with the destruction of the reactor could he turn toward another project, the destruction of Arafat's PLO in Lebanon.

Saddam Hussein, who had killed and plotted his way to the leadership of Iraq, was a hugely ambitious man, and in a sense politics had very little to do with his overweening ambition. An implacable enemy of Israel along with almost all of his Arab brethren, he also plotted against fundamentalist Iran for dominance in the Persian Gulf.

It was as a prominent leader of the Arab Rejectionist Front that Israel, and especially Menachem Begin, viewed Hussein with a wary and jaundiced eye. Israel watched Iraq's military growth and buildup with increasing concern. Iraq, with the help of the Soviet Union as well as some Western European nations, was growing militarily at an almost unprecedented and dangerous rate.

By 1979, the military took up $3.5 billion of an $18 billion gross national product. Iraq fielded an army of 190,000 men organized into 12 divisions, which included 2,200 tanks and 450 attack planes, a formidable arsenal to field against any potential foe.

Most alarming, from an Israeli point of view, was the distinct realization that Iraq was moving toward building a nuclear capability. At Osirak, a nuclear reactor was being built with technical and physical help from the governments of France and Italy.

Labor governments in Israel had tried in vain to dissuade the Western Europeans from helping Iraq, but Labor's policy toward the Iraqi nuclear buildup was basically non-confrontational. All that changed when Begin came to power.

For Begin, the prospect of an Iraqi nuclear capacity, indeed, *any* Arab nuclear capacity, was totally and irrevocably intolerable. It was a devastating weapon that he had no doubt would eventually be used to try and destroy the Jewish nation, a holocaust in the flick of an eye. Begin approached the issue not only in practical terms, but from a passionately emotional and ideological stance. For Begin, a survivor of the Holocaust, Hussein was Hitler, and the nuclear reactor at Osirak was a technologically advanced version of the Final Solution.

"There will be no other Holocaust in this century," he told his cabinet and, later, the world. By October 14, 1980, he already had mustered a majority to back him in his decision to plan the destruction of Iraq's nuclear reactor. His chief supporters in the cabinet were Defense Minister Ariel Sharon, IDF Chief of Staff Rafael Eitan and Foreign Minister Yitzhak Shamir, all of them superhawks who were even more to the right of Begin.

THE TRIO DECIDE[4]

Despite its secret and unique nature, the decision to destroy the Iraqi nuclear reactor was taken in the full cabinet some time in October 1980. Decisions of this kind in Israel had been made in the past either by one person—Ben Gurion in 1956—or the informal Labor inner circle (Golda

Meir's Kitchen Cabinet) or small ministerial committees for security (which would include the Prime Minister, the Defense, Foreign and Treasury Ministers and sometimes the chief of staff and chief of IDF intelligence). It had been preceded by serious debates, discussions and efforts to turn every stone to prevent French-Iraqi nuclear collaboration. The Labor governments of Rabin (1974–77) and his Defense Minister Shimon Peres, had already agonized about the best political and diplomatic strategy to follow, and if this proved fruitless, over what military strategy Israel should adopt to prevent the creation of a military nuclear reactor in Iraq. No timing was set for D-Day, but the instruments of war—Air Force, the operations section in GHQ, and Intelligence—started planning several contingencies and training for the operation.

It was clear from the first discussions of the General Staff Senior Officer Forum, which began some time in late summer or early autumn of 1980, that the opinions of the ten to twelve officers present were almost equally divided.

The main argument of those who opposed the attack was that even if it succeeded it would not destroy the twelve kilograms of weapons-grade enriched uranium the French were known to have already supplied to the Iraqis, nor the smaller amount of enriched uranium the Iraqis may have acquired from elsewhere. It was also known that later on the French were to supply the Iraqis with yet another twelve kilograms of weapons-grade uranium which had been deposited somewhere in a heavily protected concrete pyramid (covered over by twenty-four feet of concrete) and that there was no way either to destroy or get control over this uranium. The fear of those objecting to the raid was, therefore, that even if it was successful, the Iraqis would still be able to go ahead and produce a nuclear bomb—and might in fact even have an increased incentive to do so.

Those who supported the raid replied that the amount of weapons-grade uranium in Iraqi hands was not enough to produce even one bomb. They argued that if the Iraqis were allowed to activate the reactor they would be able to acquire much larger quantities of weapons-grade uranium (perhaps up to thirty-six kilograms per year), which would be used to operate the reactor and which would finally produce a considerable amount of plutonium—enough to produce two to three bombs a year. If the reactor was destroyed *before* it was activated and *before* the additional twelve kilograms were supplied by the French, then the Iraqis would not be able to produce a nuclear bomb until they put into operation the plutonium route to the bomb. Moreover, they argued, following such an attack, the French and Italians might be reluctant to rebuild the Iraqi reactor and, if they did, would impose much stricter controls on the supply and use of the weapons-grade uranium and/or the retrieval of the plutonium produced by the reactor.

Those in favor of the attack on the reactor, including among them

Chief of Staff Rafael Eitan, finally won the debate by a small margin, and it was decided to go ahead with the planning of the operation. Around this time two Israeli engineers visited the United States and consulted American nuclear experts on what would happen to a nuclear reactor if attacked by 1000 kilogram bombs.

The debate over timing had two interrelated aspects—when would the Iraqi reactor become "hot" and when should the military option be employed? When the government's October decision became known to leading members of the Labor Party, Shimon Peres and Mordechai Gur, this external debate over timing immediately became entangled in electoral politics.

Earlier, the Labor government and its leaders had sought more time for diplomacy, although in 1977 when they had lost the election the military threat to Israel of Osirak had not as yet been determined. Peres in particular, as prime mover of Israel's nuclear reactor in Dimona from 1958–65, must have felt even in May 1981 that the Iraqi reactor was not, as yet, critical, and that the rise of President Mitterrand, a Socialist and personal friend, could prove diplomatically advantageous to Israel vis-a-vis French-Iraqi activities.

Thus in May 1980, when Peres was still leading in the pre-election polls, he wrote and sent the following letter to Begin at the traditional Sunday Israeli Cabinet meeting:

May 10

PERSONAL—TOP SECRET

Mr. Prime Minister

At the end of December 1980 you called me into your office in Jerusalem and told me about a certain extremely serious matter. You did not solicit to my response and I myself (despite my instinctive feeling) did not respond in the circumstances that then existed.

I feel this morning that it is my supreme civic duty to advise you, after serious consideration and in weighing the national interest, to desist from this thing. I speak as a man of experience. The deadlines reported by us (and I well understand our people's anxiety) are not the realistic deadlines. Materials can be changed for [other] materials. And what is intended to prevent can become a catalyst.

On the other hand Israel would be like a tree in the desert—and we also have that to be concerned about.

I add my voice—and it is not mine alone—and certainly not at the present time in the present circumstances.

Respectfully,
Shimon Peres[5]

The surprised and furious Begin, now finding that the October decision was no longer a closely kept secret, showed the letter to M. K. Moshe Arens,

Chairman of the Foreign and Security Committee. The October decision was no longer the property of a select few. In addition to Peres, former Defense Minister Weizman, a former chief of staff, Mordechai Gur, two Israeli journalists and one businessman close to Weizman were also acquainted with the projected raid.

Begin was receiving more cautionary advice from other directions, but on this issue he was adamant. He was determined to destroy Iraq's nuclear reactor installation.

There were others in the government and cabinet who were more reluctant to confront the issue in military terms. Some cautioned that there was no need for an air strike, that Iraq would not be ready to make a bomb for years. Military experts, like Deputy Prime Minister Yigael Yadin, a former (1949–51) IDF Chief of Staff, as well as the heads of Mosad counterintelligence and army intelligence were all opposed to an air strike. But Begin would have none of it. He was not about to listen to expert advice, intelligence or military, not when, as he saw it, the very existence of the state of Israel was at stake. For Begin, it was an ideological decision, a question of averting another Holocaust while weighing the issues of American and Soviet responses to an air strike.

On March 15, 1981, Begin informed his cabinet that the decision on an air strike would be made by Begin, Sharon and Shamir, and no one else. Opposition leader Shimon Peres frowned. "We are pushing the Arab world in a dangerous direction. I am not sure that what they possess is all that dangerous."[6]

But Begin saw the reactor as a clear and present danger. He also knew that it represented a political weapon which could be used against him in more ways than one. "I know there is an election coming," he told a close political adviser. "If they (Labor) win, I will lose my chance to save the Jewish people." His adviser asked what would happen if voters saw the impending air raid as a political ploy to pull the sagging Likud fortunes together. "I could also lose the election if the attack fails," Begin reminded his adviser.[7]

The last cabinet debate before the actual raid was heated but also a foregone conclusion. Yadin was worried that Iraqi forces already knew that some kind of action from the Israelis was coming; they lacked only the knowledge of the precise time and date. "They're ready for us," he warned. Sharon argued that the decision was critical, that the May timing was not a political decision but a question of time running out. Begin was calm. "Mark my words," he told Sharon. "They [the opposition] would never accept such a decision. All the responsibility of doing this will be ours. The problem is not France or the United States but the very existence of Israel."[8]

To the end, Begin remained strong and firm in his decision and in his belief about what the reactor represented to Israel and history. "We must delay this satanic plan for years to come," he said. "If we had not done this, if we had not acted, I would never have forgiven myself."[9]

TWO MINUTES OVER OSIRAK[10]

It was Sunday June 7, a beautiful clear day. The small town of Eilat, the Israeli tourist center on the Red Sea, was overcrowded with thousands of Scandinavian, German and Israeli tourists who had come perhaps to enjoy the sandy beaches of the Red Sea before they were returned to the Egyptians as part of the peace treaty between the two states. This Sunday was a "bridge day," between the Jewish Sabbath and the feast of Shavouth; it signaled in the two-thousand-year-long Jewish history in Israel, the beginning of the collection of the winter crops.

None of the tourists was aware of the special activity in the airbase of Etzion, some twenty kilometers from Eilat. For twenty-four hours one of the best and most modern airbases in the world had been unusually busy. It is a routine in Israel that most of the regular army soldiers receive the weekend off. All regular training is stopped on the Sabbath, and planes are ready to fly only in combat missions under a short alert. This particular weekend, however, all leave had been canceled, even leave to take a trip to Eilat.

It was one of the measures taken by the Army's Security Field Service, to eliminate any chance of leaking the big secret. For the same reason, all telephone communications lines, except for some special operation ones in the headquarters of the base were cut off. "The base was still closed late in the morning when a small helicopter landed near its headquarters. The Israeli chief of staff, Rafael Eitan, accompanied by Major Generals David Ivri, the commander of the Israeli Air Force, and Yehoshua Saguy, the head of the military intelligence, and some other senior officers who had been in on the planning of the operation since its inception, came out and were taken to the main briefing hall.

"Outside, in the big hangars, some of them underground, hundreds of technicians were already preparing the planes for the mission. The special ECM devices in the F-15s were checked and rechecked. Air-to-air missiles were carefully fixed to the wings of the F-16s and the fighter bombers were armed with the MK.84 iron bombs. Even at this stage, not one of these soldiers knew what the task was to be . . ."[11]

Some minutes before 1500 local time, the young pilots entered their planes and the canopies were shut from above. Few of them were nervous, having trained for so long for all eventualities and the worst possible developments. They pressed a button and the sound of roaring engines was heard all over the base. Moving forward, the long, broad runway was now visible to their eyes. Each pair of fighter bombers, loaded to full capacity, took off, using the whole length of the runway because of the heavy weight they were carrying.

The flight to Osirak was uneventful, as the pilots recalled hours later. During the many monotonous hours of the training they had undertaken, each of them had faced many possible contingencies—being discovered on the way to the target, heavier than expected antiaircraft fire, interception on the way to or back from the target by Saudi, Iraqi or Jordanian fighters, and always the possibility of some technical hitch.

Everything, however, went exactly as planned. They were flying now over the northern parts of the Saudi desert. The F-15 in the lead was navigating them to the Tammuz project through the many radar stations positioned in this part of the region. They flew very low, about thirty to sixty feet above ground level. No word was heard in their communication system, as each pilot followed the one before him, creating a large formation behind the commander of the raid.

". . . One more long and boring hour and a half was behind them when they knew that almost half of the job was over. At 1733 the leader and those who were close to him could identify the large buildings and the sixty-foot cement dome of the Tammuz project. The F-15s started climbing to a height of some thousand feet, in order to gain control over the combat area and make sure that no enemy planes disturbed the Fighting Falcons in their mission. The F-16s climbed only a few hundred feet. As preplanned long months ago they were to bomb the Iraqi reactor from a low height, mainly to avoid the antiaircraft fire of the Iraqis protecting the project.

"No antiaircraft gun had fired yet, no SAM missile had been launched, when the first pilot dived his bomber fighter, aiming at the center of the big cement dome under which the Tammuz I reactor was positioned. In less than five seconds he was climbing up again. The first two MK.84 iron bombs had hit the concrete roof, exploding it to small pieces, when the second plane was already releasing its own ammunition. One by one, with intervals of no more than fifteen seconds the Israeli Fighting Falcons bombed the reactor, while approaching it from different angles and directions. The Iraqi ZSU-23 antiaircraft guns started firing at the attacking jets. The speed and precision of the raiders and their low-level flight left the Iraqi anti-aircraft defense no chance at all."[12]

The F-16s, after dropping their bombs, were now much quicker than before. They were joined by the F-15s, and together the sixteen-plane team started on the long way back to airforce bases in Israel.

In all, sixteen MK.84 iron bombs were dropped on the reactor. The accuracy of the bombing, considering the fact that no smart bombs were used, was astonishing. All were direct hits within thirty feet from the center of the target. Later, the foreign press could claim that secret Israeli agents planted some electronic device in the reactor which enabled the bombs to home on the project. This was false, but for many journalists the accuracy was so unbelievable that some fantastic and imaginative stories were necessary to explain it.

"The planes were flying now in pairs at a very high altitude. They were well aware that this might lead to their interception, but they had no other choice. Flying just above ground level consumed much more fuel and now the jets were short of it. The pilots could only hope that no hostile fighters would intercept them on their way back home, although they trusted their proven air-superiority in dogfights and were sure that if there was a skirmish they would prove it again.

"At exactly nineteen hundred the first F-16 plane landed back in its base. In the next ten minutes the rest of the planes landed in different air bases, scattered throughout Israel. Raful was now ready. He was connected to Begin's private house where all the cabinet ministers were nervously waiting for the news. 'The mission is completed', reported the Israeli chief of staff to the worried Begin. 'All our planes returned safely to their bases.'

"The Prime Minister was relieved. He informed his colleagues of the news. A bottle of Israeli brandy was brought and they all drank a toast of 'le'haim' to the Israeli Air Force."[13]

THE BOMB AND THE ELECTION

The immediate debate of October 1980 needs to be viewed in the context of a wrangle which had been going on for over a decade. The debate over nuclear policy had originally developed when Israel's reactor went "hot," somewhere around 1968, and two schools of thought had emerged. The strategic hawks sought nuclear monopoly and superiority (it is this school of thought that has obviously triumphed). They articulated a theory of flexible response. They believed that an Israeli nuclear monopoly and superiority would eventually lead to a solution of the Arab-Israeli conflict on Israel's terms.

The strategic doves, who are usually associated with the Labor Party or the Left, saw no reason to delay proliferation of the development of nuclear capacities among the other Middle East nations. They argued that Israel could not sustain its conventional military superiority for long, that by 1985 the Arabs would have a five-to-one superiority in numbers and in military equipment. A nuclear stability or nuclear standoff, they argued, would create peace and stability. They saw a future in which borders and territories would become unimportant: Israel's technological superiority would be sufficient for survival against the Arabs.

In justifying the reactor attack, Begin reasoned that Israel was the rational state in the Middle East and could not allow an irrational state such as Iraq to have a nuclear capability. The hawkish position here was that deterrence would never be a practical weapon. The asymmetry in the nuclear equilibrium in the Middle East could work only for the rational side. The hawks, in short, preferred the static situation of an Israeli nuclear monopoly as opposed to the fluid position of the doves.

Begin's opponent in the upcoming election, Labor leader Shimon Peres, had been highly critical of the attack. He has charged that in spite of the fact that Iraqi President Saddam Hussein was indeed irresponsible, it was not necessary to bomb the reactor, that in fact Israel could have waited five years to do so. Peres argued that international pressure, meaning his close connections to France's Socialist President François Mitterrand, could have somehow obliterated the Iraqi reactor diplomatically.

In November 1980, Peres had met Mitterrand (at that time a presidential candidate), who assured him that France, under Mitterrand, would not supply Iraq with uranium. In December, Begin told Peres that he intended to bomb the Iraqi reactor. In January, Peres again met Mitterrand, who repeated his promise. On May 10 Peres sent Begin the secret letter in which he stated his opposition to the proposed raid and urged Begin to wait until after the French election, when Peres' connection to Mitterrand could be put to good use.

When the raid finally came off, Labor was divided and perplexed on how to respond. Peres urged that Labor oppose the raid and call it a political grandstand stunt. He was backed by former Chief of Staff Mordechai Gur, who called the raid unnecessary and irresponsible, and by Chaim Herzog, who charged that the Iraqis could not possibly produce atomic weapons before 1985. Labor ineptly but insistently tried to pin political motivations on Begin for the raid.

It has been assumed that Peres would not have ordered the attack, yet events and history argue otherwise. The military, political, and cultural base of Israel is such that it relies heavily on the concept of a very narrow security margin, the idea that Israel cannot afford to take *any* risks; the Iraqi reactor was perceived as a high risk as long as it existed. The belief was that for Israel to survive surrounded by aggressive Arab states such as Iraq and Libya, it must have nuclear superiority. This concept has been followed by both the Likud and Labor parties.

The pre-election polls clearly demonstrated that the tougher and closer to his historical image Begin got the better were his electoral chances. On June 2, a poll by a pro-Labor analyst clearly demonstrated that despite the narrowing of the gap between Labor and Likud, Labor was still slightly ahead of Likud.

The next poll, by Israel's leading pollster Hanoch Smith, on June 5, 1981, after Begin's attack on Chancellor Helmut Schmidt of West Germany and President Giscard of France, and after Treasury Minister Yoram Aridor's tax relief on televisions and other foreign imported goods, once more demonstrated that the tougher Begin became, the higher his electoral score.

The end of squabbling inside Likud over Begin's ability to govern was also reflected in a rise in the polls. Begin's performance ratings in the days during the Egyptian and Camp David negotiations were indeed high. However, when Weizman resigned and when Treasury Minister Yigal Horowitz warned, "I have no money," and continuously threatened to resign, polls on governmental performance sank low.

Then came the bombing of the reactor. Smith's poll between June 4 and June 11 (the bombing was on June 7) resulted in an overall 5 percent rise for Likud. Governmental support for Begin's security policy rose by eleven percent. The popularity of the government returned to the high days when the strong men were still in government (especially Weizman and Dayan).[14]

The Jerusalem *Post* polls before the raid predicted forty-five seats for Likud in late May, forty-six in early June, while forty-two seats were predicted for Labor in late May. In early June after the raid this dropped to 40. The projected distribution of Knesset seats after the raid therefore showed a remarkable turnabout—the first one since March—Likud scoring with forty-six, and Labor with forty.[15]

The contest from May was no longer between Likud and Labor but between Begin and Peres. Not since David Ben Gurion's early years (1948–56) had the electoral contest been so much of a battle between personalities. The 1981 Israeli election was in fact the first ever to have been fought not on issues but on personalities, despite the fact that issues had seemed crucial and favored Labor from the middle of 1980 to May 1981: Begin's low governmental performance, galloping inflation, the defense budget, the quality of life, and ethnic and social issues. Yet none were focused in the crucial months of May–June. As former Foreign Minister Abba Eban said early in June, "We must zero in on the 'Begin Factor'."

Begin's image as a demagogue and rebel rouser, but as an effective and supreme electoral campaigner, and his image as a strong man who would teach the terrorist Arabs and the PLO the necessary lessons, were his electoral forté. He was charismatic in the eyes of his populist electorate, whose excitement bordered on verbal violence, while he was totally detested by the intelligensia and modern middle-class Israelis.

Yet in the end, the 1981 elections centered around a personality contrast: Peres won the TV debate—but Begin won the votes.

Braced by what he could only naturally see as a victory in Iraq, Begin now prepared himself for an even more challenging and controversial task —the war which would destroy the Palestinian Liberation Organization in Lebanon, a war that would, of course, do much, much more.

36

The Second Begin Government—
Sharon's War, Begin's Demise: 1981–83[1]

It is important to examine the electoral and political background against which the second Begin government came into being. The June 30, 1981, elections presented a political, electoral and cultural revolution in Israeli politics and society. These elections signaled the emergence of a new electorate inclined toward radical nationalism and Jewish traditionalism.

Begin's coalition government represented a realignment of the new political, social and cultural forces, replacing the Socialist-Zionist center—the old progressive and nationalist alignment composed mainly of Jews of European-American origins. It was the old alignment that had dominated Israel from even before the state's creation in 1948. The second Begin government was supported by a constituency even more radical and militant than the government itself expected to be. This emerging electorate was politically aggressive, inflexible on territorial concessions, and militant in its attitude toward the PLO, much more so than the diverse and precarious governing coalition forged by Prime Minister Begin.

The second Begin government was the most hawkish government in Israel's history. The ruling quartet—Begin, Defense Minister Ariel Sharon, Foreign Minister Yitzhak Shamir and Treasury Minister Yoram Aridor—were all hawks in the Herut political tradition and philosophy, supported by National Religious Party radicals, and sustained by the Eretz Israel true-believers in the Renaissance party. The ruling Herut party, the NRP, and the Renaissance party formed the ideological base of the second Begin government's foreign policy and security policies. If Begin's narrow victory was not exactly an overwhelming mandate, it indicated that the electorate would at last allow Begin to fulfill his dream of a Complete Israel.

What is important to know about the second Begin government is that it was not a new government, that for all practical purposes, it actually had begun its operations in July 1980, when the last member of the cabinet who had any ability to restrain Begin resigned from the government. When the flamboyant Ezer Weizman resigned over the Palestinian autonomy issue, he inadvertently helped give birth to the second Begin government, radical momentum. The electoral victory of 1981 merely formalized and legitimized the process.[2]

The exchange of letters between Weizman and Begin are very revealing on what would lie in state for the second Begin government. Weizman writes:

"Dear Mr. Prime Minister,

"I hereby submit my resignation as defense minister and as a member of the Israeli Government.

"My resignation should come as no surprise to you: In recent frank conversations I have held with you, I have never made a secret of my opinions. I explained to you that the gap between our positions is growing deeper and deeper. Too many of the key issues that the government deals with have become the subject of division between us.

"My reservations about the government's peace plan, its social policy and its style of functioning have become graver. I have felt a growing realization that our paths are diverging and that soon I would no longer be able to serve in your cabinet. Now this recognition has become firmly established and my moment to leave has come . . .

"Since its independence, the nation of Israel has known times of peaks and depths, of high tides and low. But never, I believe, has there been such despondency and depression as in the last few years.

"It is not the hardships and the critical moments that have made the spirit fall. It is the leadership that sows despondency. And he who sows despondency incessantly reaps despair."[3]

Begin's reply was in his style, personal, angry and scolding:

"To Mr. Ezer Weizman, Minister of Defense:

"I hereby acknowledge with gratitude your letter of May 26, 1980, in which you inform me, as required by law, of your resignation from your post in the Government of Israel . . . Indeed it is true that recently we have held discussions in which you often threatened to leave the government. You have also done it in the past, relatively periodically . . .

"I also remember that, when we were in Ismailia holding important talks with President Sadat and his advisers, you whispered to me, during one of the important debates with the Egyptians: 'How good it is that you are Prime Minister.' And I also remember that often you found it necessary to say to me, while mentioning great names: 'You will be marked in history as the one who signed a peace agreement with Egypt . . .'

"You were given the chance, and perhaps I was among those who gave it to you, to fulfill the important post of Defense Minister in the Government of Israel in an extremely important period. Yet you, out of impatience and rashness, which are remembered by many from the history of the Herut movement, attempted to depose me, both openly—on television while I was in the U.S. on an important national mission, which included putting into effect the agreement for the engine of the 'Lavie' airplane in a special conversation with the President of the U.S.—as well as by intrigue, which could not have remained a secret, in order to replace me.

"In this attempt to undermine me, you again failed completely. You were given, Mr. Defense Minister, a rare opportunity, but you have abandoned it out of ambition that is mind-numbing.

"Sincerely, M. Begin."[4]

Dayan, having failed to persuade Begin of a new approach in implementing the Palestinian autonomy plan, resigned earlier on October 9, 1979.

Left with a government that had all the appearances of being in a political shambles, Begin replaced Dayan with former Lehi chief of operations and Knesset Speaker Yitzhak Shamir, a man more to his ideological liking. For Defense Minister, Begin picked the man with whom he had the most in common: himself—thus taking a page out of the book of David Ben Gurion. By late summer 1980, the former government and cabinet of strong individuals had changed considerably, leaving only Sharon, who finally acted, as Begin's ideological follower.

With the successful culmination of the historic Camp David Agreements, the signing of the Egyptian-Israeli Peace Treaty, and the ongoing, if desultory, autonomy talks, Begin stood on the threshold of a benign opportunity.

He had achieved what no other Israeli Prime Minister had achieved. He could, if he chose, now move to reestablish the national consensus eroding since 1973, and to bind the nation into a single political entity in a way that a Labor Prime Minister could not. He had been elected principally by the growing Sephardim electorate, and by discontented voters who had long considered themselves political outcasts in an Israel dominated by Socialist Zionists. Begin, if he chose, could now move to bridge the chasm between Ashkenazim and Sephardim, between young and old, between generations. Politically, in the wake of his gigantic international success, he could also, if he chose, move to make Likud the nation's majority party, especially now that Labor seemed to be moving into a permanent decline.

Begin was scoring one success after another: peace with Egypt, the destruction of Osirak, next the most cherished of all goals, the destruction of Palestinian nationalism. Where? In Lebanon.

Yet as we know, Begin moved in an entirely different, and eventually disastrous direction, avoiding opportunity as if it blinded him. The elections of 1981, a sparse, difficult and uphill victory for the Likud coalition, amounted to a personal triumph for Begin. Flushed with victory and a sense of vindication, Begin, never far removed in his passions from his rhetoric, now moved to fulfill his ancient dream of a complete Eretz Israel. He was moved at least in part by a feeling that his time was running out. He was sixty-seven years old and had already been felled by one heart attack. His health was at best precarious and unpredictable.

Now, instead of attempting to unite the nation by moving on domestic and political concerns, he chose to eliminate the Palestinian issue once and for all and thus make Eretz Israel an irreversible reality.

Now, he would annihilate the Palestinian Liberation Organization's state-within-a-state in Lebanon, he would destroy its political and military capital in Beirut, he would smash the momentum and force of Palestinian nationalism and he would destroy the PLO's pervasive influence in the West Bank and Gaza, thus laying the groundwork for the creation of Eretz Israel's final boundaries. In many ways, he had already signaled his intentions by a deliberate sabotaging of the autonomy talks, which got nowhere, mired in Begin's technical foot-dragging, by the specter of PLO participations in negotiations and by the even more unacceptable shadow cast by the prospect of an independent Palestinian state. "Not an inch of territory," Begin had shouted time and time again, and he meant it certainly of Eretz Israel if not Sinai, which, in any case, was never part of Eretz Israel.

There is absolutely no doubt that Begin, spurred by his rhetoric and dreams, by his unvarnished hatred of the PLO, was the father of the 1982 Lebanon war, a war that had tragic results for everyone. And his actions all but guaranteed that the war would be enlarged, would drag on and end in a disaster when he made Ariel Sharon, the newly appointed Israeli Defense Minister, the executor of his policy.

Begin's first priority in Lebanon was to destroy Palestinian nationalism and the PLO's military and political infrastructure. But he also had a secondary goal, which fit with his sense of himself as a historic peacemaker. He would emerge from Lebanon with a peace treaty with another Arab state, this time, fratricidal Lebanon itself. Both goals almost ensured that the war in Lebanon would not be a short affair, but a long, bloody and frustrating struggle.

It was perceived by Begin, and even more by Sharon, that an alliance of sorts would have to be established with the only political force in Lebanon friendly with Israel, the Christian-Maronite Gemayel family, headed by the ruthless, young, and ambitious Bashir Gemayel. The Gemayels and Maronite Christians would help the Israelis oust the PLO from Beirut and, after a victorious conclusion to the war, and the election of Gemayel to the presidency of Lebanon, would sign a peace treaty with Israel.

This goal ignored political and military realities within Lebanon and portrayed Begin's political and military ignorance about the Arab world. For instance, Begin was obviously opposed to a war with Syria, yet Syria, more than the PLO, was the dominant Arab political and military force in Lebanon. Any attempt to create an Israeli-Christian political and military order in Lebanon would, of necessity, involve the ouster of Syria's thirty thousand troops from the Beka'a Valley, or at least a serious compromising of Syria's position in Lebanon. Yet Begin wanted no war with Syria.

Begin saw the Maronites principally in terms of their Christian faith, not as the Arabs they essentially were. And Begin saw Lebanon as a potentially Christian non-Arab state, not as the Arab state that it really was. In his wishful ignorance, Begin felt that the Western, and therefore Christian nations, would come to the aid of a Christian Lebanon. Yet, the Christians in the Arab world and in Lebanon, were a small minority who could not genuinely act autonomously. Yet for Begin, who grew up in the world of Poland, a country where the Roman Catholic Church acted as protector of the nation, Christians were Christians, "goyeem were goyeem." Why shouldn't they support their brethren?

Begin, in spite of excellent intelligence from Mosad, never saw Lebanon for what it really was—not a real political entity centrally run from its capital in Beirut, but a country made up of disparate and often desperate rival factions—Suni, Shia, Maronite and Greek Orthodox Christians, Druzes, radicals and conservatives, with political strongmen controlling business interests and territory in much the manner of Sicilian mafiosos. It had no political cohesiveness, no real central government, no system of public services or governmental compassion for its population.

Sharon reveled in grand designs, and tried to achieve the unattainable —the destruction of the PLO and Palestinian nationalism, but also the ejection of Syria from Lebanon, a military confrontation with Syria, the establishment of Bashir Gemayel as President of Lebanon, and the creation there of an Israeli-dominated order. Not all these plans were ever approved either by Begin or by Israel's cabinet. They were, in the end, Sharon's goals, which dictated the tactics of the Lebanese war and its eventually tragic outcome.

It's worth for a moment taking a closer look at Sharon, who came to be seen as Begin's evil genie and the true architect of the Lebanese war. It would be hard to find two men more different in outlook, style, and background.

Sharon, born in Palestine in 1929, was raised on a private agricultural cooperative, trained in the Haganah and the IDF. He was one of the founders of Israel's elite paratroop corps, renowned as a brilliant soldier and leader, and equally, if infamously, known for his disloyalty, brutality, overweening ambition and opportunism.

Sharon's parents, Mordecai and Chaya Shienerman, came from Brest-

Litovsk. His father died when Sharon was only one year old, and so Chaya became the dominant influence in his life. She was a tough, independent, irascible farmer, an anti-Socialist who loathed the collectivists and their ideology. Sharon inherited her independence, stubbornness, single-mindedness and energy.

Sharon fought with the Haganah in the War of Independence, but when Israel and the government of David Ben Gurion, flush with victory over no less than five Arab armies, felt secure enough to prune its army of politically suspect members, he saw no future in the army and left to attend law school at the Hebrew University, emulating several hundreds of other officers and men who pursued civilian careers either in Israel or abroad.

Some hope existed that now that independence had been achieved, a peace treaty with one or more Arab nations might emerge, but that hope was soon dashed when the Arabs, who refused to accept the verdict of war, began to rearm and to instigate raids into Israel from the West Bank and Gaza.

As marauders, border raiders and terrorists struck against Israel, Ben Gurion responded by appointing Colonel Moshe Dayan as Chief of Staff in 1953. Israeli counterterror measures had so far produced minimal reduction of the casualties Israeli troops had suffered. Now Dayan set about not only reversing this trend but creating an IDF that was aggressive, daring and cohesive.

The paratroop command would become a model for the IDF. With leaders like Sharon, Mota Gur and Rafael Eitan, the paratroop command would become an elite, effective and lethal unit engaged in retaliatory raids into the West Bank, Gaza and Syria.

Sharon's rise was swift. In a matter of three years, between 1953 and 1956, he rose to the rank of full colonel in command of Paratroop Unit 101. Right from the start, he was characteristically himself, which is to say that he was both admired for his daring and command abilities, and resented for his intriguing and politicking and his willingness to ignore the chain of command.

Ben Gurion had approved Dayan's raids, and in turn Dayan had given Unit 101 almost a free hand, of which Sharon took full advantage. Undisciplined, Sharon accelerated the raids to new heights of ferocity, to the point where they created political and international problems for Israel at a time when it least needed them. In 1954, Unit 101 attacked the Arab West Bank village of Qibya, destroying it totally and violating a United Nations truce in the process.

The action was protested in the Security Council, and brought disapproval from U.S. President Dwight Eisenhower, who was trying to follow a so-called "even-handed" policy in the Middle East by forging alliances with "moderate" Arab states, who protested the Israeli raids loudly.

As a commander, Sharon was brisk, daring, ruthless, and charismatic, but his ambition continued to overshadow his more sterling qualities. Because of his daring in the 1956 Sinai war, his actions in the 1967 Six-Day War, and especially his startling crossing of the Suez Canal in 1973, Sharon emerged as an enduring hero to much of Israel, in spite of his known darker side. In his aggressiveness, he became a model for young IDF commanders. Even though he rose to the rank of general, he was at heart always a commando leader.

His entry into politics, tentatively begun in 1969, came more out of career frustration than any idealistic notions. By 1969, he realized that he would never become IDF chief of staff, then his most cherished ambition. A majority of senior officers, as well as Prime Minister Golda Meir and Defense Minister Moshe Dayan, suspicious of the depths of his ambition, simply refused to give Sharon the job, even though they, like Ben Gurion, admired Sharon's military gifts. Ben Gurion, in retirement in 1972, once asked shrewdly about Sharon. "Is Sharon still lying?" That was the perception of Sharon, that there was something tainted, untrustworthy about him, that he would at bottom do anything to pursue his personal goals.

Sharon was an opportunist in the sense that whatever organization he joined, whatever group he led, he used, abused and left it when it was expedient to do so. He splintered the paratroop unit for his own ends; he split the IDF southern command for his own glory in 1973. When he finally chose to remain in politics in 1973, he organized Likud in order to be able to use it, hopefully, as a political weapon against Begin. As a Likud man, he plotted against the Liberal party's leaders and repeatedly joined efforts to topple Begin, as we have seen previously. In 1975, as a Rabin adviser, he plotted against Peres at the Ministry of Defense. No ideologue, he supported Rabin's Kissinger diplomacy, even though it called for conciliatory new policies toward the territories.

In 1977, he rejoined Likud, when his own party, Shlomtzion, gained a minuscule, but crucial two seats in the Knesset. At this time, he also joined Herut out of expediency, even though he was neither a rabid Revisionist ideologue nor an Etzel veteran—although he was a raving annexationist. His reward was to be appointed Minister of Agriculture, which, in fact, meant minister of settlements, and he pursued the settlements policy with all the enthusiasm of a fervent annexationist. Under his ministry, more settlements were established than in any previous government.

Yet it was Begin he sought to influence, and it was the Defense Ministership that Sharon was really after. Uncharacteristically, at least for an annexationist and hard-core territorialist, he supported Begin's peace initiative. But Begin knew that the wily general wanted the top job at Defense and he refused to give it to him, perhaps because he sensed some of Sharon's naked avarice and lust for it.

Nevertheless, Begin finally succumbed, partly because people like Arens and Shamir rejected the job, knowing full well it would mean presiding over the surrender and return of the Sinai to Egypt and ousting Israeli settlers from the Sinai settlement Yamit. But Sharon didn't mind and accomplished the job in ruthless fashion. So Begin made Sharon Defense Minister in November 1981.[5]

With Sharon firm in the saddle in the Defense Ministry, the IDF was about to undergo a seismic change in mission and orientation. Some of the responsibility for this can be laid at the door of Begin, who was ambivalent about Sharon.

Part of Begin's problem with Sharon was that Begin considered Sharon to be a shining example of everything that was grand and brave in the IDF. He was dazzled by Sharon's generalship even as he was suspicious of it. In this he reflected Sharon's attitude toward the IDF, which he saw as a "Jewish army," the "army of revenge," the army of "never again." Yet Begin himself knew little if anything about military tactics, military history or military planning. And, like many of the key Herut figures, he had never been a part of the IDF or Haganah, indeed had been their enemy during the Revolt.

Begin's ambivalence was understandable. The IDF, after all, was the creation of Socialist Zionism and of Ben Gurion in particular, Begin's lifelong nemesis. It was an instrument of the partitioned state, which Begin had never accepted. IDF strategy was enveloped in Ben Gurion's concept of a state and a defense strategy.

When dealing with the IDF, even as Prime Minister, Begin remained a splendid outsider, and in many ways he never bothered being anything else. His connection to the IDF was emotional, not historical, practical or strategical. It's not surprising that Begin always spoke of the "Israeli Army" rather than the IDF, deleting the "Haganah" part of IDF. To Ben Gurion, IDF was Israel's manifest, to Begin an instrument to fulfill the dream of Eretz Israel.

As Defense Minister and Prime Minister, Begin never interfered in the actual workings of the military. Every Thursday, he would come from Jerusalem to the Defense Ministry headquarters in the Kirya in Tel Aviv to be briefed, mainly by senior civil servants and the IDF chief. As long as Major General Ephraim Poran remained his senior military aide, Begin's relations with the IDF were cordial, if never intimate. The senior officers were not in awe of Begin and to the new generation of officers he was a virtual stranger. They were aware of his lack of military knowledge and treated him accordingly. After all, Begin was more preoccupied with ideological themes, not with matters of grand strategy, and this suited the IDF High Command, which had become more and more independent in matters of strategy, mission and training.

What changed with the coming of Begin, and accelerated with the ascendancy of Sharon to the Defense Ministry, was a change in stance and mission. The very name—Israeli Defense Force—had for long defined its mission, which is to say, it followed a national policy and strategy of *defense*. For Israeli generals and planners, this meant a strategy of tactical offense in order to preserve strategic defense. Even with the occupation of the Sinai, the Golan Heights, the West Bank and Gaza, the IDF's basic mission and strategy did not change in essence.

The Likud political victory demonstrated the growing gap between military objectives and political aspirations. For Labor and for the advocates of the partitioned state, the political and military strategy of the IDF and the nation had always been complementary. For Begin and Sharon, the partitioned state was no longer valid and its politics were a dead issue. The politics of Eretz Israel and the spirit of annexationism called for a new military doctrine and strategy. Sharon, more than anyone, recognized this immediately, and began to change the IDF's mission and strategy, and to control it personally.

Sharon already had considerable influence within the ranks of the IDF High Command, made up of many officers who could be considered his allies and lieutenants, including his old paratrooper colleagues like Rafael Eitan and Chief of Intelligence Yehoshua Saguy. As a former combat officer, Sharon had considerable influence through the ranks, especially among some young officers who admired him immensely.

In order to change IDF's deeply entrenched defense strategy, tilting it toward an offensive doctrine, Sharon had to drastically change the structure and procedures of IDF's High Command. He began, in characteristic fashion, with a purge, forcing many senior officers to opt for early retirement, especially officers who were not likely to go along with a change in doctrine. He cultivated General Avraham Tamir's special National Security Unit (NSU), turning it, in Schiff's words, "into his general staff."[6]

The NSU was designed to isolate the IDF High Command and its senior officers. He removed any political issue of import and "even certain military subjects from the General Staff dominion." He waged a campaign against dissenting voices within the IDF so that in the end "most of the men surrounding Sharon gradually accommodated themselves to his demands and style".[7]

Sharon's strategy and intent were clearly enunciated in his lecture to the war college late in March of 1982. He spoke of "destroying the PLO state-within-a-state in Lebanon" as the IDF's primary mission. Moreover, he spoke of changing the political map of Lebanon as a task for the IDF. Sounding ominous, he spoke of "a new political order" in Lebanon and of using the IDF to influence Lebanese elections, which would result in the election of Bashir Gemayel as President and a hopeful Lebanese peace treaty with

Israel. Sharon spoke of "strategic cooperation with the United States," meaning that he hoped to involve the United States in a war against the PLO, or at least get a "green light" from the Reagan Administration. He went further. He spoke of ousting Syria from the Beka'a Valley and out of Lebanon entirely and of an Israeli hegemony in Lebanon.

The PLO leadership, he said, would be forced into a "gilded cage" in Damascus where it would lose all vestiges of independence, as well as its influence over Palestinians on the West Bank. Thus, moderate Palestinians would be free to deal with Israel and Begin's own emasculated autonomy plan that would be achieved without the interference of Egypt or the United States. Other Palestinians would seek a solution in Jordan which would, as Sharon hoped, become "Palestinianized."

These goals were boldly stated, and they were goals which differed radically from any previous political missions undertaken by the IDF, and certainly from Israel's historical security doctrine. The IDF, from now on, would fight wars not imperative to its security, but to fulfill Likud's ideological doctrines.

Sharon meanwhile persuaded Begin (and Shamir and Eitan) of the military purposes he was preaching. In that sense, Lebanon was Sharon's war. Even though Begin's dream of annihilating the PLO prompted the war, Begin's dream caused him to follow Sharon in the war's execution and design, much in the manner that he had followed Paglin at the King David bombing and in the *Altalena*.

Once again, Begin was being spurred by his rhetoric, which promptly turned into an uncomfortable reality. It was one thing to speak of a "free Lebanon," the "end of the PLO" and the fulfillment of the territorial goals of Eretz Israel, but quite another to deal with the realities of the complicated relationship with the Gemayels, the outraged reactions of an unpredictable United States, or the Syrian factor. Begin had envisioned a short war and had never seriously contemplated the consequences of a long, Sharon-style conflict.

Sharon, who had all along intended to capture the Beirut-Damascus road and march to Beirut, never really gained formal approval for this "Big Pines" operation, which would also draw Israeli troops into a confrontation with Syria. There were reservations all along, including some from Begin, who knew that an assault against an Arab capital would be condemned by the international community. His intelligence officers also expressed reservations, saying "We mustn't go as far as Beirut. We'll only get bogged down here . . . This is a capital of an Arab state and we have never entered an Arab capital before . . . We might find ourselves in confrontation with the United States."[8]

Nevertheless, Sharon moved ahead by readying the IDF, putting it on alert, by meetings with the Gemayels and through supplying the Phalange

Maronite forces through the Mosad. All that was needed was an excuse, a fuse that could be lit.

It came when the ambassador of Israel to the Court of St. James Shlomo Argov was shot in London. Two days later, Begin convened an emergency cabinet meeting. Although Sharon was away on a mission to Romania, his pugnacious spirit permeated the meeting. Begin didn't need Sharon to pull the trigger. He had already been informed that the shooting was in fact the work of an anti-Arafat Iraqi-based PLO faction led by Abu Nidal. "They are *all* PLO," Begin proclaimed, calling for a strike against the PLO. "Abu Nidal, Abu Schmidal, we have to strike at the PLO."[9]

Later some cabinet members would claim that they were not aware of the consequences of a raid against the PLO, that it would in effect signal the start of a war. But even Begin, and certainly Eitan and Sharon, knew that the PLO would be forced to retaliate in a major way, and that would mean an invasion of Lebanon by Israel.

One man who understood what was happening was Yasir Arafat, who was caught in a predicament of his own making. He knew that if he followed an Israeli raid with a Katuyshka rocket attack against Israeli settlements in Galilee, ending his American-sponsored ceasefire policy, he would be starting a war that he would lose. In a way, Arafat's own rhetoric, like that of Begin, was about to suffer the consequences of reality, for he could not turn back, and the rockets rained on Galilee, causing a miniexodus of Israeli settlers and bringing loud pronouncements from PLO "Foreign Minister" Farouk Kadumi, who said, "The Zionist enemy is retreating. We can proclaim the first occupation of our stolen land."

Arafat was in a precarious position. His military policy was unsupported by the moderate states, including Egypt and the Gulf states; hated by the Shia Lebanese, whom his forces abused and terrorized; and subject to the machinations of Asad in Syria. He could, in the event of war, only retreat to Beirut and somehow hope for the best.

When five hundred rockets and shells fell on the Galilee settlements, the Israeli cabinet was ready with its unanimous vote. But the vote, even then, was only for the destruction of the PLO in Southern Lebanon, not for a march to Beirut or a war with Syria. The operation was to be theoretically limited to a forty-five–kilometer scope, a distance that would ensure that Israeli settlements were out of the range of PLO guns. Asked whether Israel would attack Syrian forces, Begin replied with an emphatic "No." Sharon cynically said that "Beirut is outside the picture."[10]

The cabinet, although it did not yet know it, was moving into the direction that Sharon wanted it to move. Sharon's strategy was cunning; his position—the destruction of the PLO, peace with a friendly and dependent Lebanon and a clash with Syria—were never altogether Begin's or the cabinet's positions, yet they were being pulled along. A reluctant Begin, however, shared with Sharon only his passion to destroy the PLO.

Sharon's private planning took place within the confines of the NSU, where he plotted to go in the direction of Beirut, capture the Beirut-Damascus road and fight with Syria if necessary. The destruction of the PLO, which was expected to be attained within roughly seventy hours, would be followed by an Israeli withdrawal (only if the PLO evacuated from Beirut), and the creation of a multinational force separating the IDF from Beirut. The goal of establishing a Christian-dominated state was not even discussed, although Sharon was "encouraging" Bashir and the Phalange to establish a representative government, dominated by the Christians. (Sharon never subscribed to a Gemayel dictatorship and in fact, his staff hoped for a broad-based representative government.) The goal was to politically oust Syria from Lebanon, hopefully without recourse to military confrontation.

All of these plans and hopes were to be drastically altered by events. Their success depended perhaps too much on thin timing, on events and possibilities that never occurred.

The destruction of the PLO took over a week of hard fighting, not seventy hours. The Syrians had to be fought, but they were not ousted from the Beka'a Valley. In Beirut, Gemayel proved to be a reluctant ally, and refused to campaign against Arafat.

The expanded long war, fought on three fronts, followed by the bombing of Beirut, complicated Israel's diplomatic problems, to say the least, creating a negative image of Israel, especially in the media, where images of bombed-out civilians dominated the airwaves.

The most serious problem for Israel and Begin was the bombing of Beirut, where Arafat and his fighters, defeated militarily in the field, were digging in the hope of being rescued, of being able to save face with a last desperate stand behind civilians.

The siege of Beirut strained relations between the United States and Israel. The special ambassador Philip Habib was once again sent to Lebanon. At home, Begin's consensus for the war was also being strained by its duration, which had far exceeded the original and stated goals. With criticism mounting, especially from the Labor party, from doves and even from strategic hawks like Rabin and Gur, the true intent of Sharon's war was finally being perceived. The positive results which had been expected from this "brief" war were not forthcoming. True, the PLO was more or less destroyed militarily, and the nation breathed a sigh of relief, but Israeli troops were still in Lebanon, being killed and wounded daily. The PLO hung on in Beirut. The Syrians were tactically but not strategically defeated. The Americans were pressuring for an end to the war, even though Begin still didn't have Gemayel in power or a scrap of paper to call a peace treaty.

Even within the ranks of the IDF, opposition was growing. Although

Chief of Staff Eitan supported Sharon, many of the other senior officers were opposed to the expanded war aims. Commanders like General Avigdor Bengal, Uri Simhoni, deputy commander of the Northern Front, and his Commanding General Amir Drori, as well as Chief of Army Intelligence Saguy were all opposed to Sharon's grand design.

Begin, however, was unaware of the growing opposition. He was being kept in the dark by Sharon, who had managed to become his major contact and source of information about the war and the comings and goings of the IDF. He would report constantly to Begin, much in the manner of a regimental duty officer—details, not substance.

The war displayed Begin's ignorance of its nature. He was still enthralled by old images and by his fondness for rhetoric. There was something unreal about the way he viewed the war. He spoke of the breaking of the PLO "Maginot Line," of Zhukov's "pincers" in the Ukraine.[11] During his only visit to a frontline unit on top of the Crusader Fort Bauffre, he proclaimed that Lebanon "would be quiet for forty years," and asked the troops if they were using machine guns. One officer scoffed sadly, "These are not Etzel days." For Begin, the Lebanon war was his World War II. "No more Treblinkas," he told his cabinet.

Basically, Begin remained uninterested in military details, preferring to draw up peace plans and peace treaties with Lebanon, thus allowing himself to be deceived by Sharon and Eitan about what was actually happening. What was happening was no longer the Peace for Galilee war.

The siege of Beirut was straining United States–Israeli relations. Syria would not agree to a peace between Israel and Lebanon as a price for Israeli withdrawal. Meanwhile, Gemayel would not or could not move on the PLO in Beirut. He could no longer tell Sharon, as he had before, to "leave Beirut to me."

Habib arrived in Beirut hoping to persuade Arafat and his flock to leave Beirut peacefully. Arafat, sensing the potential for a propaganda victory, would not. "You'll have to negotiate face to face with me," he said.[12] Arafat dug into the growing rubble of Beirut in order to exploit the tragedy, in order to seek Western sympathy through the media. Arafat was trying to turn a military defeat into martyrdom.

Begin told Sharon to intensify the bombing, even as he set out on a trip to Washington. It speaks volumes for Begin's presumption that he expected a warm reception, but he was greeted by a Capitol Hill that was as chilly as winter. His rhetoric went unheeded and was unwelcome. Even friendly senators treated him with a certain amount of disdain.

On June 21, 1983, Reagan suggested to Begin that "the best course today is diplomacy."[13] Yet Begin tried to persuade Reagan that there had been a great achievement, especially militarily. He bragged how American and Israeli planes performed against Syria, but talked little about the implications of the siege of Beirut.

In a visit with Begin, after I had returned from Beirut between June 21 and June 23, meeting with Gemayel, Camille Chamoun and other Christian leaders, I talked to Begin in the halls of the Knesset. I had realized in my visit to Lebanon that the Christian Gemayels were quite willing to fight to the last Israeli, and was depressed about the situation. Begin was attentive and concerned, but his response made me wonder if he had been listening at all. He seemed elated and threw up his hands in a victory gesture. "The Jewish brain won," he said. It took me a moment to realize he was talking about the massive destruction of Syrian airplanes and SAM missiles in the Beka'a Valley. "American brains, too," I said. "That's also a Jewish contribution," he said. He never inquired about his so-called "Christian allies," or the forthcoming role of any Lebanese government.

Even though Begin, mostly at Sharon's insistence, thought he had achieved a "Green Light" from then Secretary of State Alexander Haig, the continuing bombing of Beirut was threatening to create a serious breach in relations with the United States. The initial and misleading reports Begin received from Haig in Washington encouraged Sharon to tighten his grip around Beirut.

Arafat perceived that he was now isolated. None of the moderate Arab states came to his aid. "It's up to you," he told the Moslem leaders of Beirut. "It's up to you when I depart. If you think the time has come, I will go tomorrow."[14] The intensified Israeli bombing finally forced Arafat to make a deal with Habib to "save Beirut."

Habib's compromise would assure that the PLO forces, some ten thousand strong, would evacuate Beirut under the protective umbrella of a U.S. Marine contingent, which would stay behind to guarantee the safety of the remaining Palestinian refugees within Beirut.

Gemayel was counseled to reject the proposal. Begin found it attractive because he saw that the Marines could become the nucleus of a multinational buffer force to replace the IDF in Lebanon.

It was Sharon who wanted to continue the assault on Beirut. "Southern Beirut must be destroyed, it must be razed to the ground," he said. His stand split the cabinet. Habib complained to Washington and Reagan warned of "severe consequences." Begin remained defiant. "Jews," he replied to the President, "do not kneel except to God."[15] Nevertheless, Sharon's standing in the cabinet and his position was severely "undermined."[16]

By August 7, 1982, Begin himself expressed misgivings about Sharon's behavior. He insulted Habib as well as other American diplomats in Tel Aviv and Beirut. And the bombing continued.

Finally, between August 12 and 13, Arafat announced he was ready to withdraw. Although he had dropped his conditions, he organized the PLO departure in the manner of a Dunkirk, with his forces sallying toward the Greek ship which would take them to Tunisia with arms and weapons raised in victory.

This was perhaps good stagecraft, but it rang hollow. A generation of Palestinians were born or had grown to maturity in Lebanon, Beirut was their capital and now they were leaving, most never to return. The idea or realization of a return to the "homeland" was as distant as ever.

With the PLO gone, it was time for the attempt to implement Sharon's strategy for a Christian-dominated Lebanon. Gemayel needed the Israelis to ensure electoral victory. They did and on August 23, Bashir Gemayel was finally elected President of Lebanon, even though he had no support in large parts of the country, including Tripoli, the North, the Beka'a and even West Beirut.

Now Begin had begun to realize that he was dealing with another "goy." In a meeting with Begin in Nahariyah, Israel, Bashir flatly rejected a peace treaty with Israel, although he tried to couch his refusal in conciliatory terms. "We are Christians," he told Begin, "But we are also Arabs. Politically, I am with Arabs, personally I am with you." Reiterating his father Pierre Gemayel's conversation with Sharon, he said, "As Arabs we have friends in the Arab world. We can work for you. We have connections with Saudi Arabia. We can mediate for you." "Where do we stand with a peace treaty?" Begin asked. "I cannot decide on such matters alone," Gemayel replied. Gemayel even demurred when Begin asked him to make an official visit to Jerusalem or Tel Aviv.[17]

Begin became angry and started to berate Gemayel about his failure to participate in the seizure of Beirut. "On and on he went, like a schoolmaster scolding a delinquent pupil. Bashir was insulted to the depth of his being," wrote Schiff. Begin continued to berate Gemayel about "some Phalange officials who were openly hostile to Israel and maintain 'unacceptable' relationships with Syrians." Writes Schiff, "Begin treated Bashir like a spineless vassal, not like the President of a sovereign and allied state."[18]

Begin had some reason to feel hostile and belligerent, for this was also the day, September 1, 1982, that President Reagan announced his own plan for peace in the Middle East, the Reagan Plan, which once again pitted Begin against the Palestinians. Begin violently rejected the plan. He was in no mood for a plan that called for Jordanian-Palestinian-Israeli negotiations which might include PLO participation. Here he had just defeated the PLO, and now Reagan was resurrecting it. "Here they are, plaguing me again," he told a visitor.

Plainly, the whole experience of Lebanon was beginning to gall Begin. Reagan was reviving the PLO; Bashir had betrayed him; there was no hint of a peace treaty and no end in sight of the war itself. Yet when Gemayel suggested the meeting between the two remain secret, Begin chivalrously accepted and promised not to tell.

Distressed as he was, Begin did not have the political courage or perhaps the common sense to take the most obvious course, which, with the PLO crushed, was for the IDF to gracefully leave Lebanon, its ostensible mission accomplished.

Begin could not contemplate this. After reading Reagan's cable, he said to U.S. Ambassador Samuel Lewis, "It has been a very difficult day for both of us to have reached this unpleasantry." He told his adviser Yehiel Kadishai that "it [the Reagan Plan] died the day it was born."

Events now narrowed the options and led to almost total disaster. On September 14, 1982, Bashir Gemayel, the newly elected president of Lebanon and his entire staff were killed when an explosion detonated in the apartment house where he was staying. It is quite reasonable to assume that the bombing was the work of Syrian agents. The assassination immediately changed the entire picture in Lebanon, and the entire tone and scope of Israel's Lebanon incursion.

At 9:30 P.M. Mosad's General Yitzhak Hofi informed Begin that Gemayel was indeed dead. Begin ordered an "air train" sent to Beirut International Airport and the IDF entered West Beirut, as Begin explained, to "preserve order in West Beirut." Almost immediately, this rationale would have an ironic tinge to it. By September 15, the IDF effectively controlled West Beirut.

On that same day, a Phalange battalion from Damur, a Lebanese village where Palestinians had perpetrated a particularly horrific massacre, moved into the Palestinian refugee camps of Sabra and Shatila in West Beirut. The result was a massacre of some 750 men, women and children over a three-day period while Israeli forces stood by and did little, if anything, to stop the carnage.

The result went deeper than world outrage or even Israeli outrage at home. It created a heated fissure in the Israel body politic. It resulted in Begin being forced to acquiesce in the creation of the Kahan Commission of Inquiry, which, after heated and long testimony from all ranks, including Begin himself, came up with conclusions that rocked Israel's political world.

There was never really any question that it was Lebanese, particularly Phalangist, gunmen that pulled the trigger, engineered and executed the massacre. But it was Begin and Sharon's IDF which stood by for some time, even if not in collusion with the killers, as the massacre continued.

The Commission, during the course of testimony, discovered that Sharon, who had never trusted Arafat, had received information that there were still some two thousand PLO fighters at large, hiding in the various refugee camps, including Sabra and Shatila. The Phalangists, burning for revenge after the murder of Gemayel, were in a mood for liquidation and thought the Israelis felt likewise. Sharon, brutal as he might have been, never entertained the thought of a wholesale massacre, but rather would have preferred judicious elimination of known and identifiable terrorists. But a massacre en masse was just the ticket for the Phalange, who had no taste for civilized niceties. Sharon had considered letting the Phalange be involved in a mop-up operation in the camps, but the cabinet was never called to decide this issue, nor was Begin informed.

There is a serious question about just what exactly members of the cabinet and Begin knew. Yet it is certain that the Commander of the Northern Front, Amir Drori, knew of what was termed "Operation Iron Mind," a Phalangist sweep for terrorists.

The Commission did establish that the IDF did not give the order for nor did it participate in the massacre. But the IDF command was certainly aware of the mood and intention of the Phalangists. The moral aspects of the massacre were damning for the IDF. Begin was not really aware of what was happening until the very end of the massacre, but here he was, a Prime Minister who constantly evoked the horrors of the Holocaust, castigating world leaders for standing by while Jews were sent to gas chambers, having to defend his own army, which had stood by while women and children were being murdered. Not until the following day was the IDF aware of the extent of the massacre, but still nothing was done to help the refugees or stop the slaughter.

Sharon, who had spent so many years dealing with the Phalangists, clearly knew of their eagerness to enter the camps and what they might do. He repeated his order to send them in "under the IDF's supervision."[19] There was no evidence that Sharon actually incited the Phalangists to violence. But then, there was no need to do so.

Eitan told the Commission that after the murder of Gemayel, the Palestinian blood would reach the Phalangists' knees. Sharon, his chief of staff, and the IDF officers on the scene, all knew full well of the potential for a bloodbath. There was no need for any extra imagination or knowledge about what would happen in the camps.

The question is, where was Begin and what did he do, if and when he did find out about the IDF's indirect role in the massacre?

The Commission clearly distinguished between direct and indirect responsibility in the massacre. Direct responsibility belonged to the Phalangists: "Our conclusion, therefore, is that the direct responsibility for the perpetration of the acts of slaughter rests on the Phalangist forces."[20] But indirect responsibility was laid at the door of the IDF. "The rationale for such responsibility may be found in the outlook of our ancestors, expressed in the biblical parable of the 'beheaded heifer,' to wit, 'We must wash our hands even though they didn't shed blood.' "[21]

The Commission reminded all that in dealing with indirect responsibility, it should not be forgotten that "the Jews in various lands of exile, and in the Land of Israel when it was under foreign rule, suffered greatly from pogroms perpetrated by various hooligans."[22] "In our view," the Commission added, "everyone who had anything to do with events in Lebanon should have felt apprehension about a massacre in the camps."

"The decision to enter the camps," the report continued, "was taken without consideration of the danger, which the makers and executors of decisions were obligated to foresee as probable."[23] The Commission drew a distinction between political and military responsibility. Begin was cleared of knowing about the massacre during the time it took place. "He was entitled to rely on the optimistic and calming reports of the Defense Minister that the entire operation was proceeding without any hitches and in the most satisfactory manner." But the Commission noted that Begin, on September 16, upon learning of the Phalangists' entry into the camps did not raise "any opposition or objection to the entry of the Phalangists into the camps."[24] Begin testified that he could not conceive an atrocity would be committed. According to the Commission, Begin was amply warned by his Deputy Prime Minister David Levy, who "warned of the danger to be expected from the Phalangists' entry into the camps."[25]

The Commission was "unable to accept the Prime Minister's remarks that he was absolutely unaware of such a danger." He should have "supposed" that the assassination of Bashir Gemayel would lead to a massacre and been "aware of the brutal massacres committed in Lebanon during the civil war" and "the Phalangist hatred of the Palestinians."[26] "We are unable to accept the position of the Prime Minister that no one imagined that what happened was liable to happen, or what follows from his remarks that this possibility did not have to be foreseen when the decision was taken to have the Phalangists enter the camps."[27] The Prime Minister's "indifference" would have been "justifiable," the Commission said, if they could accept Begin's position that it was "impossible to foresee the actions of the Phalangists." Thus, the Commission added, "the Prime Minister's lack of involvement in the entire matter casts on him a *certain degree of responsibility*" (italics mine).[28]

Begin stayed with his position, stated in a December 9, 1982 letter to the Commission: "It was never imagined that the Lebanese forces, who are trained and organized military units, and who were assigned the objective of fighting under difficult conditions, would want to or be able to perpetrate a massacre." But when Begin defended the IDF entry into Beirut after Gemayel's assassination, he contradicted himself on his lack of prescience. "It was to prevent bloodshed," he said. Prodded, he added, "Bloodshed between Christians and Moslims, acts of vengeance."

Sharon had taken that particular line of reasoning in persuading Begin to send the IDF into West Beirut, when he knew perfectly well the possibility of disaster. Everyone, from Sharon and Eitan to the lowest rank, knew something would happen in the wake of the assassination of Gemayel. Yet Begin insisted that he had acted correctly, that he believed he was fighting terrorism, not instigating a massacre. It was true that terrorists still remained in all the camps.

The Commission, however, insisted that Begin should have known and thus judged him. History will render its judgment, also. Sharon, on the other hand, could not pretend, as he tried to do before the Commission, that he could not conceive of the Phalangists committing a massacre. It was Sharon after all who said to the Phalangist commander Eli Hobeika, "I don't want a single one of them [PLO terrorists in Beirut] left." Hobeika asked, "How do you single them out?" To which Sharon replied noncommittally, "We'll discuss that at a more restricted session."[29]

The Commission was adamant and sure in its judgment of Sharon. "His involvement in the war was deep," they said, "and the connection with the Phalangists was under his constant care."[30] But Sharon took no measures to ensure that the IDF would supervise any Phalangist operation.

The Commission did not exactly exonerate Begin, but they did find Sharon *personally* responsible and thus recommended that the Prime Minister "after informing the cabinet of his [Sharon's] intention to do so, [that he] remove him from office."

The Commission's judgments rocked the cabinet and Israel itself. Sharon refused to leave, and Begin, loyal as ever, wavered. In the final analysis Begin had little choice but to remove the man whom he followed into the Lebanese cauldron.

Begin, his officers and the majority of his countrymen, unlike Sharon, possessed a deep respect for Israel's democratic traditions. Begin may shout that "Goyem kill Goyem and the Jews are blamed," but he also abided by the Commission's findings. Here was a country and its people who, in effect, took responsibility upon themselves, and judged themselves by strict moral standards. There was also a commission and investigation in Lebanon, but in that country there was no judgment, there was no punishment, there was no responsibility.

37
Assessment of Begin

When you look at the career of Menachem Begin, you see complexity and contradiction, you see a man whose vices are his virtues, whose negatives undermine his positives, a man who just misses the stature of true greatness, the kind acquired by David Ben Gurion, but a man who, through stubbornness and doggedness, left a much larger imprint on history.

He could combine a capacity for true leadership and statesmanship with a bottomless capacity for pettiness and spite and a penchant for needless detail. He shone as a leader during the Sezon, during the fighting years of Etzel, as the man who finally became Prime Minister and became the first Israeli leader to make peace with an Arab nation. But he was also a man who lived much of his life in obscurity, as an unnoticed toiler or a butt of the jokes of his political opponents. He could go from the summit of Camp David to the disaster that was Lebanon, where he was not the leader but the led, spurred by the ruthless and wild ambitions of his Defense Minister Ariel Sharon.

An Old-World, quintessential Diaspora Jew, he nevertheless became the leader of a new Israeli constituency, the politically deprived Sephardim, who saw Begin as they saw themselves, as outsiders. Yet he failed miserably in trying to reach the intellectuals not only of the Left, but among his own followers; they scoffed at his passionate, simplistic rhetoric. His only steadfast constituency over the years was the small group of hard-core Etzel ancients, who fed Begin's nostalgia, a quality which played a role in his failure to create new and forward-looking policies.

Begin's career was marked by long periods of quiet, unremarkable life, sparked by euphoric highs during the Etzel years and by his final march to the Prime Ministership and the great Camp David achievement, an achievement, like Nixon's rapprochement with Red China, which could perhaps only have been accomplished by Begin.

Camp David and peace with Egypt alone might have catapulted Begin to the stature of Ben Gurion. If Ben Gurion was the man who built the state, then Begin would be the man who made the peace. But Begin was led by self-deceit and the deceit of others, like Sharon, into the morass of Lebanon. His flights of rhetoric—histrionic, emotionally charged, intellectually muddy—ill equipped him at times to deal with political reality. Begin was essentially an ideological leader, and he equated Israel's security with the ideology of complete Eretz Israel.

Perhaps Begin's greatest failure, and for that matter the great failure of Revisionism, was an inability and unwillingness to understand Israel's traditional foes, the Arabs, the arch-rivals with whom Israel will have to learn to live. Israel's neighbors are not the Dutch or the Swiss, they are the Palestinians, the Arabs. In this resistance, Begin was no different from Jabotinsky or any other Revisionist. He never bothered to learn Arabic, he never read the works of Arab writers, he never bothered to search out the viewpoints of the traditional other side, nor did he care about Arab aspirations and goals. He saw them through a glass darkly, as fanatics, as terrorists. His favorite term for the PLO was from the past—Nazis. For Begin, the Arabs would forever be stooges of the British, of the Communists and terrorists. Politically speaking, there were no Arabs for Begin. They were not negotiating partners—except perhaps Sadat, whom he dealt with from the framework of the lawyer that he was—correctly, unemotionally, even deviously. How could Begin negotiate with Palestinians when his program was the total annexation of Eretz Israel?

In this, he differed from those like Ben Gurion or Dayan who were intellectually curious and open about everything, especially the Arabs. David Ben Gurion had no more empathy for Arabs than Begin. But as a realpolitiker, he carefully studied the enemy and sought, at least early in his career, a *modus vivandi* with Arab nationalism.

Begin came late to Palestine and Israel; in many ways he remained forever an outsider. He lived in Israel without really becoming a part of the land of Israel, which to him was an *idea,* not a place or an environment in which he lived. He would travel the country to speechify, but his world view always was borrowed from the Poland of Revisionism, from Betar. He lectured to the converted, not to real audiences. To Begin, Israel would remain a dream place, an idea and a symbol, not a real world.

Ben Gurion, on the other hand, wrote a book on Begin's favorite subject, Eretz Israel, as early as 1917, and Dayan wrote a book on living with the Bible, i.e. the land of Israel. Begin never walked or surveyed the land of Israel. He was the patriot of Eretz Israel without knowing its people. He never captured the imagination of the sabras, the young Israelis who worked the land, joined its political parties, worked in the kibbutzim and fought its wars. To them Begin was someone to be mocked, a social throwback, an old world, courtly Jew wearing ill-fitting clothes, speaking with a strong accent. The Israeli young thought of themselves as the new Jews, the super-Jews. They mocked and rejected their parents, and Begin, above all, was surely a parent figure. It was the Sephardim, the generation of the great immigrations of the 1950s, who adopted Begin as their own; they were more conservative in outlook, more traditional, and they shared Begin's view of the Arab world.

Begin's entire political life was a search for recognition, a reaching out for legitimacy, a process which was often fruitless, and, at moments of success, undermined.

Thus, he never gained the recognition that he so longed for from his idol, Jabotinsky, incurring his wrath at the last great Betar conference in 1938, when, even while supporting his mentor, he straddled the ideological fence. Begin opted for military Zionism, the kind being openly preached by the Sternists, who called for a war against the British Empire and who sought an alliance with Nazi Germany against Britain.

His appointment as Betar chief in Warsaw was almost an afterthought on Jabotinsky's part, not an open, warm invitation or seal of approval.

Even when finally, and rather ironically, he became head of Etzel, Begin never quite managed to attain that mantle of respectability and legitimacy. More than anything, he wanted the Revolt to become a significant act in the annals of Jewish history, but affairs like the bombing of the King David Hotel, the hanging of the British sergeants, Dir Yassin, and the *Altalena* tended to have the opposite effect and attached to Begin and his movement a pariah label.

In the years of his political wilderness, Begin constantly and fruitlessly strove to gain recognition, a place in Israel's political sun, as he went to the polls time and time again, always unsuccessfully, never quite gaining the high ground.

It was not until 1977, in what seemed a sudden blaze of glory, that Begin reached the summit after decades of failure. Here was his opportunity to go beyond Etzel, to outstrip even Jabotinsky, and he secured it by becoming the first Israeli leader to make peace with any Arab state. The Egyptian-Israeli Peace Treaty will probably secure Begin's place of importance in the history books, and in the process he resurrected Jabotinsky's image, his memory and brought Revisionism back into the foreground of the political arena.

Yet, even here, Begin undermined himself, besmirched his great achievement in the way he was moved into the darker terrain of Lebanon and Beirut by Sharon. The old patterns had repeated themselves by the time a tired, betrayed, and wounded Begin retired from public office, apparently never to speak publicly or to be seen again. Half the nation, stung by the Lebanon experience, remained unforgiving, while the hard core of his admirers remained—and remain—adoring and uncritical. Once again, Begin, like some Shakespearean tragic figure, swung between fame and infamy, between praise and degradation.

Begin may well be remembered strongly—for leading the Revolt and for Camp David, but in many ways his most remarkable achievements may have been his political survival and that of the Herut party that he created and the legacy and ideology of Jabotinsky and Betar, which he kept alive. For the years in the political desert after the Revolt were long, often unbearable, ignominious, and difficult. Begin also deserves credit for keeping the traditions of parliamentary democracy vital during his long years as a minority leader. They were years in which, election after election, Begin offered himself and Herut up to the people and was soundly rejected, years of long, arduous battling, often hopeless. Yet Begin went on, even as his old compatriots died along the way, people like Ben Eliezer, Eri Jabotinsky, Shimshon Unitchman and others, while others reviled him, bolted Herut, and joined revolts against him time and time again. By 1966, Begin was tired and Herut was decaying, its rhetoric and its symbol, the land of Israel, overwhelmed by a movement that carried its name. The flag of Begin was carried by Labor and Herut dissidents who formed LIM, and Likud, by the radical new Zionists and now by Ariel Sharon. Today, Herut's flag—the Land of Israel—is most loudly waved by Herut dissidents like Shmuel Katz, by former Chief of Staff Raful Eitan and former Lehi member Geula Cohen, and the *Ha-Techiyah* (Renaissance) Party.

Nevertheless, Begin was a populist, and a notably stubborn leader who led Etzel away from its radicals and turned it into a viable, if mostly unsuccessful, political party. He was in many ways a superb parliamentarian and coalitional politician, qualities which assured his and his party's survival.

He was never Jabotinsky's personal choice to lead the Revisionist movement, but that's exactly what he did. Perhaps no other man could have quite done what Begin did. He rescued a moribund ideology and movement and helped legitimize it, bringing it to the pinnacle of political power. But he also left it orphaned. For, after all, Herut was a one-man deed. He left no successor and left a party in disarray. His very vices—stubbornness, unwillingness to bend—matched with his virtues—devotion, steadfastness and loyalty, and passionate patriotism—and made him a political survivor.

The map of the Middle East, and Israel with its expanded frontiers, *is* different today, and the peace with Egypt, however fragile, remains. These achievements alone make him, next to Ben Gurion, Israel's greatest and most influential Prime Minister. They also make him a tragic figure. When he resigned, the nation was torn asunder by warring successors. He left Israel to taste the bitter ashes of Lebanon. Yet, perhaps another leader would have hung on, unwilling to admit his failure and inability to cope, and would have thus paved the way for a greater tragedy.

Begin's legacy is indeed mixed, and it remains, as does the man, endlessly fascinating.

Sources and
Acknowledgments

ORAL

I can't say that I have conducted "interviews" with Menachem Begin. Like other Israeli political and military leaders with whom I have established contact since 1957, I prefer to identify my several meetings with Mr. Begin between 1973 and 1983 as part of my political education about Israel. As a scholar, columnist, participant and observer in Israeli society I got to meet and know most of Israel's key political and military leaders. I have had extensive conversations with many of them, and they are: David Ben Gurion, Moshe Sharett, Shimon Peres, Yigael Yadin, Yitzhak Rabin, Moshe Dayan, Yigal Allon, Ariel Sharon, Moshe Arens, Pinchas Lavon, Yitzhak Shamir, Natan Friedman-Yellin, Israel Shayeb-Eldad, Meir Amit, Dan Tolkowski, Ezer Weizman, Avraham Tamir, Shmuel Tamir, Shmuel Katz, Hillel Kook, Gad Yaacobi, Zvi Zur, Avraham Adan (Bren), Abba Eban, Chaim Herzog, Chaim Israeli, Avigdor Bengal (Yanush), Shlomo Gazit, Aaron Yariv, Michael Bar-Zohar, Uriel Shelah (Yonatan Ratosh), Uri Avnery, Yaacov Meridor, Mordechai Gur (Mota). With several of the above, I have established lifelong friendships. In some cases I have been a witness to history.

Among Israeli journalists, most helpful to me were my friends Zeev Schiff, Shlomo Nakdimon, Shalom Rosenfeld, Moshe Zak, Ido Dissenchik, Yaacov Erez, Hanoch Bar-Tov, Yitzhak Levi-Hayerushalmi, Yoseph Harif, Uzi Benziman, Yoel Marcus, Hagai Eshed, Eliahu Amikam.

Among the Begin entourage Yehiel Kadishai, Begin's lifetime loyalist and aide and Shmuel Katz (no longer in this category) were most helpful. So were Yaacov Meridor and Chaim Landau. Arieh Naor, Begin's *chef de cabinet* was most helpful. Moshe Arens, ambassador to the United States and Minister of Defense under Begin's government is an old friend and was helpful. Pesach Gani of the Jabotinsky Institute was courteous and very helpful, as was Etzel's former chief of operations in Europe Yoel Amrami. Among former Lehi chiefs: Yitzhak (Yizernitsky) Shamir whom I have known since 1966; Natan Friedman-Yellin, who spent many days with me telling me about Vilna in 1940 and the intense Lehi-Etzel struggles; and Matityahu Shmulevitz, a Lehi hero and fighter and director of the office of the Prime Minister under Begin. Eli Tavin of Etzel was helpful, especially through his most instructive and extremely informative book. Mrs. Ben Eliezer gave me her valuable time and advice. Last, but not least, Hillel Kook, who was helpful on the Vaad, the *Altalena,* and on Begin himself.

The Jabotinsky Institute is a storehouse for the researcher. So are Yoel Amrami's private archives and Ratosh's archives. Yaacov Shavit's private archives were my best source material. The Haganah Archives was another important research tool, as well as Yad Tabenkin. My research assistants frequented all of the above. I also used the Ben Gurion Archives in Sdeh Boker.

WRITTEN

I do not feel that a complete bibliography is called for here, especially since this is my fourth book about Israel. A most extensive bibliography and footnotes apparatus is found in my book, *Israel: The Partitioned State* (Scribner, 1985). See also my *Military and Politics in Israel* (Frank Cass, 1969) and *The Politics and Military in Israel* (Frank Cass, 1978). For the reader who wants to pursue Israeli history and politics outside of Revisionism, Betar, Etzel, Lehi and Begin, the above three books offer a considerable list of documents (published and unpublished), books, and articles in English, Hebrew and Arabic. In this book I offer only a short bibliography, culled from the text, that specifically deals with Begin, his life, times, events, places and ideas.

Professor Yaacov Shavit, a friend indeed and more than that, served as my adviser, research assistant, mover of ideas and guide. Indeed without Shavit, Israel's most knowledgable expert on that country's nationalists, this book could not have been written. There are so many of his ideas and so much of his research in this book that a bounty of appreciation would be insufficient. I also thank his thoughtful wife, author and scholar Zohar Shavit. Professor Shavit collected the material for me in the Jabotinsky Institute and in the Amrami Archives, and his own archives are indeed among the best. Shavit books in Hebrew are a requirement for those who work in the vineyards of Israel's Right, Revisionism and Etzel.

My editors, Loretta Barrett and Cynthia Barrett, spared no effort to help shape this book, which is their work as it is mine. One can only revel in such dedicated editors. For their support and advice I am eternally grateful.

My appreciation also goes to Mary McCarthy and Harold Grabau of Doubleday. And I wish to thank Edward Levi. Last but not least, deep thanks goes to Ingeborg, whose typing, editing and discipline made this book a better one.

Notes

Chapter 1 BEGIN

[1] Conversation July 1977, Jerusalem.

[2] On Jabotinsky, see footnotes for chapters 4 and 5.

[3] On Ben Gurion, see Michael Bar Zohar, *Ben Gurion: A Political Biography* (Hebrew) (Tel Aviv: Am Oved, 1971–75), 3 vols.; and Amos Perlmutter, *Israel: The Partitioned State* (New York: Scribner, 1985), footnote 9 to chapter 1, p. 350.

[4] *Betar's Third World Conference—A Report,* Warsaw, September 11–16, 1938, published by Betar's High Commission in Romania, 1940, pp. 60–61.

[5] Begin, "Herzl's Funeral Oration," Yaar Herzl, Jerusalem, 1955, on the occasion of the reburial of Herzl in Israel.

[6] Conversation with author, Jerusalem, June 1983.

Chapter 2 THE COLLAPSE

[1] In addition to meeting Begin several times in 1982 and 1983, I made use of the Israeli press, especially *Haaretz, Davar, Maariv,* and *Yediot Aharonot.* I am also grateful to several of my journalist friends in Israel who supplied me with considerable information on Begin's collapse. My thanks go to Zeev Schiff, Ido Dissentchik, Yoel Marcus, Uzi Benziman, Mati Golan, Yaacov Erez, Yoram Peri, Moshe Zak, Eitan Haber. I held conversations with Begin, his alter ego Yehiel Kadishai, Arieh Naor, Eli Ben Elisar, Shmuel Katz, Mordechai Zipori, Moshe Arens and Abrasha Tamir. See also Eitan Haber, "Begin to Those Who Do Not Know," *Yediot Aharonot,* June 5, 1983; Yoel Marcus, "The National Poorman," *Haaretz,* June 15, 1983; Allen Shapiro, "Begin's Disability," Jerusalem *Post,* December 28, 1984; Yoel Marcus, "Begin's Health," *Haaretz,* July 7, 1981, and Begin's answer, "My Policy Concerning My Health," *Haaretz,* November 27, 1981; David K. Shipler, "Begin's Era in Israeli Politics: A Period of Historic Change," The New York *Times,* September 9, 1983, pp. 1 and 6; Gideon Reicher, "A Lonely and Sad Man," *Maariv,* September 7, 1983; Yehuda Moritz, "Misleading the Public," *Haaretz,* November 27, 1983.

[2] Kadishai, "Begin Reads a Lot, Eats Properly and Looks Well," *Maariv,* March 7, 1983; Moritz, "Misleading," *Haaretz,* November 27, 1983.

[3] "Begin's Health," *Haaretz,* July 7, 1983, p. 2.

[4] Begin, "My Policy," *Haaretz,* November 27, 1981, p. 2.

[5] Yanush Ben Gal to author, summer 1983.

[6] Begin to author, Knesset, Jerusalem, July 23, 1983.

7 *Report of the Kahan Commission,* (Jerusalem: Government of Israel, 1983).

8 Reporting Aliza Begin's death in *Maariv,* November 14, 1982, p. 1.

9 Ambassador Moshe Arens to the author, Washington, D.C., summer 1983.

10 Quoted in Gideon Reicher, "A Lonely Man," *Maariv,* September 7, 1983.

11 Quoted in *Maariv,* September 30, 1983.

12 Quoted in *Maariv,* February 11, 1982.

13 Ibid.

14 Reicher, op. cit.

15 Ibid.

16 Ibid.

Chapter 3   POLAND

1 The best introductory material in English on modern Poland with an emphasis on the 1920s and 1930s is found in: Norman Davies, *God's Playground: A History of Poland, 1795 to the Present* (New York: Columbia University Press, 1982) vol. 2, chapters 19 and 20, pp. 393–491; and *Heart of Europe: A Short History of Poland* (Oxford: Clarendon Press, 1981), chapter 2, pp. 109–57.

For a summary of the history of the Jews in Poland see again, Davies, *God's Playground,* Vol. 2, chapter 9, pp. 240–66. A classic history of the Jews in Poland is Simon Dubnow's, *History of the Jews in Russia and Poland,* Vol. 3, translated from Russian (Philadelphia: The Jewish Publication Society of America, 1920). Also, Joseph Rothschild, *East Central Europe Between the Two World Wars* (Seattle: University of Washington Press, 1977), chapter 2 (Poland), pp. 27–72. The best contemporary studies of the Jews in Poland are by Ezra Mendelsohn: *The Jews of East Central Europe Between the World Wars* (Bloomington, Ind.: Indiana University Press, 1983), chapter 1, pp. 11–84; and *Zionism in Poland: The Formative Years 1915–26* (New Haven: Yale University Press, 1981). For the philosophy of Polish nationalism, see Andrzej Walicki, *Philosophy and Romantic Nationalism: The Case of Poland,* (Oxford: Clarendon Press, 1982). In Hebrew the literature is vast. I recommend a series of publications of the Diaspora Research Institute, Tel-Aviv University, *Gal-Ed,* a yearly dedicated to Polish Jewry (seven volumes); see also Israel Halperin, ed., *The House of Israel in Poland* (Jerusalem: Youth Department of the Zionist Organization, 1953), two volumes; Shlomo Netzer, *The Struggle of Polish Jewry for Civil and National Minority Rights (1918–22)* (Tel-Aviv: Tel-Aviv University Press, 1980); Emanuel Melzer, *Political Strife in a Blind Alley: The Jews in Poland 1935–39* (Tel-Aviv: Diaspora Institute, Tel-Aviv University Press, 1982). An older and personal account is Yitzhak Gruenbaum's, *The Wars of Poland's Jews* (Jerusalem: Haverim, 1941). See also Martin Malia, "Poland's Eternal Return" (collective review of more than a dozen books on Poland), *New York Review of Books,* September 29, 1983. On Menachem Begin biographies in Hebrew (translated into English), see Eitan Haber, *Begin* (New York: Bantam Books, 1978); Shlomo Nakdimon and Aviezer Golan, *Begin* (Tel Aviv: Idanim, 1979); two articles by Haber in *Yediot Aharonot* (August 1983); and Teddy Preuss, *Begin.*

2 Malia, "Poland," p. 18.

3 Leon Pinsker, *Auto-Emancipation* (London: Association of Young Zionist Societies, 1932).

4 Davies, *God's Playground,* vol 2, p. 260.

⁵ Quote in Alexander J. Groth, "Dmowski, Pilsudski and Ethnic Conflict in pre-1939 Poland" *Canadian Slavic Studies* 3, no. 1 (Spring 1969), pp. 73–74.

⁶ M. Begin, "On Three Things," in *The Encyclopedia of the Diaspora,* ed. Eliezer Steinman, vol. 2, pp. 249–52.

⁷ On Begin and Hashomer Hatzair see: Zvi Wolvesky, " 'The Cub,' Menachem Begin in the Nest of *Hashomer Hatzair,"* *Maariv,* August 17, 1983.

⁸ Conversation with Ben Gurion, Tel-Aviv, 1971.

Chapter 4 LEGIONS

¹ The best literature on the Jewish legions in World War I is Yigal Elam: *The Jewish Legions in World War One* (Tel-Aviv: Maarachot, IDF Publication, 1973); on Yoseph Trumpeldor's role in the Jewish Legion, see Shulamit Laskov, *Yoseph Trumpeldor: A Biography* (Jerusalem: Keter Publishing House, 1982); see also Vladimir Jabotinsky, *The Story of the Jewish Legion* (transl. by Samuel Katz), New York: Bernard Ackerman, 1945 for a popular general account of the Gallipoli campaign, see Robert Rhodes James, *Gallipoli* (London: Batsford, 1965); on Jabotinsky and the legions, there is no new biography of Jabotinsky with the exception of Joseph B. Schechtman's *Rebel and Statesman: The Vladimir Jabotinsky Story—The Early Years* (New York: Thomas Yoseloff, 1956) vol. 1, chapters 12, 13, pp. 201–60 dealing with the legions. See also Yehuda Ya'ari and Uri Zvi Gruenberg, *Zeev Jabotinsky, His Life and Deeds* (Hebrew) (Tel-Aviv: Mizpeh, 1931) and Menachem Begin, "Zeev Jabotinsky," special issue of *Herut,* July 1950.

² Ya'ari, Gruenberg, *Jabotinsky,* p. 11.

³ Ibid., p. 5.

⁴ Ibid.

⁵ Begin, "Jabotinsky," p. 1.

⁶ Ibid., p. 11.

⁷ Ibid., p. 4.

⁸ Ibid., p. 5.

⁹ Ibid.

¹⁰ Schechtman, *Early,* p. 5.

¹¹ Elam, *Legions,* p. 13.

¹² Ibid., p. 24.

¹³ Ibid., p. 39.

¹⁴ Ibid.

¹⁵ Ibid., p. 98.

Chapter 5 BETAR

¹ The best source on the rise and evolution of Betar is the comprehensive three-volume collection of documents, letters and narrative edited by Chaim Ben Yerucham, *Sepher Betar* (The Book of Betar), *From the People,* vol 1 (Jerusalem-Tel Aviv: Publishing Committee of Shepher Betar, 1969). Also see Yaacov Shavit, *Revisionism in Zionism* (Hebrew) (Tel Aviv: Hadar Publishing House, 1978). On Jabotinsky see Zeev Jabotinsky, *Speeches 1926–35; Speeches 1927–40,* and *Speeches 1905–26* and *On the Road to the State,* in *Ktavim* (Works), (Jerusalem: Eri Jabotinsky Publishing House, 1958).

² Shavit, *Revisionism,* p. 36.

[3] Ibid., pp. 49–50.

[4] Schechtman, p. 318.

[5] Ibid., p. 229.

[6] Zeev Jabotinsky, "On Militarism," *Speeches: On the Road to the State,* Works, pp. 39–47.

[7] Schechtman.

[8] Jabotinsky, op. cit.

Chapter 6 RADICALIZATION OF BETAR

[1] On the Biryonim, the literature has been growing since 1977. The Achimeir family has reprinted most of Aba Achimeir's writings; Achimeir's dedicated son Yosi has carefully edited his father's works. Thus we have now the following (all in Hebrew): Aba Achimeir, *Revolutionary Zionism* (1966) and *Berit Habiryonim* (1972); Yosi Achimeir ed., *The Black Prince: Y. Katznelson and the National Movement in the Thirties* (Tel Aviv: The Jabotinsky Institute, 1983); *The Principles of the Biryonim* (Tel Aviv: republished by The Jabotinsky Institute, August 1953); Yoseph Achimeir and Shmuel Shatzky, *Brit Habiryonim* (Tel Aviv: Nizanim, 1978); Yehoshua Eshel Yeyvin, *From the Lion's Den* (Tel Aviv: 1954), *Jerusalem Is Waiting* (Jerusalem: Herut, 1939), *The Kingdom of Herut* (Jerusalem: 1957) and *The Blood Crime of the Jewish Agency,* 1937. For translations of some of Achimeir's representative poetry see "Danse Macabre" (translated by I. M. Lask) in the *Palestine Tribune,* June 23, 1946, and July 18, 1946; "Kings of Emek" (translated by A. M. Kline) in *The Judean,* January 1931; "To God in Europe" (translated by R. Friend) in Pnueli and A. Ukhmani, eds., *Anthology of Modern Hebrew Poetry* (Jerusalem: Wagner Press, 1966), vol 2, pp. 264–78. For a critical (and unfriendly) review of Achimeir and the Biryonim, see Zeev Sternhell, "Jewish Fascism," *Haaretz,* July 1983; also the unpublished seminar work of Yehudah Shuster, "A Theoretical Model of a Non-Governing Fascist Ideology," under the directive of Dr. E. Sivan and Dr. Z. Sternhell, Department of History, the Hebrew University in Jerusalem, July 1976; and Yael Yishai, "Intellectuals in the Revisionist Movement in Eretz Israel, 1925–35," seminar paper under Dr. A. Cordoba, Tel Aviv University, June 1977; a friendly review in English is Joseph Nedava's, "Who Were the 'Biryoni'," *The Jewish Quarterly Review,* 1972–73, Dropsie University, pp. 317–22. On the Arlazaroff Affair, see, in defense of the Biryonim, Aba Achimeir, *The Trial* (Tel Aviv: Achimeir Friends, 1968), Menachem Begin (in Yiddish), "Dr. Aba Achimeir," *Unserwelt* August 8, 1935, and Letter to Avraham Stavsky, Jabotinsky Institute, Warsaw, 1933. In defense of the left, see the new and controversial book by Shabtai Tevet, *The Assassination of Arlazaroff* (Jerusalem: Schocken, 1982). For a bibliography, see Miriam Getter, *Chaim Arlosoroff: A Political Biography,* (Tel Aviv: Hakibbutz Hameuchad, 1977). On the Hebraist and Canaanists, see the definitive study by Yaacov Shavit, *From Hebrew to Canaanite,* (Jerusalem: Domino Press, 1984), and Yonatan Ratosh, *The First Days* (Hebrew), and *Memoirs and Essays,* (Tel Aviv: Hadar, 1982).

[2] Menachem Begin (in Yiddish), *Betar and the Message: A Letter to Jewish Parents,* (Warsaw: Betar Headquarters, Kauno Press, 1933).

[3] Ibid., pp. 4–5.

[4] *Sepher Betar,* vol. 1, p. 29.

[5] *Revolutionary Zionism,* p. 5.

[6] Ibid.

[7] Letter to Stavsky.

[8] Ibid.
[9] Letter to Aba Achimeir.
[10] Ibid.

Chapter 7 BETAR & THE RISE OF BEGIN

[1] The history of Etzel has been written by David Niv of Etzel: *Battle for Freedom: Irgun Zvai Leumi* (Hebrew) began publication in 1975. There are six volumes in total. The last volume in the series was published in 1980 by the Klausner Institute and Hadar in Tel Aviv. This is Etzel's definitive history; there is no other. *Sepher Betar (The Book of Betar)*, vol 2 , parts 1 and 2 (1973, 1976) is a mine of information and documents. *History of the Haganah* (Hebrew), ed. by Yehuda Slutsky, has several chapters on Etzel. See Vol 3 part 2 chapter 4, pp. 56–67, chapters 25 and 26, pp. 470–519. On Lehi see the private publication *Lohamey Herut Israel* (Hebrew) (Tel Aviv: The Committee for Publication of Lehi, 1954), two volumes. (This is actually the whole collection of Lehi's underground paper *Hehazit* (The Front). See also, Natan Yellin Mor, *The Fighters for Freedom of Israel* (Hebrew) (Jerusalem: Shikmona, 1974). Shlomo Lev-Ami, *By Struggle and By Revolt: Haganah, Etzel, Lehi*, (Tel Aviv: Maarachot, Israel Defense Ministry Press, [no date]); Gabi Eldor, "The Life and Death of Natan Yellin-Mor," *Monitin* (September 1977), pp. 72–80.

The sources here are: letters, documents, and pamphlets dealing with Betar, Jabotinsky, and the rise of Etzel. Our best source is *Sepher Betar* (The Book of Betar), ed. by C. Ben Yerucham, Vol. 2, parts 1 and 2, (Committee on Betar Book, Tel Aviv-Jerusalem 1966 and 1969). Most revealing are the documents and debates over the relationships between Betar-Revisionism and especially Betar-Etzel. A most important document is *A Report: Betar's Third World Conference Warsaw September 11–16, 1938*, published by Betar government in Bucharest, Romania, 1940, where we find the famous Jabotinsky-Begin debate. See also, "Interview with Dr. Shayeb-Eldad," *Monitin*, September 1979, pp. 56–63, 87, 144; unpublished letters between Shimshon Unitchman and Menachem Begin in the Jabotinsky Institute, and some privately owned. Begin-Unitchman letters, written from Vilna and Tel-Aviv, 1940–41. See a few of Begin's articles in Betar papers, *Unser Welt, Die Tat* (in Yiddish) and *Hamedinah, Masuot, Betar* and *Metzuda* (in Hebrew). Most of Begin's writings at the time were in Yiddish, especially, "Unser Matone" (Our gift, i.e. Betar) *Hamedinah*, February 16, 1934, and "A Nayer Transport" (A new transport), *Die Welt*, December 1, 1933. In this period Begin wrote few anti-Socialist, anti-Left articles in Betar papers. Those are the few published pieces by Begin in the 1930s. His speeches were many, of course, but most were not recorded or published. There is an important letter written by Begin to Stavsky (the latter wrote in Russian, the former in Hebrew) to Aba Achimeir on August 14, 1935. See also on The Second Betar Conference in Cracow January 10 to January 16, 1935 in *Sepher Betar* 2, part I, pp. 395–412, where Begin for the first time sits at the Executive Committee table fourth from Jabotinsky. Here Betar proclaimed in detail its historical-nationalist mission for the first time. On Pilsudski, see Joseph Rothshild, *Pilsudski's Coup d'Etat*, (New York: Columbia University Press, 1966). On Etzel and Polish military relations, see Ada Amichal Yevin, *In Purple: The Life of Yair-Avraham Stern* (Tel Aviv: Hadar, 1986). See also Jabotinsky's "Evidence submitted to the *Palestine Royal Commission* and to the House of Lords, February 11, 1937," (London: New Zionist Press, 1937). For remembrance of Jabotinsky at the 1938 Betar Conference, see Dr. Shimshon Unitchman, "Twenty-four Hours with Jabotinsky," *Herut*, (special issue, August

1950), p. 5; in the same issue, Zalman Levenberg, "His Last Wish," pp. 7–9; B. Weinstein, "On Those Meetings," *Hamashkif* (special issue), July 17, 1947, pp. 15, 25; and Yaacov Shavit, "Between Pilsudski and Mickiewicz: Policy and Messianism in Revisionism," *Hazionut,* (Hebrew) (Tel Aviv: Hakiblutz Hameuchad and Tel Aviv University, 1985), pp. 7–31.

[2] Shavit, "Policy and Messianism," p. 7.

[3] Ibid.

[4] *Sepher Betar,* vol. 1, Cracow Conference, pp. 280–85.

[5] Quote from Amos Perlmutter, *The Partitioned State* (New York: Scribner, 1985), p. 69.

[6] Begin, *Der Tat.*

[7] Amical-Yeivin, *In Purple,* pp. 114–21.

[8] Begin, "Unser Matone," p. 3.

[9] Ibid., pp. 122–34.

[10] Amical, op. cit., p. 87.

[11] Report, Betar Third Conference, pp. 7–8.

[12] Ibid., p. 58. Some of the quotes following (see notes 13–24) are free translations, since the language of debate does not lend itself to clarity of prose.

[13] Ibid., p. 60.

[14] Ibid.

[15] Ibid.

[16] Ibid.

[17] Ibid.

[18] Ibid., p. 61.

[19] Ibid.

[20] Ibid.

[21] Ibid.

[22] Ibid., p. 62.

[23] Ibid.

[24] Ibid., pp. 92–93.

[25] Quote in *Sepher Betar.*

[26] Natan Yellin-Mor, *The Fighters for the Freedom of Israel,* (Hebrew) (Jerusalem: Shikmona, 1974), p. 46.

[27] Joseph B. Schechtman, *Fighter and Prophet: The Vladimir Jabotinsky Story* (New York: Thomas Yoseloff, 1961), p. 479.

[28] Yellin-Mor, op. cit., pp. 46–47.

[29] Schechtman, p. 480.

[30] Ibid., p. 481.

[31] Ibid., p. 483.

[32] Quoted in Ben-Yerucham, *Sepher Betar* (Hebrew), vol. 2, part 2 (Jerusalem, 1975), p. 907.

[33] Letter to Dr. Rozov, Ibid.

[34] Natan Yellin-Mor, *The Fighters,* p. 56.

[35] Yellin-Mor to author, summer 1966, Tel Aviv.

Chapter 8 WARSAW-VILNA

[1] Our best single document is indeed Menachem Begin's *White Nights* (in Hebrew, Jerusalem: Karni, 1953; in English, London, 1978, and New York: Harper & Row, 1979). Also *The Revolt* (Jerusalem: Steimatzky, 1953), chapter 1–3, pp. 1–25.

For the description of Begin's abortive efforts to leave for Palestine in August 1939, his life in Warsaw and his flight to Vilna, I used Yaacov Shavit's excellent archive and collection of oral interviews, letters and documents. Natan Yellin-Mor related to me the life of Betarim in Vilna as well as that of Begin and Aliza. Dr. Shayeb also cooperated with me in uncovering the story. See also Begin's dispatch letter to Jabotinsky written on Betar letterhead, Warsaw, March 15, 1939, found in the Jabotinsky Institute. Shavit helped me select the few letters Begin wrote to Jabotinsky, also found in Shavit's private archives: Begin to Jabotinsky, Betar, Kaunus, June 6, 1940, in the Jabotinsky Institute. See also an interesting letter from Jabotinsky to Aaron Propes, Betar's Poland High Commissioner, on his departure, that does not mention the name of his successor, Menachem Begin; likewise, Jabotinsky to Propes, Betar's government, London, April 20, 1939, in the Jabotinsky Institute. The most revealing information on Begin's thoughts during the Holocaust is found in private correspondence between Shimshon Unitchman, a senior Betar commander in Palestine and the exile in Vilna: Begin to Unitchman, Vilna, January 8, 1940; Begin to Unitchman, Kaunas, January 24, 1940; Begin to Unitchman, Vilna, February 4, 1940; also the Shimshon Unitchman speech in *Betar's Third Party Conference*, Warsaw, September 10–16, 1938, Bucharest, 1940, pp. 91–93; Unitchman to Begin, no date, probably January 1940, Jerusalem. See also, David Yotan, "How Did Menachem Find Out That OLA Immigrated to Eretz Israel," *Zot Haaretz*, September 1983. Two of the best books on the Holocaust are David S. Wyman, *The Abandonment of the Jews: America and the Holocaust 1941–45* (New York: Pantheon, 1984), and Walter Laqueur, *The Terrible Secret* (Boston: Little Brown, 1980). On the Warsaw Period, Yaacov Meridor was helpful. See also the superb book by Yisrael Gutman, *The Jews of Warsaw*, (Bloomington, Ind.: Indiana University Press, 1982), especially pp. 3–47. On Vilna see Yehuda Baur, "Rescue Operations in Vilna," *Researches in the Holocaust* (Jerusalem: 1973), pp. 177–83; Meir Dvorjetski, "Vilna Ghetto Diaries," in *Studies on the Holocaust*, ed. by Mordechai Eliav (Tel Aviv: Bar Ilan University, 1979), pp. 79–112; Dina Porat, "Causes and Circumstances for Issuing Soviet Transfer Visas to Polish Jews in Vilna in the Year 1940–41," *Shvut*, (Tel-Aviv: Tel Aviv University Diaspora Center, 1978), no. 6, pp. 55–67; Menachem Begin, "Shimshon the Friend," in A. Remba, ed., *Shimshon Unitchman: A Memorial* (Tel Aviv: Herut's World Executive, 1982), pp. 13–19; Kalman Nusbaum, "Jewish Legion or Make-Believe," *Shvut*, no. 4, 1959, pp. 45–54.

[2] Begin to Unitchman, Vilna, January 8, 1940.

[3] Letter, Unitchman to Begin, no date, probably January 1940, Jerusalem.

[4] Letter to Jabotinsky, Kaunas, June 6, 1940.

[5] Ibid.

[6] Letter, Begin to Unitchman, Vilna, January 8, 1940.

[7] Ibid.

[8] Ibid.

[9] Interview with Dr. Shayeb, Jerusalem, summer 1966.

[10] Ibid.

[11] Begin to Unitchman, Kaunas, January 24, 1940.

[12] Unitchman to Begin, probably January 1940, Jerusalem.

[13] Unitchman, in *Third Party Conference*, Warsaw, 1938, pp. 92–93.

[14] Begin to Shalom Rosenfeld, November 1939.

[15] *White Nights*, p. 7.

[16] Ibid.

[17] Ibid.

[18] Ibid.

[19] Ibid.

Chapter 9   THE POLISH ARMY

[1] For background and story of the Anders Army see Wladyslaw Anders, *An Army in Exile* (London: 1949); Stanislaw Mikolajczyk, *The Rape of Poland* (New York: McGraw-Hill, 1948); Stanislaw Kot, *Conversation with the Kremlin* (New York: Oxford University Press, 1963); Norman Davies, *God's Playground*, vol. 2, pp. 435–91. On Jews in the Anders Army, see Yisrael Guttman, "Jews in the Anders Army in the USSR," *Yad Vashem*, vol. 12, Jerusalem, 1977, pp. 171–214; Kalman Nussbaum, "Jewish Legion or Make-Believe," *Shvut*, no. 4. (1959), pp. 47–54; Klemens Nussbaum, *A Story of an Illusion: The Jews in the Polish Peoples Army in the USSR*, (Tel Aviv: Tel Aviv University Diaspora Institute, 1984); "Antisemitism in the Polish Army," in Waclaw Jedrzejewicz, ed., *Poland in the British Parliament: 1939–1945*, Józef Pilsudski Institute of America, (New York, 1959), pp. 422–94.

[2] Kot, p. 101.

[3] Guttman, p. 178.

[4] Kot, p. 153.

[5] Guttman, op. cit., p. 49.

[6] Kot, p. 62. Kot quotes Anders on Jews. In fact, it was Sikorski. Kot "improved" the document to protect the name of Sikorski, whom he admired.

[7] Nussbaum, p. 178.

[8] Ibid., p. 182.

[9] Kot, p. 182.

[10] Ibid., p. 185.

[11] Guttman, p. 229.

[12] Ibid., p. 212.

[13] Quoted, ibid., p. 189

[14] Ibid., p. 229.

[15] Kot, pp. 246–47.

Chapter 10   COMMANDER IN CHIEF

[1] On Begin's appointment as Commander of Etzel, with an emphasis on different views of the appointment, see Begin's letter to Arie Altman, August 19, 1942, on the Betar letterhead in the Jabotinsky Institute. Defending the appointment are Arieh Ben Eliezer, "Twenty Years Ago," *Herut*, August 12, 1963. Challenging the Begin loyalists' theses is former Etzel Acting Chief of Staff Shlomo Lev-Ami, in an interview with Dan Margalit: "The Complete Truth Has Not Yet Been Told," *Haaretz*, November 6, 1981, pp. 5–7. An Interview with Mrs. Ben Eliezer, summer 1983, Ramat Gan, and conversations with Yaacov Meridor, 1982, 1983 and 1984, Tel Aviv and Jerusalem. See Dr. Mark (Meir) Kahan, "It Was in the Month of February 1944," *Herut*, December 1983, p. 22.

[2] Ben Eliezer, "Twenty," p. 5.

[3] Ibid.

[4] Ibid.

[5] Ibid.

[6] Ibid.

[7] Ibid.

[8] Ibid., p. 9.

9 Information from Dr. Leopold Labedz (London, summer 1984).

10 David A. Engel "The Failed Alliance: The Revisionist Movement and the Polish Government in Exile, 1939–1945" in *Hazionout,* Vol. 11, 1980, University of Tel Aviv, Tel Aviv, pp. 333–360.

11 Ibid., pp. 350–51.

12 Ibid., pp. 346–49.

13 Ibid., pp. 352–55.

14 Ibid., p. 334.

15 Ibid., p. 333.

16 See Stefan Korbonski, "Unknown Chapter in the Life of Menachem Begin and Irgun Tsvai Leumi," *East European Quarterly,* vol. 12, pp. 373–77.

17 Shlomo Lev-Ami interview with Dan Margalit, "The Truth," p. 6.

18 Ibid.

19 Ibid.

20 Conversation with Yaacov Meridor in Knesset, Jerusalem, summer 1983.

21 Related by Dr. Yohanan Bader, Ramat Gan, summer 1983.

22 Interview with Mrs. Ben Eliezer, summer 1983.

23 Ibid.

24 Y. Shavit archives and notes.

25 Menachem Begin, *In the Underground: Writing and Documents,* (Hebrew) (Tel Aviv: Hadar, 1978) vol. 1, p. 38.

26 Ibid., p. 41.

27 Ibid., p. 42.

28 Ibid., pp. 46–47.

29 Ibid., p. 54.

30 Meeting with Yaacov Amrami, former head of Etzel Operations, March 1986, Tel Aviv.

Chapter 11 THE LOGIC OF THE REVOLT

1 On the British policy in Palestine during the critical years of 1944–48, see Amos Perlmutter, *Israel: The Partitioned State* (New York: Scribner, 1985), chapter 4, pp. 107–20 and especially footnotes to chapter 4, pp. 357–60 for a comprehensive and annotated bibliography.

2 The most authentic study, which hides as much as it reveals, is Begin's classic *Hamered* (The Revolt), Hebrew and English versions (Tel Aviv: Steimatzky, 1951), also translated into German, Arabic, and French. Next are his collected writings on the underground, *Bamachteret* (In the Underground), four volumes in two (Tel Aviv: Hadar, 1978), which contain some of the best documents on the Revolt, published as leaflets and mimeograph flyers distributed by Etzel men in the streets of Israeli cities and villages. See also David Niv, *The Battle for Freedom, 1944–46* (Tel Aviv: 1973), *The Revolt,* vol 6; Yehuda Slutsky, *History of Haganah,* (Tel Aviv), vol. 3, part I, chapters 25, 26, 27, pp. 470–546.

3 Text of the Declaration of the Revolt, in Begin, *Underground,* vol. 1, pp. 21–24.

Chapter 12 POLITICS OF THE REVOLT

1 Once again, see Menachem Begin's *The Revolt* and *In the Underground,* plus two other volumes—David Niv, *Battle for Freedom,* vols. 4 and 5; and Yehuda Slutsky,

Haganah, vol. 3, part I. A most significant document is Etzel's *Protocols,* the secret underground meetings of July–November 1944 edited and published by its former acting chief of staff Shlomo Lev-Ami: "The Protocols of Etzel's High Command: July–November 1944" in *Hazionut* (Zionism) (in Hebrew), (Tel Aviv: Tel Aviv University, 1955), vol. 4, pp. 391–452. On Lehi-Etzel controversies, see *Haganah* 3, part I, pp. 494–519, and a letter Begin wrote to Friedman-Yellin on September 3, 1944, in the *Protocols.* Two important documents are in a report by Dr. Moshe Sneh to the Haganah command on his conversation with Menachem Begin on October 9, 1944, in Yaacov Shavit: *Sezon* (Open Season) Hebrew (Tel Aviv: Hadar, 1946), pp. 150–60. Compare with Begin's report on his conversation with Sneh, in *The Revolt,* pp. 192–97.

2 *Protocols* (minutes) pp. 394–95.
3 Ibid.
4 Begin, Sneh, Golomb meeting on October 31, 1944, in Lev-Ami, *Protocols,* p. 432.
5 Ibid., p. 434.
6 Sneh, report to Haganah on Begin in Shavit *Season,* p. 150.
7 October 31, 1944, meeting in Lev-Ami, p. 432.
8 Ibid., p. 433.
9 Ibid., p. 435.
10 Sneh, report to Haganah on Begin in Shavit, p. 152.
11 Ibid., p. 153.
12 Ibid.
13 Ibid.
14 Ibid., p. 154.
15 Ibid.
16 Ibid.; see also Begin in Lev-Ami, p. 438.
17 Sneh in Shavit, p. 158.
18 Ibid.
19 Ibid., p. 159.
20 Ibid.
21 Begin, *The Revolt,* p. 194.
22 Ben Ami, *Protocols,* p. 408.
23 Ibid., p. 409.
24 Ibid., p. 415.
25 Ibid., p. 416.

Chapter 13 THE SEZON

1 The outstanding book on the Sezon is Yaacov Shavit's *Open Season* (Hebrew), (Tel Aviv: Hadar, 1957). See also Begin's *The Revolt,* chapter 9, pp. 133–43, Begin, "There Will Be No Civil War," *In the Underground,* vol. 1., December 3, 1944, pp. 169–77; *Sepher Haganah,* 3, part 1, pp. 535–43; David Niv, *In the Battle,* vol. 4, pp. 96–113. Sneh's "Report," in Shavit, *Season,* pp. 192–97 and the Sneh-Golomb-Begin meeting in Lev-Ami, *Protocols,* pp. 432–40. The best bibliographical guide to Etzel and Lehi is Yaacov Amrami (Yoel) *Practical Bibliography* (Tel Aviv: Hadar and National Institute, 1954). This is a thorough and outstanding annotated bibliography on the undergrounds. It includes a considerable bibliography in English. The debate over the Sezon flared again in Israel in the 1960s and 1970s. See Menachem Begin, "Questions by Somebody Who Is Not So Innocent" (reply to Yigal Allon), *Herut,* September 11, 1955; "A 'Glorious' Chapter in the Palmach Actions," *Herut,*

November 9, 1949; Yaacov Goren, "A Plausible Description and a Flawed Analysis," review in Likud's paper *Etgar* (September 1976); Interview with Teddy Kollek, "Why the Sezon Was Necessary," *Maariv,* June 19, 1983. See also Begin, "Prisha, Sezon, *Altalena,*" *Maariv,* August 6, 1971, pp. 13–22.

2 Shavit, *Season,* p. 88.

3 *Haganah,* p. 541.

4 Begin, "There Will Be," pp. 170–71.

5 Interview with David Ben Gurion, summer 1971, Tel Aviv and Sdeh Boker.

6 Talks with Shmuel Katz, summer 1983 in Tel Aviv.

7 Amikam Nachmani, "General at Bay in Postwar Palestine," *The Journal of Strategic Studies,* vol. 4, no. 4, December 1983, pp. 66–78.

Chapter 14   HRM

1 Once again we find two different versions for the HRM. The Haganah's position is found in Y. Slutsky, *Sepher Haganah,* vol. 3, part 2, pp. 854–88. Etzel's view is found in D. Niv, *In the Battle,* vol. 4, pp. 179–92 and in M. Begin, *The Revolt,* chapter 10, pp. 144–53. Twenty years later Begin, Sneh and others met in a *Maariv* symposium on the HRM which ran on April 4, 10, 16, 24 and 29, 1966, and was published in *Maariv.* See also Shavit, *Sezon,* Three appendices, pp. 156–74 and Moshe Sneh, "Testimony," *The End as a Start* (Tel Aviv: 1965). See also Yigal Elam, *Haganah: The Zionist Way to Power* (Tel Aviv: Zmora, 1979) especially appendix, "Who gave the order," which analyzes Ben Gurion-Sneh correspondence on the HRM, pp. 331–49 and chapter 14, pp. 195–225.

2 Yoseph Gorni, *The British Labour Movement and Zionism: 1917–48,* (London: Frank Cass, 1983), p. xiii.

3 Zvi Ganin, *Truman, American Jewry and Israel* (New York: Holmes and Meier, 1979), p. 97.

4 Sneh, in Lev-Ami, *Protocols,* pp. 438–39. See also Sneh, "Testimony," pp. 92–93. Quoted in Elam, *Haganah,* pp. 348–49.

5 Begin, *Maariv Symposium,* April 4, 1966, p. 12.

6 Ibid.

7 Ibid.

8 Ibid., p. 13.

9 Ibid., April 4, 1966, p. 19.

10 Ibid., April 10, 1966, p. 7.

11 Ibid.

12 *Maariv,* op. cit., April 29, 1966, p. 13.

13 Gavriel Cohen, "British Policy on the Eve of the War of Independence," in Y. Wallach, ed., *We Were Dreamers* (Tel Aviv: Masada, 1985), pp. 79–80.

Chapter 15   BLACK SABBATH

1 Y. Slutsky, ed., *Sepher Haganah,* vol. 3, part 2, chapter 43, pp. 889–906; for the Haganah's view of the King David Hotel bombing see pp. 898–903; for Etzel's view see D. Niv, *In the Battle,* vol. 4, pp. 273–88; For the United Kibbutz Movement view see, Menachem Naor, *Black Sabbath* (Hebrew), (Tel Aviv: Hakibbutz Hameuchad, 1981). See also *Maariv Symposium* on the Hebrew Resistance Movement. For Begin's version, see *The Revolt,* chapter 15, pp. 212–30. For a full recent

account of the attack on King David Hotel, but weak on Haganah's side, see Thurston Clarke, *By Blood and Fire,* (New York: G. P. Putnam, 1981), see also Lehi's interpretation of Lord Moyne's assassination, *The Assassination of Lord Moyne* (Lehi Publication, 1953).

2 Gavriel Cohen, "British Policy," op. cit., pp. 97–99.

3 Sneh, "Testimony," p. 95.

4 Ibid.

5 Clarke, p. 85.

6 Ibid., p. 124.

7 Ibid., p. 200.

8 Ibid., p. 100.

9 Ibid., p. 98.

10 Ibid., p. 101.

11 Ibid., p. 240.

Chapter 16   ETZEL IN GOOD AND BAD TIMES

1 On Etzel's operations 1946–48, see D. Niv, *In the Battle,* vols. 4–6. Etzel's paper and proclamations published in *Herut* are collected in Y. Amrami, ed., *Herut* (Tel Aviv: Hadar-Jabotinsky Institute, 1978). See also Amrami, *Bibliography* (Etzel-Lehi) and *Lehi,* two volumes; Jan Gitlin and Dov Cohen, *The Conquest of Acre Fortress* (Tel Aviv: Hadar, 1982); Yaacov Meridor, *Long Is the Road to Freedom* (Tujunga, Calif.: Barak Publications, 1961). On the Lehi chief of operations, see Yaacov Banai, *Unknown Soldiers* (Hebrew) (Hadar, Tel-Aviv, 1968) and Yaacov (Yashka) Eliav, *Wanted,* (Jerusalem, Maariv, 1983). The most notorious British and anti-Etzel viewpoint is John Marlow, *Rebellion in Palestine,* (London: Cresset Press, 1946) and Roy Farran, *Winged Dagger: Adventures of Special Service,* (London: Collins, 1948), describing anti-Etzel activities in which he was involved with the British Police in Palestine. Also see Edward Horne, *A Job Well Done (A History of the Palestine Police Force 1920–48)* (Palestine Police Old Commander: Anchor Press, 1982), pp. 267–314; Israel Shayeb-Eldad, *First Tithe* (Hebrew), (Tel Aviv: Hadar, 1950). On Ben Gurion's readying of the Haganah to fight the Arabs, see the most informative and excellent study by Yoav Gelber, *The Emergence of a Jewish Army* (Hebrew), (Jerusalem: Ben-Zvi Institute, 1986).

2 Amrami to author, March 1986.

3 Gelbar, pp. 1–73.

4 Begin, *In the Underground,* vol. 2, book 3, pp. 228–29.

5 *Haganah,* Vol 4, p. 927.

6 Ibid., p. 928.

Chapter 17   ASSESSMENT

1 Talk with Begin, November 1973.

2 Livneh-Begin exchange, "Symposium on HRM," *Maariv,* April 10, 1966, pp. 19–20.

3 Ibid., p. 20.

Chapter 18 END OF THE MANDATE

[1] Once again I refer the reader to consult my book, *Israel: The Partitioned State* (New York: Scribner, 1985), chapter 4, pp. 107–20 and pp. 357–60. I single out of the above bibliography two useful books: one, which is extremely unfair to the Zionists, is William Roger Louis, *The British Empire and the Middle East: 1945–51* (Oxford: The Clarendon Press, 1984); the other is Allan Bullock, *Ernest Bevin: Foreign Secretary 1945–51*, (London: Heinemann, 1984). The outstanding work on Bevin's policy in Palestine, thoroughly researched, carefully analyzed and measured in judgment, is Gavriel Cohen, "British Policy on the Eve of the War of Liberation," in Y. Wallach, ed., *We Were as Dreamers* (Hebrew) (Tel Aviv: Masada), pp. 13–179. Also, Menachem Begin's *In the Underground* vol. 2, pp. 90–332; Shlomo Nakdimon, *Altalena*, (Jerusalem: Edanim, 1978), p. 54. On the Anglo-American Committee, see Arikam Nachmani, *Great Power Discord in Palestine* (London: Frank Cass, 1986).

[2] Begin in Nakdimon, p. 54.

[3] Louis, p. 3.

[4] Gavriel Cohen, "British Policy," pp. 13–16, pp. 21–24, pp. 79–81.

[5] The latter is the favorite thesis of various American writers whose leader is former State Department head of the NEA, Evan Wilson; see *Decision on Palestine* (Stanford: Hoover Institute, 1979).

[6] Cohen, p. 90.

[7] Nakdimon, op. cit., p. 55.

[8] Ibid.

Chapter 19 ETZEL IN ISRAEL AND JERUSALEM

[1] David Dayan, "The Young Fighters of Jerusalem," and Yoseph Kister, "The Etzel-Lehi Operations in Jerusalem" in *Kathedra* 10 (1982), pp. 116–32. See the Begin-Ben Gurion debate in Menachem Begin, "Prisha, Sezon, Altalena," *Maariv*, August 6, 1971, pp. 13, 22; August 13, 1971, pp. 13, 22; August 20, 1971, pp. 14 and 17; Ben Gurion's reply, "The State and Etzel," *Maariv*, August 27, 1971, pp. 21 and 23; Menachem Begin's "Reply to Mr. Ben Gurion and Minister Galilee," *Maariv*, October 1, 1971, p. 16; Menachem Begin, "Forgotten Chapter in a Book of Memories," *Maariv*, September 20, 1975; "The Publisher of a Book of History of the Haganah," *Maariv*, September 8, 1972; Yisrael Segal, "File Dir Yassin," *Koteret Rashit*, January 19, 1983; Dubi Bergman, *Herut from Underground to Party* (M.A. Thesis, Tel Aviv University, 1978); Nathan Yellin-Mor, *The Fighters for the Freedom of Israel* (Jerusalem Shikmona, 1974), pp. 469–73; Uri Milstein, "Etzel Against Begin," *Haaretz, Magazine*, September 29, 1978, pp. 16–18.

[2] Nakdimon, *Altalena*, p. 55.

[3] Bergman, p. 12.

[4] "Letter to Fighters," Menachem Begin to Azriel Gershuni and Aaron Rousseau, February 17, 1947, quoted in Uri Milstein, pp. 16–18.

[5] Ibid., p. 16.

[6] Ibid., p. 17.

[7] FRUS, *The Near East (Israel)*, Part 3 (Washington, D.C.: U.S. Printing Office, 1976), p. 1141.

Chapter 20   DIR YASSIN

[1] Quote of Jabotinsky in Y. Shavit, "The Attitude of Zionist Revisionism Toward the Arabs" in *Zionism and the Arab Question,* ed. by S. Ettinger (Tel Aviv: Shazar Center, 1979), p. 74.

[2] Quoted in Yoseph Heller, "Between Messianism and Realpolitik—The Stern Gang and the Arab Question" in Israel Gutman, ed., *Yahadut Zémanenu* (Contemporary Jewry), A Research Annual, vol 1, 1983, p. 225.

[3] David Ben Gurion, *War Diary,* ed. E. Orren and G. Rivlin, (Tel Aviv: Defense Ministry, 1982), vol 1, p. 148.

[4] *Haganah,* vol. 3, part 2, pp. 1546–47.

[5] *The Revolt,* p. 164.

[6] Chaim Landau in Israel Segal, "File," p. 8.

[7] Ibid., p. 7.

[8] Ibid.

[9] Ibid.

[10] N. Yellin-Mor, p. 472.

Chapter 21   THE ALTALENA

[1] The most informative (pro-Etzel but well-documented) story of the *Altalena* is Shlomo Nakdimon, *Altalena* (Jerusalem: Edanim Publishers, 1978); see also Begin, *The Revolt,* chapter 11, pp. 154–65; Begin reopened the *Altalena* controversy in 1971; see his "Prisha, Sezon, *Altalena,*" *Maariv,* August 6, 1971, pp. 13 and 22; August 13, 1971, pp. 13 and 22; August 20, 1971, pp. 14 and 17; Shmuel Katz, *Days of Fire* (Hebrew), (Tel Aviv: Karni, 1966), pp. 372–447; Eliahu Lankin, *The Story of Altalena* (Tel Aviv: Hadar, 1974). For the Haganah position, see Uri Brenner, *Altalena,* (Tel Aviv: Hakibbutz Hameuchad, 1978); for Etzel-Haganah documentation on the agreement for Etzel's dissolution, see *Sepher Haganah* 3, pp. 1554–58 and Brenner, pp. 24–31, 44–60; Ely J. Tavin, *The Second Front: The Irgun Zvai Leumi in Europe 1946–48,* (Tel Aviv: Ron Publishers, 1973).

For a complete analysis of the Vaad, see Jonathan Kaplan, "The Activities of Etzel's Mission in the U.S. During the Holocaust," *Yalkut Moreshet,* vol. 30, November 1980, pp. 115–38 and vol. 31, April 1981, pp. 75–96. Next see Ben Hecht, *A Child of a Century* (New York: 1954); Peter Bergson (Hillel Kook), "You Need Only a Will," *Hahevra* 59, Tel Aviv (1945), pp. 790–811; Ely J. Tavin, *The Second Front: The Irgun Zvai Leumi in Europe 1946–48* (Tel Aviv: Ron Publishers, 1973); Yitzhak Ben Ami, *Years of Wrath, Days of Glory* (New York: Robert Speller and Sons, 1982).

[2] Tavin, p. 78.

[3] Ibid., pp. 116–17.

[4] Ibid., p. 118.

[5] Ibid., p. 119.

[6] Ibid.

[7] Ibid.

[8] Ibid., p. 125.

[9] Ibid., p. 205.

[10] Quote in Tavin of letter sent by Begin on December 27, 1947, to headquarters in Europe, p. 193.

[11] Ibid.

[12] Brenner, p. 32.

[13] Ben Gurion, *Diary,* June 11, 1948, vol. 2, p. 592.

[14] Ibid., p. 604.

[15] *Haganah* 3, p. 1557.

[16] Conversation with author, summer 1979, Jerusalem.

[17] Nakdimon, p. 180.

[18] Ben Gurion, *Diary,* June 11, 1948, vol 2, p. 488.

[19] Nakdimon, p. 278.

[20] Conversation with Yellin-Mor, summer 1966.

Chapter 22 FROM UNDERGROUND

[1] Menachem Begin, "From Underground to Party," Lecture Institute of Zionist Research, Tel Aviv University, from tapes published by Record Company, Tel Aviv, November 28, 1974, once again Begin's incomplete version of the early history of Herut. For more accurate research, see Duby Bergman, "Herut Movement: From Underground to a Political Party," (M.A. Thesis Tel Aviv University, August 1978); Yochanan Bader, *The Knesset and I* (Hebrew) (Jerusalem: Edanim, 1979); *Herut Movement: Its Foundations and Principles* (mimeographed in "In Liberated Zion," June 1948); Menachem Begin, *World View and National Orientation,* Betar High Commission in Eretz Israel (Tel Aviv, 1952), a pamphlet. On the Zohar-Herut controversy see Eliahu Galezer and Yitzhak Yellin, "A Forced Debate" (Zohar Headquarters, Tel Aviv, September 1948), a call for Herut not to split Zohar; Bnai Zeev, "A Call to Sons of Betar, Zohar and Sons of Zeev Jabotinsky, Wherever They Are," (mimeographed by Zohar Headquarters, July 1948); "Decision of Zohar 11th National Convention," September 5–7, 1948, mimeographed; Begin letter to Dr. Altman, August 20, 1948, imploring Zohar to end the fight with Herut; Shmuel Katz letter to the leadership of Zohar (Unitchman, Abrasha and Yaacov Weinshal), September 9, 1948; "Leichud," Herut's movement platform to the 11th Zohar Conference, August 1948; Meir Grosmann, "The Future of Zohar," *Hamashkif,* February 25, 1949; David Ben Gurion, *War Diary,* ed. by G. Rivlin and E. Orren (Tel Aviv: Ministry of Defense, 1982), vol 2, pp. 602–18; Kalman Katznelson, "The Legacy of Jabotinsky," *Herut,* February 13, 1949; Meir Grosmann, *Unity Versus Fragmentation* (Tel Aviv: Am Vemedinah, 1949).

[2] Bader, p. 19.

[3] Shalom Rosenfeld, summer 1984.

[4] Tavin, p. 235 (also Begin's reply).

[5] Ibid., p. 240.

[6] Begin's "Herut," p. 3.

[7] Tavin, p. 242.

[8] Quote in Ibid., p. 248.

[9] Bnai Zeev, "Call," p. 1.

[10] Ibid., p. 3.

[11] Quoted in Bergman, p. 58.

[12] Eri Jabotinsky to Menachem Begin, April 28, 1950, in Jabotinsky Institute, Tel Aviv.

[13] Ibid.

Chapter 23 BEGIN—THE PARLIAMENTARIAN

[1] On the politics of the Yishuv see: Dan Horowitz and Moshe Lissak, *Origins of the Israeli Polity: Palestine Under the Mandate* (in Hebrew, 1977; English version, Chicago: University of Chicago Press, 1978); Amos Perlmutter, *Israel: The Partitioned State,* (New York: Scribner, 1985), chapter 3, pp. 75–106; Yochanan Bader, *The Knesset and I* (Jerusalem: Edanim, 1979).

[2] Bader, p. 20.

Chapter 24 THE IDEOLOGY OF BEGIN

[1] Begin is not an intellectual-philosophical writer. His *Weltanschauung* is found in *Worldview and National View* (in Hebrew, Tel Aviv: Basaar, Betar High Commission, 1952); for the best and most concise of his ideological works see M. Begin, *In the Underground* (Tel Aviv: Hadar Publishers); also Begin's 1951–55 Knesset speeches.

[2] Begin, "Worldview," p. 4.

[3] Begin, *"Begin, Nationalism, Nationhood* (Tel-Aviv, Herut, 1965), p. 5.

[4] Begin, *Worldview,* p. 28.

Chapter 25 HOLY CANON: BEGIN VERSUS BEN GURION

[1] On Ben Gurion see Michael Bar Zohar, *Ben Gurion: A Political Biography,* vol. 3 (Tel Aviv: Am Oved); *Divrey Haknesset,* Fifth Assembly; D. Ben Gurion, *War Diary,* ed. by G. Rivlin and E. Orren, (Tel Aviv: Ministry of Defense, 1982), vol. 2.

[2] *Divrey Haknesset,* Fifth Knesset, 1955.

[3] Ben Gurion, *War Diary,* vol. 2, p. 644.

[4] Bader, p. 53.

[5] Ibid.

Chapter 26 THE UNDERGROUND AGAINST HERUT

[1] For Dr. Israel Shayeb-Eldad's "philosophy," see *Maaser Rishon* (First thite); most important is Eldad's quarterly *Sulam* (Ladder), devoted to "The Philosophy of a Jewish Kingdom," published between 1949 and 1959, especially *Sulam,* pp. 97–108, 1957–58, privately published by Dr. Israel Eldad; Shmuel Tamir, "The Minister of Treachery," *Herut,* January 7, 1952; "Warning," *Hador* (Mapai Paper); "Instigating to Murder," *Hador* (anti-Shilansky editorial) October 7, 1952; "Shilansky," *Yediot Aharonot* (editorial), October 7, 1952; "Terror Again," *Haaretz* (editorial), October 7, 1952; Dr. Yochanan Bader, "Provocation—Shame of the Court," *Herut,* October 9, 1952; Shmuel Tamir quoted in *Maariv,* December 7, 1952; Uri Avnery, "Neo-Fascism in Israel: The Undergrounds of the Past," *Haolam Hazeh,* August 23, 1953; "One Man Against the Regime," *Haolam Hazeh,* September 14, 1955. See also Iser Arel, *The Truth About the Kastner Murder* (Hebrew) (Tel Aviv: Idanim, 1985).

[2] Arel, *The Truth,* p. 47.

[3] See also Yoseph Heller, "Between Messianism and Realpolitik: The Stern Group

and the Arab Question, 1947–48," in *Yahadut Zemanenu* (Contemporary Judaism), Jerusalem: The Magness Press, vol. 2, 1984, pp. 350–56.

[4] 39. Heruti, *Sulam*, 1955, p. 3.

[5] M. Begin, "Vindicea Contra Tyrannos," *Herut*, July 12, 1952.

[6] Ibid.

[7] Tamir quoted in *Haolam Hazeh*, September 14, 1955, p. 6.

[8] Ibid.

[9] Conversation with Minister Dov Shilansky, Jerusalem, August 13, 1983.

[10] Bader, *Herut*, October 9, 1952, p. 2.

[11] Editorial, *Haaretz*, October 7, 1952, p. 2.

[12] Herzl Rosenblum (Editor of *Yediot Aharonot* and a loyal Revisionist), editorial.

[13] Ibid.

[14] Arel, *The Truth*, pp. 47–48.

[15] A series of articles on Tamir's checkered political career, even if unfavorable, are among the best investigative reporting of the weekly, *Haolam Hazeh*, Tel Aviv, September 1, 1966, September 7, 1966, August 8, 1973; "The Begin—Tamir Struggle in Herut Conference (1966)," *Haaretz*, July 3, 1966, p. 8.

Chapter 27 1955–66: TIME OF ROUTINE, TIME OF CRISIS

[1] On the Herut party conference, see *Minutes of Herut Eighth Party Conference* (Hakfar Hayarok, Herut Headquarters, Tel-Aviv, 1967); no author given, "The Last Days of Herut," *Haolam Hazeh*, January 24, 1966; "The Long Way Toward Power," *Haolam Hazeh*, June 29, 1966; "The Mysteries of the Forged Letter," *Haolam Hazeh*, September 7, 1966; Amos Elon, "First Time Since Arlazaroff's Assassination," *Haaretz*, June 28, 1966, p. 2; "Body Change in the Bodypolitik," *Haaretz*, June 29, 1966, p. 2; "Twilight of the Gods," *Haaretz*, July 3, 1966, p. 2; "To Resign or to Conquer the Mountain," *Haaretz*, June 30, 1966, p. 2.; *Haaretz* reporter, "Herut Conference Ended in a Bitter Confrontation between Begin and Tamir," *Haaretz*, July 3, 1966, p. 8.; Moshe Yizraeli, "Herut Without Revisionist Fundamentals," *Haaretz*, March 24, 1967, p. 2. On the formation of Gahal, see Arie Avnery, *The Liberal Connection*, (Hebrew) (Tel Aviv: Zmora, 1984). On the Workers National Union see: Yeshayahu Offir, *The Book of the National Worker* (Tel Aviv: National Union Workers Publication, 1983), vol 2.

[2] Conversation with Begin, October 1983.

[3] Ehud Olmert quote in Elon, "Body Changes."

[4] Elon, "The Twilight."

[5] Ibid.

[6] Quoted in Ibid.

[7] Ibid.

Chapter 28 NO INCH OF TERRITORY

[1] For a background on the decision-making process for the 1967 war, see Shlomo Nakdimon, *Zero Hour* (Tel Aviv: Ramdor Publishing Co., 1968); Amos Perlmutter, *The Politics and Military in Israel 1967–77* (London: Frank Cass, 1978); Michael Brecher, *Decisions in Crisis: Israel, 1967 and 1973* (Berkeley, Calif.: University of California, 1980).

[2] See Amos Perlmutter, *Israel: The Partitioned State* (New York: Scribner, 1985), pp. 163–87.
[3] Nakdimon, pp. 47–48.
[4] Ibid., pp. 61–62.
[5] Ibid., p. 64.
[6] Ibid., p. 69.
[7] Ibid., p. 112.
[8] Ibid., p. 174.
[9] Ibid., pp. 222–23.
[10] Ibid., p. 232.
[11] Ibid., p. 242.
[12] Ibid., p. 243.
[13] Ibid., p. 245.
[14] Ibid., p. 247.
[15] Ibid., p. 248.
[16] Ibid., p. 251.
[17] Ibid., p. 264.
[18] Begin, *Divrey Haknesset,* 101 Session, vols. 35 and 36, August 12, 1970, pp. 2862–63.
[19] Ibid., p. 2862.
[20] Ibid., p. 2863.
[21] Ibid., p. 2865.
[22] Ibid., p. 2866.
[23] *Maariv,* August 28, 1969.
[24] *Divrey Haknesset,* 104th session, vol. 36, August 25, 1970, p. 3019.
[25] *Maariv,* November 27, 1970.
[26] *Divrey Haknesset,* 167th session, March 15, 1971, vol. 20, p. 1853.
[27] Ibid., 191st session, June 9, 1971, vol 29, p. 2675.
[28] Ibid., p. 2677
[29] Ibid., 110th session, November 16, 1970, vol 3, p. 182.
[30] *Manifesto of the Land of Israel Movement, August 1967,* appended to Rael Jean Isaac, *Israel Divided,* (Baltimore: The Johns Hopkins University Press, 1977), p. 165.
[31] Perlmutter, *Israel,* pp. 197–201.

Chapter 29   THE RISE OF LIKUD

[1] Amos Perlmutter, *Israel: The Partitioned State* (New York: Scribner, 1985), chapter 7, pp. 197–221; Rael Jean Isaac, *Israel Divided,* (Baltimore: Johns Hopkins University Press, 1977); Shlomo Nakdimon, "How Likud was Forged," *Yediot Aharonot,* August 31, 1973; "Interview with Tamir and Sharon," *Maariv,* June 21, 1974; Menachem Begin, "Lets Debate on the Issues," *Maariv,* December 1, 1972; "Is Likud the Beginning of my Political End?" *Maariv,* September 20, 1973; "Birth Pains of Likud," *Maariv,* August 31, 1973; editor, "The Unfinished Symphony of Shmuel Tamir," *Haolam Hazeh,* August 3, 1973, pp. 14–17; editor, "The Blowup," *Haolam Hazeh,* September 5, 1973, pp. 13–15; Yitzhak Rabin, *Pinkas Sherut* (Memoirs) (Tel Aviv: Maariv Publishing, 1979) two volumes; Shlomo Nakdimon, "How Likud Was Organized," *Yediot Aharonot,* August 3, 1973; and Amos Perlmutter archives that include interviews, clippings, campaign literature, Knesset speeches, and memos between Sharon and Herut-Liberal leaders. See also Arie Avnery, *The Liberal Connection* (Tel Aviv: Zmora, 1984).

2 "Let Us Debate," *Maariv,* December 1, 1972, p. 9.
3 Ibid.
4 Nakdimon, "How Likud," *Yediot Abaronot,* August 3, 1973, p. 5.
5 Quoted in Avnery, *The Liberal,* pp. 130–31.
6 Ibid.
7 Quoted in Avnery, *The Liberal,* p. 132.
8 Begin, "Birth Pains," *Maariv,* September 20, 1973, p. 8.
9 Ibid.
10 Interviews with Sharon and Tamir, *Maariv,* June 21, 1974, p. 8.
11 Rabin, *Pinkas,* vol. 2, p. 490.
12 Ibid.

Chapter 30 THE 1977 ELECTIONS

1 Amos Perlmutter, *Israel: The Partitioned State,* (New York: Scribner, 1985), pp. 257–83; Howard Penniman, ed., *Israel After the Polls: The Knesset Election of 1977* (Washington, D.C.: American Enterprise Institute, 1979); Menachem Begin, "Arab Nazism and the Jewish Boy," *Maariv,* May 24, 1974; "A Massive Popular Movement," October 18, 1974. The above two articles are the most conspicuous out of some 20 articles that Begin wrote in *Maariv* in the years 1975–77.
2 Begin, "Arab Nazism," *Maariv,* May 24, 1974, p. 6.

Chapter 31 THE FORMATION OF THE LIKUD GOVERNMENT

1 Shlomo Nakdimon, "How Likud Was Organized," *Yediot Abaronot,* August 3, 1973; Menachem Begin, "Eretz Israel and Clarification with Mr. Dayan," *Maariv,* April 22, 1977; Ezer Weizman, *On Eagle Wings* (Hebrew) (Tel Aviv: Edanim, 1976); Moshe Dayan, *Breakthrough: A Personal Account of the Egypt-Israel Peace Negotiations* (New York: Knopf, 1981); Yoel Marcus, *Camp David: The Door to Peace* (Hebrew), (Tel Aviv: Schocken, 1979).
2 Begin, "Eretz Israel," *Maariv,* April 22, 1977, p. 14.
3 Yoel Marcus, *Camp David,* p. 28.
4 Ibid.
5 Ibid., p. 30.
6 Ibid., p. 25.
7 Ibid., p. 26.
8 Dayan, *Breakthrough,* p. 1.
9 Ibid., p. 10.
10 Ibid.
11 Ibid., p. 11.

Chapter 32 TOWARD ACCOMMODATION

1 See footnotes 1 for chapters 33 and 34, and Amos Perlmutter, "The Begin Strategy and the Dayan Tactics: The Conduct of Israeli Foreign Policy," *Foreign Affairs,* January 1978, pp. 357–72.

Chapter 33 SADAT IN JERUSALEM

1 I was present through 1977 and 1978 during the pre–Camp David negotiations in Jerusalem, Cairo, Washington, Leeds, and Salzburg, and as an eyewitness I met most of the major participants—Begin, Dayan, Weizman, Tamir, Sadat, Osama al-Baz, Boutrous Ghali, Tahsin Bashir, General Magdoub, Brzezinski, Samuel Lewis. These comments are based on my judgement and information, not theirs. See also Yoel Marcus, *Camp David: The Door to Peace,* (Tel Aviv: Schocken, 1979); Moshe Dayan, *Breakthrough,* (New York: Knopf, 1981); Ezer Weizman, *The Battle for Peace,* (New York: Bantam Books, 1981); Anwar al-Sadat, *In Search of Identity: An Autobiography* (New York: Harper and Row, 1978); Zbigniew Brzezinski, *Power and Principle: Memoirs of the National Security Adviser 1977–81* (New York: Farrar Straus Giroux, 1983); Jimmy Carter, *Keeping Faith* (New York: Bantam Books, 1982); Cyrus Vance, *Hard Choices: Critical Years in American Foreign Policy* (New York: Simon and Schuster, 1983); William Quandt, *Camp David* (Washington, D.C.: Brookings Institute, 1986); Uzi Benziman, *A Prime Minister under Siege* (Tel Aviv: Schocken, 1910). See also Conor Cruise O'Brien, *The Siege* (New York: Simon and Schuster, 1986).
2 O'Brien, p. 566.
3 Ibid., p. 567.
4 Vance, p. 166.
5 O'Brien, p. 572.
6 Begin to author, summer 1983.
7 Marcus, p. 246.
8 Brzezinski, p. 281.
9 Ibid.

Chapter 34 CAMP DAVID

1 See all the books referred to in footnote 1, chapter 33. See Amos Perlmutter, *Israel: The Partitioned State,* (New York: Scribner, 1985), chapter 10, pp. 265–94; Ephraim Poran, Begin's military aide, and General Avraham Tamir, member of Israel's team at Camp David were most helpful in giving me some of the personal insights from the negotiations. See also scathing criticism of one of Begin's former loyalists, Shmuel Katz, *No Daring, No Majesty* (Hebrew), (Tel Aviv: Dvir, 1981).
2 Brzezinski, p. 235.
3 Ibid.
4 Vance, p. 213.
5 Benziman, p. 67.
6 Ibid., p. 148.
7 Brzezinski, p. 236.
8 Ibid., p. 246–47.
9 Ibid., p. 237.
10 Ibid.
11 Marcus, p. 103.
12 Ibid.
13 Brzezinski, p. 253.
14 Dayan, p. 213.
15 Brzezinski, p. 253.

[16] Quote in Marcus, p. 201.

[17] Katz, p. 159.

[18] Ibid., p. 200.

[19] Ibid.

[20] Katz and author, summer 1983.

Chapter 35 OSIRAK

[1] Amos Perlmutter, Michael Handel and Uri Bar-Joseph, *Two Minutes Over Baghdad* (London: Corgi Books, 1982); Amos Perlmutter, "The Israeli Raid on Iraq: A New Proliferation Landscape," *Strategic Review,* Winter 1982, pp. 33–43; Amos Perlmutter, "The Mideast's Nuclear Question," *The Wall Street Journal,* June 26, 1981, p. 24; Zeev Schiff, "The Operation Against the Iraqi Reactor," *Haaretz,* June 9, 1981, p. 2; Shai Feldman, "The Bombing of Osiraq—Revisited," *International Security,* Fall 1982, pp. 114–42; Ehud Ya'ari, "Hi Eastward," *Monitin,* Tel Aviv, Sept. 1985, pp. 22–26. On the abortive political coup against Begin in 1979, see Arie Avnery, *The Liberal Connection* (Tel Aviv: Zmora) pp. 256–63.

[2] Some of this information is taken from Avnery, *The Liberal,* pp. 256–63.

[3] Ibid., p. 261 (italics mine).

[4] The argument is found in Perlmutter, *Two Minutes,* pp. 80–81.

[5] Ibid., p. 82.

[6] Ibid.

[7] Arie Naor to author, August 1985, Jerusalem.

[8] Ya'ari, p. 27.

[9] Ibid.

[10] Most of the information on the attack on Osirak is taken from my *Two Minutes Over Baghdad.*

[11] Ibid., p. 167.

[12] Ibid., p. 168.

[13] Ibid., p. 169.

[14] Ibid.

[15] Ibid., p. 170.

Chapter 36 THE SECOND BEGIN GOV'T & LEBANON WAR

[1] On the election, see Amos Perlmutter, *Israel: The Partitioned State* (New York: Scribner, 1985), footnote to chapter 11, pp. 370–71; for Begin-Weizman correspondence see The Washington *Post,* June 6, 1980; on the Lebanon war the literature is burgeoning. I recommend only those works specifically dealing with Israel's war in Lebanon. See especially Zeev Schiff and Ehud Ya'ari, *Israel's Lebanon War* (New York: Simon and Schuster, 1984); Itamar Rabinovitch, *The War for Lebanon: 1970–85* (Ithaca, N.Y.: Cornell University Press, 1985), revised edition; Shimon Shiffer, *Snowball* (Hebrew) (Tel Aviv: Edanim, 1984). During the war in 1982, I stayed with General Yanush Ben Gal, Commander of the Syrian Front for two weeks and related it in "A Letter From Lebanon," *Encounter,* November 1982, and in "Begin's Rhetorics and Sharon's Tactics," *Foreign Affairs* (Fall 1982). Much help was based on information from Sharon's former national security adviser, General Avraham (Abrasha) Tamir and Generals Yanush Ben Gal, Uri Simhoni and David Ivry. I met Begin several times during the war in 1982 and 1983 in Jerusalem. Zeev Schiff,

defense correspondent of *Haaretz* was of great help, as was Arie Naor, Begin's former chef de cabinet. See also Yitzhak Kahan, *The Kahan Commission Report,* (Jerusalem: Government of Israel, November 1983).

[2] Freely adopted from my *Israel,* pp. 295–96, 299, 300, 301, 302.
[3] Letter Weizman to Begin, *Washington Post,* p. 17 (English version).
[4] Letter Begin to Weizman, ibid., (English version).
[5] Simha Ehrlich to *Haaretz* reporter, *Haaretz,* July 31, 1981.
[6] Schiff-Ya'ari, p. 40.
[7] Ibid., p. 41.
[8] Ibid., p. 49.
[9] Ibid., p. 98.
[10] Ibid., p. 105.
[11] Related by Arie Naor.
[12] Schiff-Ya'ari, p. 201.
[13] Ibid., p. 202.
[14] Ibid., p. 208.
[15] Ibid., p. 221.
[16] Ibid., p. 223.
[17] Ibid., p. 234.
[18] Ibid., p. 235.
[19] Ibid., p. 254.
[20] *Kahan Commission,* p. 12.
[21] Ibid., p. 14.
[22] Ibid.
[23] Ibid., p. 19.
[24] Ibid., p. 24.
[25] Ibid.
[26] Ibid., p. 25.
[27] Ibid.
[28] Ibid., p. 26.
[29] Schiff-Ya'ari, p. 255.
[30] Ibid., p. 68.

Index